NEW AND IMPROVED

NEW AND IMPROVED

The Story of Mass Marketing in America

RICHARD S. TEDLOW

BasicBooks
A Division of HarperCollinsPublishers

Material from The Archives of The Coca-Cola Company used with permission of The Coca-Cola Company.

Song lyrics from Pepsi-Cola advertisements used with permission of Pepsi-Cola Company.

Tables 6-1 and 6-2 reprinted from Lebergott, S., *The American Economy: Income, Wealth, and Want.* Copyright © 1976 Princeton University Press. Reprinted with permission of Princeton University Press.

Library of Congress Cataloging-in-Publication Data
Tedlow, Richard S.
New and improved : the story of mass marketing in America /
Richard S. Tedlow.
p. cm.
Includes bibliographical references.
ISBN 0–465–05023–9 (cloth)
ISBN 0–465–05024–7 (paper)
1. Marketing—United States—History. 2. Marketing—United
States—Case studies. I. Title.
HF5415.1.T44 1990
381′.0973—dc20   89-18331
                                                          CIP

For Joyce

CONTENTS

ACKNOWLEDGMENTS

I wish to thank the many people who generously contributed their ideas and support to this book.

The community of business historians at the Harvard Business School has been a constant source of support and encouragement to me. The senior member of this group, Alfred D. Chandler, Jr., provided extensive and unfailingly astute comments during our Business History Seminar and over many pleasant luncheons. Moreover, Professor Chandler's attitude toward his own work has been an inspiration not only to me but to many other scholars as well. Thomas K. McCraw, like Professor Chandler a Pulitzer Prize–winning historian, lavished time and effort on this book. Professor McCraw has a special ability to bring out the best in the work of others, and his commitment to my work has been invaluable. Similarly, Richard H. K. Vietor, who read not only the completed manuscript but many earlier versions as well, was always available with ideas and helpful suggestions.

While at the Harvard Business School, I have taught not only business history, but also first-year marketing. It is my hope that the combination of the historical and the current perspectives in this book will yield a special contribution to knowledge in both fields. Numerous members of the Marketing Area at the Harvard Business School have commented on chapters in seminars, met with me in their offices, and provided written critiques. I would like to thank: Robert D. Buzzell; Frank V. Cespedes; E. Raymond Corey; Stephen A. Greyser; Theodore Levitt, who enabled me to teach in the Marketing Area; Rowland T. Moriarty; John A. Quelch, for his valuable comments on chapters in the Business History Seminar; V. Kasturi Rangan; Walter J. Salmon, for his help in focusing the retailing chapters; and Benson P. Shapiro, who served as my research dean throughout most of my work on this project.

In the Business, Government and Competition Area of the Harvard Business School, I would like to thank Pankaj Ghemawat, George C. Lodge, Richard S. Rosenbloom, Patricia A. O'Brien, Michael J. Rukstad, Steven W. Tolliday, and Louis T. Wells, Jr. Other faculty members who provided valuable advice and deserve my thanks include Andrall E. Pearson, Abraham Zaleznik, W. Bruce Chew, Michael J. Roberts, and Jeffrey A. Sonnenfeld. Also generous in his help was doctoral candidate Edward J. Hoff.

Dean John H. McArthur is a vigorous advocate of business history, and his support has helped make possible the development of scholarship in the field at the Harvard Business School during the past decade. The support of the Division of Research under the management of Jay W. Lorsch and his predecessor E. Raymond Corey has been unstinting. The Division gave me a full-time research assistant for two years and a year away from the classroom to work on this book. I would also like to extend my gratitude to Rose M. Giacobbe and to those at the Word Processing Center, who typed the manuscript in its many drafts with remarkable efficiency and good cheer. I am grateful as well to my secretary, Chris Gilbert, for her competence and good humor.

Numerous scholars at other institutions have contributed to this book as well. Among them are W. Bernard Carlson, University of Virginia; Robert D. Cuff, York University; Patrick Fridenson, University of Paris; Lawrence H. Fuchs, Brandeis University; Louis Galambos, Johns Hopkins University; August W. Giebelhaus, Georgia Institute of Technology; Leslie Hannah, London School of Economics; Stanley C. Hollander, Michigan State University; David A. Hounshell, University of Delaware; William Lazonick, Barnard College; Maurice Lévy-Leboyer, University of Paris; David L. Lewis, University of Michigan; Roland Marchand, University of California at Davis; Cheri T. Marshall, University of North Carolina; Hans Pohl, University of Bonn; Daniel Pope, University of Oregon; Susan Strasser, Evergreen State College; Peter Temin, Massachusetts Institute of Technology; Frederick E. Webster, Jr., Dartmouth College; Stephen J. Whitfield, Brandeis University; Mira Wilkins, Florida International University; and James C. Worthy, Northwestern University. Professors Fuchs, Lazonick, Marchand, Pope, and Whitfield read the entire manuscript and provided written as well as oral comments. Each in his own way enriched this book.

I have also benefited from the helpful comments of many in the business world. Active or retired executives who shared their expertise include James W. Button, formerly of Sears; Lloyd E. Cotsen of the Neutrogena Corporation; Carol Goldberg of Stop & Shop; John J. Kelly of Royal Motors; Al Kleinke of Ford; Walter S. Mack, Jr., formerly of Pepsi-Cola; Thomas W. Rivers of Ford; Ronald S. Robbins of Ford; Alfred W. Rossow of the Hingham Marketing Group; and Peter Warren, formerly of PepsiCo.

I am grateful for the help I have received from librarians and archivists.

The staff and resources at Baker Library of the Harvard Business School have been essential to my research, and I owe special thanks to the highly knowledgeable Michele S. Marram, senior business information analyst. I am indebted as well to David Crippen, Robert Isom, and Darleen Flaherty of the Ford Archives and the Ford Industrial Archives; Stacy Flaherty of the Smithsonian Institution; Philip Mooney at Coca-Cola; Manny Banayo, Mary Edith Arnold, and Victoria Cwiok at Sears; Beth Wickham at the General Motors Institute; George Wise at General Electric; and Cynthia Swank at J. Walter Thompson.

It has been a pleasure to work with Steven Fraser, my editor at Basic Books. Steve offered me a contract after reading the first experimental essay out of which this book grew. He always had faith in this project; and if the outcome has justified that faith, it is in some measure due to his own comments, criticism, and engagement.

I owe much to many friends for their help and support. Joseph P. Goldsmith, a college classmate and the best man at my wedding, generously shared the broad knowledge of business that he has acquired at Salomon Brothers. Reed E. Hundt, an attorney at Latham and Watkins and also a college classmate, read the manuscript and provided exceptionally incisive written comments. Reed's combined knowledge of the business world and of American culture were much in evidence in his shrewd observations.

At the Harvard Business School, my editor Patricia L. Denault read the manuscript with the same care that she devotes to the *Business History Review*, where she serves with particular distinction as associate editor. It has been my great good fortune to have as a research assistant during the past two years Wendy K. Smith. Wendy traveled all over the country for this project and participated in endless discussions about it. She has been committed to making this book as good as it can be.

Finally, I would like to express my gratitude to my parents, Mr. and Mrs. Samuel L. Tedlow, and to my wife, Joyce. They have never wavered in their support both of this book and of my career in academics in general. Joyce really deserves a medal for both her contributions to the book and for her attitude toward it. A psychiatrist and psychoanalyst, Joyce has helped me look at the protagonists in this volume in a richer and more meaningful way than would have been afforded solely by historical training. A loving wife, she has also put up with a lot—and given up a lot—so that this book could be successfully completed.

The many people who have contributed to this book share in the credit for whatever addition to knowledge it makes. However, I alone am responsible for any shortcomings.

NEW AND IMPROVED

CHAPTER 1

The All-Consuming Century: The Making of the American Emporium

The American As Consumer

Americans are choosers. They cherish the right to choose what they will do and what they will be. One of the enduring attractions of Benjamin Franklin's *Autobiography* lies in how it epitomizes the American notion of choosing one's very self. Thomas Mellon, founder of a great American fortune, wrote that reading Franklin's *Autobiography* was "the turning point in my life."[1] It inspired him to leave the family farm and take up finance. Another farm boy inspired by Franklin was Jared Sparks, who became the president of Harvard in 1849. The *Autobiography* "first roused my mental energies . . . prompted me to resolutions, and gave me strength to adhere to them." Astutely capturing the book's essence, Sparks explained that it "taught me that circumstances have not a sovereign control over the mind."[2]

America has been peopled by a great mass migration in which millions of individuals chose to join the nation of choosers.[3] Here they found not only freedom of religion, but also the right not to support any church established by law.[4] They found the right to choose their potential leaders in periodic elections. And they found the right to choose what to buy.

More than any other nation in the history of the world, the United States during the course of the past century has been a nation of consumers. A higher percentage of the population has been able to purchase a

greater variety of goods and services than even the most visionary dreamer
in the mid-nineteenth century would have imagined possible. In transportation and communication, in food and clothing, in entertainment, in
household appliances, and in all the other devices that make life easier and
more enjoyable, Americans have indeed been a "people of plenty."[5]

Americans fully appreciate, perhaps even overestimate, the appeal of
our ideas of civil and political liberty to people in other countries. They
underestimate the attractiveness of simply having things. Yet the opportunity to come to this New World and to be granted full membership in
society after satisfying minimal residence requirements has so often been
seized because along with it comes the chance to better one's station in
life and by so doing to own more things.[6]

Not only is consumption possible in America, it is also good. This is an
attitude that should not be taken for granted. An English Socialist once
complained of the "damned wantlessness of the poor," but that has not
been a problem in the United States. Here, wanting is approved. What
one wants and what one purchases have become an important part of
self-definition. Moreover, being in the business of catering to the wants
of the people is also good.

The emphasis on mass consumption in American society—our habit of
identifying how well-off people are with how many things they have—is
so pervasive that we tend to take it for granted. Yet mass consumption
is a rare phenomenon in the history of the world. Even in the present day,
a nation's focus on the welfare of the mass of its citizens as consumers
is not universally accepted. Japan, for example, is a rich nation. However,
since World War II it has been far more geared toward an ethos of
production and the penetration of international markets than it has been
toward delivering consumer products to its own citizens at the lowest
possible prices.[7]

There is nothing "natural" about mass consumption. It is a cultural and
social construction. One of the keystones of the edifice is the marketing
function in the modern, large American corporation.

The Three Phases of Marketing

This book is about how some of America's most important corporations
have battled for dominance in key consumer product markets during the
past hundred years. It is about how these corporations have formulated

their marketing strategies, how they have interacted with consumers, and how they have interacted with one another.

Marketing is an elusive subject, difficult to discuss because it is difficult to define. It encompasses a wide range of activities from the technicalities of logistics to the purest speculation about what people want now, what they will want in the future, and how much they will pay to have their wants satisfied. The manufacturer faces a different set of marketing problems from those of the retailer. The consumer durables manufacturer faces problems different from those of the packaged goods manufacturer, and the general merchandise retailer faces different problems from those of the food merchant. Given this welter of differences, must we abandon attempts to find useful generalizations about historical development? Or can we locate generalizations which, though admittedly imperfect, do describe general tendencies in the evolution of marketing strategy?

In broad outline, it is possible to discern a progression in American marketing through three phases that correspond to the broader evolution of the American economy and society. During the first phase, the domestic market was fragmented among hundreds of localities. The major factor dictating this fragmentation was the absence of a transportation and communication infrastructure spanning the continent. National brands were few in number, and national advertising was almost unknown. This was an era of vertical and horizontal nonintegration. Firms were small and exercised limited control over the market. The principal business strategy was to make profits by charging high prices and thus making high margins but at the expense of low volume. This, then, was the era of market fragmentation.

Toward the end of the nineteenth century, the completion of the railroad and telegraph network set the stage for the second phase of American marketing. This was the era of the national mass market, in which a small number of firms realized scale economies to an unprecedented degree by expanding their distribution from coast to coast and border to border. The profit strategy during this phase was to charge low prices, which permitted only small margins per unit but made possible greatly increased total profits because of high volume.

In Phase II, the national market was united by manufacturers in some product lines and by retailers in others. Where once there had been no national brands, now there were many. In Phase II—the unification phase—the national product market was dominated by an aggressive leading company or a small number of such companies. Through advertising and publicity, through forward integration into company-owned wholesaling, through franchise agreements with retailers, through the creation of sales programs and their implementation, and through the systematic analysis of carefully collected data, the large firm came to exercise an impact on the consumer market far greater than anything contemplated in Adam Smith's day. In the commodity world of Phase I, the market had dictated the terms of business. In the new Phase II world of brands, the market still played a key role in the sense that consumer acceptance was essential, but the firm's power to shape and mold the market was vastly increased.

Many of the consumer products discussed in this book, such as automobiles and household mechanical refrigerators, did not exist prior to the twentieth century. For these products especially, the firm had to organize and educate a mass market. This is what Ford did in automobiles and what Frigidaire, General Electric, and Sears did in refrigerators. The development of strategies for creating and competing in mass markets for such products is the heart of this book.

The third phase of American marketing has been characterized by market segmentation.[8] This era bears certain similarities to the nineteenth-century phase of market fragmentation, in that divisions in the market have become the primary focus of the consumer marketing effort rather than the unification of the market by a dominant brand or product form. But market segmentation today is far more complex than were the market divisions of a hundred years ago. Transportation costs still matter, so geography is still important. However, marketers (a term unknown in the previous century) use such additional considerations as demographics (age, income, and education) and psychographics (life-style) to create divisions in markets that they can exploit with competitive advantages. These segments have to be sufficiently large so that scale economies are obtained. The goal, however, has been not only to achieve scale economies, but also to gain the freedom to "value price"—to price in accord with the special value that a particular market segment places on the product, independent of the costs of production.

Phase II products and marketing strategies had a changeless quality about them. For instance, Coca-Cola and the Model T Ford were conceived of as the best possible answers to market needs in their respective product categories. Coca-Cola's proprietor, Asa G. Candler, was devoted to his product because of its medicinal (he believed it cured his headaches) and refreshing qualities. He wanted to share it with the nation and also with the world. Candler did not bring out a new version of his soft drink each year, nor did he experiment with diet beverages or other line extensions. Indeed, until 1955, Coca-Cola was available in only two forms—at the soda fountain and in the traditional 6½-ounce, hobble-skirted bottle.

Coke was, the company believed, perfect for everyone. There was no need to devote special attention to one group or another.

The story at Ford in the early years was similar. After the Ford Motor Company settled on the Model T as its sole market entry in 1908, it stuck with the product doggedly. Indeed, an important reason for Ford's early success was that the company seized on the idea of reducing the price of the automobile by producing large numbers of high-quality vehicles in a progressively more efficient factory. Henry Ford explicitly conceived of the Model T as the "universal" car. Market segmentation played no part in his thinking. There was no reason, in Ford's view, for anyone to buy another model.

Phase III products have attacked the Phase II strategy through change and segmentation. General Motors introduced the price pyramid with the "car for every purse and purpose" in the 1920s. Each make was supposed to appeal to a different set of customers. Each make also changed every year. There was no sense that a 1923 Chevrolet or a 1927 Buick was supposed to be a "universal" car.

Likewise, Pepsi-Cola answered Coca-Cola's Phase II strategy with a vigorous Phase III approach. Pepsi's advertisements in the 1950s did not tout the product as much as they did the context in which the product was consumed.[9] "Be sociable, look smart. Be up to date with Pepsi."

This strategy was brilliantly refined with the inauguration of the "Pepsi Generation" in the 1960s. Margaret Mead once remarked that the world was divided into two groups—those who lived through World War II and those who experienced it only as a memory. By the early 1960s, the postwar baby boomers had reached their teenage years. Perhaps never before in the history of the nation had the generation gap been so fundamental. The baby boomers' parents grew up amid depression and war. But during the 1960s, the spread of wealth in the United States put cash in the pockets of many teens who had never earned a penny. These young people sought badges of belonging in language, in hairstyle, in clothing, and in music.[10] Pepsi zeroed in on them, combining an appeal to peer approval with life-style. Unlike Coke, Pepsi was always about variety and change. When Coca-Cola tried to change its formula in 1985, there was an uproar among loyal customers. Pepsi changed its formula in the early 1930s and again in the early 1950s, and nobody cared. People expected Pepsi to change.

The three phases in the development of American marketing are outlined in table 1–1. The phases are meant to be used as a general guide to assist us in understanding the historical evolution of marketing presented in the pages that follow. I am not asserting that all industries in

TABLE 1–1

The Three Phases of American Marketing

Phase	Characteristics
I *Fragmentation*	High margin Low volume Restricted market size due to transportation costs
II *Unification*	High volume Low margin Incorporation of the whole nation in a mass market
III *Segmentation*	High volume Value pricing Demographic and psychographic segmentation

the United States have marched through these phases together. Generally speaking, however, prior to the 1880s, the United States had a Phase I business economy. Few consumer products were able to pass from Phase I to Phase II prior to the end of the nineteenth century.[11] An inadequate transportation and communication infrastructure made a volume strategy highly problematic. Only after the 1880s were some leading industries able to pass from the first to the second phase.

The transition from Phase II to Phase III is even less sharp. In some industries, such as automobiles, the era of market segmentation began in the 1920s. In others, such as soft drinks, Phase III did not begin until well after World War II. The differences in timing are associated with the differences in market size, market growth, and those elements of the infrastructure of particular importance to a specific industry. Market segmentation has been greatly stimulated in packaged goods by the advent of television. It is hard to imagine the Pepsi Generation without television advertising.

SOME HISTORICAL EXAMPLES OF MARKETING PHASES

The three phases of American marketing—from fragmentation to unification to segmentation—will help organize the complex historical narrative that follows. This basic progression recurs in the industries under study here.

Soft Drinks. The soft drink industry was in Phase I through most of the nineteenth century. There were dozens of local brands, compounded by druggists who tried to brighten the day of their customers by concocting new flavors at the soda fountain. In the early 1890s, Asa G. Candler of Atlanta gained control of one such beverage, Coca-Cola.

Candler quickly established a market presence all over the country and abroad through exceptionally heavy national advertising and, after the turn of the century, through a bottler network that relied in large part on independent franchises. Coca-Cola's advertising in the early 1900s did not attempt to segment the market. Coca-Cola was for everyone—young or old, rich or poor. It was the universal cola—a classic example of a Phase II product.

Pepsi-Cola was developed in the 1890s, but it had a checkered career until the 1930s. At that time the company attempted to segment the market but not through psychographics or demographics. Rather, Pepsi underpriced Coke in the famous "Twice as Much for a Nickel, Too" campaign. Pepsi made some headway among people watching their pennies, of whom there were many during the Depression. However, this modified Phase II strategy became impossible to maintain as the industry's costs rose in the postwar inflation. By the late 1940s, Pepsi was looking for a new *raison d'être*. This it found first with psychographic segmentation ("Be sociable") and then with the combination of psychographic and demographic segmentation (Pepsi Generation). Coca-Cola responded; and by the 1980s, with line extensions, the proliferation of packaging, and narrow market targeting, the soft drink industry had clearly entered Phase III.

Automobiles. The automobile moved through its first phase with speed. Inventors, mechanics, and hobbyists were tinkering with contraptions that can be considered ancestors of the automobile in the 1880s. As numerous companies organized themselves at the turn of the century, the usual strategy was to produce a number of different models in relatively small runs. In those early years of fragmented competition, no product design was yet dominant. Gasoline, steam, and electricity were all vying for acceptance.

Henry Ford devised a strategy that called for total concentration on a single, "universal" car aimed at everyone. With economies of scale and learning-curve advantages, Ford successfully reduced the price of the car and in the process greatly widened the market. This was Phase II—the profit-through-volume stage of the automobile industry.

In the 1920s, the automobile market grew large enough and the problems posed by the used car proved vexing enough that there was an opportunity for a new strategy of segmentation. This opportunity was seized by Alfred P. Sloan, Jr., at General Motors; and, as a result, industry leadership was seized as well.

Since the 1920s, there have been many attempts to re-create Ford's success. Most noteworthy was the Volkswagen Beetle, another changeless "universal" car that eventually outsold even the Model T. At this writing, however, the automobile industry seems to be moving, thanks to flexible manufacturing and computerization, even more firmly into Phase III with mass customization.

Grocery Retailing. The word *industry* has somewhat different meanings when we discuss retailer-centered as opposed to manufacturer-centered marketing systems. In the soft drink and automobile industries, in which the channel commander is the manufacturer, our focus is on a specific product. Our focus in retailing, however, is on more broadly defined industries—food and general merchandise.

Despite the differences in the unit of analysis resulting from the different nature of manufacturing and retailing, the fragmentation-unification-segmentation model of marketing development is still illuminating. Nineteenth-century grocery retailing was characterized by vertical and horizontal nonintegration. Chain stores were few in number with minimal impact on the market. Brands were few, and differentiation of the overall retail product offering was limited. This was an era of commodities—of crackers out of barrels, of coffee out of sacks, of flour from the local gristmill. Much of the food industry was family-centered rather than market-centered in what was an overwhelmingly rural nation.

Toward the end of the nineteenth century, however, A&P emerged as a multistore-owning grocery retailer. Just before World War I, John A. Hartford, a son of one of the company's founders, launched a discount store policy that resulted in rapid growth. Sales soared from $5.6 million in 1900 to almost $200 million in 1919 to over $1 billion a decade later. A&P stores were not in every local market in the nation, but they were present in almost all the large population centers. In many of these places, A&P achieved its dominance through vertical integration, an effective private brand strategy, and systematic management of multiple stores.

In the early 1930s, the grocery retailing industry was shocked by the rapid spread of a new kind of food store called the supermarket. Like A&P, the supermarket operators were Phase II mass marketers, but their store and branding strategies were fundamentally new and very effective. A&P was forced to respond by turning itself into a supermarket chain. It adapted so successfully that by 1945 A&P was the fifth largest industrial company in terms of sales in the United States, the same rank it held in 1929.[12] Thus, A&P was able to move from one Phase II strategy featuring numerous small stores to another characterized by a lesser number of large stores. The nature of shopping for food had been transformed by the automobile, yet A&P was able to adapt by transforming itself even though such a change meant the abandonment of what everyone thought was A&P's primary competitive advantage—its thousands of strategically placed small stores.

After World War II, however, the story was not such a happy one. During the 1950s and 1960s, A&P proved incapable of moving into a more segmented world. It stayed with its own private brands for too long, thus losing customers who were responding to national television advertising by food processors. In a Phase II industry, putting "A&P," "Ann Page," or "Jane Parker" on everything from corn flakes to cola might have been effective. But this strategy has been less successful in recent years.

Location is critically important in retailing, but A&P compounded its problems by tarrying too long in the cities while so much of the population was moving to the suburbs. It was challenged by fast-moving regional chains and discounters whose superior local knowledge led to better store site location. In 1979, after years of slow decline, A&P was sold to a West German retailer.

General Merchandise Retailing. What is "general merchandise"? The term has no precise meaning. Sears has sold almost everything at one time or another, including cars and even houses. For a number of years, it did a high-volume business in groceries (though with low, often negative, profit).

In the Phase I era of the nineteenth century, general merchandise retailing was similar to grocery retailing. Wholesalers played a key role in the marketing channel, and there was little vertical integration, no chain stores, and no brands. Toward the end of the nineteenth century, first Montgomery Ward and then Sears undertook to sell general merchandise by mail order. The core of their market was rural America, where shopping trips to cities were inconvenient and therefore few in number.

Sears moved into store retailing (in addition to its traditional mail-order business) in the 1920s. By the 1930s, it was selling nearly anything a consumer might want to purchase—except automobiles and groceries—to people across the nation. Sears conceived of the market as a diamond—the top triangle was the Gold Coast, the bottom triangle was the "junk trade," and the "middle 80 percent," Sears felt, it owned. Sears competed successfully not only against Montgomery Ward, which faded badly in the 1950s, but against branded manufacturers as well. Its masterful use of its economies of scope in distribution enabled Sears to secure a major position in such consumer durables as kitchen and laundry equipment.

Unlike A&P, which shunned the suburbs, Sears led the way to suburbanization by becoming a major mall developer. Ironically, the very malls that Sears built and anchored and to which it attracted shoppers provided the opportunity for numberless specialty stores to eat away at its "middle 80 percent." Sears also lost business to large discounters like K Mart, which it allowed to grow almost unnoticed.

Premodern Marketing

The early American market was divided into numerous geographic fragments. The American Constitution may have forged a customs union among the states, but the realities of geography spoke louder. Transportation was so arduous and expensive, information so tardy and inaccurate, that there was no national market in the modern sense. "America during the nineteenth century was a society of island communities," notes Robert H. Wiebe.[13] Politically, these communities exercised local autonomy. Economically, they were characterized by small, local monopolies. Today's world of oligopolists plotting strategy on a national scale did not exist in the nineteenth century.

In 1800, it took weeks to get from New York City to Chicago. I should say "to the site of present-day Chicago," because in 1800 Chicago did not exist. It did not exist precisely because of this inaccessibility. The shores of Lake Michigan were at the outer limits of the known world. In the words of George Rogers Taylor, travel and transportation were "surprisingly little changed from the days of the Phoenicians." Many of the roads on the American continent

> were hardly more than broad paths through the forests. In wet places, they presented a line of ruts with frequent mud holes, and, where dry, a powdered surface of deep dust. The largest stones and stumps were removed only so far as was absolutely necessary.[14]

No national marketing network could have been developed with such poor transportation facilities.

Steamboat travel on lakes and rivers and the digging of canals helped to ease the transport problem. By 1840, there were about 3,300 miles of canals and over 80,000 steamboat operating tons. Transit time to Chicago had been cut by well over one-half.[15] But inland waterway transportation by itself could not have supported the American business revolution. In what was to become the nation's industrial heartland, waterways froze for months each year and water levels fluctuated during the remainder of the year, with freshets and floods in the springtime and droughts late in the summer.

A form of transportation was needed that could be built to any part of the continental United States and that could operate on schedule even in severe weather. It had to be fast and inexpensive as well. The railroad satisfied these needs. By 1840, there were 3,332 miles of railroad in operation and more than twice that many miles a decade later. There were over 30,000 miles of track by 1860, when the trip between New York and Chicago had been cut to about a day and a half. Measured in travel time, Chicago in 1860 was closer to New York than Baltimore had been in 1800. Chicago was the city the railroads created, growing from a settlement of about a hundred in 1830 to a metropolis of more than 1.5 million by the turn of the century.[16] Its rail connections made it the logical headquarters for two of the nation's largest distributing firms: Sears and Montgomery Ward.

The full development of the consumer economy was hindered by political and economic convulsions during the 1860s and 1870s. From 1861 through 1865, the United States was engaged in the greatest armed conflict to occur between the Napoleonic Wars and World War I. In 1873, the nation was hit by a depression that took six years to struggle out of. Nevertheless, the rail network grew to more than 90,000 miles by the close of the 1870s. Further, railroad management made great strides in handling through traffic. The set of lines on a map indicating the early rail network hides the numerous on- and off-loadings caused by physical problems like differing gauged track and operational problems like accounting for the whereabouts of traffic. These and other difficulties were well on their way to solution by 1880. And with the war and the depression finally ended, the United States experienced a railroad-building boom the like of which had never been seen anywhere before and has not been equaled since. Over 70,000 miles of track were laid, bringing the total in 1890 to 166,703. The "island communities" of the nation were now linked by highways of iron, steel, and steam.

Accompanying the railroads in their march across the continent was the telegraph. Samuel F. B. Morse linked Baltimore and Washington in 1844. The telegraph was essential to monitoring the movement of trains and traffic. It also disseminated a wealth of commercial (as well as political) information. Big retail-wholesale firms in the interior now could communicate daily with their New York buying offices and directly with their dry goods suppliers in New England.

Phase I was an era of commodities; Phase II was an era of the national brand. Prior to the 1880s, most manufacturers were unknown to the people who bought their products. Manufactured goods reached the consumer through an intricate web of agents, brokers, jobbers, wholesalers, and retailers. These distributors provided warehousing services, broke bulk (i.e., purchased goods in large quantities and sold them in smaller ones), and provided credit (depending on the product). But during the 1880s, this system began to change for several reasons. First, the completion of the new transportation and communication infrastructure made it possible to distribute goods nationally more economically than ever before. Second, new manufacturing technology made it possible to produce a standardized product in large volume and, importantly, in small packages. Continuous process machinery was "invented almost simultaneously for making cigarettes, matches, flour, breakfast cereals, soups and other canned products, and photographic film." Many of the consumer product companies that first adopted such machinery remain famous today: American Tobacco, Diamond Match, Quaker Oats, Pillsbury Flour, Campbell Soup, Heinz, Borden, Carnation, Libby, Procter & Gamble, and Eastman Kodak.[17]

Most of the leading consumer product firms of the pre–Civil War, Phase I years are, by contrast, not companies we know today. One of the greatest mercantile firms of that era, John Jacob Astor's American Fur Company, went bankrupt soon after Astor withdrew from it in 1834.[18] Those antebellum consumer firms that have proved long-lived are known today more because of what they did in the 1880s than in their earlier years. Procter & Gamble, for example, was founded in 1837; but Ivory Soap did not come along until 1879.[19]

A standardized, nationally distributed product in a small package could be named by the manufacturer. What the manufacturer could name, he could advertise. The result was something more than a name. It was a kind of supername—a brand. What does a brand do? It conveys information to the consumer, thus "reducing or eliminating the need to find out about a product before buying it."[20] This information can extend beyond the physical attributes or uses of a product to include, for example, the characteristics of the person who will use it.

A classic example is David Ogilvy's famous 1950s "eyepatch" campaign for Hathaway Shirts. Ogilvy featured a photograph of a self-confident, fearless-looking mustachioed man wearing a Hathaway shirt. The most startling aspect of the picture was the patch that the man wore over his right eye. The impression conveyed was of a calm boldness, a controlled defiance. This was "The man in the Hathaway shirt."[21]

There are, of course, many other ways to advertise a shirt. One could talk about the number of stitches per square inch or about how the colors will not run. But Ogilvy wanted to create a Hathaway image through the advertisement. He wanted to associate the Hathaway brand with characteristics he believed would be admired by potential customers.

In this way, the brand name and its concomitant associations become part of the product. Many marketers believe that "a brand name should go beyond just being 'not inappropriate' to the point of being positively appropriate—and even helpful in suggesting something desirable about the product or its performance." Thus "Handi-Wrap" for a plastic wrap, "Off!" for an insect repellent, and "Mr. Clean" for a household cleanser.[22] Originally named "Brad's Drink" after its inventor Caleb B. Bradham, Pepsi-Cola was soon renamed to suggest the beverage's putative power to relieve dyspepsia and the pain of peptic ulcer. Coca-Cola's name was descriptive; the beverage contained extracts of the coca leaf and the cola nut.

Branding involves costs and risks. The costs include those incurred for advertising, packaging, and legal protection. The risk is that if a product should prove unsatisfactory, the consumer will know what manufacturer to avoid in the future. Yet the reward of branding—a consumer franchise that to some degree insulates the brand owner from price competition—makes the effort essential in today's market. Every great modern consumer product company achieved its success in part from owning established brands. Brand management is the quintessential responsibility and opportunity of the modern consumer marketer. It did not exist in Phase I of American marketing.

Business Battles and Battlers

The strategy of profit through volume is a distinctively American contribution to marketing, facilitated by both our culture and our economy. Although cultural and economic preconditions were necessary, they could not alone move an industry from Phase I to Phase II. An added element was required: entrepreneurial drive and vision.

American entrepreneurs discovered in their attempts to implement the profit-through-volume strategy that reliance solely on market relationships was impossible. They had to build an organization through which they could coordinate manufacturing and marketing. Once created, this organization could, under certain circumstances, generate large profits. It also stood as a barrier to the entry of new competition desiring to share in those profits. Potential new entrants were faced with the choice of either replicating the successful strategy of the first-mover or of finding some fundamentally new way to compete. The firms that succeeded in the long term were those that managed their organizational capabilities against the backdrop of changes in the economy and society. In other words, the strategy of profit through volume—selling many units at low margins rather than few units at high margins—historically has been the distinctive signature of the American approach to marketing. By making products available to the masses all over the nation—by democratizing consumption—the mass marketer did something profoundly American.

Examples are numerous. Personal transportation was once a signature of social privilege, until Henry Ford made it available to everyone. More recently, acetaminophen was a high-priced pharmaceutical specialty drug, marketed primarily with the help of recommendations from physicians. James E. Burke at Johnson & Johnson cut the price of the drug, advertised heavily, and distributed intensively; he thus created in Tylenol one of the biggest brands in American history. Acetaminophen started in the province of the experts. Burke democratized it.[23]

Mass marketing did not spontaneously develop because of the existence of necessary technological, economic, and social preconditions. Entrepreneurs had to have the creativity to see new business opportunities and the willingness to take the risks involved in transforming their visions into realities. The business firms that such people made the instruments of their will had to create mass markets by shaping and molding the unorganized, inchoate demand for their products.

Tylenol, for example, did not create itself. To be sure, there has always been a market for safe pain relief. Yet the market for acetaminophen was, to an important degree, created by James Burke. He saw the product's potential when others did not. He created a new company within Johnson & Johnson—McNeil Consumer Products—to pursue a vigorous consumer marketing strategy to develop the market.[24] Had he not done so, there might never have been a mass-marketed acetaminophen; and there certainly would not have been a Tylenol. This is precisely what I mean by "creating mass markets," a phrase to which I will return. Of course, if Tylenol had not been efficacious, no amount of marketing expenditure or strategizing could have turned it into a successful brand. The product had to work. But merely working would not have turned it into a successful brand either. The world would not have beaten a pathway to it. Burke's entrepreneurial insight, drive, and investment were essential to its success.

To implement the strategy of profit through volume, the entrepreneur had to create a vertical system through which raw materials were sourced, production operations were managed, and products were delivered to the ultimate consumer. Scale at one level was useless without scale at the others. Mass production demanded mass marketing. The vertical system usually involved integration within the firm of some of the steps involved and contractual relations for the others.

The early years of the Singer Sewing Machine Company illustrate the need for the marriage of mass distribution to mass production. In the 1870s and 1880s, Singer built the largest sewing machine factories in the world. If this large fixed investment were to pay off, these plants had to operate near rated capacity. Unfortunately, the independent distributors through which Singer sold made the smooth scheduling of production very difficult. These distributors failed to maintain inventories properly. They always seemed to be either overstocked or out of stock. Just as problematic, they were late in remitting payments and deficient in supplying the various services that the market for a new, complex, and expensive consumer durable required.

As a result, Singer soon realized that it had to create a company-owned marketing network. This new organization greatly facilitated the management of demand, and the company was able to convert its high fixed costs to low unit costs and benefit from an expanding market as well as achieve high earnings.[25]

The first firm to implement successfully the profit-through-volume strategy had the opportunity to reap enormous profits. First-mover profits tantalized potential competitors, but first-mover advantages confronted those potential competitors with barriers to the industry's high returns. These first-mover advantages exist in almost every industry where technology makes possible scale economies. The first few firms to make the investment in production and distribution and then in management to coordinate the two have often dominated their industries for decades, even generations.[26] What explains this enduring preeminence? The first-mover can grow very quickly with retained earnings. It can command the attention of the consumer. It can attract the best executive talent. The newcomer, on the other hand, must acquire all these assets from scratch against efficient and entrenched competition. It is no accident that for so much of the past century, the domestic automobile industry has been dominated by three firms. There has been similar leadership by a small number of firms in such other industries as chemicals, steel, rubber, aluminum, and oil.

The key strategic choice that resulted was how to attack the barriers.

The potential entrant could attempt a more proficient implementation of the same basic strategy used by the first-mover, or it could seek to exploit some strategic insight to change the rules of the game. The entrant's thrust, the dominant firm's response, the entrant's reply, and ensuing moves defined the nature of competition in a given industry over the course of decades. This competitive thrust and counterthrust are the key dynamics in modern business. Alfred Sloan of General Motors, for example, decided to attack Henry Ford's Model T not by trying to develop a similar product philosophy. The barriers to success there were too great. Sloan exploited his strategic insight that the great surge of first-time automobile buying was playing itself out during the 1920s. As a result, there was both a need and an opportunity to develop a stream of new products, which is what the annual model change was. Eventually, the Ford Motor Company had to abandon its own philosophy of the unchanging model.

Sustained success or failure in a market has been determined by how well a firm manages change. The firm itself experiences internal change, as leaders age and new executives struggle for power. Competition changes as new strategies are attempted. The market changes as the needs and wants of consumers evolve. The infrastructure changes with the development of new technologies for transportation, communication, and data processing.

This is why a historical perspective is critically important to the understanding of the individual firm and of competition. History is the study of how institutions are created and how they change over time. Its focus is as much on individual differences as on general trends. History demands that account be taken of the judgment and drive of the individual entrepreneur and of the distinctive competence and capability of specific companies.

The discussion in this subsection can be summarized and focused in a set of six propositions:

1. The strategy of profit through volume has been the keystone of many American marketing successes.
2. Entrepreneurial drive and vision have been essential to creating and organizing mass markets.
3. Mass production demanded mass marketing. It was the responsibility of the manager to coordinate this vertical relationship.
4. First-mover advantages led to high profits, but these very advantages acted as barriers to the entry of new competitors.
5. New entrants confronted the choice of either copying the first-mover's strategy or attempting something fundamentally new and different.

that is—have chosen them. In the words of Richard Wightman Fox and
T. J. Jackson Lears:

> It will not do to view [the consumer culture] as an elite conspiracy in which
> advertisers defraud the "people" by drowning them in a sea of glittering goods.
> The people are not that passive; they have been active consumers, preferring
> some commodities to others.[32]

Choice, then, is at the center of the modern American consumer
economy. Some of the choices consumers have made have been wrong.
Some choices have carried costs of which the consumers were unaware.
On the whole, however, most of their choices have been reasonable. And
the corporations that have provided American consumers with the alter-
natives from which to choose have done something worth doing.

CHAPTER 2

The Great Cola Wars: Coke vs. Pepsi

Soft drinks—that is, nonalcoholic beverages—trace their ancestry back to the mineral springs of Europe. In the nineteenth century, numerous mineral waters were sold in the United States. Druggists often flavored mineral water with various extracts, serving homemade brews of root beer or ginger ale to please the patrons of their soda fountains. By the late nineteenth century, the owners of a few such beverages were attempting to distribute them beyond their local trading areas. However, the difficulties in obtaining broad, regional distribution were considerable. Bottling technology was in its infancy, so most soft drinks were sold at the soda fountain. And there was little reason for fountain proprietors to pay for the use of someone else's drink when they could mix their own with such ease.

I call this Phase I of the soft drink industry. Few beverages were widely available. No brand had real pull. Barriers to competitive entry were low.

Coca-Cola was invented in 1886, and by the turn of the century it was making progress in achieving national distribution and brand pulling power. Coca-Cola's owners wanted to make it the industry standard. Further, they wanted everyone to drink it anytime, as their advertisements stressed. To achieve this goal, they launched a coordinated advertising and sales force drive so well executed that it created one of the most powerful brands in the history of marketing.

This was Phase II of the soft drink industry. Coca-Cola was the national brand, the dominant force, the emblem of American consumption. In the nineteenth century no barriers to entry could be built in soft drinks, but by the early 1930s Coca-Cola was being referred to in the trade press as a national monopoly. Other brands tried to compete. When, the trade press asked, would the country see the next Coca-Cola? Industry analysts were puzzled about the nature of Coca-Cola's competitive muscle.

In the 1930s, Pepsi-Cola, a brand that was invented in the 1890s but that had experienced two bankruptcies, emerged as a challenger to Coca-Cola. Pepsi's entry strategy was based on price. Coca-Cola was aimed at a mass market, but by the time of the Great Depression Coke's pricing strategy left room for a cola offering dramatically lower prices. Pepsi's strategy achieved impressive success in part because the company had a solid base of distribution through a large chain of confectionary stores.

In my view, the "twelve full ounces" era of Pepsi-Cola from 1931 through 1949 can be seen as another Phase II strategy. Pepsi did not make any claims of product superiority, nor did its advertising campaign suggest that it was best suited for a certain kind of person or occasion. Rather, Pepsi's appeal was strictly price oriented, a defining characteristic of Phase II competition.

Pepsi's strategy, however, was founded not on any cost advantage in production or distribution but on Coca-Cola's price umbrella. That price umbrella disappeared with postwar inflation. By the late 1940s, Pepsi had to raise its prices; and it lost its customers in the process. The company's very survival was in question. A new strategy was essential.

Pepsi inaugurated that strategy in the 1950s, by appealing to customers on the basis of who they were rather than what the product was. This was a fundamental change, a bold step into the Phase III world of demographic and psychographic segmentation. Market segmentation strategies now dominate the industry, which is why supermarket shelves are so crowded with line extensions. The world of the universal cola—the one brand perfect for anyone, anytime, anywhere—is now gone.

Coca-Cola As Product

Coca-Cola was invented in Atlanta on 8 May 1886 by John Styth Pemberton, a 53-year-old druggist. Pemberton had moved from his hometown of Columbus, Georgia, to Atlanta in 1869, where he became known as much for his soda fountain concoctions as for his medicinal preparations.[1] During his seventeen years in Atlanta, Pemberton had been employed at, or part owner of, nine different pharmaceutical firms. He was, according to Coca-Cola historian Pat Watters, "a druggist of the old school, thoroughly versed in the manufacturing part of the business and . . . constantly experimenting with new preparations," such as Pemberton's Extract of Styllinger and Globe Flower Cough Syrup.[2]

During the mid-1880s, Pemberton devoted most of his attention to his "French Wine of Coca," touted as an "ideal nerve tonic and stimulant."[3] The stimulation was provided by extract of coca leaf. Pemberton was determined to produce a nonalcoholic nostrum—thus a "soft" as opposed to a "hard" drink—so he eliminated the wine. Alcohol caused fatigue and upset the stomach; Pemberton was looking for an elixir to do the reverse. He added the extract of cola nut, knowledge of which had been brought to the South by slaves. It was said to be invigorating, to cure hangovers, and to have the properties of an aphrodisiac. The result of all this experimentation was a bitter-tasting liquid.

Pemberton continued his efforts until May of 1886, when he and his colleagues were convinced that they had it right. One problem remained; the new-born product was anonymous. Recalled Frank M. Robinson, one of Pemberton's partners, "It had no name in the beginning. . . . I just took Coca-Cola as a name, similar to other advertising names, thinking that the two Cs would look well [sic] in advertising."[4] Robinson's modesty belies the importance of the name he chose. *Coca-Cola* stands today as the second most widely understood term in the world, after *okay*.

Having decided that they at last had a product worth taking to market, Pemberton and his colleagues marched over in the warm spring weather to the drugstore of Dr. Joseph Jacobs. There they encountered Willis Venable, who was leasing the fountain from Jacobs. As Watters recounts the story:

> After mutual greeting and some small talk, Dr. Pemberton placed the jug of syrup on the counter and explained what he had done. Meanwhile, they were joined by Dr. Jacobs who had been working at his desk in the back of the store.
>
> Pemberton suggested to Venable that he mix some ice and plain water with the syrup in the proportion of one ounce of syrup to five ounces of water. He made three drinks and placed them on the counter. The three of them stood smacking their lips and nodding their heads in approval. However, on the second go-around, by accident, Venable put carbonated water into the glasses instead of plain water.
>
> After tasting the contents of the second glass, the three men became excited, all talking at once. Their delight and pleasure was obvious on discovering what a delicious drink was produced by the combination of carbonated water with Dr. Pemberton's syrup.[5]

Interest in the medicinal properties of effervescent mineral waters dates back many centuries, but the first commercial manufacture of artificial seltzer water was undertaken only in 1783. Paul, Schweppe, and Gosse founded their mineral water business in Geneva six years later. Jacob Schweppe moved to Bristol, England, where he and three English partners founded Schweppe and Company in 1798.[6]

In the United States, soda water was being dispensed on draught and in bottles by 1807. The U.S. Pharmacopeia listed soda water among its medicated waters in 1820, and the *Journal of Health* reported in 1830 that flavored syrups were being added to soda water. In 1831, patents were issued for counter fountain machinery; and by the end of the decade, soda water flavored with fruit syrup was being sold at apothecary shops. Soon thereafter, root beer was on the market.[7]

The census began tracking the bottled soda water industry in 1849. Table 2–1 shows the growth of the soft drink industry from 1849 through 1889. Other noteworthy developments in the industry from the mid-nineteenth century to the invention of Coca-Cola in 1886 include the first soft drink trademark registration in 1871 (for "Lemon's Superior Sparkling Ginger Ale"); the manufacture of root beer by Charles E. Hires in Philadelphia in 1876; the founding of the Cliquot Club Company for the manufacture of ginger ale and other beverages in Milles, Massachusetts, in 1881; the bottling of White Rock mineral waters in Waukesha, Wisconsin, in 1883; the purchase of space in national magazines by Hires; and the founding in 1885 of the Moxie Nerve Food Company in Boston. Also in 1885, the Dr Pepper flavor (though not yet named as such) was invented in Waco, Texas.[8]

From this brief survey we can see that the epiphany in Atlanta in 1886 did not yield a distinctive or original product. Carbonated water flavored with syrups of various kinds had been around for years, in bottled form

TABLE 2–1

Production and Consumption of Soft Drinks in the United States, 1849–1889

Year	Number of Bottling Plants	Capital Investment (in millions)	Value of Production (wholesale; in millions)	Total Cases (in millions)	Per Capita (12-oz. containers)
1849	64	$ 0.2	$ 0.8	1.0	1.1
1859	123	0.6	1.4	1.9	1.5
1869	387	3.5	4.2	5.6	4.3
1879	512	2.6	4.8	6.3	3.0
1889	1,377	10.8	14.3	17.4	6.6

SOURCES: John J. Riley, *A History of the American Soft Drink Industry: Bottled Carbonated Beverages, 1807–1957* (New York: Arno, 1972), 251–57; *Beverage Industry 1985 Annual Manual* (Cleveland, Ohio: Harcourt Brace Jovanovich, Sept. 1985), 24.

as well as at the druggist's fountain. Such soft drinks had always been thought to have curative properties of various kinds—note, for example, the Moxie "Nerve Food" Company. Coca-Cola had been predated by what would in the twentieth century become major national brands; and one of these, Hires, had already begun national advertising. Moreover, Pemberton and his friends had entered a rapidly growing market. Total cases of soft drinks shipped increased by more than 175 percent in the 1880s. It is tempting to ascribe this growth to temperance sentiment, especially in the South; and indeed, by 1905 Coca-Cola was being advertised as "The Great National Temperance Drink."[9] Yet even though case shipments increased from 113 to 182 million (or 61 percent) during the Prohibition decade of the 1920s, they skyrocketed to 322 million (a leap of 77 percent) during the Depression years of the 1930s, despite the repeal of Prohibition in 1933.

The soft drink market has responded to all outside influences by growing, making it one of the great dream markets in the history of consumer products in the United States. Shipments of 4.6 billion cases with a wholesale value surpassing $22 billion in 1984 represent increases by orders of magnitude from 1889. In 1984, the typical American consumed an average of 469 12-ounce containers of soft drink, up more than 7,000 percent from the 1889 figure of 6.6 containers.[10]

What, then, was distinctive about Coca-Cola? Flavor chemists abroad had been experimenting with cola drinks for a decade, and Pemberton, as well as others, had long been familiar with coca. But according to J. C. Louis and Harvey Z. Yazijian in *The Cola Wars*, "Pemberton's decision to blend the two was boldly original, for it brought together two of the most massive stimulants known to preindustrial cultures."[11]

Much has been said of the "magic formula" for the syrup, especially about the ingredient known as Merchandise 7X. Charles Howard Candler, son of Asa Griggs Candler (who bought the company from Pemberton), and himself a Coca-Cola executive, wrote in 1950 that for some years the syrup was made only by Asa Candler and his partner Frank Robinson. The formula was later transmitted to a few trusted employees, but only "by word of mouth." "[O]ne of the proudest moments of my life," the younger Candler recalled,

came when my father, shortly after the turn of the century, initiated me into the mysteries of the secret flavoring formula, inducting me as it were, into the "Holy of Holies." No written memorandum was permitted. No written formulae were shown. Containers of ingredients, from which the labels had been removed, were identified only by sight, smell, and remembering where each was put on the shelf. . . . To be safe, father stood by me several times to insure the integrity of the batches and to satisfy himself that his youthful son had learned his lesson and could be depended upon.[12]

The Coca-Cola Company received an object lesson in the magic of the formula as late as 1985. On April 22 of that year, in what proved to be the most flamboyant miscalculation in the company's ninety-nine years, management announced that it was changing the product's original formula. The result was a blizzard of protest so intense that within three months the original formula was brought back. Said one trade journalist, "The company didn't fathom the depth of the emotional commitment to Coke," and a Coke bottler observed that "some consumers were mad. It was almost a psychological thing."[13]

The Coca-Cola formula, of course, produced the taste, about which devotees have waxed rhapsodic—the "sweet-and-bitter taste of first love," in the words of one.[14] The drive to crack the secret code dates back at least to the turn of the century, when the *Druggists Circular and Chemical Gazette* ran an advertisement offering five dollars for the "Secret Coca-Cola flavor formula." A number of years ago, Coca-Cola's vice-president for quality control explained that outsiders trying to discover the product's makeup would face an "extraordinarily difficult, if not downright impossible," task. Even chemists trained in the use of techniques like infrared spectrum analysis could not easily break down the mixture of citrus oils into its component parts.[15]

Those who are not commercial chemists and who do not know the precise ingredients of the formula are not in a position to evaluate how mystifying it is. However, one must be skeptical about the role that the Coca-Cola formula played in the product's success. How really different was this product from other colas in taste? Further, does it not seem likely that Coca-Cola in the early years varied as much from region to region, perhaps even from fountain to fountain, as it did from similar soft drink products? According to a 1931 *Fortune* magazine story, Coke syrup contained up to 99 percent sugar and water, and the drink itself was made up of one part syrup to five parts carbonated water. Therefore, the ratio in each glass of Coca-Cola was 599 parts sugar and water to one part essential components.[16] The constitution of water varies throughout the country, thus affecting taste. And when Coca-Cola is served at the soda fountain, the server also affects the mix.

These thoughts suggest that the attention paid to the secret formula of Coca-Cola has not been without hyperbole through the years. Alfred Steele, who spent ten years at Coca-Cola before becoming president of

Pepsi in 1950, noted, "Their chemists know what's in our product, and
our chemists know what's in theirs. Hell, I know both formulas."[17] Roger
Enrico, president of Pepsi-Cola at this writing, planned in 1985 to bring
out the original Coca-Cola formula after Coke took it off the market. He
has written that "It didn't take us long to crack the Merchandise 7X
code."[18]

One therefore doubts that the inherent chemical and physical composition of Coca-Cola—the core product—can be given the principal or even
a significant share of the credit for the company's great success. Coca-Cola
had to create its market. If the drink had remained in the hands of John
Styth Pemberton, it would have gone the way of his Extract of Styllinger
and Globe Flower Cough Syrup.

But Coke did not stay in Pemberton's hands.

Coca-Cola As System

Pemberton sold his two-thirds interest in Coca-Cola in 1887 for $283.29,
of which $76 was for advertising paraphernalia.[19] Asa G. Candler ac-
quired some company stock in 1888 and complete ownership by 1891.[20]
Born in Villa Rica, Georgia, in 1851, Candler moved to Atlanta in 1873,
where one of the first places he applied for work was the Pemberton-
Pulliam Drug Company (there was no opening).[21] He was already a
prosperous businessman when he bought the Coca-Cola Company for
$2,300. In 1916, he gave almost all of his stock to his sons, who in turn
sold it to a consortium of banks headed by Atlanta businessman Ernest
Woodruff in 1919. The price was $25 million, two-fifths of it in cash, and
it was the biggest business deal in the South up to that time. Table 2–2
charts the growth of the company until its purchase by the Woodruff
interests in 1919.

Coca-Cola was able to grow as it did because of its success in gaining
national distribution. The obstacles to this achievement were considerable. The product sold for only a nickel, and its ingredients were bulky and
heavy. Further, a beverage such as this was a convenience good *par
excellence.* Coca-Cola may have been selling syrup, but the consumer was
buying the quenching of thirst.[22] It is a rare consumer who will save his
or her thirst for twenty or thirty minutes in order to find a Coca-Cola or

TABLE 2–2

Coca-Cola's Unit and Dollar Sales, Profits, and Industry Growth, 1886–1919[a]

Year	Unit Sales (in thousands of gallons)	Dollar Sales (in thousands)	Before-Tax Profit (in millions)	Total Wholesale $ Shipped in Soft Drink Industry (in millions)	Total Cases Shipped in Soft Drink Industry (in millions)
1886	0.025	$ 0.035			
1887	1.5	1.5			
1888	1.9	2.7			
1889	2.2	3.0		$ 14.4	17.4
1890	8.9	12.4			
1891	19.8	27.8			
1892	35.4	49.5			
1893	58.4	67.8			
1894	64.3	90.1			
1895	76.2	106.7			
1896	117.6	164.7			
1897	163.3	228.6			
1898	214.0	299.6			
1899	281.1	393.5		23.3	28.9
1900	370.9	519.2			
1901	466.4	690.0			
1902	677.5	963.6			
1903	881.4	1,229.0			
1904	1,135.8	1,547.4			
1905	1,549.9	2,064.8			
1906	2,107.7	2,767.4			
1907	2,558.8	3,363.1			
1908	2,877.7	3,830.1			
1909	3,486.6	4,628.2		43.5	41.4
1910	4,190.1	5,505.9			
1911	4,815.7	6,287.9			
1912	5,505.0	7,274.4			
1913	6,767.8	8,837.2			
1914	7,231.6	9,398.3	$2.4		
1915	7,521.8	10,252.1	2.4		
1916	9,715.9	13,182.9	2.3		
1917	12,019.4	16,355.5	2.6		
1918	10,314.7	13,632.9	2.7		
1919	18,730.2	24,291.0	4.6	135.3	112.8

[a]There are a variety of sources for the data in this table. Unfortunately, these sources disagree at numerous points and provide little information concerning the basis for the data they present. The differences with regard to unit and dollar sales are, however, not great enough to raise questions about broad trends. Profit data are difficult to find for the early years. Formal income statements were not presented until 1920. "Before Tax Profit" from 1914 to 1919 is taken from *Moody's Manual of Industrials. Moody's* provides no profit figures prior to 1914. The National Soft Drink Association defines a *case* as 288 ounces.

SOURCES: Coca-Cola *Annual Reports*, 1892–1915, 1917, and 1929 (the 1929 report was published; the others are available in typescript at the Coca-Cola Archives in Atlanta, Ga.); *Moody's Manual of Industrials*, 1921, 387; *Beverage Industry 1985 Annual Manual*, 26.

any other specific soft drink. Since a thirst unquenched by Coca-Cola was a sale lost forever, Coke had to be everywhere, or, in the words of a company executive in the 1930s, "within arm's-length of desire."[23]

What were the means by which Coke's ubiquity was achieved? Five factors stand out: the vision and entrepreneurship of Candler and of his successor, Robert Winship Woodruff; the company's aggressive sales force; the system of franchised bottlers; the advertising program; and the legal right to defend the trademark together with the wit and resources to carry out the defense.

ENTREPRENEURSHIP

Asa Griggs Candler was profoundly devoted to the Methodist Church. He was baptized in June 1869, at the age of 17, and "[f]rom that day on," according to his son,

> the Christian religion became the central purpose of Asa G. Candler's life. His ambition for success and his keen competitive instinct led him to take pleasure in the conduct of his business affairs, it is true. But at no time was the accumulation of wealth an end in itself to him. . . . He had a profound reverence for his Creator, an abiding faith in the revealed word, a complete reliance on the Blood of the Cross, and an unbounded love for his fellow man.[24]

Candler's commitment to religion carried a number of implications for his entrepreneurship. First, he saw a close relationship between faith and business achievement. "Religion in the soul," he said, "raises the productive forces of any life to its highest power. It quickens intellectual facilities, arouses industry and inspires inventiveness. This fact explains why the Christian nations of the world are the richest nations on earth."[25]

Candler believed in Coca-Cola with a fervor rarely matched by the executive of today's diversified firm. In his later years, he said that Coca-Cola's success might appear like "a wonderful romance, but if people knew the good qualities of Coca-Cola as I know them, it would be necessary for us to lock the doors of our factories and have a guard with a shotgun" to control the people who wished to buy it.[26] Candler lavished on Coca-Cola a marketing effort that was not provided for his other products, such as Botanic Blood Balm or Dr. Biggers' Huckleberry Cordial ("The Great Southern Remedy for all Bowel Troubles & Children Teething"). "My experience," he said, "is that the public does not value one's wares higher than [the proprietor himself] does."[27] Candler's commitment to Methodism also meant that the thought of doing business in

Asa Griggs Candler: Owner and Chief Executive of Coca-Cola from 1891 to 1916, Candler's commitment and devotion to his product transformed it from a local brand to a household word all across the United States.

far-flung places was not alien to him. He was involved in nationwide religious work as well as international missionary efforts.

Candler was also an ardent Southerner. The Civil War had been a disaster for his family. Wrote his son:

> The fact of the war and its crushing impact on his family represents a climactic point in my father's life. It carried two of his brothers into uniform and off to far away battlefields. It reduced the standard of living of his father's home from that of near affluence to one of base subsistence. It resulted in financial ruin and loss of everything but the land, almost completely denuded of anything animate or inanimate which might have been of service to marauding bands from both armies. It meant the death-knell of Father's hopes and those of my grandfather for a medical career for him. More than that, it meant that he had . . . almost no formal education beyond the elementary grades.[28]

Despite his Confederate sympathies, Candler readily adopted a national point of view for Coca-Cola. As early as 1892, he made arrangements for its sale in New England and soon thereafter for its manufacture in Chi-

cago and Philadelphia. Coca-Cola was advertised in national magazines
by 1904. In 1909, Candler sent a dirigible plastered with Coca-Cola
advertising over Washington, D.C.

Unlike his top sales and advertising executives, Candler was apparently
neither an inspirational speaker nor a glad-hander. Ross Treseder, an early
Coca-Cola salesman, recalled that Candler

> only came to the sales meetings I attended to greet everybody in the kindest
> southern hospitable manner. I can remember very vividly his coming to the
> last day of the sales meeting when it was about to close and all of us would
> be packing our bags and catching our trains returning to our territories.
>
> In his rather high-pitched voice he wanted to wish us a "God Speed" and
> in closing his remarks he asked all of us to rise and join him in singing "Onward
> Christian Soldiers."[29]

Judging from his early annual reports, Candler appears to have been a
frank and straightforward person with more than a hint of combativeness.
These reports, unmediated by the hand of public relations and reflecting
Candler's basic honesty, are a pleasure to read today. One typical selection
from 1908 follows:

> When I wrote my first annual report, December 2, 1892, I thought all presi-
> dents of industrial corporations made reports in full detail to stockholders.
> Since then I have learned much. I now know that such reports are not often
> given stockholders. I believe they are entitled to know exact conditions and
> how well or bad their investments are being managed. And so we will have
> this report.[30]

Perhaps Candler's most outstanding attribute as an executive was his
superior management of the problem of commitment and flexibility. He
had the ability to change when his judgment told him change was called
for. Although Candler was originally attracted to Coca-Cola because it
cured his headaches, for example, he was astute enough to observe that
customers prized it more as a beverage than as a medication. He was able
to learn from his customers and to reposition the product.[31]

THE SALES FORCE

The sales force was of critical importance in achieving national distribution for Coca-Cola.[32] Coca-Cola under Candler relied heavily on a personal, face-to-face selling approach. Although there are other ways to
reach the customer—such as mass-media or direct-mail advertising—

personal selling has the advantages of high impact on the customer and flexibility. The salesperson can tailor the message to the individual customer, answering questions and responding to objections. At Coca-Cola, management worked to maximize sales force performance in such subtle exchanges. "Sales demonstrations can be staged," explained a Coca-Cola vice-president at a 1923 bottler convention, "one salesman taking the part of a merchant and the other taking the part of a salesman. Questions can be asked, ideas can be brought out, and a general discussion of territories can be gone into."[33]

This customization of the selling message sharply differentiates interpersonal from mass communication. Mass-media advertisement is the lowest common denominator appeal, designed to speak to as many potential customers as possible. This reach is achieved, however, by sacrificing knowledge and awareness of individual needs. Although prior to the broadcasting era advertising was often referred to as "salesmanship in print," the absence of a two-way selling exchange marks advertising as fundamentally different from personal selling.[34]

Shrewd salespersons not only talk but listen. They can bring market intelligence back to the regional office. The Coca-Cola Company was relentless in its desire for market information. "Know thy customers," proclaimed vice-president and director of sales Harrison Jones in a speech to the bottlers:

> Know them intimately. Know them well. Have a daily tab on them, and this is where your duplicate card that you keep in the home office fits in. If a record of purchases is kept tabulated at all times, daily, in your office, you yourself or your sales manager, has constantly at hand a record of what every customer is doing and above all, a record of what he is not doing. It is the pulse of your business, and the only way to feel the pulse of your entire business at one time. It enables you to intelligently analyze and to describe and to prescribe remedies.[35]

Coca-Cola also wanted its sales force to be everywhere. In the view of its executives, every conceivable outlet should carry the product. The Coca-Cola sales force sold not only to soda fountains, where the syrup was mixed with carbonated water on site, but also to bottlers, independent entrepreneurs under contract to Coca-Cola who marketed the beverage in bottled form to retailers. By 1928, the chief executive officer of Coca-Cola, Robert Woodruff, was convinced that the most intensive fountain distribution possible had been achieved: "We can count on our fingers the soda fountains in the United States that do not serve Coca-Cola."[36] For the bottlers, on the other hand, total distribution was a goal that could

never be achieved: "How many people can handle Bottled Coca-Cola?"
Harrison Jones asked the bottlers in 1923. Here was his answer:[37]

Bakers	Grocers
Barbers	Hat-cleaning and shoe-shine
Bowling alleys	parlors
Cafés	Homes
Cigar stands	Hospitals
Clubs	Hotels
Colleges-schools	Ice cream parlors
Confectioners	Markets
Construction jobs	Manicure parlors
Dairy depots	Military organizations
Dancing academies	Parks
Delicatessens	Places of amusement
5¢ & 10¢ stores	Police stations
Filling stations	Pool rooms
Fire engine houses	Railroad offices
Fish, game, poultry, meats	Restaurants
Fraternal orders	Tea rooms
Fruit stands	Telegraph offices
Garages	Telephone offices
General merchandisers	Wiener stands

Jones told the bottlers that their success would be based on their ability
"to make it impossible for the consumer *to escape* Coca-Cola."[38] William
C. D'Arcy, who owned the advertising agency that handled the Coca-
Cola account (and who had been set up in business by Asa Candler and
Samuel Candler Dobbs in 1904), echoed Jones in the same year: "Gentlemen, there is no place within reach, by steps, elevator, ladder, or derrick,
where Coca-Cola can be sold, but what should be reached by a Coca-Cola
salesman, or that salesman should be fired."[39]

Intensive distribution was more than a strategy at Coca-Cola. It was an
obsession. Coca-Cola executives felt that accounts could not be visited too
often. "The trade like to be cultivated," advised Samuel Candler Dobbs,
"they must be cultivated. . . . *See your trade, know your trade, like your
trade,* and they will like you."[40] Said Harrison Jones:

Repetition cuts through. A drop of water will wear through a rock. Continual
chewing will enable you to digest your food. If you keep hitting the nail on
the head it will drive up. Salesmen should keep calling unremittingly on their
prospects.[41]

New York City Salesman: The sales force was of critical importance in achieving national distribution for Coca-Cola. Prior to the acquisition in 1901 of a motorized delivery truck, such as the one pictured here, the force made their rounds on foot and by trolley.

And from William D'Arcy:

> No matter how many times you have talked to a dealer about Coca-Cola, there is always something new to say. Repetition convinces a man. A merchant buys so many different things that a persistent salesman wins an opening where a casual order-taker never makes an impression.[42]

The names of some early salesmen—Charles H. Candler, Asa G. Candler, Jr., Ezekiel Candler, Samuel Candler Dobbs—show that where possible the company made use of Asa Candler's immediate and extended family for sales help (as it did for legal services as well). But a great many more people were needed to achieve the scope and frequency of coverage that Coca-Cola managers envisioned. The seasonal nature of the selling effort during the first fifteen or more years of the company's existence provided a staffing opportunity. Soda fountains were closed during the winter, and the sales force was on the road from four to eight months a year outside the South. Recalled Charles H. Candler:

Probably the most effective salesmen we had were cotton buyers who were not actively engaged in their ordinary avocation during the summer months and were consequently available for what might be termed part-time employment by an institution like the Coca-Cola Company, which felt that it was necessary to put forth intensive efforts only during the summer months. These were men usually of robust health, affable personality and hard workers.[43]

Charles Howard Candler joined Coca-Cola's sales force in 1899, when the company had fifteen salespersons on the road at peak season. He has given us a glimpse of how the company approached the task of sales-force training:

A man employed as a salesman was brought to Atlanta, and after several weeks during the late winter or very early spring was informed and instructed, as opportunity afforded the time, concerning the policies of the Company, its problems and its plans by my father, Mr. Robinson and Sam Dobbs. If he was not already sold on Coca-Cola, he was thoroughly acquainted with its merit, and was afforded the opportunity of watching its manufacture, particular attention being called to the quality of ingredients used; the profit to be derived by a retailer in dispensing Coca-Cola was demonstrated to him; the various pieces of advertising material were displayed to him and he was taught how best to use them. He was also informed respecting a selling plan to both wholesalers and retailers, known as the rebate contract plan, and impressed with our preference that, as far as possible, all sales be made through jobbers. His attention was called to any customers on his proposed route who were not in good credit standing, and specific instructions were given him as to how these customers might be best approached and handled.[44]

An important part of the training process was the sales force convention in Atlanta. The first convention took place in 1905, with twenty-nine people in attendance.[45] Management addressed the salespeople on sales strategy, advertising strategy, and the mission of the company. These meetings were designed to increase the flow of information from the home office about retailer lists, advertising strategy and material, and expenses and from the sales force about customer performance, sales and advertising productivity, and expenses. Equally important, the salespeople had the opportunity to meet and learn from one another.

Moreover, the location of these conventions in Atlanta, where Coca-Cola sales were phenomenal, did not fail to make an impression on the ambitious salesperson. Recalled Treseder of his first convention in 1914:

My first trip to Atlanta was also my first journey to the deep South. I had heard so much about the great popularity of Coca-Cola and of the big volume fountains were selling. Although Coca-Cola was nationally known and available in the Western States that I covered, the sales of Coca-Cola at fountains were "peanuts" as compared to the deep South. . . .

There was a fountain in the Candler building on Peachtree Street very close to my hotel which was dispensing approximately a barrel of Coca-Cola syrup a day, meaning several thousand glasses of Coca-Cola a day. It was unbelievable to me. . . .

To me, one of the greatest impressions I gathered from the other salesmen was the potential possibilities of Coca-Cola in my western territory.[46]

The enthusiasm of such meetings was infectious and enduring. Six decades later, Treseder recalled that on the completion of his first meeting, "I felt like a new man."[47]

The decision to focus all its efforts on one product greatly eased Coca-Cola's sales management problems. The sales force was deployed geographically, and by the 1920s it was organized into a system of regions and districts that other soft drink companies have since copied and still use today. Coca-Cola's traveling sales force dealt solely with soda fountain operators; its mission until 1928 can be stated succinctly: open more accounts.

In the early or mid-1890s (Asa Candler was unclear on the date), the company "undertook to interest certain prominent dispensers in large places all over the country giving to each one who sold a certain amount of Coca-Cola, stock in the company."[48] By the 1900s, the traveling sales force no longer had that particular incentive to offer a prospective customer. They did, however, have premiums to offer to the new account, such as cash drawers, eight-day clocks (i.e., clocks that run for eight days on one winding so that they only need to be wound once a week), and dispensing urns.

Under another promotional plan, a salesperson sold a 5-gallon keg of syrup to a fountain operator for the regular price of $8.75. Then the salesperson mailed to at least 100 names on a list provided by the fountain operator a complimentary ticket entitling the recipient to a free glass of Coca-Cola at the fountain specified. The fountain operator sent the tickets off to Atlanta and received $5 from the company in return. This promotion provides a glimpse of the economics of the Coca-Cola business for the retailer. One gallon of syrup produced 100 glasses of Coca-Cola, which retailed at the fountain for 5 cents each, so a 5-gallon keg costing $8.75 should produce $25 in revenue for the retailer, or a 65 percent gross margin. The plan had a number of inviting aspects from the trade's perspective. First, it reduced the risk involved in getting acquainted with the new product. Second, the plan pulled consumers into the retailer's establishment, thus demonstrating Coca-Cola's power to generate traffic.

From the company's point of view, the promotion gave the salespeople something to talk about to the new accounts in order to overcome the natural skepticism about a new product. One story recounted the trials of a salesman who tried to sell a 50-gallon barrel of syrup to a fountain proprietor who had never heard of Coca-Cola. The proprietor simply laughed at him. The salesman tried again with a 10-gallon barrel, with no result. Finally: "Well how about buying a one-gallon jug? Anybody can sell a gallon of Coca-Cola." Came the reply: "Well, mister, you ain't done it yet."[49] The promotion gave the salesperson the chance to cut price on a one-time-only basis and also to distance the price cut by a number of steps—distribution and redemption of tickets—from the purchase of the Coca-Cola syrup itself. "One of the cardinal principles of the house, which was very thoroughly drilled into all salesmen," wrote Charles H. Candler, "was a positive stand that our card prices must be maintained."[50]

The sales force left the Atlanta conventions armed with lists of towns, their populations, and rosters of prospective customers doing a fountain business therein, including druggists, confectioners, grocers, and restaurateurs. Credit ratings (from Dun's) and purchases the previous year, broken down by month, accompanied the names of these merchants.[51] The sales force visited retailers. The retailers, however, did not purchase direct from the company, but rather from wholesalers.

The salespeople rode into their assigned towns like well-equipped shock troops, heavily armed with quantities of advertising material as well as complimentary tickets and circulars, which they carried with them in a large trunk. They attempted to sell not only syrup, but also glasses with the Coca-Cola trademark and, for a time, Coca-Cola chewing gum and cigars. The gum and cigars met with little success, but the glasses sold better, despite some resistance caused by the trademark.[52] The overwhelming effort, however, was to sell the syrup, to show customers how best to serve it, to reacquaint them with the company's selling plan, to hang advertising signs wherever possible, and to negotiate with the local bill poster. All this selling, promoting, and educating had to be done quickly, since the typical salesperson seldom remained in a town longer than twenty-four hours.[53]

A good deal of the information that we would like to have about sales force management at Coca-Cola has, unfortunately, not survived. We do not know, for instance, how the company established compensation, evaluated productivity, or managed career paths. Indeed, we do not even know how many salespeople the company fielded, except for occasional years. Statistics have survived on jobbers and fountains handling the product; these are presented in table 2–3. The rate of increase in accounts

TABLE 2–3

Number of Jobbers and Fountains
Handling Coca-Cola, 1910–1929

Year	Jobbers	Fountains
1910	543	
1911	659	
1912	808	
1913	930	
1914	950	
1915	1,017	
1916	1,134	
1917	1,173	
1918	1,631	
1919	1,684	75,696
1920	1,871	78,375
1921	—	81,959
1922	2,000	88,246
1923	—	93,984
1924	2,371	98,420
1925	2,312	101,172
1926	2,248	108,038
1927	2,229	—
1928	2,227	107,245
1929	2,182	105,897

SOURCE: Black Book, Coca-Cola Archives, Atlanta, Ga.

slowed during the 1920s. From 1919 to 1924 the total number of soda fountains served increased by more than twenty thousand, or 30 percent. From 1924 to 1929, total fountain outlets grew by about one-third that number.

Robert Woodruff observed not long after he became CEO of the Coca-Cola Company in 1923 that a new sales approach was needed. The object was no longer to gain national distribution. That job had been done. The new goal was to ensure that Coca-Cola stayed on top. The more intensive development of business through existing retailers should therefore replace opening new accounts as the company's primary objective. He explained:

It requires a higher order of merchandising to maintain volume than to gain new volume.

Many salesmen offering slow-moving goods are on the job. Every retailer is continually the object of much strong selling. As a result a peculiar condition constantly threatens the successful product. The retailer may drift into a habit of pushing the various products which obviously need pushing with the thought that an article like Coca-Cola pushes itself.[54]

Woodruff felt that a reorganized sales department was needed to implement this new philosophy. The previous sales structure had provided inadequate supervision for the field force of a nationally distributed product. In the old system, as *Fortune* described it, there was "hardly anything except large stretches of geography" between the salesperson and the home office in Atlanta.[55] With the new approach, control and monitoring would be increased. In place of the former system, in which one sales department with headquarters in Atlanta supervised all selling activities in the United States and Canada, Coca-Cola adopted a decentralized structure. Two subsidiary sales corporations, wholly owned by the parent, were set up for the United States and Canada. The United States was divided into five sales divisions, which were then subdivided into a total of sixteen (increased to twenty by 1929) district offices. The divisions were to be the new focus of attention. Meetings were to be held and agendas set at that level rather than in Atlanta. Woodruff hoped that greater regional autonomy would lead to intensified contact with retail outlets.[56]

In 1927, Woodruff carried out another dramatic change in the sales approach, which he presented in a particularly striking fashion. He called the sales force to Atlanta and announced that the sales department had been abolished and along with it their jobs. At the same time, he told them to attend a meeting the following day concerning their future with the Coca-Cola Company. After what must have been an anxious night for these people, Woodruff announced that the company was creating a service department in which each of them was being offered a job.[57]

The old plans and old formulas for selling no longer applied in the late 1920s, Woodruff asserted, because they were based on the strategy of increasing distribution.[58] Now, however, distribution had been secured. Almost every fountain in the nation had standing orders for the syrup and served it as a matter of course. A salesperson could perhaps push an extra unit of product on the retailers and might even get an order more quickly than otherwise, but

the approach of a salesman, whose object it is to sell [the retailer] more of something he already has and which he will buy anyway when he needs it, is likely to be somewhat tiresome to him and to impress him as a rather useless procedure. He continues as a customer of the company; he may even give the salesman an order then and there. But his feeling toward the salesman, and even toward the Coca-Cola Company itself, is one having within it the elements of resistance. He feels, some way or other, that his interests and ours are somewhat divergent; that we are trying to force on him more of our goods than he really needs or wants at any one time.[59]

Thus, the focus of the Coca-Cola sales effort would shift from selling merchandise to dealers to helping dealers sell merchandise for themselves. The members of the field force were being transformed from salespeople to teachers:

> The serviceman is schooled in the fine points of refrigeration, carbonation and sanitation. He is in no sense a repair man or plumber. But he is able quickly to look over the mechanics of a fountain and point out any faults. The result . . . is a high quality of drink. . . .[60]

Not only the mechanics of serving the product but also such concerns as the optimal arrangement of dealer help advertising now fell within the purview of the new "serviceman."

In changing the focus of Coca-Cola's selling effort, Woodruff was acting on the adage that "The time to make a change is when you don't have to," rather on the one that holds, "If it ain't broke, don't fix it." The company set sales records every year from 1925 through 1930. No one would have faulted it in 1927 for maintaining the sales system that had achieved successive records in 1925 and 1926. But Woodruff anticipated the need for change.[61]

THE BOTTLER NETWORK

The Coca-Cola Company began its corporate history as a manufacturer of a syrup sold to soda fountains located predominantly in drugstores. The fountain proprietors mixed the syrup with carbonated water at the point of sale and sold it to the customer. When bottling of Coca-Cola began is unclear. Some evidence suggests that bottling occurred as early as 1887 in Atlanta, but if so, the original venture was not long-lived.[62]

The company usually cites Joseph A. Biedenharn as the first Coca-Cola bottler. Biedenharn, who operated a family-owned wholesale and retail confectionary business, certainly agreed with this view. In a profile published in the *Coca-Cola Bottler* in 1959, he stated:

> I know it is a fact that I am the first bottler of Coca-Cola in the world because when I began there wasn't anybody bottling at that time. The soda water bottlers didn't want to bother with it; besides, they said, the price for Coca-Cola was too high. They were merely content to make soda water.[63]

Biedenharn first became interested in Coca-Cola in 1890, when Samuel Candler Dobbs, then a Coca-Cola traveling salesman, "placed a five-gallon keg of Coca-Cola syrup on the counter of Joe's store and explained what it was." Biedenharn sold a lot of syrup in the succeeding years and felt he could greatly increase business by "bringing the product to the customer. I wanted to bring Coca-Cola to the country people outside the limits of the fountain."[64]

Biedenharn's bottling operations began in 1894. "I did not say anything to Mr. Candler about it," Biedenharn recalled, "but I did ship to him the first two-dozen case of Coca-Cola I bottled. Mr. Candler immediately wrote back that it was fine."[65] Thus originated one of the Coca-Cola family bottling dynasties. Biedenharn had six brothers, all of whom, with their children, went into Coca-Cola bottling.

The subject of bottling was again raised with the company in the summer of 1899, when two lawyers from Chattanooga, Benjamin Franklin Thomas and Joseph Brown Whitehead, tried to interest Candler in the potential of this form of distribution. The idea of bottling came to Thomas while he was serving as a clerk for the military in Cuba during the Spanish-American War. Piña Fria, a carbonated pineapple drink in bottles, was well received there. Thomas approached Whitehead about the idea, and Whitehead was receptive. He liked to go to baseball games, and he was annoyed that he could not enjoy his favorite drink at the park. If it were bottled, Coca-Cola would be far more accessible to consumers than if it were permanently exiled to soda fountains.[66] Despite the enthusiasm of Thomas and Whitehead, and despite whatever success the Biedenharn operations may have experienced by that time, Candler apparently was not impressed by the idea of bottling.

The reasons for Candler's point of view are not known precisely; perhaps, having been a druggist all his life, he naturally thought in terms of the rest, refreshment, and camaraderie of the soda fountain. Or perhaps he was concerned about safety and purity. The technology of bottling carbonated beverages was still at an early stage. Not infrequently, bottles exploded. The bottle seal most commonly used was the Hutchinson stopper—a cork attached to the inside of the bottle with a wire. This contraption was not effective in keeping the beverage fresh much longer than ten days. Crown Cork and Seal had been marketing the bottle cap since 1892, but the new device did not gain complete acceptance for a number of years.[67]

Despite his reservations, Candler granted Whitehead and Thomas a franchise to bottle and sell Coca-Cola everywhere in the United States except in New England, Mississippi, and Texas, where prior distribution arrangements (such as the one with Biedenharn) had already been made. The contract provided that Thomas and Whitehead would bottle soft drink made from syrup provided by Coca-Cola; Coca-Cola granted them sole use of the trademark on their bottles and furnished labels and adver-

Predecessors of the Crown Closure: Prior to the invention of the Crown seal in 1892—a type of seal which is still in use today—the bottling of carbonated beverages was a chancy venture. Leakage was a major problem. Between 1850 and 1900, dozens of devices for sealing bottles were patented in the United States. An important reason for Asa Candler's underestimation of the potential sales of Coca-Cola in bottles was his long familiarity with the inadequacies of so many of the stoppers pictured above. Stoppers, from left to right, are: (1) Cork; (2) Cork Fastener—1857; (3) Matthews Gravitating Stopper—1865; (4) Codd Ball Stopper—1873; (5) Lightning Stopper—1875; (6) Hutchinson Stopper—1879; (7) Klee Stopper—1880; (8) Bernardin Bottle Cap—1885; (9) Joly Stopper—1885; (10) Twitchell Floating Ball Stopper—1885; (11) Bottle Seal—1885; (12) Crown–1892.

tising matter.[68] This franchise cost Thomas and Whitehead a grand total of one dollar—which was never actually collected. "If you boys fail in the undertaking," historian Watters quotes Candler as having said, "don't come back to cry on my shoulder, because I have very little confidence in this bottling business."[69]

Soon thereafter, Thomas and Whitehead parted company; and Whitehead, realizing that he did not have the $5,000 he needed to set up his own bottling operations, brought in another Chattanooga businessman, John Thomas Lupton. These two firms (Thomas's and Whitehead and Lupton's) set up four more so-called parent bottlers.[70] The primary activity of the parent bottlers soon ceased to be the bottling of Coca-Cola and became instead the franchising of a whole network of bottlers to whom they wholesaled Coca-Cola syrup. It was estimated in 1960 that three-fourths of the fortunes made in Chattanooga derived from Coca-Cola or related businesses, such as the production of bottles, crates, and coolers.[71] Table 2–4 provides data on the number of plants bottling Coca-Cola from 1905 through 1929.

The decision to franchise bottling thus established a second kind of Coca-Cola fortune (the first being the syrup fortunes). A *Fortune* article described the system in 1931:

> The Coca-Cola company supplies parent bottlers with syrup at $1.35 . . . a gallon. Now let us suppose that a bottler puts up 500,000 gallons a year (which is about the production of the New Orleans bottler). This amount of syrup makes about 2,167,000 cases of Coca-Cola, with twenty-four bottles to a case. The retailer pays eighty cents a case, so the bottler receives $1,730,000 on a syrup investment of $675,000. He must, of course, buy his carbonic gas and maintain his bottling plant, but (provided he gets back his empty bottles to refill) he makes on his business a very fine profit. Indeed, his franchise to bottle Coca-Cola is a privilege upon which he can borrow money at the bank, and which he can sell at from $7 to $12 per gallon bottled per year. In other words, our New Orleans bottler has a franchise worth (at a $10 a gallon median figure) some $5,000,000; and a franchise which any New Orleans bank would accept as good collateral.[72]

TABLE 2–4

Number of Plants Bottling Coca-Cola,
1905–1929

Year	Number of Plants	Year	Number of Plants
1905	241	1918	948
1906	201	1919	1,069
1907	268	1920	1,095
1908	290	1921	1,115
1909	374	1922	1,123
1910	493	1923	1,142
1911	611	1924	1,186
1912	691	1925	1,203
1913	504	1926	1,221
1914	562	1927	1,228
1915	636	1928	1,263
1916	948	1929	1,235
1917	1,020		

SOURCE: "The Coca-Cola Company: Distribution of Bottled Coca-Cola," 22 Mar. 1940, Black Book, Coca-Cola Archives, Atlanta, Ga.

Had Candler not franchised bottling, those profit dollars would have found their way to the bottom line of his company's income statement. Moreover, company ownership of the bottling operations would have greatly enhanced the freedom to price and would have facilitated the process of working out coordinated marketing programs. But such considerations were for a distant future. In 1899, the bottling of Coca-Cola did not seem nearly as important or as lucrative as it was to become.

Further, the bottlers did essential work in market development, and their success can be attributed at least in part to Coca-Cola's perpetual licenses. Commitment to the business was heightened by the bottlers' right to sell their franchises if Coca-Cola approved the purchaser or to bequeath them to their children. By 1960, a number of franchises spanned four generations.[73]

Despite his entrepreneurial abilities, Candler failed to foresee the impact of Coca-Cola in bottles. Yet he might not have done better had he foreseen it. Although there has been a marked trend recently at Coca-Cola and in the industry generally toward the purchase of bottlers by the syrup or concentrate manufacturers, it is not clear that Coca-Cola could have expanded so quickly had it tried to do all the work itself.[74]

Perhaps the franchised bottler system was the best method for Coca-Cola to achieve the intensive nationwide distribution essential to its success. One suspects, however, that Candler might not have allowed the two-tiered franchise system to develop had he appreciated the importance of the bottle. In fact, this system has been terminated, and Coca-Cola now owns all the parent bottlers and sells syrup directly to the bottler network. Also, Candler might have been more concerned about payment for the franchise. Coca-Cola literally gave away an element of its distribution system that it has cost the company many millions to buy back. Yet another change might have been in the duration of the franchises. "Perpetuity" is a long time. In 1920, a year after the Woodruff interests took control of the company, they tried to rewrite the bottler contracts to make them terminable at the wish of either party. When the bottlers heard about the plan, they countered by refusing to agree to an increase in the price of syrup. The issue wound up in the courts, which eventually decided that Coca-Cola could pass along higher costs of raw materials to its bottlers in return for agreeing that the bottler contracts were indeed "perpetually perpetual."[75]

The tensions of this distribution system are worth considering. Coca-Cola and its bottlers had one basic goal in common, the sale of Coca-Cola. But for the company, profit resulted from the drink's sale in the glass as well as in the bottle; for the bottler, sales and profits came only from bottled sales. Thus the company to an extent competed against its own distribution system. Many Coca-Cola bottlers believed, in the words of the president of the Coca-Cola Bottlers Association in 1923, that the company

> was their strongest competitor, and in some cases there was actual antagonism. The Coca-Cola Company's salesmen would try to convince customers of the bottlers that it was more advantageous to handle the fountain product, and the bottler would try to convince customers of the Coca-Cola Company that it was better to handle Coca-Cola in bottles.[76]

On the other hand, the bottlers could (and many did) bottle other carbonated beverages—such as soda water—that were not directly competitive with Coca-Cola, though the company discouraged the practice. Speaking for the company, advertising man William D'Arcy estimated that in the early 1920s, one-third of bottler output consisted of drinks other than Coca-Cola:

> Now, some fellow starts a company out of his imagination. He wants to get into the soft drink business. He thinks it is profitable. The first customer he thinks of is the Coca-Cola bottler. . . .
> You know your trade. You understand your credits. You have the plant and you have the trucks to make deliveries. This gazebo waltzes up to the Coca-Cola bottler because the Coca-Cola bottler is a national figure; he is part of one of the best organizations in the country; his credit is good; his customers know him and have confidence in him. This salesman says: "I'll give you a cheaper price per gallon. I'll put twelve salesmen on your trucks and send them out with your salesmen and keep them at it for a week. For one week, mind you, when there are fifty-two weeks in the year. I will send them into your merchant's store whom you give credit and sell this merchant merchandise that won't turn over."
> You wouldn't let a burglar walk into your home and take what he wants! Why does it happen so often that this fellow walks in and walks away with the results of your investment, with your good will? I tell you it is not right— from your standpoint or from Coca-Cola's standpoint—for they are one and the same.[77]

In the management of its bottling network, Coca-Cola tried to convince the bottlers that their interests and the company's were indeed one and the same. To that end, company executives made presentations to the bottlers designed to show that sales by the glass and by the bottle could and did increase together, that one did not take share of a stagnant market from the other.[78] The company also expended considerable effort in schooling the bottlers in how to motivate and manage their own sales forces and how best to utilize the company's national advertising efforts. In 1923, sales vice-president Harrison Jones said that "inevitably the progress of Coca-Cola from now forward will more largely depend on you men, the bottlers, than on any other one branch of the Coca-Cola family."[79] He was right. Since the fountain outlets were becoming saturated, the effort to make Coca-Cola available everywhere would have to focus on the bottle.

Indeed, Jones was more right than he could have known. In 1922 or 1923, the six-bottle carton was first developed. This device proved an important wedge into grocery outlets and into the homes of consumers.[80] If a consumer bought six bottles at a time, the number of times during the course of a year that she or her family made a decision concerning what beverage to buy decreased, and the opportunities for a competitive brand to penetrate Coca-Cola's market were reduced. And with Coca-Cola always in the home of the consumer, consumption was bound to increase. Meanwhile, new coolers were being developed for retail sale of the product, and electric home refrigeration was just around the corner.[81] In 1928, Coca-Cola sales in bottles surpassed fountain sales for the first time.[82]

THE ADVERTISING PROGRAM

"The trade of advertising is now so near to perfection," Dr. Johnson wrote in 1759, "that it is not easy to propose any improvement."[83] Most consumer product marketers in 1900 (and doubtless most today as well) would have taken issue with the good doctor on this point.[84] We are so accustomed today to branded product manufacturers spending heavily on advertising that it takes some effort to realize that such expenditures were new in the 1880s, 1890s, and early 1900s. To be sure, advertising itself is almost as old as communication, but the expenditure of hundreds of thousands and soon millions of dollars on advertising in sustained campaigns year after year by large corporations is a development of the twentieth century.[85]

The corporate advertising manager at the turn of the century could have proposed numerous improvements in the advertising trade as he knew it, Dr. Johnson to the contrary notwithstanding. Perhaps the first would have been better information. The advertising manager would have asked the same six questions that today's managers ask (questions that are still rarely answered to the advertiser's satisfaction):[86]

1. What is it precisely that I should be trying to do with my advertising? Is it designed actually to sell the product? Or rather is my real goal simply

to make consumers aware of the product so that when they see it the salesperson will be able to close the deal at the point of purchase?

2. To whom should I advertise? Whom should I be trying to reach?
3. What should I say to the target market and how should I say it?
4. Where should I place my advertisements to achieve maximum impact?
5. How much money should I spend?
6. How should I measure the extent to which my advertising is working?

Coca-Cola was advertising incarnate. Remember that Frank Robinson chose "Coca-Cola as a name, similar to other advertising names, thinking that the two C's would look well in advertising." Everyone knew from the beginning that advertising would play a big role in this product's future. Coca-Cola advertising was designed not only to sell the product to the end consumer, but also to defend Coke against the many charges that it contained dangerous amounts of cocaine, alcohol, or caffeine.[87]

Coca-Cola advertising was also aimed specifically at the trade, to convince druggists that the company would treat them fairly and well. The company's commitment to consumer advertising was very early used as a talking point in advertising to the retailer. Coca-Cola told the drug trade in 1913 that it would spend over $1 million that year in advertising.[88] The company used consumer advertising to excite the bottlers about their sales prospects, as this passage from Harrison Jones's speech to a bottlers' convention demonstrates:

> Thank God for a Board of Directors and heads of a business that came 100 per cent clean and said, "You need the ammunition, and here she is," and they gave us a million dollars more than we have ever had in this world for sales and advertising. [Applause.] And they could have kept it for profits—but they didn't do it; they gave it to us, and, believe me, with your help and God's help we are going to get them in 1923. [Applause.][89]

The basic goal of Coca-Cola advertising was to make customers think of Coca-Cola when thirsty and to assure them that the beverage would satisfy their thirst better than any other. But how did Coca-Cola define the customer? At whom was its advertising primarily aimed?

An observer today would expect to find in the marketing of a product such as Coca-Cola a market segmentation scheme designed to discover the desires of groups of potential customers and to speak as directly as

Advertising Gallery: "Pretty Girls," such as those pictured (right), presented an ideal of femininity. Young women aspired to be like the girls in the advertisements; young men aspired to date them. And these girls drank Coca-Cola. By drinking Coca-Cola—for only a nickel a bottle—Americans could associate themselves, in their own minds at least, with the world in which winsome girls such as these seemed to dwell.

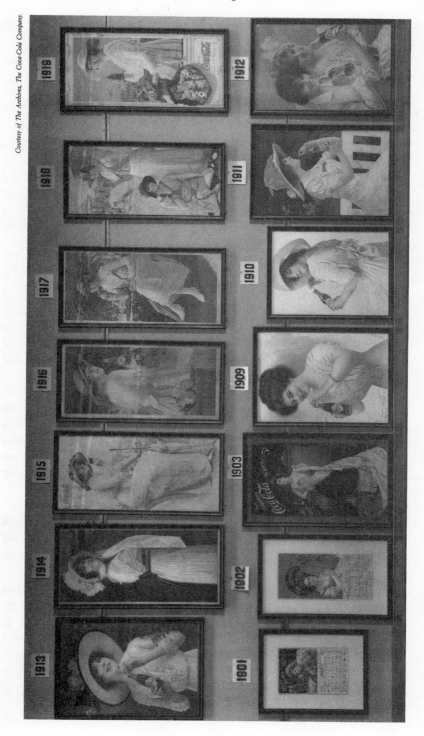

possible to them. Modern market segmentation is, however, something for which the researcher will seek in vain during the early history of this company. Here, for example, is an advertisement that appeared in a national magazine in 1905:

> Coca-Cola Is a Delightful, Palatable, Healthful Beverage. It Relieves Fatigue and Is Indispensable for Business and Professional Men Students, Wheelmen and Athletes Relieves Mental and Physical Exhaustion and, Is the Favorite Drink for Ladies When Thirsty, Weary, Despondent.[90]

This advertisement covers a lot of ground, and it is not atypical. Each time a Coca-Cola executive began a statement suggesting a modern segmentation scheme (e.g., "To formulate a proper selling plan, one must analyze the class of people whom he is desirous of reaching"), another statement followed, suggesting that the segment comprised everyone (e.g., "In other words, our advertising must be an appeal to each class of people").[91] Coca-Cola was looking for thirsty throats. If you had one, no matter who you were, where you were, or what season of the year it was, you were the market.[92]

Coca-Cola spent freely to reach its market. It was ready, as Harrison Jones said, to put into advertising money that could have been profit dollars. From the beginning, Coca-Cola looked on advertising as a long-term investment. In 1892, Asa Candler had noted in his annual report that "We have done very considerable advertising in territory which has not as yet yielded any returns." But even during those years in which Candler "would be grateful if we could only claim solvency," he was willing to wait. "We have reason to believe that it [the advertising that had not yet yielded results] will show good returns during the ensuing year."[93] As table 2–5 shows, Coca-Cola advertising expenditures increased rapidly from 1892 to 1929. Although other companies matched Coca-Cola's advertising expenditures in 1892, by 1901, Coca-Cola's outlays topped $100,000.[94] This sum probably placed the company among the top thirty advertising spenders. And all this money was being devoted to a single product. By 1912, the year that the Advertising Club of America declared Coca-Cola to be the best-advertised product in the United States, advertising expenditures had increased to almost $1.2 million, a figure greater than total sales in 1904.[95]

What did all this money buy? A list of where these dollars went in 1913 is reproduced in exhibit 2–1. The data are startling. Five million lithograph signs! Where were all these signs hung? Were five million more signs put up the following year? Coca-Cola was doing its part to see to

Drink
Coca-Cola

MISS MARION DAVIES

"Spunky, funny, beautiful" is how film critic Pauline Kael described actress Marion Davies (in *The Citizen Kane Book,* 1971). Here she is seen posing for a Coca-Cola advertisement in 1919. William Randolph Hearst found Davies irresistible and she became his life-long mistress. She is best known today through the caricature of her as Susan Alexander in the motion picture *Citizen Kane.*

it (to borrow Harrison Jones's phrase) that it was impossible for the consumer to escape Coca-Cola.

TABLE 2–5

*Coca-Cola's Advertising Expenditures, Percent Increase from Previous Year,
Advertising per Dollar of Sales, and Advertising per Gallon Sold, 1892–1929*

Year	Advertising Expenditures (in thousands)	Percent Increase from Previous Year	Advertising per $ Sales	Advertising per Gallon
1892	$ 11.4		23.0 %	$.32
1893	12.4	8.7 %	18.3	.26
1894	18.5	49.6	20.6	.29
1895	17.7	(4.3)	16.6	.23
1896	23.2	30.8	14.1	.20
1897	52.4	125.7	22.9	.32
1898	43.9	−16.3	14.6	.20
1899	48.6	10.7	12.3	.17
1900	84.5	74.0	16.3	.23
1901	100.3	18.7	14.5	.22
1902	149.6	49.2	15.5	.22
1903	200.9	34.3	16.4	.23
1904	281.0	39.8	18.2	.25
1905	356.6	26.9	17.3	.23
1906	486.6	36.5	17.6	.23
1907	550.8	13.2	16.4	.22
1908	624.1	13.3	16.3	.27
1909	675.0	8.2	14.6	.19
1910	853.3	26.4	12.3	.20
1911	978.3	14.6	15.6	.20
1912	1,182.3	10.8	16.3	.21
1913	1,186.2	0.3	13.4	.18
1914[a]	1,570.9	—	6.7	.22
1915	1,561.1	−0.6	15.2	.21
1916	1,717.9	10.0	13.0	.18
1917	1,608.7	−6.4	9.8	.13
1918	883.5	−45.1	6.5	.09
1919	1,956.6	121.5	8.1	.10
1920	2,330.7	19.1	7.2	.12
1921	1,790.1	−23.2	6.3	.11
1922	1,948.8	8.9	9.3	.13
1923	2,616.9	32.3	10.8	.15
1924	2,413.1	−7.8	9.5	.14
1925	2,625.2	8.8	9.2	.13
1926	2,999.0	14.2	10.0	.14
1927	3,478.5	16.0	10.7	.15
1928	3,455.4	−0.7	10.0	.14
1929	3,832.4	10.9	9.8	.14

[a]The advertising data from 1914 are taken from one of the Black Books in the Coca-Cola Archives. Those data for the years prior to 1914 did not agree with the annual reports. The latter were used for 1892 to 1913. However, from 1914 to 1929 the only source is the Black Book data. There is no figure for percent increase from the previous year in 1914 because of this discontinuity.
SOURCES: Coca-Cola *Annual Reports*, 1892–1913; and "The Coca-Cola Company—Advertising Expenditures in Dollars," Black Book, Coca-Cola Archives, Atlanta, Ga. The reader should be warned that there are numerous estimates for advertising expenditures during the years covered by this table. The ones used here seem reasonable.

TRADEMARK DEFENSE

The problem of "bogus substitutes," "unscrupulous pirates," "miserable little substitutes, little mushroom beverages that rise up at every morning's milestone and wither before the day is done," and "contemptible, white-livered hound[s]," as company organs variously described them in the 1890s, had plagued the Coca-Cola Company from the beginning.[96] Retailers, bottlers, and manufacturers all over the nation tried to cash in on

EXHIBIT 2–1

Advertising Material Distributed by the Coca-Cola Company in 1913

Units	
200,000	4-head cutouts for window display
5,000,000	Lithograph metal signs from 6" × 10" to 5' × 8'
10,000	Enamel metal signs 12" × 36", 18" × 45"
60,000	Fountain festoons
250,000	Special signs for bottlers 12" × 36"
50,000	Cardboard cutouts for window display
60,000	4-head festoons for soda fountains
10,000	Lithograph metal display signs
20,000	Lithograph metal display containing reproduction of bottles
50,000	Metal signs for tacking under windows
200,000	Fiber signs for tacking on walls of refreshment stands
2,000,000	Trays for soda fountains
50,000	Window trims
250,000	5-head window displays and mirror decorations
1,000,000	Japanese fans
50,000	Christmas wreaths and bell decorations for fountains
50,000	The Coca-Cola Company song
1,000,000	Calendars
50,000	Thermometers
10,000,000	Match books
50,000,000	Doilies (paper)
	24-sheet posters for billboards 10' × 20'
	Oil-cloth signs for storefronts
10,000	Large calendars for business offices
144,000	Pencils
	Transparent signs for windows and transoms
20,000	Blotters
10,000	Framed metal signs for well displays
5,000	Transparent globes, mosaic art glasswork
	Art glass signs
25,000	Baseball score cards
	Celluloid display cards
$300,000	Newspaper advertising
	Magazine, farm paper, trade paper, religious paper ads
	Other forms of advertising

SOURCE: Testimony of Samuel Candler Dobbs as preserved in the Coca-Cola Archives, Atlanta, Ga.

Coca-Cola's reputation and consumer recognition in a bewildering variety of ways.[97]

The most common problem was caused by companies that tried to convince the customer that their product was essentially the same as Coca-Cola and a court—in the suit that inevitably followed—that their product was essentially different.[98] Here is a partial list of brand names against which the company took action:

Taka-Kola	Afri-Cola
Chero-Kola	Star Coke
Espo-Cola	Co Kola
John D. Fletcher's Genuine Coca and Cola	Coke-Ola
Takola	Kos-Kola
Klu-Ko Kola	Cafa Cola
Crescent Coca Cola	Sola Cola
A.D.S. Ext. of Coca and Cola	Carbo-Cola
Caro-Cola	Celro-Zola
Coke	Celery-Cola
Koke	Okla-Cola

Some of these brands suggested by their very names the segmentation strategies contemplated by their producers. Thus Afri-Cola was aimed at the African-American market while Klu-Ko Kola apparently targeted the bigot market.[99] In 1926, a business journalist reported that there had been more than seven thousand cases of trademark infringement against Coca-Cola.[100]

Protecting the trademark was a multifaceted activity. It included prosecuting those who adopted names such as those in the preceding list. It also meant navigating the treacherous course between the charge that the name Coca-Cola was merely descriptive—a generic phrase not worthy of capitalization that any producer could use to describe his wares—and the charge that the name was deceptive, depriving the company of the right to be protected.[101]

The most important date in the long history of Coca-Cola's defense of its trademark was 6 December 1920, the date of the victory over the Koke Company of America in the Supreme Court. Coca-Cola had sued Koke for trademark infringement and won in Federal District Court only to see the decision reversed in the Ninth Circuit Court of Appeals. Harold Hirsch, the firm's general counsel and a law partner of Asa Candler's brother, litigated Coca-Cola's case before the Supreme Court. Writing for the majority was Oliver Wendell Holmes, Jr.:

Since 1900 the sales have increased at a very great rate corresponding to a like increase in advertising. The name now characterizes a beverage to be had at almost any soda fountain. It means a single thing coming from a single source, and well known to the community. It hardly would be too much to say that the drink characterizes the name as much as the name the drink. In other words Coca-Cola probably means to most persons the plaintiff's familiar product to be had everywhere rather than a compound of particular substances. . . . [W]e see no reason to doubt that, as we have said, it has acquired a secondary meaning in which perhaps the product is more emphasized than the producer but to which the producer is entitled.[102]

In the view of the Supreme Court and of millions of consumers as well, Coca-Cola had, by 1920, succeeded in establishing its brand. The process of decommodification had been completed.

Even if Coca-Cola meant more to the consumer than "a compound of particular substances," the company still had to employ chemical tests to determine whether the beverage being sold at a soda fountain was Coca-Cola or a substitute. Protection of the trademark also included ensuring that suppliers, such as fountain operators, did not substitute a brand that was more profitable for them to serve when the consumer asked for Coca-Cola. Given the number of soda fountains in the United States, this problem presented a detection challenge. To discover which fountains may have been cheating, the company hired teams of investigators to order Coca-Cola where substituting was suspected.

Yet another aspect of trademark protection concerned how and where the name Coca-Cola was used. "It's amazing how few books there are that don't mention Coca-Cola," an executive once commented.[103] The company encouraged employees to read widely and to flag possible trademark violations in the process. Was the spelling correct? Were the words capitalized? This was not mindless worry. Should the company not take care in this area, the chances were increased that it would lose its protected trademark.

Coca-Cola As Concept: Robert Woodruff

Gradually, beginning about 1914, Asa Candler started to lose interest in Coca-Cola. Advertising manager Frank M. Robinson retired that year, thus terminating an enduring and happy partnership. New federal taxes and rules limiting executives' latitude in managing the assets of their firms left Candler feeling constrained. As his son put it, "He could no longer conduct his business in the way he believed it should be conducted to assure its best progress and to realize its potential greatness."[104] A major, ongoing irritant was the litigation both to preserve the company's trademark and to defend it against federal prosecution instigated by the Food and Drug Administration concerning its use of caffeine.[105] Yet another factor was Candler's election to the mayoralty of Atlanta in 1916. On Christmas of that year, just before taking office, Candler divided among his wife and five children almost all of his Coca-Cola stock. The death of Candler's wife in February 1919 plunged him into a depression from which he apparently never fully recovered. He spent much of the decade that remained of his life in a state of painful confusion. He was informed only after the fact of the sale of the company in September 1919 to a consortium of entrepreneurs headed by his neighbor, Atlanta financier Ernest Woodruff.

Woodruff, described by *Fortune* as "gruff, much feared . . . , relentless," was a deal maker. "He originally made money . . . by assembling small companies into big ones, capitalizing the whole at greater than the sum of the parts, and taking a generous cut on the deal."[106] The price for Coca-Cola was $25 million, $10 million in cash and the rest in preferred stock. Woodruff proceeded to issue a half million shares of new common stock, which he and his associates bought up for $5 a share. By the end of World War II, each share was worth $900 (adjusting for splits) and had generated $475 in dividends.[107]

The company's onward march was not without detours. Indeed, Coca-Cola's performance soon after World War I gave those associated with it deep cause for concern. Samuel Candler Dobbs, the new president, made a major purchase of sugar at $.28 a pound in 1920. The price soon collapsed to $.07, and eventually to under $.02. These fluctuations almost bankrupted Woodruff and his partners, who had to borrow over $20 million to stay in business.[108] Also in 1920, a dispute arose with the bottlers that lasted eighteen months because the company wanted both to raise the price of syrup and to change the terms of the bottler franchise. The bottlers claimed fraud and bad faith on the part of the company, and they took their complaints to court.[109]

Meanwhile, unit and dollar sales were softening ominously, as table 2–6 indicates. For what must have been the only time in the company's history, a complaint was published in an *Annual Report* (for 1921) about the "attitude of many bottlers who allowed themselves to become discouraged and get into a state of lethargy insofar as pushing the sale of Coca-Cola was concerned."[110]

TABLE 2–6

Coca-Cola's Unit and Dollar Sales,
1919–1922

Year	Unit Sales (in millions of gallons)	Dollar Sales (in millions)
1919	18.7	$27.3
1920	18.7	32.3
1921	15.8	28.5
1922	15.4	21.1

SOURCES: Coca-Cola *Annual Reports* and *Moody's Manual of Industrials,* 1920, 1922, 1923, and 1929.

If we recall Frederic William Maitland's dictum that things now in the past were once in the future—if we remember, in other words, that in 1923, when Ernest Woodruff with the support of the Coca-Cola board of directors prevailed upon his son, 33-year-old Robert W. Woodruff, to leave his vice-presidency at White Motors in Cleveland to become Coca-Cola's CEO, no one knew what Coca-Cola was to become so soon thereafter—we realize that during these crisis years the game appeared to be over. A *Fortune* article later recalled that: "It seemed then that Coca-Cola had perhaps reached its peak. Weak from losses on sugar and having suffered drops in gallonage sales for three successive years, Coca-Cola looked indeed as if it might at last have reached senescence."[111] So intense was the crisis that a decade and a half afterward—long after Coca-Cola had made millions of dollars for her own family and many others—Ernest Woodruff's wife, Emily Winship Woodruff, could still say, "I never wanted Ernest to buy that company and I've been sorry ever since that he did."[112]

Robert W. Woodruff was not cast in the Horatio Alger mold. In the words of W. C. Bradley, chairman of Coca-Cola's board in the 1920s and a heavy investor in the company, "Bob's grandfather made a lot of money and kept it, Bob's father made a lot of money and kept it, Bob has made a lot more than either of them and kept it. A *wonderful* family."[113]

Robert Woodruff was born in Columbus, Georgia, on 6 December 1889. In the six-plus decades from his accession to Coca-Cola's presidency in 1923 to his death in 1985 at the age of 95, Woodruff was the company's chief executive, *éminence grise,* icon—he was the company's great man.

Despite his family's wealth, the younger Woodruff did not enjoy an easy road to success. His relationship with his father appears to have been a difficult one. Ernest Woodruff "constantly needled" him and "with one hand [would give] him many advantages, such as a 10,000-mile trip in the private rail car of his railroad friend C. A. Wickersham, but with the other [would take away his] cash allowance."[114] Woodruff attended but did not graduate from Emory University in Atlanta. His father refused to honor his college debts, and to pay them off he got a job as a laborer in a foundry. From there he went to the General Fire Extinguisher Company, where he soon became a salesman.

Selling turned out to be Woodruff's special talent. He was

> tall, dark-haired, dark-eyed, quiet, and self-assured. He was not the shake-hands-with-my-friend drummer who expects to be discounted, but the rare and more valuable salesman who can act naturally and make a person feel at ease before he gets to the matter at hand.[115]

By one acquaintance, he was described as "a *retirin'* showman." Another remarked: "His personality is so *gratifyin'* men actually like to be out-smarted by him."[116]

Woodruff's next move was to one of his father's combinations, Atlantic Ice and Coal. While there, in the early 1910s, he bought a fleet of White Motor trucks to replace horse-drawn wagons. His father was upset by the expense of the transaction, but Walter White, president of the trucking concern, was sufficiently impressed by Woodruff's negotiating skill to hire him. Woodruff was thus vice-president and general manager of White Motors when he was summoned back to Atlanta to do something about Coca-Cola.

One of the things that Woodruff did not do was change the product. The unchanging nature of the core product and the consistency of advertising appeals used to sell it are among the most remarkable aspects of Coca-Cola history. Coca-Cola experienced major changes in distribution and packaging from 1886 to the Depression, but the product did not change. Its advertising was also basically consistent. The 1925 slogan "Six Million a Day" is not that different from the one used in 1917, "Three Million a Day." As late as the 1950s, the company was proclaiming on television that "Fifty million times a day, at home, at work, or on the way, there's nothing like a Coca-Cola, nothing like a Coke."

Coca-Cola is distinctive in the constellation of consumer products. All major consumer durables sold between 1886 and 1929 experienced substantial changes in their core product, and these changes have con-

Robert Winship Woodruff, the dominant personality at Coca-Cola from 1923 until his death in 1985:
Woodruff's strategy was founded upon his belief in a single, unchanging product. Diet Coke was not
introduced until 1981, the year Woodruff retired as Chief Executive Officer. New Coke appeared
on the market only after Woodruff's death.

tinued through the twentieth century. Automobiles, radios, cameras,
phonographs, and the host of electrical products whose introduction was
just over the horizon in 1929—such as televisions, air conditioners, and
dishwashers—underwent dramatic changes in the course of any given

decade. Indeed, some of these products, driven by both technological and market considerations, changed every year. Yet, as a *Fortune* article commented in 1945, "Unlike the auto or refrigerator or electrical-goods maker, Bob [Woodruff] would be properly horrified at changing his."[117] Such rapid change was not confined to the world of technology-intensive hard goods. Any products with a high fashion content, including apparel and such semidurables as luggage and furniture, were in a constant state of flux. Even food products were changing, especially with the creation and development of quick freezing during the Depression and World War II.[118]

Although Coca-Cola was remarkable in its unchanging core product, it was not unique. Other consumer products, such as some soaps and detergents, remained essentially the same for years. Yet it is worth noting that most of these were manufactured by companies that were constantly changing their overall product offering. Hence, though a bar of Ivory soap may have remained unaltered between 1886 and 1929, Procter & Gamble as a company did not. It marketed an increasing variety of soaps, and foodstuffs as well.

Coca-Cola also experimented with product diversification at the turn of the century, trying to sell Coca-Cola Chewing Gum and Coca-Cola Cigars.[119] Management, however, decided to stick with what it knew best and to stay away from other markets. Through the 1960s, well into the era of the multiproduct firm, Coca-Cola consistently opted not to exploit its superb distribution system and advertising economies to market other convenience goods.

The company's ability to succeed with a single, unchanging product in the tumultuous world of twentieth-century consumer marketing leads to speculation about the true nature of Coca-Cola. It was, of course, a beverage; but, as we have argued, its core nature was not special. It was also a service, but the quick quenching of thirst could be provided by many other products.

Roberto Goizueta, CEO of Coca-Cola from 1981 to this writing, said in 1988:

> There is not another company in the world like the Coca-Cola company, not one. I'm not saying we're better, I'm not saying we're worse. I am saying that there is none other like it. If proof is needed, all you have to do is go back again to the summer of 1985 [the time of the abortive formula change]. It was then that we learned that if the shareholders think they own this company, they are kidding themselves. The reality is that the American consumer owns Coca-Cola.[120]

TIME
THE WEEKLY NEWSMAGAZINE

WORLD & FRIEND
Love that piaster, that lira, that tickey, and that American way of life.

Coca-Cola Makes the Cover of *Time* Magazine: Although Robert Woodruff had decided by the late 1920s that it would be necessary to expand internationally, World War II opened the way for rapid growth of existing plants and expansion into new territory. During the years that followed the war, Coca-Cola became "the Global High Sign." The company's achievements were recognized with a cover story in *Time* in May of 1950. Opponents of American influence abroad sometimes specifically objected to what they labeled "Coca-Colonization."

How did Coca-Cola achieve this unique status?

Robert Woodruff's answer was, "We've always tried to be decent in our advertising. We've tried to practice what I guess they call the soft sell. . . . We've tried to do with our advertising what we always try to do inside and outside the company—to be liked."[121] Coke was your friend, your good friend, always there when you needed it. Not only was Coke your friend; when you drank it, you became friends with other Coke drinkers. And they were the right kind of people—well-dressed, well off, happy.

There was also a luxurious aspect to Coca-Cola. It was a mystical, dark compound of magical ingredients with indeterminate powers. But the miracle of the product was that Coca-Cola made this luxury available to everybody for only 5 cents. Americans like equality; but they have always tried to achieve it by leveling up, not by giving anything up.[122] A luxury, yes . . . but a democratic luxury.

Thus a key aspect of Coca-Cola's competitive advantage lay with neither the product nor the service but with the concept that had found its way into the hearts and minds of American consumers. Woodruff understood this better than anyone, as his direction of the company during World War II was to illustrate. Soon after the attack on Pearl Harbor, during which four Coca-Cola coolers were shot up at Hickham Field, Woodruff announced that Coca-Cola would be available to all members of the armed forces, wherever they might be stationed.[123] In the process, he managed with remarkable success to identify this product with America and Americanism. Consider the following passage from a letter written by an American private in Burma during World War II to his aunt:

> To my mind, I am in this damn mess as much to help keep the custom of drinking Cokes as I am to help preserve the million other benefits our country blesses its citizens with. . . . May we all toast victory soon with a Coke—if flavored with a little rum, I am sure no one will object.[124]

Could such a letter have been written about any other product?

Robert Woodruff succeeded with Coca-Cola so well in part because he understood the cultural resonance the product had achieved.[125] After his arrival in 1923, he guided the company back to solid ground. His achievement is illustrated by the data in table 2–7.

An admirable record. How was it achieved?

Coca-Cola was a mature product in a mature product category by 1930. It was over forty years old. We have already seen how, in the soda fountain segment, where both the trade and its patrons were thoroughly familiar with Coca-Cola, Woodruff redefined the role of the sales force. In this case, he emphasized what he described as "the pull of better merchandis-

TABLE 2–7

Coca-Cola's Unit and Dollar Sales and Profits
After Taxes, 1923–1930
(in millions)

Year	Units	Sales	Profit
1923	17.3	$24.3	$ 4.5
1924	17.5	25.4	5.7
1925	20.1	28.6	7.9
1926	21.2	30.1	8.4
1927	22.8	32.5	9.2
1928	24.2	34.7	10.2
1929	27.0	39.3	12.8
1930	27.8	41.3	13.5

SOURCE: Coca-Cola *Annual Reports,* 1923–1930.

ing" rather than "the push of sales pressure."[126] On the other hand, in those markets where growth potential existed, the company moved forward in the spirit of what might be called vigorous conservatism. Potential sales of Coca-Cola in bottles were virtually without bounds, and the company worked creatively with its bottlers to help them develop this business. Important innovations during the 1920s included new coolers for vending the bottle, the six-bottle carton, and increased penetration of grocery stores.

Expansion abroad was also of great importance. Foreign operations can be traced to the nineteenth century, but it was only under Woodruff that systematic expansion was undertaken. He was, as he explained, taking a long-term view of the company's well-being:

> The opening of foreign markets is a costly undertaking and during the early years of development promises to parallel our domestic experiences with regard to the protection of our trade-mark and the development of consumer acceptance with the manifold problems involved. Successful prosecution of these undertakings will require time, courage, and patience, as well as large expenditures.[127]

But Woodruff felt it worthwhile to develop the foreign business as opposed "to adopting a policy that might result in increased net earnings for the immediate future at the expense of the Company's later and continued growth."[128]

By 1929, Coca-Cola was on sale in seventy-six countries, more than twice the number only three years previously. Export sales grew 118 percent in 1927, 82 percent in 1928, and 32 percent in 1929.[129] Perhaps the most encouraging news was from Canada, where sales increased 20

Coca-Cola on Guam: During World War II, Coca-Cola made a big push abroad. It was Woodruff's policy to make the product available for a nickel to all members of the armed forces, wherever they might be stationed. By 1943, General Dwight D. Eisenhower called for the installation of ten separate bottling machines in different localities, each equipped to produce twenty thousand bottles per day, to meet the demand for Coca-Cola. Our military leaders much preferred to see our soldiers and sailors consuming "soft" rather than "hard" drinks. The bottling plants followed the battle fronts, and by the end of the war, Coca-Cola had, in the eyes of some at least, come to represent America itself.

percent in 1926, 35 percent in 1927, and 33 percent in both 1928 and 1929.[130] In the words of a securities analyst in 1930:

> The increase in Canadian business has been phenomenal. Entirely under company management, the product has been distributed in a foreign country within the course of a few years only, to a point where it has attained a per capita consumption in the large cities of Montreal, Toronto and Winnipeg, which is in excess of the average for the United States where Coca-Cola has been sold for over forty-three years.[131]

If the largest Coca-Cola bottling plant in the world in 1928 was in New Orleans, the second largest, with an annual output of almost forty million bottles, was in Montreal. The company saw such statistics as proof that, as the 1928 *Annual Report* stated, "Contrary to a generally prevalent belief, our experience in marketing Coca-Cola indicates that climatic, geographical, and racial factors exercise relatively small influence upon our sales over a reasonable period of time."[132]

By the early 1930s, Wall Street analysts had come to appreciate the remarkable performance of the Coca-Cola Company. Here are some of the points that seemed to make the deepest impression:

- Sales and profits had increased steadily since 1923. Both had, by 1929, set records in five consecutive years.[133]
- Profit after taxes in 1929 was equivalent (after dividends on class A stock) to $10.25 a share on the outstanding one million no-par common shares. Earnings could have been considered higher because $2.2 million was deducted for contingent and miscellaneous operating reserves. Had this been added back, earnings per share would have been about $12.50.[134]
- Income and expenses had been managed with skill, system, and predictability.[135]
- Almost $40 million in sales and over $12 million in profits (with conservative accounting) were generated in 1929 with an investment in property, plant, and equipment of only $6.3 million.[136] Gross sales equaled 6.2 times the value of this investment. Earnings (with the special reserves discussed above added back) equaled 2.4 times total plant investment.[137]
- The company's current ratio was 17.7 to 1.[138]
- As one analyst explained, a holder of Coca-Cola common "possesses an advantage over stockholders in most companies having large tangible assets, for he does not have to wait his turn at the end of a long line of senior security holders, because neither the Coca-Cola Co. nor its subsidiaries have any funded debt."[139]
- There was no labor problem because there were very few laborers. *Barron's* reported in 1932, "Manufacture is simple, and the Atlanta plant, which makes approximately 7,000,000 gallons of syrup annually, employs only about 75 laborers, chiefly unskilled, many of them making containers."[140] In the approaching era of labor strife, Coca-Cola was in the virtually unique position among manufacturers of being able to hire almost a complete new labor force in a day.
- Coca-Cola's low price of 5 cents put it within reach of nearly every consumer, and repeat purchases occurred quickly because the product could be consumed rapidly. It therefore was not greatly affected by general economic declines.[141]
- The company was uniquely important to the trade through which it sold its product. *Barron's* noted, "Evidently, of every 100 persons entering a drugstore, 61 patronize the soda fountain, and of these, at least 22 buy Coca-Cola. These startling figures . . . impress [the retailer] with the public

preference for Coca-Cola, and discourage his active pushing of any competitive drink."[142]

· Management had a proven track record. "The success which this company
has attained is a remarkable tribute to its management. It shows that it
has been progressive and efficient."[143]

As for competition, all agreed that there simply was no other product
in Coca-Cola's class. Eleven hundred trademarked soft drinks were said
to have come and gone since the 1880s, while Coca-Cola flourished.
Coca-Cola was viewed by trade analysts as "virtually a monopoly."[144] The
ubiquity of Coca-Cola, both as a product and in advertising, they believed,
"created an asset in the trade name 'Coca-Cola' of very great value. This
is an asset which could not readily be duplicated."[145]

In July of 1924, Robert Woodruff asserted that the fundamental reason
for Coca-Cola's unique position in the commercial world

> lies in the fact that Coca-Cola was placed on the market at 5 cents at a
> time when the nickel was adequate to pay for ingredients of the highest
> quality, despite an infinitesimal volume. Thus it was possible to establish
> the highest standards of purity, and this fact coupled with sound principles
> in merchandising has enabled Coca-Cola to survive hundreds of carbonated
> beverages. . . .
> This feat could not be duplicated today without enormous capital.[146]

By 1929, sales of the Coca-Cola Company and its subsidiaries were
$39.3 million. The company's total assets were $55.1 million (counting
the $21.9 million carried on the books for "formulae, trade-mark, and
goodwill"). The company was among the 175 largest in the United States
in assets and among the 125 largest in sales.[147]

The Coca-Cola Company manufactured one product—syrup for the
beverage that gave the firm its name. In 1929, this syrup was produced
at 13 plants in the United States, Canada, and Cuba. It was warehoused
at 38 sites, from which it was distributed to 105,000 fountain retailers by
2,200 jobbers and to some 600,000 bottle retailers by 1,250 bottlers. The
company sales force operated out of 5 regional offices, 20 district headquarters, and 150 sales territories in the United States. Company "service-
men" traveled 2.2 million miles to call on retailers in 1929.[148] If ever a
manufacturer's brand had achieved national distribution, Coke was it
indeed. This small-ticket item with such an unfavorable ratio of value to
weight and bulk was available in more than 700,000 different locations
in the United States, Canada, and Cuba. And Coca-Cola's empire
stretched beyond the seas, where the drink was available in more than

seventy countries. Coke may well have been the most conveniently available product in the world during the 1920s.[149]

In its product category, Coca-Cola was in a class by itself. In a 1920 consumer survey conducted under the auspices of the New York University Bureau of Business Research, it was mentioned by more of the 1,024 college students polled than any other soft drink brand, and by more than four times as many as the runner-up, as indicated in table 2–8. Coca-Cola achieved this recognition level not only by a ubiquitous physical presence but also by a massive advertising campaign.

Coca-Cola ranked 55 in a list of advertisers purchasing space in a selection of thirty nonfarm and nontechnical nationally circulated magazines in 1929. The company spent $515,750 to buy advertising space in those publications that year; the leader, Procter & Gamble, spent $3.6 million (with sales of $202 million).[150] Numerous companies ranking above Coca-Cola at that time, including Procter & Gamble, Colgate-Palmolive-Peet, General Foods, and others, spread their advertising over many products. Coca-Cola's total budget was devoted to just one product. Moreover, a list including only thirty magazines hardly does justice to the full advertising presence of Coca-Cola. The company customarily spent

TABLE 2–8

Number of Mentions per Soft Drink Brand in a 1920 Survey

Brand	Mentioned by Men	Mentioned by Women	Total
Coca-Cola	186	167	353
Cliquot Club	60	25	85
Bevo	62	13	75
Hires	17	34	51
Moxie	25	6	31
Whistle	14	16	30
Howdy	—	26	26
Beech-Nut	6	—	6
Welch	5	2	7
Miscellaneous brands	69	61	130
Names apparently not brands:			
Ginger ale	—	12	12
Grape juice	4	10	14
Pop	3	6	9
Sarsaparilla	—	5	5
Blanks	61	129	190
Total	512	512	1,024

SOURCE: George B. Hotchkiss and Richard B. Franken, *The Leadership of Advertised Brands* (New York: Doubleday, Page, 1923), 216.

four to five times more on signs, point-of-purchase displays, and various other promotional devices than on advertisements in the print media.[151] These signs, displays, and other paraphernalia do not constitute national advertising in the same sense that a magazine campaign does. Yet they were everywhere. As early as 1895, the company's *Annual Report* claimed, Coca-Cola was "sold and drunk in every state and territory in the United States."[152] But even on the basis of national magazine advertising considered alone, the company was in a class by itself when compared to its direct competition, as the data in table 2–9 indicate.

All this effort was not without results at the consumer level. The company sold nearly 27 million gallons of syrup in 1929, which translates into an annual consumption of 27 bottles and glasses per person in the United States—an all-time high.[153]

By the time of the Depression, the first-mover advantages cited by Woodruff seemed more formidable than ever. The distribution system was running smoothly. The company was hurt by the Depression, but only briefly. By 1935, when Coca-Cola was the highest priced industrial listed on the New York Stock Exchange, profits were well over $15 million.[154] The company had proven that it could cope not only with the Depression but also with the repeal of Prohibition, which some had thought was going to deal Coca-Cola a major setback.[155]

How could one compete with a product and a company like this?

TABLE 2–9

Advertising in Thirty Nationally
Circulating Magazines by Coca-Cola and
Its Competitors, 1929

Product	1929 Advertising Expenditure
Beverage bottlers	$157,500
Canada Dry	144,000
Cliquot Club ginger ale	95,800
Coca-Cola	515,750
Hires soft drink and extract	57,350
Mineral water and ginger ale	29,800
Orange Crush soft drink	27,500
Rexall soft drink	2,500
Sanitary straws	24,000
Vermouth	13,081
Vichy Celestins	7,375

SOURCE: *National Markets and National Advertising* (New York: Crowell, 1930), 102.

The Competitor

In 1931, when Coca-Cola was the envy of the world of soft drinks and one of the most worry-free profit machines in the history of business in the United States, Pepsi-Cola was declared bankrupt for the second time in its history.[156] In 1987, PepsiCo, Inc., with sales of over \$11 billion, ranked 29 in *Fortune*'s list of the nation's 500 largest corporations.[157] One analyst asserted in 1986 that PepsiCo "has emerged as perhaps the single best consumer products company that exists today."[158] Coca-Cola's sales in 1987 were \$7.7 billion, which placed it 54 in the *Fortune* 500.[159]

Both companies were diversified by the mid-1980s. About 70 percent of Coca-Cola's sales and almost 85 percent of its profits, however, were still derived from soft drinks, with the remainder coming from the food and entertainment divisions.[160] The variety of soft drinks available from the company had increased dramatically since the 1930s, when Coca-Cola was available either at the fountain or in the famed 6½-ounce, hobble-skirted bottle. By 1985, the consumer could purchase Coca-Cola, Caffeine-Free Coke, Coca-Cola Classic, Diet Coke, Caffeine-Free Diet Coke, Cherry Coke, Sprite, Diet Sprite, Tab, Caffeine-Free Tab, Mello Yello, Fanta, Fresca, Mr. Pibb, and others in a great range of sizes, in cans or bottles, and in different kinds of vending machines as well as through the restaurant and fast-food trade.[161] The distinction between fruit juice and soft drinks was broken down with the introduction of such products as Minute Maid Orange Soda, in response to Pepsi-Cola's Slice.[162]

Thirty-nine percent of PepsiCo's 1985 income and 31 percent of its profits were derived from soft drinks.[163] It too had a wide variety of soft drinks: Pepsi-Cola, Diet Pepsi, Mountain Dew, Slice, and others in a truly bewildering variety of packages and with or without various ingredients, such as caffeine.[164] PepsiCo's soft drink offering accounted for 27 percent of the sales of the \$39 billion domestic retail soft drink business in 1985, up from 21 percent a decade earlier. During the same years, Coca-Cola's share had increased from 33 to 39 percent.[165] Thus, Pepsi's dream of reaching and surpassing Coca-Cola in the soft drink business has yet to be achieved.[166]

Nevertheless, Pepsi's success has been remarkable. Coca-Cola had been a virtual monopoly in the nationally distributed cola business when Pepsi-Cola was bankrupt. But by 1985, Pepsi-Cola had succeeded, where thousands of other soft drink producers had failed, in giving Coca-Cola all the competition it could handle. Indeed, Pepsi-Cola in 1985 had the largest sales of any individual soft drink brand in the United States.[167]

The monopoly was now a duopoly. How had this happened?

Pepsi-Cola: The Early Years

Like Coca-Cola, Pepsi-Cola was invented by a southern druggist. Caleb D. Bradham was born in Chinquapin, North Carolina, in 1867.[168] Bradham's lifelong ambition was to practice medicine; but after his second year of medical school his father's business failed, and he was forced to find work. For two years he taught school in New Bern, North Carolina, but his dream of practicing medicine lived on; and when the chance came for him to buy the local drugstore, he did so.

Bradham's two years of medical education qualified him to become a pharmacist. In addition to preparing prescriptions, he also liked to mix the various nonalcoholic beverages that he sold at his soda fountain. From making drinks according to directions found in pharmaceutical publications, Bradham soon moved on to creating entirely new mixtures. Sometime during the 1890s, he began offering a mixture that his friends labeled "Brad's Drink" in his honor. By 1898, Bradham was calling it "Pepsi-Cola" in recognition of his belief that the drink could relieve dyspepsia (upset stomach) and the pain of peptic ulcers.[169] Believing that the drink had promise as a business proposition, Bradham hired a manager to run his drugstore, filed for registration of the trademark with the U.S. Patent Office in 1902, and set about to make his soft drink company grow.

Grow it did. Operating out of the back room of his drugstore, Bradham mixed and sold 2,000 gallons of Pepsi-Cola in the first three months after the formation of the Pepsi-Cola Company at the end of 1902. Total sales for 1903 came to 7,968 gallons, all of which were sold to soda fountain operators. Bradham managed advertising as well as production and sales. The first known advertisement for Pepsi-Cola appeared in the February 25, 1903, issue of the New Bern *Daily Journal*. The tiny notice read:

Pepsi-Cola
At Soda Fountains
Exhilarating, Invigorating
Aids Digestion

Pepsi-Cola's advertising budget in 1903 totaled $1,888.78.[170] That same year, Coca-Cola spent over $200,000 in advertising and sold over 880,000 gallons of syrup.[171]

Although dwarfed by Coca-Cola, Pepsi-Cola grew quickly. In 1904, Bradham moved out of the quarters he had been renting since leaving the back room of his drugstore and bought Bishop Factory in New Bern for $5,000. He equipped this factory with machinery not only for manufacturing syrup but for bottling it as well. Unlike Asa Candler, Bradham early saw the potential of bottling. In addition to his own bottling works, he began to franchise other entrepreneurs to bottle his syrup. The network grew speedily: 40 bottlers in 1907; more than twice that many the following year; and by 1910, 280 bottlers operating in twenty-four states.

The scale of the operation also increased rapidly. A new building was completed in 1908—one so grand that it was featured on postcards of New Bern—and motorized trucks began to replace mule-drawn delivery wagons. The following year a New York advertising agency was hired to professionalize the company's advertising, but "the material they turned out still smacked of the Gay Nineties."[172]

Sales skyrocketed, passing the 100,000-gallon mark in 1907, only five years after Bradham set up the business. Bradham, the once penniless schoolteacher, was by 1915 the president and general manager of a company with assets surpassing $1 million. He was active and popular, even mentioned in the press as a gubernatorial candidate for North Carolina. A touching photograph has survived of an exceptionally handsome Caleb Bradham at the age of 46, trim and proud in the uniform of captain in the North Carolina Naval Militia, with his young son seated at his feet.[173]

In 1920, however, disaster struck the Pepsi-Cola Company as a result of fluctuations in the price of sugar following World War I—the same price movements that disrupted even the far better established Coca-Cola Company and led to a change of ownership.[174] With price controls lifted, sugar prices soared to over $.25 per pound, two and a half times what the industry could accept and still keep its retail prices at $.05 per unit. Like Samuel Candler Dobbs at Coca-Cola, Bradham bought heavily at these ruinous prices, only to see Pepsi lose over $150,000 as a result of price declines in 1921. Bradham tried desperately to find the working capital needed for a comeback. He obtained a mortgage from an insurance company, and he sold off real estate and various other assets. He finally surrendered control of the firm to the Wall Street investment house of R. C. Megargel and Company. By January 1922, with Pepsi-Cola's balance sheet showing current assets of $53,008 and current liabilities of $249,536, Bradham was out of the soft drink business forever. He returned to his drugstore in New Bern for a time but soon sold out. A series of other disasters overtook him during the next decade, and he died in obscurity in February 1934, at the age of 67.[175]

By July 1923, Roy C. Megargel had acquired the business, trademark, and goodwill of the Pepsi-Cola Company from its previous creditors for $35,000. Megargel closed the North Carolina operation; and from 1923 to 1931, Pepsi-Cola concentrate was manufactured and shipped from Richmond, Virginia. But apparently not very much was shipped—or at least not enough to turn Pepsi-Cola into a force to be reckoned with. Megargel was a financier in a company that needed a marketer. Although he took an interest in the company and apparently invested substantially in it, his efforts were met by a wall of massive public indifference.[176] The company continually lost money, and it could not survive the Depression. Thus, on 8 June 1931, Pepsi-Cola was bankrupt for a second time.

The lack of evidence forces us to leave unanswered the question of why Pepsi-Cola grew as quickly as it did early in the century. The product must have tasted good. Bradham did not sell 100,000 gallons in 1907 solely to friends who liked to gather at his New Bern drugstore. Distributed in half the states in the Union by World War I, Pepsi in its early years—though still only a fraction the size of Coca-Cola—could be termed with only slight exaggeration "a nationally important entity in the soft-drink field."[177]

If Pepsi-Cola seemed to have been making an impression in the 1910s, it was thoroughly engulfed in a miasma of consumer apathy following World War I. The company lost money even during the decade of Prohibition, which was supposed to be beneficial for soft drinks. Pepsi-Cola was not even mentioned in the study of brands conducted at New York University in 1920 (see table 2–8), and it appears in no compendia of advertising expenditures.[178]

In the 1920s, Pepsi-Cola simply was not in the traffic. There was no indication that Pepsi rather than, say, Canada Dry Ginger Ale would become the long-awaited "second Coca-Cola."[179] Canada Dry's sales in 1928 were more than $12.5 million, over one-third those of Coca-Cola.[180] Its ginger ale was distributed only east of the Mississippi at this time, but management had ambitions to open further territories around the nation and to increase its business internationally as well. In 1928, Canada Dry showed total assets of $7.6 million.[181] When Pepsi-Cola was bought out of bankruptcy for the second time in 1931, the price was either $10,500 or $12,000 (depending on which source one chooses to believe).[182] The company was worth only a third of its previous bankrupt value eight years earlier.

The Road to "Twelve Full Ounces"

In 1931, the Pepsi-Cola Company was purchased by Charles G. Guth in a complex financial transaction worked out in association with, and at the instigation of, Roy Megargel. Guth was born in the mid-1870s and apparently had spent most of his life prior to the Depression as a fairly successful entrepreneur in the soft drink and confectionary industries. He joined Loft, Inc., a chain of confectionary stores, in 1929; and the following year he became president.[183]

Loft's performance had been mediocre for years. In 1921, its net after-tax profits were $0.73 million, and in 1925 its sales had reached $8.2 million. In 1928, on the threshold of what was to prove a decade of management tumult, sales were only $7.3 million, and net profit after taxes had dropped to $0.19 million.[184] One year later sales dropped again, by almost $30,000, and Loft lost over $150,000. On 1 April 1929, a new management team took control of the company and found itself, as they reported, "confronted with financial and operating conditions of a most unsatisfactory nature requiring the immediate development of ways and means for placing the finances of the Company on a sound basis and for increasing sales to such a volume that the business would again be placed on a profitable basis."[185] The new managers raised money in the capital markets, closed stores, and developed new manufacturing processes for the candies Loft sold.

Whether or not this program would have proven successful we will never know, for Guth took over the company in a proxy fight on 18 March 1930. Pepsi executive Milward W. Martin's later description of the organizational arrangements Guth instituted at that time speaks volumes about the new CEO. Guth's board members were all handpicked, and at least one was required to tender a signed resignation in advance. Guth's salary was fixed at $25,000 plus 1 percent of increased sales, with no requirement for increased profits. He had the power to name the salaries of all other officers and employees and to change them without notice. He delegated as little authority as possible, dealing directly with everyone from board members to clerks.[186]

Guth had every intention of using his new power to enrich himself. He had much need of enrichment. He was almost continuously in financial difficulty during the first half of the 1930s. Banks were calling in his loans; he was borrowing on his insurance; he was substituting Loft for the banks as his creditor.[187] Though he did not have much money, Guth did have Loft. And even though it was not doing very well, Loft did have assets of over $13 million in 1931. The company's sales that year exceeded $14 million, although profits came to only $0.37 million (one remembers the terms of Guth's employ).[188]

The Delaware Court of Chancery, before which the question of the ownership of Pepsi-Cola was litigated in 1938, described Loft in 1931 as a "substantial company." It operated 115 stores in major cities in the Middle Atlantic states; and its subsidiaries, the Happiness and Mirror chains, operated approximately 85 additional stores. These stores sold candy, ice cream, soft drinks, and light lunches.[189] Loft also had a large manufacturing plant across the river from Manhattan in Long Island City that turned out many of the products sold in the stores and did a wholesale business with other retailers as well.[190]

The Pepsi-Cola Company had first come to Guth's attention in 1928, when Megargel tried, unsuccessfully, to interest him in it. As chief executive of Loft in 1931, Guth renewed his interest in Pepsi from a different perspective, as a memorandum that he wrote to one of his vice-presidents attests: "Mr. Robertson: Why are we paying the full price for coca-cola? Can you handle this, or would you suggest our buying Pebsaco [Pepsi-Cola] at about $1.00 per gallon? C.G.G."[191]

Guth felt that Loft had a right to a discount on Coca-Cola. In 1929, 1930, and the first eight and a half months of 1931, Loft was moving an annualized average of 31,584 gallons of Coca-Cola syrup, or more than 1 percent of Coca-Cola's sales.[192] Robertson replied: "We are not paying quite full price for Coca-Cola. We pay $1.38 instead of $1.50, but we pay too much. I am investigating as to pepsi-cola. V.O.R."[193] Although Robertson was correct in saying that Loft received a discount, his numbers were incorrect. Loft was paying $1.48 for the syrup, the standard wholesale price of which for the big buyer was $1.60. (As the volume purchased declined, the per-gallon price of Coca-Cola rose as high as $2.00.)[194] Guth's point remained, however. If Loft kept its retail fountain prices constant, purchased Pepsi instead of Coke, and suffered no decline in sales as a result, a substantial additional sum would fall to the bottom line.[195]

The week after Guth's memorandum to Robertson, Pepsi-Cola was declared bankrupt. Megargel quickly contacted Guth to suggest that the two combine to buy Pepsi out of bankruptcy. Guth agreed, using $7,000 of Loft's money as part of the $12,000 purchase price.[196] Having expressed a mild interest in Pepsi syrup, Guth suddenly found himself owning the entire company.

Saying that Guth owned the whole company was, however, not saying much. Pepsi in 1931 was, in the words of the Delaware Chancery Court, "a corporation which in point of actual fact was a mere shell of a corporation with practically nothing in the way of assets except a formula and trademark and the franchise as a corporation to engage in the work of erecting a business thereon." The company, furthermore, "completely lacked any executive force of its own to direct its affairs." As if all this were not enough, when Guth finally sampled a drink compounded from the formula he had purchased, he declared it "unsatisfactory."[197]

Pepsi, however, did have an asset in Guth—an owner who was the chief executive of another company whose resources he was happy to exploit for Pepsi's benefit. Loft supplied Pepsi with personnel from common laborers to skilled workers to white-collar employees to executive talent.[198] Loft's laboratory was at Pepsi's disposal. Indeed, it was in Loft's laboratory that a Loft's chemist, Richard Ritchie,

> experiment[ed] with the formula with the view of producing a drink which would have a competitive resemblance to Coca-Cola. Ritchie spent about two or three weeks . . . trying out different changes in the formula. When he thought he had a result which was satisfactory, he notified Guth who said it was about right.[199]

Pepsi also had in Loft a customer. From 1931 through 1933, Loft purchased $50,300 worth of Pepsi syrup, almost half of Pepsi's sales.[200] The results at the fountain were predictable. Coca-Cola was well known, whereas Pepsi was not. Precisely how much Loft lost by selling Pepsi instead of Coke is not known, but one account estimates that the soft drink volume of Loft slipped from an annual average of over 31,000 gallons to 21,000 gallons.[201] The complainants against Guth in the 1938 Delaware Chancery Court case calculated that from 1931 to 1935, Loft's total loss in profits came to $322,631.[202]

As late as 1933, Loft's Pepsi-Cola experiment was considered a "complete failure." Pepsi-Cola, in the judgment of the Delaware Chancery Court in 1938, "was in a condition of undoubted insolvency"; it was "confessedly an unadjudicated bankrupt."[203] Guth made an unsuccessful attempt to sell the company to Coca-Cola that year.[204]

Sometime late in 1933, however, Guth made a product policy decision that reversed the failing company's fortunes decisively. He decided to price 12-ounce bottles to the trade in such a way that they could be retailed at the same price as the standard 6- or 7-ounce bottle. The Pepsi customer would thus receive twice as much product for the same price as the Coke customer—and this in the middle of the Depression.

Although Pepsi was primarily a fountain product when Guth bought it, soon thereafter he began bottling operations, both company-owned and franchised. By 1932, he was experimenting with a 12-ounce bottle for 10 cents, but "the sales volume was so totally unimpressive as to be discouraging."[205] Perhaps a 6-ounce bottle for 3 cents compared to the competition's 5-cent bottle was the answer, an idea that was considered but rejected. Finally, out of a series of conferences in late 1933, the concept emerged, apparently inspired by the presence of the bottle itself, of selling the 12-ounce bottle for 5 cents. Bottles were to be sold to candy jobbers for 50 cents per 24-bottle case. The jobbers were to resell them to their retailers for 75 cents per case, and the retail price was to be 5 cents per bottle or $1.20 per case. Credit for the idea and for the pricing structure must go primarily to the chief Loft candy salesman, Frank Burns.[206]

The product took off. By 30 June 1934, Pepsi-Cola had, in the words of the Delaware Chancery Court, "turned the corner."[207] Guth was not the type to hesitate when there was money to be made, and so he moved with vigor to ensure that Pepsi would not be merely a local brand. Enfranchising bottlers as quickly as possible was the key, because Pepsi did not have access to the capital necessary to develop a fully company-owned bottling operation. Fortunately, there were enough bottlers looking for additional brands to carry to make rapid franchising possible.[208]

One of the first to be called, in November 1933, was Joseph LaPides, whom Guth had known through previous business dealings in Baltimore. LaPides did not at first believe that a 12-ounce bottle could be retailed profitably for a nickel. Guth persisted and promised to cover any losses LaPides might incur. By April 1934, LaPides was selling a thousand cases of Pepsi-Cola in one day.[209] Soon thereafter he became a Pepsi representative, with responsibility for enfranchising bottlers in one of four huge territories. Territorial representatives received a royalty of 2 cents per case of Pepsi sold in their area. For at least two of those contracts, the remuneration quickly soared above a half million dollars a year.[210]

In 1936, Pepsi posted net after-tax profits of nearly $2.1 million. In 1937, profits reached $3.2 million, and the company had a network of 313 domestic franchised bottlers, five company-owned bottling plants, and the beginnings of a foreign business.[211]

By 1935, Guth was clearly getting bored with Loft, where things continued to deteriorate. Profits were $65,340 in 1933 and $21,280 in 1934; the following year the company lost $229,551.[212] In October 1935, Guth tried to lower wages and salaries in an economy move. In response, angry employees surrounded his office, and Guth was able to leave only with the assistance of a police escort. Guth asked himself why, owning 91 percent of the Pepsi-Cola Company (now worth a fortune), he needed this kind of aggravation. He couldn't come up with an answer, so he resigned from Loft to devote himself full-time to Pepsi.

Guth departed from Loft under a complicated agreement that he hoped would soon allow him to oust his successor, James W. Carkner, and to replace him with an executive to whom he could give orders. Carkner declined to play the assigned role. He knew that the only chance for Loft to reverse its deteriorating position and for him to survive professionally was to obtain financing for Loft, to keep Guth's influence and appointees out of the company, and, most important, to obtain control for Loft of Guth's 237,500 shares of Pepsi-Cola stock.

Although the chances of achieving even one of these goals seemed very slim in November 1935, Carkner achieved all three. The developments leading to this result are complex, but we can focus here on those elements most important to our story. Carkner contracted with two New York law firms to develop Loft's case for Guth's Pepsi stock in return for $10,000 to cover expenses and a contingency fee of one-quarter of everything recovered.[213] Financing came from the Marine Midland Trust Company and also from a Wall Street investment firm, the Phoenix Securities Corporation. With Phoenix came the remarkable Walter S. Mack, Jr., who was to serve as Pepsi-Cola's CEO for more than a decade.

But before we proceed to Walter Mack's years at Pepsi's helm, we should first analyze Pepsi-Cola's transformation. How did Pepsi move from unadjudicated bankruptcy to a valuable prize, able to command the time and effort of talented lawyers and the capital of banks on the chance that they might obtain a share of it?

The first piece of the Pepsi puzzle is Charles G. Guth himself. Pepsi did not simply survive and grow by itself in response to the needs of an impersonal market. It was envisioned and energized by Guth. It was Guth's refusal to do business on Coca-Cola's terms in the first place that saved Pepsi from the dustbin of business history. Negotiation expert Chester Karrass has written about people who are "simply less willing to be dominated than others and would rather do without than be exploited" even if an agreement is in their best interest.[214] Judging from how Pepsi-Cola performed for Loft from 1931 at least through 1933 (and probably well beyond—remember that it was Pepsi in bottles that took off, not Pepsi at the fountain), both Loft and Coca-Cola would have been better off if Loft had purchased Coke at the asking price. It was a so-called win-win situation. Yet Guth did not give Coke what was best for both of them because he refused to be dominated by an unyielding negotiating opponent. Moreover, Guth had the fundamental insight that Pepsi would never succeed as a me-too product. Coke was simply too strong. A dramatic gesture was needed, and what more dramatic gesture could there be than offering twice the product for the same price? That idea had originated with Frank Burns, not Guth; but Guth saw its value.

Indeed, the supposedly impregnable wall of the "brand beyond competition" was breached with remarkable ease. The battering ram was neither a magical taste nor a mystical advertising appeal; it was value, an especially attractive attribute in the middle of the Depression.

Guth immediately recognized that once a hole was poked in the enemy's battlements, he had to move quickly to consolidate Pepsi's position. He, like Candler long before him, had a nationwide vision. He was determined to make his brand grow, even at the price of royalty agreements that in hindsight appear overgenerous. Guth had been around long enough in the confection and soft drink industries to know some of the young, aggressive, bold distributors—like Joseph LaPides. Guth also moved to develop a system that would bring active distributors into his camp in areas where he did not know them personally.

Quick expansion was important. Competing on price—unlike, for example, pouring a fortune into an advertising campaign—was a strategy that Coke did not want to copy. As market leader, it did not want to educate the public to expect twice as much for the same price. New entrants could copy the Pepsi strategy because they had nothing to lose. That was why it was important for Pepsi to expand aggressively.[215]

Another key to Pepsi's success was Loft or, more precisely, Guth's willingness to exploit Loft for Pepsi's benefit. He not only used Loft's property and executive personnel, but he also viewed Loft as a captive market of considerable size for Pepsi. Pepsi at this time was more a retailer's than a manufacturer's brand. And it was probably also helpful that Loft was so prominent in New York City, where a large market could be reached without the daunting problems of transporting soft drinks over long distances.[216]

The final key to the rise of Pepsi, ironically enough, was Coca-Cola. The leader was so profitable—its price umbrella was so high—that a competitor could afford to sell twice as much cola for the same price and still make a considerable profit. Further, Coca-Cola was already confronting a problem that would bedevil it in later years. The company's extensive distribution system had developed incrementally over many years, and the network was composed of firms that operated with varying degrees of efficiency. Coca-Cola wanted to protect all the players, including the inefficient, and thus its system was becoming inflexible.

The company was, moreover, attempting to maintain prices during the greatest depression in American history. Prices of so many commodities dropped so sharply that the cola market was being invaded by intertype

competition. Decreases in citrus and milk prices, for example, were leading to greater sales of orange juice, orange drinks, and milk shakes. Soda
fountains were changing as well; they were turning into luncheonettes. A
survey of luncheonettes toward the end of the 1930s indicated that many
were devoting less display space to Coca-Cola and were instead using that
space to advertise their own daily food specials.[217]

Coca-Cola was making some adjustments, such as developing new
methods of distribution like the automatic vending machine, which was
installed in the territory of the Coca-Cola Bottling Company of New York
in 1937.[218] And, of course, it advertised vigorously. Price competition,
however, was another matter. Because of its success, because of its profitability, and because of its rigidity, Coca-Cola unwittingly helped call
Pepsi-Cola into being.

From Buccaneer to Entrepreneur

Walter Staunton Mack, Jr., who was to succeed Guth as chief executive
of Pepsi-Cola in 1939, was born in his parents' brownstone in New York
City on 19 October 1895. Mack's father, who was in the woolen business
in New York, made a good living, though the family was not wealthy.
Mack was raised in New York City, attending Public School 87 and
DeWitt Clinton High School. He graduated from Harvard in 1917, and
from there took an officer candidate's course at Annapolis, where he
graduated third in a class of three hundred. After active duty in World
War I, Mack returned to New York. He worked for a time in his father's
company, became involved in politics and community affairs, and married
a wealthy woman. Toward the end of the 1920s, he took a position with
a small investment trust called Chain and General Equities, which invested in such chains as Safeway and Kroger.[219]

Mack caught the eye of financier Wallace Groves, who made him chief
operating officer of Groves's Phoenix Securities Corporation in 1932 or
1933.[220] Mack told Groves that he "was really only interested in reorga-
nizing and rebuilding companies" rather than in buying and selling securities. Groves said that his interest also lay in that area, which was why he
had chosen for his company the name Phoenix, "the legendary bird that
grows out of its own ashes."[221]

Mack was visited at Phoenix in 1936 by James W. Carkner. The new
CEO of Loft needed money to stave off bankruptcy. Phoenix agreed to

provide funds in exchange for options to purchase Loft stock at an attractive price. Loft's situation was becoming critical, as sales continued to drop and losses to mount. But the suit against Guth for control of Pepsi made Loft attractive to a gambling man.

Loft's suit against Guth came to trial in November 1937, and the judge issued his opinion the following September. That opinion was an unmitigated victory for the Loft forces. Guth elected to appeal, precipitating a managerial morass in which three directors represented the Guth forces, three the Loft forces, and a seventh served as a disinterested mediator.

Mack, one of the directors, became president, but Guth stayed on in the position of general manager. Here is Mack's description of how that arrangement worked out:

> I remember my first day in the office at Pepsi's plant in Long Island City. It was a chilly day in October, but I was far from chilly. The general manager, Mr. Guth, had assigned the president, me, an office which was a cubbyhole directly above the boiler room. I looked around the space, which didn't take very long, there was nothing there. No paper, no pencils, no nothing. I called my secretary and said I wanted some office tools so that I could start working, and she said she was sorry but that Pepsi employees had been instructed by the general manager not to supply us with anything, since there wasn't anything in the court order requiring them to give me a pencil. A little later in the day I wanted to go to the men's room but it was locked, and I was told that only Mr. Guth had the key, which he handed out personally to whomever he saw fit. Well, I knew that was hopeless, so I found a little restaurant around the corner and used their john for the next six months.[222]

Mack let neither this rather dispiriting situation nor the constant uproar at directors' meetings bother him; he concentrated instead on "straightening out the company."[223]

Guth was finally forced out of both Pepsi and Loft in 1939, when it was discovered that he had purchased another cola company (Noxie-Cola) and had started spiriting away people in the Pepsi organization to run it. Soon thereafter, the Delaware Chancery Court's decision against him in *Loft* v. *Guth* was upheld in the Delaware Supreme Court.[224] Charles Guth thus passed into history, last seen trying to get Guth Cola—a 12-ounce bottle selling for 3 cents—off the ground in Pittsburgh. He did not leave Pepsi empty-handed, however. He took with him an estimated $3 million—an impressive accomplishment in Depression values for someone who had begun the 1930s flirting with bankruptcy.[225]

Guth's departure was an important step forward for Pepsi. In order to get started, the company had needed someone like Guth who could think the unthinkable and who was willing to skirt the edge of propriety, to put the best face on his activities, to make something out of nothing.

But Guth was not the man to make the company grow. He seems to have been in business strictly for himself, with no concept of institution building. He was untrusting and, judging from his actions at Loft and during the period when he was general manager at Pepsi, not always trustworthy. Guth never could have understood what Coca-Cola knew so well—the social role that soft drinks, and especially a cola, play in the United States and abroad. With Walter Mack, on the other hand, Pepsi acquired as its chief executive a more legitimate entrepreneur. Mack had access to high society, he was active politically, and he knew the money men. He was a very persistent individual. He combined a well-developed sense of propriety with the spirit of a street fighter. Walter Mack was precisely what Pepsi needed in 1939.

What was the Pepsi-Cola Company when Mack took it over, and how did it stand in the world of soft drinks? Reliable data on Pepsi sales in the late 1930s are difficult to obtain. However, profit data are available; and, as table 2–10 shows, they tell a happy story. Although neither Pepsi-Cola nor Coca-Cola reported sales figures publicly in the 1930s and 1940s, they did provide figures for "gross profit on sales," or sales minus cost of goods sold. In 1941, gross profit on sales for Pepsi was just over $26 million.[226] If gross profit on sales bore the same relation to profits during the years 1936 through 1940 as it did in 1941, then we can estimate Pepsi's gross profit on sales for these six years as shown in table 2–11. Pepsi's balance sheet on 31 July 1939, showed total assets of $13.9 million, of which $4.6 million represented fixed assets and $1.5 million trademarks, formula, and goodwill.[227] One estimate asserted that the combined total investment of Pepsi and its bottlers in 1939 was $20 million.[228]

The company had enfranchised 341 bottlers by 1939, but their morale was low. Many of the bottlers had little confidence in the mercurial Guth, and they had many other problems as well—"lack of funds, lack of facilities, lack of equipment, lack of personnel," in the words of Joseph LaPides.[229] "In those days," LaPides recalled, "many bottlers were 'hungry.'" They wanted to increase their volume, because "they could then give their route salesmen a higher wage for selling more merchandise off the same trucks."[230]

Bottler relations were clearly going to be a key factor in Pepsi's future, and Mack at first excelled in this aspect of the business. By the end of 1940, the company had enfranchised 415 bottlers. That number increased by 54 the following year. "[T]here is scarcely a franchise bottler of Pepsi-Cola in the United States who has not made some improvements in

TABLE 2–10

*Pepsi-Cola's Profit Before
Taxes, 1936–1941*

Year	Before-Tax Profit (in millions)
1936	$ 2.1
1937	3.2
1938	4.0
1939	6.0
1940	8.5
1941	14.9

SOURCES: Pepsi-Cola *Annual Report,* 1941, 2. The reader should be warned that there are as many estimates for Pepsi-Cola profits during these years as there are sources for them. See, for example, Milward W. Martin, *Twelve Full Ounces* (New York: Holt, Rinehart & Winston, 1962), 82, 84, 104; Ko Ching Shih and C. Ying Shih, *American Soft Drink Industry and the Carbonated Beverage Market* (Brookfield, Wis.: W. A. Krueger Co., 1965), 70–71; "Pepsi-Cola Co. (and subsidiaries)," *Commercial and Financial Chronicle* 149 (14 Oct. 1939): 2375–76. The trends in all these sources are, however, similar; and the company's *Annual Report* would appear to be the most reliable source.

equipment, trucks and manufacturing facilities during the year," observed the Pepsi-Cola *Annual Report* for 1941.[231] In some instances that investment was made possible by loans from Pepsi.[232]

In our discussion of Pepsi's success during its early years, we asked why people bought the product and found that to be a question without an easy answer. From 1933 until 1946 (when economic forces began to

TABLE 2–11

*Pepsi-Cola's
Estimated Gross
Profit on Sales,
1936–1941*

Year	Gross Profit on Sales (in millions)
1936	$ 3.6
1937	5.6
1938	7.0
1939	10.4
1940	14.8
1941	26.0

SOURCES: Calculated from Pepsi-Cola *Annual Report,* 1941, and Table 2–10.

compel Pepsi to abandon the nickel price for a 12-ounce drink), the appeal of Pepsi-Cola is more easily identified. Pepsi attracted the price-conscious consumer.[233] "During the Depression," Pepsi-Cola advertising executive Philip Hinerfeld recalled, " 'Twice as much for a nickel too' meant a hell of a lot. . . . [T]he availability of the 12-ounce bottle of this good quality cola versus the 6-ounce bottle of Big Red" made Pepsi's success possible.[234]

If a firm is able to supply a product at a cost lower than the competitor, serving the price-conscious segment can be a successful strategy. Some great American industrial fortunes—those of Rockefeller, Carnegie, Ford, and Hartford—were built on this principle. The problem is that price-conscious consumers view the product in question as a commodity. Charles Revson once remarked that "in the factory we make cosmetics. In the store we sell hope."[235] There are limits to what can be charged for chemicals, whereas there is no standard markup on hope. Price buyers are, in the unlovely term of more than one trade, "whores," since money is the only desideratum. Pepsi had proven by 1941 that it could build a profitable business by selling for less than Coca-Cola. But what would happen if the company was no longer able to sell twice as much as the market leader for the same price? To what extent does a consumer products company permanently taint itself by basing its appeal on the most prosaic buying motive and perhaps as a result attracting the most prosaic—and least prestigious—consumers?

These were questions with which Coca-Cola—"Big Red"—did not have to concern itself in 1940. If Pepsi-Cola remained a "dynamic speculation," Coca-Cola was adjudged a "solid investment."[236] As table 2–12 indicates, Coca-Cola was not unscathed by the Depression. Sales volume dropped 21.8 percent from its record high in 1930 to 1933. Profit before taxes and net profit declined 16.2 and 19.8 percent, respectively. Coca-Cola, of course, was not alone. During those years the GNP declined 22 percent (28.9 percent from 1929), and the CPI (consumer price index) declined 22.5 percent (24.6 percent from 1929). From 1933 to 1941, however, Coca-Cola's recovery was most impressive. Gross operating profit increased almost threefold. If the company's gross margin in 1941 matched that of 1939 (36 percent), then sales that year were over $133 million, more than four times those in 1933. Analysts remained puzzled "that a company should be able to earn in a year an amount equivalent to three times the total physical assets of the business. Certainly it is most unusual. . . ."[237] This puzzlement notwithstanding, Coca-Cola was one of the darlings of Wall Street. Commented *Barron's* during the so-called Roosevelt Recession year of 1938: "You could have bought Coca-Cola

Pepsi and Pete: In the 1930s, the Pepsi-Cola Company introduced a pair of "crazy-cop" comic strip characters, known as Pepsi and Pete, to advertise their product. The madcap adventures portrayed in the strip usually climaxed with Pepsi and Pete downing a Pepsi-Cola to give them the necessary energy to complete some heroic act, such as rescuing pretty women marooned on a rock. Note the final frame, with its boast of 12 full ounces for only a nickel.

stock at the top price of 154½ in 1929, carried it through a major depression and the latest business recession, sold it at the low this year and you would have had, including dividends, a profit of approximately 225%."[238]

Coca-Cola had not maintained its great success through magic or blue smoke and mirrors. The company by 1940 boasted a network of 1,084 bottling plants operated by an efficient and well-trained corps of bottlers, many of whom had been involved with the product for over a generation and some of whom had been made millionaires by it. The bottlers serviced almost a million outlets, and Coca-Cola's jobbers sold syrup to a hundred thousand soda fountains.[239]

Universal distribution had always been the keystone of Coca-Cola's strategy of dominance. Supporting that keystone was, among other things, a well-conceived, well-executed, and well-funded advertising program— "mammoth, unflinching," in the words of *Barron's*. [240] (The company's advertising expenditures through the Depression are presented in table 2–13.) A trade magazine comparison of major corporation advertising expenditures ranked Coca-Cola thirty-ninth in the nation in 1937, but documents in the Coca-Cola Archives indicate that published estimates sharply underestimated Coca-Cola's advertising outlays.[241] My own esti-

TABLE 2–12

Sales and Profits of Coca-Cola, 1930–1941
(in millions)

Year	Sales	Gross Operating Profit	Before-Tax Profit	Net Profit
1930	$41.3	$25.8	$15.3	$13.5
1931	40.3	26.1	16.1	14.0
1932	33.6	22.2	12.5	10.7
1933	32.3	21.8	12.8	10.8
1934	39.8	27.1	16.9	14.3
1935	45.5	31.3	19.0	15.8
1936	58.0	39.6	25.4	20.4
1937	70.4	47.1	30.1	24.7
1938	78.1	50.7	31.7	25.6
1939	90.5	58.1	36.4	29.0
1940	n.a.	64.9	41.4	28.9
1941	n.a.	85.4	55.2	28.9

SOURCES: Coca-Cola *Annual Reports*, 1930–1941. Sales figures for 1931 and 1932 are from annual reports. Sales figures for 1932 through 1939 are from Black Book, Coca-Cola Archives, Atlanta, Ga.

TABLE 2–13

*Advertising
Expenditures of the
Coca-Cola Company,
1930–1939*[a]

Year	Expenditure (in millions)
1930	$4.6
1931	4.9
1932	5.0
1933	4.4
1934	4.9
1935	5.4
1936	5.7
1937	7.0
1938	7.1
1939	8.0

[a]Exclusive of expenditures by in-
dividual bottlers.
SOURCE: Black Book, Coca-Cola
Archives, Atlanta, Ga.

mates place Coca-Cola among the top twenty-five national advertisers
throughout the Depression.

The company was a leader in utilizing radio, the most potent new
development in advertising since the invention of printing.[242] Coca-Cola
charted the listenership of the programs on which it advertised as early
as 1927, and it was mastering the art of building a total merchandising
program around its radio effort by 1931 and perhaps earlier.[243] The fact
of Coca-Cola's sponsorship of popular radio programs was featured in
other Coca-Cola advertising, as well as in material provided to the "ser-
vicemen" (remember, Coca-Cola no longer had an official sales force) and
of course to the bottlers.[244]

Coca-Cola's enormous popularity, its degree of brand recognition, and
its widespread presence created an impression of invincibility. It was
commonly referred to in trade and financial journals as late as 1937 as a
"worldwide monopoly." This putative position was thought to be highly
beneficial to its advertising strategy, because almost all of Coke's advertising dollars could be spent on increasing consumption rather than on
convincing consumers to drink Coca-Cola rather than competitors.[245]

If the trade press was slow to notice the threat Pepsi posed, Coca-Cola
certainly was not. Not long after the introduction of Pepsi-Cola into Loft
stores, Coca-Cola brought suit, not for trademark infringement—the
reliability of that time-honored attack having been called into question by

the loss of the Roxa Kola case in 1930—but for substitution.[246] Coca-Cola's corps of detectives had determined that Loft patrons were still asking for Coca-Cola but were surreptitiously being served Pepsi-Cola instead. Pepsi's expenses for this and other early litigation with Coca-Cola came to more than $28,000, at a time when total annual sales reached only $100,000. The legal fees would have meant the end of the beverage altogether had it not been for the financial backing of Loft.[247] Having lost the substitution case, Coca-Cola began trademark litigation in 1939, which concluded only with Pepsi's final victory in 1942.[248]

Walter Mack has written that Robert W. Woodruff himself offered Mack the presidency of White Motors (Woodruff's former employer) to spirit him away from Pepsi. He was willing to pay Mack five times the $50,000 salary he was then earning. "Thank you very much, Bob," Mack recalls replying, "but I've just started this job and I can't walk out on it now. Money doesn't mean that much to me, but doing the job means a lot."[249]

Coca-Cola's assault on Pepsi, however, was apparently not always as polite as formal courtroom confrontations or executive recruitment luncheons. Recalls Walter Mack:

> The people at Coca-Cola . . . went after us every which way. For instance, they would start rumors that our product was no good and that it was filled with chemicals, which, of course, was completely untrue; but worse than that, they physically got very rough. One of their tactics was to follow our deliveries into one of the big chain grocery stores like A&P. After we had set up our supply of Pepsi in cases and displays, the Coca-Cola truck would arrive, they'd pull our signs down, and they'd stack their cases right around ours so that the customers couldn't even see Pepsi. The Coke franchise in New York was run by a fellow named Jim Murray, and one day I went into one of the stores and watched what they were doing. The next day, I dressed a couple of our boys in A&P uniforms and stationed them in the A&P with cameras. When the Coca-Cola boys came in to do their stuff, we took pictures of them in action and I gathered the evidence together and went down to Mr. Murray's office and told him that unless it stopped immediately he was going to be faced with a lawsuit for tampering with other people's property. Needless to say, that particular harassment tactic was dropped immediately, but Coca-Cola had a bundle of other tricks up their sleeves, which they would pull out regularly over the next few years.[250]

One wishes that a lawsuit had been brought, because it would have made it possible to document this charge and to define the boundaries of competition from Coca-Cola's point of view. It might also have helped us learn what tactics Pepsi was employing in return.

Despite Coca-Cola's efforts, Pepsi-Cola clearly had become a player in the cola game by the close of the 1930s. In 1938, Guth's last full year with the company, Pepsi's gross profit on sales was just over $7 million, about 14 percent of Coca-Cola's. By 1941, Pepsi's gross profit had increased nearly threefold, to over 30 percent of that of Coca-Cola. Statistics for the unit share of market of the six leading soft drink producers in 1940 are provided in table 2–14.

The growth of Pepsi can also be observed through the changing share of sales of bottles of various sizes, as table 2–15 illustrates. Sales of 12-ounce bottles throughout the industry increased sharply in only five years, and Pepsi's 12-ounce bottle unquestionably was a major contributor to this trend. By 1939, one bottle of carbonated beverage in four was of the 12-ounce size. Despite this trend, financial analysts still reported in 1940 that "The very active research department of the Coca-Cola Co. has . . . determined by tests that the average person who buys a drink is completely satisfied with the 6 ounce bottle and in fact does not want more than that at a clip."[251]

In its ability to execute well today precisely what had been done yesterday, Coca-Cola's distribution system was incomparable. Introducing a new bottle size to a varied distribution system of over a thousand independent businesses, however, was not seen as an opportunity to be embraced but rather as a problem to be avoided. Coca-Cola bottlers had millions invested in the 6½-ounce bottle. A new bottle size meant that

TABLE 2–14

Case Sales of Six Leading Soft Drink
Franchise Companies, 1940

Brand	Number of Cases (in millions)	Percent of Market
Coca-Cola	291.8	53.0%
Pepsi-Cola	59.4	10.8
7-Up	58.3	10.6
Canada Dry	50.6	9.2
Royal Crown	17.6	3.2
Dr Pepper	10.0	1.8
All others	62.7	11.4
Total	550.4	100.0%

SOURCE: Ko Ching Shih and C. Ying Shih, *American Soft Drink Industry and the Carbonated Beverage Market* (Brookfield, Wis.: W. A. Krueger, 1965), 72. This study, which has been used as an authority by the Federal Trade Commission and by soft drink companies, does not cite sources for the data in this table.

TABLE 2–15

Carbonated Beverage[a] Sales of Bottles of Various Sizes,
1935–1939
(in billions)

Bottle Size	1935	1937	1939
6–7-ounce	3.3	5.4	6.5
Percent of total	75.0%	69.2%	61.3 %
8–10-ounce	0.4	0.5	0.5
Percent of total	9.0%	6.4%	4.7 %
12-ounce	0.3	1.2	2.8
Percent of total	6.8%	15.4%	26.4 %
16-ounce	—	0.1	0.1
Percent of total	—	1.3%	0.9 %
Other sizes[b]	0.4	0.6	0.7[b]
Percent of total	9.2%	7.7	6.6 %
Total	4.4	7.8	10.6

[a]The term *carbonated beverage* encompasses more than the cola business and more even than soft drinks (so-called cereal beverages, for example, are also included).
[b]"Other sizes" in 1937 and 1939 include bottles that are 24 ounces or larger.
SOURCES: U.S. Department of Commerce, Bureau of the Census, *Biennial Census of Manufactures, 1935,* "Beverages, Nonalcoholic," Table 5, p. 51; ibid., *1937,* Part 1, "Beverages, Nonalcoholic," table 5, p. 54; Bureau of the Census, *Sixteenth Census of the United States: 1940; Manufactures, 1939,* Vol. II, Part I, "Nonalcoholic Beverages," table 4, p. 209.

much of that investment might have to be written off. As a result, Coca-Cola did not introduce king- and family-sized bottles to accompany "our old reliable, the Standard Package" until 1955, by which time it was perceived as copying Pepsi.[252]

Walter Mack viewed Coca-Cola as well entrenched but muscle-bound.[253] It had, in other words, the defects of its virtues. In the situation he faced, Mack believed that his best bet was to "pick the hole in the cheese. In other words, go into areas where they weren't."[254] Mack's advertising budget was reported to have been $600,000 in 1939, when Coca-Cola's was over thirteen times as large.[255] How could Pepsi make an impact in this most advertising-intensive of product categories, given this disparity in resources?

One way was to try skywriting. "A fellow named Sid Pike," Mack later recalled,

had an exclusive patent on a little plane that would spell things out with smoke. I made a deal with him that if he could keep the Pepsi name up in the air and legible for three minutes, I'd pay him $50; if it didn't stay, he wouldn't get a thing. Sid started out in Florida, spent about three weeks there, and then moved with the sun to other densely populated areas, spending from two to three weeks in each before going on. Some days it was windy up there and Sid didn't make much money, but most of the time there it was, all over the country, up in the air, the words "Pepsi-Cola" . . . [I]t made a huge impression. Not only had most people never seen skywriting before, but most had never heard of Pepsi-Cola. They made a beautiful team. . . .[256]

Skywriting was a clever idea and is indicative of Mack's creativity. Yet its efficiency obviously was limited, and not only by the vicissitudes of meteorology. Skywriting could provide only announcement; there was no opportunity for selling appeal. Thus skywriting, though it exploited twentieth-century technology, was really a throwback to the early days of advertising.

Pepsi needed to break into radio in a big way. But how, outspent as it was by Coca-Cola by more than ten to one? The answer came in a moment of inspiration—ranking with Guth's adoption of the 12-ounce bottle. The answer was a jingle.

In 1939, "a couple of odd-looking fellows . . . wearing white shoes, open shirts and no coats" presented themselves at Mack's door, claiming to have the solution to Pepsi's advertising dilemma.[257] They were Bradley Kent and Austin Herbert Croom, and their idea was to set the following verse to the tune of an English song called "Do Ye Ken John Peel."

Pepsi-Cola hits the spot.
Twelve full ounces, that's a lot.
Twice as much for a nickel too.
Pepsi-Cola is the drink for you.[258]

Mack liked the jingle because it was "something different. It was amusing, entertaining and catchy—although at the time I had no idea just how catchy—and it was short. . . ."[259] Apparently the first jingle ever aired in a radio advertisement was "Have You Tried Wheaties?" which General Mills placed on the *Jack Armstrong* radio program in 1929.[260] But probably no jingle had ever been handled as this one was.

The networks in the late 1930s usually sold advertising air time in five-minute blocks. Mack felt that this was too long and "dismissed radio advertising as a waste of time. . . . I found that when it came time for the commercials, everybody got up and went to the bathroom or started talking and nobody listened."[261] Mack wanted to run the Pepsi jingle without an accompanying sales pitch. Thus he told his agency, Newell Emmett, to "clear away the spinach" and to buy thirty- and sixty-second spots.[262] The system—meaning both the agency and the networks—disagreed with Mack's judgment. The agency claimed that the product needed extensive explanation of all its advantages. For their part, the networks did not want to sell time in such small blocks.

As he did so often when the "system" said no, Mack found a way around it. "I went out to some little radio stations in New Jersey that weren't making much money; I was able to buy my thirty- and sixty-second spots from them, and they were the first to put the jingle on the air."[263] The sales results were apparent in only two weeks. "I heard people humming it," Mack said. "It came echoing back in full force."[264] By 1941, the jingle had been broadcast almost 300,000 times over almost 470 stations. The following year it was orchestrated and 100,000 copies were distributed.[265] If readers wish to test the extent to which this jingle penetrated the consciousness of the American public, they should ask anyone who was ten years of age or older in 1939 to hum it.

The jingle was effective not merely because it was unaccompanied by a hard sell or because the tune was particularly catchy. It told a great advertising story, simple and easily understood. When you buy our product, you get more for less. No image, ambience, or *nouvelle vague*. The jingle worked like magic, which is precisely what Pepsi needed.

The jingle story typifies Mack's approach to business. He found a way to do what he wanted. Examples abound, but there is one that is particularly on point. When the United States entered World War II, Coca-Cola executive Ed Forio became the industry's consultant to the beverage and tobacco section of the War Production Board, presenting Coke with an opportunity to stifle Pepsi quietly through manipulation of the sugar quota. Mack circumvented the sugar quota by building a syrup plant in Monterrey, Mexico, and importing his sugar in syrup form. When Forio tried to put a stop to that, Mack, who was a shrewd political operator in his own right, went to the War Production Board and threatened to go public with the question of how sugar was being rationed.[266] A public airing of an issue like this in wartime would have served neither the government nor Coca-Cola well. This was a round Mack won.

Surveying the whole of Mack's tenure, we can see that Pepsi's most dramatic gains took place in his early years as CEO. In 1939, the first year of Mack's services as CEO, Pepsi's before-tax profit increased almost 50 percent, and the following year it jumped an additional 43 percent. On the basis of the indicators presented in table 2–16, the year 1941 can be considered Pepsi's best during the Mack era. Gross profit on sales topped $26 million, 7.3 percent higher than in 1949, although substantially lower than in 1942 and 1943. Income before taxes in 1941 was 75 percent higher than in the previous year, 270 percent higher than in 1938, and just under 75 percent higher than in 1949. Net income after taxes was more than 75 percent higher than in 1949. Table 2–17 provides

Coca-Cola data for these years for comparative purposes. When we compare the data in the two tables, we see that Coca-Cola set successive records in 1947 through 1949, whereas Pepsi showed encouraging signs of growth in 1946 and 1947 but then experienced menacing declines in 1948 and 1949, despite an expanding market for soft drinks generally. What went wrong?

After World War II, Pepsi-Cola found it impossible to maintain concentrate prices at a level commensurate with the retail sale of the 12-ounce bottle for 5 cents. In its 1946 *Annual Report,* the company noted that the suggested retail price was now 6 cents, "only" a 20 percent increase over prewar prices, "small . . . compared to the average increase in the price of sugar of 86% over the same period, and compared to the increase in the prices of most sugar-containing products such as candies, jams, jellies, and the like." The company hoped that when sugar rationing was completely removed, prices would decline, and "Pepsi-Cola in the big 12-ounce bottle will be again selling at 5 cents."[267] Meanwhile, Coca-Cola was continuing to sell its "old reliable, the Standard Package" at the old, reliable price of 5 cents. Pepsi-Cola was about to learn a lesson in the problems of trying to act like a price leader when a company has a small market share and no cost advantage.

Late the following year, in an attempt to recapture the 5-cent retail price, Pepsi slashed its concentrate prices below prewar levels. The result

TABLE 2–16

*Gross Profits on Sales, Income Before Taxes, and Net
Income After Taxes of Pepsi-Cola, 1939–1949
(in millions)*

Year	Gross Profit on Sales	Income Before Taxes	Net Income After Taxes
1939	$10.4[a]	$ 6.0	n.a.
1940	14.8[a]	8.5	n.a.
1941	26.0	14.9	$9.4
1942	26.3	14.8	6.3
1943	30.5	12.6	6.4
1944	26.7	13.0	5.9
1945	25.0	10.8	5.2
1946	25.0	10.0	6.3
1947	29.8	10.3	6.8
1948	25.0	5.1	3.2
1949	24.1	3.9	2.1

[a]Estimated.
SOURCES: Pepsi-Cola *Annual Reports,* 1941–1942 and 1946–1949; *Moody's Manual,* 1943–1945.

TABLE 2–17

Gross Profits on Sales, Income Before Taxes, and Net Income After Taxes of Coca-Cola, 1939–1949
(in millions)

Year	Gross Profit on Sales	Income Before Taxes	Net Income After Taxes
1939	$ 58.1	$36.4	$29.0
1940	68.9	41.4	28.9
1941	85.4	55.2	28.9
1942	78.2	50.5	23.3
1943	87.7	55.7	25.5
1944	94.9	55.7	25.0
1945	81.5	41.4	25.1
1946	76.2	38.3	25.4
1947	99.2	54.0	33.0
1948	126.0	59.4	35.6
1949	127.7	63.5	37.8

SOURCE: Coca-Cola *Annual Reports,* 1939–1949.

was an unprofitable final quarter for 1947; the bottlers, moreover, did not respond as hoped. Half of them continued to sell at a price level commensurate with a 6-cent retail price and half of them at 5 cents.[268]

In 1948, a new slogan—"Twice as Much for a Penny More"—and a new 8-ounce bottle for 5 cents were introduced.[269] Neither was successful. By this time, the full impact of the concentrate price cut combined with demoralization among the bottlers led to a drop in gross profit on sales of almost $5 million, or over 16 percent. Income before and after taxes was cut in half.

In its 1948 *Annual Report* (published in March of 1949), Pepsi-Cola provided the data shown in table 2–18 to illustrate to its stockholders the cost pressure it was facing. "Such things," commented the report, "as magazines, street cars, buses, etc. had long since abandoned the nickel. There was, therefore, no basic reason why the soft drink industry should not also receive a fair price for its products to offset some of its increased costs."[270] Fair or not, consumers simply did not look at the matter the same way the company did.

At the end of the 1940s, Pepsi launched yet another slogan—"More Bounce to the Ounce." This slogan was designed to claim that Pepsi was a bargain not only in volume but in qualitative terms as well, that it had more punch and provided more energy than its competitor.[271] The slogan commanded no credibility among consumers.

Soft drink sales are not, of course, merely a matter of advertising

TABLE 2–18

Cost Pressure on Pepsi-Cola in 1949

	Price		Percent Increase
	1939	1949	
Sugar (pound)	$ 0.0403	$ 0.0784	95%
Bottles (gross)	2.87	5.35	86
Wooden cases (unit)	0.35	0.80	128
Trucks (1-ton Diamond T)	700.00	1,500.00	114
Freight (per unit)	6.58	11.50	75
Labor (average weekly wage in the food industry)	24.10	51.47	114

SOURCE: Pepsi-Cola *Annual Report*, 1948, 4.

sloganeering. They depend preeminently on a distribution network of independent bottlers. These bottlers, collectively, have a very large investment in plant, machinery, inventory, transportation equipment, and, crucially, in a field force that services accounts, opens up new ones, places signs, other advertising material, coolers, vending machines, and other such items, and sees to it that customer inventory is properly maintained. In the Pepsi system, the bottlers were even more important than they were at Coke, because they had responsibility for distribution to fountain operations in addition to managing the bottled beverage. They also had greater production responsibilities because, unlike bottlers in the Coca-Cola system, they supplied the sugar.

By the late 1940s, the bottlers had become "dissatisfied, disillusioned, and confused."[272] They were concerned about the obvious problems in sales and profits. They were wondering why, with things going so badly, the company was indulging in what could be perceived as superfluities, such as college scholarships, the sponsorship of art shows, and other cultural and community activities. The bottlers perceived a basic problem in leadership and organization at headquarters.

Walter Mack was described by a journalist in 1950 as a man "who is apt to weary of his philanthropies once they become routine."[273] One feels similarly about his attitude toward the cola business. Forging the bottler network, circumventing the sugar quota, and advertising and publicity—such activities were exciting and, in the case of advertising and publicity, they had a novelty about them that could attract and hold the attention of a restless intellect. Other problems, not so attractive, seem to have been finessed.

Mack later asserted that he wanted to move Pepsi forward by creating a company-owned distribution system and by moving into canning. To achieve this objective, he needed a new board of directors, and he claimed that the bottlers would have supported him in a proxy fight, but that he chose to leave the company rather than create a struggle that would have proven damaging to everyone involved.[274]

The weight of the evidence, however, suggests that Mack had lost the support of key people in the company and among the bottlers.[275] In 1950, the cadre of bottlers had enormous power within the Pepsi-Cola Company, and by then Mack no longer held their confidence. The company had fallen on hard times. New thinking and new action were urgently needed if the situation was to be turned around.

On 23 March 1949, Mack hired Alfred N. Steele as a vice-president. Steele's salary was set at $85,000 per year, with an option on 16,000 shares of Pepsi stock and a seat on the board. Steele said that "When I arrived at Pepsi the other vice presidents figured I had come to liquidate the company." Instead, as a journalist commented, "What Steele liquidated was Mack."[276] In the midst of a losing first quarter, Steele went to the board to demand control of the company. The board made him president and chief executive on 1 March 1950. Mack was elevated to the largely ceremonial board chairmanship, departing from the company soon thereafter and bearing a grudge against Steele ever since.[277] Steele then proceeded to make the company over anew.

Out of the Kitchen and Into the Living Room

Alfred N. Steele was born in Nashville, Tennessee, in 1901. He graduated from Northwestern University and worked for the Chicago *Tribune*, Standard Oil of Indiana, and the D'Arcy Advertising Agency before joining Coca-Cola as vice-president for bottle sales.[278] Steele clashed with Woodruff just as he later did with Mack. Aggressive, flamboyant, and domineering, Steele wanted to wield power alone. One colleague said of him, "If he connected he could be magnificent. If he flopped, nothing flopped worse."[279] Steele had the quality, which he shared with so many great American businesspeople, of being utterly undiscouraged by his failures. When he came to bat, he swung for the fences. At Pepsi, Steele hit a grand slam, as the data in table 2–19 illustrate. By 1959, Pepsi case sales had risen by 182 percent from 1950, whereas case sales in the industry and the nation's population were increasing only 48 percent and 17 percent, respectively. More than four hundred bottling plants set

TABLE 2–19

*Sales, Gross Profits on Sales, Income Before Taxes, and Net Income After Taxes of Pepsi-Cola, 1950–1959
(in millions)*

Year	Sales	Gross Profit on Sales	Income Before Taxes	Net Income After Taxes
1950	n.a.	$ 23.8	$ 2.5	$ 1.3
1951	n.a.	30.2	4.2	2.6
1952	n.a.	35.0	7.8	3.9
1953	n.a.	45.4	11.4	5.5
1954	n.a.	51.8	12.7	6.2
1955	n.a.	62.8	18.9	9.5
1956	n.a.	69.1	17.9	8.9
1957	n.a.	85.6	19.7	9.6
1958	n.a.	98.4	24.0	11.5
1959	$157.8	113.6	30.2	13.9

SOURCE: Pepsi-Cola *Annual Reports*, 1950–1959.

production records in 1959. Seventy sold more than one million cases each, compared to thirteen that did so in 1950. Case sales in December 1959 were greater than those for the traditionally peak summer months of July and August just five years earlier. Twenty-one new bottling plants were opened abroad during the year, bringing the total to two hundred. Pepsi-Cola was now available in eighty countries. Earnings per share had skyrocketed almost 900 percent, from $0.22 in 1950 to $2.17 in 1959, and stockholders' equity had more than doubled from $22.4 to $54.6 million.[280] Gross profit on sales had increased each year under Steele's leadership. Earnings had declined only once, in 1956, after a costly strike, unusually cool summer temperatures, and international currency problems.[281]

Table 2–20 presents comparative data for Coca-Cola in the 1950s. In 1950, Pepsi-Cola's gross profit on sales, income before taxes, and net income after taxes were 20, 4.5, and 4 percent, respectively, of those of Coca-Cola. In 1959, these percentages increased to 57.9, 39.1, and 41.3 percent.

Alfred Steele understood how to bring about the rebirth that Pepsi-Cola once again needed. He took what was best about the company—the best of its executives, its strongest bottlers, and, perhaps most important, the feistiness and creative potential inherent in being the underdog in the industry—and built on it. He also took what was most problematic—including production, product research and quality control, packaging, administrative systems, bottler relations, and advertising and product positioning—and, by using his exceptional abilities and matchless energy

TABLE 2–20

Sales, Gross Profits on Sales, Income Before Taxes, and Net Income After Taxes of Coca-Cola, 1950–1959
(in millions)

Year	Sales	Gross Profit on Sales	Income Before Taxes	Net Income After Taxes
1950	n.a.	$118.6	$56.8	$31.8
1951	n.a.	123.5	58.9	26.1
1952	n.a.	133.0	59.3	27.3
1953	n.a.	139.5	61.1	28.2
1954	n.a.	137.7	54.8	25.9
1955	n.a.	144.7	58.2	27.5
1956	n.a.	153.6	60.9	29.2
1957	n.a.	165.3	65.5	29.9
1958	n.a.	174.5	65.4	30.0
1959	$342.3	196.3	77.2	33.6

SOURCE: Coca-Cola *Annual Reports*, 1950–1959.

(he traveled 100,000 miles a year) as well as the tricks of the trade he had learned at Coca-Cola, brought about major transformations.

Production. In 1949, the Pepsi-Cola Company operated three domestic and three overseas syrup and concentrate plants. By 1958, the last full year of Steele's tenure, nine more foreign plants had been constructed and two of the existing operations had been moved to more modern facilities. American operations had also been expanded. Domestic Pepsi plants shipped over 24 million gallons of concentrate, finished syrup, and fountain syrup in 1958, compared to 9.5 million gallons in 1949. Foreign plants produced about 1.2 million gallons of regular and export concentrate compared to about 230,000 gallons in 1949.[282]

Product Research and Quality Control. Steele established Pepsi's research department in 1951 and, as a sign of his support for its activities, he held the directors' meeting in its library the following year. By 1958, the company employed twenty scientists investigating new flavors, glass composition and color, and bottle design.[283]

In a 1954 speech, Steele said:

People used to write to us and call us and tell us that Pepsi-Cola was too sweet, that it was too watery, that it was too highly carbonated, that it was not carbonated enough, that it was nondescript. Some even said that it was tasteless.

Well, the trouble is that all too often all these things were true. . . .

Pepsi-Cola once varied from place to place. You got a sweet Pepsi in one city, and a tart one in another.[284]

To correct these problems, Steele put seven mobile laboratories into the field by the end of 1951 to assure that Pepsi-Cola became a standardized, truly national product.[285]

Packaging. In the words of Steele:

> We inherited cases of all kinds and conditions. Some were so bad that the more you stacked in a store, the less Pepsi-Cola you could hope to sell. They were, at best, an advertisement of our poverty and of our despondence. Today [1954], we have a clean, good-looking case that can be built into a display in a store with a certain expectancy of improvement in sales. We have a case that a man or woman can carry without tearing their clothes, that can go into a kitchen without carrying a hatful of roaches with it.[286]

Under Steele, Pepsi pioneered in introducing bottles of various sizes. In 1949, the product was distributed in 8- and 12-ounce bottles. The 10-ounce bottle came in 1950, followed by the 26-ounce "hostess" bottle in 1955 and, at last in 1956, the 6½-ounce single-drink size that Coca-Cola had been using for so many years. By 1958, all these bottles were manufactured in Pepsi's distinctive swirl style with baked-on labels rather than the pasted-on paper variety.[287]

Administrative Systems. Steele instituted a decentralized administrative system at Pepsi that was designed to maximize company assistance to bottlers and to increase understanding of the various business situations the local bottlers faced. In 1955, the eight existing regions were further organized into four divisions, each headed by a vice-president.[288]

Aware that systems are no better than the people who run them, Steele staffed Pepsi by raiding Coca-Cola of some of its best people. He lured them to Pepsi by the simple expedient of paying them significantly more than Coca-Cola did. Systematic training programs were developed to enable Pepsi to get the most from its employees, and Steele instituted the company's first stock-option program.[289]

Bottler Relations. Steele's own words best express his attitude toward and achievements in bottler relations at Pepsi:

> [W]e brought to Pepsi-Cola Company a new point of view, a new idea—that the bottler was not our market, but our partner; that our job was not to sell him something in the hope that he could sell it, but that our true *forte* was to help him to move more goods at a profit. . . .
>
> Our Creed says that ". . . our Bottler is our customer and our friend. He likes us and we like him. He owns his own business.
>
> "Our job with our Bottler is to help him—to help him make Pepsi-Cola the most popular beverage in his community, to help him make money with the

aim of building the Pepsi-Cola franchise into a real estate for his family and himself."[290]

In 1950, soon after becoming CEO, Steele told the bottlers that he wanted to take them out of their Fords and put them into Cadillacs. He told them they could save their way into bankruptcy or spend their way to prosperity. He presented to them a plan by which the company would attack the market locality by locality, starting where it was already strongest. These twenty-six "push markets" would form the core for further expansion. Steele asked the bottlers to have faith in his policies and programs. He would find the best equipment and make it available to them. He would reconceptualize the advertising and see to it that every cooperative dollar the bottlers invested would be well spent. The bottlers backed him, and Steele came through for them.[291]

In 1954, he told them:

> In 1950 and 1951, many of you had franchises for sale. Some were ready to be given away—and didn't even have any takers. Today, there are not many Pepsi-Cola franchises that can be bought, and those few that are offered, because of death or family reasons, are worth as much as ten times what they were in in 1950. . . .
>
> There were many among you in 1950 who told me yourselves that you were afraid of going broke. Today, I am proud to say that there are many among you who are millionaires. You not only own Cadillacs, but you can afford them.[292]

So much of managing a franchise relationship is the creation and maintenance of goodwill. At this, Steele was the master, as even Mack admitted.

Advertising and Product Positioning. Steele's achievements in advertising and product positioning were the greatest and yet the most difficult to understand. Positioning is the determination of a product's *raison d'être*—the art of giving the consumer a reason to purchase the product. From the time Guth bought Pepsi-Cola in 1931 until late in 1933, no real effort was made to establish an identity for the product in the consumer's mind. People drank Pepsi because they were in a Loft store for other reasons, and because they wanted a Coke. They asked for Coke and got Pepsi because that was the only cola the store sold, just as patrons of Howard Johnson's used to drink Ho-Jo Cola because it was all they could get. People did not visit Howard Johnson's because they wanted Ho-Jo as opposed to Coke or Pepsi.

From 1933 until 1950, however, Pepsi established a clear consumer image. It was the cola that gave you more. This price appeal was superbly advertised. The company had something to say and said it with great effectiveness. In the late 1940s, Pepsi was forced to abandon its simple price appeal. We asked earlier what would happen if Pepsi were no longer able to sell twice as much for a nickel. The answer is that the company began to fall apart. It tried to hold the price line and failed, alienating bottlers in the process. It tried to maintain the same basic price appeal with modified slogans and failed.

We also asked to what extent a company can permanently taint itself by choosing as a positioning the most prosaic appeal—price—and thereby attracting the least loyal of customers—the price buyer. This was the trap from which Steele had to extricate the Pepsi-Cola Company. His aim was to achieve that most difficult of marketing feats, trading up. We must remember that Pepsi was, in 1950, well known as the bargain cola. It was the brand served to children. People actually bought Pepsi and secretly poured it into Coke bottles in the kitchen before serving it to guests. With the help of his advertising people, Steele determined to move Pepsi out of the kitchen and into the living room.

There is, in business, a phenomenon known as the "monkey law": If you let go of one branch before gripping the other, you will find yourself on the forest floor. With its decision to trade up, Pepsi's former segment of price buyers was let go. That part was all too easy. But how could the company get a grip on the next branch? Why would anybody who could afford to choose buy Pepsi instead of Coke? All of Steele's other initiatives, impressive as they were, were without purpose unless this question could be answered. Strategic insight was needed to move the company to the next branch.[293]

Steele's first step toward this goal was the reformulation of the product. A new, lighter taste was combined with a calorie-reduced formula. "We actually brought out an early diet cola," observed advertising man Philip Hinerfeld.[294] Since sugar was expensive, the new formula had the added advantage of being cheaper to manufacture. Pepsi formerly had been positioned as similar to, but cheaper than, Coca-Cola. Now it was being marketed as something just as expensive but fundamentally different from Coke, something that some people would prefer. Which people? "The theme of 'Light Refreshment,' " a Pepsi spokesperson remembered, "was beamed directly at the home market's principal purchasing agent, the American woman."[295]

The new Pepsi was thus differentiated in terms of taste and calories. Another dimension of the company's segmentation strategy is also suggested by the previous quotation. Steele aimed first at the "home market," which meant selling through grocery stores. Efforts were steadily increased in the fountain area as the 1950s progressed; but Coca-Cola had always been, and indeed remains, very strong there. Long before Pepsi's modern era, Coca-Cola had been installing equipment with its logo in soda fountains and luncheonettes all over the country. That equipment came with contractual obligations that the distributor put only Coca-Cola in it. Whereas first-mover advantage was considerable in that channel, it was less significant in retail groceries, where the needs of literally thousands of different brands competed for limited shelf space. Here, better terms offered by a more flexible Pepsi could result in more prominent retail display, of great importance for a low-ticket impulse item. Also, the consumer had a choice in the grocery store that he or she did not have at the fountain, and Pepsi could combine pull with push to good effect.

Yet another aspect of Pepsi's new positioning dealt with age. In the 1960s, Pepsi used an age-segmentation strategy brilliantly with its creation of the Pepsi Generation campaign. Age was not as clearly emphasized in the 1950s, but there was an implicit message that Pepsi was the beverage of the youthful or, at least, of the young at heart. The "Sociables" jingle clearly contained these elements:

Be Sociable, look smart
Keep up-to-date with Pep-si.
Drink light, refreshing Pep-si
Stay young and fair and debonair,
Be Sociable, have a Pepsi![296]

This appeal was quite different from the contemporary efforts of Coca-Cola, which consistently portrayed itself as timeless and ageless rather than trendy.

Pepsi's life-style appeal was middle to upper-middle class. The women in the advertisements were young, well-dressed, chic, and definitely New York rather than country. On 10 May 1955, Steele married the actress Joan Crawford, and she was used extensively by the company as a sort of first lady to lend an aspect of elegance to the product.[297]

Steele said that with his regime, Pepsi had "cease[d] to operate by hunch, by guess, by looking for the miracle, or by some supposed plan put together with spit and string. . . ."[298] He did not hope to revivify the company with a new slogan alone. Rather, he attacked the market with a total program. He targeted specific localities so that he could score gains battle by battle rather than attempting to win the whole war at once. He never could hope to match Coca-Cola's reserves, but he could muster a considerable field force at the point of contact. He had a specific consumer in mind—the young American woman purchasing for her family. He had a specific channel through which to reach her—the grocery store.

Joan Crawford at a Pepsi Board meeting, 7 May 1959. At left is Herbert Barnet, who became President of Pepsi following Alfred Steele's death on April 19. Crawford was elected to the Board at this meeting and remained with the company until 1973.

He changed the product so that she would find it more appealing. He changed the advertising to alert her to this transformation. He inspired the bottlers to spend heavily in support of his programs. And he managed to keep even those bottlers whose territories were not targeted as push markets loyal to the company.

Alfred Steele died of a heart attack at his home on 19 April 1959, just a few days short of his fifty-eighth birthday.[299] In the last decade of his life, Steele transformed himself from a washed-up executive of the second rank, exiled to the Siberia of Coca-Cola with "no mail, no phone calls, no meetings," into an internationally known entrepreneur married to a legendary woman of glamour.[300] He had made extravagant promises to the Pepsi bottlers and had kept them. All his multiplicity of talents had been available to Coca-Cola, where he had held an executive position for five years. But Coca-Cola did not know how to use him and, according to Walter Mack, Woodruff was glad to get rid of him.[301] When Woodruff lost Steele, he lost more than Steele alone, because Steele hired some of Woodruff's best executives away.

Steele assured Pepsi a permanent place in the American corporate landscape. The low-price strategy when market share is relatively small and there are no clear cost advantages is precarious, as the company discovered in the late 1940s. Steele made possible competition on a new basis.

Afterword: Cola War and Cola Peace

The first use of the phrase "Cola War" that I have found is in a 1950 *New Yorker* essay about Walter Mack.[302] Since then the phrase has often been used to describe the competition between Coca-Cola and Pepsi-Cola. From the beginning, Pepsi cultivated the image of itself as David versus Coca-Cola's Goliath. Coca-Cola, for its part, clung tenaciously to its image as the "brand beyond competition" for many years, hardly acknowledging the existence of Pepsi-Cola, although forced to deal with it as a business reality. The intensity of what might be called Coca-Cola's product focus has been demonstrated on numerous occasions between Steele's time and today.[303] When Coca-Cola decided to bring out a diet cola, the company named it Tab, because it felt that the name Coca-Cola must be reserved for one product and one product only. When Pepsi wanted to bring out a diet drink (which it did two years earlier than Coca-Cola), it called that drink Diet Pepsi. Similarly, when Pepsi came out with a light formula before Coca-Cola, the company again used its brand name. Pepsi periodically changed its formula. At Coca-Cola, the formula was sacred.

Beginning in the mid-1970s, Coca-Cola has swung from the extreme of rigidity in which it seemed to regard itself as akin to a utility, supplying the population with a great-tasting soft drink out of concern for the national welfare, to a competitive actor. Indeed, when the concept of change came to Coca-Cola, it came with a rush and included renegotiated bottler contracts and numerous efforts to leverage brand-name equity, such as the extremely successful Diet Coke in 1982, Caffeine-Free Coke and Caffeine-Free Diet Coke the following year, and Cherry Coke in 1985. Coca-Cola has even franchised its name and logo for use by apparel manufacturers. Having instituted so many changes with such speed and success, the company lost a sense of limits.[304] Its executives came to feel they could do anything, which explains a lot about the formula change in 1985 and how it was handled.

Pepsi for many years and Coke in recent years have accepted the existence of a competitive relationship characterized by the phrase "Cola War." But what does this phrase mean? Roger A. Enrico, president and CEO of the Pepsi-Cola division of PepsiCo, recently described the Cola Wars as follows:

> There are no final defeats. The ammunition we fire at one another is often damn silly stuff. But for all that, our battles are very real.
>
> Tens of billions of dollars are at stake. And "market share"—the sales performance of a soft drink compared to others in its category. And something intangible, but no less important: pride. . . .
>
> At Pepsi, we *like* the Cola Wars.
>
> We know they're good for business—for *all* soft drink brands.
>
> You see, when the public gets interested in the Pepsi-Coke competition, often Pepsi doesn't win at Coke's expense and Coke doesn't win at Pepsi's.
>
> Everybody in the business wins.
>
> Consumer interest swells the market. The more fun we provide, the more people buy our products—*all* our products.
>
> The catch is, the Cola Wars *must* be fun. If it ever looks as if one company is on the ropes—as if it's been dealt such a run of bad fortune that it won't recover—the air will go out of the game faster than the fizz leaves an open can of soda.
>
> The warfare must be perceived as a continuing battle without blood. All the interest lies in keeping the public curious: "Okay, Pepsi did *that* today—what do you think Coke will do tomorrow?"[305]

I would assert that on the national level the relationship between Coke and Pepsi should be characterized—with one important exception—as "Cola Peace" rather than "Cola War." Ever since Pepsi abandoned its "Twice as Much for a Nickel" campaign, these two companies have appealed to the public almost exclusively in terms of psychic benefit. Coca-Cola has tried to associate itself with motherhood, the flag, and "country sunshine."[306] Pepsi has tried to tie itself to feistiness, youthfulness, and California girls.[307] The success that both firms have had in associating products with such images speaks well for the conception and execution of their advertising programs and public relations events.

There has been one instance in the recent past in which Cola Peace really did break out into war. It began when a Pepsi executive named Larry Smith went to Texas to do something about Pepsi's wretched situation there—a 6 percent share compared to 35 percent for Coca-Cola and 25 percent for otherwise lowly Dr Pepper. "This image stuff is great," Smith told the executives in Purchase (the home office at the time) about the Pepsi Generation campaign, "but we're being outsold eight to one. We've got to have a campaign that will move the needle."[308]

The plan that Smith and others devised was even simpler than "Twelve Full Ounces." They conducted taste tests that showed a consistent majority preferring Pepsi. The Pepsi Challenge hit the air in Dallas in May 1975, and things began to happen. Pepsi's share skyrocketed from 6 to 14 percent there, although most of that gain seemed to come not from Coke but from other competitors. Coca-Cola was shocked. For all its millions of dollars invested in research over the years, it had never conducted tests against other brands. "It wasn't allowed," explained an executive.[309] For the first time since "Twice as Much," there was a rational basis for selecting one cola over another. Why buy a trademark when Pepsi actually tastes better?[310]

Pepsi made extensive use of the Challenge, which was eventually aired in 90 percent of the American market.[311] Two aspects of the Pepsi Challenge story surprise the critical observer, however. First, neither Coke nor apparently Pepsi had ever conducted competitive taste tests prior to 1975. Both companies had gone through such contortions to demonstrate various psychic benefits that the most elemental competitive weapon at their command—how the product tasted—had been overlooked.

The second surprise is that the Challenge was never embraced by Pepsi with the glee one would have expected. It was used essentially as a local marketing device and was never made the basis of a national advertising blitz. One reason was that Pepsi liked advertising that focused on the consumer rather than on the product. Roger Enrico, the man who discontinued the Challenge altogether, offered another reason:

All during the exceptionally hot and dry summer of 1983, I watched our commercials. "More people prefer the taste of Pepsi to Coke," they said. And as you'd see people taking the Challenge, you'd hear, "They pick Pepsi, time after time after time." Then the music would come on, reminding you once again that now *is* the time for Pepsi.

The hot weather was great for our business; sales surged throughout June and July. But despite the glowing reports I received from our sales team every week, I had an uneasy feeling about the effectiveness of our advertising.

They were about as well done as semi-Challenge, semi-imagery commercials ever could be. But they weren't exciting—by trying to sell with both product superiority and imagery, they didn't do much of a job with either. It was clear we weren't going to find the answer here. Nobody could make truly wonderful advertising pulling this heavy a ball-and-chain around.[312]

The real problem with the Challenge was that it was potentially too explosive. What would have happened if Pepsi had gone national in 1976 with a heavy-hitting campaign designed to prove that Pepsi tasted better than Coke? What would have happened to Coke's belief in Merchandise

7X? What would have happened to its fountain business? What would have happened abroad? Coca-Cola might have been forced to give away some of the fat margins it had so lovingly guarded for so long in favor of deep discounts to marketing channel members. The Pepsi Challenge might have put Coca-Cola in the position that Pepsi occupied in the 1940s. Might Coke have to say that it might not taste quite as good but it cost less? Might it have become less appropriate to serve such a brand to guests?

The Pepsi Challenge, if managed differently, might have resulted in a real Cola War, one that was price-based. This, however, is precisely the kind of competition both companies want to avoid. If price competition does take place, it is kept on a local market level. These two firms have not yet figured out how to excise this competition completely from their market, but they clearly prefer brush-fire wars to a full-scale nuclear exchange. These firms prefer Cola Peace to Cola War.

Are there winners and losers in this kind of competition? In its public statements, Pepsi consistently declares that everybody wins in the Cola Wars. In a sense that is not true. If Pepsi did not exist, it is hard to believe that Coca-Cola would not have higher sales and profits than it does today. On the other hand, the Pepsi people are correct in pointing to the market development that the peaceful cola warfare has stimulated. And though it is hard to tell this story without making Coke appear as being bested, the Coca-Cola Company has been selling sweetened, carbonated water at handsome profits for a century now. Along with Pepsi, it has kept the leadership of this industry in American hands to an extent that many other manufacturers must envy.

And Coca-Cola still has the largest share of soft drink sales in the world—a market far larger than anyone a hundred, fifty, or even twenty years ago ever thought it would be.

Conclusion

Of all the products discussed in this book, soft drinks are the least essential. Today's world would be no different had they never been invented, as modern soft drink company executives cheerfully and frankly admit. All people must consume liquids to quench their thirst and maintain their health. There is, however, no reason for anyone to pay for Coca-Cola or Pepsi-Cola when they can quench that thirst for nothing with water. Yet in 1988, Americans drank more soft drinks than they did water.

This very aspect of superfluity makes the soft drink business an appropriate place to begin a book on the creation of mass markets. The market did not create these firms. It was the other way around.

In this chapter, we have seen how the soft drink industry evolved from a fragmented, ill-defined collection of small local enterprises to the national monopoly enjoyed by Coca-Cola, to today's duopoly that Coke shares with Pepsi. Our six propositions from chapter 1 can help explain the nature and causes of this progression: (1) profit through volume; (2) entrepreneurial vision; (3) vertical system; (4) first-movers and entry barriers; (5) the competitor's options; and (6) managing change.

PROFIT THROUGH VOLUME AND ENTREPRENEURIAL VISION

Coca-Cola from the 1890s pursued a volume strategy. The firm sought sales all over the country very soon after it passed into Asa Candler's hands. Why?

I believe Candler when he said that he wanted to make the benefits of what he viewed as such a wonderful product available to all his fellow Americans, North and South. The Civil War had destroyed his state and his city. It had injured his very family. But the product he was pushing was designed to be a nationally uniting force. Politics might divide, but all Americans could agree on the benefits of Coca-Cola. Candler wanted to extend these benefits abroad as well. Very much like his brother the Methodist bishop, Candler was a preacher; but he was a secular preacher and Coca-Cola was his gospel.

Now it seems to me that Candler was, to extend the metaphor, worshiping a false god. Coca-Cola's medicinal properties could not have been really exceptional. It is also difficult to believe that it was more refreshing than the scores of similar products on the market. I doubt that Candler would have been able to identify his own beverage in a blind taste test.

But all this is not the point. The point is that Candler really believed his product was something special, and he was able to infuse that belief into his organization. It was not by accident that "Onward Christian Soldiers" concluded sales meetings. Coca-Cola was a company with a mission extending beyond profit.

VERTICAL SYSTEM

Candler was thus essential to colas, but equally essential was his business organization. He built a sales force that had at its core his family. Coca-Cola systematically trained its salespeople. Not only did it invest in them, it invested in advertising to make their job easier.

Coca-Cola depended on the railroad to transport both its salespeople and its syrup to soda fountains all over the country. Shipping the syrup alone and having the druggist mix it with carbonated water was the key to Coca-Cola's logistics. Only the most valuable ingredient had to bear the shipping costs. As bottling technology developed, the bottle, too, became a key to Coca-Cola's ubiquity.

Although Coca-Cola owned some bottling works, most of its bottlers were franchisees. The company was not vertically integrated, but it did captain a vertical system that shepherded the product to the consumer and that kept other products away from that consumer. If fountain operators had Coca-Cola dispensers on their counters, they were supposed to sell only Coca-Cola through them. If bottlers had Coca-Cola franchises, they were prohibited from bottling any other cola.

FIRST-MOVERS AND ENTRY BARRIERS

Thus by the late 1920s, Coca-Cola had both created the Phase II unification era in soft drink history and mastered it. There was nothing inevitable about these developments. Business executives made them happen through the instrument of a well-structured organization. By means of a combined policy of heavy pull through massive advertising and heavy push through a well-trained sales force and through partners in the distribution system who were rewarded with high consumer demand and restricted by contracts from pushing competing products, Coca-Cola had created a brand.

Business analysts had been familiar with barriers to entry since the railroad boom of the nineteenth century (although the phrase itself is relatively recent). However, traditionally such barriers had been conceived of in terms of property, plant, and equipment. In Coca-Cola's case, this kind of barrier was small. The force that kept other companies out of Coca-Cola's lucrative field was invisible and did not appear on the company's balance sheet. By 1930, Coca-Cola had advertised nationally for four decades. It had constructed an intricate web of contractual relations. Here was its real power. The brand name itself, "Coca-Cola," is among the most valuable assets in the corporate world today.

The first of this book's six propositions describes a profit-through-volume strategy made possible by low prices and low margins. These propositions are generalizations that do not apply equally to all industries, and here we have an example of an exception. Coca-Cola was always a volume company, but that volume was achieved through advertising and intensive distribution rather than through a sacrifice in margins. The ability to keep margins high made Coca-Cola as profitable as it was. Apparently the unit price to the customer was so low—5 cents either for a glass at the fountain or, as bottling took hold at the turn of the century, for a 6½-ounce bottle—that cheaper beverages could not win a substantial portion of Coca-Cola's business by selling for, say, 4 cents. A more dramatic price difference was required.

THE COMPETITOR'S OPTIONS

In the 1930s, Pepsi-Cola intruded on Coke's strategy. After Charles Guth bought Pepsi in 1931, it had a distribution base because Guth was also the president of Loft. Just as Sears—as we shall see in chapter 5—competed against General Electric and Frigidaire in refrigerators through a different distribution system, so did Pepsi attack Coca-Cola through backward integration. Had Pepsi remained tied to Loft alone, it could not have expanded beyond the New York metropolitan area. If it went into bottles, however, it would have to have some power to overcome Coca-Cola's. The necessary strategic insight was the price approach. We must emphasize that this was executed with particular drama—"Twice as Much"—and during the most price-sensitive decade in the twentieth century.

Thus we have seen how Coca-Cola erected barriers to entry and how Pepsi combated them in the 1930s. I have characterized Pepsi's approach as Phase II in nature because Pepsi was using the oldest method in history to gain market participation—price. There was no demographic or psychographic segmentation involved. In fact, I have encountered no reference to research of any kind in association with Pepsi's marketing moves in the 1930s.

Price is the most consistently effective tool at the marketer's command; but if a price strategy is based on a competitor's price umbrella rather than on a cost advantage, it is always in jeopardy. Pepsi lost its price advantage and its customers at the end of the 1940s. It would have gone bankrupt had it not inaugurated a new, Phase III era of life-style product positioning in the industry. Steele brought Pepsi out of the kitchen and into the living room by using new advertisements to make it a respectable drink for middle-class Americans to serve their guests.

It was under Donald Kendall, however, that differentiation through demographic and psychographic segmentation made Pepsi the near equal of Coke. Kendall, the recently retired CEO under whose leadership PepsiCo has become one of the great multinational consumer product marketers, brought Pepsi out of the living room and into the rec room, into

Donald M. Kendall is the man who transformed Pepsi-Cola, which at Alfred Steele's death seemed once again to be heading into a nose dive, into a prospering multinational. Kendall joined Pepsi as a salesman in 1947. He rose through the international division. He is pictured above (far left) in 1960, drinking Pepsi-Cola with Khrushchev and Nixon in Moscow.

the stadium, onto the dance floor, and onto the beach. The Pepsi advertisements of the 1960s are so different from those of the 1950s that it is only with difficulty that one recognizes that they are for the same product.

MANAGING CHANGE

With the exception of the Pepsi Challenge, competition has been on a Phase III basis ever since the 1960s. There, my guess is, it will continue. Phase III competition in the soft drink industry is defined not by economics but by imagination.

Through most of the twentieth century, Coke—the universal cola, the classic Phase II product—was the most changeless of America's consumer goods. It was only available in one bottle size as late as the mid-1950s.

Today, both Coca-Cola and Pepsi-Cola play in the Phase III world of segmentation and line extension. The transition was easier for Pepsi because it had less to lose. To some extent, Coca-Cola's strategic flexibility was hindered by its "marketing mind-set," a kind of mobility barrier not encountered in textbooks but important in the real world. The Coca-Cola

Company does indeed seem to have viewed its great product as a "brand beyond competition." When a competitor finally arose, Coke was slow to recognize it.

Phase III Comes to the Cola Business: The invention of the "Pepsi Generation" constituted a major initiative in soft drink marketing. The Pepsi Generation was a segment defined by a set of shared demographic and psychographic characteristics.

CHAPTER 3

Putting America on Wheels: Ford vs. General Motors

In chapter 2, we described and analyzed the history of marketing strategy in the soft drink industry from the point of view of the manufacturers. Our focus was on Coca-Cola and Pepsi-Cola, not on the fountain operators, the food stores, or even the bottlers, though they were essential to the distribution of soft drinks and made money from the industry.

Our treatment of the automobile industry in this chapter also focuses on the manufacturer's point of view. To be sure, we will discuss the role of the independent retail dealer, just as we discussed the independent franchised bottler in the previous chapter. However, our attention will be primarily on the automobile manufacturers because they have been the leading members of the marketing system, the commanders of the marketing channel.

Soft drinks and automobiles have this "manufacturer leadership" in common, but they share very little else. The automobile is the most expensive nationally branded consumer item. For most repeat purchasers, it is a trading item because the used car retains some of its original value. The purchase of an automobile can be bundled or unbundled in a seemingly endless variety of ways (e.g., with air conditioning, power windows, and the like). For all these reasons price is typically a matter of negotiation at the point of sale. The availability and expense of consumer financing can also be an issue. The performance of the product from a technical standpoint is a key factor in sales, but the automobile is also a style item with a not insignificant fashion content. The mass manufacture of the automobile is one of the great marvels of the twentieth century, and the balance between output and demand is a long-standing problem in the history of the industry. And, finally, a vast legal, social, and economic infrastructure was a prerequisite for national automobility.

None of this is true of soft drinks. These two products bracket the extremes of consumer marketing.

Despite their differences, however, one can discern an evolution through phases in the automobile industry similar in many ways to what happened in soft drinks.

Phase I in soft drinks dates back hundreds of years. In the automobile industry, Phase I began far more recently, with the invention of the first automobile-like conveyances in France and Germany in the 1880s. This phase was marked by fragmentation caused by a lack of a dominant product design among steam, electricity, and internal combustion and, equally important, by the lack of a winning marketing idea.

It was Henry Ford who had that idea. He showed the industry the power of a single, unchanging model of high quality turned out in ever greater numbers at ever lower costs. The Model T was the "universal" car, and with its hegemony the Phase II world was established. Although Coca-Cola could be attacked with some success on Phase II grounds, as Pepsi proved in the 1930s, no sane business executive could have hoped to beat Ford at his own game. Ford's very strength drove potential competitors to seek a whole new way to compete against him.

That is what Alfred Sloan did with the "car for every purse and purpose" and the annual model change in the 1920s. He brought the Phase III world of market segmentation to the automobile industry. One major attempt, at least, to return to a "universal car" was successful—the Volkswagen Beetle. The basic direction in recent years, however, has been further into a Phase III world of market segmentation and "mass customization."

The Automobile As a New Product

"Distance divides, and that which sets distance aside begets acquaintance, which in the end ripens into friendship." These were the words of Asa G. Candler in 1909. Candler was not only the owner of Coca-Cola at that time; he was also the president of Atlanta's Chamber of Commerce. In that capacity he addressed a group of northern businesspeople in town to attend the first automobile show in the South. Among those visiting for the show that autumn were John N. Willys and Ransom E. Olds. Also there was Henry Ford.[1]

Did Candler and Ford speak to each other at some time during the course of the show? We do not know. We can say that both might have benefited from a chat. The man who commercialized the universal cola had a lot in common with the creator of the universal car. Neither was provincial. Both thought in nationwide and, indeed, in international terms. Neither had an interest in market segmentation. Both believed in finding the one best version of a product and then selling it to everybody. They were true mass marketers, although they relied on different elements of the marketing mix to create their mass markets; that is, Ford featured price whereas Candler emphasized advertising—a difference easily explained by the different kinds of product they sold. Neither believed in change once the one best product had been invented. (Given their views, one is tempted to say "discovered.") In other words, Candler and Ford were classic Phase II businessmen.

Candler was an automobile booster not only because he thought that distance divided and propinquity begat friendship. He shrewdly saw in the automobile a key to southern economic development. He wanted Atlanta to benefit fully from the future as he saw it. Moreover, transportation costs were a major expense item not only for Coca-Cola but for its franchised bottlers. Trucks and all-weather, surfaced roads for them to travel on would help nicely in that area. Coca-Cola bottlers were, not surprisingly, early investors in trucks. With their advent, the reach of bottler distribution was extended because delivery routes were lengthened.

So Candler and Ford would have had a lot to talk about. But then again, everyone in the country would by World War I have had a lot to talk about with Ford. The automobile had a fundamental impact on grocery retailing and on general merchandise retailing, as we will see in chapters 4 and 5. Indeed, it penetrated every cranny of the economy and affected every citizen's interests as did nothing else in this whole century with the possible exception of electricity.

If the automobile business was the key industry in the twentieth century, the United States was, until recently, the key country in the automobile industry. The key companies in this country were Ford and General Motors, and the key men in those companies were Henry Ford and Alfred P. Sloan, Jr. This chapter is about how the Ford Motor Company became dominant but then lost its leadership to General Motors. To introduce this saga, let us look at the industry in 1900, before either company was founded.

"What is an automobile and what does it do?" Any child could answer that question today. No one could give a fully satisfactory answer to it in 1900. The automobile at that time was new. Every product is new at its birth, and every product is new only once. Newness is often a time of great uncertainty, great eagerness, and great dreams. It is just as often followed by great disappointment. All this was true of the automobile.

The automobile can trace its ancestry as far back as the mid-seventeenth century, when two French missionaries in China tinkered together a pair of self-propelled, steam-powered vehicles.[2] However, it was not until the 1880s that a series of technological developments led to the vehicles constructed by Karl Benz and Gottlieb Daimler in Germany, which have been called the "lineal ancestors" of the modern gasoline-powered automobile.[3]

By the mid-1890s, the industry had gotten under way in France, by then the leader, and Germany. The Peugeot and the Panhard and Levassor companies each produced 72 cars in 1895 and Benz produced 135.[4] Britain, still shackled by the Red Flag Act, which limited the speed of "road locomotives" to 2 miles an hour in cities and required that such vehicles be preceded by an individual carrying a red flag by day or a red lantern at night, lagged.[5] The United States lagged, too, "still a long way from the best European practice."[6] No large American firm had by 1895 yet taken an interest in automobile production. The field was fast becoming crowded with eager young entrepreneurs, a select few of whom would be heard from again.

In 1899, the automobile made it onto the United States census of manufactures for the first time. It ranked 150 out of 150 industries on the list in terms of value of product. It was still unranked in terms of wage earners, total wages paid, cost of materials, and value added by manufacture. By 1925, the U.S. industry ranked third in number of wage earners and first in the other four categories.[7]

Predictions of the future greatness of the automobile industry were easy to find at the turn of the century and even earlier. In 1895, for example, Thomas A. Edison stated in a newspaper interview that "the horseless vehicle is the coming wonder. . . . It is only a question of time when the carriages and trucks in every large city will be run with motors."[8] Albert A. Pope, an early entrant into the industry and a large bicycle manufacturer, said in 1900 that there would within a decade "be more automobiles in use in the large cities of the United States than there are now horses in these cities."[9]

Such observations make it appear almost inevitable that the automobile industry would become a dominant force in the nation. This impression was buttressed by the fact that soon after the turn of the century a wave of panic buying developed. "Now the demand for automobiles here is a perfect craze," said an early Ford partner in 1903. "Every factory here . . . has its entire output sold and cannot begin to fill orders. . . ."[10] Scores of firms were scurrying into the industry. The surge of demand was the great attraction, and there was nothing to keep potential entrants out. Little capital was needed. If parts were purchased with 30 to 90 days to pay, and if an advance deposit and the balance on delivery were demanded from the dealer, automobile manufacture became virtually self-financing.[11]

This description, however, glosses over the great hurdles this industry had yet to jump at century's turn. Many of these hurdles related to the question posed earlier: What really was this new thing, this automobile? Was it a plaything for the rich? Many early automobiles had tillers rather than wheels. Perhaps the yacht was the proper analogy, a yacht that drove on the land. Was the automobile, by contrast, a product designed for the middle class? If so, how would they use it and what would they use it for?

Was the automobile a product for the masses? Who precisely are the masses? How many people do we mean? Was gasoline sufficiently widely distributed to power mass-marketed automobiles?[12] Where would owners have their cars serviced? What would they drive them on? American roads were atrocious at this time; less than 10 percent of the mileage was surfaced.[13] Weather was severe in many parts of the United States during much of the year, making the roads impassable. The early automobiles

Courtesy Lazarnick Collection, Motor Vehicle Manufacturers Association, Detroit.

The first Glidden Tour covered 870 miles—from New York to Bretton Woods, New Hampshire, and back. Here we see the cars participating in the Tour at the Mt. Washington Hotel in Bretton Woods. Tours were a feature of the automobile world when the car was still something of a novelty. The setting depicted here well reflects the upper-class aura surrounding auto travel in its early years.

were not enclosed, so they were of limited use in bad weather. And how were the masses going to buy the automobile? With all the great wealth of the American mass market, per-capita realized national income adjusted by the cost of living was under $500 in 1900.[14] How cheaply could a car be profitably produced and sold? It is fine to talk about tremendous demand in 1903, but in that year there were only 11,235 automobiles sold. Would the market someday support sales ten times that great? A hundred times that great?

It is true that there were predictions about the automobile replacing the horse. "But horses were everywhere, pulling surreys . . . , buggies, cabs, delivery wagons of every sort on Main Street, and pulling harvesters on the tractorless farms out in the countryside."[15] Horses also provided fertilizer for those farms. Could the internal combustion engine do that? There were 21 million horses in the United States in 1900 (and only 76 million people).[16] How many of these horses could the automobile be expected to replace? In the words of journalist Mark Sullivan, "That a time should come when horses would be a rare sight on city streets seemed, in 1900, one of the least credible of prophesies."[17]

True, the great Edison had predicted the success of the automobile. But the great Edison also predicted that he would develop an improved storage battery that would lead to the dominance of the electric vehicle over gasoline power. According to *Motor Age* in 1908, "Mr. Edison's bunk has come to be somewhat of a joke—a real joke."[18] True, Pope had predicted the triumph of the automobile, but he was betting on the electric as well. The doom of the internal combustion engine was that, as Pope explained, "You can't get people to sit over an explosion."[19]

Predictions are cheap. We tend to remember only those that turn out to be correct because we have the benefit of hindsight. For contemporaries, on the other hand, discerning the true trend of events amidst the welter of conflicting views is no easy task. If one wanted to make a case against the possibility of a mass-marketed automobile from the viewpoint of an analyst in 1900, there are plenty of arguments near at hand. Many of these have already been mentioned—the lack of consumer purchasing power, roads, gas stations, repair facilities. To this list we might add the absence of rules of the road, of useful maps, of an insurance system, of licensing.[20] In short, the whole infrastructure—both corporate and governmental—that we take for granted as members of an automobile-ized society was absent.

All of this assumes that the problem of actually producing a rugged, versatile vehicle at a price within the reach of the masses could be solved. The statistics show that during the years 1903 through 1907 (the year

One way early automobile manufacturers got publicity for their industry, their companies, and themselves was through racing. We see above one of Ford's early racers, the 999, with Henry Ford standing next to it, and the soon-to-be-famous race car driver Barney Oldfield at the tiller.

before the Model T was introduced), prices were rising, not dropping. Unit sales of automobiles priced under $1,375 increased during these years, but share of market decreased sharply (see table 3–1).

In 1906, Henry Ford was still defending the automobile against the charge that it, like the bicycle during the 1890s, was little more than a fad.[21] That same year Woodrow Wilson, at the time the president of Princeton, is said to have remarked that the automobile was likely to serve

TABLE 3–1

Passenger Car Sales and Price Levels, 1903–1907

Year	Total Sales	Percent Sold for $1,375 or Less	Units Sold for $1,375 or Less	Percent Sold for Greater than $1,375	Units Sold for Greater than $1,375
1903	11,235	68.7%	7,718	31.3%	3,517
1904	22,130	71.0	15,712	29.0	6,418
1905	24,250	48.3	11,713	51.7	12,437
1906	33,200	40.9	13,579	59.1	19,621
1907	43,000	36.2	15,566	63.8	27,434

SOURCE: Ralph C. Epstein, *The Automobile Industry: Its Economic and Commercial Development* (Chicago: A. W. Shaw, 1928), 335–37, 341.

as a stimulus to socialism because it was obviously desirable but only the rich would ever be able to afford it.[22] Two years later the founder of General Motors, William C. Durant, said to the shrewd Morgan partner George W. Perkins that the time would come when the automobile industry would turn out a half million cars a year. Perkins is said to have later remarked that "If that fellow has any sense, he'll keep those observations to himself when he tries to borrow money."[23]

Michigan machine shop owner Ransom E. Olds believed in the low-priced automobile enough to bring one out. Actually he had no choice. His Detroit factory burned down on 9 March 1901, and only one, single-cylinder, curved-dash vehicle was saved. The company concentrated its efforts here, and these efforts were rewarded. The "Merry Oldsmobile" became the "first car in the world to be produced in really large quantity over a period of years."[24] Six hundred vehicles were manufactured in 1901 and 5,000 in 1904, accounting for more than a fifth of the market. These statistics testified to the vigor of the demand for a $650 vehicle and lead to the question of whether this car could have become the great mass-marketed vehicle. Most automobile historians think not because Olds's car was not much more than a motorized buggy rather than the heavier vehicle that would have been required for family use. We will never know the answer, because Olds got into an argument with his financial backers and was forced to leave the company that bore his name. Without Olds, the proprietors of the Olds Motor Works de-emphasized the small, cheap car in favor of a heavier and more expensive one. Olds himself founded another company, REO, which also did not pursue the low-priced market.[25]

In 1907, Alanson P. Brush made an effort to penetrate the low-price market with his Brush Runabout, which he sold through 1912. At $500, it was attractively priced. The problem with the Brush Runabout was that, like the curved-dash Oldsmobile that preceded it, it was not only inexpensive, it was cheap. It used cheap, buggy-type construction, substituting wood for metal wherever possible, prompting its owners to complain that it had a "wooden body, wooden axles, wooden wheels and wooden run."[26]

Thus, by 1908 there was no example either in the United States or abroad of a company that had successfully combined low cost with high quality through concentration on the volume production of a single model.[27] This is what Henry Ford did. We should be absolutely clear on this point. The market did not do it. Public opinion did not do it. The Europeans did not do it. Ford did. It was Ford who made the necessary investment in production and who organized distribution to awaken the demand that many people suspected in a vague way might exist for a good quality, low-cost automobile. All this seems inevitable only in retrospect. Remember what George Perkins said about William Durant's forecast in 1908, the very year the Model T was introduced.

Because of his determination, because of his abilities as a problem solver, but most of all because he understood the true answer to the question of what an automobile really was, Henry Ford placed himself— along with Einstein, Freud, Lenin, and a very few others—in that class of people who exercised a decisive impact on the history of the twentieth century. Woodrow Wilson had feared that the automobile would lead to socialism because only the elite would be able to afford one. Ironically, this is precisely how the automobile culture has developed in Socialist countries. There only the elite can obtain cars. In the West, by contrast, cars were democratized. In the United States today, a large percentage of those wanting automobiles own them.[28] The Ford Motor Company led the way.

Breakthrough at Ford

"I will build a motor car for the great multitude," Ford said early in his career, "constructed of the best materials, by the best men to be hired, after the simplest designs that modern engineering can devise . . . so low in price that no man making a good salary will be unable to own one—and enjoy with his family the blessing of hours of pleasure in God's great open spaces."[29] That was the goal. Its achievement was Ford's life's work.

Born in 1863 on a prosperous farm in Dearborn, Michigan, just outside Detroit, Ford served an apprenticeship in a Detroit machine shop while spending his evenings as a watch repairman. After completing his apprenticeship in 1882, he got a job operating a traction engine for Westinghouse while helping his father on the farm when laid off. In 1891, Ford became an engineer with the Detroit Edison Illuminating Company and also began his experiments with internal combustion engines. Five years later, he produced his first automobile; and in 1899, he founded the Detroit Automobile Company, which lasted only until 1901. This was followed by the short-lived Henry Ford Company, which was succeeded in turn by the Ford Motor Company.

The Ford Motor Company was incorporated on 16 June 1903, shortly before Ford's fortieth birthday. Nominal capitalization was $150,000. One thousand shares of stock at a par value of $100 per share ($50,000

Henry Ford in his first automobile, the quadricycle. The year is 1896; Ford is 33. There is room for two (just barely) on the single seat above the box containing the engine. For steering, there is a tiller, not a wheel.

was held as treasury stock) were divided among twelve people. Ford and his principal financial backer, Detroit coal merchant Alexander Y. Malcomson, took 255 shares each. James Couzens, the Canadian-born son of a grocery clerk who would later serve in the United States Senate, took 25 shares, and 50 shares each went to the two proprietors of one of Detroit's best machine shops, brothers John F. and Horace E. Dodge. Total paid-in capital amounted to only $28,000.[30]

In the 1905–1906 model year, the Ford Motor Company sold 1,599 cars. Income for the fiscal year ending on 30 September 1906 was close to $1.5 million. In 1920–1921, Ford sold 933,720 passenger cars, with sales for calendar 1921 in excess of a half billion dollars.[31]

A great deal has been written about Henry Ford, perhaps more than about any other businessperson. A number of years ago, a historian observed that more had already been written about Ford than could be read in a lifetime.[32] Most have been struck by the contradictions about the man, one author entitling a chapter "Genius Ignoramus."[33] Another scholar asked, "[W]as he a simple man erroneously assumed to be complex, or an enormously complex individual with a misleading aura of simplicity?"[34]

David Riesman has suggested that the "control equipment" of the twentieth century has been radar, with which modern man senses signals from others and molds himself accordingly. In the nineteenth century, by contrast, Riesman's ideal type was equipped with a gyroscope, which permitted him to keep on course no matter how life knocked him about.[35] Preeminently, Henry Ford was the gyroscope type. The course he set for himself was to build a "car for the common man," for the "great multitude," a "universal" car that would be sufficiently versatile to serve for every occasion. This car would be durable, and it would be inexpensive both to purchase and to operate. Ford wanted to sell a high-performance vehicle for under $600 that was inexpensive but not cheap.[36]

As we have seen, other automotive pioneers believed in the mass market. Brush and Olds tried to tap it, but they approached the problem from the wrong direction. Their first thought was to design a car that could be built cheaply. The result was a light-weight, flimsy buggy. "Only Ford realized that the first requisite was to formulate the qualities that a 'universal' car must possess and design the vehicle accordingly; after that the problem of low-cost production could be attacked."[37]

Ford's partner Malcomson did not share Ford's view of the low-price market. He wanted to do the same thing in 1905 that Olds's partners had done the previous year—follow the market up by bringing out a heavier, more expensive automobile. Ford had left the Henry Ford Company in 1902 because, as he later wrote, "I found that the . . . company was not a vehicle for realizing my ideas but merely a money-making concern . . ."[38]

uncertainty, great eagerness, and great dreams. It is just as often followed by great disappointment. All this was true of the automobile.

The automobile can trace its ancestry as far back as the mid-seventeenth century, when two French missionaries in China tinkered together a pair of self-propelled, steam-powered vehicles.[2] However, it was not until the 1880s that a series of technological developments led to the vehicles constructed by Karl Benz and Gottlieb Daimler in Germany, which have been called the "lineal ancestors" of the modern gasoline-powered automobile.[3]

By the mid-1890s, the industry had gotten under way in France, by then the leader, and Germany. The Peugeot and the Panhard and Levassor companies each produced 72 cars in 1895 and Benz produced 135.[4] Britain, still shackled by the Red Flag Act, which limited the speed of "road locomotives" to 2 miles an hour in cities and required that such vehicles be preceded by an individual carrying a red flag by day or a red lantern at night, lagged.[5] The United States lagged, too, "still a long way from the best European practice."[6] No large American firm had by 1895 yet taken an interest in automobile production. The field was fast becoming crowded with eager young entrepreneurs, a select few of whom would be heard from again.

In 1899, the automobile made it onto the United States census of manufactures for the first time. It ranked 150 out of 150 industries on the list in terms of value of product. It was still unranked in terms of wage earners, total wages paid, cost of materials, and value added by manufacture. By 1925, the U.S. industry ranked third in number of wage earners and first in the other four categories.[7]

Predictions of the future greatness of the automobile industry were easy to find at the turn of the century and even earlier. In 1895, for example, Thomas A. Edison stated in a newspaper interview that "the horseless vehicle is the coming wonder. . . . It is only a question of time when the carriages and trucks in every large city will be run with motors."[8] Albert A. Pope, an early entrant into the industry and a large bicycle manufacturer, said in 1900 that there would within a decade "be more automobiles in use in the large cities of the United States than there are now horses in these cities."[9]

Such observations make it appear almost inevitable that the automobile industry would become a dominant force in the nation. This impression was buttressed by the fact that soon after the turn of the century a wave of panic buying developed. "Now the demand for automobiles here is a perfect craze," said an early Ford partner in 1903. "Every factory here . . . has its entire output sold and cannot begin to fill orders. . . ."[10] Scores of firms were scurrying into the industry. The surge of demand was the great attraction, and there was nothing to keep potential entrants out. Little capital was needed. If parts were purchased with 30 to 90 days to pay, and if an advance deposit and the balance on delivery were demanded from the dealer, automobile manufacture became virtually self-financing.[11]

This description, however, glosses over the great hurdles this industry had yet to jump at century's turn. Many of these hurdles related to the question posed earlier: What really was this new thing, this automobile? Was it a plaything for the rich? Many early automobiles had tillers rather than wheels. Perhaps the yacht was the proper analogy, a yacht that drove on the land. Was the automobile, by contrast, a product designed for the middle class? If so, how would they use it and what would they use it for?

Was the automobile a product for the masses? Who precisely are the masses? How many people do we mean? Was gasoline sufficiently widely distributed to power mass-marketed automobiles?[12] Where would owners have their cars serviced? What would they drive them on? American roads were atrocious at this time; less than 10 percent of the mileage was surfaced.[13] Weather was severe in many parts of the United States during much of the year, making the roads impassable. The early automobiles

The first Glidden Tour covered 870 miles—from New York to Bretton Woods, New Hampshire, and back. Here we see the cars participating in the Tour at the Mt. Washington Hotel in Bretton Woods. Tours were a feature of the automobile world when the car was still something of a novelty. The setting depicted here well reflects the upper-class aura surrounding auto travel in its early years.

Here Henry Ford, in his later years, revisits the brick shed in which he built his first automobile, the quadricycle, in 1896. This picture well illustrates the "cottage industry" stage of the business prior to the turn of the century. Within just a few years, an enormous capital investment would be required to hold a significant position in this industry.

This time, with the help of the Dodge brothers, Ford was able to buy Malcomson out; and the company became his in fact as well as in name.

Ford now had the power to turn his idea of the universal car into a reality. But how? Here, too, Ford had a basic concept of how to get the job done. "The way to make automobiles," he told one of his partners in 1903, "is to make one automobile like another automobile, to make them all alike, to make them come from the factory just alike—just like one pin is like another pin when it comes from a pin factory, or one match is like another match when it comes from a match factory."[39]

It took five years and eight models (the A, B, C, F, K, N, R, and S) before the precise configuration of this particular "pin" was settled on. Ford also had to fight the many industry forces that sought, through patents, law suits, and agreements of various kinds, to restrict output and keep prices high.[40] These attitudes were vestiges of Phase I thinking, which were soon swept away from the industry by the tide of Fordism.

Finally, on 1 October 1908, the world and the Model T Ford were introduced to one another.[41]

The most famous automobile ever built, the Model T was an unquestionable value for the price. It was the product of the hard work of many talented people guided by the vision, the commitment, and the indomitable spirit of Henry Ford. In Ford's words, the "universal car had to have these attributes":

1. Quality in material to give service in use. Vanadium steel is the strongest, toughest, and most lasting of steels. It forms the foundation and superstructure of the cars. It is the highest quality steel in this respect in the world, regardless of price.
2. Simplicity in operation—because the masses are not mechanics.
3. Power in sufficient quantity.
4. Absolute reliability—because of the varied uses to which the cars would be put and the variety of roads over which they would travel.
5. Lightness. With the Ford there are only 7.95 pounds to be carried by each cubic inch of piston displacement. This is one of the reasons why Ford cars are "always going," wherever and whenever you see them—through sand and mud, through slush, snow, and water, up hills, across fields, and roadless plains.
6. Control—to hold its speed always in hand, calmly and safely meeting every emergency and contingency either in the crowded streets of the city or on dangerous roads. The planetary transmission of the Ford gave this control, and anybody could work it. That is the "why" of the saying: "Anybody can drive a Ford." It can turn around almost anywhere.
7. The more a motor car weighs, naturally the more fuel and lubricants are used in the driving; the lighter the weight, the lighter the expense of operation. The light weight of the Ford car in its early years was used as an argument against it. Now all that is changed.

The design which I settled upon was called "Model T." The important feature of the new model—which, if it were accepted, as I thought it would be, I intended to make the only model and then start into real production—was its simplicity. There were but four constructional units in the car—the power plant, the frame, the front axle, and the rear axle. All of these were easily accessible, and they were designed so that no special skill would be required for their repair or replacement. I believed then, although I said very little about it because of the novelty of the idea, that it ought to be possible to have parts so simple and so inexpensive that the menace of expensive hand repair work would be entirely eliminated. The parts could be made so cheaply that it would be less expensive to buy new ones than to have old ones repaired. They could be carried in hardware shops just as nails or bolts are carried. I thought that it was up to me as the designer to make the car so completely simple that no one could fail to understand it.

That works both ways and applies to everything. The less complex an article, the easier it is to make, the cheaper it may be sold, and therefore, the greater number may be sold.[42]

The original price of the Model T was $850 for the "touring car," and $25 less for the "runabout." This was, obviously, well above Ford's goal of $600. But with the production miracle that he and his people engineered, prices plummeted while sales skyrocketed. Table 3–2 shows the declining retail price of the Model T touring car as well as the increase in sales (including both the touring car and the runabout). By 1914, when the moving assembly lines at Ford's Highland Park plant were achieving astonishing economies and making possible the manufacture of a thousand vehicles a day, the Model T's closest competitor in terms of product quality sold at twice the price.[43] Exhibits 3–1 and 3–2 provide graphic representations of the outcome of Ford's price and product quality strategy. In exhibit 3–1, we see that the price of the Model T dropped as average annual income increased. In exhibit 3–2, we see the result: the American public gave the Ford Motor Company dominance in the automobile industry.

To set the stage for the changes that were to take place at Ford, we need to review briefly the story of the coming of mass production. An "alchemy of circumstances" accounted for the success of the Ford factory. Ford and his people were not shackled by preconceived notions about the

TABLE 3–2

Prices of the Model T Touring Car and
Sales of All Model Ts, 1908–1916

Calendar Year	Touring Car Retail Price	Unit Sales
1908	$850	5,986
1909	950	12,292
1910	780	19,293
1911	690	40,402
1912	600	78,611
1913	550	182,809
1914	490	260,720
1915	440	355,276
1916	360	577,036

SOURCES: Allan Nevins, *Ford: The Times, the Man, the Company* (New York: Scribner's, 1954), 646–47; "Ford Motor Company Automobile Sales in Calendar Years," Accession 96, Box 10, Ford Archives, Dearborn, Mich.; David A. Hounshell, *From the American System to Mass Production, 1800–1932* (Baltimore, Md.: Johns Hopkins University Press, 1984), 224.

EXHIBIT 3–1

Retail Price of the Model T Touring Car Compared to per Capita Realized National Income, Adjusted by the Cost of Living, 1908–1916

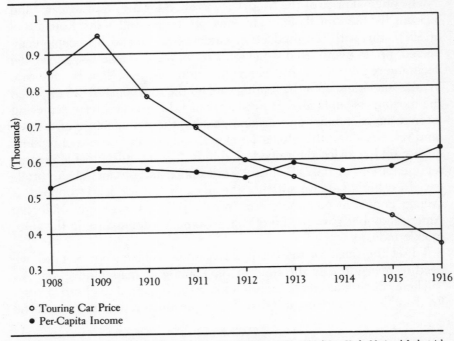

o   Touring Car Price
●   Per-Capita Income

SOURCE: Robert F. Martin, *National Income in the United States, 1799–1938* (New York: National Industrial Conference Board, 1939), 6–7, table 2.

best way to make a car, and there was a great deal of freedom in experimentation. The result was a high rate of scrapping of machine tools and of discontinuing processes. But Ford, like Carnegie before him, understood that as long as the goal was clearly in mind, this scrapping was progress, not waste. Unwittingly, Ford had stumbled into a mode of operations that engaged creative and gifted young people and got the very best out of them. In the words of historian of manufacturing David A. Hounshell, "Henry Ford possessed an uncommon gift—or was unusually lucky—in attracting to his company well-educated mechanics who believed that 'work was play.' "[44] Ford saw that for maximum efficiency it was necessary to take "the work to the man" rather than "the man to the work." At first, production at the Highland Park plant was carried out by carefully arranging the order in which men moved from one work station to the next. By the summer of 1913, a series of conveyors, rollways, and gravity slides enabled the assembly of magnetos on moving lines. A bottleneck was still occurring at the final stage of production, but, by the fall of 1913, the chassis had been put on a moving line as well. The average labor required to assemble a chassis declined from 12 hours and 28 minutes prior to October 1913 (when the chassis was put on a moving assembly line) to 1 hour and 33 minutes in the spring of 1914.[45] At its peak in 1924, Highland Park employed 68,285 workers. It was soon to be dwarfed, however, by the gigantic industrial complex Ford was putting up on the River Rouge, where more than a hundred thousand people were employed by the end of the decade.[46]

Ford thus managed to deliver to the consumer a quality product at a low price, pay the highest wages in the industry, and at the same time become the nation's second billionaire (after John D. Rockefeller). Indeed, at the height of his success, Ford may have been the richest person in the history of the world.[47]

Consider what Ford had done. He had reconciled seeming opposites.

EXHIBIT 3–2

Model T Unit Sales Compared to Total Passenger Car Unit Sales, 1908–1916

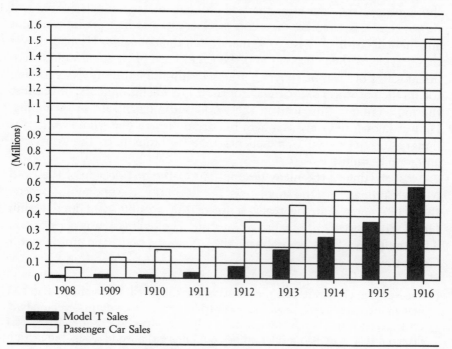

■ Model T Sales
☐ Passenger Car Sales

SOURCES: Calculated from data in Allan Nevins, *Ford: The Times, the Man, the Company* (New York: Scribner's, 1954), 646–47; "Ford Motor Company Automobile Sales in Calendar Years," Accession 96, Box 10, Ford Archives, Dearborn, Mich.; and Ralph C. Epstein, *The Automobile Industry: Its Economic and Commercial Development* (Chicago: A. W. Shaw, 1928), 336–37, 345.

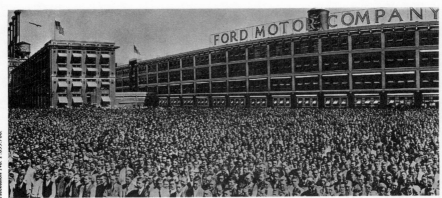

The Highland Park Plant in 1913: It was here that the moving assembly line was introduced and the five-dollar day was inaugurated. This was an expensive photograph to take because the 12,000 employees were paid while posing. As the size of this plant clearly illustrates, the automobile industry became a big money game very quickly. Large capital investment was essential to obtain market share.

He had shown that high quality and low price were not antithetical. On the contrary, the two were married through mass production. He had shown that high volume, precision production, and high wages were not antithetical. In his system, one made the other possible. He had shown that service to the consumer and the acquisition of personal riches were not at war. Ford was no robber baron, selfishly and unproductively levying toll on the pathways to progress. For these great achievements, he became the most famous American in the world and a legend in his own time. He was known not only as a man but as an "ism." The whole world was hungry for the production benefits that he brought to the American automobile industry.

Most striking in the many descriptions of the first decade of the Ford Motor Company are the suppleness, the flexibility, the open-mindedness, the excitement, and the ready sense of the possible contained within Henry Ford's gyroscopic sense of mission. The hallmark was eclecticism. The result? As Ford biographer Allan Nevins put it, the Ford Motor Company

> had not merely developed the most successful of all automobiles, but had inaugurated a new epoch in the industrial history of modern society. Many centuries before, Archimedes, exulting in his invention of the lever, had declared that if he had a fulcrum he could move the world. Mass production furnished the lever and fulcrum which . . . shifted the globe.[48]

The introduction of the Model T in 1908 and the opening of Ford's huge Highland Park plant on the first day of 1910 helped set a new course for the automobile industry as a whole. As table 3–3 shows, sales took off, and the share of lower-priced models led the way.

To produce all these vehicles, big business came to the industry. The era of entry on a shoestring was over. As one manufacturer noted in 1910, "Henceforth the history of this industry will be the story of a conflict among giants."[49] Automobile manufacture became preeminently a volume business, with the growth of large factories and the accompanying high fixed costs. In 1917, just fourteen years after it was founded and three years after the completion of the moving assembly line, Ford was the

From the collection of Henry Ford Museum & Greenfield Village. Accession No. P.O.3342.

Inside Highland Park, the Miracle of the Moving Assembly Line: Bringing the work to the man rather than the man to the work vastly increased productivity, making possible low prices for a high quality motor vehicle, the Model T Ford.

TABLE 3–3

Passenger Car Sales and Price Levels, 1908–1920

Year	Total Sales (in thousands of units)	Percent Sold for $1,375 or Less	Sales (in thousands of units)	Percent Sold for Greater than $1,375	Sales (in thousands of units)
1908	63.5	43.3 %	27.5	56.7 %	36.0
1909	127.7	45.0	57.5	55.0	70.2
1910	181.0	52.3	94.7	47.7	86.3
1911	199.3	58.9	117.4	41.1	81.9
1912	356.0	62.9	223.9	37.1	132.1
1913	461.5	67.0	309.2	33.0	152.3
1914	543.7	81.3	442.0	18.7	101.7
1915	896.0	74.7	669.3	25.3	226.7
1916	1,525.6	91.0	1,388.3	9.0	137.3
1917	1,740.8	90.0	1,566.7	10.0	174.1
1918	943.4	86.7	818.0	13.3	125.7
1919	1,657.7	75.2	1,246.6	24.8	411.1
1920	1,905.6	68.2	1,299.6	31.8	606.0

SOURCE: Ralph C. Epstein, *The Automobile Industry: Its Economic and Commercial Development* (Chicago: A. W. Shaw, 1928), 336–37, 345.

eighth largest industrial company in the country in terms of sales. By 1929, it ranked third, and General Motors had climbed to second (just behind Standard Oil of New Jersey).[50]

Automobile Marketing in the Era of Hyper-Demand

The story of Ford's production achievement in the "glory days" from the founding of the Ford Motor Company in 1903 to the rebirth of General Motors in 1921 has received a great deal of scholarly attention, and for good reason. In no other industry have the problems been more daunting or the triumph more dazzling.

Marketing, by contrast, has been relatively neglected.[51] One can search the literature on the industry, the company, and the man and find rather little about how Ford brought its product to market; and what little there is, is often contradictory.

Why has early marketing at Ford and in the industry as a whole received such limited attention? The answer is that it has been viewed as unimportant. The demand for a low-priced, reliable automobile was so great, many commentators believe, that Ford's factory could hardly keep up with it. Remember that the whole country was buying its first car. In such a business environment, marketing seemed to be little more than a formality rather than a strategic variable presenting problems and offering opportunities.

In my opinion, marketing mattered very much, even in the pre–World War I era of hyper-demand. I believe that sustained study of early marketing at Ford is essential to an understanding of the development of the automobile industry.

It is true that Henry Ford himself showed relatively little interest in the mechanics of marketing. He shared the prejudices of rural America with regard to merchants. In his opinion, retailing was essentially "speculation" in things already manufactured and, therefore, could fairly be labeled "more or less respectable graft."[52]

So it would appear that Ford largely turned the distribution problem over to others. The tasks these executives had to perform were difficult. The questions they had to answer were weighty. The models after which they could pattern their strategy were of limited usefulness. The system they eventually developed was not without flaws. Nevertheless, by the time of America's entry into World War I in 1917, Ford had the best distribution system in the industry.

Only by understanding Ford's marketing achievement prior to World War I can we properly appreciate the magnitude of its failure during the 1920s. That failure was not merely the aging of a product, the Model T; it was also the dissipation of the capabilities of a once-great business organization. As an avenue into this subject, let us outline some of the basic problems involved in automobile marketing. Let us then proceed to a description and analysis of how Ford dealt with these problems.

The first problem was that for every single automobile produced, there had to be a purchaser. Ford manufactured over a half million Model Ts in 1916. A mere four years later, it manufactured about a million. By the time Model T production was discontinued in 1927, over fifteen million had been manufactured. Each unit manufactured had to be sold. If it were not, it was worthless. "A product," Theodore Levitt has observed, "is something people buy. If they don't buy it, it's not a product. . . . It's a museum piece."[53]

An increase in volume meant an increase in fixed costs but a decrease in unit costs. But how could consumption be "massified"? Production could be standardized. But what about the consumer? Was it possible that in the process of carrying out so many individual sales, the cost of distribution per automobile could be reduced? Or was it inevitable that as the unit costs of production dropped, the unit costs of distribution would rise? The first consumers were likely to be those most interested, most well informed about the product, and most adventurous. They were also more likely to have the necessary funds. To reach successive classes of consumers, would it not be necessary to incur greater costs for selling and perhaps financing as well?

For production reasons, it was essential that the mass manufacture of automobiles be concentrated geographically. That the Detroit area should become its home was understandable when one considers the city's proximity to supplier industries, its accessibility to the transport of commodities, and its thriving community of skilled machinists and craftsmen.[54] There was no reason, on the other hand, for consumption of automobiles to be centrally located; and, of course, it was not. The Ford Motor Company early knew that it had to reach consumers all over the nation (and even before World War I, abroad as well). Automobiles first gained acceptance in cities; but they (and the Model T in particular) quickly became popular in rural areas also.[55]

How was this big, bulky, 1,200-pound item to be spread over the landscape? How much of the work of distribution should Ford undertake? At what point should the vehicle be turned over to other businesses or to the end user? When should money change hands for the vehicle, and how should payment be arranged? What kind of guarantees should be provided? What service arrangements should be made?

What role, if any, should salesmanship play in automobile marketing? What did good selling mean? Who should do it? How should the salespeople be trained? How should they be evaluated? What were reasonable expectations for the selling force? How did the company know when the sales force was doing a good job?

These were all questions of enormous complexity. They brought into sharp relief the problem of what precisely a corporation is, how it interacts with other businesses, and how it relates to its markets. Possible solutions ranged from selling the vehicle directly to the consumer to consigning annual output to one or more distribution companies at the factory gate. Firms tried these extremes as well as variations between them.[56]

The automobile was not the first machine to be mass marketed in the United States. Far from it. It was preceded by sewing machines, typewriters, cash registers, bicycles, farm equipment, and others. Each of these products presented marketing problems similar in certain respects to those of the automobile.[57] Some were complex, which meant that when they broke down professional help might be required for their repair. Some were expensive, which meant that customer financing might be required. Some were produced in huge factories, which demanded full and steady production. The marketing methods of all these other industries were well known to automobile pioneers. International Harvester, in fact, began automobile manufacture in 1907. John H. Patterson of National Cash Register was the mentor for Chevrolet sales chief Richard Grant (as well as for IBM's Thomas Watson).[58]

The differences between automobiles and these other consumer durables are, however, at least as striking as their similarities. Bicycles were intensively distributed, but they were much less complicated and less expensive. Moreover, their manufacture did not require giant works; and, with lower fixed costs, the problem of balancing production and distribution was less intense. Sewing machines were complex precision machines that did require a large factory for cost-efficient production. But they were far less expensive than automobiles; and the provision of parts and service was rendered easier by the fact that they were stationary. Sewing machines did not break down on the road. Some types of farm equipment, such as harvesters, were large, expensive, complex machines requiring a large factory for efficient production. Like automobiles and unlike sewing machines, harvesters were moving vehicles. Like cash registers and typewriters, however, harvesters were really more an industrial than a consumer product. Although individual families did purchase them, they did so as a business investment, suggesting a different kind of analysis and selling approach from one that would have been appropriate for the automobile. Moreover, the harvester was less intensively distributed than the automobile. There was not much of a market for them in cities.

Thus, there were marketing models for the automobile industry to learn from, just as there were production models. However, as was the case with production, the industry had to blaze its own marketing trail to an important extent. What trail did Ford blaze?

Early marketing at Ford seems to have been haphazard and unsystematic. In general charge of the marketing effort was James S. Couzens. Hard-driving, hard-bitten, incapable of discouragement, Couzens began his life in Canada as the son of an English grocery clerk and completed his career as a millionaire senator from Michigan. Neither Couzens nor his partners apparently wanted the company to own its whole distribution system down to the retail level. Ford was, however, willing to do business directly with the consumer if the opportunity presented itself. In March of 1904, the company established a large sales facility in Detroit to handle visiting buyers. Out of town, however, the company did business through independent dealers.[59]

Who were these dealers? At first, "anybody with cash enough to pay a deposit on a few cars could represent the company," but toward the end of 1904, Couzens began making selections with more care. Commissions and discounts were also standardized. Dealers taking over 150 cars re-

ceived a 25 percent discount. Territories were assigned, with Couzens—
"the field dictator"—expending every effort to see to it that territorial
boundaries were respected. Terms of payment were a $100 advance de-
posit and the balance on delivery.[60]

By the fall of 1905 there were an estimated 1,250 automobile dealers
in the country and 1,545 the following year. Ford's selection among those
1,545 was limited by the fact that many refused to deal with the company
because of a pending patent infringement suit. Despite this handicap, the
company, according to Allan Nevins, "never met any difficulty in selling
all the cars it made. . . ."[61]

The story of William L. Hughson, by some considered Ford's first
dealer, is illustrative of early dealer arrangements. Hughson was born in
Buffalo in 1868 or 1869 and attended Bryant & Stratton Business Institute. He became an agent for a bicycle company in 1886 and soon
thereafter opened a hardware store with a partner. When that burned
down in 1889, Hughson opted for the romance of the West, selling
bicycles to finance his trip to San Francisco.[62]

Along with a partner, Hughson opened a hardware distributorship in
San Francisco. The year 1902 found him in Chicago visiting a bicycle
show in search of new products. There he encountered what looked to
him like a "four-wheeled bicycle." The man there to explain that this was
"a motor carriage—an automobile" was none other than Henry Ford
himself. Ford must have talked a good game because Hughson agreed to
become an agent and placed a substantial initial order. "I didn't draw up
a contract with Mr. Ford. It was just a little scratch of the pen. . . . That
was the whole thing. And a handshake. The terms were cash on delivery
and 10% down." Hughson's territory included the entire West Coast,
Alaska, and Hawaii.[63]

The following year, Hughson came to Detroit with $5,000 of borrowed
money and took twelve automobiles back to San Francisco. The best he
was able to do with these vehicles was to rent them out. The people of
San Francisco did not believe in them enough to make purchases. (The
intensity of demand spoken of earlier was obviously not shared equally
throughout the nation.) Fortunately, Hughson continued to run his hardware agency as well as a battery factory and was able to survive financially
what must have appeared a disastrous investment.[64]

It was not until 1906, with the successful performance of the six of
Hughson's vehicles that survived the great earthquake, that Ford purchasing activity began to quicken on the West Coast.[65] Operating as a wholesaler as well as a retailer, Hughson began to establish relations with other
distributors up and down the coast. "The dealers ordered from us. We

would sell to them at the regular dealer's discount and then the Ford Motor Company would pay us 5%."[66]

Hughson was typical of other early dealers in several respects. He came to cars from the bicycle and hardware business, and he added cars to the goods available at his existing store. He managed to remain solvent during the early, uncertain years of the industry by relying on his other enterprises, and he was quick to capitalize on the situation by establishing himself as a wholesale distributor when the demand for cars exploded. His early arrangement with Ford was informal, sealed simply by a handshake. Apparently, Ford never sold on consignment. Even in 1902, before the Ford Motor Company had been incorporated, Ford required a deposit and the balance on delivery. When Hughson came to Detroit in 1903, he paid cash for the dozen Ford cars he took back to San Francisco. Moreover, although Hughson's original territory was vast, it was quickly subdivided among other dealers as Ford's production increased.

Hughson managed subagents at least into the 1920s if not beyond, but his activities as a wholesaler were probably somewhat circumscribed by the establishment of a company-owned branch in San Francisco in October of 1911.[67] This was one of many branches established by Couzens's successor as Ford sales manager, Norval A. Hawkins, to assist in supplying the growing demand for the Model T. The branch was originally a 7,500-square-foot establishment operated by a staff of fifteen. Automobiles were shipped to San Francisco by rail in the "knocked-down" condition designed by Hawkins to cut down on transportation costs. At first, the branch was not a full-scale assembly plant. It was responsible for preparing the cars for dealer delivery, a process that included putting the wheels on and checking the headlamps, the water, and the gas. The cars would then be turned over to the dealer, and many of them went to Hughson.[68]

The branch soon became more involved in both manufacturing and retailing in the San Francisco area. William S. Knudsen set up a full-scale assembly operation, and the first car rolled off late in 1913. Meanwhile, the 37-year-old branch manager, John B. Lund, began to spend his time on the road signing up new Ford dealers. Lund would remark at the end of a week of this: "Well, I now have a schoolteacher in Salinas who is going to be a Ford dealer, and I'll have a funeral director in some other place who is also going to be a Ford dealer." There simply were not enough automobile people to go around. Nevins asserts that dealers were "selected with scrupulous care," which may have been true as far as financial backing and standing in the community were concerned (and even this can be questioned) but could not have been true in the area of product knowledge. The average California funeral director in 1910 knew little, one would imagine, about the workings of the internal combustion engine.[69]

The Ford branch at San Francisco not only assembled and wholesaled vehicles; it sold them at retail in 1913 and possibly earlier. Retail sales accounted for 197 out of 2,875 vehicles sold during the first five and a half months of 1913 and 343 out of 4,090 vehicles sold during the comparable period in the following year.[70]

Some time between 1913 and 1915, Ford began to establish company-owned and operated retail outlets geographically separated from the main branches that it was setting up in San Francisco and elsewhere around the nation. The company is reported to have sold for the same prices and on the same terms as the dealers, but prospective customers nevertheless believed they could get a better bargain directly from Ford. Dealer opposition to the company's retailing activities was said to be strong. Then, in November 1916, the company announced its decision "to discontinue the further sale and delivery of cars at retail by or through our branch houses. . . ." From that point on, retail orders taken at the branch

> will be turned over by us to the special agent in the locality nearest where the customer resides, and . . . such agent will deliver the car and will receive full credit for the sale. . . . This ruling applies to public utility companies and all other so-called wholesale concerns that have been purchasing cars at retail through our salesmen or branch houses, including the Standard Oil Company, various city departments, the Western Electric Company, and any concerns classed as wholesalers or jobbers.[71]

The situation in San Francisco was similar to that in other parts of the country. At the turn of the century, few if any manufacturers required exclusive representation (Hughson himself dealt not only in Fords but also in the Kissel Kar), nor did they show much interest in the dealer's facilities or assign specific territories. In fact, dealers were not obliged to do anything more than to try to sell cars.[72] The mass of dealers appear to have been small businesspeople interested in taking on another line. These small entrepreneurs were often familiar with moving vehicles such as bicycles or wagons or with plumbing or other aspects of the hardware trade. Industry expert Charles C. Parlin divided early retailers into three categories: "bicycle men, nephews of rich uncles, and men seeking new connections."[73]

Early in its history, Ford began to develop a marketing system that, although no one in the company thought in these terms (an attitude that would later carry a price), had the capacity to serve as a powerful competitive tool. The company moved closer to the consumer, especially as the pulling power of the Model T became clear, by integrating forward into wholesaling and by establishing relationships with a growing number of dealers.

There are as many estimates for the number of Ford dealers as there are sources for those estimates. The data presented numerically in table 3–4 and graphically in exhibit 3–3 are drawn from internal Ford Motor Company documents that appear, but cannot be said definitely, to be authoritative. The data force us to ask two questions: (1) what explains the sharp increase in dealerships in September of 1916, and (2) why was there a trend toward an increase in the number of dealerships from 1920 to 1925? Let me turn to the first of these questions.

Ford's official announcement that it was exiting the retail business was issued in mid-November of 1916, but its plans were well known as early as August. As soon as they became known, the retail salespeople at the sales branches knew they were out of their jobs. Many of them decided to open their own Ford dealerships.[74]

The drop in the number of dealerships by September of 1917 is less easily explained. It may have been the result of the failure of some of these

TABLE 3–4

*Dealer Population of the Ford
Motor Company, 1908–1925*

Month and Year	Number of Dealers
September 1908	215
September 1909	859
September 1910	1,091
September 1911	1,400
September 1912	2,049
September 1913	3,738
September 1914	4,497
September 1915	5,046
September 1916	8,468
September 1917	6,167
September 1918	6,861
September 1919	6,778
September 1920	6,326
September 1921	7,855
September 1922	8,501
September 1923	9,451
September 1924	9,738
September 1925	9,751

SOURCE: Accession 260, Ford Motor Co. Auditing Branch Report. Archives & Library, Henry Ford Museum & Greenfield Village, Dearborn, MI.

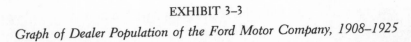

EXHIBIT 3-3

Graph of Dealer Population of the Ford Motor Company, 1908–1925

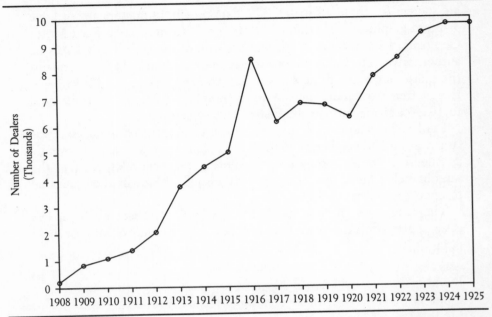

SOURCE: Accession 260, Ford Motor Co. Auditing Branch Report. Archives & Library, Henry Ford Museum & Greenfield Village, Dearborn, MI.

new entrants or of some of the weaker dealers who were already in business. It may also have been caused in part by the general dislocation associated with America's entry into World War I.

As the number of dealers increased from 1903 to 1917, so too did the number of company-owned wholesale sales offices. According to my estimates, there were 30 such sales branches attached to branch assembly plants in 1917 and another 39 that were freestanding. Thus, there seem to have been at least 69 wholesale sales offices in 1917.[75] Atop the branches were six branch supervisors who reported to Detroit concerning the branches within their purview. These supervisors were often branch managers themselves on leave from their normal responsibilities to troubleshoot for the home office. They, in turn, reported first to Norval Hawkins, sales manager from 1907 to 1918, and then to his replacement William A. Ryan as well as to Edsel Ford, Henry's son.[76]

How much money did this massive marketing effort cost? To answer this question we must categorize the expenses. The most general category is company versus dealer expenses. Company expenses include the cost of the sales force and its administration, various transportation costs, and advertising.

I have not located a comprehensive estimate of Ford marketing costs, but some statistics can be put together from various years to give an idea of the expenses involved. In 1922, William Ryan estimated salaries and expenses of the "roadmen" alone (those people who spent most of their time on the road visiting and evaluating dealerships) at $2 million.[77] To this number should be added some percentage of the salaries of the branch managers, assistant managers, chief clerks, and assistant chief clerks of those branches attached to assembly plants and sales and parts offices and all the salaries at the branches that were solely sales offices. Salaries of sales and marketing staff at the home office must also be considered. These salaries might have amounted to an additional half million dollars. Any estimate for expenditures for office space and transportation would be pure guesswork.

Advertising expenditures varied from year to year. Henry Ford had mixed feelings about advertising, conceding that it was "absolutely essential to introduce good, useful things" but "an economic waste" for products already on the market.[78] The result was, in the judgment of historian David L. Lewis, lower expenditures than those of any other major consumer firm of the 1910s. In 1916, the company invested a grand total of $16,000 on paid advertising. From 1917 to 1923, it spent not a penny advertising the Model T.

This policy was facilitated by two circumstances. The first was that, although the Ford Motor Company did not advertise the Model T during these years, the automobile benefited from advertising nevertheless. The company imposed its advertising expenditures onto its dealers, who were required to finance them under the terms of their contracts. The company thus benefited from an estimated $3 million a year in advertising, an enormous sum for the time, during years in which it paid for no space at all. The second reason that Ford was able to spend so little on advertising was the huge amount of free publicity that the company and Henry Ford personally commanded.[79]

If the first of the two general categories of expenses involved in getting the vehicle from the factory to the customer was undertaken by the company, the second was undertaken by the dealer. The dealers incurred expenses for occupancy, inventory, transportation (the drive-away from the branch plant), advertising and the purchase and posting of signs, and salaries and associated personnel expenses. What did this come to? The answer varies widely from the established big-city agencies to some in rural areas that were little more than shacks with no paid sales force and precious little inventory. Clarence Bullwinkel, assistant manager of the

San Francisco branch, reported in 1922 that a dealer required on the average about $5,000 to get started out in the country.[80] If we take that as the average dealer capital investment (and it is probably on the low side because of the bias in Bullwinkel's estimate toward rural dealerships), we do, I think, get one important clue concerning why the Ford Motor Company did not integrate forward into retailing. That clue is money. If Ford's 8,501 dealers in 1922 required an investment of $5,000 each, the total dealer investment in marketing Fords came to over $42.5 million. The investment represented by the 9,751 dealers in 1925 would have equaled over $48.75 million. If the average investment were increased to, say, $6,500, to take urban dealers into account, the totals for 1922 and 1925 would have been over $55.25 million and just under $63.4 million, respectively. In 1919, when Ford took his company private, it was valued at $255 million.[81] That year Ford had 6,774 dealers; at $5,000 per dealership, that represents an investment of $33.87 million. Independent businesspeople thus had made an investment equal to almost 15 percent of the value of the company and far more than Ford itself had invested in the marketing function. These dealers furnished a selling force of probably between 15,000 and 20,000 people located throughout the nation.

It should be noted that there are many reasons in addition to capital investment that Ford and the other major automobile manufacturers exited retailing, have stayed out of it, and at this writing do not show an interest in getting involved in it. Local dealers give the manufacturers an intimate knowledge of the situation in their markets that might otherwise be difficult to attain. Further, although trade-ins did not become an important factor until the 1920s, trading did take place on a small scale from the beginning. Trading is different from manufacturing, and it is perhaps true that entrepreneurs make better traders than do salaried managers.

The manufacturers decided that retailing was fundamentally different from what they did best. It was not in selling to the end user that their competitive advantage lay. It seems to me that an important reason for this decision was the sheer size of the capital investment required for an effective dealer network. It is true, of course, that this capital earned a return. But many other kinds of capital investments competing for the manufacturers' attention also earned a return. Retailing, it was felt, was best left to others.

Let us now briefly review the development of marketing at Ford, from the founding of the company in 1903 to 1917. These years can be divided into two periods: 1903–1907 and 1907–1917.

In the first period, James S. Couzens was in charge. Important steps were taken in shaping the company's marketing program. Couzens established a number of sales branches around the country and hired some able executives who were to remain part of the Ford marketing system for years. He made an effort to see that the dealers were properly supervised.[82]

Couzens had too many other responsibilities, however, to give the marketing network the time and attention it demanded. In the fall of 1907, the sales department was turned over to Norval A. Hawkins. Hawkins was trained as an accountant, and this background helped him to establish standards of performance both for the company-owned branches and for the dealers they supervised. He could feel the pulse of the market thanks to the information system he devised and monitored. Hawkins also made a major contribution to marketing logistics. It was he who worked out the system of shipping complete knocked-down units to branch assembly plants, thus saving on freight rates.

Combined with his sense of system was Hawkins's spirit. He had the soul of a salesperson, always pushing for more results, often providing encouragement (it was he who founded *Ford Times*, a celebratory house organ for branches and dealers), and tough when he had to be.[83]

It was under Hawkins that the Ford marketing method and organization were most clearly defined. In the early days, Ford seems to have sold to customers in a variety of different ways. By 1916, however, retailing, as we have seen, was eliminated. Wholesaling, on the other hand, was to be owned and managed by the company. Most other firms had to rely on independent distributors. Ford, however, had the consumer pull and the volume to enable it to afford to build its own branches and to staff them.[84] (Exhibit 3–4 diagrams the reporting relationships in the Ford marketing system in 1917.)

The task, then, for Ford was to control this great host of dealers without ownership through the use of its salaried sales organization. To get an idea of the techniques used to reach this goal, let us take a close look at the operations of one branch in one year: Atlanta, Georgia, in 1917.

The Ford Motor Company opened its first Atlanta office in 1907.[85] By 1911, this office had grown, and a new manager, Robert S. Abbott, was appointed to run it. Abbott had joined the Ford Motor Company in March 1907 as a salesman at the huge Chicago branch. When he resigned from Ford in 1930, his monthly salary was $2,975 compared to $175 in Atlanta in 1911.[86] Similarly, Abbott's assistant manager in Atlanta, George I. Banks, rose from salesman at $100 a month plus bonus in March 1914 to assistant manager in 1915. By 1917, Banks, not yet 30 years of age, had become the manager of his own branch, albeit a small one, in Jacksonville, Florida. His monthly salary as of 1 August 1918 was $450, representing more than a fourfold increase in only four years.[87] The careers of both men are indicative of the quick advancement in position

EXHIBIT 3–4

Reporting Relationships in the Ford Marketing System, 1917

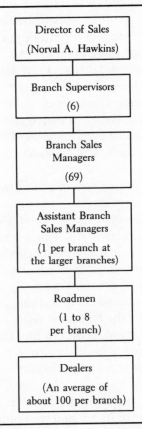

SOURCE: Richard S. Tedlow, "Automobile Marketing in the Context of American Business History," in *Business Management in Historical Perspective*, ed. Maurice Lévy-Leboyer and Patrick Fridenson (Cambridge, England: Cambridge University Press, forthcoming). Used by permission.

and salary available in the early days of Ford. Unlike smaller automobile companies, Ford was big enough to afford to pay talented people to staff its own wholesale network.[88]

In addition to Abbott and Banks, administrative personnel at the Atlanta branch included a chief clerk and a superintendent, as well as office staff members and assembly managers. The branch also served as the home base of a force of about a half dozen roadmen who, with Banks and Abbott, were responsible for visiting approximately 185 limited agencies in Georgia, Alabama, and Tennessee.[89]

Soon after Abbott became manager, more space was rented for the branch, and a repair and parts department was opened. In 1915, an assembly plant was established in the city. This facility was a four-story structure on two and two-thirds acres with 151,327 square feet.[90] An operation that had originated as a small sales office eight years earlier was in 1917 a multiservice outlet, offering sales, service, repair, a parts store, and an assembly plant turning out almost 12,000 cars annually.

For the Ford Motor Company as a whole, on the basis of unit and dollar sales, the fiscal year from 1 August 1916 to 31 July 1917 was a spectacular success. Unit sales hit 730,041, up more than 50 percent from the previous year. Profits were down 40 percent from the previous year, due to a steep price cut from $440 to $360 on the touring car. Nevertheless, the company made more than $30 million.[91] In the territory supervised by the Atlanta branch, business was booming. Numerous agencies reported that they had more orders on hand than cars to fill them. It is against this backdrop of Ford's prosperity that we discuss the activities of the Atlanta branch and the state of the dealers it supervised.

One is immediately impressed by the blizzard of paperwork generated as the branch employees attempted to maintain contact with the dealers in their territory. Roadmen were visiting perhaps five or six dealers a week.[92] The manager himself was supposed to take trips out into the territory "several days of each week" and was expected to visit every dealership at least once a year, as was the assistant manager.[93]

Each visit led to a report covering the population of the dealer's territory and the taxable property therein, an analysis of the local economic situation, an estimate of the capital invested in the agency and the credit the owner could command, the value of the parts inventory (no one in the territory at this time was holding on to Model Ts themselves, which were sold when shipped), and comments on the agent and the employees concerning character and connections, sales ability, advertising, exclusivity, and actual sales compared to plan.

These reports were only the beginning of the paperwork. Whenever an agent had a conflict with the branch or the home office, correspondence was created. There was a constant stream of letters from headquarters on matters ranging from new prices to the fact that one C. D. MacKenzie, former office boy from the New York branch, "has been traveling through the country representing himself as a roadman by the name of C. D. Marsh and obtaining funds from hotels on our Light Draft Form."[94]

On 27 March 1917, branch supervisor E. T. Backus sent his evaluation of the Atlanta branch to Norval Hawkins in Detroit. Backus personally visited seventy-eight dealerships, which he categorized from Class A ("proper building interior and exterior, good location, tools, machinery, equipment, separate show room, garage and shop—proper stock room— retail record, car record, price schedule, accounting system—order forms—Clean in all departments") to Class E ("Poor building, no equipment, disorderly or dirty—fair or poor stock arrangement, no records—not inclined to follow suggestions made—place amounts to merely a stock of parts, outside service arrangement—irregular contract, question as to whether should be continued—after pressure has planned to build a place in order to hold contract").[95] Backus classified only 4 agencies as "A," whereas 27 were "E," with 7, 10, and 30 in the "B", "C", and "D" categories, respectively. He found that various agents needed to be put on different contracts, that some subcontractors were claiming to provide representation that they were not, and that some agencies should be terminated. As for the branch management, Backus asserted that not enough emphasis was being placed on sales techniques and record keeping, that too much time was being spent with agencies "in good shape" to the neglect of those "who really needed attention," and that Abbott had not visited all of the agencies (although Banks had).[96]

On May 8, Hawkins, having received and analyzed the Backus letter, wrote Abbott. His letter did not acknowledge that the Atlanta branch was selling more cars than it could get its hands on or that Abbott was a rising star in the organization. Instead, it contained two and a half pages of orders delivered in a peremptory tone: "1. Arrange at once to call on all agents and sub-agents in your territory. . . . 2. See that roadmen spend the proper time with all agents," and so forth. Hawkins wanted some contracts changed, more effective visits by roadmen, and "a stop put immediately" to the practice of some agents carrying lines other than Ford.[97]

Abbott responded to Hawkins immediately in an artful five pages of submissiveness and exculpation. He regretted that he had not been to some agencies at the time Backus wrote his letter, but between that time and this (May) he had been almost everywhere "with the exception of a few minor small agencies which agencies I will cover immediately." There have, however, "been some agencies which I have seen three or four times already. I just wanted to mention this to show you that I have not been neglectful this season in calling on our agents. . . ."[98] Abbott then proceeded to a point-by-point discussion of the fourteen observations in the Hawkins letter. In each instance, he either regretted less than adequate performance, asserted that solutions to the problems were under way, or expressed uncertainty concerning what precisely the home office's policy was.[99] Apparently, Abbott's responses and actions were satisfactory. The Atlanta branch flourished; and he himself went on to a successful career in distribution at Ford for more than a decade afterward.

There were indeed problems with the Ford system, as illustrated by the Atlanta story. Too many agencies were Class E and too few Class A. Too few had adopted the customer prospecting system that the company was pushing. Too many either handled other cars or spent too much time with other businesses. There were too many varieties of contractual and sub-contractual arrangements and too many agents and subagents who were not living up to their terms. Too many dealerships looked down at the heels. Too little parts inventory was carried. Too little advertising was done. Too many selling opportunities were being missed due to lack of aggressiveness or poor management.[100] Too few roadmen were working hard enough or smart enough. Too much time was spent with dealers who did not need help, and perhaps in the process the roadmen were "compromising their positions as representatives of our company by accepting hospitalities on the part of dealers, even going so far as taking dinner with them in their homes and remaining there over night instead of putting up at the hotel, where they should."[101]

The roadmen were the company's eyes and ears, the key to the Ford strategy of control without ownership. And yet, who guards the guardians? The dealer was near, the branch office far away, and the home office farther away still. Were the roadmen telling the branch office the truth about the dealer? Was the branch manager in turn telling the true story to the home office? And how reliable was the report of a man like Backus, who probably saw himself as being in competition with Abbott for promotion in the Ford marketing system? What was Hawkins to believe? By the time this great mass of information got to him from two dozen branches, it was a jumble of names and numbers. Hawkins could not have had firsthand knowledge of more than a very small percentage of Ford's thousands of dealers.

For all these difficulties, though, Ford's early marketing system was in many ways impressive. The company had settled on a structure that had much to recommend it. The Model T was represented all over the country. The great American automobile mass market did not merely spring out of thin air. A lot of the work of market development—of explaining what a car was, of providing service and parts when it broke down, of envisioning for the potential purchaser a network of as yet unconstructed roads on which it could be driven—was successfully undertaken by Ford through its management of its retail network. Many of the right questions were being asked of the dealers. The company was developing a philosophy about going out and prospecting for customers that is more aggressive than that used today. Despite distortions, it was accumulating information that, if properly used, could enable it to make a reasonable estimate of the number of automobiles per unit of population it should expect to sell under given market conditions. No other automobile company had anything comparable.

By World War I, the Ford Motor Company had created a total approach to the automobile business through which it was able to thrust itself into a position of leadership—a position that appeared unassailable. The elements of that total approach included:

1. First and foremost, a great product—the Model T Ford.
2. Long runs in efficient plants. Few variations on this great product. A stringent policy of cost minimization.
3. A policy of company-owned branches, unlike the practice in much of the rest of the industry. Clear standards for and close supervision of the branches.
4. Intensive distribution at the dealer level.
5. Far closer supervision of dealers than was the case with any other firm in the industry. A large sales force capable of covering almost every town with a population greater than 2,000 in the United States.
6. Consumer pull, made possible by the value of the product, the fame of the CEO, and millions of dollars in dealer advertising. This pull enabled the company to control the distribution channel. The dealers—forced to advertise—were unwilling conspirators in their own manipulation.

The data in table 3–5 are both the illustration of and the reason for the success of this policy. When a consumer purchased a Model T in 1913, 62 percent of the retail selling price was pure car. If the consumer wished to buy the $1,000 grade, he or she paid 82 percent more money ($550 to $1,000) but received only 62 percent more car ($340 to $550). Distribution costs for the $1,000 car were $250 as opposed to a mere $90 for the Model T. Yet odds are that Ford's superior distribution system actually delivered more value even for the small sum than did the $1,000 competitor.

TABLE 3–5

Estimated Comparative Automobile Costs, 1913

	$550	RSP[a]	$1,000	RSP	$2,000	RSP	$4,000	RSP
Material and labor	$340	62%	$ 550	55%	$1,050	52.5%	$1,900	47%
Advertising, selling, and overhead	20	4	100	10	250	12.5	550	14
Wholesale and retail selling costs	90	16	250	25	500	25	1,200	30
Manufacturer's profit	100	18	100	10	200	10	350	9
Cost to consumer	550		1,000		2,000		4,000	

[a]RSP = Retail Selling Price
SOURCE: Allan Nevins with Frank E. Hill, *Ford: The Times, the Man, the Company* (New York: Scribner's, 1954), 651. Reprinted with permission of Charles Scribner's Sons, an imprint of Macmillan Publishing Company. Copyright 1954 Columbia University; copyright renewed © 1982 Meredith Nevins Mayer and Anne Nevins Loftis.

General Motors: From "Fabulous Billy" Durant to Mr. Sloan

General Motors was founded on 16 September 1908, by William Crapo Durant. Durant was born in Boston on 8 December 1861 to a family well known in both Massachusetts and Michigan. Choosing Flint, Michigan, as his home, he went into the carriage business with J. Dallas Dort and was a millionaire by the time he was 40. But Durant was not satisfied with mere riches, and as the carriage business "settled down into stodgy matter-of-factness," his "natural bent toward commercial adventure" led him to automobiles.[102]

Like Ford, Durant was a visionary. The *Detroit Free Press* observed soon after his death: "To him the immediate future was remote; the remote future near and vivid." Said a banker, "Durant is a genius and therefore not to be dealt with on the same basis as ordinary businessmen. In many respects he is a child in emotions, in temperament, and in mental balance, yet possessed of wonderful energy and ability along certain other well defined lines."[103] Unlike Ford, "Fabulous Billy" Durant was, above all, a plunger, with General Motors and with his own personal finances.[104] He nearly bankrupted the company on two occasions and finally succeeded in bankrupting himself in 1936, when he listed his debts as $914,231 and his assets as his clothing, valued at $250.[105] But for a time, he loomed as the second great man of the automobile industry. Like Henry Ford, Billy Durant believed in the automobile.

Durant entered the auto business by taking control of the troubled Buick Motor Car Company in Flint, Michigan, in 1904. In 1907, he attempted to form a combination of four major manufacturers: Buick, Maxwell-Briscoe, REO, and Ford, but the deal fell through when Ford demanded that Durant's $3 million offer be paid in cash. However, Durant was determined to form an automobile conglomerate. Following its creation in 1908, General Motors acquired Oldsmobile and Cadillac, in addition to Buick, as well as several other motor vehicle companies and an assortment of parts and accessory manufacturers. Except for Cadillac, for which the price was $4.4 million in cash, most of the companies were paid for in General Motors stock. Durant renewed his effort to buy Ford, but Ford raised his price to $8 million, still in cash, leading Durant to the conclusion that Ford had no intention of selling his company.[106]

Although they shared a belief in the future of the automobile, Durant and Ford tried to meet this future in opposite ways. Ford was certain that the Model T was the permanent answer to the nation's transportation needs, whereas Durant was convinced that no one could know what the car of the future would be. As a result, he acquired many different companies simply to protect himself should one of these makes prove to embody the technology of the future. As he himself explained it, ". . . how was anyone to know that Cartercar wasn't to be the thing? It had the friction drive and no other car had it. How could I tell what these engineers would say next? . . . I was for getting every kind of car in sight, playing it safe all along the line."[107]

Durant lost control of General Motors to bankers in 1910 during a cash crisis brought on by his acquisition strategy. He bounced back quickly, however. The following year, he bought the fledgling Chevrolet Motor Car Company and proceeded to build it into a large, profitable competitor. With the backing of the du Pont family, Durant returned to the presidency of General Motors in 1916, bringing Chevrolet with him.

Once again, Durant pursued a strategy of rapid growth. Through the exchange of stock he absorbed a variety of suppliers, including manufacturers of roller bearings, rims, radiators, horns, and starting, ignition, and lighting systems. With Delco came the brilliant engineer Charles Kettering; with Hyatt Roller Bearings came Alfred P. Sloan, Jr.

Durant hoped that his many acquisitions would provide insurance against the vicissitudes of the fast-changing auto business. They did not provide a hedge against business cycles and technological uncertainty, however, because Durant's product line strategy was poorly conceived and executed. He had little interest in automobile engineering, so he bought companies indiscriminately and saddled GM with many weak cars that could make little contribution in either technology or sales. Since there was no overall plan, his automobile divisions competed with, rather than complemented, one another. Further, GM, as constructed by Durant, lacked organizational capability. The company did not "systematically constrain or integrate divisional operations," as Arthur J. Kuhn has shown in his valuable study. "Neither performance improvements nor even results were transmitted horizontally or vertically. With his minuscule central staff, Durant was unable to provide for the discovery and communication of the best technique of auto design, production, and marketing among his divisions."[108]

In the case of strong acquisitions, Durant was often unable to hold on to the most talented executives. When he took over General Motors for the second time in 1916, he hired Walter P. Chrysler as president of the Buick division at an annual salary of a half million dollars. Chrysler called Durant a genius and found him charming, but he eventually had to get out, saying, "I just can't stand the way the thing is being run."[109] Finally, GM under Durant suffered from a lack of data about consumer needs and desires. As Kuhn aptly observed, "Durant's telephones were connected to the stock market, not the automobile markets. . . . Who knew what might catch on with the fickle automobile public? Durant certainly did not, as he made no attempt to find out what consumers desired."[110]

"Look at All THREE!

BUT DON'T BUY ANY LOW-PRICED CAR UNTIL YOU'VE DRIVEN THE NEW PLYMOUTH WITH FLOATING POWER"

THOUSANDS of people have been waiting expectantly until today before buying a new car. I hope that you are one of them.

Now that the new low-priced cars are here (including the new Plymouth which will be shown on Saturday) I urge you to carefully *compare* values.

This is the time for you to "shop" and buy wisely. Don't make a deposit on any automobile until you've actually had a demonstration.

It is my opinion that the automobile industry as a whole has never offered such values to the public.

In the new Plymouth we have achieved more than I had ever dared to hope for. If you had told me two years ago that such a big, powerful, beautiful automobile could be sold at the astonishing prices we will announce on Saturday, . . . I'd have said it was absolutely impossible.

I have spent my life building fine cars. But no achievement in my career has given me the deep-down satisfaction

A Statement by
Walter P. Chrysler

that I derive from the value you get in this 1932 Plymouth. To me, its outstanding feature is Floating Power. We already know how the public feels about this. Last summer it was news, but today it is an established engineering achievement.

It is my opinion, and I think that of leading engineering authorities, that any new car without Floating Power is obsolete. Drive a Plymouth with Patented Floating Power, and note its utter lack of vibration . . . then drive a car with old-fashioned engine mountings and you will understand what I mean. *There's absolutely no comparison.*

We have made the Plymouth a much larger automobile. It is a BIG car. We have increased its power, lengthened the wheelbase and greatly improved its beauty.

In my opinion you will find the new Plymouth the easiest riding car you have ever driven. Yet with all these improvements we have been able to lower prices.

Again let me urge you, go and see the new Plymouth with Floating Power on Saturday. Be sure to look at all THREE low-priced cars and don't buy *any* until you do. That is the way to get the most for your money.

FIRST SHOWING NEXT SATURDAY, APRIL 2nd, AT DESOTO, DODGE AND CHRYSLER DEALERS

The Last Great American Entrepreneur in the Automobile Industry: Walter P. Chrysler. He ran Buick when General Motors was headed by William Durant. Chrysler rebelled against Durant's lack of organization, however, and left the company. He formed the corporation bearing his name in 1925 and managed to make a success of the Plymouth, which was launched just as the Great Depression commenced. Chrysler is seen above in an early example of hard-hitting comparative advertising.

Durant's irresponsible stock market speculation and gross mismanagement during the depression following World War I led his bankers, Morgan and Company, to the conclusion that he was "totally incompetent" to manage the corporation. A series of investments by the du Pont family and associates and by the Du Pont Company climaxed in the 1920 ouster of Durant from GM, this time permanently. Pierre du Pont, GM's new owner, reluctantly agreed to take on the presidency himself.[111]

The depression of 1920 was a disaster for General Motors. Alfred P. Sloan, Jr., described the bleak situation facing the corporation at the time of Durant's forced resignation:

> The automobile market had nearly vanished and with it our income. Most of our plants were shut down or assembling a small number of cars out of semifinished materials in the plants. We were loaded with high-priced inventory and commitments at the old inflated price level. We were short of cash. We had a confused product line. There was a lack of control and of any means of control in operations and finance, and a lack of adequate information about anything. In short, there was just about as much crisis, inside and outside, as you could wish for if you liked that sort of thing.[112]

In addition to the company's internal problems, its major competitor was the Ford Motor Company. We must keep in mind that GM executives did not know in 1920 and 1921 what the future held for Ford. Both man and company were, in those years, at the height of their prestige. In an industry in which market share has always been a key to profitability, every other automobile sold in the United States in 1921 was a Model T. Ford's 55.67 percent share that year represented 845,000 vehicles. Although General Motors was the second firm in the industry, its unit sales of 193,275 were just 22.87 percent of Ford's and only 12.73 percent of the industry as a whole.[113] GM sales toward the end of 1920 had slumped disastrously. Car and truck sales for the final quarter came to 43,532, well under half the number sold during the comparable period the previous year. From April 30 to October 31, inventories soared almost 25 percent to $209 million. The current ratio at the end of 1920 was 2.24:1 compared to 3.84:1 and 5.5:1 at the close of 1919 and 1918, respectively. The stock price in 1920 had dropped from $27.625 on May 29 to $13.25 by Christmas.[114]

Yet there were pluses, too. With its ownership of some of the best-established names, such as Oldsmobile, Buick, and Cadillac, General Motors had a major presence in the automobile industry. And if, like John Jacob Raskob, Du Pont treasurer and financier, one chose to define Ford out of the segment in which General Motors competed (that company, he explained, produced "a special car in very large quantities and is not considered by us a competitor"), then General Motors could be considered a leader.[115]

Along with acquiring famous names, General Motors had invested great sums in assembly plants and in suppliers. Total assets at the end of 1920 were almost $605 million. Nearly $70 million of that represented investments in suppliers, and about $250 million was carried under property, plant, and equipment.[116] The arrival of the Du Pont interests meant that men of exceptional ability were available to manage these resources. The challenge was to ensure that the firm did not lose more people like Walter Chrysler, to attract more talent if possible, and, most important, to devise a way to make the huge organization answer to the will of those trying to run it.

The individual most responsible for the achievement of this goal was Alfred P. Sloan, Jr. Sloan was born in New Haven in 1875, where he lived for ten years. His father, a coffee and tea importer, then moved the family to Brooklyn. "I am told," Sloan wrote in 1963, that "I still have the accent."[117] He attended the Brooklyn Polytechnic Institute, where he developed his interest in mechanics and engineering, and went on to the Massachusetts Institute of Technology, where he graduated with a B.S. in mechanical engineering in 1895, one year ahead of his class and five years after his future colleague in the management of General Motors, Pierre S. du Pont.

In 1895, the country was in the midst of a depression, and Sloan could not find work. "My discouragement was stronger because I had worked so hard at college. As I look back [from 1941], I believe it to be the most discouraging point of my whole life. I had been a grind. I had worked every possible minute. . . ."[118] His discouragement was not long-lived.

His father gave Sloan an introduction to a sugar magnate named John E. Searles, who pointed him to a firm in which Searles had an investment, the Hyatt Roller Bearing Company, located in a "gloomy, machinery-cluttered loft in a building on Market Street in Newark." Sloan got a job in the drafting room at $50 a week.[119]

Sloan did not see much of a future at Hyatt. The firm was running at a loss; and its backer, Searles, was beginning to tire of what appeared to him to be throwing good money after bad. Sloan wanted to get married and felt he could improve his prospects by joining the Hygienic Refrigerator Company in Manhattan in 1898. This company was founded by an inventor who was "trying to make a mechanical icebox twenty years ahead of his time." Sloan got married on the strength of this new position, but "in a short time, there was a jolt." The refrigerators the company sold all broke down, their inventor died, and his company failed.[120]

Sloan was not precisely back on the street again. He approached his father who, along with another investor, bought Hyatt from Searles for $5,000. Existence was hand to mouth for a short while; "Payroll worry has whitened a lot of hair in this country, mine included."[121] But the firm was soon on its feet. Hyatt had been doing about $2,000 a year in volume and unprofitably so; but it made a $12,000 profit in Sloan's first six months.[122] His father's faith in him had been justified.

The firm's founder, John Wesley Hyatt, had told Sloan that he "should find a market for antifriction bearings anywhere there was a turning wheel." Most of Hyatt's business had been in industries "where line shafting was used in the mechanical transmission of power, [but] we knew the field was going to disappear" as electric power revolutionized the factory.[123] The solution was suggested in 1899 by a letter from Elwood Haynes in Kokomo, Indiana, who wanted to know whether Hyatt bearings might be of better use than greased wagon axles on his automobiles.[124]

Hyatt grew with the auto industry. In the process, Sloan learned much about precision and product quality, about punctuality, and about selling to the industry that was to become Hyatt's great customer.[125] By 1916, Hyatt had become a large company with some 4,000 employees, and both marketing and production capacity had grown. There were three sales forces: one in Newark for mine cars, shafting, and other industrial machinery; another in Chicago for servicing the farm equipment industry; and the third, of course, in Detroit. Hyatt had contracts with more than a dozen of the leading names in the automobile industry and with suppliers of axles, transmissions, and electric starters.

But there was, amidst all this, an obvious problem:

> [O]ne dismal fact was revealed by our accounting: More than half our business came from Ford, and our other big customer, General Motors, dwarfed the remainder. If either Ford or General Motors should start making their own bearings or use some other type of bearings, our company would be in a desperate situation.[126]

For this reason, Sloan was receptive when Durant expressed an interest in purchasing Hyatt. The agreed-on price was $13.5 million, handsomely repaying the initial investment of $5,000 by Sloan's father, who with his son owned 60 percent of the company's stock.

Durant made Sloan the president of United Motors, the parts and accessories company of which Hyatt became a division. Sloan put together a general office to coordinate the activities of the units so that the firm could function as more than a holding company. He created a division to manage sales and service and thus to assure "better coordination between marketing and manufacturing, [to permit] his divisions to exploit the replacement trade more effectively, and [to help] provide General Motors' dealers with a reliable supply of parts and accessories."[127] Sloan also developed control systems to increase his understanding of what precisely the organization was doing.[128]

Not surprisingly, Sloan had little tolerance for Durant's approach to management. Durant was a "big picture" man. Some would call him intuitive; others, less charitable but more to the point, sloppy. Durant was, in fact, a good example of strategy without implementation. According to Sloan, Durant "never felt obliged to make an engineering hunt for facts." Sloan, in contrast, was convinced that "facts are precious things, to be eagerly sought and treated with respect."[129]

By the end of 1919, Sloan "had become increasingly disturbed by the trend of affairs inside General Motors," and he wrote a report on the firm's organization for Durant.[130] Durant had neither the time nor the inclination for such matters, and Sloan was considering an offer to join the investment firm of Lee, Higginson when Durant lost control of the company.[131]

Pierre S. du Pont was 50 years of age in 1920 when he assumed the presidency of General Motors. It was a job he did not want. From as early as 1910, du Pont had wanted "to take time to realize his childhood dream," the development of the magnificent Longwood estate.[132] He needed neither the money nor the aggravation that would attend the rescue of General Motors, but his prestige in the business community and among the bankers involved necessitated his taking the job, if only briefly.[133] He soon realized that Sloan, who had become vice-president for operations, was the most outstanding among his subordinates. General Motors came to life through Sloan's guidance even before he assumed the presidency in 1923.

In 1920, when the du Pont team took control of GM, Sloan was 45 years of age. He was almost 6 feet tall, but weighed only 130 pounds. His manner was "formal, even remote."[134] The contrast with Durant was striking:

> Durant was a small, lively, warm man. Nearly everyone called him "Billy." Mr. Sloan was tall, quiet, and cool. Increasing deafness heightened his reserve. Nearly everyone called him Mr. Sloan.[135]

Sloan's marriage was childless, and he had no hobbies. "He was, rather, totally absorbed by the challenge of running GM, dedicated, as he put it, 'perhaps to a fault.' "[136] An associate likened him to the product he manufactured at Hyatt, the roller bearing: "self-lubricating, smooth, eliminates friction and carries the load."[137]

Sloan's qualifications for his position were manifest. He was an engineer and a production man who had been closely associated with the automobile industry since its inception. He knew all the pioneers and indeed had corresponded with Henry Ford before the turn of the century. Despite being a production man and despite his admiration for Ford, Sloan had none of Ford's "artisan mentality." He did not try to run his business by rote, and he understood the critical necessity of changing with the times.

Like Durant, Sloan was a man of daring, imagination, and vision. "I have always believed in planning big," he announced in his autobiography; and "I put no ceiling on progress."[138] On the other hand, Sloan was a consummate believer in reality—in finding out what it was and acting accordingly. Sloan thus embodied the virtues of Ford and Durant without their shortcomings; and he brought an additional strength to the scene that neither of them possessed—an acute understanding that excellence in organization was the prerequisite for success in the automobile industry.

The Changing Postwar Market

By the end of World War I, the automobile had been a commercial reality for twenty years, and people understood that it was here to stay. The automobile was still a potentially dangerous machine, but now people were underestimating rather than overestimating its hazards. Roads were much improved, and the cars themselves were easier to operate. The electric starter was introduced in 1912 and was standard equipment within two or three years. Only 10 percent of cars were built with closed bodies in 1919; but more than half were enclosed by 1925, making them far more comfortable.[139]

The rate of fundamental technological change slowed considerably in the 1920s. The reasons are not altogether clear, but one factor undoubtedly was the capital required to build the huge plants that Fordism had made the order of the day. In 1926, Ford's total assets were $898,986,071 and those of General Motors, $920,894,106.[140] Since without enormous assets the game could not be played, the 1920s became the era of the great shakeout. According to one count, there were 88 firms in the industry in 1921, but by 1929 that number had dropped to 20.[141] Although the number of firms and makes declined, factory capacity more than tripled from 1.4 million units in 1921 to 4.4 million units in 1927.[142] At the same time, the operational life span of the automobile was increasing. Estimates gave the average automobile manufactured in 1918 five years of usefulness; by 1927, the estimate was over seven years, with Fords above the average.[143]

Table 3–6, which provides data on car sales, total registrations, and number of households from 1920 to 1930, shows that the number of available first-time buyers for the automobile was rapidly diminishing. Indeed, the trade and general business literature of the early 1920s was filled with reports of the "saturation" of the automobile market.

An industry that had been "geared to sell automobiles to a car-less population" was now face-to-face with an experienced market.[144] The market was not only experienced in terms of knowledge but in terms of ownership. Since the automobile lasted longer, many potential purchasers already owned one with some life left in it. These buyers might be convinced to try a new or different car, but they wanted something for their "old" car. Thus was born the market for used cars and the practice not merely of buying at a dealership but of trading there.

The distribution system was unable to accommodate this transformation. Manufacturers maintained the practice of shipping vehicles to dealers in accord with a quota determined by what was needed to keep the factory running full and steady rather than by what consumer demand actually was. Dealers created sales the only way they could—they gave

TABLE 3–6

Number of Car Sales, Registrations, and Households, 1920–1930

Year	Car Sales (in thousands)	Passenger Car Registrations (in thousands)	Total U.S. Households (in thousands)	Total Passenger Car Registrations as a Percentage of Households
1920	1,905.6	8,131.5	24,467	33.2
1921	1,468.1	9,212.2	25,119	36.6
1922	2,274.2	10,704.1	25,687	41.6
1923	3,624.7	13,253.0	26,298	50.3
1924	3,185.9	15,436.1	26,941	57.2
1925	3,735.2	17,481.0	27,540	63.4
1926	3,692.3	19,268.0	28,101	68.5
1927	2,936.5	20,193.3	28,632	70.5
1928	3,775.4	21,362.2	29,124	73.3
1929	4,455.2	23,121.0	29,582	78.1
1930	2,787.5	23,034.8	29,997	76.7

SOURCE: Harold Katz, *The Decline of Competition in the Automobile Industry, 1920–1940* (New York: Arno, 1977), 41.

generous allowances for used cars. In 1922, when the used-car problem
at the dealer level became unbearable, dealers allowed an average of
$332.88 for a used car but were able to realize only $276.67 on its sale.
Thus they absorbed on average a $56.21 cash loss for each used-car
transaction, even if they were able to sell the car (and this figure leaves
out selling, reconditioning, and overhead expenses). Since the dealer
markup on a new car averaged only $132, the sacrifice on the used car
represented almost half the dealer's profits on sales to first-time buyers.
The stock of used cars in dealer hands doubled, from 200,000 to 400,000,
in 1922 alone.[145] Moreover, the cash flow situation turned around almost
overnight, because potential buyers wanted their used cars to serve as part
of their down payment. Disgruntled dealers generally agreed that the
"best automobile salesman" in the business was the "prospect with an old
car to trade in."[146] As table 3–7 shows, used-car sales exceeded those of
new cars for the first time in 1927, and they continued to do so into the
Depression.

In the post–World War I era, dealers began to fail, and dealer distress
was widespread. For the first time, the automobile industry began to take
a sustained and intensive look at the panoply of tools of the modern

TABLE 3–7

Number and Proportion of Used-Car Sales, 1919–1935

Year	New-Car Sales (in thousands)	Used-Car Sales (in thousands)	Ratio Used to New	Installment Percent New	Sales Percent Used
1919	1,851	1,087	58.7	64.9%	44.5%
1920	2,057	1,337	65.0	61.6	47.6
1921	1,553	1,093	70.4	63.9	50.7
1922	2,414	1,663	68.9	63.7	51.6
1923	3,798	2,598	68.3	65.0	54.8
1924	3,312	3,021	91.2	70.4	57.4
1925	3,569	3,526	98.8	68.2	62.8
1926	3,614	3,231	89.4	64.5	65.2
1927	2,951	3,497	118.5	58.0	63.6
1928	3,481	4,073	117.0	58.1	60.8
1929	4,407	5,350	121.4	60.9	64.7
1930	3,036	4,654	153.3	61.1	64.6
1931	2,222	3,791	170.6	62.8	60.4
1932	1,277	2,374	185.9	54.6	47.0
1933	1,740	3,097	178.0	56.8	66.8
1934	2,293	3,671	160.1	54.4	57.9
1935	3,255	5,136	157.8	58.0	62.6

SOURCE: Harold Katz, *The Decline of Competition in the Automobile Industry, 1920–1940* (New York: Arno, 1977), 54.

marketing manager.[147] These included more rational and systematic advertising strategy, more comprehensive consumer research, and better training for sales managers and the sales force at both the manufacturer and the dealer levels.

Manufacturers began to publish lengthy manuals for the purpose of sales force education. Ford, for example, created the six-volume, 747-page *Ford Products and Their Sale* in 1923. We concede that some of the advice therein must have been of questionable value to the salesperson. For example, *Book Six* contains a section entitled "How to Read Human Nature and Fit Your Selling Talk to the Man." Under subsection seven, "Proportionate Shape of Head," we learn:

> *High head* leaves room for a larger development at the very top. This is the idealistic area of the brain. Thus we find the high headed man comparatively idealistic and should be appealed to with that thought in mind. The medium height of head is more commercial and must be reached accordingly. The extreme *low head* has its widest build just over the eyes and at the base of the brain, but with little above that, meaning a purely physical type, and he must be reached through the sense of the physical, through seeing it, and through a grosser appeal.
>
> Henry Ford is a wonderful example of the head ideally high plus the broad commercial belt. Hence his great success in combining the ideal with the practical.[148]

A look at dealer manuals gives us an idea of how difficult the used-car problem was for the average salesperson. *Automobile Salesmanship* is the earliest manual I have found that mentions the used car. Published in 1915, it describes the "second-hand problem" as the "bane of the automobile business" but then devotes only 3 out of 121 pages to it. As was to become typical of such discussions, the used car was viewed as a problem, not an opportunity, although the manual does note that used-car shoppers could become new-car buyers if treated properly and therefore should be tracked. In an interesting commentary on the job of the car salesperson, the manual cautions against being "influenced, in the slightest degree, by what the second-hand owner says. He is the seller in this case, even if he is trying to make a trade deal, so it is well to discount most of the claims."[149] The implication is that the wise prospect would do well to discount the claims of the salesperson. A *Cadillac Dealers Manual* for the 1920s asserted that the "automobile dealer's success really hinges on his ability to handle his used car department properly." The *sine qua non* for proper management of used cars was the avoidance of the "evils of overallowances," because "all the used car trouble can be traced to mistakes in buying." Paperwork helped in the process of squeezing out "[e]very minute of delay" prior to having to name an allowance. "[A]s much formality as possible [should] be thrown around the appraising of the used car. The used car appraisal form will not only aid you, but will also impress the customer."[150]

But after all the forms had been filled out and all the delaying tactics possible had been employed, the magic moment at last had to arrive. The appraisal "does not enable the dealer to determine how much the car is worth, it merely permits him to ascertain its condition. . . ." A trade-in's "worth is determined by the amount the dealer can get for it."[151] After the allowance has been determined,

> there follows a real battle of wits. The slightest sign of weakening on your part is sure to be observed by your prospect. So you must be as keen to observe any sign of weakening on his part, and when you see it—be quick to utilize it.[152]

These instructions call for a lot of finesse on the part of the salesperson, who must be capable of concealing some considerable tension behind an insincere smile. He has to postpone constantly a straight answer to a reasonable question, and he knows that his eventual answer to that question will displease the prospect. It is not surprising that this task was so poorly executed and that so many dealers failed because of so much capital tied up in overvalued used-car inventories.

Such was the state of the automobile industry in the early 1920s, when General Motors offered only modest competition to the seemingly invincible Ford Motor Company. As it turned out, however, Alfred Sloan had one great advantage over Henry Ford: he knew GM was in trouble, whereas Ford had no inkling of the vulnerability of the Ford Motor Company. Perhaps it was this circumstance that led Sloan to feel in later years that he had been given too much credit for the success of General Motors and Henry Ford not enough.[153]

Ford in the 1920s: Omitting the Buyer

The force that drove all others at the Ford Motor Company was Henry Ford's determination to produce the Model T in ever greater numbers at progressively lower prices. In this goal he was completely successful: by December 1924, the Model T touring car was available for $290. The result of this success was disaster, because it blinded Ford to changes taking place in the industry. The car's meaning to the consumer was changing. The relationship between supply and demand was changing. The average car was lasting longer, and the Ford lasted longer than the average. The consumer had to be given a reason to purchase a new vehicle, and price could no longer be the sole appeal. And there was a limit to how low even Ford could price a car. In the fiscal year ending 29 February 1924, the Ford Motor Company showed a profit of $82,260,000, but only $4,110,000—under 5 percent—resulted from car sales; the rest came from other sources such as parts. The Ford Motor Company was making a profit of $2 per unit on its cars. The Model T was being sold almost at cost.[154]

According to James Couzens, before the era of mass production of the Model T, "[i]t was thought that selling started with the customer and worked back to the factory—that the factory existed to supply what the customer asked for." The result, said Couzens, was that the automobile company found itself absorbed in meeting "the needs and even the whims of the buyer," which made the advantages of standardization and mass production impossible to achieve.[155]

> What the Ford company really did—although not in so many words—was to reverse the process. We worked out a car and at a price which would meet the largest average need. In effect, we standardized the customer. We set the price of the car as a goal to reach and depended for profit upon the economies that we might effect in volume manufacturing. . . .[156]

Ford made a huge investment in production facilities, but they were single-minded, special-purpose works dedicated to an unchanging Model T. By the 1920s, "the whims of the buyer," to use Couzens's phrase, were beginning to make themselves felt. In the early 1900s, Henry Ford's vision of the needs of consumers for an inexpensive, reliable transportation vehicle matched reality, but during the 1920s, automobile marketing came to involve more than providing customers with an appliance to take them from place to place. By then, however, Ford had come to believe that he was in the business of building Model Ts. In fact, like every other businessperson, he was in the business of satisfying consumers. He mistook the product for the service it performed. Here is how Alfred Sloan analyzed the situation:

> The old master had failed to master change. Don't ask me why. . . .
> Mr. Ford, who had had so many brilliant insights in earlier years, seemed never to understand how completely his market had changed from the one in which he had made his name and to which he was accustomed.[157]

In this new environment, the role of the dealers was rapidly changing. A greater emphasis on marketing, not merely distribution, was required. The dealers' role had expanded from selling to trading. They needed guidance in managing this difficult transition because the business skills required were greater. Ford unfortunately remained steadfast in the principle on which his production system was built. Since the company intended to "omit the individual buyer from our calculations," as Couzens had put it, the home office had little patience with dealer complaints about recalcitrant consumers.[158]

To meet the challenges of the "New Era," organization was essential. The company needed a structure that would act as an avenue toward rather than as a barrier to the formulation and implementation of well-conceived strategy. And it needed to attract the best executive talent possible to make the organization work. Ford did not believe any of these things. Indeed, he deliberately chose the reverse of them. He marched in place during the postwar period, unwilling or unable to admit that the world of automobiles had moved on. Why was it that this company—which in earlier years could be described as supple, flexible, and open-minded—turned to the opposite of such things? The answer lies in the personality of Henry Ford.

Ford's perspective changed as his fame increased. Historian David L. Lewis locates the turning point in Ford's self-image and in his view of the world at the outpouring of public adulation following the announcement of the five-dollar day (i.e., a daily wage of $5 for his factory workers) in 1914. The publicity surrounding that event turned his head.[159]

Ford was the victim of his own success. Back at the turn of the century, he had stubbornly held fast to his vision of a car for the masses in the face of a lot of advice and pressure. For this he had been rewarded, not only with fabulous wealth but also with the sense of power derived from seeing his ideas become reality. This simple, unsophisticated mechanic from the midwestern backwoods had lived to see his name become an "ism" all over the world. It is not that hard to understand how a man in such circumstances could lose perspective.

As Ford began to believe his own press notices, it became impossible for him to tolerate favorable publicity for anyone else in his organization. Surely one reason he hated the very concept of organization and literally vandalized the offices of those keeping the records that were so essential to the management of a company even a tenth Ford's size was that he came to believe that no record, no evidence, no research could solve a problem as effectively as his own inspired intuition.[160] If he did not become hard of hearing as he passed his sixtieth birthday, it may fairly be said that Ford became hard of listening.

The exodus of talented and experienced executives from the Ford Motor Company was impressive indeed. James Couzens left in 1915, Norval Hawkins in 1919, and in 1921—the greatest blood-letting of any year—Ford's European representative, the head of advertising, the assistant secretary and general attorney, the treasurer, the head of the Sociological Department (personnel), the chief auditor, and William S. Knudsen, head of manufacturing. As members of his management team left, Ford eliminated the systems they had tried to put into place. "It is not necessary for any one department to know what any other department is doing," he said. "[T]he Ford factories and enterprises have no organization, no specific duties attaching to any position, no line of succession or of authority, very few titles, and no conferences. . . . [W]e have no elaborate records of any kind, and consequently no red tape."[161] He saw the intrusion of management tools into his world as an attempt to steal his company from his personal control and oversight.

Ford's drive for complete control of his industrial empire led to the decision to take the company private. In 1916, Ford announced that special dividends would be discontinued in order to begin work on the monumental installation on the River Rouge. John and Horace Dodge filed a suit aimed at forcing the company to pay dividends to its shareholders. A year later they won, and the company had to pay out almost $20 million. The loss of this suit was an important reason for Ford's decision to buy out the minority stockholders and to merge all his ventures into one giant private enterprise. The cost of this buy-out to Ford was almost $106 million, of which $60 million was borrowed money. The transaction was completed on 11 July 1919.[162]

Ford's decision to go private was directly contrary to the trend in business at the time. No entrepreneur had ever owned all of an enterprise the size of the Ford Motor Company. Ford's decision to eliminate the cadre of professional managers in the ranks of his company was also swimming against the stream. Ford thought he could run a company that numbered its dealers in five figures, its employees in six, its customers in eight, its assets in nine, and its sales (at their peak) in ten as if it were a mom and pop shop.

As Ford was buying out the minority shareholders, he was also undertaking unprecedented expenditures to build the Rouge. He might have been able to execute both these maneuvers had the prevailing assumptions about continuing good car sales in 1920 and 1921 been correct. In fact, in those years the automobile industry endured its first depression. Sales for 1921 were off almost 23 percent from 1920, and the situation was particularly bad in the fall of 1920 and the winter of 1921. For Ford, the slump could not have come at a worse time. Through April 1921, Ford

had liabilities totaling between $50 and $60 million, and his company had
about $20 million with which to meet them. The day before Christmas
in 1920, the Highland Park plant closed; and rumors spread that Ford
might have to seek loans.[163]

Ford was convinced that Wall Street was out to wrest his company
from his control, a not entirely unfounded view. The president of the
Bankers Trust Company of New York, a Morgan bank, had stated in 1915
that the Ford Motor Company was far more than "the ordinary manufacturing proposition. . . . It is, in effect, a very large and important financial
institution, and it needs the guiding hand of a man with . . . balance and
sound judgment"—qualities in which most bankers found Ford sorely
deficient.[164] When Highland Park closed, several banks offered Ford
loans, on the condition that they could name the company's treasurer.
One, the Liberty National Bank of New York, wanted power to name one
of the directors as well.[165] Determined to remain in control of the company, Ford imposed his illiquidity on his dealers. He decided to convert
his raw material and work-in-process inventories into finished product
and, along with the stock of automobiles he already had, ship the cars off
to dealers. These vehicles were shipped on standard terms—the dealers
paid cash.

Thus Ford's 6,400 dealers found themselves with new consignments of
automobiles, totaling about 90,000 units, to dispose of during the worst
depression in a quarter of a century. Ford's dealers had to borrow so Ford
would not have to. Of course, dealers could refuse to accept shipments,
but those who did so forfeited their franchises. Historian Allan Nevins,
in a charitable interpretation of this episode, explained that the company
did its best to help dealers dispose of their bulging inventories. William
Ryan told the sales force to "Wipe out the cloud of pessimism hovering
over the dealer who has not sold a car or tractor lately by staying with him
and closing a few sales."[166] In this era of increased marketing competition, however, there was a need for something more than cheerleading.
A manufacturer could greatly enhance the effectiveness of individual
dealers by pooling their experiences and using the information gathered
as a tool to teach them how to operate more effectively. But Ford had no
tradition of give and take with dealers and continued, as it had in Norval
Hawkins's day, to issue peremptory orders rather than to work coopera-
tively.

In addition, the company was unprepared for a market in which the
Model T was no longer technologically superior. After the outlay of capital
and the planning that went into the River Rouge facility, it became much
more difficult for Ford to convert its production processes to accommodate design changes. Despite the experimentation that had gone into the

development of the car originally, Ford felt that his Model T, now perfected, would remain the industry standard forever. He therefore saw no danger in being locked in to the production of a single car.

By 1927, the necessity of bringing out a new vehicle had penetrated even Ford's impenetrability. Sloan, for one, thought a change was long overdue. "There is a legend cultivated by sentimentalists," he wrote, "that Mr. Ford left behind a great car expressive of the pure concept of cheap, basic transportation. The fact is that he left behind a car that no longer [by 1927] offered the best buy, even as raw, basic transportation. . . ."[167]

The conversion of the River Rouge facilities created a tremendous strain. It idled tens of thousands of workers and cost an estimated $100 million.[168] Ford's market share collapsed to under 10 percent in 1927; and though it rebounded when the Model A came on line, Ford's market dominance was gone forever.[169] Predictably enough, Ford proceeded to handle the Model A exactly as he had the Model T, as another unchanging standard. The same system of special-purpose production was instituted, ending few of the company's real difficulties.

As the Model T became outmoded during the early 1920s and therefore began to lose ground to the competition, the company blamed its dealers. What was needed, the company believed, was more competition at the dealer level. Continuing its policy of subdividing territory and pushing the car closer to the consumer, Ford increased the number of its franchised dealers by over 50 percent from 1921 to 1924, to 9,800.[170]

Trade-ins were apparently not as severe a problem in the early 1920s for Ford dealers as they were for those selling more expensive vehicles. The Model T was more likely to be a starter purchase, and its creeping obsolescence made it less likely that a customer would trade in a more advanced vehicle to purchase one. "[G]ear-shift cars," according to the Federal Trade Commission, "were seldom traded in the purchase of Model T cars."[171]

Nevertheless, by the middle of the 1920s, even Ford dealers were having trouble with the trade-in business, and Ford's response was not particularly helpful. Other firms came to believe that the used-car business needed a flexible policy on the part of the manufacturers. As late as 1925, in contrast, Ryan published a letter in *Automotive Industries* asserting that those Ford dealers who were losing money on their used-car business had been engaging in "unfair competition" with other dealers. If a dealer did not make a "gross profit of at least 20% on used cars, the same as you receive on new cars," that dealer was a "poor merchandiser." Warned Ryan, "We have already started to closely check the activity of our dealers so as to properly classify each dealer as either a 'good' or a 'poor' merchandiser, and summary action will be taken in the elimination of Ford dealers who persist in being 'poor' merchandisers of Ford products."[172] In the face of such treatment, there are indications that the older, more experienced dealers began to switch to Essex, Dodge, and Chevrolet as the decade progressed.[173]

By 1927, with no management organization at the top and a disconsolate dealer organization in the field, the Ford marketing program, which less than a decade earlier had been the envy of the business world, was a shambles. Worst of all, Henry Ford seemed unaware of any difficulty. As late as 1929, he was of the opinion that "we do not have to bother about over-production for some years to come, provided our prices are right."[174]

While Ford was refusing to admit any of these changes in the automobile industry, Alfred Sloan was using his understanding of them to create at General Motors one of the great success stories in American business.[175] The essence of Sloan's accomplishment was his creative approach to the problem of how to combine a degree of decentralized responsibility with centralized control. Under his aegis, the relationship of the divisions to the corporate office was defined—not only for General Motors but also for a legion of imitators in a host of industries.

The task of running the business and of achieving a specified return on the investment entrusted to them was placed in the hands of the division general managers. These managers were measured against standards established by Donaldson Brown, GM's vice-president for finance, and patterned on Brown's work at Du Pont. Executives who exceeded their goals were cut in on a handsome bonus plan; those who failed to meet them and could not provide an acceptable explanation might well find themselves looking for work.

The responsibility for setting standards, for evaluating performance, for making major decisions concerning personnel, and for forecasting future demand lay with GM's central office. The central office established policy and the divisions administered it. The divisions were charged with serving distinct market segments, thus boldly leading the automobile industry into Phase III of its history. Divisional operations were coordinated through a masterfully designed committee system.[176] And at the pinnacle of the central office was the iron fist within the iron glove of Sloan, whose prestige and power increased with each successful year.

Sloan employed a variety of tools to compete in the marketplace rather than relying on a single element in the marketing mix. This variety gave General Motors the flexibility that Ford lacked. In the process of formulating and implementing this approach, Sloan showed how supple a huge firm with enormous fixed costs serving a consumer market could be.

The Old Competition vs. the New: Postwar Marketing at Ford and GM

In the world of neoclassical economics, the business landscape was studded with anonymous small producers and merchants; and the consumer had perfect information. Buyers did not know other buyers; buyers did not know sellers; sellers did not know other sellers. No seller could, without collusion, raise price by restricting output. All he could do was lose business. This was a world of commodities. All products were undifferentiated. Competition was through price. Prices were established through the mechanism of an impersonal market—the "invisible hand" that ensured consumer welfare.[177] Producers in an untrammeled market system had no choice but to accept "the lowest [price] which can be taken."[178] In Adam Smith's world, businesspeople did not lose sleep over the issue of whether or not to compete on price. Price was competition's defining characteristic.

Conditions approximating this description may have existed in the United States prior to the railroad revolution of the 1840s.[179] With the building of the railroad network, however, the context of business activity began to change. First in the transportation infrastructure, then in the distribution sector through economies of scope, and finally in production in those industries in which scale economies obtained, a small number of firms with high fixed costs grew to dominance.

With the development of high concentration in manufacturing during and after the 1880s in the United States, businesses began to work out new ways to compete. These firms—such as Standard Oil, Du Pont, Singer, International Harvester, and Swift—experienced reduced operating costs per unit with the increased scale of their works and were thus able to offer quality merchandise at very low prices and still make more money than any businesses ever had.[180] But price as a competitive weapon now had to share the stage with a number of other tools. Competitors in oligopolies had to make a threefold investment in production, distribution, and an organization of managers to administer their facilities. With these assets and capabilities, these firms

competed or negotiated for market share through functional and strategic effectiveness; that is by improving their product, their process of production, their marketing, their purchasing and their labor relations more effectively than did their competitors; or they moved more quickly into new and growing markets, and out of older and declining ones.

Such rivalry for market share and profits normally increased the enterprise's functional and strategic capabilities and therefore its organizational capabilities as a whole.[181]

Thus was born the new competition of the twentieth-century oligopoly, the competition that Henry Ford never understood. Alfred D. Chandler, Jr., has characterized the historical development of highly concentrated industries as "ten years of competition and ninety years of oligopoly."[182] This was surely the case for the automobile. In 1896, Henry Ford could build a quadricycle in a shed and be in the car business. Within a decade and a half, that was no longer the case. The advent of the Model T and especially the opening of the plant at Highland Park signaled the "conflict among giants." At first, a certain operational sloppiness and arrogance could be tolerated because of the great demand the Model T tapped as Ford cut its prices. By 1921, however, Ford's strategy of competition strictly on the basis of price was beginning to lose its power. The era of the automobile's newness—the time of the great surge of first-time buying—was drawing to a close. In 1908, when the Model T was introduced, there was one automobile registered for every twenty households in the nation. In 1920, the ratio had dropped to one in three.[183] The world of automobiles had changed.

Let us look at how Ford and GM competed in this new environment. We have already seen Sloan's mastery of organization and Ford's disdain of it and how both companies made huge investments in production. What remains to be discussed is marketing. The marketing function offers a variety of competitive tools to the firm. These can be considered under four headings: product policy, price, communication, and distribution.[184]

Product Policy.   The first question marketers must ask is what markets they elect to serve with what products.[185] Three aspects of General Motors's answer to this question—the product line, the annual model change, and style—are most relevant here.

Sloan's product policy is clearly enunciated in *My Years with General Motors:*

> We said first that the corporation should produce a line of cars in each price area, from the lowest price up to one for a strictly high grade, quantity production car, but we would not get into the fancy price field with small production; second, that the price steps should not be such as to leave wide gaps in the line, and yet should be great enough to keep their number within

reason, so that the greatest advantage of quantity production could be secured; and third, that there should be no duplication by the corporation in the price fields or steps.[186]

Sloan observed that the idea for what came to be known as "the car for every purse and purpose" did not, in hindsight, seem revolutionary—no more startling than, for example, a shoe manufacturer deciding to sell shoes in more than one size. Nor was the idea original with the Sloan regime. Durant had tried a similar approach, but as Sloan said, GM under Durant had "no concept to guide our actions."[187]

This product-line strategy was not predominant in the industry in the early 1920s. The pattern was rather to depend heavily on one winning entry, the most successful example obviously being the Model T. Indeed, the single product had been the keystone of Ford's strategy; and that strategy represented a clear shift from the predominant product policy in the early history of the industry in both the United States and Europe, which was short runs of numerous models.

The addition of vehicles to a company's offering greatly increased the complexity of the business, and it required Sloan's organizational genius to make it possible for General Motors to achieve the goal Durant had set for it, insulation from the vagaries of the consumer market. It is easy to envision the goal of decentralized authority with central control. But the actual adjudication of the relationship among the divisions and between the divisions and the market was extraordinarily difficult and became the very stuff of management. General Motors was enabled to achieve the security it needed—mid- and high-priced cars in good times and the Chevrolet in the Depression—while being sufficiently united through its committees and the central office to gain the advantages of scale economies.

General Motors introduced the annual model change, the second element of product policy under discussion, after 1923, although the system was not fully operational until the 1930s.[188] This was the innovation no one wanted. It put tremendous pressure on the production facilities and increased costs enormously. It demanded a major commitment to the management of style and fashion, which are inherently somewhat unpredictable. It put a strain on the sales force, with a constant need to educate the dealer about the new features of each model and its (supposedly) superior attributes. Chevrolet sales manager Richard Grant was opposed to the annual model policy.[189] Social commentators have regularly condemned it as a wasteful manipulation of the consumer.[190]

Sloan said, "[W]e are all against yearly models, [but] I don't see just what can be done about it."[191] Yearly models meant that the changes taking place in the product could be programmed on a regular basis. Major changes, for example, could be timed to take place every three years, to coincide with the life expectancy of the dies. More important, the model change was the ideal device to stimulate new-car sales. The auto manufacturers in the 1920s needed to convince consumers that the cars they presently owned were obsolete, regardless of their running condition. In 1941, Sloan wrote that "Today, the appearance of a motorcar is a most important factor in the selling end of the business—perhaps the most important single factor because everybody knows that all cars will run."[192]

The annual model change, problematic though it may have been, had a major virtue from GM's point of view. Smaller makers did not have the resources to compete in this way. Writing of the 1920s, Robert Paul Thomas has asserted that "no small firm could have survived and played the annual model change game. Either a firm grew larger or failed."[193] Most important, however, was the inability of the Ford Motor Company to deal with the annual change concept. Henry Ford was opposed on principle to any model change, let alone an annual one. Ford made no concession to consumer self-expression. Because he felt so strongly that people *should not* want anything more than basic transportation, Ford with characteristic paternalism attempted to limit the choices for an increasingly demanding public. In a world in which the automobile could be taken for granted, basic transportation had become less of an issue. Moreover, Ford lacked the organizational capability to institute change smoothly. The company's production system was geared to continuity. For all these reasons, the annual model change was a master stroke of competitive strategy in Sloan's effort to overcome Ford's hegemony.

If technological change was to be limited in order to control costs, General Motors was confronted with the problem of how to define the change that its models were to undergo from one year to the next. It found an answer in style. In his autobiography, Sloan explained the function of style changes and also the difficulty of calibrating them properly:

> The degree to which styling changes should be made in any one model run presents a particularly delicate problem. The changes in the new model should be so novel and attractive as to create demand for the new value and, so to speak, create a certain amount of dissatisfaction with past models as compared with the new one, and yet the current and old models must still be capable of giving satisfaction to the vast used car market. Each line of General Motors cars produced should preserve a distinction of appearance, so that one knows on sight a Chevrolet, a Pontiac, an Oldsmobile, a Buick, or a Cadillac.[194]

The inspiration for formalizing styling as a staff function came, appropriately enough, from Los Angeles, where custom car bodies were produced for Hollywood movie stars. Harley Earl was the man who came east to Detroit to head up the new Art and Color Section. Appointment and appearance became the keystone of GM's product policy during the 1930s and remained so until recent years.[195]

Price. Reviewing the prices of the ten cars that General Motors produced in 1921, Sloan was struck by the "irrationality" of the pricing strategy. GM had "no position in the big-volume, low-price field," but "in the middle, where we were concentrated with duplication, we did not know what we were trying to do except to sell cars which, in a sense, took volume from each other."[196]

Sloan's idea was to throw an array of cars at strategically selected price points within specified price ranges. GM's entry in each group would appeal to the consumer looking for a lower-priced car on quality and to the consumer looking for a more expensive car on price. These price points had to be sufficiently separated to prevent the company from competing primarily against itself.

In 1922, the conventional wisdom among manufacturers was "that to endeavor to compete against Ford you might just as well go against a brick wall."[197] Sloan agreed, but he nevertheless devised a plan to take market share away from the Model T. Here is Sloan's analysis:

> In 1921, Ford had about 60 percent of the total car and truck market in units, and Chevrolet had about 4 percent. With Ford in almost complete possession of the low price field, it would have been suicidal to compete with him head on. No conceivable amount of capital short of the United States Treasury could have sustained the losses required to take volume away from him at his own game. The strategy we devised was to take a bite from the top of his position, conceived as a price class, and in this way build up Chevrolet volume on a profitable basis. In later years, as the consumer upgraded his preference, the new General Motors policy was to become critically attuned to the course of American history.[198]

In this particular, as in so many others of the GM strategy, Ford was attacked not head-on by doing what he did best, but in a flanking maneuver by which GM refused to play Ford's "own game."

General Motors not only worked out a rational price strategy for its product line; it also worked to change the meaning of price to the consumer by devising a new institution, the General Motors Acceptance Corporation (GMAC). As an expensive, mass-marketed durable, automobiles called for assistance in their sale through financing, for both dealer

The Machine that Made Ford Great: The Model T. The most famous car in the history of the world and the very essence of a Phase II product.

inventory and consumer purchase. Reliance on bank financing alone would have slowed industry growth. General Motors dealt with this problem at John J. Raskob's suggestion in 1919 with the establishment of the wholly owned GMAC. Financing in itself was not unprecedented. "Makers of durable goods for a mass market, like sewing machines, typewriters, and agricultural implements, had many years before worked out ways to finance dealers and consumers so that purchases could be made on time or [through] installment plans."[199] But General Motors was the first to establish a wholly owned subsidiary for this purpose in the automobile industry.

Once again, Henry Ford's staunch opposition helped make a GM innovation an important competitive plus. The only concession Ford made to time payment was the Ford Weekly Purchasing Plan, inaugurated on 7 April 1923. This was more like a Christmas Club than an installment plan, however. The consumer did make small, regular payments toward the purchase of an automobile, but he or she could not take possession of the merchandise until it was completely paid for. The Ford plan was not very successful.[200]

Terms for the average installment purchase in 1925 were one-third down with the remainder payable in twelve equal installments, including finance charges. More than three cars in four were sold on the installment plan in 1925 (including Fords, where outside financing was available), compared to fewer than one in three 5 years earlier.[201] The attraction of installment buying was obvious, especially for Chevrolet, which was trying

The Machines that Made General Motors Great: A—Chevrolet; B—Pontiac; C—Oldsmobile; D—Buick; E—Cadillac. These were the cars for every purse and purpose. This was the beginning of Phase III—which would not reach its full fruition until the 1960s—in the automobile industry.

to enter Ford's market from above. The impact of price as a selling point was diminished.

For Ford, as we have seen, price was the sum and substance of strategy, but there was a limit to what price, unconnected to the other strategic variables, could do. Ford was making $2 per unit in 1924. A price cut of $1, which would have been meaningless to the consumer, would cut profit per unit in half. Twice as many cars would have to be sold to achieve the same profit dollars. A price cut of more than $2 would be an admission by the company that it could not make money on cars but only on parts and accessories. Further, the Model Ts were being undersold by used cars that had gear shifts, shock absorbers, and other features the consumer was coming to think of as standard equipment; and the sale of new cars on credit made Ford's low prices less important. By the mid-1920s, Henry Ford had pushed the price strategy as far as it could go. Indeed, further. General Motors surpassed Ford in terms of both profit and market share in the 1920s and outperformed Ford in profit every year from 1925 until 1986.

Communication. At General Motors, institutional advertising and public relations programs were undertaken at the corporate level, and product advertising was carried on by the divisions.[202] The most impressive aspect of GM's advertising program was its sheer size throughout the 1920s. There was a variety of media available for the company's messages, including newspapers, magazines, and, as the decade progressed, radio. There is no compendium of advertising expenditures encompassing all available media, but we can get indications of GM's presence from statistics on leading national magazine advertisers during the 1920s.

In 1928, the automotive industry ranked third behind food and beverages and slightly behind drugs and toilet goods in national magazine advertising expenditures.[203] General Motors was dominant, with $3,240,800 (excluding Frigidaire) out of $9,108,510, or more than one-third of the expenditures among major auto advertisers (i.e., those among the top seventy-five magazine advertisers). Indeed, General Motors became the largest national magazine advertiser in 1923 (counting all its divisions), and it has remained at or near the top of national advertisers in all media throughout the twentieth century.[204] Moreover, because of the annual model changes GM's advertising had something new to bring to the consumer's attention. Ford, by contrast, was not even on the list of the top national magazine advertisers for four of the eight years between 1921 and 1928.

Advertising was only one aspect of GM's comprehensive communications programs. Each division had its own sales force, led in the early years by Ford alumnus Norval Hawkins. Hawkins's successor was Richard Grant, "Dynamic Dick" the "Little Giant." Massachusetts-born and Harvard-educated, Grant came to General Motors by way of the National Cash Register Company, where his mentor was the famous John Henry Patterson. Patterson, like Hawkins, firmly believed that selling success called for a careful mix of system and spirit. His use of comprehensive checklists and manuals was leavened by public demonstrations and rewards for leadership performance.[205] He pioneered in contests, quotas, and the staging of sales force conventions. Grant left Patterson's tutelage at National Cash Register in 1915 for Delco-Light, which became part of General Motors three years later. Following dramatic success in marketing Frigidaire refrigerators, which had become part of Delco-Light in 1921, Grant moved on to Chevrolet in 1924.

In Sloan's plan, Chevrolet was going to be the division through which General Motors would attack Ford; but the division's performance had been erratic through 1924. It was the leading division in the company in 1920, accounting for 42 percent of total car sales, but the following year Chevrolet sales were almost halved. In 1923, sales reached a record high but then fell off badly the following year.[206] With Grant running sales, Chevrolet grew dramatically, and sales set records each year from 1925 until 1929, when volume reached 988,191 passenger vehicles, a three and a third increase over 1924. Grant put together what *Fortune* described in 1931 as the "most costly and far-reaching dealer organization in the automotive world."[207] The result of this performance was a corporate vice-presidency for Grant. Executives whom he had trained at Chevrolet disseminated the Grant approach throughout the other GM car divisions.[208]

Grant, working with Chevrolet division president William S. Knudsen, made an effort to bring the "whims of the buyer" back into the equation of automobile distribution. There could be no question about endangering the scale economies achieved through mass production; the "American idea of profit through volume" had to be maintained.[209] But within this context, Grant made an effort to consider consumer tastes and desires, particularly through an emphasis on choices in color and trim. Even more important, Grant brought demand into the process of production scheduling: "[I]nstead of Mr. Grant's adapting his sales programs to the number of cars Mr. Knudsen could make for him, Mr. Knudsen began to set his production schedules on the basis of advance sales estimates—one month firm and two months tentative. . . ."[210]

The making of these estimates required another dimension to the General Motors communication program. The company had not only to talk to the market but to listen to it as well. Research at General Motors meant market as well as product. The company in the 1920s systematically developed data on the "market and its potential in terms of population, income, past performance, business cycle, and the like."[211]

Distribution. Part of Sloan's genius as a businessman was his ability to direct his energies toward the most pressing problems. Dealer relations would be high on any such list in the 1920s. "When I was chief executive officer of General Motors," he wrote in 1963,

I gave a large part of my attention to dealer relations, amounting at times, you might say, almost to a specialization. . . . I made it a practice throughout the 1920s and early 1930s to make personal visits to dealers. I fitted up a private railroad car as an office and in the company of several associates went into almost every city in the United States, visiting from five to ten dealers a day. I would meet them in their own places of business, talk with them across their own desks in their "closing rooms" and ask them for suggestions and criticisms concerning their relations with the corporation, the character of the product, the corporation's policies, the trend of consumer demand, their view of the future, and many other things of interest in the business.[212]

GM's attitude toward its dealers was more helpful and conciliatory than Ford's. In its 8 October 1925 meeting, for example, the general sales committee of General Motors agreed that "the Ford policy, whereby the dealer is required to make money on the used car end, is unsound, at least as applied to our business."[213]

General Motors never seriously considered owning its retail outlets. Although individual dealers were small businesspeople, the dealer organization as a whole, just as in the case of Ford, represented a huge capital investment. In 1939, GM had contracts with 17,000 dealers, with a total of 125,000 employees. The dealers bought and stocked the spare parts and provided the service shops to make repairs. This represented a lot of capital and human effort that GM could rely on others to provide. The most important reason militating against GM's forward integration dealt with the company's conception of what it was—a manufacturer that made money from the efficient exploitation of scale economies. The techniques of which it was the master could not easily be applied to the dealer's tasks, especially with the advent of the used car. According to Sloan:

> When the used car came into the picture in a big way in the 1920s as a trade-in on a new car, the merchandising of automobiles became more a trading than an ordinary selling proposition. Organizing and supervising the necessary thousands of complex trading institutions would have been difficult for the manufacturer; trading is a knack not easy to fit into the conventional type of a managerially controlled organization.[214]

The dealer-manufacturer relationship has a number of inherent stresses. To some extent, the interests of dealer and manufacturer converge—both want to sell the company's vehicles. But the dealer wants to sell the cars he stocks through his agency. His interest is in the health of his particular business. The manufacturer wants to sell cars it manufactures and is less concerned about the particular dealership through which they move. Two conflicts immediately arise out of this situation, dealer location and sales quotas.

Neither Ford nor General Motors solved these problems. The difference between the two in the 1920s was that GM under Sloan was organized to think about these issues, to ask the right questions, and to try to use the answers to come to some accommodation with its dealers. What was the optimum number of dealers in a particular area? In the manufacturer's view, more dealers meant more competition among dealers, more missionary sales work, and better service. From the dealer's viewpoint, intense competition through dealerships selling the same vehicle threatened his investment with disaster. How many vehicles should the manu-

facturer expect the dealer to sell? How could the manufacturer be sufficiently well informed to establish reasonable standards? How could consumer demand be predicted accurately? How did the manufacturer know
when the time had come to terminate a franchise?

Sloan liked "win-win" situations—"I have never been interested in
business relationships that are not of benefit to all concerned," he declared.[215] The Ford Motor Company treated its dealers without consideration because it never really understood the contribution they made to its
success. During the 1920s, the changed market situation meant that
dealers' aggressive cooperation was even more important. Instead of working to make them team players, however, Ford succeeded only in transforming them into a group of embittered and rebellious adversaries.

Afterword

As a result of Sloan's mastery of Phase III competition and of Ford's
adherence to the principles of Phase II in a Phase III world, General
Motors became the most successful automobile manufacturer in the twentieth century. In the decade from 1927 to 1937, which included some of
the worst years in the history of the industry, GM made money every year.
Its net profit for those eleven years was almost $2 billion, compared to the
almost $100 million in losses over the same period for Ford.[216] GM stock
became one of the great holdings in the history of investment. The
company has been the largest auto manufacturer in the world from the
1920s to the present.

Large though the company still is, General Motors is no longer viewed
as the paragon of corporations. As much as any company in the United
States, its decline into disarray has epitomized the entropy that has crept
over so much of America's industrial heartland.

Japan has become the world's preeminent automobile-producing nation, a turn of events that no one would have predicted forty or even thirty
years ago. Ironically, the Japanese have done to American manufacturers
precisely what GM did to Ford, the principal difference being that the
first "bite" they took was from the bottom rather than from the top of
the market. The principal similarity was that they attacked seemingly
overwhelming competition at its Achilles heel and then watched theirs
become the policy "critically attuned to American history."

In retrospect, it is less surprising that the United States has lost its leadership than it is that we held it for so long. By the 1950s, our automobiles had become technologically outdated, impractical, and unsafe cathedrals of chrome manufactured sloppily and sold using methods that can only be described as shameful. A journalist in 1958 wrote of American cars as "overblown, overpriced monstrosities built by oafs for thieves to sell to mental defectives."[217] One automobile analyst described the Buick and Oldsmobile of that year as follows:

> When reckoning time comes at the end of the era of the automobile, anthropologists will look upon these two cars as prime examples of the age of excess. Huge, vulgar, dripping with pot metal, and barely able to stagger down the highway, they were everything car people hated about the American automobile.[218]

Another critic called the average American automobile of the 1960s "a true ocean liner of the road," bringing to mind an early characterization of the turn-of-the-century automobile as a land yacht.[219]

Most egregious was failure in safety. Over two and a half million Americans have been killed in automobile accidents, a fantastic total, and millions more have been maimed. Given the nature of driving, many of these accidents were unavoidable. Nevertheless, there should have been greater concern with this dreadful problem on the part of the industry. Detroit had convinced itself that style would sell and safety would not. Even evidence close to home of the price paid for that point of view—the son of a GM executive vice-president suffered permanent brain damage in one Corvair accident, and in another the son of the general manager of Cadillac was killed—failed to change minds.[220] Much of the sometimes wrong-headed interference of government in safety, pollution, and other matters has been summoned up by the industry's own irresponsibility.

The world of GM's greatness was one in which the government was not a key player in the industry (except through such stimulating programs as road-building); in which the desire for safety was unfocused; in which the consumer purchased his or her automobile on average more often so that he or she was more willing to live with a machine that was not built to last; in which, therefore, product quality was relatively less important and thus worker cooperation on the plant floor was relatively less urgent; and in which the consumer did not have as a viable alternative the option of purchasing a variety of foreign, most importantly Japanese, cars that are produced under a set of constraints and expectations far different from those that have prevailed in the United States.

That world is now gone. It could be argued that GM today needs to

Published with permission of Arnoldo Mondadori Editore S.p.A.

The Unthinkable: Foreign penetration of the industry America thought it owned became notable with the Volkswagen Beetle. This German version of the "universal" car is the only vehicle ever to outsell the Model T. In more recent years, Americans have been unable to meet the Japanese combination of price and quality.

do what Ford did after World War II: institute massive change. In the words of H. Ross Perot:

> We've got to nuke the system. We've got to throw away Sloan's book [i.e., *My Years with General Motors*]. It's like the Old Testament—frozen thousands of years ago. We still believe that we can find the right page and paragraph to give us the answer to any questions we have today.[221]

How the company responds to the new reality will be its test as the twenty-first century approaches.

Conclusion

Automobiles have been as essential to the world of the twentieth century as has electricity. They have been the signature of our age. Let us discuss the automobile industry in terms of our propositions from chapter 1.

PROFIT THROUGH VOLUME

There was at the turn of the century a tremendous demand for a personal, nonanimate conveyance in the United States, where transportation has always been a center of national attention. Further, the wealth of the nation was great, growing, and democratically distributed, which meant that the demand was effective. Given these two key facts—that everyone wanted a car and that a lot of people could afford one—is it fair to say that anyone really created a mass market in this industry? We saw at the beginning of this chapter how the Phase I stage in the automobile industry was brief. The fragmented era of tinkerers lasted only a few decades, and the attempt by a patent pool to keep prices high and output low lasted only a few years. If Henry Ford and his company had not dragged this industry into the Phase II world of profit through volume, can we not say that it was inevitable that someone else would have?

The short answer to this question is "yes." Or, at least, "in all probability." The automobile as a mass-marketed product was more inevitable, if one can think in such terms, than was the soft drink. If Asa Candler had not brought the soft drink industry out of Phase I and into Phase II and if Robert Woodruff had not saved Coca-Cola in the 1920s, it is quite possible that there would be no Coca-Cola today and perhaps no international cola business at all. By the same token, Charles Guth, Alfred Steele, and Donald Kendall were essential to the cola business becoming a duopoly. Without them, Pepsi probably would not have survived. The word "create" is less applicable in automobiles than in soft drinks for these reasons.

ENTREPRENEURIAL VISION

Nevertheless, to declare something to have been inevitable (relatively speaking) is to deny many of the lessons that the history of the automobile industry has to teach us about the molding and the mobilizing of a mass market. Further, we must ever keep in mind that what seems to have been inevitable in hindsight rarely so presents itself to contemporaries. Ford had to fight for control of his company, and he had to fight legal battles with outsiders as well to make the car he wanted the way he wanted to. The idea of a single, high-quality model produced in giant works on a moving assembly line for ever lower prices was original with Ford. Other people glimpsed it, and other people implemented part of it. Ford, however, had the whole picture and built a vertical organization to make it happen.

In so doing, Henry Ford touched greatness. It would, however, be a mistake in my view to deduce from this that great men and women are the sole explanation for corporate success in the modern world. Corporate success is determined by the interactions among the guiding intelligence of the firm; the capabilities of the firm itself including its executives, its work force, and its tangible assets; and the nature of the times in question.

VERTICAL SYSTEM

To take Ford as an example, Henry Ford did provide the strategic insight that led to the Model T. But that insight would have been of no value had he not made the investment in the plant at Highland Park and had he not been able to gather around him all those engineers for whom "work was play." Equally important was Ford's marketing system with its managerial infrastructure. All these things needed to be combined with a reasonably receptive market.

The story of the automobile industry, or of any industry, is not the story of how one of these factors may be more important than the others. It is, rather, the story of how they interact to produce success or stagnation. In the same sense that a great biography must be the complex interweaving of life and times, the history of success not only in marketing but in any other business function or in the corporation as a whole must be about individuals and institutions. The contribution that the historian can make is to delineate these interactions in a manner as free as possible from preconceived notions.

FIRST-MOVERS AND ENTRY BARRIERS

By World War I, Ford, his team, and his firm as a whole dominated the automobile industry. The Model T was more important than any other automobile before or since. The barriers to entry Ford had erected were formidable both in manufacturing and in marketing. The company owned a great plant, a great vertical system, and a great name.

THE COMPETITOR'S OPTIONS

The Ford Motor Company lost them all with startling speed. Alfred Sloan supervised the reorganization of General Motors with the help of Du Pont, the best-managed company in the world at the time. He never launched what we would call a Phase II attack on Ford because the barriers were simply too high. Instead, he came up with the segmentation strategy.

Once again, this may sound like a great man story; but it is not. Sloan without his organization would not have merited our attention. If Sloan had tried to enter another industry, he might not have made the impact that he did on American business history. Indeed, he tried his hand at electro-mechanical refrigeration at the turn of the century and abandoned the field after two years because the time was not right. Man and hour must meet.

To a degree, Ford's very strength drove General Motors into a Phase III strategy. Even so, there was nothing inevitable about the move; and it was hotly debated within the firm at the time it was taken. Richard Grant, the marketing man, was opposed. It was not intuitively obvious that changing models yearly and selling five different makes was the best product strategy. After all, Ford's success was based on the opposite approach. In 1919, James Couzens had said that the greatest lesson he had learned from the Ford Motor Company was to omit the buyer rather than to cater to him, which is what a segmentation strategy suggests.

In the other three industry studies in this book, the Phase III segmentation strategy did not become the focus of the industry's attention until the late 1960s. In automobiles, however, we are speaking about Phase III by the mid-1920s. Phase II in the cola business lasted from the 1890s to the 1950s. In the automobile industry, it lasted only from 1908 to 1927, the dates of the Model T. Why the difference?

First, all industries are different. Used cars created for the automobile industry a kind of problem that no other industry under study in this book has had to face to the same degree. Second, Ford's very strength forced a fundamentally different competitive response. Finally, it should be pointed out that the segmentation scheme that General Motors implemented was not, in all respects, modern. The firm described its segments in terms of price. To be sure, it seemed clear that an individual who could afford a Cadillac had a different life-style from one who could afford only a Chevrolet. But neither life-style nor demographics appeared to be uppermost in GM's definition of its consumer segments.

Some automobile firms did make an effort to compete through psychographic segmentation (although the term was not used) during the 1920s. The classic example is the Jordan Playboy. In one of the most famous of advertisements, Edward S. Jordan wrote:

> Somewhere west of Laramie there's a broncho-busting, steer-roping girl who knows what I'm talking about. She can tell what a sassy pony, that's a cross between greased lightning and the place where it hits, can do with eleven hundred pounds of steel and action when he's going high, wide and handsome. The truth is—the Playboy was built for her. . . .[222]

The whole advertisement adopted this tone. It was not about the product at all; rather, it was about a fantasy world in which the product played a part.

One can clearly see psychographic segmentation assuming a more prominent role in the product offering of the major automobile manufacturers in the mid-1960s. The "muscle" cars like the Pontiac GTO and the "pony" cars like Ford's Mustang were designed with life-style uppermost in mind.[223] These were the cars for the Pepsi Generation.

MANAGING CHANGE

Success in business is about the management of change. For many years, General Motors managed change as well as any company could. In fact, it programmed change; it brought us the future according to its own schedule.[224]

Even after the shocking downfall of the Model T, the Ford Motor Company still did not understand the new competitive world. It replaced the Model T with the new Model A, which was conceived of as another "universal" car. Thus Ford responded to a Phase III attack with another Phase II product.

The Model A was very successful but only for a limited time. It took years for Ford to understand that it would no longer be able to manage a Phase II approach with success in this industry. An important reason for this vital delay was Henry Ford himself. He was incapable of changing gracefully with the times. Instead of preparing his company for the future, he cleaved to the past. As was the case with Robert Woodruff at Coca-Cola, Ford's longevity impaired his firm's responsiveness to the market and to the challenge of competition.

CHAPTER 4

Stocking America's Pantries: The Rise and Fall of A&P

In this chapter we focus not on the manufacturer but on the retailer. A&P has been one of the most important retailers of the twentieth century. It grew powerful by organizing and managing a vertical marketing system with skill and efficiency. It succeeded as a mass marketer despite strong forces pulling its market apart.

The Phase I era of food retailing lasted throughout the nineteenth century. Almost all food merchants based their business on high margins and low turnover. They were small shops, inefficiently run. They had market relations with independent wholesalers who, in turn, had market relations with independent suppliers.

This is the world A&P organized and industrialized. It brought high volume and low prices into food distribution, especially with the launching of its economy-store program just before World War I. It cut out market relations with wholesalers, taking over the wholesaling function. Its well-designed warehouse network saved money. In some product lines, such as coffee, baked goods, and fish, A&P integrated all the way back to processing.

The firm's multiple-store network gave it a fund of knowledge about store site location and management. By 1930, A&P was running more stores than any other chain-store company in any product line has done before or since. These stores did not cover the whole nation; for example, the company had no presence in the mountain states and in some of the plains states. Nevertheless, A&P was unquestionably the nation's leading food merchant. Indeed, it was the largest retailer of any kind until overtaken by Sears in 1965.

To complete the Phase II picture, A&P was committed to its own private labels. It sought to put names that it owned on a wide variety of foods. As a result, the company often was in conflict with manufacturers that owned brands, including the Coca-Cola Company in the 1920s.

In the 1930s, A&P was faced with a fundamental challenge to its business strategy when a new store format—the supermarket—invaded its trading areas. The supermarket struck at one of the pillars of A&P's power—its store network—by changing the scale of the food outlet. The new stores were enormous. They eliminated services altogether and depended on nationally advertised manufacturers' brands to sell themselves.

This, in my view, was a Phase II challenge. The supermarkets were trying to do to A&P what Pepsi tried to do to Coca-Cola in the 1930s, and what Sloan said he could never have succeeded in doing against Ford—beat it at its own game. The supermarkets had even higher volume, higher turnover, and lower margin than A&P. Theirs was a mass-market strategy based on a major change in the transportation infrastructure, the automobile.

A&P responded to the supermarket challenge by becoming a supermarket company by the close of the 1930s. However, it was unable to maneuver successfully in the postwar world. A nationally dominant food retailer with a location strategy rooted in older cities and a product strategy firmly opposed to nationally distributed manufacturers' brands became an anachronism. While Phase III food manufacturers segmented the market with ever greater precision and force, A&P kept trying to sell everybody everything using its own private label. Specialty retailers and local chains took a different view, and their strategies, combined with the exceptionally poor management of A&P, led to the downfall of this once-great firm.

The Rural Merchant in the Nineteenth Century

The United States was an overwhelmingly rural nation in the early 1800s. Slowly but inexorably, the balance between rural and urban population changed during the course of the nineteenth century. In 1800, the nation's population was 5.3 million with only 322,000 (or 6 percent) living in "urban territory," which the census defined as settlements with a population of 2,500 or greater. By 1900, there were 76 million people living in the nation with 30 million (or 40 percent) living in urban areas. Only with the census of 1920 do we find a majority (51.2 percent) of the

U.S. population living in cities; and even that late the census defined a city as having a population of only 8,000 or more.[1]

These demographic realities had important implications for nineteenth-century retailing. On the farm, many of life's necessities could be obtained without recourse to a formal market. The household unit could produce furniture, clothing, and shoes. A family could grow a variety of foodstuffs for its own consumption, and it could barter the remainder for other goods or services within the local area or sell to a local dealer for shipment to a distant market.[2]

The general store at the rural crossroads of a small village carried a bewildering variety of merchandise in very cramped quarters, often as small as 400 square feet. Tea, flour, sugar, liquor, shoes, axes, kegs of nails, spices, and saddles were crammed into the available floor space; harnesses and a host of other goods were hung from the rafters.[3] One not atypical early store in Arrow Rock, Missouri, in the 1820s was located in a clearing shared with deer, snakes, and other denizens of the nearby woodland. The simple two-room structure was built of logs held together by clay and lime. One room, windowless, was used to store goods; the other, used as a salesroom, had bolts on the door and windows to foil robbers.[4] There was little organization in such stores:

> A great deal of time was wasted in looking for articles that were not in place or had no place. . . . Flies swarmed around the molasses barrel and there was never a mosquito bar to keep them off. There was tea in chests, packed in lead foil and straw matting with strange markings; rice and coffee spilling out on the floor where a bag showed a rent; rum and brandy; harness and whale oil. The air was thick with an all-embracing odor, an aroma composed of dry herbs and wet dogs, or strong tobacco, green hides and raw humanity.[5]

One authority has estimated that $5,000 to $6,000 was sufficient for the pre–Civil War frontier merchant "to purchase a good stock, and much of this could be obtained on credit."[6] Merchants often traveled to large cities such as New York and Philadelphia in the East and Chicago and St. Louis in the West to obtain their wares. Difficulties caused by the primitive state of transportation lent an element of risk to the acquisition of inventory.

The pace of business in the country store was slow in the early 1800s. A day might not see more than a dozen customers. Because of the absence of an adequate currency, trade was often carried on by a system of money-barter, whereby customer and merchant would exchange goods with money equivalents used as a standard of value. Price was a matter for negotiation, and if sharp dealing was not the rule, neither was it the exception. Phineas T. Barnum, who admittedly may not be the best authority on a question such as this, remarked of his experience keeping store in Connecticut in the 1820s: "the customers cheated us in their fabrics, [and] we cheated the customers with our goods. Each party expected to be cheated if it was possible."[7]

The merchant's relationship with the manufacturer was a distant one. There was little if any direct buying. Purchases were made from wholesalers or jobbers, and the daunting logistical problems were also solved through recourse to a thick and intricate web of middlemen. National brands were not completely unknown; for example, it is said that Walter Baker's Chocolate was stocked by the store Abraham Lincoln tended in New Salem, Illinois, in 1833, and branded patent medicines were ubiquitous.[8] But only with the growth of the big consumer packaged-goods firms in the last two decades of the nineteenth century did manufacturers begin their concerted effort, through national advertising and preemption of shelf space, to develop a marketing program combining both pull and push.[9]

Until that time, merchants dealt primarily in undifferentiated commodities, and their advertising was largely restricted to announcing the availability of products.[10] Advertising, in a setting characterized by a poor communication infrastructure and commodity products, offered scant assistance. Writing in 1939, historian Lewis E. Atherton observed that the "primary aim" of advertising before the Civil War was "to give the location, business, and services of a store, or to acquaint the public with any unusual changes occurring in the life of the firm. Little effort was spent in trying to increase sales through creating new desires for goods."[11] Advertising had yet to become an active tool for selling.[12]

It has been observed that the "nearest thing we ever have had to monopoly in grocery retailing was the old village grocery store," but this observation is accurate only for certain settings.[13] If there was but one store accessible to a wide trading area, consumers were indeed confronted with the choice of buying goods there, making the goods themselves, or going without them. On the other hand, this "vast network of minuscule monopolists" could be disrupted by the presence of more than one store in a village.[14] For farmers who traveled twenty miles over country roads for their provisions, it made sense to shop as many stores as were easily accessible. Competition would then take place on the basis of price, because such modern nonprice allures as are today grouped under "shopping experience" did not play a significant role. Distinctions between shopping and convenience goods, so central to retail strategy today, were largely irrelevant to the rural dweller of the nineteenth century.[15] Every trip to a store took planning and effort. Even the rural merchants appreciated the importance of access to the consumer insulated from competition, as was evidenced by their attempts to open additional stores when problems of capital, communication, and control could be overcome.[16] A great deal of traveling selling was also carried on.

The picture that emerges of the nineteenth-century country store, then, is of an institution without most of the tools at the command of today's retailer. Storekeepers' access to merchandise was sporadic and inconsistent. Their stores were general indeed, more likely to carry whatever goods were available from suppliers than those that the customer wanted. The pace of business was so slow that merchants had to rely on margin rather than turnover as the key to their financial success. Merchants located in proximity to competition lost control over their prices. The necessity of extending credit to customers whose ability and willingness to pay their bills were questionable put the merchants' solvency at risk. They received minimal help in selling from the wholesalers from whom they bought or from the manufacturers from whom the wholesalers bought.

The Urban Merchant

In the smaller cities, especially before the Civil War, one could find stores that did not differ radically from the rural, general stores. Indeed, even in the larger cities as late as the early twentieth century, some of the elements of rural merchandising—the confusion and disorganization especially—were present. Some urban merchants sold a wide variety of goods. Retailers have always run their businesses to make a profit rather than to facilitate the task of the analyst or census taker.[17]

Nevertheless, we can discern overall trends in urban retail merchandising that differentiated the city store from the country store. Of these, the most noteworthy was specialization in lines of merchandise offered. Ralph M. Hower, a historian of Macy's, observed that in urban retailing around 1850

> the principle of specialization dominated the scene: Both retail and wholesale trades were split up, by types of merchandise, into single line or specialty stores. . . . A 'gent's furnishings' store could thrive on Broadway in 1850, but in a small community in 1800 the owner of such a specialized store would have been idle and hungry most of the year.[18]

The retailing of food was also specialized. Produce, dairy products, meat, fish, baked goods, tea, coffee, other beverages both alcoholic and nonalcoholic, and various specialty items such as candy were retailed through specialty stores in large cities.

Location was a problem faced by all these specialized retailers. Household appliances for the efficient storage of food were not widely available. The old-time icebox provided safe storage of perishable products for only a few days. Mechanical refrigeration made possible the storage of food without a noticeable decline in quality for longer periods, but refrigerators were not sold in significant numbers until the late 1920s. Freezers were not marketed until after World War II.[19]

With the possible exception of the newsstand operator, grocers historically have seen their customers more often than any other type of retailer. In January 1988, the average shopper visited the supermarket 2.3 times per week.[20] It is likely that the average shopper of seventy-five years ago, especially if an urbanite, visited a food store even more often. Thus transportation to and from the food store was a matter of great concern to the nineteenth-century customer. For the majority of consumers until relatively recent times, driving to a food store was not an option. Consumers could walk to the store if it was nearby, or they could resort to public transportation. They could also use the telephone to place orders for delivery, a practice sufficiently common by 1929 to provoke a complaint that it was leading to higher food-distribution costs.[21] Whether the store was contacted in person or by telephone, groceries were usually delivered to the consumer's home seventy-five years ago. Thus ease of transportation was a concern to the expense-wary grocer as well as to the customer.[22]

The narrow specialization of food retailers meant that customers might have to shop a half dozen different stores to satisfy their basic food needs. One way to mitigate this inconvenience was to locate food stores near one another in a large, central marketplace. Such markets date back to the earliest days of European settlement in North America. One source reports that the "first public marketplace in our city, without a direct gain to the public coffers" was established on Pearl Street in downtown Manhattan in 1656. Two years later, Boston also established a central market. New York's Catharine Market was established in 1766, and a century later it contained sixty enclosed stalls as well as open-air vendors.[23] By the early twentieth century, central markets were recognized as playing an important role in efficient food distribution.[24] According to a report submitted to the House of Representatives in 1901 by the Industrial Commission on the Distribution of Food Products:

Such markets as those which prevail in the towns of eastern Pennsylvania make the expenses of living materially lower than the system of expensive corner stores, whose proprietors the community supports because there is no foresight in the municipal policy.

On the whole, nine-tenths of our cities are behind the distributive experience of the best-fed communities for want of proper facilities for bringing producers and consumers together at some convenient place or places at regular times.[25]

Unfortunately, we have no data indicating the total volume of foodstuffs sold through public and private central markets, so we cannot estimate the "share of stomach" of this method of distribution. However, the census reported that in 1918, 128 of 227 U.S. cities with a population greater than 30,000 maintained municipal markets. The total number of such markets was 237, of which 174 were retail, 14 wholesale, and 49 a combination of the two. Sixty-seven of these markets had been founded since 1914.[26]

A&P and the Chain Store Revolution

"In the United States," retailing expert Malcolm P. McNair wrote in 1931, "the major scene of the industrial revolution has definitely shifted from production to distribution." Over the preceding thirty years, the focus of consumer marketing had been changing from small-scale shopkeepers to "a large-scale, fully capitalistic business."[27] McNair had in mind not the supermarket—neither the concept nor the name had any meaning at the time he was writing—but the chain store. When industry experts spoke of a "revolution in distribution" in the 1920s and early 1930s, it was chain ownership and management of retail outlets and the backward integration often accompanying this development that they found most striking.[28] The growth of chains was not confined to groceries but encompassed general merchandise, apparel, and drugs as well.

The first chain store to make a lasting impact on the distribution of food in the United States was the Great Atlantic and Pacific Tea Company (A&P). Founded in 1859 by George Francis Gilman, the company at first sold hides and leathers.[29] By 1862, it had begun to specialize in the tea trade. Gilman was operating four tea stores in downtown Manhattan in 1865, and by the end of the decade he had opened an additional seven stores. One of his most productive clerks was George Huntington Hartford, who in 1866 was rewarded for his performance by promotion to cashier. The following year Hartford became a junior partner. In 1878, Hartford took over operational responsibilities for the firm, which had greatly enlarged the scope of its activities and had changed its name from the Great American Tea Company to the Great Atlantic and Pacific Tea Company.[30] The Hartford family both owned and managed the firm through the 1950s, and it made them one of the richest families in the world.

A&P's early success was based more on its mail-order distribution arrangement known as the Club Plan than on its branch stores. As an 1866 advertisement in *Harper's Weekly* explained, "all towns, villages or manufactures where a large number of men are engaged, by clubbing together, can reduce the price of their Teas and Coffees about one-third by sending directly to the Great American Tea Company."[31]

The reason for the lower prices of the company's tea are not altogether clear. The direct-mail distribution system eliminated some of the participants in the traditional channel.[32] The practice of quoting prices f.o.b. New York (transport costs not included) made prices appear lower than they really were in comparison with the local grocers' price lists. Club organizers, who received complimentary packages in recognition of their efforts, helped overcome "that inertia of buyers which is always a handicap in securing mail orders. . . ."[33] And, finally, the size of the coverage order received through mail order was greater than that received by the competition. Offsetting these economies were the costs of promoting the mail-order program. Records of expenditures have not survived, but A&P invested in a great deal of periodical advertising and also distributed circulars.

Published with permission of The Great Atlantic & Pacific Tea Company.

This is the way Vesey Street in Manhattan looked in the earliest days of A&P.

Tea was a particularly inviting item for an ambitious grocer to concentrate on because standard practice in the trade was to price it high. A rural nation could grow much of its own food if store prices got out of hand, but tea was a specialty product for which this was not an option. The high price of tea subsidized more competitively priced commodities like sugar, salt, and flour.[34]

What A&P did, in modern terms, was to "cherry pick" and then to mass market. Tea served a specific purpose for the standard food merchant. It was the high-priced, high-margin item designed to generate big profit dollars. However, A&P looked at tea not from the viewpoint of the average grocer's profit but from the consumer's perspective. Consumers wanted tea at a lower price, and they would be likely to buy more of it at a lower price. A&P thus realized that it could make profit through volume on tea. The company's original strategy was to expand its distributive network for tea and coffee by increasing the number of its stores—to about one hundred in 1881 and to about twice that many in 1901—and by developing a system of peddler routes that would bring the product directly to the customer.[35] Toward the end of the nineteenth century, A&P began to broaden its product line. "I think it was about '90 or '91," recalled John A. Hartford, the younger son of A&P owner George Huntington Hartford, many years later, that "[w]e first got into baking powder

The exterior of an early A&P.

and then into extracts. . . . We got into the grocery business gradually."[36] At first, the company purchased its groceries from wholesalers but soon began to assume the warehousing function itself. In 1911, an A&P store in New York City, for example, was carrying about 25 different product categories, in a total of 270 varieties, ranging from 23 different kinds of tea to single selections of butter, baking powder, and cornstarch. A quarter of a century earlier, a similar A&P carried only six product categories.[37]

In 1900, one year before the firm's incorporation, A&P's sales had reached $5.6 million, and profits during the preceding three years had averaged $125,000 on an investment of $936,000. Economist Morris A. Adelman, an expert on the company, describes its progress to that time as being "not spectacular."[38] Its share of the total retail food market remained quite small. Nevertheless, it was clearly the industry leader by a wide margin.

The first years of the twentieth century brought rapid growth for A&P. By 1907, sales had increased almost threefold to $15 million. In 1913, the company embarked on a new strategic course. Up to that time, A&P had made extensive use of premiums and trading stamps, and it had also provided customers with the full range of services common to most retail grocery outlets of the era. The new format, in contrast, was described by an officer of the company as follows:

> In our so-called "Economy Stores" we do not make any deliveries, we have no telephone communication, we close the store when the manager goes to lunch, we sell strictly for cash, we give no premiums, trading stamps or other inducements. In our regular stores we do give trading stamps, we do make deliveries, we have telephones, in some instances give credit. . . .[39]

The cost of food was a significant issue during the first fifteen years of the twentieth century. Retail food prices increased by more than a third from 1900 to 1912; and although income for some occupational groups was keeping pace, others were falling behind. The high cost of living was the subject of investigations at the state and federal level in 1911 and 1912, and it became an important political issue.[40]

Though the economy-store format was not original with A&P, the company pushed it harder than any other food retailer. John A. Hartford was convinced that trading stamps and other frills were driving the company's prices too high. For him, A&P had one dominant mission—to sell quality food at low prices. "I have always been a volume man," he later said. "[U]nless we can operate in the future along economy lines, I do not believe I can put my heart in the business."[41] Hartford's unswerving devotion to this tenet helped the company solidify its position as the nation's preeminent mass retailer.

Inside early A&P stores, customers were served by clerks. These clerks obtained what the customers asked for from the shelves and often made suggestions concerning what to buy.

A&P's new economy-store format lowered operating costs, and part of these savings were passed along to the customer. The Cream of Wheat Company refused to deal with A&P because the price per package of its well-known cereal was $0.12 in the economy stores as opposed to $0.14 in the standard stores.[42] Because A&P did its own wholesaling, it could sell the cereal for less than competitors could. Complaints can be found in the trade press against similar low prices on such well-known brands as Campbell's soups and Bon Ami cleanser. Competing retailers found themselves under pressure to adopt the new store format themselves.[43]

To set up an economy store, $1,000 in up-front investment was required for equipment, stock, and cash.[44] Operating expenses, by one estimate, were as low as 12 percent of sales. These expenses included rent, ice, light and heat, delivery to store, insurance and interest, and salary. The latter was set at $12 to $13 per week plus 1 percent of sales over $200 per week.

Having established its new formula, A&P embarked on a policy of saturating its major markets by opening stores at a rate that was unprecedented in the history of American retailing. From 1914 to 1916, George and John Hartford opened 7,500 stores, and closed over half of them to weed out the weakest. They made all the A&Ps look as similar as possible, both in architecture and in the layout of goods inside. By 1920, as Morris A. Adelman noted, "although some of the old type of stores were still being operated, the economy line *was* the A&P."[45] A&P growth in terms of number of stores, sales, and profits was impressive, as table 4–1 indicates.

Economy operation and rapid branching were pursued vigorously by other grocery retailers as well. Table 4–2 shows the number of stores operated by the five leading food retailers from 1919 to 1937. Table 4–3 provides data on sales and market share for the same group of chains. However, A&P firmly established its leadership in this chain-store race. From 1919 to 1930, its sales increased almost four and a half times. Profits skyrocketed from $4.8 million to $35 million. In terms of sales, A&P was in 1929 the fifth largest industrial corporation in the United States and by far the largest chain organization in the world, with sales $173 million greater than those of Sears, Ward, and Penney combined.[46] It owned and operated over 15,000 stores, most of which were located in the densely populated eastern half of the nation (see exhibit 4–1). More than three-

EXHIBIT 4–1

A&P Retail Operations in 1933

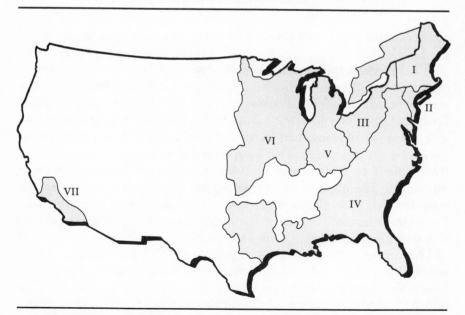

TABLE 4-1

Number of Stores, Sales, and Profits of A&P, 1914–1930

Year	Number of Stores	Sales (in millions)	Before-Tax Profit (in millions)
1914	650		
1915	1,500		
1916	3,250		
1917	3,782		
1918	3,799		
1919	4,224	$ 194.6	$ 6.7
1920	4,600	235.3	4.8
1921	5,200	202.4	8.4
1922	7,300	246.9	8.8
1923	9,300	302.9	11.2
1924	11,400	352.1	13.2
1925	14,000	440.0	13.8
1926	14,800	574.0	16.2
1927	15,600	761.4	21.3
1928	15,100	972.8	27.5
1929	15,400	1,053.7	29.0
1930	15,700	1,065.8	35.0

SOURCES: Morris A. Adelman, *A&P: A Study in Price-Cost Behavior and Public Policy* (Cambridge: Harvard University Press, 1959), 26, 434, 438; Godfrey M. Lebhar, *Chain Stores in America, 1859–1962* (New York: Chain Store Publishing Corporation, 1963), 395. The number-of-stores data for 1917–1919 are taken from Lebhar; all other data are from Adelman.

quarters of the company's two million shares were held by a single family, the Hartfords.[47]

What explains the remarkable performance of grocery chain stores in general and of A&P in particular? This question can best be answered by asking another one: What do consumers look for when they shop for food? Each year, the Food Marketing Institute, the industry's trade association, asks a sample of consumers to describe what they consider the most important criteria in selecting a supermarket at which to shop. Of the twenty-eight attributes listed in 1984, good/low prices was most often mentioned. The importance of price appeal is further apparent when one considers that four other attributes (items on sale; money-saving specials; items clearly marked for price; coupons; and generic/unbranded products) also strongly suggest price consciousness.[48]

This concern with price is not surprising. In 1983, total consumer food expenditures (both at home and away from home) amounted to $365.1 billion. Total personal consumption expenditures that year were $2,155.9 billion.[49] Thus, the fraction of disposable income devoted to food expenditures was about 16.9 percent.

If spending more than $0.17 out of every disposable dollar for food helped make the consumer price-sensitive in the 1980s, the consumer in the 1920s may have been more price-sensitive still. In 1921, 1925, and 1929, expenditures on food and beverages equaled 27.4, 27.3, and 25.3 percent, respectively, of total consumption expenditures.[50] Prior to World War I, Clyde Lyndon King of the Wharton School estimated that "Probably half of [urban dwellers] now spend annually nearly half of their income on food."[51]

Studies of the question in the interwar years usually concluded that price was the most important factor that chain-store patrons cited for their choice of retailer. In a survey of the shopping habits of Floridians, for example, Theodore N. Beckman and Herman C. Nolen found that 28 percent of the 4,435 responses to why 1,496 chain shoppers bought most of their groceries from chains was lower price. The next largest number of responses was 15 percent for convenient location. In contrast, only 12 percent of the 3,357 responses of 1,151 independent store patrons as to why they bought from independents was lower price.[52] The Beckman and Nolen results are shown in table 4–4.

TABLE 4–2

Number of Stores Operated by the Five Leading Food Retailers, 1919–1937

Year	A&P	Kroger	American Stores	Safeway	First National
1919	4,224		1,175		
1920	4,600	799	1,243		
1921	5,200	947	1,274		
1922	7,300	1,224	1,375	118	
1923	9,300	1,641	1,474	193	
1924	11,400	1,973	1,629	263	
1925	14,000	2,599	1,792	330	
1926	14,800	3,100	1,982	673	
1927	15,600	3,564	2,133	840	1,681
1928	15,100	4,307	2,548	1,191	1,717
1929	15,400	5,575	2,644	2,340	2,002
1930	15,700	5,165	2,728	2,675	2,549
1931	15,670	4,884	2,806	3,264	2,548
1932	15,427	4,737	2,977	3,411	2,546
1933	15,131	4,400	2,882	3,306	2,705
1934	15,035	4,352	2,859	3,228	2,653
1935	14,926	4,250	2,826	3,330	2,623
1936	14,746	4,212	2,816	3,370	2,556
1937	13,314	4,108	2,620	3,327	2,473

NOTE: There are as many variations in these statistics as there are sources from which they can be drawn. For example, Godfrey M. Lebhar (see source note below) gives 1,050 as the number of Safeway Stores in 1925 on one table (p. 56) but a mere 330 on another (p. 397). However, the broad trends illustrated by Lebhar and by other authorities are essentially similar.

SOURCES: Godfrey M. Lebhar, *Chain Stores in America, 1859–1962* (New York: Chain Store Publishing Corporation, 1963), 393–97; Safeway *Annual Report,* 1934.

TABLE 4-3

Sales and Market Share of Five Leading Food Retailers, 1919–1937

(in millions)

Year	Estimated Total Food Sales, All Stores	The Great Atlantic & Pacific Tea Co.	The Kroger Grocery and Baking Co.	The American Stores Co.	Safeway Stores, Inc.	First National Stores, Inc.	Total Sales of Large Chains	Market Share of Large Chains
1919	$6,470.5	$ 194.6	—	$ 76.4	—	—	$ 271.0	4.2%
1920	7,132.2	235.3	$ 50.7	103.1	—	$ 9.9	399.0	5.6
1921	5,441.1	202.4	44.9	86.1	—	9.6	343.0	6.3
1922	5,735.2	246.9	53.8	85.9	$ 12.5	10.5	409.6	7.1
1923	6,249.9	302.4	74.3	94.6	19.9	11.5	502.7	8.0
1924	6,249.9	352.1	90.1	98.2	28.5	12.5	581.4	9.3
1925	6,544.0	440.0	116.2	108.9	38.7	49.0	752.8	11.5
1926	6,985.2	574.1	146.0	116.9	50.5	59.1	946.6	13.6
1927	6,985.2	761.4	161.3	120.7	69.6	64.4	1,177.4	16.9
1928	7,352.8	972.8	207.4	137.3	103.3	75.5	1,496.7	20.4
1929	7,352.8	1,053.7	286.6	143.3	213.5	107.6	1,804.7	24.5
1930	6,544.0	1,065.8	267.1	142.8	219.3	108.2	1,803.2	27.6
1931	5,955.8	1,008.3	244.4	135.2	246.8	107.6	1,742.3	29.3
1932	5,294.0	864.0	213.2	115.5	229.2	103.9	1,522.8	28.8
1933	—	819.6	205.7	109.4	220.2	105.8	1,460.7	—
1934	—	842.0	221.2	114.4	243.0	111.3	1,531.9	—
1935	6,352.4	872.2	229.9	115.9	294.7	119.6	1,632.3	25.7
1936	—	907.4	242.3	113.4	346.2	120.9	1,730.0	—
1937	—	881.7	248.4	114.6	381.9	124.3	1,750.9	—

SOURCE: Adapted from A. C. Hoffman for the Temporary National Economic Committee, *Large-Scale Organization in the Food Industries*, monograph no. 35 (Washington, D.C.: GPO, 1940), 8.

TABLE 4-4

Reasons Why Consumers Bought Most of the Family Groceries from Chains or from Independent Merchants

	Buying from Chain Stores		Buying from Independent Stores	
	Number of Reasons Given by 1,496 Persons	Percent of Total Reasons Given	Number of Reasons Given by 1,154 Persons	Percent of Total Reasons Given
Lower price	1,248	28.14%	416	12.39%
Convenient location	698	15.74	675	20.11
Better quality	631	14.23	487	14.51
Wider selection of goods	832	18.76	247	7.36
Pleasing personality	320	7.22	518	15.43
Credit	48	1.08	403	12.00
Delivery	104	2.34	235	7.00
Sanitary and clean	152	3.43	117	3.49
Advertising	231	5.21	51	1.52
Good store appearance	67	1.51	37	1.10
Other reasons	104	2.34	171	5.09
Total	4,435	100.00%	3,357	100.00%

SOURCE: Theodore N. Beckman and Herman C. Nolen, *The Chain Store Problem: A Critical Analysis* (New York: McGraw-Hill, 1938), 169. Reprinted by permission of McGraw-Hill.

Although these findings confirm our preconceptions, the subject is more complex. A study of almost 1,000 Springfield, Ohio, families, completed in 1937, indicated that chain shoppers advanced convenient location a good deal more often than lower price (25.6 to 16.8 percent) as their reason for patronizing chains. Just as surprising, the same study found that independent store patrons gave lower price for their choice more often (17.1 percent) than did chain shoppers for patronizing chains. This startling result led Beckman and Nolen to conclude that the "magnetic force of price has been overemphasized."[53]

It is instructive to reexamine the data in table 4-4 with these comments in mind. Although lower price was the response most often advanced by chain shoppers, 71.86 percent of the total responses were unrelated to price. Moreover, 3.42 percent of the reasons for chain shoppers choosing chains were credit and delivery, although many chain outlets did not offer these services—one of the reasons their prices were low.[54]

In my view, the grocery retailing revolution in the interwar years was based predominantly but not solely on price.

This is a complicated story, and one aspect of that complexity is price comparison. How different were chain and independent grocery store prices? Almost all authorities during the interwar years (and most postwar authorities as well) agree that grocery prices were lower in chain stores than in independents.[55] Such complete agreement does not exist, however, concerning the meaning of that statement.

For example, which items are the relevant ones for price comparison? Is it essential that all items compared be "branded, packaged, or otherwise carefully identified through specifications in order to assure uniform quality and absolute comparability"?[56] This procedure limits discretion and minimizes error in the field, but some chains specialized in private brands. Should these be ignored because of the impossibility of precise comparison, even though their quality might be virtually indistinguishable from branded merchandise? Should a "market basket" rather than an item-by-item approach be employed? Which prices are the most relevant? How should sales be taken into account? And how should "loss leaders" be treated? Which stores should be investigated? Until 1951, the census defined a chain as a retailer operating four or more stores. (In that year, the requisite number of stores was increased to eleven.) Apparently, the anomalous findings from Springfield, Ohio, referred to above resulted from the fact that most of the chain business in that city was carried on by local chains, which might have been less price-competitive than the nationals.[57]

A comparison of fifteen studies analyzing chain and independent store prices in the interwar years reveals that prices at the chains were significantly lower than at the independents—never less than 3 percent and often as much as 10 or 11 percent lower (see table 4–5). If $0.25 of the disposable dollar was spent on food and the chain shopper could save 10 percent of that amount by patronizing the chain, the savings were noteworthy. Second, the difference between the prices of chains and independents tended to narrow during the 1930s. This trend becomes more apparent if one examines the three sets of studies carried out by the same authors in the same towns in different years. Malcolm D. Taylor found that the chain advantage diminished from 13.79 percent in Durham in 1929 to 11 percent in 1933; Charles F. Phillips found that the chain advantage diminished from 12.3 percent in central New York State in 1930 to 10.2 percent in 1934; and Paul D. Converse found for Champaign-Urbana that the chain price advantage decreased from 11.5 percent in 1931 to 6.5 percent in 1937. Converse's results derived more from an increase in chain prices than from a decline in those of independents. Whereas the annual per capita cost of groceries purchased from an independent store increased only slightly between 1931 and 1937, from $122.29 to $123.41, the cost of a year's groceries from a chain store rose from $109.39 to $115.36.[58]

These observations lead naturally to two questions: (1) what explains the difference in price between chains and independent groceries, and (2) why did this price spread apparently narrow during the 1930s?

Chain and Independent Grocery Prices: Some Thoughts on the Differences

There are a number of possible explanations for chain stores' ability to offer lower prices to the consumer than did independent grocers. First, the chains may have been more willing to accept lower profits. Second, the nature of their operations, including their efficiencies in retail management, their policy on service, their backward integration into wholesaling and (in some instances) processing, may have permitted them to charge less while making more. Finally, the volume of their operations may have enabled the chains to extract extraordinary discounts from suppliers and thus charge less because they themselves paid less.

The first explanation—that the chains were willing to accept lower profits—can be quickly dismissed. The chain grocery business in the 1920s was a profitable one. The rate of return on invested capital for A&P between 1921 and 1927 never fell below 20 percent, and in 1928 it was 26.2 percent. Four other large chains earned a 17.5 percent return on investment in 1928, and an FTC sample of chain groceries (also selling meat) earned 20.8 percent. These returns on investment were considerably better than the average of all corporations for that year, which was 14.8 percent.[59] Juxtaposed against these generous returns was the situation—one is tempted to use the word "plight"—of the independent food retailer.

One is immediately struck by how small so many of the independents were. Of all grocery stores without meats, 52.4 percent had a volume of less than $10,000 per year; of those also selling meat, 48.2 percent had a volume under $20,000. The census does not tell us how many units by size were chain-affiliated, but most of the small stores were probably independents. In 1929, for example, the average sales per store of single-store independents in Chicago were $16,753, whereas average sales per store for sectional and national chains in Chicago were more than $60,000.[60] Nationwide, the average sales per chain grocery store were $43,836.[61] In 1939, when 958,972 retail outlets (for all commodities) had an annual sales volume of under $10,000, 943,533 of those, or 98.4 percent, were independents.[62]

TABLE 4-5

Prices in Chain and Independent Grocery Stores, 1929–1938

Author of Study	Site	Year Published	Year Data Were Gathered	Principal Findings
R. S. Alexander	New York City	1929	1929	Chain prices 4.56 percent lower than those of independents for items under $0.10. Chain prices 0.93 percent lower than those of independents for items over $0.20.
Einar Bjorklund and J. L. Palmer	Chicago	1930	1930	Chain prices 13 percent lower[a] for items under $0.10. Chain prices 10.22 percent lower for items over $0.25.
E. Z. Palmer	Lexington, KY	1930	1930	Savings of 14 percent if the lowest price available at chain stores is compared to average prices on 58 items.
Malcolm D. Taylor	Durham, NC	1930	1929	Average savings at chain stores on 60 items of 13.79 percent.
Charles F. Phillips	Five towns in central New York State	1931	1930	Average savings at chain stores of 12.3 percent on 63 items compared to independents. Voluntary chains[b] undersell independents by 3.1 percent.
Paul D. Converse	Champaign-Urbana, Illinois	1931	1931	Chain prices 11.5 percent lower.
Dorothy W. Dowe	Two New York City neighborhoods and four suburbs of the city	1932	1931	Average savings at chain stores of 8.53 percent on 48 items.
Federal Trade Commission	Washington, DC	1933	1929	Chain prices 6.8 percent lower on 274 items.
Federal Trade Commission	Memphis, TN	1933	1930	Chain prices 5.6 percent lower on 193 items.

TABLE 4-5 (Continued)

Author of Study	Site	Year Published	Year Data Were Gathered	Principal Findings
Federal Trade Commission	Detroit, MI	1933	1931	Chain prices 6.7 percent lower on 183 items.
Federal Trade Commission	Cincinnati, OH	1933	1929	Prices at large chains 6 percent lower on 120 items. Prices at small chains 5.4 percent lower on 120 items.
Malcolm D. Taylor	Durham, NC	1934	1933	Chain prices 11 percent lower on 60 percent of items.
Charles F. Phillips	Five towns in central New York State	1935	1934	Average savings at chain stores of 10.02 percent on 52 items, compared to independents. Voluntary chains undersell independents by 3.6 percent.
Paul D. Converse	Champaign-Urbana, Illinois	1937	1937	Chain prices 6.5 percent lower on 66 articles.
Theodore N. Beckman	Numerous communities in Florida	1938	1935	On 124 items, chains with more than 15 stores 4.8 percent less expensive than independents. Chains with 11–15 stores, 4.1 percent. Chains with 7–10 stores, 3.4 percent. Chains with 2–3 stores, 3.3 percent.

[a]When the comparison is unspecified (i.e., when the finding reads "Chain prices x percent lower"), the stores to which the chains are being compared can be assumed to be predominantly traditional, single-unit independents.

[b]Voluntary chains have been defined as "unit stores independently owned but in varying degrees centrally controlled and managed. . . . Such aggregations are held together by contracts or by licenses." Paul H. Nystrom, Economics of Retailing, vol. 1 (New York: Ronald Press, 1930), 16.

SOURCES: See note 55.

Noting that well over half of the independent retailers sold less than $10,000 each in 1939 and that the annual store mortality rate was at least 7 percent, political scientist Joseph C. Palamountain observed that "The economic existence of these small merchants, if not solitary, certainly tends to be 'poor, nasty, brutish and short.' "[63] The smallest stores found survival the most difficult. Of the twenty-six independent grocers analyzed in a special Commerce Department survey in 1928, four of the five with annual sales under $10,200 lost money.[64] Among the various retail trades, grocers were the most vulnerable. Their economic life expectancy was less than half that of retail druggists.[65]

Thus, chain grocers offered lower prices than independents not because they were satisfied with making less money.

Were chain price advantages, then, made possible by retailing efficiencies and backward integration? Many of the smaller independent retailers in early twentieth-century America did not operate their businesses as professionally as they should have, often neglecting the most elementary requirements. Some did not keep books or even figure their costs at all. As one retailer put it, "What's the use? I have no one to account to but myself."[66] And as for those who did make an attempt to keep records, the Harvard Business School Bureau of Business Research remarked in 1919 that many retail grocers kept no records of profits or expenses and so "did not know even approximately where they stood financially." Many never took inventory, and even those who did made no provision for the salary of the proprietor or of store goods appropriated for family use. "This," pronounced the bureau in a concluding observation with which few would disagree, "is not sound business management."[67]

Writing in 1979, Theodore Levitt observed:

> The owner-manager of a small variety store with some 3,000 stockkeeping units . . . has a far more difficult and demanding task than the head of K Mart with his 1,492 stores. The owner-manager has to do everything, including the bookkeeping, purchasing, selling, repairs, even janitoring. The head of K Mart does none of these. Division heads and department heads under him each do only one of those tasks. Their job may be big, but it's relatively simple compared with the owner-manager's. By subdividing work, K Mart has become simpler, more manageable, and thus bigger.[68]

Chain-store publicists were fully aware of the advantages of expertise and of the subdivision of tasks. Store location was only one of many examples to which they pointed to illustrate the contributions of staff experts. Unlike the random site selection of an inexperienced independent merchant, the chain accumulated experience as it grew, knowledge that it could codify into standard business practices, which added both speed and acumen to its site selection decisions.[69]

The United Cigar Stores Company, for example, employed traffic counters from its real estate subsidiary to

> stand at promising corners and check off the traffic on tabulators they can carry in the palm of one hand. They check it off at different hours of the day, on different days of the week, at different seasons, and on different sides of the street. It was found by the company that the busiest street corner in America was at State and Madison Streets, Chicago, which 142,000 people passed between the hours of 7 A.M. and midnight.[70]

The company learned from such research that consumers were more likely to purchase their cigars on the way home from work than when rushing to their jobs in the morning, and that they would probably be waiting for transportation on a corner, rather than in the middle of a block.[71]

The advantages of "scientific management" extended beyond accounting and location. It comprehended store layout and design, skilled professional buying based on the best information, better communication with the consumer through research and advertising, and more astute management of human resources in general.[72] Few of the 300,000 independent grocers were able to match the resources possessed by the chain experts to meet these needs.[73]

Now, too much can be made of the "science" of chain management. One of the most striking aspects of the history of A&P between the world wars was the company's resolute refusal in certain instances to do what its chief operating officer, John Hartford (who was also one of the principal owners), wanted it to do. "Sometimes," Hartford remarked in 1931, "the body gets so large that the pulsations fail to reach its extremities."[74] This is one kind of control problem that the single-store independent merchant did not have.

Nevertheless, the chain grocers did apply science to retail management in the 1920s to a greater extent than earlier grocers had. Multiple stores meant the rapid acquisition of experience from which the chains greatly benefited. And the enormous volume of the chains allowed them to spread the cost of staff expertise over so many units that its impact on price was negligible.

In addition to these management practices, the chains were able to offer lower prices because they made a basic policy decision to offer fewer services than did the independent grocer. The most expensive of these services were credit and delivery. It is difficult to determine precisely how much these two services cost. There are as many estimates as there have

been estimators, but Malcolm P. McNair's calculation—that they accounted for about 3.65 percent of the sales of the independents offering
them in 1924—seems reasonable and has been cited by others.[75] In a
business in which typical return on sales varies from 1.5 to 3 percent, this
is a significant outlay. The contemporary perception in the interwar years,
that chains tended not to offer credit and delivery or to take telephone
orders, is supported by the data. Under 5 percent of chain store grocers
granted credit; just over 30 percent made deliveries; and slightly more
than a fifth accepted telephone orders. And if we look at chain groceries
that also sold meat, such services were provided significantly less often.[76]

The largest grocery chains offered the fewest services. But even they
made exceptions where particular market or competitive conditions warranted them. Thus from A&P:

> Our general rule is not to make deliveries. However, with so many stores
> operating under so many different circumstances, no such rule as this can
> universally exist without some exceptions. . . . The only real exception to the
> rule today is the metropolitan district of New York, where from stores in the
> higher class residential neighborhoods delivery is made in a minor way from
> handouts.[77]

And from Kroger:

> We have no store delivery system, no wagons, or any hired deliveries, but in
> a number of neighborhood stores, high school boys, after school, will deliver
> for customers when necessary. It is not the company's policy to deliver
> goods, but in some neighborhoods where the housewife demands it and is
> willing to pay for it we give that service. One out of every ten stores has a
> delivery boy. . . .[78]

There are, unfortunately, no similarly comprehensive data concerning
the number of independent stores that offered these services. One indication of practice among independents can be found in the Harvard
Business School Bureau of Business Research's report on independent
grocers in 1924. Of the 389 grocery stores surveyed, 110 reported
charge sales accounting for 75 percent or more of their total sales; only
46 reported cash sales accounting for 75 percent or more of their total
business.[79]

Clearly, then, management expertise and policy on service did play
significant roles in the capacity of chains to offer consumers lower prices
than the independents could.

Let us now turn, in this search for the sources of chain price advantages,
to the question of vertical integration. Traditionally, numerous middle-

We do not know precisely when this picture of an A&P delivery wagon was taken, but it was probably around the turn of the century. Soon thereafter, John Hartford's "economy store" movement would greatly reduce the amount of delivery service the company provided.

men of various descriptions stood athwart the pathway of foodstuffs as they made their way from farmer to consumer. The charges levied by these intermediaries for the performance of their services were the targets of reformers eager to control the cost of living. In 1913, for example, Clyde Lyndon King asked "Can the cost of food distribution be reduced?"[80] He was convinced that the length of the channel and transportation difficulties made food cost more than it should. Examining food distribution costs for unprocessed farm produce in Philadelphia, King found that differences in the price received by the farmer and that paid by the consumer varied from 67 to 266 percent (depending on the product) after payments to transporters, terminal operators, jobbers, and wholesalers.[81]

The first authoritative, nationwide count of wholesaling activity in the food trades was taken by the U.S. Census for 1929. The results show that in groceries, confectionery, and meat, 15,224 merchant wholesalers did $5.4 billion in business. The first employment figures available are for 1935, and these show 164,486 persons engaged in this work. The census treats farm products (defined to include fresh fruit and vegetable wholesal-

The Kroger Company was an early chain store competitor of A&P. Here we see a showplace of the Kroger chain at 530 Main Street in the headquarters city of Cincinnati soon after the turn of the century.

ers and poultry and dairy-product distributors) separately. The corresponding figures in this category are 8,972 wholesalers doing almost $3.1 billion in business and employing 89,043 people in 1935.[82] In 1929, by comparison, there were 481,891 stores in the food group doing $10.8 billion in business and employing close to 1.2 million people.[83]

Thus, a fundamental characteristic of the chain store in the food industry was its vertical integration. The trend during the 1920s was for chains to do a diminishing percentage of their business through independent wholesalers.[84] This was especially true of the largest and most important companies in the industry.[85]

Exhibit 4–2 illustrates graphically how the chains were redrawing the geography of product movement in the interwar years, using fruits and vegetables in New York City as an example. By the mid-1930s, slightly more than 50 percent of the fruits and vegetables purchased by the chains in New York City were distributed without the assistance of wholesale markets. But New York was not unique. The chains in Boston and Philadelphia received direct at their warehouses 55 and 57 percent, respectively, of their fruits and vegetables. The biggest chains were the most committed to backward integration. A&P, for example, bought "almost nothing from the terminal produce wholesaler in many cities."[86] But why did the large food chains like A&P backward integrate into wholesaling? The visible hand of managerial coordination was able to guide products from producer to consumer less expensively than was the invisible hand of market relations. To understand how much less, we must compare the margins and expenses of chain stores with those of the independent retailers and wholesalers combined. We are not really making a comparison between two different kinds of stores here, but rather between two different distribution systems.

Malcolm P. McNair attempted to quantify the differences between these two systems. He explained that this attempt was "illustrative rather than factual" and was not offered "as being in any sense final or conclusive."[87] Lack of data forced McNair to make numerous assumptions. However, his assumptions seem reasonable, and his work stands as the closest approximation of the key financial data of these two systems that we are ever likely to have. (Table A–1 is derived from McNair's data and is analyzed in detail in appendix A.)

On the basis of McNair's data, we can calculate that consumers spending $100 took home $71.80 worth of merchandise at wholesale prices if they shopped at a traditional, independent, single-unit grocer. That same $100 bought $80.60 in merchandise at a chain grocery store. To understand how such savings were possible, we must explore the problem of inventory management. Precisely why was it that administrative coordination through backward integration into wholesaling was more efficient than were market relations between retailers and wholesalers?

In a study of business logistics, James L. Heskett, Nicholas A. Glaskowsky, and Robert M. Ivie divided inventory into five categories:

1. Cycle stocks—stocks needed to satisfy basic demand under conditions of certainty.

EXHIBIT 4-2

Flow of Fruits and Vegetables in the New York Metropolitan Area Markets, 1936

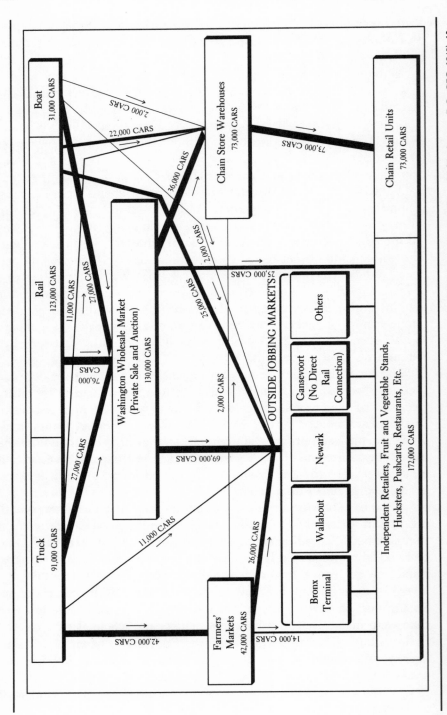

SOURCE: A. C. Hoffman for the Temporary National Economic Committee, *Large-Scale Organization in the Food Industries*, monograph no. 35 (Washington, D.C.: GPO, 1940), 13.

2. In-transit stocks—stocks in the process of moving from one location to another.
3. Safety stocks—stocks held in excess of cycle stocks due either to uncertainties or to time required for replacement.
4. Speculative stocks—stocks acquired in anticipation of shortages, because of price opportunities, or for other such reasons.
5. Dead stocks—stocks for which there appears to be no demand.[88]

In each of these categories, the integrated system of the big chain could boast marked advantages over the independent system. Accounts of the independents give the impression that many did not have a clear idea of what their cycle stocks should be. The independent was served by numerous wholesalers but might do as little as $20 of business per month with an individual supplier. Even for these, the independent had to serve "as chairman of the entertainment committee" when the salesperson called, thus wasting time. Grocers received small orders, inconsistently timed, and their product offering suffered from a lack of coordination of their lines. A 1930 *Forbes* article complained:

The typical independent grocer who buys here, there and everywhere, is not often very much of a merchandiser. . . . Almost inevitably, the man who scatters his buying in this way buys more of some things than he should, and less of others. . . . A persuasive or insistent salesman [says]: "Buy this!" And the merchant . . . [yields]. Anyhow, he "thought he could sell it."[89]

The contrast with A&P's operations is clear. Its stores were visited only by A&P representatives and inventory was managed in a systematic fashion, minimizing waste. Twice a week A&P grocery managers filled out order sheets for their stores. Each order was processed at an A&P warehouse, where goods were arranged in the same sequence as they were listed on the sheet. A handtruck labeled with the store's number was used to collect each order in a system that for its time was a marvel of efficiency.[90]

An idea of the differences in the management of in-transit stocks can be achieved by referring to exhibit 4–2. More than half of chain produce in New York City, and all of that destined for A&P, circumvented the Washington Wholesale Market. This meant lower mileage; lower charges for on- and off-loading, storage, order processing, and labor; and less shrinkage. These wholesale markets were unlovely places. According to a Federal Trade Commission investigation, collusion to fix charges among the various handlers of goods who controlled the limited receiving and marketing facilities was commonplace. Produce was sometimes destroyed to keep prices high. New entrants were excluded by "rules that were occasionally enforced by threats, sabotage, and even violence."[91] The chains avoided these problems. It was estimated that in the chain system the average laborer assembled and delivered twenty-four carloads of produce per year, whereas in the independent system the average laborer handled only ten carloads.[92]

If retailers had no clear idea of what their cycle stocks should be, they could not accurately plan safety stocks. Nor could they speculate intelligently. With the well-run chain, management of these inventory problems was far more rational.

The advantages of the vertical system are perhaps most dramatic in the category of dead stocks. Let us take an example. Suppose a customer entered a small independent grocery shop in 1930 and asked for goat cheese. That grocer probably did not keep this item in stock and would have had to order it from the wholesaler. If the wholesaler also did not carry the item, he would have to order it from a producer. Now it may have been that goat cheese was not shipped in less than carload lots. The wholesaler, then, would face the dilemma of either buying a carload of goat cheese or not satisfying the retail customer. If the wholesaler purchased the carload, he might not be able to sell more than the single order to the single grocer who asked for it. The remaining cheese would become dead stock. In the words of a man who decided to leave the wholesale grocery business in the mid-1920s, the wholesaler's "contacts with the consuming trade have been negligible. He has had no way to sense a demand except by the indirect means of feeling out his customer—the retailer. . . ."[93] On the other hand, in the chain system the wholesaler and retailer were combined. This meant that the wholesale end of the chain-store business had access to far better information than did the independent. For example, a grocer with fifty stores in a metropolitan area would be better able to sense if the request for goat cheese was uncommon or if it was part of a general trend among consumers. This knowledge, then, would help determine whether a carload of a particular product was worth purchasing and would mitigate the problem of dead stock.

Efficiency in inventory management among chains was also the result of greater certainty in their business operations. An A&P store could not only respond to demand as a result of its superior information but could also, to a degree, create demand through coordinated programs because of its impact on the market. Thus, as we shall see, A&P was able to move commodities in a glutted market with greater efficiency than could the independent system.

The large food chains integrated backward beyond wholesaling (see table 4–6). A&P, through its subsidiary the American Coffee Corporation, was the largest coffee merchant in the world in 1930, controlling the commodity from Brazilian plantations to the consumer. Another subsidiary, Quaker Maid, owned and operated canneries and even employed salmon fishermen in Alaska. "In Brooklyn," according to a 1930 *Fortune* article,

> a vast Quaker Maid factory packs a vast assortment of foods: 72,000 pounds of jams and preserves ooze into jars every day; 70,000 pounds of cereals; and hundreds of thousands of pounds of baking powder, rice, lentils, and split peas are put into dated paper packages every day. Veritable conduits of mayonnaise, vats of olive oil, cauldrons of pickles and cauliflower (for relish) are jarred.[94]

A&P also baked bread—a half billion loaves per year.[95]

Why did the food chains integrate backward into manufacturing? The Federal Trade Commission surveyed twenty grocery, grocery and meat, and meat chains in 1932 to ascertain their reasons for integration into manufacturing. Among the 44 reasons that companies gave for backward integration, the one most often cited was a desire to obtain "higher quality and control of quality" (11 times). The ability to sell a brand exclusively and to provide better value to the consumer was also frequently men-

TABLE 4–6

Number of Plant Facilities Owned and Operated by the Five Leading Grocery Chain Systems in the United States, 1936

Type of Facility	The Great Atlantic & Pacific Tea Co.	Kroger Grocery & Baking Co.	Safeway Stores, Inc.	American Stores Co.	First National Stores, Inc.
Retail stores	15,427	4,250	3,277	2,822	2,653
Warehouses, total	111[a]	[b]	79	10	[b]
Bakeries	40	13	21	9	1
Meat-packing plants	—	2	—	—	[b]
Milk plants[c]	13	5	4	1	—
Coffee-roasting plants	8	4	—	[b]	—
Canning plants	6[d]	—	—	1	—
General factories	9	1	1	—	1
Printing plants	1	1	—	—	1

[a]A&P operated warehouses for produce (39), meat (12), fish (5), butter (3), and general goods (52).
[b]Indicates that facilities were operated but the number of them is unknown.
[c]Includes condenseries, creameries, cheese, and miscellaneous dairy products.
[d]Salmon canning. Also operated a fishing fleet.
SOURCE: A. C. Hoffman for the Temporary National Economic Committee, *Large-Scale Organization in the Food Industries,* monograph no. 35 (Washington, D.C.: GPO, 1940), 12.

tioned.[96] Kroger, the second largest food chain next to A&P in 1932, gave the FTC five reasons for having company-owned and company-operated manufacturing facilities:

1.   To enable us to operate our business with a smaller investment in inventories of finished goods.
2.   To assure absolutely fresh merchandise, such as baked items and roasted coffee, in our stores.
3.   To deliver to the ultimate consumer merchandise of equal or better quality at a lower price.
4.   To attract customers to our stores to obtain merchandise which can be purchased only at our stores.
5.   To identify uniform quality merchandise with our name.[97]

A&P, the most vigorous backward integrator, had processed tea and coffee since the Civil War era, and a variety of other products since 1885.[98] But it was not until the 1920s, as table 4–7 shows, that the firm took up manufacturing seriously.

A&P told the FTC that it was forced to go into manufacturing because food processors were withdrawing from the private-label business in favor of the development of their own nationally advertised brands. The firm discovered also that it could deliver certain products to the consumer more cheaply through its own plants than by relying on independent suppliers.[99]

But there was at least one other important reason, this one not volunteered to the FTC. Manufacturing by A&P or, at least, the threat to manufacture a given product, was a powerful club to use in keeping even

TABLE 4–7

A&P Manufacturing Operations in 1920 and 1930

Manufacturing Operation	1920	1930
Coffee-roasting plants	3	7
Bakeries	2	35
Food factories	2	9
Cheese warehouses	1	3
Condenseries	0	9
Creameries	0	1
Salmon canneries	0	6
Total	8	70

SOURCE: Federal Trade Commission, *Chain Stores: Chain Store Manufacturing*, 73d Cong., 1st sess., S. Doc. 13 (Washington, D.C.: GPO, 1935), 14.

the largest suppliers in line. In the late 1930s, for example, Ralston Purina, then a 90 percent private-label supplier, sold 60 percent of its corn flakes to A&P. Ralston tried, unsuccessfully, to have inserted in its contract with A&P the phrase, "Whereas, the Purchaser . . . , indicating that it could advantageously manufacture its own flakes, . . . has declared its intention to do so unless it is adequately compensated for its forbearance; . . ."[100]

A&P was neither a manufacturer nor a wholesaler; it was a retailer. Other operations existed to serve the retail outlets. And it is arguable that backward integration to processing among chain grocers was limited rather than extensive. FTC documents reveal that 12.1 percent of grocery and meat chain sales in 1930 were goods manufactured by chains. The great majority of sales, in other words, were from independent processors. And much of this manufacturing was of commodities that were highly perishable, such as milk or bread, as table 4–7 shows. Even so, manufacturing was not a losing proposition undertaken solely for narrow reasons like product perishability. The visible hand of managerial coordination was profitable when it reached back past wholesaling to manufacturing. In fact, according to Morris A. Adelman, A&P's manufacturing returns were quite high. The company's plants, he explained,

> run steadily at the most economic level of operations, as near to the equating of marginal revenue and cost as a manufacturing business can come in practice. They sell all their output at the current market price. Goods move steadily into consumption, and there are no inventories (except for those physically necessary) to spoil or be marked down. Above all, there are no selling or advertising costs. . . . In bakery products, which are the local oligopoly situation par excellence, combined selling-advertising costs were nearly five times the net profit; in cereal preparations, biscuits and crackers, and fruit and vegetable canning, selling-advertising costs at least exceeded net profit. This suffices to explain the showing of the A&P facilities: they avoided much of the cost of transfer between manufacturing and distribution. In part it was a saving on making contact, which is a cost even under pure (but imperfect) competition; in part the profit was the return from A&P advertising, which built up the A&P brands and enabled the retail stores to charge prices nearer or even equivalent to the advertised brands. . . .[101]

To impute these savings from vertical integration to either manufacturing alone or to distribution alone, concluded Adelman, is no more sensible than to impute a child to the father or mother alone.[102]

There remains in our examination of lower chain prices the question of whether the chains could sell for less because they could buy for less.

Chain grocers unquestionably purchased goods for less than the independents could, but for how much less and why? And how important were the discounts? A Federal Trade Commission report concluded "that lower selling prices are a very substantial, if not the chief, factor in the growth of chain-store merchandising, and that lower buying prices than are available to independents are a most substantial, if not the chief, factor in these lower selling prices."[103] This opinion was shared by many merchants, by many Americans not specifically involved in trade, and by many politicians. Yet it is difficult to reconcile this assertion with the data collected by the FTC. Analysis of the data reveals that approximately 15 percent of the chains' price advantage resulted from lower purchasing costs, but that the remainder must be attributed to lower margins and operating expenses.[104]

How could the FTC have misinterpreted its own findings? We have no direct evidence, but it is difficult to escape the suspicion that politics were involved. The evolution of food distribution in the interwar years is a business situation that demands the perspective of political economy rather than of economics alone.

The Political Problems of the Grocery Chains in the 1930s

In some ways, the situation of the grocery chains in 1930 could hardly have been better. A&P was the leader, but other large chains were also doing well. These companies had constructed a system through which they could deliver value to consumers, and consumers rewarded the chains with their patronage. Once their business formula had been worked out, the chains made a massive commitment of their resources to exploiting it. They opened thousands of stores. They greatly reduced and in some lines eliminated their reliance on wholesalers. They owned and operated scores of plants and warehouses. And they made the commitment in human resources necessary to make the system work.

Yet the chains faced great challenges in the 1930s. One such challenge was political—and predictable: the voice of the past crying out against the present. Another challenge, economic in nature, was more difficult though not impossible to predict. In contrast to the political challenge, the economic challenge represented the future. The antichain store laws, the Robinson-Patman Act, the antitrust case against A&P—all these developments had their origins deep in American political culture. As Richard A. Posner has pointed out in his discussion of the Robinson-Patman Act, "The roots of [this legislation] lie in the late nineteenth century, the era of the great 'trusts' . . . that were formed roughly between 1875 and 1905. The best known of these was John D. Rockefeller's Standard Oil Trust. . . ."[105] We must, therefore, turn to a discussion of these developments to understand the twists and turns of public policy vis-à-vis the chains in the 1930s.

Alfred D. Chandler, Jr., has demonstrated that the "modern multiunit business enterprise replaced small traditional enterprise when administrative coordination permitted greater productivity, lower costs, and higher profits than coordination by market mechanisms." Numerous mergers could be and have been attempted in American industrial history, yet they were successful only "if they were in industries where mass production could be integrated with mass distribution and if their organizers created the managerial hierarchies necessary to assure effective administrative supervision and coordination of the processes of production and distribution."[106] Business, in other words, became big when it delivered value to the customer. Big business failed in those industries in which it failed to provide value.

Although the ability of big business to benefit the consumer is clear to us now, it was understandably unclear to contemporaries. Woodrow Wilson declared in the presidential campaign of 1912 that "I deny the fundamental proposition. I deny that big combinations are inevitable. . . . And when these gentlemen say that these big combinations are necessary for economy and efficiency, the only answer I can think of that meets that suggestion is: Rats! Go and tell all that to the Marines."[107] For Wilson and for many of the voters who twice elected him to the presidency, big business meant stock watering, manipulation, secret covenants secretly arrived at, "dirty deals," and, above all, brute force to bring these great institutions into being. Charges such as these help explain why public attitudes toward big business were never less favorable, even during the 1930s, than they were in the 1890s and during the Progressive Era.[108]

Perhaps the most successful of American corporations in the age of enterprise was John D. Rockefeller's Standard Oil. The public reaction to this company epitomized the antipathy to bigness in business, and the nature of the polemics against it illustrates well some general themes.

Standard Oil dominated its industry through its skill in exploiting the scale economies inherent in oil refining. The per-barrel cost of a refinery with a 500-barrel daily throughput was $0.06 a gallon; with a capacity of 1,500 barrels it was $0.03 a gallon; and so forth. Standard benefited from this technological reality because under Rockefeller's leadership it became a consolidated, integrated enterprise with a skilled team of managers capable of guiding the product from production through refining and wholesaling.[109]

Standard was a fierce competitor. Among the most controversial of its business practices were its dealings with railroads. The company was granted rebates (reduced rates) by the railroads, which were nothing more than quantity discounts. It was Standard's volume of business that made the railroads willing, indeed anxious, to offer the rebates.[110]

Yet this is not how critical contemporaries saw it. In the greatest muckraking tract of the Progressive Era, *The History of the Standard Oil Company*, Ida Tarbell asserted that "the country was a unit against the rebate system" until "Mr. Rockefeller and his friends" undermined the drive toward equal railroad rates.[111] Standard Oil did receive rebates, but they were the result, not the cause, of Standard's power. The cause was the cost advantage of scale. Standard was not the first to corrupt the railroads. The country was never "a unit against the rebate system," as Tarbell claimed. To the contrary, "rate cutting was universal," as one railroad historian has argued. The railroads had always been "one big oriental bazaar" when it came to rates.[112]

However, it was more comforting to those entrepreneurs whom Standard put out of business (such as Ida Tarbell's father) to believe that Standard Oil was successful not because it delivered its product to the consumer at a lower price but because it represented a malevolent approach to business. If the railroads shipped Standard's oil at rebated prices, that was unfair in the eyes of competing shippers no matter what the reason. This view had important consequences. Standard Oil was broken up on antitrust grounds in 1911. Even Theodore Roosevelt, who was not a doctrinaire foe of big business, condemned it as a "bad" trust. The Federal Trade Commission Act, designed to prevent "unfair methods of competition," was passed in 1914.[113] The FTC conducted the studies that served as the basis for the Robinson-Patman Act.

The more radical opponents of big business attacked it not only because of its supposedly unfair advantages over smaller businesspeople but also because of its very "bigness." For Louis D. Brandeis, foremost expositor of this school of thought, bigness per se was a "curse." "I have considered and do consider," he wrote, "that the proposition that mere bigness cannot be an offense against society is false, because I believe that our society, which rests upon democracy, cannot endure under such conditions." In his thinking, Brandeis made an explicit connection between the chain stores and Standard Oil because of their successful strategies of vertical integration; and he opposed them both, whether they delivered goods to the consumer more efficiently or not. He opposed quantity discounts—they were supposedly "fraught with very great evil"—even, apparently, if they were accompanied by cost savings to the supplier.[114]

Many of the proponents of "fair trade" (i.e., the right of manufacturers to fix retail prices) and the opponents of chains had aims similar to those of Brandeis, if for different reasons. Brandeis wanted to put a stop to bigness whether it was efficient or not because he felt it threatened democracy. Most other chain opponents wanted to put a stop to bigness precisely because the big chains were so efficient that they were putting the small merchant into an untenable economic position.

But how could these interests make their case to the American people? Had they marched under the Brandeis banner with its slogan that might be caricatured as "Spend more for your necessities—it's good for our democracy," their adherents would have been few. They could not make a politically attractive case against the visible hand in a nation devoted to mass consumption. They could, however, make a case against what we might call the "visible fist." Thus, Ida Tarbell dwelt not on economies of scale but on nefarious rebates. The Federal Trade Commission looked not at the economies of vertical integration and the consumer benefits resulting therefrom, which its own research had documented, but at buying power. Taken by itself, this buying power seemed as unfair in the 1930s as did railroad rebates in the 1870s. Why should the small merchant not be able to buy the same goods at the same price as the big one? But neither rebates nor quantity discounts can be taken by themselves. Both are the results, not the causes, of economic power.

Before discussing the political problems that the more than one million independent retailers posed to the chains in the interwar period, let us pause to consider the point of view of the small merchant. An interesting book published in 1922 entitled *Meeting Chain Store Competition* begins with the following:

> Every retailer who has to meet chain store competition thinks he needs no one to tell him what a chain store is. To him it is a cut rate competitor managed from the outside by a soul-less corporation. What the principles behind it may be he neither knows nor cares. He is confronted with conditions, not theories, with the necessity for keeping trade which shows a persistent tendency to drift over to the chain store which shouts loudly and continually for business with colored window banners and multitudinous price cards.[115]

It is easy—perhaps too easy—to dismiss the problems of the small, inefficient independent merchant. I remember being told by my mother how my immigrant grandfather, who operated a small newsstand and candy store by the railroad station in Montclair, New Jersey, in the interwar years, felt when he learned that an A&P was opening across the street and that it would be selling cigarettes. People like him all over the country had carved out settled lives and some respect and standing in their own eyes. What would happen to them? Where would they go? What would they do?

Isolated, such people were helpless. But organized, their potential power was notable:

> When the chain store comes into your territory, you are not the only interested party. Your banker who is carrying your paper and depending upon your continuance in business to make that paper good, is going to wonder right away what that will mean to your financial standing. The jobber who is supplying you with goods will wonder whether he will be paid as promptly as before, whether you will buy as much and continue to discount your bills, whether perhaps that old bill that was changed into a note may not remain unpaid to the end of the chapter. Your landlord may feel anxious about you remaining as a prompt paying tenant, or even remaining at all.
>
> In addition to all those who are financially interested in the matter, you have many friends and relatives . . . [who] will all be ready to boost your business, against the chain store, if you give them a chance to do it.[116]

This web of relationships could be multiplied by over a million independent merchants who were potential victims of the chain store.

Organized opposition to chain stores occurred as early as 1922, when the suggestion was made at a convention of the National Association of Retail Grocers that there should be legal limitations on the number of chains in any community.[117] The following year, Missouri considered a tax on chains designed to redress what were viewed as chain-store tax advantages.[118]

In 1925, two state legislatures considered but rejected laws discriminating against chain stores. In 1927, however, fifteen states considered such legislation. That year, Maryland prohibited expansion of chain stores within its borders, and Georgia and North Carolina levied taxes graduated according to the number of units.[119] By 1929, there were local organizations fighting the "chain store menace" throughout the nation.[120]

Legislative activity quickened as the Depression set in. In 1931, one journalist remarked that "wherever a little band of lawmakers are gathered together in the sacred name of legislation, you may be sure that they are putting their heads together and thinking up things they can do to the chain stores."[121] In 1933, some 225 antichain bills were introduced in 42 state legislatures; 13 were passed. Chain taxes had been passed in 27 states by 1939, although not all were still in force that year.[122]

It can be argued that chain taxes were essentially ineffectual. The chains' share of total retail sales nationwide increased from 20.3 percent in 1929 to 21.7 percent in 1939. Results in individual states confirm this ineffectuality. In Indiana and Maine, for example, the chain stores' share of market in many lines increased more quickly than elsewhere despite the taxes.[123] Congressman Wright Patman proposed a national chain store tax that would have devastated the larger chains. This bill was nicknamed the chain "Death Sentence" bill. Under its provisions, A&P would have had to pay $524 million in taxes on its 1938 sales of $882 million. The proposal never made it beyond the House Ways and Means Committee.[124]

The opposition to chain stores was not very successful. The most threatening proposals were not passed, and the less threatening ones did not cripple the power of the chains. This, however, is a judgment shaped by hindsight. How did antichain agitation look to chain-store managers at the time? We have already touched upon much of what they saw: dozens of bills in state legislatures, a groundswell of local agitation, and the web of friends and business connections of the independent merchant all spelled potential trouble. It was suggested by the National Association of Retail Grocers that "there are in the United States literally thousands of individuals interesting themselves [in attacking chains] purely for the money they can make out of it for themselves."[125]

Chain-baiting, in other words, was becoming a popular movement and an industry. A number of its entrepreneurs made effective use of the new medium of mass communication, the radio. Of these, one of the most successful was William K. "Old Man" Henderson. Based in Shreveport, Louisiana, Henderson could be heard throughout the South and Midwest over his "Hello World Broadcasting Company," the flagship of which was his own KWKH. This is the sort of thing he told his listeners each evening:

> American people, wake up! We can whip these chain stores. We can whip the whole cockeyed world when we are right. . . . I'll be your leader. I'll whip hell out of them if you will support me. We can drive them out in thirty days if you people will stay out of their stores.[126]

The price of Henderson's leadership was a $12 fee payable to his "Merchants' Minute Men," which he organized over the air.[127]

All this agitation was worrisome to chain executives. And surely it must have been demoralizing to employees as well, who no doubt heard the attacks just as independent grocers did. Once again, one thinks of the Standard Oil experience. Similarly attacked, one of the company's executives said:

> We are quoted as the representation of all that is evil, hardhearted, oppressive, cruel (we think unjustly), but men look askance at us. We are pointed at with

contempt. . . . None of us would choose such a reputation. We all desire a place in the good will, honor and affection of honorable men.[128]

Antichain agitation does not seem as serious in retrospect as it did at the time because the chains did alter their activities to combat accusations. They took action on a number of fronts, including their own image and their relations with farmers and with organized labor. It is possible that their pricing policy may have been influenced as well.

A good example of the new willingness of the chain to tell its story was A&P's approach to publicity during the Depression years. Early in the 1930s, the firm adopted a take-it-or-leave-it attitude when trouble arose. Thus, when its Cleveland stores were struck by the Teamsters, "it simply closed up shop, announcing dourly through the local press that conditions no longer favored its presence."[129]

In 1937, however, A&P hired the public-relations firm of Carl Byoir and Associates to fight a proposal for chain-store taxes in New York State. Byoir believed that "it is not what a client says about himself that scores, but what another person, whom the public regards as an outstanding authority, says about him, that carries weight." He explained the interest-group approach of his efforts as follows: "We went out to farmer organizations, cooperatives, and labor organizations, and civic groups, women's clubs, consumer organization [sic] . . . and preached the distributive method of the chain store. . . ."[130] A&P retained Byoir to fight the Patman "Death Sentence" Bill of 1938. The company invested about a half million dollars in his efforts, which probably did contribute to the measure's defeat.[131] There was a real story to tell to each of the groups Byoir targeted. The consumer story was obvious—lower prices. The farm story was dramatized in 1936 and 1937 in California and Florida:

> The 1936–1937 grapefruit crop was 30 percent larger than in any previous year. Ruinous prices and a glutted market loomed. A powerful promotion drive by A&P moved 1,425 carloads in eight weeks—three and a half times normal sales—[and] helped raise shipping-point prices 20 percent. The same formula has worked with canned peaches, dried fruit, midwinter lamb [and] turkeys—[and has] made thousands of farmer friends for the chains. And the chains need friends.[132]

In the twelve months following May of 1936, the chains engineered eight "Producer-Consumer Campaigns," with "most gratifying results to all concerned."[133]

The chains made certain that the farm lobby was fully aware of these services, and the farmer responded at the ballot box. California rejected a chain-store tax law by a two-to-one margin statewide in 1936, but the margin was three to one in agricultural areas. In Maine, pressure by farmers was instrumental in securing chain tax repeal.[134] Independent merchants also made efforts to relieve the problems of commodity gluts, but the nature of their operations made them less effective in helping hard-pressed farmers with sufficient dispatch.[135]

The chains had also taken action toward the end of the 1930s to conciliate unions. As noted earlier, A&P had simply shut down operations threatened by organized labor in Cleveland earlier in the decade. As late as 1937, the American Federation of Labor passed a resolution condemning various chain practices. But then A&P launched a campaign to woo the unions, and in 1938 and 1939 the company signed a series of collective bargaining agreements with AFL unions. When the Patman "Death Sentence" bill was debated, many union locals and state federations of labor, as well as national AFL affiliates, opposed the bill's passage vigorously.[136]

Here are the five key points that the president of Amalgamated Meat Cutters, with a membership of 120,000, made about the chains:

1. Chains were easier to work with than independent merchants.
2. Chain stores paid higher wages for shorter hours.
3. Union members were consumers as well as employees, and chain prices were lower.
4. The demise of the chains would mean more proprietors but fewer employers and therefore fewer employees.
5. Unions themselves were threatened if chains were singled out for special taxation because "the largest operator of the chain unit system in the world is organized labor itself."[137]

The chains were concerned enough about antichain agitation to be willing to make significant changes in their business practices in order to build constituencies they could rely on for defense against damaging legislation. The chains may have allowed antichain agitation to influence pricing policy, just as they allowed such agitation to influence their labor relations and commodity purchases.

Earlier in the chapter we saw that the difference between chain and independent prices was narrowing in the interwar years, primarily because chain prices were rising. Were the chains pricing more closely to the independents to quell the public outcry against them? If so, it was not the first time a market leader like A&P allowed its prices to float up to protect itself politically. In the first quarter of the twentieth century, the chief executive of United States Steel pursued a live-and-let-live pricing policy. The result was loss of market share, but, understandably, much praise from the competitors over whom Big Steel held a price umbrella. This policy probably preserved the company from dismemberment in Sherman Act proceedings. Standard Oil followed no such passive policy and lost the antitrust action the government launched against it.[138]

There are two more chain political problems in the 1930s that deserve our attention: the Robinson-Patman Act and the antitrust case against A&P.

The year 1986 was the golden anniversary of the passage of the Robinson-Patman Act. It was not an occasion for those believing in an efficient economy designed to maximize consumer benefit to celebrate. The original Patman Bill was drafted in 1935 by H. B. "Judge" Teegarden, counsel for the United States Wholesale Grocers Association.[139] Wright Patman, who once remarked that "one certain concern had really caused the passage of this Act, the A&P Tea Company," explained to Congress that "This bill has the opposition of all cheaters, chiselers, bribe takers, bribe givers, and the greedy." The bill's supporters, he claimed, believed "that the policy of live and let live is a good one" and "that greed should be restrained and the Golden Rule practiced."[140]

Emanuel Celler, Democratic representative from New York, set forth the opposing view:

> The advocates of this bill include many independents unable to meet competition which is easily met by their efficient fellow dealers, and as well wholesale grocers catering to such small dealers handling the basic necessity, food, and asking for unnatural restraints upon their most efficient competition. They searched high and low when they had the N.R.A. for ways and means to the same selfish end.[141]

Celler went on to declare that consumers "owe no business a living; laws like the instant one intended to preserve any business at the expense of the consumer will in the end prove harmful."[142]

What were the goals of the Robinson-Patman Act and what did it achieve? These questions are difficult to answer because the legislation is difficult to understand. The Supreme Court labeled it "singularly opaque and illusive,"[143] and University of Chicago Law School Dean (and later Attorney General) Edward H. Levi said that the legal profession's opinion of the act was so low that commentary had degenerated into "a contest of witticisms to relieve an otherwise dreary picture."[144] Supposedly the law's goal was to strengthen the Clayton Act (to which it was an amendment) by proscribing price discrimination that might "injure, destroy, or prevent competition." Further proscribed were discounts in lieu of brokerage, discriminatory advertising discounts, and the provision of greater service to some customers than to others.[145] These proscriptions opened the door to intricate and sterile debates about what constitutes discrimination and under what circumstances cost savings justified lower prices. One school of thought (to which I adhere) is that the act was really aimed not at price discrimination but at price difference and that it was designed to eliminate those differences whether they reflected genuine cost savings or not.[146]

The most threatening aspect of the bill to the chain grocer was the prohibition of discounts in lieu of brokerage in Section 2C. A&P and the other large chains had internalized the brokerage function rather than buying through independent merchants and brokers. Because they did so, they felt justified in demanding lower prices than those paid by independent retailers. The savings achieved by this method of operation are detailed in table A–1, appendix A. At least some of these savings would be eliminated by Robinson-Patman, and consumer prices would therefore be increased. It is ironic that such a measure was smuggled into law as an amendment to an antitrust statute, considering that the antitrust enterprise was supposedly designed to keep prices low through prohibition of price-fixing.[147] If the Robinson-Patman Act did make chain operations more difficult, it fell far short of causing their demise. First, one could always break the law by negotiating face-to-face deals in which the absence of brokerage fees was silently passed on in lower prices.[148] Second, the chain had the option of increasing its reliance on its own manufacturing capabilities and, concomitantly, on private labels.[149] Here we have yet another instance of the paradox of antitrust. Designed to cripple big business through indirect means, it succeeded only in encouraging further vertical integration.[150]

This is not to say that the chains escaped from the Robinson-Patman assault unscathed. *Fortune* estimated in 1938 that brokerage fees and advertising allowances were worth $8 million to A&P.[151] The firm's pretax profit that year was $19.4 million.[152] Although *Fortune*'s estimate may be high, it does indicate the kind of money at stake.

Ironically—although in light of the previous history of antitrust one is tempted to say "predictably"[153]—the principal impact of the law fell not on the center firms it was supposed to disable but on the small merchant it was supposed to protect, because it prevented independent merchants from forming associations to obtain volume discounts.[154]

The final political problem faced by chain grocers in the interwar period was the antitrust case against A&P. Although a full analysis of this case is beyond the scope of this book, we should make one important point.[155]

The National Association of Retail Grocers petitioned for an investigation of A&P in June 1939. The outcome of the investigation that ensued was a criminal action under Sections 1 and 2 of the Sherman Act, which the Antitrust Division of the Justice Department filed on 26 February 1944. Pausing briefly to remark that this seems an odd way for a government in the midst of the greatest war in the history of the world to expend its energies, it can be said that this trial turned into a judicial extravaganza. Counting transcript, exhibits, briefs, and appendices, the total record ran to some 50,000 pages.[156]

In September 1946, A&P lost its case in federal district court. It appealed to the Seventh Circuit in Chicago and lost there in February 1949. The company paid fines in the amount of $175,000. The following September, the government launched a civil suit, which threatened A&P's existence. The government asked that "A&P be dismembered by divorcing the manufacturing plants, dissolving Acco [i.e., the Atlantic Commission Company, A&P's subsidiary in charge of the purchase of produce], and dividing the retail establishments into seven parts corresponding to the seven divisions."[157] At last, in the more congenial atmosphere of the Eisenhower administration, the company offered a consent decree to the Justice Department. The two parties formally entered into it on 19 January 1954, eleven years after the criminal action had begun.[158] The consent decree, in the view of Morris A. Adelman,

> was a sweeping victory for the A&P Company. Their sales policy and manufacturing integration were almost untouched. Their buying operations were restricted only in one significant way: they, and the cooperating jobbers, could no longer enjoy the economies of bulk transactions and resale in produce. This was an obvious restriction on competition and a social waste.[159]

We have seen in this review of the political problems faced by chains in the interwar years how the economic success of the chains was challenged by the political power of those whose economic interests they were injuring. There were literally millions of voters whose livelihood was threatened by the chains. Through merchant trade associations and other voluntary organizations, these people argued that if the chains were selling for less, it was only because something fundamentally unfair had happened in the economic system. Certain distributors—the chain stores— were able to obtain goods at lower prices than were available to the independents. Chains also received advertising allowances, which critics viewed as extortion.

The political initiatives of the independents posed a genuine threat to the chains. They emerged bloodied but unbowed. Their success was due in part to their own flexibility. A&P made important changes in its labor practices, its sourcing, perhaps its pricing, and certainly its general approach to its constituencies through public relations. As one commentator remarked, "An A&P which recognizes unions and assumes some responsibility for aiding distressed farmers is a changed organization."[160]

Another reason for chain survival was the difficulty of framing laws that the chains could not circumvent. Cheating on Robinson-Patman was possible; indeed, the act stimulated vertical integration rather than leading to smaller chain organizations. Its impact fell with unexpected force on the very group it was designed to protect. The state antichain measures were predominantly based on taxation by number of units, which only encouraged the chains to build larger stores. As Joseph Palamountain observed, "Chain taxes did no more than somewhat hasten the adoption of supermarkets and other large grocery units. Thus these taxes had no lasting effects on grocery chains."[161] If anything, the bigger stores proved to be even more fearsome competitors.

In two instances the nation did have the opportunity to strike at the vitals of the chains. First, the aptly nicknamed Patman "Death Sentence" proposal would have put the largest chains out of business. Second, the antitrust case against A&P would have destroyed it. But the nation was unable or unwilling to take such decisive steps. The Patman "Death Sentence" measure was defeated, thanks to the skillful lobbying of the chains and to the fact that the interests of consumers were beginning to assert themselves. The consumer was the sleeping giant of American politics, huge in potential but immobile. A noteworthy consumer movement did develop in the 1930s, partially in response to which the Federal Trade Commission broadened its regulation of advertising to include not only competitive injury but consumer welfare.[162] The antitrust attack against A&P failed because it proved too blunt an instrument. The company was able to follow a strategy that has since become traditional in actions such as this, that of delaying until the advent of a more sympathetic administration.[163] It is important to emphasize that although A&P lost the criminal antitrust suit and settled the civil suit through a consent decree, the many catastrophes that later visited this once-proud corporation should not be traced to these antitrust actions.

This set of problems was described earlier as historical in nature. The problems were "blasts from the past" in that they expressed the efforts of the distribution system in place to avoid being superseded by a more efficient one. These conflicts were predictable because the history of change in business is a history of the old struggling against the new. The attacks on Standard Oil by its less efficient competitors were similar in nature to those launched against A&P. We could go back further in American history to cite other examples of the old fighting the new, such as the delays that Erie Canal–biased state legislators imposed on railroad building in New York, or the efforts of the captains of sailing vessels to ram steamboats when they were first used on American rivers.[164] And antichain taxation was not limited to the United States. Such taxes were levied in Germany and France prior to World War II.[165] In the interwar period, the "movement against the chains was worldwide, and hostility to chain stores was a tenet of Nazi economic policy. . . ."[166] In other ways as well, this kind of opposition to chain stores was born of the past. We see here reenacted the battle between small proprietor and professional manager, with all that has entailed in so many industries.

The Challenge from the Future

In 1930, at the age of 46, Michael J. Cullen was a "food merchandiser of unique capacity,"[167] working in a small town in southern Illinois for the second largest chain grocery-store operator in the United States— Kroger. That year, Cullen wrote to the president of Kroger, proposing the creation of a new kind of food store and asking for an interview to explain his views further. His letter describes with prescience the type of retail food outlet that would soon come to dominate the nation (a large section of the letter is reproduced in appendix B).

The data that Cullen provided give us an idea of the kind of store he wanted to build (see table 4–8). Although his data on the meat business

The leading figure in the supermarket movement in the 1930s was Michael J. Cullen. He revolutionized the business by building far larger stores than the chains and locating them away from high traffic and high rent areas. The resulting savings enabled him to claim legitimately to be the "World's Greatest Price Wrecker."

were less clearly broken down than were the grocery data, we do know that Cullen expected to net out 3 percent on meat, which, on a weekly volume of $2,500, would yield $75. Cullen thus projected a $325 weekly net profit from each of the five stores he was proposing, or $16,900 per year on a total volume of $650,000, or a return on capital of 56.33 percent in the Depression years.

The keystone of Cullen's strategy was low price.

When I come out with a two-page ad and advertise 300 items at cost and 200 items at practically cost, which would probably be all the advertising that I would ever have to do, the public, regardless of their present feeling towards chain stores, because in reality I would not be a chain store, would break my front doors down to get in. It would be a riot. I would have to call out the police and let the public in so many at a time.[168]

TABLE 4–8

Cullen's Proposed Food Outlet, 1930

Start-up costs	
Grocery equipment	$ 2,500
Meat equipment	4,500
Beginning inventory	23,000
Total start-up costs	$30,000
Operating Costs (weekly basis for groceries)	
Help	$ 250
Rent	58
Investment on money (interest)	30
Insurance	10
Light-heat-water	7
Taxes	10
Depreciation	10
Supervision	20
Paper, bags, etc.	75
Income tax	30
Hauling	20
Advertising	50
Buying	40
M. J. Cullen	40
Total operating costs per week	$ 650
Projected weekly grocery volume	10,000
Estimated cost of goods sold	9,100
Gross profit	$ 900
Operating expenses	650
Net profit	$ 250

SOURCE: M. M. Zimmerman, *The Super Market: A Revolution in Distribution* (New York: Mass Distribution Publications, 1955), 32–33.

Other important aspects of Cullen's strategy included that (1) the store would be "monstrous," between 5,200 and 6,400 square feet;[169] (2) all sales would be made in cash; (3) there would be no delivery service; (4) the store would be located in a low-rent area or warehouse district and would have ample parking;[170] and (5) a wide variety of goods would be made available—100 percent branded and nationally advertised merchandise.[171]

King Kullen stores were strictly self-service. They relied on the recognition of nationally advertised brands (as opposed to private labels) to stimulate business. Here we see Michael J. Cullen standing next to a large, end-aisle display of Hellman's Mayonnaise.

How did Cullen's format and strategy compare to the food retailing approach common in 1930? Table 4–9 compares an income statement for a chain grocery outlet in 1929 with Cullen's proposal in table 4–8. (If Cullen's estimates for his meat business are included as well, the net profit comes to 2.6 percent.)

Let us push the comparison between Cullen's proposition and a typical chain store further. We can estimate the sales of a typical A&P retail outlet in 1930 at about $67,000, with a net per-store profit of $1,577. (This gives us a return on sales of 2.35 percent, which would make A&P's performance significantly better than that of the average chain outlet cited in table 4–9.) My estimate for capital investment per store would be $5,062, yielding a return on the capital invested per average A&P store of 31.16 percent.[172] (Although these calculations are rough, they would have to be incorrect by a wide margin to make a significant difference.) Cullen estimated that he could do almost ten times the volume of the average A&P, make slightly more than ten times the net profit, and return over 25 percent more on the capital required to make this proposal a reality. And A&P's numbers were far better than those of the average chain grocer.

Cullen's letter (see appendix B) suggests to me that there was something of the megalomaniac in him—"I would lead the public out of the high-priced houses of bondage into the low prices of the house of the promised land."[173] However, if Cullen's projection proved accurate, his prediction that he "would be the 'miracle man' of the grocery business" would be justified.[174]

TABLE 4–9

*An Average Chain Grocery Unit Compared to
the Cullen Proposal
(for groceries only)*

	Average Chain Store	Cullen's Proposed Store
Retail selling price	100%	100%
Cost of goods sold	80.6	91
Gross margin	19.4	9
Total expenses	17.93	6.5
Net profit	1.47%	2.5 %

SOURCES: Malcolm P. McNair, "Expenses and Profits in the Chain Grocery Business in 1929," *Bureau of Business Research Bulletin*, no. 84 (Cambridge, Mass.: Murray Printing, 1931); M. M. Zimmerman, *The Super Market: A Revolution in Distribution* (New York: Mass Distribution Publications, 1955), 32–33.

There are other contrasts between Cullen's approach and that of the traditional chain. Cullen's store was to be 5,200 to 6,400 square feet, whereas the *Progressive Grocer*'s model combination grocery and meat store in 1931 had 1,134 square feet of selling space and another 81 square feet of back room.[175] Cullen would provide no credit or delivery services, whereas the chains did provide these services under some circumstances and the independents did so more often. But the absence of service extended beyond the avoidance of credit and delivery.

Cullen's store would significantly reduce clerk service. In the traditional grocery store, there was always a clerk behind the counter to help consumers with their purchases. It is worth putting ourselves at the point of sale in such a store to see what the purchase process was like. Prior to the supermarket, in both independent and chain groceries, customers did not *buy* merchandise; rather, products were *sold* to them. Prices were not marked on the goods, which were stacked behind the counter, accessible only to the clerks or proprietors, who could then control the sale—usually pushing their own private brands, which carried a higher profit margin. In supermarkets, in contrast, customers were left on their own. Since goods were openly priced and openly displayed on shelves, consumers could, for the first time, make their own choices about food purchases without pressure or the potential of having to admit to a clerk that for financial reasons they did not want to purchase the more expensive brand he was pushing.[176]

Thus what had originally loomed as a necessity—the emphasis on price appeal meant that the supermarket could not afford a lot of help in the store—became unexpectedly an important competitive weapon. The early supermarkets emphasized in their advertising such slogans as "Pick Out the Merchandise You Like Best," "Pick Your Own National Brands," and "Serve Yourself and Save." Best of all from the store operator's perspective, when the customer "served herself" she didn't save. "[W]hen left to herself, the average housewife sold herself far more than the best clerk behind the counter did in his palmiest days."[177] Although today we supposedly live in the era of the services revolution, food shoppers received far more service a half a century ago than they do now.

The in-store, self-service approach confronted the store operator with numerous logistical problems that had to be solved for this new format to succeed. One problem was where the food should be placed on the shelves. In the traditional chain, only the merchant and clerk had to know where items were shelved, since they collected them for customers. With in-store self-service, however, customers had to locate the items themselves, which became even more difficult in the larger stores. In the early self-service stores, the few clerks there were "spent more time answering questions than they had previously needed to wait on customers."[178] One self-service operator solved this problem by arranging food alphabetically.[179] Traffic flow through the store now became a key to productivity. The first self-service mass distributor recognized the importance of traffic flow so clearly that he patented his store design.[180] Shelf space and facing also became matters of the utmost importance. Since well over half the items purchased in a supermarket were bought on impulse, "Unseen, therefore, is unsold."[181]

Another problem was how consumers would physically handle prospective purchases while in the store. Operators hoped consumers would buy in quantity, but food products are heavy and bulky. The early supermarkets coped with this problem by providing hand-held wire baskets. However, these baskets became full and heavy very quickly. Clerks were thus instructed to help customers who had full baskets of groceries by arranging for the baskets to be picked up later on at a designated checkout counter and by supplying customers with empty baskets.[182] This procedure left much to be desired.

The solution was devised by Sylvan N. Goldman, an Oklahoma grocer who went on to become one of the richest men in the nation. In a moment of inspiration, Goldman saw in a folding chair the basis of a solution for overburdened shoppers. By raising the chair's seat a few inches, one could add a second seat below, making two platforms on which baskets could be placed. Wheels attached to each leg made the chair mobile, and the back of the chair was adapted to push the cart.[183]

Goldman, certain that his elegant solution would meet with an enthusiastic consumer response, placed advertisements announcing the new "No Basket Carrying Plan." He was disappointed at the result:

> I got down to the store about 10 o'clock in the morning waiting for the time when people'll start coming in, and this was right on a . . . Saturday when its your biggest day, and I knew that I'd be seeing people lined up at the door to get in to get the merchandise and see what the dickens it was. And when I got there, I went to our largest store, there wasn't a soul using a basket carrier, and we had an attractive girl by the entrance that had a basket carrier and two baskets in it, one on the top and one on the bottom, and asked them to please take this cart to do their shopping with. And the housewives, most of 'em decided, "No more carts for me. I have been pushing enough baby carriages. I don't want to push anymore." And the man would say, "You mean, with my big strong arm that I can't carry a darn little basket like that?" And he wouldn't touch it. It was a complete flop.[184]

Only after Goldman hired people of various ages and both sexes to push the carts filled with merchandise around the entrance to his stores was he

Photograph © Arnold Newman.

The shopping cart became one of the symbols of American abundance, as this 1955 cover from *Life* magazine indicates. *Life* used the phrase "Mass Luxury," which has indeed been an enduring theme of the American consumer culture of the twentieth century.

able to convince shoppers that "the carts weren't wheeled monsters."[185]

Problems such as this represent more than merely charming anecdotes. They illustrate unanticipated difficulties requiring creative solutions. Further, they show us how the boundary between retailer and consumer was changing. It has been said that "a sharp separation between the functions of distribution and production has to be more or less arbitrary."[186] These incidents show how the tasks of distribution itself could be reallocated. When grocery stores delivered, delivery was charged and the appropriate markup was taken. When they provided in-store service, this too was charged and marked up. With the supermarket, however, consumers drove to the retail outlet, and once there they pushed a cart around and assembled the merchandise they wished to buy. Rarely have attempts been made to impute a dollar value to the transportation costs the consumers thus incurred and to their time.[187]

The final line in Cullen's letter to Kroger's president asked "What is your verdict?"[188] The verdict was "No." In fact, Cullen did not even get a hearing from the president. He resigned forthwith[189] and, with the backing of a vice-president of the Sweet Life Foods Corporation, opened the first unit of the King Kullen Grocery Company in August 1930, at 171st Street and Jamaica Avenue in Queens, New York. Information on Cullen's success is sketchy, but indications are that he did well. *Business Week* reported in 1933 that Cullen had eight stores, averaging more than $1 million in volume per year. This represented, according to the magazine, a 15 percent increase in sales over the previous year despite a drop of 20 percent in average prices.[190] When Cullen died in 1936, he had at least fifteen stores in operation.[191]

We have more information on the Big Bear supermarket, which was opened by two entrepreneurs with the backing of a food wholesaler. Robert Otis and Roy Dawson leased a vacant Durant Motors automobile plant in Elizabeth, New Jersey, in 1932. The plant was huge—the first floor (the only part of the building used) was 50,000 square feet. They converted this space into a

circus-like emporium, with a food department as the hub, surrounded by eleven other specialty departments, such as auto accessories, paints, radios, hardware, drugs, soda fountain, lunch, etc. Only 30 percent of the total space was devoted to the food department.[192]

On 8 December 1932, full-page advertisements announced that "Big Bear," the "Price Crusher," "Crashes into New Jersey." In the first three days, sales were $31,861.71,[193] almost half the volume of an average A&P store for one year. The income statement for the first year of Big Bear's operation is shown in table 4–10. On an investment of slightly more than $10,000, the promoters of Big Bear had in one year earned $166,507.47.[194]

Before discussing the success of the supermarket in the 1930s and the chain grocers' reaction to it, we should devote some further effort to

TABLE 4–10

Statement of Sales and Expenses for Big Bear, 1933

Grocery Department Sales		$2,188.4
Gross Profit		262.8

Overhead Expenses	Percent of Profit	$ Thousands
1. Rent (all space and parking lots)	0.709 %	15.5
2. Payroll	3.635	79.5
3. Light and heat (all space)	0.351	7.9
4. Advertising (grocery dept. only)	1.324	29.0
5. Handling and wrapping	0.930	20.4
6. Administration and supervision	0.514	11.2
7. Clerical	0.316	6.9
8. Postage, insurance, stationery, telephone, and telegraph	0.161	3.5
9. Miscellaneous	0.341	7.5
10. Taxes	0.050	1.1
11. Depreciation	0.010	.2
Total expenses	8.341	$ 182.7
Net Profit—grocery department	3.669	80.1
Rental income from tenant departments		86.4
Total Net Profit		$ 166.5

SOURCE: M. M. Zimmerman, *The Super Market: A Revolution in Distribution* (New York: Mass Distribution Publications, 1955), 43.

exploring its history. How novel was the proposal that Michael J. Cullen made to the president of Kroger in 1930?

Even Cullen was of two minds on this question. On the one hand, "[N]obody in the world ever did this before. Nobody ever flew the Atlantic either, until Lindbergh did it." On the other hand, "The reason that I know that this proposition can be put over is that I have already put over a similar proposition right here in Southern Illinois."[195] Cullen's ideas had plentiful precedent. A small number of very large food stores already existed in the United States on the eve of the Depression. Even as far back as 1896, a food store gigantic by the standards of the times was opened in New London, Connecticut. It featured a wide variety of food and nonfood items, had prices marked on the items, and gave consumers the choice of self-service shopping for less. In 1916, Clarence Saunders founded his famous Piggly Wiggly chain in Memphis, Tennessee. Piggly Wiggly was a complete self-service operation in which consumers used large handbaskets to carry the items they selected from the shelves to the checkout counter, paid for them in cash, and then took the groceries home themselves. Piggly Wiggly's success was phenomenal. At its peak, the company was operating 2,660 stores and posting sales of more than

$180 million a year. But Saunders lost control in a famous Wall Street bear raid, and his company was soon carved up and sold off.

In Denver, Detroit, Houston, and especially southern California through the 1910s and 1920s, numerous entrepreneurs experimented with formats similar to those of the later supermarkets. These stores offered plenty of parking space and featured self-service shopping. Some of these "food coliseums" were far larger than the average food store.[196]

Thus, in one sense, it is not accurate for the supermarket industry to look to 1930 as the date of its birth, which it does to this day.

Nevertheless, it was only through the success of Cullen and then of Big Bear that the supermarket concept captured the imagination and support of the public and of other entrepreneurs. In his first speech as president of the newly formed Super Market Institute in 1937, William H. Albers, referring to Cullen, said:

> Yes, I know that California had large markets, had the advantages of climatic and other conditions, and I know there were large markets in practically every city in the country. However, I say there was only one man who had the vision and the confidence to back up and build what is today, ladies and gentlemen, the Super Market Industry. I say that with full credit to what any of you have done in this business.[197]

The big news in food retailing in the 1920s had been the growth of the chains. Those big food stores that existed seemed to flourish because of anomalous local circumstances. Supermarketing became a movement that proved it could penetrate the heavily populated Northeast and Midwest only in the 1930s. Why is it that the time had come for this innovation in the 1930s but that supermarket predecessors prior to 1930 were before their time?

There are a number of reasons, the first of which deals with the issue of price. The supermarket was built on price appeal. In June 1933, an investigator checked prices of well-known branded items in Big Bear and in a chain store. He found that chain prices were 12.8 percent higher.[198] As suggested earlier, one reason chain prices floated up during the interwar period was in reaction to political problems. But there were other reasons as well.

Henry C. Bohack, Jr., vice-president of a 435-store grocery chain, argued in 1928 that "the American household is again seeking service. . . . We are getting back to the prewar days when quality and service took precedence over price."[199] Bohack saw that in some cases his stores were being outperformed by independent merchants who emphasized service.

It seems likely, however, that the chains wanted to de-emphasize price competition because they were competing not only against independents but also, more frequently toward the end of the 1920s, against each other. In 1929 the five leading grocery retailers together were operating 27,961 units. These firms were beginning to invade one another's territories, and as a result they were competing their margins away. One analyst noted that it was not surprising that companies were trying to "shift competition to a less suicidal basis and that increasing emphasis is being laid upon the soundness of a unit pricing policy based at least upon cost plus service."[200]

Writing in 1931, Malcolm P. McNair noted that "where grocery chains have been longest established the competition of chains with chains has contributed to increased operating expense ratios."[201] McNair went on to suggest a seminal thesis in the history of marketing thought:

> To venture a broad generalization, it seems to be characteristic of new types of distributive enterprise that in the first stage of their development they gain a foothold primarily by means of low prices, in the second stage they "trade up" the quality of the merchandise carried, and in the third stage they compete by offering services.[202]

The danger for companies in this third stage was that they might lose control of their costs. By 1958, McNair was prepared to assert that this phenomenon extended beyond chain retailing in food to retailing in general, and he developed his famous metaphor of the "wheel" to describe it:

> [W]hat do we see going on in the distribution sector of our competitive high-level economy? What are the dynamics of the institutional changes which we can see taking place? It seems to me that there is a more or less definite cycle in American distribution. The wheel always revolves, sometimes slowly, sometimes more rapidly, but it does not stand still. The cycle frequently begins with the bold new concept, the innovation. Somebody gets a bright new idea. There is a John Wanamaker, a George Hartford, a Frank Woolworth, a W.T. Grant, a General Wood, a Michael Cullen, a Eugene Ferkauf. Such an innovator has an idea for a new kind of distributive enterprise. At the outset he is in bad odor, ridiculed, scorned, condemned as "illegitimate." Bankers and investors are leery of him. But he attracts the public on the basis of the price appeal made possible by the low operating costs inherent in his innovation. As he goes along he trades up, improves the quality of his merchandise, improves the appearance and standing of his store, attains greater respectability. Then if he is successful comes the period of growth, the period when he is taking business away from the established distribution channels that have clung to the old methods. Repeatedly something like this has happened in American distribution. The department stores took it away from the smaller merchants in the cities in the late 19th and early 20th century; the original grocery chains

took it away from the old wholesaler-small retailer combination, the supermarkets then began taking it away from the original grocery chains to the extent that the latter had to climb on the supermarket bandwagon. And today the discount houses and the supermarkets are taking it away from the department stores and variety chains.

During this process of growth the institution rapidly becomes respectable in the eyes of both consumers and investors, but at the same time its capital investment increases and its operating costs tend to rise. Then the institution enters the stage of maturity. It has a larger physical plant, more elaborate store fixtures and displays, and it undertakes greater promotional efforts. At this stage the institution finds itself competing primarily with other similar institutions rather than with old line competitors. The maturity phase soon tends to be followed by topheaviness, too great conservatism, a decline in the rate of return on investment, and eventual vulnerability. Vulnerability to what? Vulnerability to the next fellow who has a bright idea and who starts his business on a low-cost basis, slipping in under the umbrella that the old-line institutions have hoisted.[203]

The application of McNair's "wheel of retailing" thesis, both to the food industry specifically and to retailing in general, has attracted a good deal of discussion and a fair amount of criticism.[204] Many of these criticisms have merit. But the great value of McNair's idea is that it focuses our attention on the upward pressure on the expense ratio, which can force retailers to raise their prices or change their product mix, not to meet consumer needs or the competitive situation, but to cover operating costs. Both A&P and Sears, the nation's leading merchants through most of the twentieth century, started as price cutters but wound up holding the price umbrella.

Trading up is dangerous. Its danger for the chains was recognized by commentators at the time they were doing it. Wrote a Harvard Business School professor in 1931, "The greatest single danger doubtless is that the chains will allow increasingly keen competition to express itself in added service rather than in efforts to reduce costs and improve values."[205]

The chains in the 1930s forgot where they had come from. They had won their customer base through low prices. There was no reason to believe that they could compete successfully with high-margin independents whose survival depended on personal service and many reasons to believe that they would be unable to do so. These chain organizations were created to deliver low prices. Their very nature—specifically the fact that they were managed by employees rather than by proprietors with deep roots in the communities they served—made higher margin and higher service a difficult segment to penetrate. And of all the decades in American history to decide to trade up, the 1930s was the worst. During the decade 1930–1939, outlays for food and beverages as a percentage of total consumption expenditures were 25.7, 24.4, 23.4, 25.2, 27.7, 29.1, 29.8, 30, 29.5, and 28.7 percent, respectively.[206]

There are two other reasons that the time had come for the supermarkets in the 1930s. The first of these is the automobile. There were over 8 million automobiles registered in the United States in 1920. By 1930, that number had risen to 23 million, and it continued to rise even during the Depression.[207] Mileage of surfaced roads had also increased dramatically, from 387,000 miles in 1921 to nearly 1.1 million in 1935.[208] It is not hard to imagine the impact of these developments on retailers who had located their outlets in accord with the practices favored by the chains in the 1910s. The automobile meant that a food market could draw on a larger trading area than ever before. It meant that parking was essential and that therefore the whole meaning of convenient location had changed. Stock-up trips now became more important, and such trips were becoming progressively more practical because of the increased availability of refrigerators. The total number of refrigerators sold prior to 1930 was 1.9 million; in the years 1930 to 1941 inclusive, over 20 million were sold.[209]

The second major reason, although of lesser impact than the automobile, was the development of national branding strategies by the big food manufacturers. These strategies were facilitated by the commercial use of radio, which came into its own in the 1930s.[210] This new tool for the pull strategy had been fortuitously placed in the hands of the Procter & Gambles, the Kelloggs, and the like. And it was a tool they used skillfully. While traditional chains were becoming more committed to private labels for both competitive and legal reasons, the supermarkets welcomed strong national brands with open arms. They wanted the manufacturers to do their selling for them, and the manufacturers were more than willing.

A&P and the Supermarket Revolution

Earlier in the chapter, we observed that A&P and the other big grocery chains seemed to be in a strong position as the 1930s began. We noted that A&P had won marketing leadership through its commitment to a system that enabled it to deliver superior value to the consumer. With the benefit of hindsight, we know that the company was less securely situated than it appeared. It owned and operated over 15,000 stores. But what Cullen, the Big Bear entrepreneurs, and the dozens, and soon scores, and

New supermarkets, based upon automobile transportation as is clearly visible here, sprang up all over the country during the Depression. A number of different companies—not only the one in New Jersey—adopted the name "Big Bear." Pictured here is a Big Bear store in Columbus, Ohio, in the 1930s. This picture typifies the look of many such early supermarkets.

soon hundreds of Big Chiefs, Big Tigers, Big Bulls, and so forth that sprouted up everywhere proved was that the A&P stores were in the wrong locations and in the wrong format. Writing in 1933, a business journalist observed:

> Basically, the supermarket represents the complete antithesis of all the important factors that have been considered essential to success in retailing. Its location is generally far removed from established trading centers. Vacant lots in the neighborhood are desirable to facilitate parking. Large floor space on a side-walk level is considered essential, but the exterior appearance of the building seems to be of no importance so long as it will serve as a base for huge signs.[211]

Interiors were uninviting, but practical, and they were kept well-stocked with merchandise. The help of sales clerks was replaced by goods, with prices conspicuously marked, within easy reach of customers.

Here seemed to be a fundamentally new way of doing business. Had A&P, the world's greatest food-distribution system, suddenly become obsolete? How would the company alter its system to deal with this new method of competition?

The supermarket was more than a new kind of store. Some operators were experimenting with a new marketing philosophy. According to a Big Bear advertising manager, the grocery department was designed to be a traffic builder. The real money was made through the concessions.[212] Big Bear originally had eleven concession departments, including such nontraditional grocery-store products as electrical and radio supplies, auto accessories, and paints and varnishes.[213] Thus, there was the possibility that this new kind of food store would treat the bulk of A&P's product offering as a loss leader.

What was more, some of the new supermarket operators vertically integrated wholesaling and retailing. Big Bear, for example, was founded in part by the American Grocery Company, a wholesale grocer that had already organized a chain of six hundred independent retail grocers for the purpose of pooled buying.[214] A key aspect of chain operations could be and was being copied.

A&P was caught in a dilemma. Should the company go into supermarkets itself? There were indications that the supermarket would become the store of the future. It was receiving plentiful publicity throughout the 1930s. Perhaps by moving quickly A&P could nip the movement in the bud. It was surely possible, with its market expertise and organization, for A&P to become the leader in the low-price field. The company had traded down before, when it created its economy-store program. The man who had managed those stores was John A. Hartford.[215] And yet, A&P had much to lose. One cornerstone of its success was its multitude of stores. If it went into supermarkets, it might by its very decision enhance the new format's chances of success. We must keep in mind that while the ultimate success of the supermarket is clear to us today, it was understandably less clear at the time. Giant food stores had existed before 1930 and some had succeeded, but they had not captured a significant share of the retail food market. To the executives of the established chains, the supermarket seemed a creature of "hype," a "circus" that people would grow tired of soon.

Faced with a retail format that "could profitably sell goods at prices which would be ruinous to a conventional store,"[216] A&P's initial reaction was one of paralysis. "We did not take it very seriously at first,"[217] Hartford recalled in 1945. The implications of the supermarket were so startling that a head-in-the-sand attitude developed. What A&P's executives lacked, to borrow a phrase from Henry James, was "the imagination of disaster."[218]

Such imaginings were coming more readily to mind as the decade progressed. There were approximately three hundred supermarkets in operation in 1935; the following year saw a fourfold increase in their number.[219] Nearby A&P units were suffering as a result. "We had a demonstration in Brooklyn," Hartford testified in 1945, of what this competition really meant to us. We had a competitor there by the name of King Kullen, and a great many independents, who opened these stores very fast and very rapidly. We had had a very profitable operation in Brooklyn. In a very short space of time, they priced that Brooklyn [store] into deep red figures.[220]

Something had to be done, but what? Should A&P pound on expenses and improve its logistics to make certain it could not be undersold even in its present stores? Should it experiment with deep discounts? Should it stick to an "everyday low price" policy?[221] Should it close stores? If so, which ones? Should it open supermarkets? If so, would these be like the King Kullen or the Big Bear operation? Where should they be located? Should the policy of heavy advertising and emphasis on national brands, both of which were part of the supermarket movement, be copied along with the store format? Who would run these new stores? What would be the overall strategic plan? And once that plan was established, would this gigantic company be able to move?

A&P began experimenting with different pricing possibilities on a store-by-store basis as early as 1935. Some stores were divided into two parts—one continuing as usual, the other offering greatly reduced prices in a self-service area. Others opened a grocery "bargain basement," operating their ground floor as in the past but establishing a lower-priced, self-service section in the basement.[222]

In 1935, the so-called "Baby Bear" program, featuring everyday low prices and plentiful publicity, showed heartening results. But A&P did not vigorously pursue this option. Sales increased in 1936, and the sense of urgency was blunted.[223] There was confusion in the central office about the road the company should travel. In October of 1936, George Hartford complained of overemphasis on volume at the expense of margins. To John Hartford's dismay, the divisional president expressed a "ready acceptance" of his brother's view.[224]

For John Hartford, A&P had always meant and could only mean high volume and low prices:

> It has always been our idea—we have been volume. We thought it was sounder business to sell two hundred pounds of butter at a cent a pound profit, than one hundred pounds at two cents. That was our theory.[225]

In 1936, A&P opened 20 supermarkets, but there were net closings of 180 stores—from 14,926 in 1935 to 14,746. In 1937, the company operated 282 supermarkets, and there were net closings of 1,432 stores.[226] Then, in 1938, the Great Atlantic and Pacific Tea Company took the basic strategic decision to transform itself into a chain of supermarkets.

Reluctantly at first, but wholeheartedly after 1938, A&P turned itself into a supermarket company. Here is an early example.

By this time, even John Hartford's conservative older brother George had become "completely convinced that Mr. John's plan is the only salvation."[227]

The sense of tension in the company over this decision was palpable. John Hartford well understood that massive store closings would "involve many heartaches."[228] Observed *Fortune* magazine of the new policy:

> [I]n those years of building "Mr. George" and "Mr. John" developed a paternalism toward their employees that has become, in the case of "Mr. John" at least, an obsession. It has taken the tangible form of high wages (currently $30 a week average for managers and clerks, which compares favorably with the Department of Labor figure of $22 for all retail stores). And it has left hundreds of marginal stores open when unsentimental business judgment would have closed them.[229]

A&P was now willing to transform itself because the crisis it had long faced had at last become clear. In the words of Morris A. Adelman, "Perhaps it was this realization that the world could come to an end that accounts for the urgent, even anxious, tone of the divisional presidents' meetings during that year [1938]; and for John Hartford's constant adjurations to speed things up."[230] By 1941, A&P was operating 6,170 stores, 1,594 of which were supermarkets.[231]

How can we best evaluate A&P's management of the supermarket revolution? A useful way to judge the company's response is to note the activities of its competitors. And a good index of competitive response to the supermarket is sales per store. Higher sales per store do not necessarily mean that a company has built supermarkets. Sales through the standard small store could be greatly increased through lower prices and more publicity, as A&P discovered in its Baby Bear experiment. On the other hand, if increasing sales per store were accompanied by a decrease in the number of stores and an increase in total sales, the assumption that a firm was building supermarkets would be warranted.

Table 4–11 shows that A&P moved more quickly than its four largest rivals. In 1930, A&P sales per store ranked second behind Safeway among the five top firms. The latter's base of operations was the West, where large stores had appeared earlier than in the East. However, by 1941, A&P sales per store were 25 percent higher than Safeway's. A&P sales per store had increased by well over a factor of three while its number of stores had dropped more than 60 percent. Net store closings at Safeway from 1930 to 1941 were a mere 15, while at A&P they were 9,567. (Net store closings at Safeway measured from the peak number of stores in 1936 were 710.)

Safeway had experimented during the Depression with a middle term between its traditional business and the total transformation to a super-market organization. This middle term was a separate division called Pay-N-Takit, which sold no Safeway private-label merchandise.[232] Eventually, Safeway's president felt that this half measure was insufficient; the company terminated the experiment and converted all its stores to a low-price policy with the Safeway name.[233] It is not known precisely when this decision was taken, but as late as 1940, *Fortune* observed that "Safeway sticks to neighborhood stores . . . , regarding great supermarkets as unsound because they serve the customer no better and often make him travel farther."[234]

Kroger, which was not directly competitive with Safeway because it was located in the Midwest, asked to use the Pay-N-Takit name. The stores it opened under this name were designed to fight the Albers supermarket chain, which was making inroads into Kroger sales. Unfortunately, Pay-N-Takit stores "caused more damage to Kroger's own neighborhood stores than to Albers, which continued to expand and prosper."[235]

As the per-store sales figures in table 4–11 suggest, neither American Stores nor First National Stores had become heavily involved in supermar-

TABLE 4-11

Total Sales,ᵃ Number of Stores, and Sales per Store of the Five Leading Grocery Chains, 1930–1941

Year	A&P Total Sales (in thousands)	A&P Number of Stores	A&P Sales per Store	Safeway Total Sales (in thousands)	Safeway Number of Stores	Safeway Sales per Store	Kroger Total Sales (in thousands)	Kroger Number of Stores	Kroger Sales per Store	American Stores Total Sales (in thousands)	American Stores Number of Stores	American Stores Sales per Store	First National Stores Total Sales (in thousands)	First National Stores Number of Stores	First National Stores Sales per Store
1930	$1,065,807	15,737	$67,726	$219,285	2,675	$81,976	$267,094	5,165	$51,712	$142,770	2,728	$52,335	$107,635	2,549	$42,226
1931	1,008,325	15,670	64,347	246,784	3,264	75,608	244,371	4,884	50,035	135,225	2,806	48,192	108,197	2,548	42,464
1932	864,048	15,427	56,009	229,173	3,411	67,186	213,160	4,737	44,999	115,454	2,977	38,782	107,634	2,546	42,276
1933	819,617	15,131	54,168	220,157	3,306	66,593	205,692	4,400	46,748	109,387	2,882	37,955	100,893	2,705	37,299
1934	842,016	15,035	56,004	242,966	3,228	75,268	221,175	4,352	50,831	114,355	2,859	40,002	105,813	2,653	39,884
1935	872,244	14,926	58,438	294,698	3,330	88,498	229,908	4,250	54,096	115,867	2,286	50,685	111,324	2,623	42,441
1936	907,371	14,746	61,533	346,178	3,370	102,723	242,273	4,212	57,520	113,388	2,816	40,266	111,575	2,556	46,782
1937	881,705	13,314	66,224	381,868	3,327	114,778	148,444	4,108	60,478	114,566	2,620	43,727	120,683	2,473	48,800
1938	879,000	10,900	80,642	368,255	3,227	114,117	231,296	3,992	57,940	109,853	2,416	45,469	124,295	2,350	52,891
1939	990,400	9,200	107,652	385,882	2,967	130,058	243,357	3,958	61,485	114,824	2,272	50,539	124,223	2,244	55,158
1940	1,115,774	7,230	154,326	399,322	2,671	149,503	258,115	3,777	69,255	124,839	2,157	57,876	131,041	2,137	61,320
1941	1,378,147	6,170	223,363	475,124	2,660	178,618	302,766	3,477	87,077	157,677	2,130	74,027	142,681	1,923	74,197

ᵃFor the sake of consistency, total sales, rather than retail sales, are used. The difference is negligible.

SOURCES: "Annual Reports of A&P, Safeway, Kroger, American Stores, and First National Stores, 1930–41," Godfrey M. Lebhar, *Chain Stores in America, 1859–1962* (New York: Chain Store Publishing Corporation, 1963), 393–97; A. C. Hoffman for the Temporary National Economic Committee, *Large-Scale Organization in the Food Industries*, monograph no. 35 (Washington, D.C.: GPO, 1940), 8.

kets by 1941. In fact, it was the smaller chains that spotted the trend the earliest and moved the fastest. In 1933, Union Premier Stores (which later became Food Fair) operated twenty-six neighborhood stores, with average sales of about $62,500 per unit. By 1937, all neighborhood stores had been closed and the company was operating twenty-two supermarkets, averaging about $600,000 each in annual sales.[236] Stop & Shop in Boston moved a bit later but with similar resolution.[237]

Relatively speaking, then, we can say that A&P moved reasonably quickly. It was not as fast as the smaller chains that could show greater flexibility because they were less committed to the traditional system, but it was faster than those chains that were in positions similar to its own. John Toolin, president of A&P's Central Western division, once observed in a letter to John Hartford that "It is easy to build up a complicated and expensive structure, but very difficult to adjust and reduce it to the demands of time and conditions."[238] But A&P met the challenge—it was the nation's leading food retailer well into the postwar period.

A&P's ability to change was enhanced by the vision of its chief operating officer, John Hartford. Many in the chain grocery business and indeed many in A&P itself, not the least of whom was John's older brother George, had, to use a phrase employed earlier, forgotten where they had come from. John Hartford held to the idea that 2 pounds of butter at 1 cent was a better business than 1 pound at 2 cents. That view, combined with his power as part-owner of the firm, enabled him to institute the changes required.

Despite its success, however, A&P could and should have done better. During the Depression, A&P was too committed and insufficiently flexible. It managed for the present. A leader must manage for the future.

A company wins market leadership by devising a method to deliver superior value to the consumer. The well-managed company then proceeds to commit itself to this system with all the skills and resources at its command. In the process, the company puts distance between itself and the competition. This is what Rockefeller did with Standard Oil, what Ford did in automobiles, and what the Hartfords did in food distribution.

Ironically, just at the time when a market leader appears most firmly ensconced at the top of its industry, it may be vulnerable. Its system may be so superior that potential competitors may decide that it is hopeless to compete against it on its own terms. Tidewater Pipeline chose to compete with Rockefeller not by trying to achieve better railroad contracts than he had, but by innovating a whole new way to transport oil.[239] Alfred P. Sloan, Jr., chose to compete against Henry Ford not by building a better Model T—Ford built the best such car imaginable—but by redefining the market for automobiles through the "car for every purse and purpose," the price pyramid, and the annual model change.[240] And the supermarket entrepreneurs competed against A&P not by doing better what A&P was the best company in the world at doing, but by doing something that A&P did not want to do at all. The greatest entrepreneurial failure in this story is Kroger. This company was second in the market, and one of its own employees knew how to make it first. Kroger executives did not listen. Perhaps it was lack of imagination or perhaps, like the executives at A&P, those at Kroger also had too much invested in the standard way of doing business. If the executives at A&P endorsed the supermarket revolution, they were ruining their own distribution system. That is why they sat by paralyzed, unable to act until it was almost too late. In the end, A&P had little choice. The company could ruin its own system or see others do it.

Thus, in addition to a commitment to delivering value to the consumer, marketing leadership demands flexibility. When flexibility is lost, leadership is lost with it. The reason is that things change, things over which the individual firm may have no control.

John Hartford showed the flexibility the company needed, albeit a little tardily. In the view of former A&P executive William I. Walsh, John Hartford did not conceive of himself as managing a set of stores of a certain configuration or a distribution system of a certain description. Rather, he believed he was managing an idea: providing the most good food for the money. During the 1930s, the supermarket revolution shook the company "to its roots." Hartford felt that the company was not its 15,000 small stores. It was the idea. If the furtherance of that idea meant the abandonment of the small stores and the building of 4,000 big stores, so be it.[241]

Corporate Suicide

In 1950, the Great Atlantic and Pacific Tea Company, with sales approaching $3.2 billion, was the second largest industrial company in the United States in sales. Only General Motors was larger. A&P was the largest privately owned company in the United States—larger even than Ford—and the largest retailer in the world. Its profits of over $32 million were $5 million greater than the combined profits of the second and third largest grocery chains, Safeway and Kroger. Its sales were over $1 billion greater than theirs. Geographically, A&P was still concentrated east of the

Mississippi with an enclave in southern California; so its direct competition with West Coast–headquartered Safeway was limited. It was well over three times the size of Kroger, which was the biggest chain with which it shared a larger number of trading areas. In the metropolitan areas in which it was the strongest—the Northeast and the Midwest—A&P was the dominant force in the industry.

John and George Hartford, the brothers who ran the A&P business, were 78 and 86 years old, respectively, in 1950. They both had joined the firm upon finishing high school, well before the turn of the century, and had spent their whole lives with it. John and George were featured on *Time* magazine's cover on 13 November 1950; this is how the article described them:

> Both brothers are widowers; both live only for the A&P. But there the similarity ends. John is thin, George is plump. John is bold and expansive, George cautious and conservative. John is gregarious and full of quips, George shy and sober-sided. John stands and talks; George sits and listens. Plain and unpretentious George, in his drab black suit, sedate tie and stiff collar, could easily be taken for a retired motorman dressed up for Sunday.
>
> Nobody would make that mistake about John, who looks the merchant prince from the tip of his elegant shoes to the top of his wavy-maned, handsome head.[242]

John was the merchant; he ran the company while George kept his eye on the numbers. These two immensely wealthy and successful men did not look on themselves nor were they looked on by others as brilliant. "We're just a couple of grocery boys trying to do an honest business," Mr. George, as he was known in the company, once said. John ran the company in accord with a few simple but clear principles—high volume, lowest possible prices, low margins, high turnover. "The secret of chain store profits lies almost entirely in a rapid turnover of merchandise," he asserted, "and a rapid turnover simply means unceasing attention to the needs and the buying habits of your customers."[243]

Let us contemplate A&P's power at mid-century. The company had an excellent distribution system that had proven itself over the years. It had a first-class executive corps and a private-label program as well executed as any in the industry. Its market leadership made it possible to amortize fixed expenses such as newspaper advertising over a larger volume of sales than any other firm in the industry. It had a simple but shrewd corporate mission. It had a debt-free balance sheet making new investments well within reach. And it had what money can't buy—a reputation for nine decades of giving customers their money's worth.

Yet this great company came to grief. What went wrong?

The dapper John L. Hartford (left) and his more conservative brother George L. Hartford are pictured here beneath the portrait of their father, George Huntington Hartford, one of A&P's founders. The brothers look self-satisfied, and well they should. Their ownership of A&P made them among the world's wealthiest men. After John's death in 1951, however, the company began a long slow decline which ended in its purchase by a West German firm in 1979.

A&P was not done in by some clever thrust from a competitor. The company was not afflicted by some massive change in the nature of the market. It was not clobbered by some ferocious foreign competitor. Nor was there some new technological innovation that shattered its competitive advantages. This company was milked.

The Hartford brothers had chosen an able executive named David T. Boffinger to succeed them, but Boffinger died suddenly of a heart attack in December of 1949. Their next choice was Ralph W. Burger. Burger was the secretary of the company, for which he had worked since youth. He was very close to the Hartford brothers. What he was not was an operating executive who had worked his way up by making a division grow. Burger was a pedestrian man, without vision or imagination. But he had great power in the company. In addition to being its president, he was also president of the Hartford Foundation, which was soon to hold 40 percent of the company's stock.[244]

On 20 September 1951, John Hartford attended a meeting of the Chrysler board at the Chrysler Corporation offices, a few blocks from A&P's Graybar Building headquarters in midtown Manhattan. In the elevator after the meeting, he had a heart attack. He never regained consciousness and died at the age of 79. In obituaries he was, appropriately, compared to Henry Ford and John D. Rockefeller. Six years later, George, who had continued to serve as treasurer but who devoted little of his attention to operations or strategy, also passed away. He was 92 years old and had worked for A&P for eighty years.[245]

By some measures, Burger's presidency was proceeding well. Sales topped $4 billion in 1954 and $5 billion in 1958. Profits increased every year from 1951 through 1958, setting records each year from 1954 and topping $53 million in 1958.

Underneath these positive developments were danger signals. New stores rather than improved performance from existing stores were accounting for the lion's share of sales increases. Although sales were obviously growing, they were doing so at less than half the industry average. A union agreement was signed in which the company may have given away more than it had to in order to maintain peace. The result was that New York metropolitan-area stores "were saddled with the highest labor contracts in the area." In the words of an executive, "Retail food has always been a labor-intensive business. Store wages constitute the largest controllable expense by far. Without effective control of labor costs it is impossible to operate a store effectively."[246] Add to this a clumsy effort at centralization and the introduction of inappropriate productivity measures and one has many of the ingredients for trouble.

A&P went public in 1958. Because of Ralph Burger's presidency of the Hartford Trust and his relations with the Hartford heirs, he controlled 60 percent of the stock. Sales and profits fell in 1959 and grew irregularly through 1962. Over 90 percent of the quarter billion dollars in profits earned during those years was paid out in dividends. In 1962, when A&P had a third of the volume and 36 percent of the number of stores of the total for the top ten grocery chains, it accounted for only 18 percent of the total capital investment of those chains. With less than half of A&P's volume and number of stores, Safeway invested twice as much in store development in 1962.[247]

"While most of its customers were signing long-term home mortgages," an executive later observed, "A&P simply refused to make a reasonable financial investment in the nation's future."[248] Like Montgomery Ward, A&P was always waiting for the next depression. Unlike Montgomery Ward, however, A&P was the market leader. It was a far stronger company with greater resources and a greater margin for error. As we will see in chapter 5, Montgomery Ward's CEO Sewall Avery failed in 1945 to foresee the growth in the West. Ralph Burger failed to see it in 1960. A&P had stores in southern California and Washington State; but instead of widening this wedge, the company abandoned the West Coast completely by the end of the decade.

This was just one of a long list of errors. The industry was moving to larger stores. A&P was not. The country was moving to the suburbs. A&P was not. Under the impact of television advertising, nationally branded grocery products were increasing in demand. But A&P, with its heavy investment in manufacturing facilities, was strongly committed to Ann Page, Jane Parker, and its other private labels. Other big chains began to carry nonfood general merchandise, higher margin lines that could offset the brutal competitive pressure on groceries. Once again, A&P, stuck in its small stores with their limited shelf space, lagged.[249] In 1947, *Fortune* had written that "Grandma," as A&P was referred to in the trade, "has rarely been an innovator, leaving such risky stuff to the more daring independents."[250] There are limits to this attitude, and in the postwar era A&P transgressed them.

Worst of all, A&P lost its sense of strategic direction. Trading-stamp programs gave way to experiments with discounting. The manufacturing arm was mismanaged. The company did not properly handle its buying from branded suppliers, thus sacrificing trade promotion funding in untold amounts. The animating idea that had answered questions and given direction in the past was gone, and nothing had grown to replace it. At the core of this company was now a void.

Sales in 1970 of $5.7 billion were actually below 1952 levels on a tonnage basis. The following description of the stores—one that will ring true to readers who shopped A&P at this time—helps explain why:

These stores had few customers and did little business, but were open long hours, often seven days and six nights. These stores were obviously short of help, shelves were poorly stocked. What carriages were on hand were usually out in the parking lot. Only one of six checkstands was operating, with no bagger to help shorten the checkout wait. Advertised sale features were often missing from the shelves, dairy, produce and meat cases. Most times, and particularly at night, no employees were available to assist customers seeking a cut of meat not available on display, or to check backroom stocks for sales items missing from shelves, or even to scale and price produce items or grind A&P's bean coffees. Cleanliness and courtesy standards, freshness and quality control standards, shelf stocking and checkout standards, and store morale all deteriorated at the same grinding steady pace.[251]

The essence of A&P's policy had always been extremely simple: Sell more good food for less money, and keep the margins as low as possible so the prices can be kept as low as possible. This is a great strategy, but it depends absolutely on the maintenance of a low-cost structure. As John Hartford put it in 1925, "I am a firm believer in getting this business into a position whereby we can sell goods cheaper than any concern in the country. I have always been a volume man and it is hard to divert my mind to any other policy. . . ."[252]

The greatest failure of Ralph Burger's presidency was that he allowed A&P's low-cost position slowly to erode. When his successors tried to return to the discount strategy with which John Hartford had built the company before World War I, they did not have an organization that gave them the economic firepower to make the strategy a success.

William J. Kane, a long-time A&P executive, took the helm in 1971 determined to improve performance. During that year, one of the company's Philadelphia stores had adopted a discount strategy and had generated favorable results. For the company as a whole, however, the fifty-two-week period ending 26 February 1972 was, to use Kane's words in the *Annual Report*, "disappointing in many aspects." Sales fell more than $100 million, and profits plummeted from $50.1 million to $14.6 million.[253]

Kane believed that what had worked for one store in Philadelphia on an experimental basis might point the way to the company's future. The result was the WEO (Where Economy Originates) price war of 1972. A&P slashed its prices. Competitors responded and the already razor-thin margins in grocery retailing became thinner still. If A&P had launched a price war fifteen years earlier, it would have beggared the whole industry and doubtless have run afoul of the antitrust laws. By the early 1970s, its competitive advantages had disappeared. Its labor costs were among the industry's highest. Too many of its stores were in the wrong locations and of the wrong size. Other chains, even much smaller ones, had learned how to match A&P's savings from integration back to wholesaling. The company's manufacturing arm was proving a hindrance, committing the stores with their limited shelf space to stock what A&P produced rather than what the advertising-sensitive consumer wanted.[254] Table 4–12 provides a comparison of store data for the leading grocery chains in 1971.

John Hartford believed in "getting this business into a position whereby we can sell goods cheaper. . . ."[255] But in the 1970s, A&P tried to sell goods cheaper without being in a position to do so, as the data in table 4–12 make clear. In the words of William I. Walsh, an A&P executive at the time,

> to arbitrarily reduce prices in stores already losing money, where there was little or no potential for attracting compensating new sales volume, or to order hundreds of poorly operated small stores into battle in price wars against larger competition with much higher shares of local markets seemed to challenge reasonable odds and reduce chances for success of the WEO program.[256]

Commented an analyst, "It's absurd. If they can't make money with regular prices, they certainly can't make money this way."[257]

And they couldn't. Competition struck back, cutting prices to match or increasing service. For the fifty-two weeks ending 24 February 1973, the company lost a staggering $51.3 million. True, sales did increase by over $860 million.[258] But A&P had not proven that it could win a price war. It had only proven that it could give away the store. In the fifty-two weeks ending 23 February 1974, sales did edge upward; and the company was back in the black.[259] Unsurprisingly, however, Kane was replaced in 1975.

The new CEO was Jonathan L. Scott, and his selection represented a

TABLE 4–12

Store Data for the Five Leading Grocery Chains in 1971

Grocery Chain	Sales per Store (in thousands)	Sales per Employee	Store Size (sq. ft.)	Inventory Turnover
A&P	$1,300	$48,320	8,900	12.2%
Safeway	2,300	54,983	19,000	14.2
Kroger	2,000	71,206	16,600	13.9
Food Fair	3,100	64,273	15,500	11.9
Jewel	2,200	87,555	18,000	14.0

SOURCES: Eleanor Johnson Tracy, "How A&P Got Creamed," *Fortune*, January 1973, 105; *Fairchild's Financial Manual of Retail Stores* (New York: Fairchild, 1973), xi.

real break with A&P's past. The company had always been run by older men, but Scott was only 44. It had always exuded formality, but everybody called Scott "Scotty." Most important, Scott was an outsider. A&P had always been governed by leaders who had grown up in the company. When Kane took over in 1971, he and the other three top executives represented among them 138 years with the company. Kane himself started as a store clerk.[260] Scott was the CEO of the Idaho-based Albertson chain, where he had the perhaps unique experience of rising to the presidency after divorcing the boss's daughter. Scott brought with him executives from Albertson and other firms.[261]

Scott launched a comprehensive program to turn A&P around. The most important aspect of this program was store closings. A&P would have to get small before it could get big again. The size of individual stores, in terms of volume and square footage rather than the total number of stores, was to be the new emphasis. Scott closed more than a third of the company's 3,500 stores. "We must move ahead," Scott explained, "to effect a transition which other chains have completed long ago."[262]

In order to finance this transition Scott established a pretax reserve of $200 million. As a result, the income statement for the fifty-two weeks ending 22 February 1975 showed a loss of over $157 million. Despite store closings, however, sales actually edged upward, and profits began to respond to the new "Price and Pride" campaign. In the fifty-three weeks ending 28 February 1976, the company was back in the black.[263] Performance steadily improved as articles with titles such as "Price, Pride, and Profitability" began to appear in the business press.[264]

This was, however, a false dawn, as losses quickly reappeared. Many years earlier, A&P executive John Toolin had written John Hartford about the ease with which one could build a complicated structure and the difficulties of reducing and changing it when that became necessary.[265] That was the very lesson Scott learned.

Scott was confronted with a basic dilemma in his store-closing program: Should he move store by store and warehouse by warehouse or should he hack off whole divisions? Scott chose the site-by-site approach, but that did not go far enough. It is easy to imagine the problems involved in opening a store, but few realize how difficult and expensive it can be to close one down. "The shutting of a single store can have significant ramifications on a marketing area's distribution costs, its warehousing operations, its advertising expenses, and its labor situation, as well as on the A&P manufacturing facilities that are deprived of an outlet for their products."[266] The labor situation was especially thorny. Union contracts mandated that when a store was closed in a given market area, the senior employees were to be moved to other stores and the junior employees "bumped" off the payroll. The company had to retain higher-priced and often less-productive employees while firing its future.[267]

By the end of 1978, it was again time for a change at the top at A&P. Donald M. Kendall, chief executive officer of PepsiCo, was acquainted with both Scott and Erivan Karl Haub, chairman of the Tengelmann Group, West Germany's largest food retailer. The two were introduced through Kendall's good offices; and in early 1979, Tengelmann bought 42 percent of A&P's 24.9 million shares for $7.38 a share or about $77 million.[268] The Great Atlantic and Pacific Tea Company—one of the oldest firms in the United States and, as recently as 1950, the nation's second largest industrial company—was now owned by West Germans.

With the change in ownership came a change in management. Scott was replaced by James Wood in April. Wood, an Englishman, had begun his career as a grocer's apprentice at the age of 16. He headed Cavenham, Ltd., a British food retailer, before coming to the United States in 1973 to run Grand Union.[269]

A&P's problems were no easier for the new managers than they had been for the old ones. The company in 1982 was being described as "Tengelmann's Vietnam"—Wood and Haub were disagreeing publicly, and Haub was quoted as saying that "If we had it to do over again, we wouldn't do it."[270]

With the help of a massive store-closing campaign and an unexpected cash windfall from an overfunded pension plan, A&P's results improved during the 1980s. Sales for the 52-week period ending 25 February 1989 were slightly over $10 billion.[271] Such sales made A&P large indeed. However, they also meant that A&P occupied a position in the American business economy in no way comparable to its situation three decades earlier.

It was through good management that A&P grew to one of the great corporations of the world by 1950. It was mismanagement that killed it. Good management can build it up again (although never, in all likelihood, to its previous preeminence).

Conclusion

Let us now locate the A&P story in the context of the propositions this book presents.

PROFIT THROUGH VOLUME AND ENTREPRENEURIAL VISION

Unlike the other products discussed in this book, food is an absolute necessity for every person. That has not changed from the Stone Age down to the present. Neither is the need for food specific to any one nation or culture. There is nothing peculiarly American about eating in the sense that there is about drinking Coca-Cola. Thus, we cannot speak about creating a market for food in the way we can for Coca-Cola. We can, however, speak about creating a way of mass marketing standardized grocery products, and that is what the Great Atlantic and Pacific Tea Company did.

A&P is the oldest company discussed in this book. It was founded in 1859, deep in the Phase I era of premodern marketing. For years thereafter, it was not only a store-centered company but a mail-order business as well. Moreover, it was not a full-line grocer; it concentrated on a specialty item, tea. This was an ideal product for A&P to build a business on. Most suppliers charged high prices and high margins to subsidize their business on items more generally available and difficult to differentiate. But A&P's founder George Gilman and his young partner George Huntington Hartford applied the "American idea of profit through volume" to tea. They cut margins and prices and sold not only through their stores but also through peddlers and the mail. With the distribution system they built up, Gilman and Hartford realized they could reap what are today called economies of scope. By the turn of the century, they were in the grocery business.

Young John A. Hartford applied the same profit-through-volume strategy to the stores that his father had applied to tea. The result was the economy-store program, which built A&P into a position of real power. A&P was the leader of the chain-store movement in the 1920s, bringing system and science to a sector of the economy that had up to that time seen little of either.

VERTICAL SYSTEM

The high cost of living in general and of food distribution specifically were matters of public debate at the turn of the century. More than any other company, A&P attacked both by bringing the grocery retailing business into Phase II of its development. The company's tools were the profit-through-volume strategy and the vertical system it designed. Integrating back into wholesaling, it cut out brokers' commissions and inefficiencies. Integrating all the way back into food manufacturing, A&P assured itself of supplies that it could market under its own name. From the turn of the century, the company fought running battles with manufacturers of national brands. But its vertical strategy gave it greater freedom to negotiate with manufacturers or to choose to do without them.

FIRST-MOVERS AND ENTRY BARRIERS

Retailing is local in nature. If an A&P store is occupying a particular site, no other store can occupy that location. Food stores are visited by their customers more often than other types of retail stores, and some store sites are more convenient to consumers than are others. Think of A&P's system in 1929: more than 15,000 stores in the most heavily populated parts of the country. Many of these store sites were carefully selected by a staff that had a lot of information on the subject. There were a limited number of such sites in any locality; and in some cities, A&P had hundreds of stores. A&P's first-mover advantage stood as a powerful barrier to the entry of competition.

THE COMPETITOR'S OPTIONS

There were two ways to compete against A&P. The first was to attempt to construct a vertically integrated chain-store system of one's own. Some firms experienced considerable success in this effort. A&P was big, but the market for food was huge. All during the 1920s, chains could attack independents, not just one another; and their competitive advantages were sufficient so they could do well. These chains could do especially well if their principal market was in an area where A&P's presence was relatively weak. Safeway, for example, was based on the West Coast, where A&P had few stores.

The second way to attack A&P was to try to use the company's own strength against it. Throughout the 1920s, America was becoming a nation on wheels; yet the implications of automobility did not seem to register at A&P until the supermarket entrepreneurs had made their presence felt unmistakably.

The supermarket was foreshadowed by a number of large food stores, especially in the West. But the supermarket movement did not get under way as a major factor in eastern population centers until Michael Cullen started it in 1930. In my view, the supermarket as conceived in the 1930s was essentially a Phase II institution. Cullen and the others did not try to use research to create a demographic or psychographic segmentation scheme. To the contrary, they figured simply that they could use a change in the infrastructure (the automobile) and the availability of store space resulting from the Depression to beat even large chains of small stores at their own game. If A&P profited through volume, the supermarkets would make far more profit from far more volume. If A&P marketed to the masses, the supermarkets would market to even greater numbers, drawing trade from as much as a 50-mile radius. The biggest difference in philosophy between A&P and the supermarkets related to national brands— A&P fought with them, but the supermarkets exploited their consumer recognition to cut down on store service expenses. Food prices have always been important, but never were they more vital than during the Great Depression. In that atmosphere, the supers set out to show the world what an economy store could do.

A&P responded slowly. Turning itself into a supermarket operation meant abandoning part of the formula that had made it great. It also meant firing a lot of store managers, always a difficult task but especially painful for a paternalistic company in the middle of the Depression.

Slow though it may have been, A&P's response was effective. I believe the fundamental reason for this success was that John Hartford understood price appeal. He had built his company on it since before World War I. Thus, if the supermarket format generated the lowest prices, the supermarket format was what A&P would adopt. John Hartford had a Phase II mentality, and he could understand a Phase II challenge.

A&P not only had to deal with competition from the business world in the interwar years, but it also had to cope with a challenge from government. As has so often happened in the history of antitrust, the effort to stifle A&P was motivated not by complaints from consumers— A&P was the best thing that ever happened to the American grocery shopper—but by objections from other businesspeople who were unable to compete with it. In the *U.S.* v. *A&P* case, antitrust was an attack on Phase II methods of doing business.

MANAGING CHANGE

After World War II, food marketers had new challenges to face. John Hartford's death in 1951 robbed A&P of a highly creative business mind, and the company fell into the hands of a series of executives who viewed their responsibilities as fundamentally passive and trustee-like in nature.

The country was booming after the war; and it was on the move, too, as population shifted to the suburbs, the South, and the West. Another major change in the commercial infrastructure—television—came into almost every household in the nation. With it came enhanced power for national advertisers.

Into this new environment came a proliferation of grocery-store formats, ranging from giant superstores of 75,000 square feet to small convenience stores. This variety of formats is a notable change in food retailing from the "cookie cutter" chain systems of the late 1920s, in which one firm could manage thousands of stores in a highly centralized, programmatic fashion.

Price is still a key factor in modern food retailing, and it always will be. However, especially during the past quarter century, food retailers have also used such other variables as product quality, assortment, convenience, service, and ambience to segment the market.

The concept of segmentation was absent, as far as I can tell, from the world of A&P's leadership. In my research, I did not see the company's executives thinking in such terms. They always wanted to sell everything to everybody under their own name. The combination of television advertising and the demise of fair trade, however, has increased the difficulties involved in A&P's traditional strategy.

Yet another change has been the growth in the power of independent wholesalers in recent years. This development has been caused to some degree by the importance of capitalizing on the complexity of the deals that food manufacturers now offer to the trade. Wholesalers have been able to supply their customers more economically than previously because of their ability to buy on a deal-to-deal basis. The health of wholesaling compared to retailing in recent years also derives from the wholesalers' insulation from the vagaries of the consumer market. They do not have to bet on a store format as do retailers. Finally, the leading food wholesalers now supply sophisticated consulting services to their retail customers. The leading firms do not have the rather sleepy relationships common in the 1920s and described earlier in this chapter.

Like the Ford Motor Company in the 1920s, A&P in the quarter century following John Hartford's death suffered from exceptionally myopic management, which must bear much of the responsibility for the firm's collapse. Nevertheless, the recent poor performance of a number of other large chain grocery retailers suggests there is a phenomenon that is not specific to A&P but instead is overtaking the industry as a whole. Inflexibility and programmed, unexciting stores—stores that offer nothing special in ambience but that have lost the power to deliver lower prices—have constituted the bane of the large chain grocer in recent years.

CHAPTER 5

Bringing the Mass Market Home: Sears, Montgomery Ward, and Their Newer Rivals

Like grocery retailing, modern general-merchandise retailing emerged from a Phase I world of low volume, low turnover, and high margin. There were no chain stores selling general merchandise in the nineteenth century, and there was no vertical integration. Market relations prevailed among manufacturers, wholesalers, and retailers.

Montgomery Ward was the first firm to build a national retail business in general merchandise—that is, in any product that could be sold at a profit. Ward used the mail to advertise its wares and to receive orders, and it used the railroads to ship its goods. In the 1880s, Richard W. Sears began selling watches through the mail. By the 1890s, he too had branched out into numerous lines of goods and by the turn of the century had surpassed Ward in volume.

The heart of the market for the two mail-order giants was rural America. The arrival of the catalog—often known as the "wish book"—was eagerly awaited by farm families all over the nation. Sears especially, with its highly touted money-back guarantee, became a symbol of reliability and honesty. The company's name, not those of the manufacturers who supplied it with goods, became the important one for the customers to whom it sold. And Sears, Roebuck became the most trusted name in the nation.

In the new high-volume world that Sears helped bring into being, vertical-channel organization was essential to keep prices low and quality high. Sears was its own wholesaler, and it made many investments in manufacturing operations. It also worked out channel relationships in which it sometimes owned the supplier and often performed certain essential functions for it, such as purchasing.

In the 1920s, Sears, followed quickly by Ward, moved into store-centered retailing. With this move, Sears firmly established itself as a Phase II company. It had a nationwide reach, including cities as well as rural areas. Most important, the company brilliantly anticipated population movement by making a major commitment to the development of stores with parking lots in suburban areas. Whereas A&P waited for independent supermarket operators to demonstrate the importance of mass automobility to American retailing, Sears led the way in this respect.

Sears aimed its product offering at the middle-class family man with a home and a car. In this chapter, we take an extended look at the marketing problems and opportunities presented by one such product, the refrigerator. The refrigerator is among the most important new products in the twentieth century, both in terms of its dollar volume and its impact on the way we live. Sears was able to enter the refrigerator market in the 1930s, in competition with some of the best-managed companies in the country, and has remained a major player to this day. This industry gives us a chance to describe and analyze Sears's power in detail.

Montgomery Ward fell by the wayside during the 1950s, but Sears roared through the 1960s as one of the most powerful firms in the nation. During the 1970s, however, a malaise began to overtake the firm, a set of intractable problems that have yet to be solved.

Some of these problems, perhaps most of them, stem from the impact of Phase III in general-merchandise retailing. New specialty stores arose, targeting demographic and psychographic market segments in narrowly defined product categories. Ironically, the success of many of these specialty stores was facilitated by the crowds that Sears drew to the malls it developed and anchored. Other problems were Sears's continuing commitment to the private label in a world of nationally televised manufacturers' brands and its rising cost structure which, combined with a certain myopia, allowed K Mart and other discounters to steal business that Sears once considered its own. And, finally, the top leadership—so brilliant from Richard Sears to Julius Rosenwald to Robert Wood—seemed incapable of reconstituting the company in the face of these external challenges.

Sears, Roebuck and the Promise of American Life

It is said that when Franklin D. Roosevelt was asked what American book he would place in the hands of every Russian should such an opportunity arise, his response was not a biography of one of our great political leaders—Washington, Jefferson, Lincoln. Neither was it a poetic or novelistic treatment of American themes by such as Hawthorne, Twain, or Whitman. Nor was it a scholarly examination of the themes defining the American experience. Possible choices here might have included works by Turner, Parrington, Beard, Henry Adams, or even by his own fifth cousin once removed, Theodore.

Roosevelt's selection was not really a book at all. It was the Sears catalog.[1]

His choice was profound.

No single document better dramatized the American cornucopia from the end of the nineteenth century through World War II than the Sears catalog.[2] This was the Baedeker of the consumer economy; and it was this, Roosevelt may have felt, that showed better than anything else what the American way could provide for the average person. The greatest contribution of Greece to the world may have been in the realm of politics, of Britain in drama, of Germany in philosophy, of Austria in music, of Russia in literature, of Italy in art. America, on the other hand, has given the world things. Good things. Things that make life easier, nicer, or more fun. Things that work (or you get your money back). In the words of the best history of the company, Boris Emmet and John E. Jeuck's *Catalogues and Counters:*

> Sears guaranteed his $11.96 cookstove to cook. It cooked. And it cooked for years and years. Sears's plows would plow, and Sears's washing machines would wash. That was what farm families wanted; and that was what they got from Sears, Roebuck.[3]

Sears was about "the humbling of products."[4] Some products may have been available only in certain areas, but Sears brought them everywhere. Other products may have been technically complex or expensive machines, previously sold only to the elite. Sears pushed the price down and sold them to the average citizen. In the process of humbling these products, Sears, in a sense, and, to be sure, for a profit, ennobled the consumers of those products. And that, perhaps, was what Roosevelt had in mind when he selected the Sears catalog as his book of choice for the Russians.

Richard W. Sears: American Salesman

Richard Warren Sears was born on 7 December 1863—about five months after the birth of Henry Ford—in the small town of Stewartville, Minnesota. His father, James, was a man who dared much but achieved little. He prospected for gold with the forty-niners but returned home empty-handed. He saw action in the Civil War, and the grim realities of the conflict impressed him far more deeply than did the purportedly idealistic goals for which it was being waged.

After the war, James Sears returned to Minnesota to pursue his blacksmithing. At one point, he apparently accumulated a considerable sum of money but lost it in a speculation. It would appear that most of Richard Sears's early life was spent in modest if not actually poverty-stricken circumstances. Sears and his mother Eliza coped with this bleak domestic setting through a lifelong mutual devotion.[5]

Sears's entrepreneurial flair evinced itself early. He earned his first wage at the age of 7, and in his early teens, he "amused and astounded his family by constantly answering advertisements offering free booklets and other enticements. He ordered trinkets and notions of all sorts and traded them to other boys in the neighborhood."[6] Young Richard's mother "sensed that the boy did not like farming and had no taste for it."[7] The railroad offered a possible way out. At the age of 16, Sears struck a deal with the station agent at Huron Lake, Minnesota, in which he would undertake manual chores around the station in return for telegraphy lessons. He mastered the code quickly and the following year was running his own station.

Sears may have worked briefly in the auditing department of the central office of the Minneapolis and St. Louis railroad in St. Paul, but he was no happier on a salary than he had been on a farm. He was a born entrepreneur; and he requested and received another station agency, this time at North Redwood, Minnesota. His freight and express responsibilities took little of his time in that outpost, so he developed a trade of his own in a variety of commodities.

Perhaps more important than his early mercantile forays, Sears's position gave him access to information on the prices of many items through catalogs and deliveries that passed through his hands. He found the prices of watches particularly noteworthy, since they were selling at a very high markup. One day, delivery of a consignment of watches was refused by a local retailer. The wholesaler that had sent them out may not have even had an order for them. These watches fell into Sears's hands. The wholesaler offered them to him for $12 a unit if he would dispose of them. Sears informed station agents up and down the line that they could have as many of these watches as they wanted for $14 per unit and they could keep the difference between that and what they could sell them for. The standard price for these items was $25. Six months of this activity netted Sears $5,000.

Sears was not a reflective man, and whatever thoughts he may have had during those six months are lost to us. One imagines that he must have been astonished. Brought up through most of his life in modest circumstances, he had succeeded in a mere half year in making what at the time was a considerable sum of money. And it had been relatively easy. He had begun his career, like Andrew Carnegie, by mastering the two forces most responsible for the transformation of the nineteenth century—the railroad and the telegraph. Like John D. Rockefeller, he instinctively understood the critical importance of up-to-date information in business. Like both Rockefeller and Carnegie, and like Henry Ford after them, he understood that nothing could compare to a dramatically low price to generate big sales. And like every great entrepreneur, Sears was not a man to let grass grow under his feet when there was money to be made.

No wonder he left the railroad to found the R. W. Sears Watch Company in Minneapolis. He was 23 at the time. The year was 1886. Earlier that same year the Coca-Cola Company had been founded in Atlanta.

Sears's office, its staff, and the company's paid-in capital were minimal. The business was created "out of thin air . . . , on less than the proverbial shoe string."[8] Success was immediate. Sears began by selling through bonded railway agents. In 1887, he started advertising directly to customers through newspapers and soon followed that with a highly successful direct-mail postcard campaign.[9]

He was always looking for new ways to promote and to source his product. Sears's philosophy was profit through high volume leading to high turnover made possible by low prices, which were themselves made possible by low margins. By March of 1889, Sears was able to sell his company for at least $60,000 and perhaps as high as $100,000. "At twenty-five years of age, Richard Sears retired from the mail order business with a fortune possessed by few men of his age at that period."[10]

Sears went into banking, but that was boring. He quickly returned to selling, using names for his company other than his own because of a three-year, noncompete agreement into which he had entered with his purchasers in 1889. With the expiration of that agreement, his firm was named Sears, Roebuck and Company on 16 September 1893. (Alvah Curtis Roebuck was a watch repairman who had joined forces with Sears in 1887. He left the company prior to the end of the century but would return during the Depression in a public relations role.)[11]

From 1891, the first year for which figures are available, to 1908, the year Sears left the company, Sears, Roebuck grew into one of the most successful merchandising organizations in the world. Sales and profits climbed from $137,743 and $30,293, respectively, in 1891 to $40,843,866 and $2,034,796, respectively, in fiscal (ending June 30) 1908, a depression year.[12] Sears received $10 million when he sold his interest in the business in 1908. When he died at the age of 50, six years later, his estate was valued at $17.5 million.

What explains Sears's achievement? There are many answers to this question. First, despite cyclical fluctuations, the basic trends in the United States were toward an ever-richer nation. Population increased by well over a third, from 64,361,000 in 1891 to 88,710,000 in 1908. The primary mail-order markets were rural areas, and population was growing there as well (if at a slower rate), from 40,841,000 in 1890 to 49,973,000 in 1910. Along with the growth in population, per capita income was also increasing.[13] Second, new technologies from the 1880s onward were placing before consumers a wider variety of goods on which to spend their money than at any time in history. Third, by 1890, the basic railroad and telegraph infrastructure was at last in place. There were 166,703 miles of railroad trackage in the United States that year and 679,000 miles of telegraph wire.[14] This new transportation and communication network created the potential for linking producer and consumer more directly than ever before. And, finally, the traditional merchant was not well positioned to reorganize the distribution system of which he was a part. Wholesalers, jobbers, retailers, and middlemen lived in a world of limited vision and market intelligence, a world characterized by the Phase I philosophy of low volume, high margin, high price, low turnover, and, in general, sharp trading.[15] The second industrial revolution and the completion of the transportation and communication infrastructure knocked the underpinnings from this system, but most distributors were too close to it to see that the world had changed.

Although these facts illustrate the kind of opportunity that awaited the enterprising merchant toward the end of the nineteenth century, they do little to explain why Sears succeeded. These general conditions were the same for all players and potential entrants. Why was Sears uniquely successful in exploiting them?

The sum and substance of Richard Sears's strategy was volume. He wanted to do as much business as possible as quickly as possible. All of his efforts were geared toward that end.

The most important decision that any firm makes, as we have noted previously, is what markets it elects to serve with what products. Sears started off in the mail-order watch business, but he immediately defined himself as being more in the business of mail order than in the business of watches. Thus, in 1893, the company "issued a small 6 × 9 catalogue, hardly more than a booklet, of 64 pages." Among the items featured were watches, jewelry, silverware, clothing, guns, sewing machines, and a variety of other goods.[16]

A great deal flowed from this decision. First, it facilitated a far greater volume than would otherwise have been possible. The company could not have done $40 million worth of business in 1908 in watches alone. It was through scope—the variety of different items that the company handled—rather than through scale—the intensive exploitation of a single product through a large plant—that Sears would seek its fortune.[17] Louis E. Asher, a turn-of-the-century business associate of Sears, later wrote that:

A phrase of the day was: "Mr. Sears raised a flock of sheep from a pet lamb." The pet lamb was, of course, the first watch that he sold by mail. The flock of sheep numbered thousands of items in the catalog that brought him business.[18]

Further, the decision to be a mail-order house rather than a retail store operator freed Sears from the constraints of geography. The word "market" had until the late nineteenth century usually referred to a place where goods were bought and sold. The mail-order method of doing business, by contrast, spelled the conquest of geography.[19] An Oregonian and a Virginian who wanted to purchase a shotgun could now constitute part of a shotgun market, even though they lived thousands of miles apart.

Sears was selling general merchandise, an appropriately vague description of a vaguely delimited set of products, to the general public. But why was the general public buying? The answer was price. Richard Sears was "firm in his belief that the strongest argument for the average customer was a sensationally low price."[20]

Experience demonstrated the accuracy of this judgment time and again. Take sewing machines. Sears machines were priced at $15.55 to $17.55 at a time (1897) when branded, nationally advertised machines were priced three to six times higher. Other mail-order competitors were in the vicinity of Sears's prices with their own nonbranded makes, but as Sears's catalog proudly and loudly trumpeted, the "world's cheapest supply house" was "the great price maker." The price on the $16.55 model was cut by $3.05 in September of 1897. An avalanche of orders followed immediately.

> Sears was intoxicated. He persuaded the manufacturer to lower his price to the company by one dollar per machine, down to $9.50. Then Sears, Roebuck likewise chopped its price—to $12.50. In October 19,000 orders made their way to the company.[21]

By the turn of the century, Sears was selling sewing machines for $7.65.

This was fun, and Sears was always on the lookout for other products on which to cut price and, in the phraseology of a later generation of Sears buyers, to "sell the hell" out of. Alvah C. Roebuck believed that the sewing machine price-cutting experience

> was the most important step toward the future great success of the business. This policy was quickly extended to the sale of buggies, harness[es], wagons, bicycles, cream separators, baby carriages, stoves, etc. and with this done, the growth of the business was phenomenal.[22]

Of the products Roebuck mentioned, none was more successful than the cream separator. Sears, Roebuck was already selling cream separators when Sears himself first realized the product's potential. It could save the farmer hours of drudgery and aggravation. Those who could afford it apparently felt that the $100 price of the standard model was not unreasonable. Sears, Roebuck's own cream separator was selling at the highly competitive price of $62.50; but it was not, in 1902, selling well. The company was actually losing money on it.

However, once Sears saw firsthand what this product meant to the American farmer, he was ablaze with excitement over the prospects. Just by looking at the machine, he could tell how much more cheaply it could be sold. Where competitors saw the opportunity for a skimming strategy (no pun intended), Sears saw the chance for a coup through penetration pricing. He brought out three sizes in 1903 at $27, $35, and $39.50. The prices caused a sensation, and sales and profits skyrocketed.[23] Table 5–1 compares the sales and profits of the cream separator to those of the company in general from 1902 to 1908. This product had become a bulwark of the company in less than a decade. In the words of Louis E. Asher:

TABLE 5-1

*Sears Cream Separator Sales and Profits Compared to Company Sales
and Profits, 1902–1908
(in thousands)*

Year	Cream Separator Sales	Company Sales	Cream Separator Net Profit	Company Profit
1902	$ 272.3	$15,945.4	$ − 17.0	$1,215.8
1903	474.6	23,252.6	5.5	1,768.6
1904	696.0	27,692.7	18.8	2,276.8
1905	1,533.1	37,789.4	103.3	2,868.1
1906	1,865.4	—	244.1	—
1907	1,582.9	50,722.8[a]	192.9	3,238.5[a]
1908	1,316.2	40,843.9[a]	375.2	2,034.8[a]

[a]Fiscal year ending June 30.
SOURCE: Boris Emmet and John E. Jeuck, *Catalogues and Counters: A History of Sears, Roebuck and Company* (Chicago: University of Chicago Press, 1950), 112, 172.

There is an inner logic in the fact that the two outstanding triumphs in merchandising were the sewing machine and the cream separator; time and labor-saving devices for the home and the farm. Valuable customers—the housewife and the farmer. Potent markets—the home and the farm.[24]

"In a real sense," Boris Emmet and John E. Jeuck observed, "the cornerstone of the business was a low-price policy."[25] How were these prices achieved? How was Sears, Roebuck able to sell merchandise profitably at prices below the costs of the traditional competition? The answer is through deals to get the goods, through the elimination of the middleman, and through huge volume made possible by the catalog.

RELATIONS WITH MANUFACTURERS

Sears took the risk out of manufacturing because its marketing muscle guaranteed steady demand. As a result, the manufacturer could increase his fixed investment in property, plant, and equipment, secure in the knowledge that his plant would run full and steady. With this increased investment, unit costs dropped. In addition, the manufacturer incurred no marketing expenses—there was no need for a sales force, market research, or advertising. The manufacturer's marketing function was assumed by Sears, one of the greatest marketing machines of all time.

There were a variety of arrangements with manufacturers. For example, in the early 1900s, Andrew Fyrberg, a gunsmith in Worcester, Massachusetts, came to the attention of the company. Fyrberg produced about fifteen single-barrel shotguns a day, which he sold through a jobber. Having learned of Fyrberg through his buyer, Sears went to Worcester to meet him and look over his shop and also invited Fyrberg to Chicago. It was there that the deal was struck. "The business interview," according to Asher, "went something like this":

> "Mr. Fyrberg, have you enough capital to finance yourself for an output of 50 guns a day—or even 100 guns a day?" "No, Mr. Sears—unless I sell some property which is bringing me in a good income."
>
> "How much capital would you need to increase your product to 100 guns a day?" Sears asked.
>
> Fyrberg figured with pencil and paper, considered the cost of new machinery, dies, tools, jigs—"$25,000," he said.
>
> "How much for 200 a day?" Sears asked.
>
> "Oh, $35,000 to $40,000."
>
> At this point, Sears explained to Fyrberg that should Sears put up the money to enable Fyrberg to turn out 200 guns a day, he would have to incorporate the business, make a stock company, issuing stock to himself for the value of his plant and stock to Sears, Roebuck for their capital. As Sears explained what a stock company was, Fyrberg began to grasp what it would mean to him to have a new factory building large enough to make at least 200 guns a day and the machinery to make the guns. On the basis of cost plus 10%, Fyrberg accepted the offer, with the additional benefits of a salary for himself, as general manager, at $5,000 a year, and salaries for his two sons who were to receive $2,500 a year each.[26]

Not long afterward, Fyrberg's daily output was 300 single-barrel shotguns, 300 revolvers, and 50 double-barrel shotguns.[27]

What we have here is the coming of the twentieth century to another product and its manufacturer. A small plant is scaled up. Stock is issued. A proprietor becomes a salaried manager. Costs drop. Volume grows.

Sears did the same for other manufacturers as well. The company assumed a financial interest in at least nine factories by 1906, and that number grew to over thirty by the end of World War I.[28] This partial backward integration was undertaken because in some instances manufacturers were reluctant to sell to Sears in fear of pressure from their other customers and in other instances because the goods Sears wanted to sell simply were unavailable. Thus, the visible hand of managerial coordination did reach backward from Sears to the manufacturer, but it did so more out of necessity than as part of an aggressive hunt for profit opportunity. For the most part, moreover, Sears preferred not to take a manufacturer's complete output because it wanted the market to discipline the supplier.

ELIMINATING THE MIDDLEMAN

When it came to the distributive process itself, however, Sears willingly took complete control. Its capacity to cut costs was striking. Although this capacity varied according to product line, an analysis, published in 1916 and approved by Sears, provides a general picture of the company's impact on the distribution discount structure (see tables 5–2 and 5–3). By this calculation, Sears, through internalizing wholesaling functions formerly performed by smaller independent merchants in market transactions, could deliver a product to the consumer for 22 percent less.[29] This was an impressive achievement of the administrative coordination of the flow of a large volume of goods.

TABLE 5–2

Retail Price of an Article with a Manufacturer's Selling Price of $1.00 Sold Through the Traditional Distribution System

Cost to wholesaler or jobber		$1.00
Net profit to wholesaler or jobber		
(5 percent of cost)	$0.05	
Expenses of wholesaler or jobber		
(15 percent of selling price)	0.18	0.23
Cost to retailer		$1.23
Net profit to retailer		
(10 percent of cost)	0.12	
Expenses of retailer		
(23 percent of selling price)	0.40	0.52
Retail price		$1.75

SOURCE: Reprint of Theodore H. Price, "The Mail Order Business," *The Outlook*, 26 Jan. 1916, in Julius Rosenwald papers, University of Chicago, p. 3.

TABLE 5–3

Retail Price of an Article with a Manufacturer's Selling Price of $1.00 Sold by Sears

Cost to retail mail-order house		$1.00
Net profit to mail-order house		
(10% of cost)	$ .10	
Expense of mail-order house		
(20% of selling price)	0.27	0.37
Retail price		$1.37

SOURCE: Reprint of Theodore H. Price, "The Mail Order Business," *The Outlook*, 26 Jan. 1916, in Julius Rosenwald papers, University of Chicago, p. 3.

The mail-order catalog was the most effective means of mass selling in the rural United States prior to the development of network television in the 1950s. Selling through the mails was not new in the 1880s. In colonial America, wealthier settlers sometimes bought by mail from abroad. Purchase by correspondence was also not unknown in the early nineteenth century to Americans moving westward. In 1870, E. C. Allen invented the mail-order journal, which contained, in addition to its editorial matter, advertisements for various items available from Allen through the mail.[30] Two years later, Aaron Montgomery Ward, working from a 12-by-14-foot office over a livery stable in Chicago, issued a 1-page handbill listing the few items he was selling. This handbill was followed by nine more until he published his first genuine catalog in 1874.[31]

The Ward catalog measured 3 by 5 inches and was a mere 8 pages in length, but it grew to 72 pages in just two years. Its cover succinctly declared Ward's policy: "Cheapest Cash House in America . . . Grangers, Farmers, Mechanics, Supplied with a Full Line of Dry Goods, Clothing, Hats, Caps, Boots, Shoes, etc., etc., At the Lowest Wholesale Prices."[32] Ward was the true pioneer in this business. His catalog made him the first great mail-order merchant.

Purveying goods by mail had a number of advantages. These included a larger-sized potential market and the ability to offer a wider variety of goods to farmers and residents of villages or small towns (the population of which constituted the great majority of Americans throughout the nineteenth century) than these people could ever have purchased without traveling great distances. In the words of an advertisement for a catalog as late as 1923, "This Book Brings New York to Your Door."[33] The catalog was a key device in bringing market relations to rural America.

There were also problems in mail-order selling. Some of these are aptly summed up by Daniel Boorstin:

> Montgomery Ward's business depended on the confidence of a buyer in a seller whom he had never seen. . . . [I]t had been the farmer's custom to buy his store goods from an old acquaintance, the country storekeeper, and even then only after close inspection. A. Montgomery Ward built his business on his hope for a revolution in farmers' buying habits.[34]

To gain the trust of its market, Montgomery Ward secured the endorsement of the National Grange of the Patrons of Husbandry. Founded in 1867, the Granger movement was a farm-based pressure group. It agitated on such issues as railroad and warehouse regulation and also sought to increase the efficiency of the marketing of farm products and to lower the costs of the goods farmers purchased. By the mid-1870s, the Grange boasted 800,000 members, heavily concentrated in the Midwest. Signed testimonials from officers in the Grange adorned Ward's catalog and flyers. The first picture in the catalog was of the official Granger hat.[35]

The Ward guarantee was another method of establishing that the firm was trustworthy. The first leaflet carried the phrase "Satisfaction Guaranteed—or your money back." The company offered to pay handling charges both ways. Another technique to inspire trust in the company was what would today be called an effort to humanize it. Catalogs contained pictures of the company's founders, of its executives, and of the buyers of individual lines, and the product guarantees were signed by these individuals. In addition, Ward made an effort to respond specifically to the letters of inquiry it received.

Such letters about products were often predictable, but some of the correspondence that the company received is quite startling to the modern reader. For example:

> I suppose you wonder why we haven't ordered anything from you since the fall. Well, the cow kicked my arm and broke it and besides my wife was sick, and there was the doctor bill. But now, thank God, that is paid, and we are all well again, and we have a fat new baby boy, and please send plush bonnet number 29d8077. . . .[36]

It is probably safe to say that no one at Ward was actually spending any time wondering why this particular customer had not ordered anything since the fall. The letter strikes one as mildly ludicrous but also rather touching in both tone and content, because the author was transferring a community attitude that would be quite appropriate when dealing with a local country storekeeper to the context of a mass-selling situation in which the merchant neither knew the purchaser nor cared about him or her as an individual.

By the time Sears issued his first catalog, Ward had been in business for a decade and a half and had already established its consumer franchise. Other firms such as Spiegel, Macy's, May, Stern, and the National Cloak and Suit Company were going into mail-order selling in the 1880s.[37] But Sears and Ward were in a class by themselves in terms of volume of business, variety of merchandise, and extent of geographic focus. Stores like Macy's, May, and Stern were city-based. They did not really understand the rural market. To them it was an afterthought. Those mail-order houses that did make a major effort to serve the rural market usually sold a narrow line. National Cloak and Suit, for example, specialized, as the name suggests, in apparel.

Sears was able to surpass Ward because he managed his catalog with greater skill and *élan*. Sears was in love with his catalog, and no moonstruck lover ever studied his mistress's habits with greater care and concentration. He loved the catalog because it brought him that which he loved above all else—sales—and the thrill of persuading people with whom he did not even have the advantage of face-to-face contact to do what he wanted them to do. Not just the money, but this psychic conquest was, one senses, the true reward Sears wanted from his company. When forced to choose in 1907 and 1908 between yet greater volume at the cost of operational chaos or retrenchment and system, he opted unquestioningly for the former. "In my humble opinion we must have volume—whether it be easy in the boat or not. Our very life *Demands Volume*—and if one hot fire doesn't get it I would build more fires."[38] This was at a time when sound business judgment called for retrenchment. But there was no thrill for Sears in that.

Most of the policies Sears pursued were known in the mail-order trade prior to his taking them up. Others guaranteed their goods, but none promoted their guarantees with Sears's panache. Sears not only guaranteed his watches, he guaranteed the parts therein. He is said to have once replaced a watch that a streetcar conductor had dropped with the declaration: "We guarantee our watches not to fall out of people's pockets and break."[39] Apocryphal? Perhaps. But the circulation of such stories said much about people's affection for the company.

Other companies advertised low prices, but Sears could promote items with skill matched by few. He had a shrewd sense for the dramatic price cut on big-ticket durable items like the cream separator and the sewing machine.

Others sold C.O.D., but none were as proud of it as Sears. And none understood what an important gesture it was to the consumer. Sears knew that he had to trust the customer before he could ask for trust in return. Montgomery Ward was grudging in its C.O.D. policy.[40] But Sears told the world in numberless advertisements to "Send No Money." Sears executive Louis E. Asher said the company was built on those "three simple words":

The "Send No Money" advertisements violated every rule of good advertising except one—the advertisements pulled! As Sears once said, "They almost pulled the ink off the paper." They were unattractive to the eye, set in crowded five-point type that was hard to read. There was no white space. But every ad carried the magic three-word message in heavy black type: "Send No Money," followed by the simple directions: "Cut out and return this ad."[41]

The Sears Catalog: One of the greatest selling tools in the history of marketing. The cover reprinted here is from a turn-of-the-century edition, proudly touting Sears, Roebuck as the "Cheapest Supply House on Earth."

Others advertised their wares in publications in addition to the catalog, but none spent the way Sears did. The *Mail Order Journal* asserted in 1901 that Sears was the largest mail-order advertiser in the nation.[42] It may have been the largest advertiser of any description. Expenditures of $400,000 in 1898 climbed to $1.5 million in 1902 and to $3.5 million six years later.

Other catalog merchants sought a wide circulation for their big books. Both Sears and Ward distributed their catalogs without charge beginning in 1904. But Sears's various schemes led to a greater circulation than any competitor. In 1905, Sears tried an experiment in Iowa. He shipped two dozen catalogs to each good customer who agreed to act as a distributor. Each of these distributors passed out the catalogs to twenty-four neighbors and supplied the names of those neighbors to the company. The distributors received premiums based on how much the new customers ordered. Thus the distributors were encouraged to act as personal salespeople for the company.

This worked so well that Sears decided to "Iowaize," as he put it, the nation. Circulation of the general catalog was 318,000 in 1897; in 1902, that figure (including both the spring and fall books) was 1,591,727; in 1905, 3,800,724 catalogs were distributed; and in 1908, 6,582,542 books were mailed out.[43] The business life of Sears was a parade of deals— scores, hundreds, thousands of deals—with customers and suppliers after the fashion of this Iowa-ization scheme.

And, finally, other catalogs featured selling copy. But no copy sold like Sears's. Said Henry Goldman of Goldman, Sachs, "I think he could sell a breath of air."[44]

From Sears to Rosenwald

Whether or not Sears could sell a breath of air, he could and sometimes did sell what he had not yet bought. When suit salesman Sam Hayman of the New York clothing firm of Newborg, Rosenberg and Company called on him, Sears placed an order for 10,000 suits, a huge number. Hayman told Sears it would be best to deal with the firm's Chicago branch, Rosenwald and Company.[45] Similarly, when Sears went to Arnold Schwinn to order 50,000 bicycles, Schwinn thought he meant 5,000. Sears told Schwinn just to worry about making them, he would take care of selling them.[46] The same sort of thing happened when Sears went to Julius Rosenwald's shop. Could he possibly sell so many suits, Sears was asked. The role of buyer and seller was being reversed, with the seller the one urging caution. The suits were sold already, Sears replied. And often they were. Sears believed in "Get[ting] the orders first, don't worry about delays and the warehousing."[47]

Rosenwald had heard about Sears and his business prior to their encounter in 1895, but it was the size of these suit orders that dramatized for him the fact that Sears, Roebuck was turning into something big and important. He and his brother-in-law, Aaron E. Nusbaum, bought in. On 23 August 1895, Sears, Roebuck was reincorporated under an Illinois charter with a capitalization of $150,000. Sears held 800 shares; Nusbaum and Rosenwald each held 350 shares, for which they each paid $35,000. Three years later, each of the three partners held 500 shares. After much acrimony, Sears and Rosenwald bought Nusbaum out for $1,250,000 in

1901. For Rosenwald, though, Sears stock was to mean accumulation of one of the great American fortunes.

There was always a sense of tension about Richard Sears. He seemed to feel he was only as good as his last deal or his last great ad. He had difficulty believing in the longevity of his business.[48] Where had all this money come from? It had come out of his own imagination, out of the advertisements he wrote down on pieces of paper. In *King Henry the Fourth, Part One,* Owen Glendower says to Hotspur: "I can call spirits from the vasty deep." To which Hotspur replies: "Why, so can I, or so can any man; but will they come when you do call for them?" At the turn of the century, the United States was full of men summoning spirits. Richard Sears was one of the very few for whom they came when he did call for them. But would they keep coming? What if they stopped? Richard Sears was the marketing equivalent of Henry Ford. Ford focused on manufacturing to the neglect of management. Sears focused on marketing to the neglect of management. When management became essential because of the huge number of orders Sears's advertisements were generating, he left the company and seemed to lose interest in it altogether.

Julius Rosenwald was a different kind of man with a different agenda. Rosenwald was born in Springfield, Illinois, in 1862. His father and mother were German Jews who had emigrated in 1854 and 1853, respectively. Both had lived their early years in the rear of their families' clothing stores. Samuel Rosenwald met Augusta Hammerslough in Baltimore. He had been a peddler on the Winchester trail in Virginia, while her family had already established a clothing business in Baltimore. A month after their marriage in 1857 the couple went West, with Rosenwald acting as a representative of his in-laws' family firm, eventually settling in Springfield.

Julius Rosenwald thus grew up in the clothing trade. He was apprenticed to reasonably well-established relatives and quickly learned retailing, wholesaling, and manufacturing. It was a tough business, and during the 1880s and 1890s, Rosenwald experienced his share of failure as well as success.[49]

In his mid-30s, Rosenwald probably would not have struck an observer as a particularly noteworthy man. He was smart but not brilliant, decent but not, it would seem, terribly warm. He was ambitious but not extravagantly so. In the 1890s, he remarked to a business associate that his goal was to have an annual income of $15,000, to be devoted in equal part to personal expenses, saving, and charity.[50] This was not a small sum, but it was a mere pittance compared to the enormous fortune he eventually accumulated. His ambition was to be a burgher, and he wound up a prince.

Yet Rosenwald did exhibit a number of traits that were to serve him well through the trials of his business life. One was his intense sanity and grip on reality, a critical corrective to the dream world of Sears. The picture that comes down to us of Sears is of a child surrounded by vast quantities of orders for goods he had advertised but did not own. Could these goods be delivered profitably? Could they be delivered at all?[51] Stories of operational confusion were endless. There was the customer who wrote to complain that the goods ordered had not been shipped, only to have the company respond by mistakenly shipping a dozen sewing machines, or bicycles, or whatever the case may have been. These would, of course, be returned, but at company expense. And such sloppiness wrought havoc with inventory records. Then there was the customer letter which, though fictitious, said a lot about the firm's efficiency:

> We are still waiting for the special $5.95 baby carriage we ordered for our little son. Better change the order to a single barrel shotgun and a plug of chewing tobacco. The kid is growing up.[52]

Unlike Sears, Rosenwald was a systematizer and institution builder. The development of the mail-order business, he said in 1923,

> has been made possible through the cooperation of a large corps of trained experts. Organization, efficiency, system—they are the mainstays of the structure that has been built up in the last few decades. It has not been necessary to push the business; but it has frequently required much effort to keep up with it.[53]

A key architect of Sears's efficiency was Otto C. Doering. It was Doering who worked out the famous schedule system that made it possible during the early 1900s to process 100,000 pieces of mail per day with dazzling speed. How fast? In the words of an instruction booklet, "No order must be held longer than 24 hours for any reason."[54] Here is how the 1905 catalog described the great Chicago mail-order processing plant, then nearing completion:

> Miles of railroad tracks run lengthwise through, in, and around this building for the receiving, moving, and forwarding of merchandise; elevators, mechanical conveyors, endless chains, moving sidewalks, gravity chutes, apparatus and conveyors, pneumatic tubes, and every known mechanical appliance for reducing labor, for the working out of economy and dispatch is to be utilized here in our great Works.[55]

Many people came to Chicago to inspect this modern marvel. One of them, it is said, was Henry Ford.[56]

Rosenwald did not share Sears's view that the mail-order business could be run only by lighting one "hot fire" after another. Consumers bought from the company not because it had cast a spell over them but because it sold what they wanted to buy at a price they were willing to pay and delivered the goods promptly. Because Rosenwald understood the needs of the company, he was able to modulate his strategy in the face of different circumstances. Sears, on the other hand, knew but one command: attack.

Another of Rosenwald's key traits was his ability to withstand severe interpersonal conflict in the service of his company's goals and of his own. His decision in 1901 to join with Sears to buy out his brother-in-law Aaron Nusbaum (with whom neither he nor Sears could get along) was a difficult one. He felt he owed Nusbaum much for bringing him into the company. And having to endure Nusbaum's enraging demand for more money after he and Sears thought the deal had been agreed on was a dreadful trial.[57]

Equally difficult was the deterioration of Rosenwald's relationship with Sears. True, Sears had shown himself to be a man who, by 1907, was unable to comprehend what the business that bore his name had become. The contempt he showed for the elementary demands of good business—an attitude similar to, if not quite as noxious as, Henry Ford's in the 1920s—was inexcusable. Nevertheless, it is one of the most difficult things in business and perhaps in life to part from a man with whom one has worked for over a decade and with whom one has made a vast fortune. Rosenwald succeeded as a businessman by "appreciating his own limitations, and surrounding himself with experts."[58] Rosenwald was no advertising copywriter, and in Sears he had as a partner the expert of experts. But, as with Nusbaum, the break had to be made; and as with Nusbaum, Rosenwald persevered. He was "a good man in a storm."[59] The depression of 1921 would have ruined the company had he not saved it. And he had to pledge his personal fortune to do so.

Another trait, in addition to Rosenwald's level-headedness and personal toughness, that helped him emerge as a great leader of the firm was the high standard of conduct to which he held his firm and himself. Richard Sears understood the importance of trust in business, and he did much to build it up between customer and company. "Honesty is the best policy," he used to say to Rosenwald. "I know because I've tried it both ways."[60] Early in his career, Sears had run advertisements that were misleading and, in some instances, plainly untrue. Some of his customers in the late 1880s must have wondered whether he was a merchant or a

Some catalog items in the early years were of questionable efficacy, for example the "Bust Developer and Bust Cream" (above), the "Electricating Liniment" (below), and the "Blood Builder" cancer cure (opposite page).

ELECTRICATING LINIMENT.

A NEW AND GREAT DISCOVERY.

NOTHING BEFORE HAS BEEN KNOWN LIKE IT. By a newly discovered process this liniment is electrically charged by a powerful current of electricity, whereby the ingredients undergo a powerful change which, when applied to the most severe cases of Rheumatism, Sprains and Bruises, effects immediate relief. It never fails in its Magical Effect.

Certain cure for Rheumatism, Cuts, Sprains, Wounds, Old Sores, Corns, Galls, Bruises, Growing Pains, Contracted Muscles, Lame Back, Stiff Joints, Frosted Feet, Chilblains, Etc. Persons suffering from partial paralysis of arms and legs will be rendered great benefit by its use, frequently regaining complete use of these members, also an application to the Throat and Chest and externally for Lung Troubles; great relief will be experienced by rubbing the chest with this, the most penetrating liniment in the world. TRY IT.

No. D1550.   Price, bottles, 29c; per doz. $3.00

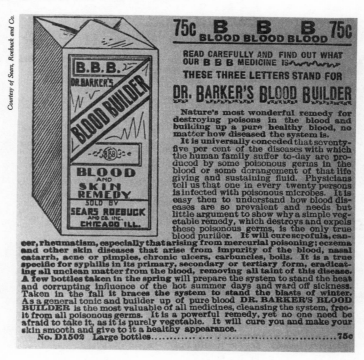

practical joker.[61] Rosenwald, by contrast, was honest not because it was the best policy. Nor had he tried it both ways. He was honest because he did not know how to be otherwise, which is why he set about to expunge from the catalog unconscionable products.[62]

Under Rosenwald, sales and profits grew strongly, if irregularly, because of the postwar disaster suffered by so many American firms, as table 5–4 indicates. By the time Rosenwald terminated his active involvement in the firm, after three decades of service (more than half of it as chief executive) Sears, Roebuck had become established as the nation's leading mail-order house and leading purveyor of general merchandise. New factories had been purchased. New distribution branches had been opened.[63] An organizational structure reasonably well suited to the demands of the business had been fashioned. A great crisis—the postwar depression—had been weathered.

To be sure, failures had been experienced. But the numbers in table 5–4 speak louder than they.

TABLE 5–4

Sales and Profits of Sears, 1908–1925
(in millions)

Calendar Year	Net Sales	Net Profit or Loss
1908[a]	$ 40.8	$ 2.0
1909	51.0	6.2
1910	61.3	6.8
1911	64.1	7.0
1912	77.1	8.3
1913	91.4	9.0
1914	96.0	9.1
1915	106.2	11.1
1916	137.2	16.5
1917	165.8	14.1
1918	181.7	12.7
1919	234.0	18.9
1920	245.4	11.7
1921	164.0	−16.4
1922	166.5	5.4
1923	198.5	11.5
1924	206.4	14.4
1925	243.8	21.0

[a]Fiscal year ending 30 June 1908.
SOURCE: Boris Emmet and John E. Jeuck, *Catalogues and Counters: A History of Sears, Roebuck and Company* (Chicago: University of Chicago Press, 1950), 301. Copyright 1950 by the University of Chicago. All rights reserved.

The 1920s: Decade of Decision

Two decisions were taken in the 1920s that continue to influence Sears to this day. One was that Robert E. Wood was chosen to be chief executive officer. The other was that Sears would open retail stores.

ROBERT E. WOOD

Julius Rosenwald spent most of the period from late 1916 to early 1920 away from the firm. He served on the Advisory Commission of the Council of National Defense during World War I, and his mission to France in 1918 at the request of the Secretary of War took a toll on him.[64] Despite Rosenwald's absence, Sears did well, benefiting from wartime prosperity. At its height in 1920, Sears stock reached $243 a share.

The following year, however, the bottom fell out. Prices collapsed, leaving mail-order concerns, which operated on long-term contracts and whose method of business made it difficult to take markdowns on a timely basis, severely exposed. Sales volume plummeted, inventories skyrocketed, and so did losses. Robert E. Wood later said that living through this experience "made Mr. Rosenwald an old man."[65] During the worst of it, Rosenwald was further saddened by the death of his mother. The company pulled through, thanks in part to Rosenwald's donation to its treasury of 50,000 shares of his stock. (He took an option to buy them back at par of $100 a share within three years.)[66] By the end of 1922, the crisis was abating, providing a weary Rosenwald with the welcome opportunity to begin thinking about retirement.

Rosenwald's views on executive succession reveal much about what he thought was most important for the future of his firm. He set out to find a man who was young, so that the company could benefit from continuity of leadership, and who was not yet rich, so that he would have the incentive to drive himself and his employees. These qualifications were sensible enough, but the remaining requirement—that the successor come from the railroad industry—is more surprising. Not only did Rosenwald want to go outside the company for a successor, he wanted to go outside the industry.

He turned to the railroads because of his World War I experience, in which he had been impressed with the administrative skills of the railroad executives whom he had met during those years. Thus, his analysis of what had gone wrong with Sears during the 1920–1921 depression and the challenges the future held led to the belief that coordinating the vast enterprise that Sears had become was the key task facing the next generation of leadership.

Sears had become a complex business. Branch mail-order plants had been established in Dallas in 1906, Seattle in 1910, and Philadelphia in 1920.[67] The number of product lines the company handled had vastly increased, as had overall sales. This expansion was made possible by the high degree of independence allowed to the buyers. Rosenwald and his colleague, company treasurer Albert Loeb, conceived of the firm as a "federation of merchants."[68] Decentralization was critical to expansion because it put the responsibility for working out the details involved in bringing tens of thousands of different products to market on the shoulders of those closest to the situation. On the other hand, the lack of central coordination heightened the danger of inventory crises and made it difficult for the firm to present a consistent image to the consumer. In Rosenwald's view, the company needed a manager, not a merchant, to cope with such problems. This is a clear indication of how far he felt it had come since the "hot fire" days of Richard Sears.

The man chosen to do this big job was the 44-year-old executive vice-president of the Illinois Central Railroad, Charles M. Kittle, who took up his new responsibilities on 1 November 1924. Kittle was an able man in many ways but difficult to deal with. He "was brusque and ruthless. He treated Rosenwald and other executives of the company with little respect. . . ."[69]

The company grew quickly under Kittle's regime. New mail-order plants were established in Kansas City, Atlanta, Memphis, and Los Angeles. Twenty-seven retail stores were also established. Sales increased by 1927 to over $277.5 million and profits to more than $25 million.[70] Suddenly and unexpectedly, though, on the second day of 1928, Kittle died of septicemia following an operation for gallstones. He was 47.[71]

Rosenwald was once again confronted with the problem of executive succession. This time he turned not to the railroads but to a man he had hired simultaneously with Kittle as the new vice-president of factories and retail stores, Robert E. Wood.

In his early life, Robert Wood had many of the best experiences that an America entering its early adulthood had to offer a strong-willed, well-disciplined, virile, and unafraid young man. He was born on 13 June 1879, in Kansas City, Missouri, to a mother whose father had emigrated from Ireland and a father who had served as a captain in the Civil War, prospected for gold in the West, and finally settled down to a rock-ribbed Republican life as a coal and ice merchant.

Due to the state of the family's finances, Robert attended West Point (which was tuition-free) rather than Yale. In 1900, he graduated thirteenth in a class of fifty-four and was immediately shipped off to the Philippine insurrection. Two years later, he was back in the United States, at Fort Assiniboine, Montana. For a young man, he later recalled

> it was a fascinating life. You could drop your reins on your horse's neck and you could ride 100 miles in any direction with no fences. We were only 15 miles from the Canadian line . . . , and the country was all virgin prairie. The plow had never touched it. We used to ride up to a mountie post at Medicine Hat. But there were no people there. Plenty of game, geese, prairie chickens. . . .[72]

Wood craved adventure, and the place for that was not in Montana but on the isthmus of Panama where the government of the United States was undertaking its biggest project since the defeat of the Confederacy. Panama was a deathtrap, as the French had learned in the 1880s and the

Americans were in the process of learning in the 1900s.[73] A variety of dreadful diseases were taking away thousands in the prime of life. In the summer of 1905, as Wood was heading south, three-quarters of the Americans at work on the project were heading in the opposite direction back home. To health warnings, Wood jauntily replied, "I don't intend to get sick."[74]

Clearly, Wood did not care much about physical comfort. He could be equally at home without complaint in Montana and in Panama. Just as clearly, he was far more intrigued by opportunity and adventure than he was frightened by the attendant hazards. Lastly, he had that for which there is no substitute in life—luck. No one who went to Panama intended to get sick. Many did. Many died. Wood did not. Doubtless, Wood's remark about his intentions was meant in jest. But one wonders the extent to which it suggests a man with an iron confidence in the power of his intentions over the forces of the world, natural as well as human.

In the Army on the Canal, Wood learned business:

> Without knowing it, I was getting a wonderful education . . . I had the whole supply system of the Canal. I was chief procurement officer. . . . I was buying steel rails, locomotives, cars, and spare parts and I learned the principle of handling inventory.[75]

Wood loved the work. Indeed, of all the executives discussed in this book, Wood appears to have enjoyed life more and to have been less careworn than any of the others.[76]

Wood, at the time a major, retired from the Army to begin his career in business in 1915. A brief stint with Du Pont was succeeded by a position with the General Asphalt Company. Wood rejoined the Army with America's entry into World War I, serving under General George W. Goethals, who had been his boss on the Canal. Goethals made him acting quartermaster general.

In March of 1919, Wood retired from the Army for the second time, and his first job offer was not long in coming. Robert J. Thorne, the president of Ward, wanted Wood for his firm. At first glance, Wood's qualifications for a position at Ward were not obvious. He had no experience in the industry nor did he have any of those instincts retailers prize so much and with which Richard Sears, for example, was so richly endowed. In 1951, Wood himself observed that

> I must confess I fall very far short in some of the qualifications of a successful retailer—I have no style sense, no eye for display, and am no judge of advertising copy, either catalogue, radio or newspaper. . . .[77]

On the other hand, as his biographer James C. Worthy has observed, Wood may have learned through his war work "more than any man then living about merchandise sources, mass buying techniques, and supply logistics."[78] Robert Thorne had worked with Wood during the war and observed his organizational expertise and ability. His idea was to put them to work for his firm.

Thorne's idea was a good one. In fact, it might have resulted in the transformation of Ward from a perennial "also-ran" to market leader. But Wood was unable to get along with Thorne's successor, Theodore F. Merseles; and he was fired in 1924.

Wood shared the prejudices of his background and, when first approached about Sears, worried to a friend about getting involved in "a Jewish family firm."[79] He was reassured, perhaps with the help of a generous compensation package; and he joined the company on the same day Kittle did as vice-president for factories and retail stores (of which at the time there were none).

On 11 January 1928, nine days after Kittle's death, Rosenwald made Wood president. News of this appointment brought two resignations: that of Otto C. Doering, the creator of the incomparable scheduling system, and of Max Adler, a brother-in-law of Rosenwald who had joined the company in 1898 and worked his way up to the vice-presidency of merchandising. The careers of both these men spanned Rosenwald's tenure as CEO and reached all the way back to Richard Sears. Both were men of unquestionable ability. They were affronted at being passed over in favor of Kittle and found it intolerable to be passed over again. With their departure, strong ties with the Richard Sears years were severed. Perhaps it was just as well. The company was about to embark on uncharted waters.

RETAIL STORES

In the 1920s, both Sears and Montgomery Ward made major investments in stores. Writing in 1962, Alfred D. Chandler, Jr., asserted that the entrance into direct retailing was "the most significant step in Sears's history."[80] Why did this constitute such a momentous move? What was so different about selling a customer a jacket, a screwdriver, or a bicycle in a store as opposed to through the mail?

In terms of efficiency and ease of operation, mail order has some noteworthy advantages over store-centered retailing. The selling job is undertaken by the catalog rather than by salespeople. The mail-order customer "practically waits upon himself" by making his selection from

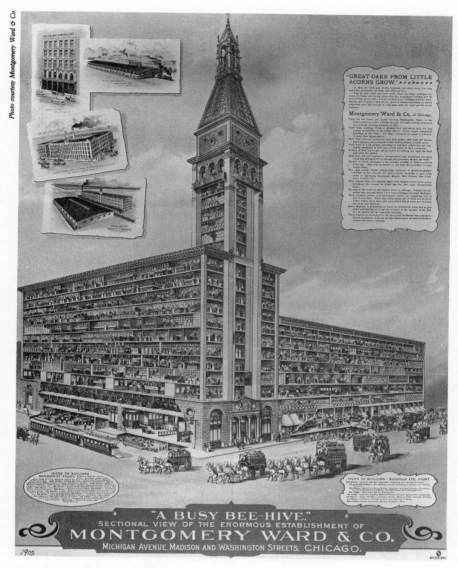

The headquarters of Sears's traditional rival, Montgomery Ward, in Chicago.

the catalog and filling out an order blank, which the mail-order house uses to process the goods and sometimes even returns to the customer as an invoice.[81] This system facilitates impressive economies in processing transactions. In the words of Julius Rosenwald:

> A continuous stream of customers in the shape of orders are in line to be waited on from 8 a.m. till closing time; their purchases selected in advance. . . . The

clerk has merely to take the goods from the shelf and have them wrapped. No high salaried salespeople, but 10 to 20 customers can be served in the time one would be in an "over-the-counter" retail store, and with only a fraction of [the] expense for rent.[82]

Second, the mail-order house, through a small number of large plants, could serve the whole nation rather than merely a metropolitan area. This made possible a greater volume than had been achieved by any other general merchandiser in the early 1900s (although, in the grocery line, A&P had far higher sales volume in the 1920s than did Sears). As a result of this volume, Sears's relations with its suppliers were fundamentally different from those of the store-centered merchant. "The buying of all large-volume items," Wood said in a 1932 speech,

> is based on a thorough knowledge of manufacturing costs, with actual inspection of factories, rather than on price comparisons brought in by manufacturing salesmen. . . .
> With [Sears's] quantities, to get uniform, reliable quality, with proper specifications, it is obviously impossible to flit from manufacturer to manufacturer wherever a lower price is presented; it is essential to ascertain in the beginning the best and lowest cost source, and to plan with and work with that source over long periods.[83]

In the case of the mail-order house, instead of a factory salesperson seeking a market for his goods, the distributor's buyer was seeking goods for his market. He knew more about those goods than a factory salesperson would be likely to tell him. Indeed, he often helped in the design of the goods and even in the purchase of the raw materials for their manufacture. This was specification buying. And Sears supported a laboratory to be certain that the goods purchased met the specifications agreed on.

A third advantage of mail order also derived from the size of the market served. Mail order was not "compelled to 'pinpoint' its operations to a particular city or even to a particular state. What mattered to a mail order plant was how any given item sold within its whole region. . . ."[84] Thus, extraordinary local occurrences, such as a crop failure or the failure of a major employer, might be less damaging to the mail-order house than to a store-centered retailer.

A whole constellation of other problems with which store-centered retailers had to cope and that mail-order operators were spared dealt with real estate. Where, precisely, did the store belong? How large should it be? Where should it be located vis-à-vis present and possible future competition?

Yet another set of dilemmas that the mail-order operator was spared concerned physical design. How should the store be laid out? What merchandise should be placed where? How much space should be allocated to each line? How similar should one store be to another?

Lastly, but probably most important, was the question of management. Every store has to have a manager capable of making merchandising and personnel decisions and of dealing with customers and with the local community. Where was this cadre of managers to come from? In the words of a Montgomery Ward pamphlet published around 1920:

> It is noteworthy that chain stores have been most successful when handling lines of low-priced merchandise which normally carry a large profit and which yield fair margins after the regular price has been cut. It is doubtful if a large chain of general merchandise stores can be successfully operated. The difficulty of securing a man of executive and merchandising ability for each store at a salary which the business would justify would be all but insurmountable. Men of this type are usually found to be engaged in business for themselves and could be employed, if at all, only at salaries that would endanger the success of the enterprise.[85]

The freedom from the need of such high-priced talent was thought to be a major operational advantage of mail order.

The mail-order method of merchandising was well suited to the rural market it served, especially in times of relative economic stability with prices neither rising nor falling quickly. The farm and village population constituted "an essentially conservative clientele" that was purchasing "staples and necessities."[86] The demand for style items was limited, and that which existed could not be satisfied by local merchants. In some rural areas, there were no local merchants; and those who did exist were probably less fashion-right than the goods in the Sears catalog. Mail-order merchandise, like the Model T Ford, appealed to a simple world, a world where commodities were purchased for their utility. In American cities in the 1920s, the merchant faced a very different customer. In this market, the mail-order operator had to cope with the defects of what in the rural context were virtues.

In the early 1930s, Sears was issuing two large catalogs annually, which had a circulation of five to seven million, and two small catalogs, which carried only 10 to 15 percent of the items in the big books and which had circulations of nine to twelve million. Before it received an order, the mail-order house invested $3 to $6 million up front in the catalog. Even "the simplest kind of a bulletin from the mail order house carrying only a limited number of items of merchandise costs into the hundreds of thousands of dollars."[87]

The lengthy lead times required by the mail-order merchant made pricing, in Wood's view, the "most difficult problem of the business."[88] Distribution of the spring catalog was scheduled to begin on January 15. The pricing for this book began in mid-October of the previous year and had to be completed by November 15. This book remained in circulation until August 15.

Thus, the mail-order house had to live with a fixed price for nine months. Unfortunately, the world rarely stood still for that long. What if commodity prices rose rapidly after the catalog prices were settled? A number of things could happen, none of them good. The buyer could try to renege on his contract with the manufacturer. He could tell the customer, anxious to buy his goods because the published catalog prices were so much lower than currently competitive offerings, that he was out of stock. Or the merchant could continue to make ever-increasing sales and ever-increasing losses. This is why, as Wood said, a "period of rapidly rising prices is the test of integrity and good faith for the mail order merchant."[89]

The mail-order merchant was equally ill-suited to manage in a falling market. Merchandise with high prices published in the catalog could not compete with the lower-priced goods of the store-based merchant, who could go back into the market and purchase goods for resale at the prevailing lower prices. The result was a decline in unit sales for the catalog, albeit with a higher gross profit. This is precisely what took place in the post–World War I cataclysm.

> In 1920, the initial drop in prices began in July and in September, when the book was in the hands of the customers, prices had fallen all the way from 20% to 60%. Catalog prices were too high, and the two great mail order houses were forced to sit by, with heavy inventories and rapidly declining sales and resulting enormous losses.[90]

The big-city department store was far more nimble. It did not price its goods many months in advance in accord with a plan worked out with the manufacturer. Its prices could be changed with a newspaper advertisement.

Sears was completely unfamiliar with this mode of operation. Its buyers may have been great, but they were mail-order buyers. They knew neither the urban customer nor the department store mode of operation. During the course of its history, Sears had undertaken sundry, desultory experiments with stores; but these had not come to much. Ever since Richard Sears had decided in the 1880s that he was not primarily a watch salesman who happened to do a lot of business by mail but rather primarily a salesman of mail-order merchandise who happened to do a lot of business in watches, Sears had defined itself as a mail-order company. What strengths did Sears bring to this new business to compensate for its weaknesses? Why would it be more successful than the firms already in the business?

A final caveat, if one was needed, concerning the proposal that Sears move from catalogs to counters was the mediocre performance of those companies that attempted to move in the opposite direction—from counters to catalogs. Macy's, for example, entered the mail-order business just after Montgomery Ward did and more than a decade before Sears. Eventually, Macy's catalog reached 460 pages in length. But it was consistently underpriced by Sears and "seems to have been eternally conscious—even plaintively envious—of the success" of the two mail-order giants.[91]

The differences in the two businesses were just as important from the department store's perspective as they were from the view of the mail-order firm. With the catalog, merchandise and price were etched in stone for more than half the year. Changes in style, however, made it "advantageous to dispose rapidly of stocks of goods carried for over-the-counter trade and to supplant those stocks with new styles."[92] The result was that department stores usually found themselves with separate stocks and different merchandising plans for their mail-order business. What was originally conceived of as building on a company's strengths by generating plus business at very little cost more often than not meant entering a new field altogether with no competitive advantage. Given such problems, it is not surprising that Macy's exited mail order in 1912.[93]

Robert Wood was the person most responsible for moving Sears into retail stores.[94] His accomplishment is impressive testimony to the ability of a determined and talented visionary to change the course of a business. To us, today, accustomed as we are to Sears stores throughout the nation, nothing seems more natural than that Sears should manage stores. Yet, we must keep in mind Maitland's dictum that things now in the past were once in the future. Sears's entry into retail appeared to mail-order executives in 1920 to be anything but inevitable. Indeed, in 1921, Ward's new president, the able Theodore Merseles, pigeonholed Wood's retail memorandum and three years later, in the biggest single mistake in the history of a firm that has been no stranger to mistakes, fired Wood.

If Wood had not been hired by Rosenwald, Sears's entry into store-centered retailing might well have been delayed. If Sears had not entered stores by 1930, the Depression might have made such a move far more difficult than it was in 1925. Table 5–5, showing the increase in the number of stores from 1925 to 1935, illustrates how the rate of growth slowed early in the Depression. If Sears had not built the stores in the

Depression, it is likely there would not have been any stores built during World War II. In actuality, the number of stores declined from 617 in 1941 to 604 in 1945.[95] Without the stores, the Depression would have been far more grim for Sears than it was in terms of sales, although the profit record in the early Depression is not as clear-cut. Table 5–6 compares the sales results of Sears's retail stores and the mail-order catalog from 1925 to 1935.

Available data do not provide a clear picture of store and mail-order profitability in the early years of the Depression. Mail-order profits declined, and combined factory and retail profits increased in 1931.[96] The following year was the worst year of the Depression. Sears reported a loss of over $2.5 million, the only loss the company had shown since 1921. Reflecting the collapse in farm income, mail-order sales declined to their 1915 level, when the company had three mail-order plants rather than ten. Nevertheless, mail order reported a profit of over $3 million.

Retail, on the other hand, suffered a loss of over $4 million in 1932. These losses were the result of heavy, one-time charges associated with various store openings and closings. The government did not allow some of these charges, and thus the company in 1932 reported losses while the government required that it pay taxes on over $1 million in profits. Further, the *Annual Report* cites the decline in commodity prices as causing heavy retail markdowns, but it is not clear why that would have been harder on the retail than on the mail-order operations.[97]

We do know that after 1932, the stores did much better, as did the company as a whole. Indeed, the Depression was over for Sears after that year. Net sales exceeded the pre-Depression high in 1936. They topped one billion in 1945. In the first full year of peace, net sales passed $1.6

TABLE 5–5

Number of Sears Retail Stores, 1925–1935

Year	Number of Stores	Year	Number of Stores
1925	8	1931	378
1926	9	1932	374
1927	27	1933	400
1928	192	1934	416
1929	319	1935	428
1930	338		

SOURCE: Boris Emmet and John E. Jeuck, *Catalogues and Counters: A History of Sears, Roebuck and Company* (Chicago: University of Chicago Press, 1950), 487. Copyright 1950 by the University of Chicago. All rights reserved.

TABLE 5-6

Sears's Gross Sales, Mail Order vs. Retail, 1925-1935
(in millions)

Year	Mail-Order Sales	Retail Sales	Total Gross Sales	Percentage of Retail
1925	$246.5	$ 11.8	$258.3	4.5 %
1926	249.3	23.0	272.3	8.5
1927	253.1	40.0	293.1	13.6
1928	240.1	107.2	347.3	30.9
1929	266.0	174.6	440.7	39.6
1930	209.6	180.8	390.4	46.3
1931	161.9	185.3	347.2	53.4
1932	116.7	159.0	275.7	57.7
1933	120.3	167.9	288.2	58.2
1934	133.1	204.1	337.2	60.5
1935	171.7	243.3	415.0	58.6

SOURCE: Boris Emmet and John E. Jeuck, *Catalogues and Counters: A History of Sears, Roebuck and Company* (Chicago: University of Chicago Press, 1950), 653, 344–46. Copyright 1950 by the University of Chicago. All rights reserved.

billion and profits climbed above the $100 million mark (at $100,098,516) for the first time.[98]

This was a performance few companies could match, and it would have been impossible without retail stores. Retail stores would have been impossible, or at least far more difficult, without Wood. All of which is to say that this could easily have been a story of failure rather than of success. Perhaps historians would be writing that the decline of Sears, Roebuck was "inevitable" because of the decline of farm income.

Wood may have been aware of some of the difficulties that a mail-order firm might face in the chain-store business, but he was not as frightened of them as were many people with more experience in the industry. Sometimes, Wood later said, "It's a good thing for a man not to have been in business. I mean, you can see things that men who are very close to the business don't see."[99] To be sure, Wood was very knowledgeable about purchasing and logistics,

> But buying for the government and buying for retail are two different things. In Panama and in France, the soldier and the worker had to take your goods, but outside, it was the customer that determined things.[100]

This very lack of experience may have freed him from the constraints of the conventional wisdom.

Whether or not he fully appreciated the potential problems in the retail

From Catalogs to Counters: Sears entered the retail store business in the 1920s. This is a picture of the interior of the first such store.

strategy, Wood abundantly understood the opportunities it presented as well as the risk involved in doing nothing. During those long, lonely nights in the Panama Canal Zone, Wood had developed an "odd passion" for poring over the *Statistical Abstract of the United States.* [101] Like so many other great figures from American business history—Morgan and Rockefeller, for example—Wood had a talent for and an enjoyment of mathematics, evident even from West Point.[102] He was one of those fortunate few to whom numbers spoke. They were not rows and columns of inert markings. They dramatically evoked a compelling tableau.

The numbers in 1920 were telling Wood and Wood was telling Montgomery Ward that the era of rural America was drawing to a close. Its waning meant the shrinking of a market that had been "a virtual monopoly for the two large [mail-order] houses" for more than a quarter of a century.[103] The United States was born in the country and moved to the city, and that movement was well under way by 1920. Farm income in 1919 was about $14.6 billion, accounting for more than a fifth of national income. Ten years later, farm income stood at just over $11.3 billion, and its share of national income had dropped to under 13 percent. It would not reach its 1919 level again until 1943, when it accounted for 8.6 percent of national income.[104]

That is not all the figures said. They also told Wood that automobile sales and registrations were on the rise as was the mileage of improved roads. He put these two facts together and deduced that the trading area of a well-located, well-advertised, and well-merchandised store could be greater than ever before.

There were more figures, these on the activities of other distributing companies. James C. Penney became the manager of and one-third partner in a Golden Rule Store in Kemmerer, Wyoming, in 1902. By 1920, his company was running almost three hundred stores, and by 1928, more than a thousand. Penney's success proved that the chain-store system was not necessarily restricted to groceries.[105] He was targeting large towns and small cities for its outlets. If the mail-order houses did not grasp this historic retail opportunity, others surely would.

Ward began experimenting with stores soon after new management took over in 1921, and it immediately faced the same sort of problem that so many manufacturers encountered when they attempted to integrate forward into retailing. That is, what precisely were these stores supposed to do for the company? Were they designed primarily to satisfy the customer in the competitive context of the retail environment? Or were they designed to get rid of what the manufacturer had made too much of (or, in this instance, what the mail-order house had bought too much of)?

At Ward in the early 1920s, the answer was the second of these two options. The company's stores were "outlets" for its overstocks. Those established as adjuncts to its mail-order distribution centers were successful, whereas those set up as freestanding stores were not.[106]

On 28 October 1921, Wood wrote a memorandum asserting that retail expansion, and not on an outlet basis, offered an inviting opportunity to

Ward. This comprehensive memorandum provides an excellent overview of Wood's evaluation of the competitive situation and is therefore worth quoting at length.

> We must realize that we have a keener competition to face than ever before. In the parcel post lines, we have Sears, Chas. Williams, The National Cloak & Suit Company, Bellas Hess, Standard Mail Order Company, Phillipsborn, Leonard Morton and the Chicago Mail Order. In the eastern cities, Altmans, Wanamakers and Gimbles [sic] have developed extensive mail order departments. The western department stores have not gone so extensively into this business, the Boston Store of Chicago being the only one which maintains any real mail order department and that being largely confined to shoes. In the heavy lines, Sears Roebuck is our only large competitor, but there are a number of mail order concerns dealing in specialties. In the furniture and rug line there are Spiegel, May, Stern, and Hartman. . . . There is the Kalamazoo Stove Co. doing a mail order business on stoves and the Monmouth Plow Company on implements. There is a Pittsburgh concern doing a large mail order business in wall paper. There are two western concerns that are doing an extensive mail order business in auto supplies. . . . Schmelzer of Kansas City does a mail order business in sporting goods. There are any number of concerns operating a jewelry mail order business. Larkin has a large business on furniture, rugs and other house furnishings. However, our mail order competition in the heavy lines is nothing like as severe as in the parcel post lines.
>
> The keenest competition of all that we have to face is the chain store competition. Beginning originally with the grocery chains, they have extended their field first to drugs and then to general textile lines and shoes, such as the lines handled by the Penny [sic] stores. . . . It is true that with the exception of the grocery chains and the Penny [sic] stores, there are relatively few chains operating in the small towns or cities. Successful small town merchants are buying out their competitors or combining with other local merchants and making local chains of small department stores. The chain system is even extending into some of the heavy lines like roofing. Lumber companies running a chain of lumber yards through small towns are adding to the lumber line, hardware, roofing, paints and other building materials and are securing the jobbers' discount and retailing at low costs.
>
> The great strength of the chain store system appears to be that their volume gives them as good purchasing power in many lines as a mail order house and that, particularly in the case of the Penny [sic] stores, they can operate more cheaply than the mail order houses. These two advantages, combined with the tremendous advantage of allowing the customer to see what he buys make them formidable competitors and furnishes competition that will grow keener as they become better organized and more firmly established.
>
> There are two weak spots in connection with the chain store, the first being that with the exception of the old established grocery chains like the A and

P. they have no distributing warehouse system. For a multitude of small stores, they must, at some place and some time, perform the function of jobbers for themselves, that is assembling goods in carload lots and distributing them. Many of these chains have not had the foresight to so group their stores so as to work out a good system of warehouse distribution. The other weak spot is that when the guidance of the original founder is lost, the problem of personnel in 200 or 300 widely scattered stores becomes acute. The problem of supervision and inspection becomes great. J. C. Penny [sic] wisely provided for this weakness in his original scheme by which he made his managers partners and gave them an ever present incentive to manage and operate their stores profitably and economically.

I feel, however, that if we are so inclined we can beat the chain stores at their own game, that we have certain advantages which they do not possess and that we can easily and profitably engage in the chain store business ourselves with a relatively small amount of capital. We have four splendid distributing points; we have an organized purchasing system; we have a wonderful name if we choose to take advantage of it and we ought to be able to build up as good or better an organization than the chain stores themselves and without harming our mail order business.[107]

Wood had an imperial vision for Ward's mail-order future: groups of forty to fifty stores clustered around each of the four mail-order distribution plants and doing a total of $20 million in business. However, Wood did not get along with Merseles and could not sell his plan to Ward's top management. With much ill-will on both sides, Wood was fired in September of 1924; and his office files, including his retail plan, were seized.[108] The next stop was Sears.

At Sears, as at Ward, there was skepticism about retail stores. The company was doing well. The crisis of the post–World War I years had abated. The company was profitable. There was no pressing need to change. Why borrow trouble? "I took issue with this philosophy," Wood recalled in 1950, "for a company is like a man, it cannot stand still, it must move forward; if not, it begins to move backward."[109]

As table 5–5 indicates, Sears entered retailing immediately after the Kittle-Wood team moved into control. With Wood as CEO in 1928, expansion accelerated dramatically. By 1930, the company had 338 stores. In 1941, that number had risen to 617, through which flowed 68.4 percent of the company's sales.[110]

The problems of staffing these stores, of merchandising them, of buying for them, and of integrating them with the mail-order operations were numberless. The managerial problems were so difficult of solution that both Sears and Ward seriously contemplated merger with J. C. Penney in 1929 in order to exploit the wealth of Penney's store personnel and experience. The feuding between retail and mail order at Sears reached "a bitterness approaching the 'fighting' point."[111]

To cope with such problems, top executives took to the road. In addition to Sears's ten mail-order branches and hundreds of suppliers, there were now hundreds of retail stores to be visited and to be analyzed merchandise line by merchandise line. James M. Barker, who was appointed retail administrative vice-president midway through 1932, later recalled spending two-thirds to three-quarters of his time on the road with little opportunity for vacation:

> Most of the evenings as I traveled were taken up with meetings at the hotels with the senior men from the store and from the district. We started early, motored all day inspecting stores, got in late and worked later. It was an extremely strenuous period of my life.[112]

For such men, Sears became more than an employer—it became their community, their family. They devoted themselves to it with a passion exceptional in corporate America. The company bound its executives and employees to it not only through their salaries and through a very successful profit-sharing program, but also by providing psychic income in the form of pride in working for an honest company, for a company that brought the future to the lives of middle-class America, for the Great American Company.[113] It was this sense of fealty that turned Sears into the company nobody quit and that made the changes of the 1970s and 1980s so wrenching.

The stores that Wood conceived and that men like Barker helped to perfect were varied in nature, ranging from the small "C" stores up through the huge, 100,000-square-foot, full-line "A" stores. There was much confusion within the company through the early 1930s "about what the retail stores would really be." Wood said that early on, "We had a 100% record of mistakes . . . we hadn't overlooked a single mistake. . . . We made them all."[114] Nevertheless, Wood believed that Sears's retail success illustrated that "Business is like war in one respect—if its grand strategy is correct, any number of tactical errors can be made, and yet the enterprise can prove successful."[115]

Wood did bring to the store business a basic belief that Sears should not try to compete directly against the big-city department stores in terms of either geography or product offering. The department stores were strongest in the central business districts of the biggest cities in the East and the Midwest. They had been built up in the era of urban rail transport. The science of store site location required that the stores be located near the hub of the hub-and-spoke system, in areas of maximum pedestrian traffic.

Wood, with his ability to see not only what was but to foresee what very well might be, opted to buy large parcels of land near highways removed from the central city. At such places, far away from the congestion and high rents, Sears could build stores that sprawled over the landscape and that were accompanied by vast parking lots. At first, these locations were a "source of great amusement and wonderment to the department store world,"[116] Wood observed with pardonable pride, but, in fact they were critical. The parking lots were

the most important of all, the one thing that contributed most to the success of the stores. . . . As time went on, as the number of cars increased, as the lack of parking in the down-town shopping sections grew more pronounced, as the congestion in the streets and highways became more overwhelming, the importance of this one basic factor became greater and greater. It largely nullified our own initial mistakes, the superior cleverness of many of our competitors, and enabled us to grow at an astounding rate and to make very large profits.[117]

Here was the retailing strategy designed to capitalize on the suburban world of the auto-industrial age.

The suburban housewife, Wood later explained, "can't take her car downtown and park it and take the children with her. Out in the periphery, they could do it, and that helped our stores a good deal."[118] Part of the novelty of these stores, however, was that they were not aimed solely or even primarily at women. The market for stylish clothing and accessories was the heart of the downtown department and specialty stores. Sears made a major effort to appeal to the man by selling fishing tackle, hunting gear, sporting goods, and a wide variety of tools for the do-it-yourself market blossoming in the suburbs, hardly product lines likely to be featured in Macy's, Gimbel's, or Filene's.

Another set of products in which Sears made a major statement and which department stores and other chain stores tended to neglect clustered around the automobile. The customer traveled to Sears by car, a car he or she probably owned. Those cars needed grease; they needed oil; they needed batteries; they needed radios. Sears sold them all.

The cars needed tires, and that was a product in which Sears scored a tremendous success. Robert Wood understood tires. In his years at Ward, he increased unit tire sales by a factor of ten. He explained his philosophy on this product in a 17 August 1920 letter to Ward interim president (and later board chairman) Silas H. Strawn:

> It should be our policy to develop the sale of tires, for although this is a low profit division and will tend to bring down the average gross profit of the house, it is a high net profit division, which after all, is what we are really interested in. It is also a spring and summer line and brings business when we need it most.[119]

By the time Wood left for Sears, Ward's tire sales were well over twice those of Sears in dollar terms. In the stores at Sears, Wood made tires a featured item. Wood "put one tire on top of another until he had a tower of tires near the cash register with the biggest savings he could offer."[120] For years, according to one report, sales per square foot were greater on tires than on any other item in the stores. In 1928, Sears tire sales stood at over $3.2 million compared to just over $2 million for Ward.[121] Thus, these few years in the history of one product line stand as eloquent testimony to Wood's mercantile ability.

Finally, the cars Sears's customers drove to its stores needed to be insured. The idea that Sears should go into the insurance business was first proposed to Wood by the individual who handled some of his own personal insurance. Insurance was not a natural fit with the company's business. Unlike products such as tires, which were charting the company's future, insurance was an intangible. "Nothing is sold in such a transaction except the promise of protection and of the performance of an accompanying service if and when needed; the customer simply buys that protection and, through it, perhaps peace of mind."[122] The name for the insurance subsidiary was borrowed from Sears's tires: Allstate. It developed into one of the company's most productive investments. In fact, in 1980, in the depths of Sears's worst merchandising crisis since 1921, Allstate would make more than twice as much money as the rest of Sears.[123] Thus, in many different ways the automobile, which could have constituted a great problem for Sears, was turned into a major source of profits.

Sears stores also became the dominant suppliers to the nation of the big-ticket items that young couples needed as they set up house, such as furniture, plumbing and heating equipment and fixtures, laundry equipment such as washing machines, and kitchen equipment such as stoves and refrigerators.[124] The company had made a major statement in such items since the great days of the cream separator and the sewing machine. These products, with their big-dollar margins, made a critically important

Courtesy of Sears, Roebuck and Co.

A Moment of Triumph: Robert Wood (left) and Julius Rosenwald are pictured here with the ten-millionth Allstate tire. Automobile accessories have long been a mainstay of Sears's business.

impact on the income statement. We shall see below how the Sears system for one of them—refrigerators—worked.

Sears, to be sure, did an enormous business in shoes, apparel, and other soft lines. Nevertheless, it was the statement made in hard lines and big-ticket items that set it apart from distributors differentiating themselves on the basis of fashion. From the beginning, Wood said, Sears "gave its stores an appeal to the man—the family—the home—the car—and relatively little appeal to style."[125] These were the years when Sears staked its claim to its "core customer"—"the guy who walks in and says he's just had his first kid and just bought his first house, and he needs a washer, dryer, and a lawn mower, and tools."[126] Wood defined the company's target this way:

> Just who [sic] do we cater to? Sears, Roebuck and Company does not cater to the deluxe trade—the Gold Coast—nor do they cater to the junk trade. They cater to the 80% or 90% of the population in between those two classes.[127]

It was the allegiance of this customer that helped Sears weather the Depression so well and that positioned it for its explosive growth after World War II.

The Competition

When Robert Wood, addressing the Sears Congress of Merchants at the "On to Chicago" conclave in 1950, used the phrase "our competitor,"[128] no one in the audience needed to be told what company he was referring to. It was Montgomery Ward. Eventually, the Sears-Ward duo came to be looked on as a trio with the addition of Penney. As late as 1982, the daily stock prices of Ward and Penney were displayed in foyers of many of the floors of the Sears tower in Chicago along with the quotes for Sears itself.[129]

This concentration on Ward is understandable. Ward predated Sears by about two decades (depending on what date one chooses for the founding of Sears). Both companies were headquartered in Chicago, the best location from which to exploit the rural market; and the early history of Sears reveals an intense concentration on its cross-town rival.[130] By the 1890s, when Sears was struggling to establish itself, Ward was already a nationally known institution. The partnership of Aaron Montgomery Ward and his brother-in-law George Thorne was converted to a corporation in 1889, with a capital of a half million dollars. That year sales exceeded $2 million and profits $115,000. Ward's profits in 1889 were about $22,000 less than Sears's sales in 1891, the first year for which such data are available.[131]

Another reason for Sears's concentration on Ward was Ward's importance as a mail-order house. Both these businesses defined themselves not in terms of what they sold (e.g., cream separators, suits, or Granger hats) but in terms of how they sold (i.e., by mail order and exclusively by mail order). The mail-order efforts of department stores at the turn of the century were not perceived as major threats.[132]

The early rivalry between Sears and Ward bears a certain resemblance to the competition between Coca-Cola and Pepsi-Cola in the 1930s and 1940s, with Ward playing the role of Coca-Cola. Like Coca-Cola, Ward viewed its rival as beneath notice. Ward was making an effort in the 1890s to gain respectability by toning down its advertisements and letting its prices rise. To the five Thorne brothers, sons of George Thorne who assumed control of the company at the turn of the century, Richard Sears was a fanatic vulgarian, a throwback to the era of uncivilized merchandising.

The Sears sales story in the 1890s is remarkable. Sales grew from $137,743 in 1891 to $745,595 in 1895, the year Rosenwald and Nusbaum bought into it, managing operations and freeing Richard Sears for the promotion that was his first love. In 1900, sales topped $10.6 million, leading Ward for the first time. Never again would Sears fall behind.

What explains Sears's early victory? We cannot point to a single key thrust such as "twelve full ounces" or "the car for every purse and purpose." Sears seems to have succeeded by beating Ward at its own game. Its aggressive pricing was probably a critical factor. Sears developed a more efficient buying system than Ward, and that system probably made lower consumer prices possible. In one of his first speeches to the merchants of Ward in May 1919, Wood said that

> sellers drew very unfavorable contrasts between the buying methods of Montgomery Ward & Company and Sears, Roebuck & Company. The seller, when he came to Montgomery Ward & Company, submitted his samples and possibly after a delay of two or three weeks was informed that he would get an order but was not given the quantity of the order or the exact class of merchandise; in other words, the seller was embarrassed as to how to cover. Moreover, there was procrastination and delay, in some cases extending over a considerable period. The seller, when he went to Sears, Roebuck and Company, had his samples examined and usually had the confirmation of an order in his pocket within a week; in other words there was quick decision and action. As a result the prices quoted to Montgomery Ward & Company were never as close as to Sears, Roebuck.[133]

Sears's product line also contributed to its success. The company stressed hard lines such as the cream separator to a greater extent than did Ward, and its dramatic price promotions on a C.O.D. basis on these items were undoubtedly effective. Finally, Sears laid greater emphasis than Ward on advertising. And in Richard Sears, the company had one of the greatest copywriters in history.

Ward, in general, became too mature and too polite too soon. Sears, by contrast, was hungry.[134] Ward grew smartly in the early years of the new century but at nothing like Sears's pace. By 1913, Ward's sales reached almost $40 million, an increase of almost four and a half times from 1900. Sears's sales in 1913 were over $91 million, an eight and a half fold increase from 1900. From 1913 through 1921, Ward never captured as much as one-third of the total business of the two companies, as table 5–7 indicates.

Montgomery Ward was clobbered during the post–World War I depression. Sales hit an all-time high of over $100 million in 1920, but heavy inventory losses and other problems led to a loss of more than $7.8 million.[135] Debt hung heavily on the balance sheet, and a consortium of bankers headed by J. P. Morgan took control of the company. Robert Thorne was forced from the presidency; and, in January 1921, Theodore F. Merseles took his place.[136] Ward was a family-managed firm no longer.

Theodore Merseles was a talented man. For eighteen years, he had served as an executive of the National Cloak and Suit Company (later known as National Bellas Hess).[137] This firm was the third leading mail-order house in the nation, with sales climbing from $10.9 million in 1912 to $47.7 million in 1920, Merseles's last year.[138] Sales had reached almost half those of Ward and were closer to Ward than Ward was to Sears.

Merseles was convinced that Ward's goal should be to exploit more fully the rural market it knew so well. He saw plenty of room for growth. In order to achieve it, he overhauled the company. New research was undertaken so that Ward could better understand its customer. New copywriting standards were designed to communicate more effectively.

TABLE 5–7

Comparative Sales of Sears and Ward, 1913–1921

Year	Sales (in millions)			Percent of Total	
	Sears	Ward	Total	Sears	Ward
1913	$ 91.4	$ 39.7	$131.1	69.7 %	30.3 %
1914	96.0	41.0	137.0	70.0	30.0
1915	106.2	49.3	155.5	68.3	31.7
1916	137.2	62.0	199.2	68.9	31.1
1917	165.8	73.5	239.3	69.3	30.7
1918	181.7	76.2	257.9	70.5	29.5
1919	233.9	99.3	333.2	70.2	29.8
1920	245.4	101.7	347.1	70.7	29.3
1921	164.0	68.5	232.5	70.5	29.5

SOURCE: Boris Emmet and John E. Jeuck, *Catalogues and Counters: A History of Sears, Roebuck and Company* (Chicago: University of Chicago Press, 1950), 295. Copyright 1950 by the University of Chicago. All rights reserved.

TABLE 5–8

Comparative Sales of Sears and Ward, 1921–1924

Year	Sales (in millions)			Percent of Total	
	Sears	Ward	Total	Sears	Ward
1921	$164.0	$ 68.5	$232.5	70.5 %	29.5 %
1922	166.5	84.7	251.3	66.3	33.7
1923	198.5	123.7	322.2	61.6	38.4
1924	206.4	150.0	356.5	57.9	42.1

SOURCES: Boris Emmet and John E. Jeuck, *Catalogues and Counters: A History of Sears, Roebuck and Company* (Chicago: University of Chicago Press, 1950), 295. Copyright 1950 by the University of Chicago. All rights reserved.

The quality of the catalog was improved. Merseles made an effort to infuse a new, winning spirit in the firm, at the same time eliminating employees who could not make the transition he was trying to engineer.

Merseles's first year was a tough one. Sales dropped by a third as the bottom fell out of the mail-order market. Losses mounted to $9.9 million. The following year, however, the company's golden jubilee, the situation began to turn around. By 1924, Ward seemed to be conducting a sustained assault on Sears for the first time, as the data in Table 5–8 show.

In the whole long history of Montgomery Ward from 1872 to the present, the most important single moment came in September 1924. That was when the tensions between Merseles and Wood resolved themselves by Wood's dismissal. The ideas of the two men on the future of mail order were fundamentally different, and a series of highly publicized meetings that Wood had been holding with Ward's manufacturing sources were generating more personal attention for Wood than Merseles liked. "It came to be common talk in Chicago business circles, and probably elsewhere as well, that Wood would be the next president of Ward's, perhaps in the near future."[139]

It has been said that one of the toughest aspects of management is accepting not the weaknesses but the strengths of one's colleagues and subordinates.[140] Accepting weakness takes magnanimity; accepting strength demands an inner sense of security and self-confidence. The latter are in as short supply as the former. It was Wood's ability, rather than whatever shortcomings he may have had, that led to the break with Merseles.

Merseles wanted to do better at what his company was already doing well. Wood wanted to strike out in the direction of something new. Merseles did well, but in this instance the good was the enemy of the great. The retail initiative was a historic opportunity to beat Sears not at its own game but by a flanking maneuver. Had Merseles grasped it, there is reason to believe that this chapter would be dealing with Ward rather than Sears. As it was, Wood arrived at Sears with full knowledge that although Ward had not yet committed itself to retail stores, it might choose to do so in the future.[141]

Ward moved into stores soon after Sears. The example of Sears and the demands of Ward's own customers weighed more heavily than the assertions, like those at Sears, that Ward was by nature a mail-order firm.[142] Wanting to avoid competition with department stores, Ward targeted towns of between 5,000 and 50,000 in population. Sears's own plan called for targeting larger metropolitan centers.[143]

Retail proved as important to Ward as it had been to Sears, with sales exceeding mail order in 1930. Profitability was a problem, however, as the deepening Depression engulfed the company. Merseles had departed in 1927 to assume the presidency of Johns Manville. His handpicked successor, George Everitt, was replaced as CEO by Sewell Lee Avery in November 1931.[144]

Avery was born in Saginaw, Michigan, in 1873. Bright and intense, he graduated from the University of Michigan and took a job at the Alabaster Company in the 1890s, one of the founders of which was his father. This company was among the firms that merged in 1901 to form United States Gypsum. Avery became chief executive in 1905 and successfully piloted the firm through the panic of 1907 and the depression of 1920. Avery predicted the Great Depression and positioned U.S. Gypsum so well that it made a handsome profit in 1930 and increased its market share sharply. He became known as the "rich boy who made good."[145]

Avery was reluctantly persuaded to take control of Ward by its bankers. He set about systematically to revivify the company and did so with such skill that he gained national note. Three hundred executive positions changed hands. By 1935, two-thirds of Ward's 35,000 employees had been hired since Avery's arrival. It was essentially a new firm. Stores were relocated and redesigned. New packaging was developed as was new advertising. The catalog was restyled. Inventory was written down. And all this was undertaken while Avery retained his post as president of U.S. Gypsum.[146]

Ward once again was able to mount a credible challenge to Sears. Sales in 1931 were over $200.4 million, about 38.5 percent of the total for Sears and Ward; and the company lost more than $8.7 million. In 1938, in the depth of the "Roosevelt Recession," sales reached nearly $414 million, 45.2 percent of the combined Sears and Ward total. Sears's sales exceeded Ward's that year by less than $90 million. Ward's profits surpassed $19.6 million.[147]

It was during these years that a tone of concern, even of apprehension—so different from his usual expansive optimism—crept into Wood's statements to his managers about Sears's duel with Ward. In 1936, he told his buyers that Ward had "improved the quality of their buying organization very greatly during the past three years. Even with our splendid showing of today, we must not fall into the fundamental error of underestimating the ability of our competition."[148] By 1938, things had, from Wood's standpoint, gotten worse. "We come to the present year," he told his buying and cataloging forces in August, "and thus far it presents a melancholy picture. The statement we put out two weeks ago was the first statement of which I felt ashamed."[149] In the first seven months of 1938, Wood went on, Ward made greater dollar and share gains than at any time since 1924 (Wood's last year there).

> I believe there still lingers in some, not all, of Sears's buying force a trace of that feeling of smugness or superiority which was quite noticeable ten or fifteen years ago. Ward's volume fifteen years ago was nearly half of Sears's; today it is 80% of Sears's. If you have such a feeling, get rid of it, for you don't deserve it after 1937 and 1938. Learn from your competition, examine yourself to see what are your weak spots, and see if you can't discover new ways in your line to make sales and profits.[150]

Ward was already doing as much or more mail-order business than Sears if the Southeast (where Sears was dominant) were excepted, Wood warned. Ward had developed new credit policies, had made impressive inroads in soft lines and style items, and was putting out a strikingly effective catalog in an all-out campaign "to wrest the title of the World's Biggest Store away from us."[151] Management, Wood said, was willing to accept its share of the responsibility for Ward's progress. It was time for all to work together to stop it.[152]

The changes Wood instituted and the spirit he instilled had their effect. The two companies would never again be so near one another in terms of sales or market share as they were in 1938.

The Story of One Product: The Refrigerator

Sears conceived of Ward as its primary competitor, eventually to be joined by Penney and K Mart. However, in terms of the individual lines that Sears sold—and there were approximately 100,000 in the catalog by the end of World War II—at one time or another in its history, Sears has competed against more firms than any other company in American history. Despite Wood's own focus on Ward, he well knew that "we have to compete with everybody, every day, in every article we sell."[153] Sears, for example, sold suits. So did Ward. So did hundreds of department stores and thousands of specialty stores. Sears sold those suits under its own label. It thus competed against every manufacturer that sold suits under the manufacturer label. Some of those manufacturers may have supplied Sears with suits in addition to selling their own branded merchandise. Thus, Sears competed with some firms whose products it also distributed. This was true of thousands of product lines.

What follows is a story that conceives of Sears as a competitor not on the corporate level but from the viewpoint of a single product line: the refrigerator. This product is particularly important because it provides a prime example of how manufacturer-centered and distributor-centered marketing systems compete within the same product line. In addition, it illustrates the role that Sears played in helping to make available to a wide market one of the great advances in comfortable living of modern times.

THE INDUSTRY BEFORE SEARS

Interest in household refrigeration dates to the early nineteenth century in the United States. A Maryland farmer named Thomas Moore invented a refrigerator to enable him to transport butter to market and preserve it until sold. This refrigerator was an oval-shaped cedar tub within which was a metal container surrounded by ice. In a pamphlet, Moore asserted that refrigeration could be useful for home food storage as well as for transportation. "Every housekeeper may have a refrigerator in his cellar, in which, by the daily use of a few pounds of ice, fresh provisions may be preserved, butter hardened, milk or any other liquid preserved at any temperature. . . ."[154]

It was not until after the Civil War, however, that the demand for ice as a refrigerant to preserve food in private homes began to climb sharply. In 1856, for example, New York City consumed 100,000 tons of ice for all purposes. In 1860, Boston and New Orleans used 85,000 tons and 24,000 tons, respectively. In the year from 1 October 1879 to 30 September 1880, by contrast, New York consumed almost a million tons, Chicago over 575,000, Brooklyn and Philadelphia more than 300,000 tons each, and Cincinnati and St. Louis more than 200,000 tons each. Total consumption was between 5 and 5.25 million tons.

The ice industry had become big business, and the demand for home refrigeration was one of the driving forces behind it. About half the ice sold in New York City, Baltimore, and Philadelphia in 1879–1880 was sold to households. The increasing population (especially in cities) and changing dietary habits (i.e., away from salted meats and toward fresh beef and dairy products) accounted for this trend. Industrial uses of ice included the transportation of beef in refrigerated railroad cars and in the brewing of beer.[155]

Demand for natural ice tripled in the quarter century following 1880. To satisfy it, harvesting took place in growing amounts on northern lakes and rivers. However, ice manufacturers steadily made inroads into the business. Interest in ice manufacture was especially strong in the South, where the obvious problems in logistics and storage made ice expensive and sometimes unavailable in the needed quantities. This lack of a refrigerant was a drag on the region's economic development, restricting the variety of crops that could be grown commercially because of spoilage in transit and also the kinds of farm products that could be processed. By 1889, there were 165 ice plants in the region.[156]

By the end of the nineteenth century, ice manufacturing was spreading through the North as well. Polluted lakes and rivers were giving rise to questions about the possible health dangers of natural ice. Warm winters from 1888 to 1890 led to two successive summers of ice shortages and a boom in ice manufacture. There developed "an unprecedented demand for refrigerating machinery, not only for ice making, but for all industries which required low temperatures."[157] Within two decades, there were more than two thousand plants in the United States using coal-fired steam engines to manufacture ice.

In addition to its industrial uses, ice was distributed regularly to iceboxes in millions of American homes. The "iceman" placed a block of ice on the top shelf of a cabinet, and the melting of the ice cooled it. The Sears catalog of 1897 devoted two pages to its refrigerator department. The opening price point model—"Our Acme Single Door Refrigerator," "manufactured of kiln-dried ash lumber, beautifully finished antique brass lock, fancy surface hinges, anti-friction casters"—contained about 8.75 cubic feet of space, weighed 100 pounds, and cost $5.60. The top of the line—"Our Highest Grade Acme Dining Room Sideboard and Refrigerator Combined," "made of selected kiln-dried quarter sawed oak, rubbed and polished," which contained "all the improvements of our celebrated Acme, and is one of the handsomest pieces of dining room furniture furnished in the country"—contained 22.75 cubic feet of space, weighed 500 pounds, and cost $50.[158] The value of product of the domestic refrigerator-manufacturing industry increased from about $4.5 million in 1889 to over $26 million three decades later.[159]

There were obvious and insoluble problems associated with domestic refrigeration that depended on ice, whether it was natural or manufactured. Ice melted. The water thus produced had to be disposed of. Because ice melted, it had to be replaced, which meant frequent visits from the iceman. This worthy, the butt of much humor, "was apt to be a rough, uncouth individual whose route across the kitchen floor was marked by dirty footprints and puddles of water and who too often would fail to make delivery when need was greatest."[160] Add to this the facts that ice was expensive or at least so perceived, that its distributors had a reputation for giving short weight, and that ice as it melted failed to produce a constant temperature and the stage was set for a mechanical answer to the demand for domestic refrigeration.[161]

A number of start-up companies in the 1910s were trying to overcome the technical difficulties surrounding practical domestic refrigeration. The Kelvinator Corporation of Detroit, founded as a partnership of two men with experience in the automotive industry, apparently began experiments in 1914. It sold its first refrigerator in February of 1918. Kelvinator has been credited with the development of an automatic-control device, which was essential to the maintenance of constant temperature in the refrigerator cabinet.[162]

Another early entrant was the Guardian Frigerator Company, also of Detroit. This company was founded by a mechanical engineer named Alfred Mellowes. In the two years from its founding in the early spring of 1916, Guardian sold thirty-four refrigerators, all in the Detroit area. Mellowes personally serviced each of these units and "kept in close touch with the purchasers, visiting each of them every two or three weeks."[163]

Guardian's customers were pleased with its product, so much so that a number of them became investors. As investors, they were, alas, less pleased. By June of 1918, the company had accumulated a deficit of $34,162. At that time, it was purchased by William C. Durant for $56,366.50, much to the relief of all who had invested in it. In May of 1919, Durant sold the company to General Motors for the same price. "It was a small enterprise of no great substance," Alfred P. Sloan, Jr., later recalled.[164]

Why did Durant purchase a refrigerator company? Charles F. Kettering, the engineer whose Delco-Light division would soon be charged with manufacturing and marketing the product, thought Durant simply wanted to boost General Motors stock. John L. Pratt, long-time senior GM executive, suggested another reason: that Durant was looking for a product that his automobile dealers would be able to market when automobiles themselves became unavailable during World War I.[165]

The thought that an automobile dealership might be an appropriate place to sell a refrigerator sounds strange indeed today. We must remember, however, that in 1918 the refrigerator was a new product. Like the automobile in 1895, some visionaries thought it had a future from a mass-marketing standpoint, but no one understood how the marketing task could best be carried out. From a production standpoint, the refrigerator was not as far removed from automobile manufacture as we think of it as being today.

As an automotive producer General Motors was . . . a specialist in metalworking—casting, forging, machining, stamping, pressing, heat-treating, and assembling parts made of metal into useful and complex products. . . .

Moreover a refrigerator [in 1918] had many parts that resembled quite closely the parts of an automobile engine—such as the crankcase, pistons, cylinders, cam shafts, pulley and fan in the compressor. Like the automobile the refrigerator had an electrical system and a cooling mechanism.[166]

General Motors began manufacturing the Model A by Frigidaire (the new name Durant chose for the Guardian) in a Detroit plant. Problems abounded. In Sloan's words:

Our miscalculation about the product's suitability for mass consumption was speedily brought home to us. Model A and its successors in the first few years remained a luxury product. What was worse, we could not get the "bugs" out of the machine, which broke down repeatedly. Our efforts to introduce a sales and service organization into a number of cities outside of Detroit were unsuccessful. It appeared that the machine really needed the kind of steady personal service that Mr. Mellowes had provided his small group of customers; but this kind of service was obviously impossible in a product intended for a mass market.[167]

General Motors gave serious thought to jettisoning Frigidaire during the 1920–1921 cash squeeze. Instead, Sloan turned the company over to Delco-Light, with the abundant electrical engineering expertise of Charles F. Kettering and the sales abilities of Richard Grant.

The first technical problem that Delco had to solve dealt with the refrigerator cabinet. Frigidaire cabinets were manufactured by the Grand Rapids Refrigerator Company, which used first seaweed and later cork for insulation. Neither worked well. They left air spaces that rendered the insulation less effective. Yet a more serious problem was the moisture from the cabinet's interior, which condensed on the insulation and on the paraffin sealant. The moisture absorbed food odors, and the refrigerators thus insulated became known as "stinkers." Frigidaire worked with Armstrong Cork to solve this problem.[168]

The most serious of the problems Frigidaire had to solve dealt with the refrigerant. Frigidaire used sulphur dioxide, a toxic compound that often

escaped, causing great distress to salespeople, servicepeople, and customers alike. Dangerous enough in a household environment, the presence of
sulphur dioxide made refrigeration off-limits for any place that could not
be quickly ventilated. The major alternative as a household refrigerant was
methyl chloride, less toxic but also odorless and therefore difficult to
detect. The dangers of toxic refrigerants were illustrated by a disaster in
1929, when over a hundred people died in a Cleveland hospital as a result
of a leak in the refrigeration system.[169]

In 1928, Frigidaire launched a concerted campaign to find a better
refrigerant. Charles Kettering, by then a director of General Motors
Research Laboratories, asked his former colleague Thomas Midgely, Jr.,
to go to work on the problem. Midgely, a mechanical engineer by training,
had worked with Kettering on refrigerants a decade earlier. In the meantime, Midgely had become well known for his discovery of the antiknock
fuel, tetraethyl lead. Midgely and his associates began experimentation
with derivatives of fluorine. The eventual result was Freon 114, which had
a suitable boiling point, was neither toxic nor flammable, and had a
distinct but not unpleasant odor.

There was concern about the safety of this new compound. When
Freon is exposed to an open flame, free fluorine is liberated; and some
competitors tried to use that fact to influence various localities to pass
ordinances against its use. Midgely dramatized his own belief in its safety
by publicly inhaling it at a 1930 meeting of the American Chemical
Society. Not until the end of 1933, however, did the new compound gain
general acceptance. At that time, competitors joined Frigidaire in purchasing Freon from Kinetic Chemicals, Inc., the Du Pont/General Motors joint venture that manufactured it.[170]

General Motors turned Frigidaire over to Delco-Light in 1921, both
because of Delco's electrical manufacturing capability and because of the
hope that Delco's distribution system for its home-lighting plants would
be able to handle it. As it turned out, the marketing needs of the home-
lighting plant and the refrigerator were altogether different. Delco distributors were located in cities but the dealers tended to be in small towns
to serve the farms that had not yet been reached by power lines. The
refrigerator, by contrast, was a specialty item, costing on average almost
twice the price of a Model T Ford in 1924. The market was among rich
urbanites, and the need was for a well-trained missionary sales effort.

In the early 1920s, Frigidaire began to develop its own organization of
distributors and dealers. There were nine factory branches and forty
independent distributorships in 1924. The company preferred not to
integrate forward but found itself forced to do so. As the business grew,
some independent distributors balked at making the investment that

Frigidaire felt was needed to serve the growing market. During the 1930s, lack of venture capital made it difficult to replace distributors who dropped out of the system. By 1949, there were twenty-two factory-owned sales branches and only twenty-one independents.[171]

It was in 1926 that General Motors made the decision to scale up refrigerator operations. Ground was broken for a $20 million plant to manufacture and assemble refrigerators at Moraine City, four miles south of Dayton. The plant became fully operational the following January. In April of 1927, Alfred Sloan addressed a sales convention there: "In the past five years," he said, "Frigidaire Corporation has grown from one of the smallest GM divisions to the third place in the volume of sales, exceeded only by Chevrolet and Buick." This success had not been the result of any synergies that Durant or others thought might exist between automobiles and refrigerators. In the early 1930s, Sloan observed that "It goes without saying that [Frigidiare] has nothing to do with the automotive industry. . . ." Nevertheless, its profits as well as its sales were amply appreciated.[172]

Frigidaire became the generic term for refrigerator early in the industry's history. But the company did not have the market all to itself. Its rival, General Electric, had been involved in commercial refrigeration since before World War I. In March 1923, a GE scientist, Dr. Alexander R. Stevenson, was assigned to make a report on the household market. Stevenson said that the refrigerator would fit well into GE's product line. In his words, it would "complete the string of appliances" for the salesman and thus maximize the sales from his "contact with the customer." Stevenson called for the designing of a hermetically sealed, air-cooled unit. In his view, the "General Electric Company cannot hope to get more than 20 percent of the business, and probably will not reach even that figure before 1934."[173]

GE scaled up in 1927, just months behind Frigidaire. On the first day of that year, the company authorized millions of dollars for plant and $1 million to promote the new product. The Monitor Top, as GE's refrigerator was called, took the industry by storm. The sealed case at the top of the unit, which enclosed the complete motor and compressor, lent an air of mystery. The quietness of the unit in operation was heavily stressed and represented a clear and demonstrable advance. The five-year warranty was also stressed. In the words of a Frigidaire executive, "the ordinary household salesmen and many industry sales executives were thrown into a panic." For years after 1927, Frigidaire veterans regretted their sluggishness in responding to GE's move.[174]

General Electric's strength in the refrigerator market did not derive solely from its product. Its refrigerator's most important characteristics

Courtesy of General Electric Co.

The General Electric Monitor Top refrigerator, which spearheaded GE's entry into the industry in the 1920s.

could be and soon were equaled by Frigidaire. But General Electric had an important marketing edge that was much harder to replicate. Complicated and expensive though it may have been, the refrigerator was, after all, just another electrical appliance to a distribution system built around electrical appliances. In Alexander Stevenson's terms, it completed the string of appliances. General Electric had scope economies in marketing that neither Frigidaire nor Kelvinator could match. Refrigerators were a seasonal business; and GE's water heaters, ranges, and other electrical appliances gave the distributors and dealers plenty to do when the refrigerator business was slow. Westinghouse had the same kind of advantages, and they helped it capture almost 6 percent of the market in 1931, the year it entered.

The need for scope economies in marketing was so great that Frigidaire was eventually forced by its distributing organization to broaden its product line. In 1936, the company sent a questionnaire that asked its dealers "Should Frigidaire manufacture additional appliance products?" Ninety-nine percent said "yes." By 1954, Frigidaire was selling ten kinds of appliances. This strategic decision was taken not because of a new product advantage or to satisfy consumer demand, but strictly to keep a marketing system intact. More than 58 percent of Frigidaire volume in 1954 was still accounted for by the refrigerator, even though the product accounted for only 34.6 percent of the total dollar volume for these ten products industry-wide. Frigidaire was never able to equal in these other fields—in which it was a latecomer with no *raison d'être* from the consumer's view—the success it experienced in refrigerators, where it had been a first-mover and technological leader.[175]

Table 5–9 provides data on the growth of the refrigerator industry from 1920 to 1928 and Frigidaire's share of market. As the data in the table show, during the 1920s, the household refrigerator market boomed as the price dropped. Meanwhile, average income grew. Of critical importance, moreover, was the growth in household electrification. One-third of American homes had electrical service in 1920; two-thirds had it in 1930.[176] Table 5–10 shows a market-share breakdown of the household mechanical refrigerator market from 1929 through 1933. The table shows

TABLE 5–9

Refrigerator Sales and Prices, 1920–1928

Year	Total Units	Average Price	Frigidaire Units	Frigidaire Share of Market
1920	10,000	$600	—	—
1921	5,000	550	399	8.0%
1922	12,000	525	1,808	15.1
1923	18,000	475	2,753	15.3
1924	30,000	450	4,436	14.8
1925	75,000	425	15,960	21.3
1926	210,000	390	95,915	45.7
1927	390,000	350	136,110	34.9
1928	560,000	334	187,006	33.4

sources: "Frigidaire Household Refrigerators," 27 Jan. 1949, 79-10.1-44, Box 3, Frigidaire papers, GMI Alumni Foundation's Collection of Industrial History, Flint, Mich.; *1935 Refrigeration and Air Conditioning Market Data* (Detroit, Mich.: Business News Publishing Co., 1935), 37.

TABLE 5–10

Share of Market of Household Mechanical Refrigerators, 1929–1933

Company	1929		1930		1931		1932		1933	
	Number of Units	Percent of Market	Number of Units	Percent of Market	Number of Units	Percent of Market	Number of Units	Percent of Market	Number of Units	Percent of Market
Frigidaire	308,733	38.6%	207,703	24.5%	227,823	23.1%	174,085	20.4%	224,246	21.0%
General Electric	243,600	30.4	289,430	34.1	275,419	27.9	117,065	13.7	150,311	14.0
Kelvinator/ Leonard	99,415	12.4	66,477	7.8	69,850	7.1	102,221	12.0	149,937	14.0
Westinghouse	—	—	—	—	58,227	5.9	57,540	6.7	81,391	7.6
Norge	6,140	0.8	13,986	1.7	64,386	6.5	68,197	8.0	82,541	7.7
Sears	—	—	—	—	14,000	1.4	20,000	2.4	20,000	1.9
Servel	47,862	6.0	57,508	6.8	80,680	8.2	55,784	6.5	66,302	6.2
Others	94,471	11.8	213,404	25.1	196,295	19.9	258,892	30.3	297,574	27.8
Total	800,221	100.0%[a]	848,508	100.0%	986,680	100.0%	853,784	100.0%	1,082,302	100.2%

[a]Numbers may not total 100% due to rounding. There are a number of arithmetic errors in the original table, which I have corrected.

SOURCE: Frigidaire Marketing Research Department, 9 Mar. 1949, 79-10.4-352, Box 43, Frigidaire papers, GMI Alumni Foundation's Collection of Industrial History, Flint, Mich. Used by permission.

the refrigerator market growing sharply, with the exception of 1932. It also shows volatility in terms of share. Frigidaire and General Electric dominated the industry with more than two-thirds of the business in 1929. In 1933, their combined share was not much more than one-third.

The industry was controlled by manufacturers selling through company-owned branches or independent distributors, which in turn sold through dealers. Table 5–11 outlines the dealer structure of Frigidaire.

Could a distributor organize a marketing system in this industry? That was the question Sears posed in the 1930s.

COMPETITION THROUGH DISTRIBUTION: THE COLDSPOT

Sears's interest in mechanical refrigeration dates back to 1922, but its early efforts to develop its own private-label supplier did not meet with success. Sales were not the problem. Midway through 1927, the supplier—a combination of two companies called Hercules and Servel—had an estimated 15 percent of the market, trailing only Frigidaire and Kelvinator. "Unfortunately, the pressure upon the factory for such an output resulted in complete demoralization of operating control, together with imperfect or undeveloped design, resulted in a wave of failures in operation and a tremendous volume of returned refrigerators."[177]

A review of the documents of the Sears/Hercules/Servel story provides impressive testimony to how difficult it was for a company distributing tens of thousands of lines of merchandise to engage in the manufacture of one of them, especially when, as was the case with refrigerators, manufacture was a matter of some technical complexity.[178] Not until the early 1930s did a dominant design in domestic mechanical refrigeration

TABLE 5–11

Frigidaire Dealers in 1936

Outlet	Number of Dealers	Percent of Dealerships	Percent of Units Sold January–July
Department stores	265	5.2%	13.3%
Furniture stores	656	12.8	11.7
Public utilities	142	2.8	18.7
Appliance dealers	4,074	79.3	50.3
Sales by distributors, headquarters offices, and unclassified	———		6.1
Total	5,137		

SOURCE: "Operating Report, Frigidaire Division," 31 Aug. 1937, p. 7, 79-10.1-52, Box 4, Frigidaire papers, GMI Alumni Foundation's Collection of Industrial History, Flint, Mich. Used by permission.

emerge. Sears itself was undergoing dramatic changes and opening retail stores during these years. A company selling solely through the mail had different needs in a refrigerator from one selling through stores.

Sears was drawn into difficult financial and managerial questions concerning Hercules and Servel. Wood's letters to Kittle show an acute awareness of the problems of these companies as early as 1925. Problems of efficiency and of trust seemed intractable if Sears retained a minority stockholding in Hercules. It increased its holdings in this firm not to maximize opportunities but to minimize the losses it otherwise feared it would suffer.[179] Although the Hercules/Servel combination sold refrigerators, and although Sears owned a large fraction of Hercules/Servel, it is unclear whether Sears itself actually sold any of these or any other mechanical refrigerators except in small lots on an experimental basis. Refrigeration for Sears meant the use of ice until 1931.

The 1920s drew to a close with Sears having little to show for the effort it had invested in mechanical household refrigeration. Nevertheless, Donald M. Nelson, the company's senior merchant, persisted in the belief that Sears had a role to play in this industry. Nelson was one of those able individuals from the hinterland who chose to devote themselves to the building up of this all-American company and who grew with it. He was born in Hannibal, Missouri, in 1888 and was educated as a chemical engineer. He taught for a brief period before joining Sears's testing laboratory in 1912. His first assignment was to assure the quality of the company's textiles; and, to educate himself about the industry, he took the full course of study at the Lowell Textile School in Massachusetts and then served as an apprentice at four different textile mills in the Northeast before returning to the laboratory.[180]

Once there, Nelson launched a campaign for quality merchandise and truth in advertising that met with some resistance. The chief of the harness department, for example, had this to say about Nelson's testing of his horse blankets: "What difference does it make to the horse? He doesn't know what the catalogue says."[181] But Nelson was able to turn such skeptics into believers by demonstrating that the most expensive product in the horse-blanket line offered the least value.

Nelson served as manager of men's and boys' clothing from 1921 to 1926 and was an assistant in the general merchandise office in 1926 and 1927 before rising to the post of senior merchant.[182] He thus had firsthand familiarity with production, marketing, and quality issues; and that background, combined with his knowledge of chemical engineering, must have played an important role in his decision that Sears should do something exciting in refrigeration.

Nelson, W. I. Westervelt, who was the head of the merchandise development division, Eddie Gudeman, and the newly hired Herman Price went to work to turn things around. Another key man was Dr. Adolph J. Snow. Austrian born, Snow was educated at Ohio State and Columbia. He came to Sears in 1928, at the age of 34, and quickly made a name for himself in product design and engineering for items as diverse as stoves and roller skates. He was instrumental in hiring Price from Goldblatt's department store.[183]

Price went to Evansville, Indiana, where new arrangements were entered into for refrigerator manufacture. William A. Carson, the chief executive officer of the Sunbeam Domestic Appliance Company, had a plant well equipped for appliance manufacture but did not have a contract. Sunbeam's washing machine business had recently been discontinued. Price selected Sunbeam as Sears's supplier.[184] Sunbeam was not equipped to manufacture the refrigerator cabinets, so these would be sourced from a Sears supplier in Minneapolis called Seeger. Sears made a financial investment in the Evansville factory and signed a contract in 1931 calling for 10,000 units per year for ten years.[185]

The new Coldspot, as the Sears machine was named, made its debut in the catalog in 1931. The Spring/Summer general catalog devoted five pages to refrigerators that year (the first three of which were given over to ice cabinets). Prices for the Coldspot ranged from $137.50 for the 4-cubic-foot model (or $151.25 on the $10 down and $10-a-month time-payment plan) to $205 for the 7.5-foot model. Electric refrigeration was described as "Proven—Time Tried," and the advertisement asserted that the Coldspot had been "thoroughly tested in actual operation for five years"[186] (although it is not clear how that could have been true). There was a thirty-day home trial, and letters of praise from satisfied customers were published. Every attempt was made to reassure the risk-averse potential customer.

Reassurance to the contrary notwithstanding, the product simply did not work. The Coldspot introduction was little short of disastrous. Sales greatly exceeded expectations, and the plant could not cope with demand. Given the production problems that both Frigidaire and General Electric had experienced, the difficulties encountered by a converted washing-machine plant are not surprising. William Carson later recalled of the early 1930s that "we had more service employees than production workers."[187]

Things rapidly went from bad to worse. In the words of a Sears executive:

1932 was a black period in the history of the Coldspot refrigerator. Faced with an inventory of almost 30,000 refrigerators that were returned as unsatisfactory

almost as fast as they were sold; with rebellious retail store managers refusing
to stock them because of the trouble they caused; with sub-normal business
conditions throughout the country; and with Sears's lower price advantage
destroyed because of the decreased price of competitive manufacturers, Sears
officials seriously debated whether to continue to try to sell electric refrigerators or to leave the field to more successful, established competitors.[188]

In 1932, Sears sold about 20,000 refrigerators. Frigidaire enquired about
the possibility of supplying Sears, and Carson was pleading for patience.
The following year, as industry sales climbed from 850,000 to over one
million units, Sears's sales were flat. The company actually lost share.

It must have looked to everyone like failure. Twelve years of interest
in electric refrigeration had yielded nothing but executive effort wasted,
money lost, and customers disappointed. Exiting from the business was
under active consideration at the company. But Price, Snow, and Gudeman refused to give up. They undertook more research and experimented
with different models. A new, easily removable electrical unit was designed. New, inexpensive, rust-proof shelving was installed. The well-
known industrial designer Raymond Loewy was commissioned to redesign
the cabinet. "He removed it from the ugly square box on legs to a thing
of beauty with gently curving edges and attractive horizontal lines," said
one executive. "He gave it symmetry and grace without sacrificing utility
or size."[189] Coldspot design was changed each year during the Depression.

The real breakthrough, however, dealt with product-line pricing. Standard practice in the industry in the early 1930s was to promote the
4-cubic-foot model at low prices through heavy advertising but to talk the
customer up through pressure selling in the store to, at least, the 6-cubic-
foot model. As was true with automobiles, small refrigerators, small profits, . . . big refrigerators, big profits. Selling up was facilitated by the fact
that many consumers felt the 4-foot model offered inadequate space.

Theodore V. Houser, who succeeded Nelson as senior merchant in
1939, cited the refrigerator as an illustration of Sears's superior merchandising methods. The standard buying method, used by department stores,
was to shop around among various manufacturers, comparing their goods.
This led to a "personal competition" in which the buyer competed "with
his shrewdness, his judgement, his trading ability against those same
qualities in competing buyers." The Sears system, by contrast, called for
something to be added beyond these personal trading abilities. "That
something is the economic power possessed by this firm when the selling
of our goods and the production of our goods can be harnessed together."[190]

This harnessing called on the buyer to have knowledge of production processes and raw material costs as complete as any engineer in the factory. Maurice Tippett, Herman Price's predecessor, bought refrigerators with an "arbitrary differential" based on "the pricing conventions of the industry." But Price and A. J. Snow did not accept the price the industry offered. Their analysis told them that through their own suppliers they could deliver far more value to the consumer and still capture a handsome profit.[191]

This knowledge and this sourcing arrangement, combined with its power as a huge distributor, made it possible for Sears to shock the refrigerator industry in 1934. It put a 6-foot model on the market at the 4-foot price. Moreover, Sears fielded a far narrower product line than its principal competitors. General Electric offered sixteen models in 1934, and Frigidaire offered fourteen. Coldspot offered three.[192] Herman Price said in 1936 that Sears was attempting to do for the refrigerator what Ford did for the automobile.[193] By offering fewer models, Sears could reap increased scale economies and lessen inventory problems.

The market was moving to Sears. According to one estimate, about two-thirds of the "prestige group" of buyers (e.g., business executives and professionals) owned refrigerators in 1936, whereas only about one-third of wage workers did.[194] The leading branded manufacturers underestimated the strength of the demand among people with lower incomes. According to a Frigidaire market study in 1936, "80% only of wired homes should be regarded as the potential market for electric refrigerators, because the other 20 percent have little purchasing power and are not regarded as financially responsible. . . ."[195] Sears had been selling to these people for almost half a century. The company believed they would pay their bills even in a depression. And it believed that because they were good, honest Americans, they deserved to own refrigerators.

The Sears refrigerator strategy was announced in the 1934 Spring/Summer catalog (see exhibit 5–1).

The resurrection of the Coldspot provided a vivid illustration of the differences between catalog and store selling. The catalog operation was centralized. Price and Gudeman could guarantee themselves space if they could convince Nelson and others in top management that they had a story to tell. Getting the Coldspot into the stores, however, was far more difficult. By 1934, many store managers had reached the end of their patience with the refrigerator. They were persuaded to cooperate in the new program "only with the greatest difficulty." Various methods of persuasion were used, including letters and personal visits to store managers that combined cajoling with veiled threats.

Despite the problems involved in gaining distribution through the

EXHIBIT 5–1

Coldspot Advertisement, Sears Spring/Summer Catalog, 1934

HERE'S REAL NEWS

For Families of 4 or More Who Have Been
Considering an Electric Refrigerator

$124 $\frac{50}{\text{cash}}$

6 Cubic Feet Net

Sears is determined to keep refrigerator prices in line with cubic foot capacity! That's welcome news to families of 4 to 6 who are being asked to pay a high price for a 6 cubic foot electric refrigerator. Either they've had to pay the high price of a refrigerator large enough for their needs or else they've had to buy the smaller size, which was totally inadequate. Sears now comes to the rescue with a genuine NEW COLDSPOT of full 6 cubic feet net capacity at a price within reason—in fact, it's no higher in price than you are now asked to pay for many "4's". This is refrigerator news as important as we've ever printed. You get extra size at no extra cost.

SOURCE: Sears *Catalog,* Spring/Summer, 1934, p. 626.

stores, their cooperation was critical to the success of the Coldspot program. The electric refrigerator was new to most Americans in the early 1930s. It was mysterious. It was also a planned purchase and a major investment, which meant that the potential customer was likely to shop around. Sixty-three percent of those questioned in a survey who purchased a refrigerator from Sears or Ward in 1940 looked at one other brand at least. The average number of brands shopped was 2.7.[196] Moreover, by the end of the 1930s, a great many refrigerator purchasers had an old one to trade. This meant that there might be bargaining at the point of sale, and the company accepting the trade-in would need a way to dispose of it.[197]

It would have been impossible for Sears to have become a force in this business had it not gone into stores. By 1939, less than 5 percent of refrigerator sales came through the catalog.[198]

The 1934 program achieved sales of 59,000 units, well above twice the previous year's mark. The following year sales more than doubled again to 138,000 units. Sales climbed to 216,000 units in 1936, accounting for almost 10 percent of the market.[199] (Sales and market share of the industry for 1934 to 1941 are given in table 5–12.) Even though Sears lost share in 1941 (for reasons that will be given presently), the company can definitely be said to have muscled its way to the table in competition against some of the best-managed firms in the country and on their own turf. How did it accomplish this?

Prior to 1934, as the history of Kelvinator, Frigidaire, General Electric,

TABLE 5-12

Market Share of Household Mechanical Refrigerators, 1934–1941

Company	1934 Number of Units	1934 Percent of Market	1935 Number of Units	1935 Percent of Market	1936 Number of Units	1936 Percent of Market	1937 Number of Units	1937 Percent of Market	1938 Number of Units	1938 Percent of Market	1939 Number of Units	1939 Percent of Market	1940 Number of Units	1940 Percent of Market	1941 Number of Units	1941 Percent of Market
Frigidaire	242,325	17.5%	300,976	17.4%	443,940	20.1%	503,574	19.6%	259,103	18.2%	338,259	16.0%	621,730	22.0%	722,397	19.1%
Montgomery Ward	—	—	—	—	23,181	1.0	57,019	2.2	72,358	5.1	95,682	4.5	98,231	3.5	133,323	3.5
Total: Frigidaire and Montgomery Ward	242,325	17.5%	300,976	17.4%	467,121	21.1%	560,593	21.8%	331,461	23.3%	433,940	20.5%	719,961	25.5%	855,720	22.6%
General Electric	202,333	14.6	251,007	14.5	263,091	11.9	373,760	14.6	192,604	13.5	329,638	15.6	448,196	15.8	635,636	16.8
Hotpoint	—	—	—	—	21,905	1.0	52,014	2.0	44,546	3.1	61,673	2.9	89,295	3.2	151,125	4.0
Total: GE and Hotpoint	202,333	14.6%	251,007	14.5%	284,996	12.9%	425,774	16.6%	237,150	16.6%	391,311	18.5%	537,491	19.0%	786,761	20.8%
Kelvinator/Leonard	218,565	15.8	201,757	11.6	257,894	11.7	246,643	9.6	95,533	6.7	138,904	6.6	281,185	9.9	489,414	12.9
Westinghouse	105,783	7.6	143,640	8.3	174,160	7.9	249,279	9.7	93,179	6.6	193,549	9.1	266,184	9.4	311,153	8.2
Norge	143,509	10.3	175,714	10.1	234,279	10.6	198,969	7.7	92,343	6.5	108,218	5.1	111,813	3.9	187,594	5.0
Crosley	—	—	122,765	7.1	119,322	5.4	84,256	3.3	48,764	3.4	76,982	3.6	83,544	2.9	158,920	4.2
Sears	59,000	4.2	138,000	8.0	216,000	9.8	295,000	11.5	200,000	14.1	290,916	13.7	329,625	11.6	307,322	8.1
Philco	—	—	—	—	—	—	—	—	—	—	50,000	2.4	100,000	4.7	152,000	4.0
Servel	105,450	7.6	164,347	9.5	215,751	9.8	257,836	10.0	169,437	11.9	218,823	10.3	228,690	8.1	283,551	7.5
Other	311,485	22.4	234,141	13.5	242,228	11.0	249,486	9.7	155,570	10.9	216,179	10.2	170,197	6.0	251,116	6.6
Total	1,388,450	100.0%ᵃ	1,732,347	100.0%	2,211,751	100.2%	2,567,836	99.9%	1,423,437	100.0%	2,118,823	100.0%	2,828,690	101.0%	3,783,551	99.9%

ᵃNumbers may not total 100% due to rounding. The original table contains a number of arithmetic errors, which I have corrected.

SOURCE: Frigidaire Marketing Research Department, 9 Mar. 1949, 79-10.4-352, Box 43, Frigidaire papers, GMI Alumni Foundation's Collection of Industrial History, Flint, Mich. Used by permission.

and Westinghouse all demonstrate, competition in refrigeration "was entirely a matter of improving your product, reducing your manufacturing costs and so your prices, and of devising an ingenious and productive sales technique."[200] Sears expressed pride in the Coldspot's various features and in its appearance—"out of the ordinary in design . . . years ahead of any other refrigerator in beauty and style."[201] However, Sears's main claim for its refrigerator was that it was no worse than the competition's: "The truth is that there are many good Electric Refrigerators. Size for size, most first-class refrigerators are much alike in quality and cost of production."[202]

How, then, consumers could reasonably be expected to ask, could Sears offer its unit for $40 to $50 less—a savings of 25 to 33 percent—than units of comparable quality from well-known manufacturers? The company's answer was that it competed through distribution:

> The Coldspot is offered at a lower price than any of the others, *not* because it costs less to build but because its COST OF DISTRIBUTION is so much less.
>
> That's the whole story of Coldspot's extra value. There is no huge advertising allowance to be included in the price you pay for the Coldspot, no sales organizations of any kind. Those savings go to you.[203]

In the conventional, manufacturer-centered distribution system, the manufacturer shipped the refrigerator to a distributor. The distributor shipped the product to a retail dealer, from whom the consumer purchased. In the Sears system, the Sunbeam factory shipped directly to Sears stores (or to the catalog warehouse for the small percentage of sales that traveled that route). Table 5–13 provides quantitative data on the expenses of the different systems in 1939.

Table 5–13 clearly illustrates why Sears persevered through more than a decade of failed experimentation and supplier difficulties. Although no documents have survived from the 1932 meeting at which Sears executives considered exiting this business, calculations like those in the table must have weighed heavily on the side of staying in. The calculations are startling. The customer paid $2 more in manufacturing costs in the manufacturer-centered system. These added costs did not result, claimed Sears, from better product but from scheduling problems. Such scheduling problems did not exist in the Sears system, because Sears guaranteed Sunbeam, its supplier (two-fifths of which Sears owned), a steady, year-round volume of business.

In the manufacturer-centered system, the manufacturer spent $18 per unit, or 10 percent of the retail selling price, to persuade the customer

TABLE 5–13

*Comparison of Manufacturer-Centered and Sears-Centered Refrigerator
Distribution Systems for a 6-Cubic-Foot Unit, 1939*

	Manufacturer-Centered		Sears-Centered	
	Costs Per Unit	Percent of Retail Selling Price	Cost Per Unit	Percent of Retail Selling Price
Manufacturing costs	$ 55.00	30.6%	$ 53.00	41.0%
Sales costs	7.00	3.9	none	—
Advertising and sales promotion	11.00	6.1	none	—
Administration	6.00	3.3	4.00	3.1
Excise tax	4.00	2.3	3.00	2.3
Manufacturing profit	9.50	5.3	4.50	3.5
Distribution expenses	21.50	12.0	4.50	3.5
Dealer expenses	52.50	29.2	41.50[a]	32.0
Dealer profit	8.00	4.5	14.00	10.8
Warranty charge	5.00	2.8	5.00	3.9
Retail selling price	$179.50	100.0%	$129.50	100.0%

[a]This figure includes about $7 for advertising.
SOURCE: "The Nudes Have It," *Fortune*, May 1940, 111. Copyright © 1940 Time Inc. All rights reserved.

to buy the product and the distributor to stock it. These costs were nonexistent in the Sears system. The manufacturer had no marketing costs in its Sears business; no sales costs because there was no sales force; no sales promotion costs because it was not selling to an independent distributor in a pure market transaction but rather to Sears, which owned 40 percent of it; and no advertising costs because it was Sears's name, not Sunbeam's, that mattered. Manufacturing profit in the Sears system was less in percentage terms and far less in dollar-per-unit terms. But volume was high, and throughput steady. About 40 percent of that profit accrued to Sears. Distribution expenses in the manufacturer-centered system came to 11.5 percent of the retail selling price. These expenses, in addition to occupancy, would have included inventory carrying costs as well as the costs of providing credit and service. Distributors also had to support a sales force. There were in 1934 an estimated 1,100 distributors selling to 25,000 dealers.[204] The major item of dealer expense in the manufacturer-centered system was salesperson commissions. These were usually 10 percent. Sears paid only 5 percent. This lower percentage rate on a lower unit price was made possible by Sears's greater volume.

The manufacturers fully recognized the threat posed by Sears's cost structure. In 1930, a Frigidaire vice-president assured his salespeople that price competition would not pose a problem. By the mid-1930s, however,

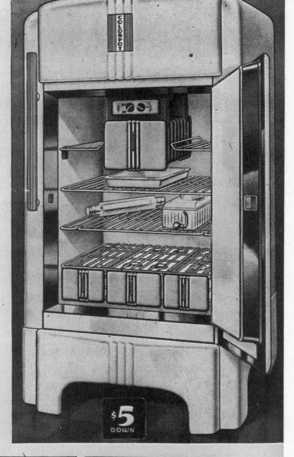

Sears's market entry was made possible by the dramatic success of its Coldspot in the 1930s. This is the 1935 model.

Sears was being described as an "important price disturber." In a report to the General Motors Executive Committee, Frigidaire executives stated that "our method of distribution is such that we cannot match the mail order houses on price. . . ."[205]

In 1939, Sears sold 290,916 Coldspots at an average price of

$131, accounting for $38,109,996 or over 6 percent of the company's $617,414,266 in sales that year.[206] At a dealer-profit rate of 10.8 percent, those sales yielded $4,115,880 in before-tax profits, or 11 percent of Sears before-tax profit that year. A spectacular performance, indeed, but not surprising in light of the data in table 5–13. The only surprising thing about the Coldspot is that it did not do even better.

What conclusions can we draw from the remarkable merchandising success of the Coldspot?

First, this is another example of how administrative coordination of mass production with mass marketing can be more efficient than arm's-length, market-mediated transactions. Factories needed guaranteed volume to run full and steady. Sears could provide this for Sunbeam without the heavy expenses for advertising and selling that the manufacturer-centered system depended on.

Second, refrigerators provide a striking illustration of the importance of Robert Wood's move into stores. Had the company not had a big chain of stores up and running in 1934, it never would have been a factor in this business and would have lost share in other home appliances, which, along with other big-ticket and hard-line items, constituted the heart of Sears's postwar expansion.

Third, this product shows Sears making an impact in what might be thought of as an industry of the future while Ward played a far lesser role. In 1939, Ward posted sales of $474,882,000, 77 percent of Sears's, but its refrigerator sales were a third of Sears's. In 1942, *Fortune* criticized Sears for being "overbalanced on the side of hard lines" compared to Ward.[207] Such overbalance might indeed have been a problem in light of war-induced restrictions and shortages.[208] But it positioned Sears perfectly for the postwar boom, at which time Ward's conservative approach and problematic store-location policy would injure it mortally.

Fourth, we can see Sears playing an important part in what we might call "the refrigeration of America." Sears did not invent the mechanical refrigerator; recognition for that goes to numerous experimenters. Nor did it develop the self-contained unit; General Electric did that. Sears did not innovate in refrigerants. It was still using sulphur dioxide when Frigidaire was using Freon. Nor did it initiate the downward trend in prices. The average price of a refrigerator had plummeted from $600 in 1920 to $170 in 1933, the year before Coldspot's major market impact.

What Sears did succeed in doing was pushing the price down further, thereby disciplining the industry as a whole. The industry was forced to respond to Sears's pressure by cutting its prices further and faster than it would otherwise have done.[209] This price pressure, combined with Sears's strong endorsement of the product, brought refrigeration to more people more quickly than otherwise would have been the case. The proportion of families with electricity owning refrigerators increased from 19.2 percent in 1934 to 62.8 percent in 1940.[210] Although this increase cannot be attributed solely to Sears, a significant proportion of it can be.

Our examination of the refrigerator during the 1930s also serves to illustrate a common pattern of competition in the American economy. The industry was dominated by manufacturers as the decade began. Chief among these were Kelvinator, Frigidaire, General Electric, and Westinghouse. The entrepreneurs who founded Kelvinator and Frigidaire during the 1910s had as their model the automobile industry. Kelvinator remained independent until 1937, when it became part of Nash. Frigidaire became part of General Motors under Durant, but it was Sloan's management team that made it number one.

If Kelvinator and Frigidaire came out of the Detroit motor tradition, General Electric and Westinghouse came out of the electric tradition. Both firms had technical competence and market knowledge, and both produced electric appliances other than refrigerators. Both, moreover, competed in selling electrical generation equipment to utilities; and both, therefore, shared an interest in selling appliances that increased the household consumption of electricity.[211]

All four of these firms had, by the early 1930s, captured scale economies in manufacturing. All four had worked out marketing arrangements that, for the most part, called for sale to an independent, noncompany-owned distributor, who then sold to a dealer.

Given this oligopoly, how could a new player enter the business? The barriers to entry in terms of capital and market knowledge made this an unattractive proposition for an entrepreneurial start-up, and no such firm played an important role during the 1930s. A new entrant had to have some special competence or advantage that gave it a chance against the established players.

For Sears, that advantage was an efficient distribution system that cut out one level of market transactions. But that was not all. Sears also had experience dating back almost half a century in how to sell consumer durables. It knew how to manage shotguns, sewing machines, and cream separators. At the time it entered the refrigerator industry, Sears was selling plenty of such products, and that is key to understanding its success. The refrigerator was just one more product for Sears to sell. It was an add-on. It was plus business for the distribution system. That is one reason why its expenses were so low. For example, Sears spent about $7 per unit advertising the Coldspot in 1939. This was less than competitors because Sears advertised the product primarily to inform the consumer rather than to hold a distribution system together.

To be sure, Sears had to make a major investment to capture the scale economies in manufacturing, but these expenditures were easily within reach. Sears's competitive advantage, as it admitted, lay not in manufacturing. It claimed only to be as good as the others. Its advantage lay in what Alfred D. Chandler, Jr., calls economies of scope. The breadth of the product line Sears already distributed made refrigerators an inviting addition.

Coldspot's success was so impressive that the other firms had to strike back. This they did by integrating forward and slashing their own prices. The leader was Kelvinator, the firm that had been most hurt by Sears's share gains. In 1939, Kelvinator sold through 135 distributors to 4,300 dealers. The following year it sold to 3,800 dealers through 65 distributors, 29 warehouses, and 13 factory branches. Sixty percent of sales went from factory branches to several hundred dealers. This new distribution system enabled Kelvinator to cut $40 off the retail selling price of its 6-cubic-foot refrigerator. The result was a price war, in which Sears yielded share. The price war was halted when World War II put the industry on hold.[212]

After World War II, Sears refrigerator sales did not rebound as quickly as did those of its competitors. The reason is not clear, but it may be traceable to manufacturing difficulties and to the aggressive growth of "brown-goods" manufacturers in this "white-goods" industry. Apparently, companies like Philco were able to use their radios and televisions after World War II to gain distribution. Philco was also a very heavy advertiser. Through the first nine months of 1949, for example, it outspent Frigidaire 1.6 to 1 in advertising and 2 to 1 in advertising on radio and television.[213]

To be sure, Sears sold a lot of refrigerators after World War II. But the share loss annoyed Wood, who, as late as 1953, wrote Sears's president that "I hope every effort will be made to regain this business."[214] Whatever these efforts were, they eventually proved successful. By 1969, Sears accounted for 20 percent of the industry, compared to 21 percent for General Electric plus Hotpoint and 15 percent for Frigidaire.[215]

The history of the refrigerator between the wars is the story of how American industry delivered to the average citizen a product that provided dependable year-round refrigeration. The wealthy had enjoyed the benefits of refrigeration well before the twentieth century. By 1940, in the United States, the majority of citizens could enjoy a cold cabinet in their homes that was more reliable than anything possessed by the richest people of a century earlier.

A former luxury had become an everyday necessity. A product had been democratized. Nelson, Snow, Gudeman, and Price had sensed in the refrigerator an analogue of the cream separator. The refrigerator was more difficult to manufacture and to market. The competition was tougher. But the profit dollars the Coldspot generated rewarded their faith.

Sears and the Postwar World

Robert E. Wood was in his sixty-sixth year in 1945. He had already had two careers—one in the army and the other at Sears—either one of which most men could have pointed to proudly as a life's work. His company was in a strong position. In 1945, Sears accounted for 61.55 percent of the combined sales of itself and Ward, a showing that had been matched only once since 1923 and a marked improvement over the 54.8 percent share it held in 1938. J. C. Penney was a distant third, with a minimal catalog business. Sears's $1.045 billion in sales represented about 10 percent of the total of its own and department store sales.[216] Discounters existed at the end of World War II, but such "cat and dog" operators did not seem to loom as a major threat. S. S. Kresge was still years away from transforming itself into K Mart.

Sears's 604 stores were well located and designed to exploit the world of automobility. These stores gave Sears a national reach matched by no other retailer, a key advantage in a nation where people moved so often. In a talk to his merchants in April 1946, Wood placed special emphasis on the competitive advantage provided by the big "A" stores:

I wonder if you gentlemen have fully realized the wonderful strength of this company as a retail distributor. Sears, Roebuck and Co. has its catalog, its ten big mail order plants which serve as supply bases to its retail stores, its outlying department stores in the large cities of the country with their parking space and their service stations, its B1, A1, B and C and farm stores serving the smaller cities and towns. Sears, Roebuck and Co. has the buying organization, the sources of supply, the distributive facilities and organization for both hard lines, soft lines and big ticket items. No department store or chain of department stores, no specialty chain store organization such as the food, drug, shoe or apparel chains can match us. In fact, there is only one other organization in this country that can do so and that is Montgomery Ward & Company. But Wards, while they can meet us on equal terms in the catalog business and in the smaller cities and towns, have nothing to match our organization of A stores in the larger cities of the country which account for at least 35% of our total sales and profits, and with present land and building prices it will take prohibitive amounts of capital for them to do so. I feel as certain as I am standing here tonight that when the era of competition does come, Sears is fundamentally sounder and stronger than any of our competition. While our profits will decline, we will survive and come back stronger than any of our competition.[217]

Sears's product offering was heavily weighted toward hard-line and big-ticket items with high dollar margins. These product categories accounted for an estimated 50 percent of Sears's volume as opposed to 20 percent for department stores in 1948.[218]

In addition to its competitive strength vis-à-vis Ward, Penney's, standard department stores, and other retailers in these lines, Sears's system of basic buying and competition through distribution was well equipped to deal with manufacturer-centered marketing systems. The system that had seen such success with sewing machines, cream separators, and refrigerators was strategically designed to capture a big share of the market for those innovations like television and dishwashers, which, at war's end, everyone knew were on the point of commercialization.

The situation seemed to suggest a conservative policy of slow, programmed growth. This policy would have met with no criticism, but it was a policy Wood and Sears rejected. Here was another case of fixing something that was not broken.

In 1945, Wood "took the biggest gamble of his career" and invested $300 million in a great postwar expansion program. The decade from 1945 to 1954 saw a net increase of more than one hundred stores, many of the large "A" variety. Wood followed a policy similar to his entry into the chain-store business two decades earlier. He "raced for the big cities first." He was convinced from his analysis of population figures that the nation's future lay in Texas and California, so he spent heavily there and very little in New England. In 1949, California and Texas replaced Illinois and Pennsylvania as Sears's two biggest states.[219]

Fueling this expansion drive was Wood's innate optimism about America's future. He was completely untouched by the "depression psychosis" afflicting so many as World War II drew to a close. Where some analysts had visions of demobilized soldiers moving directly from the army to the bread lines, Wood saw young men with young families in the market for those washers, dryers, lawn mowers, and tools that were at the heart of Sears's profits. He sensed that the demand pent-up during the war would burst forth at its conclusion. There would be no return to 1929 or to 1920–1921, he believed, because with the gold standard abandoned, the control of money and credit rested with the government and "no people willingly take deflation."[220]

In just two years, sales almost doubled and profits more than tripled. Sears had become the sixth largest industrial company in the country in terms of sales and the second largest retailer, behind only A&P. It held 5 percent of the retail general merchandise market. Wood's faith was handsomely rewarded, as table 5–14 shows.

The pace of growth slowed after the postwar spurt, reflecting economic conditions in both the nation and the world. The general improvement from 1947 to 1954, the year Wood finally gave up the board chairmanship at the age of 75, is nonetheless marked. Sales and profits both increased by a half.

Philip Purcell, the former McKinsey partner who played a key role in the revitalization of Sears in the late 1970s and early 1980s, believes that great men who build great institutions try to destroy them before they leave.[221] Purcell thought this observation applied to Wood, who had arranged in 1939 to have the chairman exempted from the mandatory retirement age of 60, thus allowing himself to hold office for an extra decade and a half. Even though, as we have seen, great things were done in these years, toward the end of this period Wood was clearly in his dotage. There had always been a certain eccentricity about him. In 1937, he was quoted in *Fortune* to the effect that "A good night's sleep, a good appetite, and a sound elimination are a man's prime concern."[222] It is not the sentiment that one finds controversial or even odd here, it is their

TABLE 5–14

Sears: Sales, Profits, and Number of Stores, 1945–1954

Year	Net Sales (in millions)	Net Profit (in millions)	Number of Stores	Number of Catalog Sales Offices
1945	$1,045.3	$ 35.8		
1946	1,612.6	100.1		
1947	1,981.5	107.7		
1948	2,296.0	137.2	628	341
1949	2,168.9	108.2	647	358
1950	2,556.4	143.7	654	404
1951	2,657.4	111.9	674	479
1952	2,932.3	110.2	684	546
1953	2,981.9	117.9	694	570
1954	2,965.4	147.3	699	609

SOURCES: Boris Emmet and John E. Jeuck, *Catalogues and Counters: A History of Sears, Roebuck and Company* (Chicago: University of Chicago Press, 1950), 650, 664; *Fairchild Financial Manual of Retail Stores*, 31st annual ed. (New York: Fairchild Publications, 1958), 61–62.

expression in *Fortune*. One can hardly imagine Sloan or Woodruff talking this way for quotation, and it would be more incredible today.

"Externally," *Fortune* declared in an understatement of business reportage, "General Wood is anything but the streamlined executive of fiction."

> His necktie is forever riding up under his left ear. The only time clothes seem to matter is when he boasts that the suit he is wearing came "off the pile" at Sears. . . . He has a passion for caramels. Excited, he doesn't bother to remove the wrappers, but just gulps them down, paper and all [perhaps explaining his concern with elimination]. If a conference lingers too long, he begins to scratch his head, bounce in and out of his chair, mutter incoherently, and even munch cigarettes; if the visitors have not been unstrung by these alarming symptoms, they may find that the General, having meanwhile circled out of sight, is absent-mindedly bowing himself out of his own office.[223]

By the mid-1950s, eccentricity had become separated from the constraints of an executive of operations; and we are presented with the Gothic vision of an old man "wander[ing] the endless halls at the West Side Headquarters . . . , who drooled, ate cigarettes whole, forgot to take the wrappers off candy, and often forgot to zip his fly."[224] Retired though he supposedly was, Wood exercised a dominant influence over the selection of his successors.

> Like the Roman Emperor Hadrian, who chose Antonius Pius to follow him and Marcus Aurelius to come next, the father of the system named and blessed all of the short-term chairmen. As late as 1973, the men the General had personally culled from the pack toward the end of World War II were still coming up and taking their crack—sometimes for as little as two years— because the General, the arbiter of fairness, had said thirty years earlier that it was "the fair thing to do."[225]

Doubtless unconsciously, Wood saw to it that none had the status or was given the opportunity to develop the stature that he himself possessed.

Wood's immediate successor, Theodore Houser, bitterly resented Wood's persistent presence at the company and established 65 as the mandatory retirement age for CEOs, even though that meant limiting his own tenure to four years.[226] One man who might have proven more than an epigone was Edward Gudeman. But Gudeman was not only a Jew, he was also a Harvard graduate, the interactive effects of which may have rendered him unacceptable to the General.[227]

Wood himself recognized that he had failed to supply Sears with the leadership it needed,[228] a remarkable admission given his pride in finding

Budding talent received early exposure in the Ward catalog of the 1940s, including Susan Hayward (above), Lauren Bacall and Gregory Peck (opposite page).

and building men. He never had an inkling of the Oedipal nature of the succession situation.

If Philip Purcell's speculation about the attitude of old men toward what they build throws some light on Wood's conduct in late career and in retirement, it seems startlingly applicable to Sewell Avery at Ward. The dour Avery was a great depression manager, as the performance of U.S. Gypsum in 1908 and 1920–1921 and of U.S. Gypsum and Montgomery Ward in the 1930s attest. In 1945, however, he predicted—perhaps the wish was father to the thought—another sharp economic downturn. "This country's going into a tailspin within two years," he told Wood over lunch at the Chicago Club soon after V-J day. "Every great war has been followed by a great depression, and our charts indicate it within 12 to 24 months."229

While Sears built stores, Ward, in accord with Avery's vision, closed them. While Sears invested in inventory, Ward sold it off. Ward enjoyed a sharp increase in sales and profits immediately after the war, but its policies quickly caught up with it, as table 5–15 indicates.

These results were caused not only by Avery's mistaken belief that a depression was just around the corner but also by strategic decisions dating back to the earliest years of his tenure and indeed even predating it. Ward had built smaller stores in smaller towns instead of big stores on the outskirts of big cities because it originally conceived of its stores as an extension of its rural market base. Thus, it was not able to participate fully in the trend toward urbanization and suburbanization, as was Sears. Ward invested less in manufacturing than did Sears and was thus unable to make

TABLE 5–15

Ward: Sales, Profits, and Number of Stores, 1945–1954

Year	Net Sales (in millions)	Net Profit (in millions)	Number of Stores
1945	$ 654.8	$22.9	—
1946	974.3	52.3	628
1947	1,158.7	59.1	622
1948	1,212.0	68.2	622
1949	1,084.4	47.8	622
1950	1,170.5	74.2	613
1951	1,106.2	54.3	605
1952	1,084.6	49.6	599
1953	999.1	41.2	590
1954	887.3	35.2	568

SOURCES: Montgomery Ward, *Annual Reports*, 1945–1954; *Fairchild's Financial Manual of Retail Stores*, 31st annual ed. (New York: Fairchild Publications, 1958), 61–62.

an equally massive statement in hard goods and big tickets. Neither had Ward expanded regionally. It was a negligible factor in the South and virtually invisible on the West Coast. By 1959, Sears had seventeen stores in the exploding Los Angeles market, and Ward had not one.[230] Table 5–16 presents a comparison of Sears and Ward in 1945 and 1954.

By 1954, Ward had become so liquid that its retail business seemed on the road to liquidation. Its balance sheet showed $327 million in cash and securities, $147 million in receivables, and $216 million in inventories, amounting to $690 million in current assets. Its net worth was $639

TABLE 5–16

Comparison of Sears and Ward, 1945 and 1954

	Sears			Ward		
	Sales (in millions)	Profit (in millions)	Number of Stores	Sales (in millions)	Profit (in millions)	Number of Stores
1945	$1,045.3	$ 35.8	—	$654.8	$22.9	—
Percent of Total	61.5	61.0		38.5	39.0	
1954	2,965.4	147.3	699	887.3	35.2	568
Percent of Total	76.7	80.7		23.3	19.3	

SOURCES: Calculated from data in Boris Emmet and John E. Jeuck, *Catalogues and Counters: A History of Sears, Roebuck and Company* (Chicago: University of Chicago Press, 1950), 650, 664; Montgomery Ward, *Annual Reports*, 1945–1954; *Fairchild's Financial Manual of Retail Stores*, 31st annual ed. (New York: Fairchild Publications, 1958), 61–62.

million.[231] Here was a company preparing not for a recession or a depression but for *Götterdämmerung.*

No wonder Ward became known as the bank with the store attached. And no wonder it attracted the attention of speculator Louis E. Wolfson, who launched one of the first unfriendly takeover efforts in modern American business history. By September of 1954, Wolfson held 200,000 shares of Ward stock and was planning a proxy fight at the next annual meeting. The strategy of the Wolfson group at the 22 April 1955 meeting was a cruel but clever effort "to show up Avery as weak, confused and nearly senile, by asking [him] pointed questions and letting him hang himself. . . ." The company's lawyer, John A. Barr, protected Avery for as long as he could; but at last the old man got up to speak. After a half hour of incoherence, Barr got up again to replace him.[232] Although Wolfson failed to take the company over, Avery was finished. And so was Ward as a viable competitor for leadership in general-merchandise retailing in the United States.

Sears and Ward had competed vigorously for well over half a century by 1955. Nevertheless, the relationship between the two firms had elements of symbiosis. In 1919, just after joining Ward, Wood told his buyers that the competitive methods of Sears

> of necessity must be clean cut and honorable, and I want to encourage every division manager to become acquainted with, to get in touch with the corresponding man in Sears, Roebuck and Company, to visit him and encourage him to visit you. You may necessarily have no trade associations in the mail order house but the exchange of views on markets, conditions, prices in your various lines must be in itself mutually helpful. . . . I think you will find them disposed to meet you more than halfway.[233]

In 1936, when Wood had been at Sears for twelve years and was beginning to feel pressure from Ward, he told his buyers that

> There is a deeper conflict between Sears, Roebuck and Company and Montgomery Ward & Company than just between two great business competitors. There is a conflict between two philosophies of life and business.
>
> The philosophy of Julius Rosenwald was to share prosperity. All of you, through your stock purchase contracts, and 19,000 rank and file employees, through the Profit Sharing and Pension Fund have participated in the appreciation of values as represented by a rise from a low of 10 in 1932, to the present price of 98. I am anxious for the employees of Sears to prove to the world that our philosophy represents not alone better ethics, but better business.[234]

Despite these different philosophies, Wood was happy to share with Ward what by the mid-1930s had become a mail-order duopoly.[235] Happy, that is, as long as Sears had the lion's share of the business.

Ward stood Sears in good stead as a point of comparison and as a spur to improvement, as Wood's 1936 speech illustrates. Ward was also an important source of Sears's executive talent.[236] And Ward served as a political ally of Sears in battles against antichain state legislation. Wood himself was very supportive of Avery when the latter was forcibly removed from his office by National Guard troops in April 1944 during a labor controversy. "While the two firms are competitors," Wood wrote Avery, "in a matter of this kind we must stand together, and if there is anything that either the firm or I can do to be of assistance to you in your stand, I am at your service."[237]

By the mid-1950s, Ward was only a shadow of its former self. It would never rise again. Perhaps it had been killed too dead for Sears's own good.

While Montgomery Ward floundered in the late 1950s and early 1960s, Sears forged ahead along with American prosperity. In 1965, the company posted sales of $6.4 billion, more than twice the size of any competitor in general-merchandise retailing. (Table 5–17 gives the 1965 sales and profits of Sears and other leading general merchandisers and department stores.) Another milestone was reached in 1965, when Sears's sales surpassed those of A&P. For the first time in decades, A&P was not

TABLE 5–17

Sales and Profits of Leading General Merchandise and
Department Stores, and of A&P, 1965

Company	Sales (in millions)	Profit (in millions)
Sears, Roebuck & Company	$6,390.0	$323.3
J. C. Penney	2,289.2	78.9
Montgomery Ward	1,748.4	24.0
F. W. Woolworth	1,443.3	73.0
Federated Department Stores	1,330.7	70.5
Allied Department Stores	955.5	22.3
May Company[a]	869.2	45.9
S. S. Kresge	851.4	22.2
W. T. Grant	839.7	31.2
A&P	5,119.0	52.3

[a]Includes the results of G. Fox & Company, which became a division of May on 29 Nov. 1965, and whose figures have been combined with May on a pooling of interests principle.
SOURCE: *Fairchild's Financial Manual of Retail Stores*, 39th annual ed. (New York: Fairchild Publications, 1966), xvi–xvii. Reprinted by permission.

Ward CEO Sewall L. Avery refused to comply with War Labor Board directives during World War II. As a result, President Roosevelt ordered him bodily removed from his office.

the world's largest retailer. Sears was. It stood alone, resplendent, at the head of the table.

But, in the words of historian and former Sears executive James C. Worthy, "No business strategy is good forever."[238]

The All-American Company

The mid-1960s saw the climax of Sears's hegemony in the world of American retailing. To insiders, however, there were indications by late in the decade that all was not well. Sales kept climbing, but profit margins did not; and return on equity (ROE) was dropping, down to 9.8 percent in 1975 from 16.1 percent two decades before.[239]

Symbolic of the change that had overtaken the company were two *Fortune* articles. The first, "Sears Makes It Look Easy," was published in 1964. Its praise was unstinting. Commenting on an 11.1 percent jump in sales in 1963 (an increase in dollar terms equal to the total sales of the Gimbel's chain), coming on top of a decade boasting a compound annual sales growth of 5.6 percent, the article asked:

> How did Sears do it? In a way, the most arresting aspect of its story is that there was no gimmick. Sears opened no big bag of tricks, shot off no skyrockets. Instead, it looked as though everybody in its organization did the right thing, easily and naturally.[240]

By contrast, the second article, by Carol Loomis, "The Leaning Tower of Sears," published in 1979, questioned the competence and enthusiasm of management and the ability of the company to call a halt to the war it was fighting with itself, to establish clear and sensible goals, and to attain them. To Loomis, Sears's situation seemed "very scary." "The company obviously needs to recover its old skill and competence and do it in short order. Whether it can is a matter of considerable doubt."[241]

Nineteen seventy-nine was not a good year for Sears. When the 21 May 1979 annual meeting took place, the stock had plummeted to $19 a share. Top management had to endure public criticism of humiliating intensity. Rarely had any American management been subjected to such merciless attack. It was almost as tough as what Sewell Avery had gone through in 1955.

Many explanations for the precipitous decline of Sears have been offered. One is that Sears had simply grown too large. A second is that the post-Wood management was incapable of striking out in new directions as had the master. Another is that the nature of the market had fundamentally changed and that there were fewer of Sears's "core customers" around. Yet another is that the promotional policies of quick-moving specialty retailers living off the crowds that Sears was attracting to subur-

Photo Hedrich-Blessing.

The Sears Tower—the world's tallest building—was, at first, a symbol of the company's preeminence. In more recent years, the company's problems have forced it to put the building on the market.

ban malls were too agile for Sears to keep up with. These Phase III segmenters had carved up the Phase II mass-market world of Sears's greatness. Another possibility is that fast-growing K Mart had ambushed Sears when it was still thinking in terms only of Ward and Penney. And a final explanation is that Sears had purposely abandoned its customers— rather than the other way around—by trading up to more expensive merchandise.

Whatever the reasons, Sears undertook to strike out in new directions in the late 1970s.[242] The automobile business was considered. According to one estimate, American Motors could be had for $80 million.[243] But that was not the way of the future.

The American economy was moving toward services. Viewing itself as the embodiment of American consumption, Sears determined to move in that direction as well through the acquisition of real estate and brokerage companies. From the cheapest store to the largest, Sears was going to become the most convenient. And why not? Sears had always been an opportunistic company, selling whatever it could profitably. It had been in the insurance business since the 1930s. If customers were willing to buy insurance along with their overalls, why not homes and securities as well? In their move into this new arena, Sears executives counted not only on their firm's financial muscle but also on its meaning to the American consumer. Trust. That was Sears's real competitive advantage. ("You know what I can't get out of my head?" the CEO of Dean Witter said after an exploratory discussion with Sears. "Could you imagine actually *trusting* your investment firm?")[244]

Sears once transformed itself from catalog alone to catalog and counters. It is now trying to create stores that sell socks and stocks. How successful will it be? At this writing, there are still grave doubts about whether the company will be able to prevail in its new ventures. And doubts persist about its ability to revivify its retailing business also.

Conclusion

Let us now review the Sears story in the context of this book's propositions.

PROFIT THROUGH VOLUME

Like A&P, Sears emerged in the late nineteenth century from the Phase I world of low turnover and high margins. Along with Ward and large department stores, such as Marshall Field and Macy's, Sears played an important role in the transformation of shopping from procurement to excitement.

Sears did not move into store-centered retailing until the late 1920s, so it could not awe its clientele with great "Marble Palaces" such as Field's establishment in Chicago. Can we, nevertheless, say that shopping the Sears catalog was exciting? I think we can. Through that catalog and through the railroad and telegraph systems that made Sears's operation possible, the great expanse of rural America was brought into the matrix of the market culture. Page after page of the Sears catalog brought New York to the farmer's door. It was no accident that the catalog was colloquially known as the "wish book."

In the rural general store, the farmer had been used to bartering and bargaining. A mail-order business could not have been run on such a basis. Sears was not in the business of trading, nor could it deviate from its published prices. How could it entice the suspicious farmer to do business on this basis?

Trust became the keystone of Sears's business. The customer had to feel in his gut that he (or she) was getting his money's worth. Sears did not ask the customer to take this completely on faith. The company guaranteed satisfaction or money back.

Other retailers made refunds, but Sears certainly featured its guarantee as prominently as any. The guarantee not only reassured the customer, it disciplined Sears itself. Sears could not afford to ship shoddy merchandise, for it would find it returned to its warehouse in short order. Sears had to be an honest house to do a volume business from one year to the next.

ENTREPRENEURIAL VISION

Admittedly, we cannot reconcile this portrait with some of the merchandise that appeared in the Sears catalog prior to Rosenwald's taking control of the firm. The Sears $11.96 cookstove did indeed cook. But did the electric ring cure rheumatism? Or did the electric belt—the $18 "Giant Power Heidelberg Electric Belt"—really make you into a "new man?"[245] Of course not. Why, then, were such items not sent back by return mail? We do not know. The survival of these and similar products (descendants of which can still be purchased in our supposedly more sophisticated age) is one of the mysteries of American merchandising. Under Richard Sears, the company sold medical devices and nostrums because Sears himself could never pass up a sale and because, like so many others in the history of American selling, he was able to be both upright and less than upright simultaneously.

Rosenwald did not adopt the joking relationship that Sears did with his customers. Under his aegis, worthless products were expunged. The company's reputation for honesty was thus enhanced, and that reputation even today is among its most important assets.

Richard Sears was fascinated by the "hot fire" of volume. Profit he understood less well. He was a true marketing man. Rosenwald, the manager, put the two together. It was with Wood, however, that Sears became the complete Phase II mass marketer. His move into stores in the late 1920s meant that the company sold every consumer product except groceries and automobiles to everybody no matter where in the country they lived.

VERTICAL SYSTEM; FIRST-MOVERS AND ENTRY BARRIERS

Sears now competed no longer solely against Ward but also against every department store in America. However, Sears did not compete against these stores on their own terms. It did not, for the most part, locate its stores downtown. Further, its target was not solely, perhaps not even primarily, the woman. Sears focused on expensive consumer durables, the purchase of which the man—because of the amount of money involved and perhaps also because of his claim to technical expertise—would be involved in. Early advertisements targeted men specifically: "Articles for Men: Men! It's Easy to Shop Here—Everything for Men in One Place . . . The sort of store men have always wanted. . . ."[246]

The specific concentration on hard goods served Sears well, especially in the post–World War II boom. The hard-won successes with products like the Coldspot put the company in a perfect position to capitalize on the surbanization of America. The stores that it built with such speed in the late 1940s were ideally located to tap into this growing new market. And the reputation for trust and service that it had established through decades of honest dealing was an important asset in a nation whose population moved so often. Wherever one moved in the United States, there was a Sears, the consumer's friend, nearby.

Montgomery Ward, Sears's greatest Phase II competitor through a half century, did not adopt the Sears strategy. It was weaker on hard lines and late moving west. Its stores were smaller. By the mid-1950s, as Sears was approaching its high point as America's all-purpose merchant, Ward fell by the wayside.

Sears can be thought of as competing horizontally against Ward and, later, against department stores in that these firms were first and foremost distributors. However, Sears was also a great vertical competitor, using its economies of scope and its vertical system to compete against branded manufacturers. Throughout the first half of the twentieth century, Sears would guarantee a market to companies like Andrew Fyrberg's shotgun factory and Sunbeam's appliances, thus making it possible for them to scale up. Working with Sears, such firms made far more money than they ever could have made on their own. Problems with transfer pricing, cost allocation, and corporate focus, so critical a dilemma for vertically integrated distributors in recent years, were finessed while these relationships were growing quickly and while both parties to them were profiting handsomely. Even so, Sears did not own its suppliers except when it had to do so to gain access to goods. Otherwise, it would own some percentage of the suppliers' stock or perform some key function such as purchasing raw materials for them.

THE COMPETITOR'S OPTIONS; MANAGING CHANGE

Sears, the great all-American company, has experienced many difficulties lately. There is talk at this writing of its being a takeover target, talk that would have been dismissed out of hand just a few years ago. Potential raiders, however, believe that Sears is rife with undervalued assets, including especially the stores themselves; and they hunger to liberate that capital.

Why has this happened to this once-great company?

The short answer is that Sears is a Phase II company trying to do business in a Phase III world. Is that not, one might object, an excessively glib formulation? After all, Sears was one of the key institutions in bringing Phase II of American marketing into existence. Sears was a company that adjusted with facility to that earthquake in American retailing—the automobile. Unlike A&P, which did not begin to respond effectively to the automobile until 1938, Sears led the way into the new era in 1925. Why could not this company adjust with equal facility to Phase III market segmentation?

The move into stores in the 1920s took judgment and courage. However, it was essentially a way for Sears to reach out for additional business, because its mail-order target market had never been urban areas. The transition from a Phase II world of big stores selling private-label goods to a mass market to a Phase III world of smaller stores, many featuring nationally advertised brands and moving quickly with the changes in fashion characteristic of the age of television, was tougher for Sears because it struck directly at its greatest strengths. What could Sears do with a 100,000-square-foot store? How could it make it smaller and more flexible? What would be its new relationship with its suppliers?

Sears's physical fixed assets were predicated on a Phase II world. Its organization and marketing mind-set were geared to such a world. Its psychological contract with its consumers existed in the context of that world. Sears could put Cheryl Tiegs on its catalog cover, but it still remained Sears—honest, clunky old Sears.

CHAPTER 6

Secrets of Success: Modern Marketing in Historical Perspective

This concluding chapter is synthesized around the propositions that were introduced in chapter 1 and that have served as a theme through the course of this book. Let us first restate them and then proceed to a discussion of each.

1. The strategy of profit through volume—selling many units at low margins rather than few units at high margins—historically has been the distinctive signature of the American approach to marketing. By making products available to the masses all over the nation—by democratizing consumption—the mass marketer did something profoundly American.
2. Mass marketing did not spontaneously develop because of the existence of the necessary technological, economic, and social preconditions. An entrepreneur had to have the creativity to see new business opportunities and the willingness to take the risks involved in transforming his or her vision into reality. The business firms that such people made the instruments of their will had to create mass markets by shaping and molding the unorganized, inchoate demand for their products.
3. To implement the strategy of profit through volume, the entrepreneur had to create a vertical system through which raw materials were sourced, production operations managed, and the product delivered to the ultimate consumer. Scale at one level was useless without scale at the others. Mass production demanded mass marketing. The vertical system usually involved integration within the firm of some of the steps involved and contractual relations for the others.

4. The first firm to implement successfully the profit-through-volume strategy had the opportunity to reap enormous profits. First-mover profits tantalized potential competitors, but first-mover advantages confronted those potential competitors with barriers to the industry's high returns.

5. The key strategic choice that resulted was how to attack the barriers. The potential entrant could attempt a more proficient implementation of the same basic strategy used by the first-mover or it could seek to exploit some strategic insight to change the rules of the game. The entrant's thrust, the dominant firm's response, the entrant's reply, and ensuing moves defined the nature of competition in a given industry over the course of decades.

6. Sustained success or failure in a market has been determined by how well a firm manages change. The firm itself experiences internal change, as leaders age and new executives struggle for power. Competition changes as new strategies are attempted. The market changes as the needs and wants of consumers evolve. The infrastructure changes with the development of new technologies for transportation, communication, and data processing.

Profit Through Volume

In one of his most famous observations, Adam Smith wrote that "People of the same trade seldom meet together, even for merriment and diversion, but the conversation ends in a conspiracy against the public, or in some contrivance to raise prices."[1] Broadly speaking, this was true of business in Smith's time not only in Britain but also around the world. People struggled to find a way to cooperate toward the goal of limiting output and keeping prices and margins high. What is today called the skimming strategy was the predominant approach to business since time began. The reason is simple. Through this strategy, the businessperson could make more money doing less work.

What is new is the penetration strategy, selling as many units as possible for the lowest price possible and making money on volume. This strategy was adopted by a select group of American businesspeople during the course of the last hundred years. Unlike Adam Smith's merchants, Henry Ford did not meet with other automobile manufacturers to keep prices high. John Hartford did not meet with other grocers to keep prices high. Robert Wood did not meet with others in the refrigerator industry to keep prices high. Instead, these men figured out new methods and systems to drive prices as low as possible.

The great mass marketers have been just that—marketers to the masses. They have struggled for volume before all else. And they have not merely served markets. They have created them. Candler created a mass market for colas. Ford organized and mobilized one for automobiles. Sears, Roebuck created mass markets for a wide variety of general merchandise. It did not invent the cream separator, the sewing machine, or the refrigerator; but its aggressive penetration pricing program combined with terms of sale that featured an iron-clad, money-back guarantee drew rural America into the national market. A&P got its start by creating a mass market for a specialty food item, tea, through aggressive pricing and clever promotional schemes. Through the first half of the twentieth century, A&P made more food available to more people at lower prices than any other firm, which resulted in its control of, at one time, 13 percent of the historically highly fragmented business of retailing groceries.

A 1938 *Fortune* article used the phrase, "The American idea of profit through volume."[2] This astute phrase not only describes a business strategy; it is about American culture as well. Indeed, it links the two. This book is about the democratization of consumption[3] as a distinctive contribution of America to the world. The way to run a business is not to collude with other producers to restrict output and keep the price high. Rather, it is to run the works full and steady and push prices down so low that everyone can buy the product cheaply and conveniently.

The American business system has placed in the hands of the average citizen an unprecedented panoply of products. Table 6–1 compares the selected possessions and living conditions of all American families in 1900 to those of poor families in 1970. Table 6–2 shows that Americans owned more of the most desirable household appliances than did Western Europeans in 1970. The data in both tables show that America was the leader in that year. America democratized consumption, and foreign nations envied it and wanted to have these things as well.

America's twentieth-century revolution has been more material than ideological. Even in the worst year of the Great Depression, the French philosopher André Siegfried said, "The United States is presiding at a general reorganization of the ways of living throughout the entire world. . . ."[4] No one understood the power of the attraction of this "general reorganization of the ways of living" better than Franklin Roosevelt. That is why he wanted to give every Russian a copy of the Sears catalog. He knew that that catalog and the business system behind it were leading to the world of table 6–1, a world in which the poor had access in 1970 to what even much of the middle class did not have in 1900. Given half a chance, his hunch was that the American "wish book" could become the Russian one as well.[5]

The intellectual aspect of the creation of mass markets cannot be

TABLE 6–1

Standard of Living of all American Families (1900) and Poor American Families (1970)

Percent of Families Having:	All Families in 1900	Poor Families in 1970[a]
Flush toilet	15%	99%
Running water	24[b]	92
Central heating	1	58
One (or fewer) persons per room	48	96
Electricity	3	99
Refrigeration	18 (ice)	99 (mechanical)
Automobiles	1[c]	41

[a]Family incomes under $4,000.
[b]Data are for 1890.
[c]Data are for 1910.
SOURCE: Stanley Lebergott, *The American Economy: Income, Wealth, and Want* (Princeton, N.J.: Princeton University Press, 1976), 8.

TABLE 6–2

Percent of Population in Possession of Selected Products in the United States and Western Europe, 1970

Percent of Households Having:	United States	Western Europe
Refrigerator	99%	72%
Washing machine	70	57
Dryer	45	18
Iron	100	93
Vacuum cleaner	92	61
Dishwasher	26	2
Toaster	93	21
Television	99	75
Telephone	91	33

SOURCE: Stanley Lebergott, *The American Economy: Income, Wealth, and Want* (Princeton, N.J.: Princeton University Press, 1976), 102.

overlooked. In André Siegfried's view, the idea that life could and should be a pleasure was a "revelation," "the most fantastic innovation of all."[6] Innovation is much studied by economists and business academicians, but any analysis that omits the sociocultural matrix out of which ideas such as this emerge is incomplete.

There could have been no mass-marketed automobile before the idea of one. We forget what a staggering intellectual leap this horseless world constituted because we take it for granted. Ford and a few others had this idea at least in part—and in my view, in important part—because he and they were Americans. They grew up in a country where equality was a deeply held belief. The picture Ford had of society was not one of static, frozen classes in which some are born to serve and others to be served. It was of a fluid world, where a man was judged not on where he was but on how far he had come. Such a man, Ford believed, deserved to own his own automobile.

We are so accustomed to this democratization of consumption—the mass marketing of what previously had been seen as the property of an elite—that we can easily overlook the extent to which it continues to happen all around us. Here, for example, are the comments of John Sculley, president of Apple and former president of Pepsi-Cola, on the computer revolution:

> When Apple was founded [in 1976], there were probably fewer than 50,000 computers that had ever been built in the entire world. Today [1987], more than 50,000 computers are built and sold every day. The decade saw a hobby-ist's dream materialize into a $46 billion industry. . . .
>
> [T]he parallels between Steve [Jobs] and Henry Ford were striking. Neither man was educated as an engineer nor invented the technology behind the product that would bring him massive wealth and attention. They were, instead, leaders of a social revolution to empower the common man. Ford envisioned the automobile as a mass-produced tool that would give the average person incredible new freedom to explore the world. Steve saw the same in the personal computer.[7]

That is precisely correct, and that is why Jobs, like Ford, became a hero in this nation. Jobs did not merely make money. He did something for Americans that had a profound cultural and historic resonance.

Entrepreneurial Vision

Mass marketing was not made by preconditions. Men made it; men of vision, taking risks.

The energizing, animating force of the entrepreneur is nowhere more evident than in the Coca-Cola story. There was a soft drink market prior to 1886, when Coca-Cola was invented—Schweppes, Hires, Cliquot Club, Moxie, Dr Pepper, and others were already in business—but there was not a defined market for cola. Further, the market for soft drinks was local by nature. The product was heavy and bulky. Production was suffi-ciently simple so that scale economies could be achieved in a fairly small syrup plant. Unlike the automobile industry, a soft drink manufacturer did not have to have a national market to run an efficient plant.

Coca-Cola became a mass-marketed product for one reason—because Asa Candler wanted it to be. He felt sure he had the right product. He loved Coca-Cola because it cured his headaches. He was sure that if people really knew how wonderful this product was, he would have to "lock the doors of our factories and have a guard with a shotgun to make people line up and buy it."[8] Candler had a breadth of vision by virtue of the missionary religious activities of his family. That same religious fervor was brought to the company, where "Onward Christian Soldiers" concluded the sales meetings. It was not easy for Candler to find salespeople. The job was difficult, demanding weeks of travel far from home on the nation's newly completed rail network. It was not a full year's employment, because soda fountains were only open seasonally.

Candler solved such problems first by employing his family members and later by using people like cotton buyers, who were seasonally employed at other tasks. None of the people he hired had a business school education. We know this because there were no business schools. Coca-Cola had to establish its own training program for young recruits such as Ross C. Treseder. They had to be informed about the past performance of the accounts in their territory and about the coming season's promotion plans, and they had to be taught how to negotiate. Once on the road, early salespeople met with doubt about this new product. To lessen skepticism, Candler invested in advertising. As early as 1892, he was spending "considerable" sums "in territory which has not as yet yielded any returns."[9]

Candler did not *have* to do what he did to mass market Coke. He did not have to send salespeople north, to meet with skepticism when trying to open up new territory for an unknown southern beverage. He did not have to invest in advertising to make the beverage better known. Spending that money meant taking a chance. How could Candler have known whether these advertising expenditures would generate sufficient returns? Why didn't he just take the money out of the company and spend it to build himself a big house? That is what Coca-Cola inventor John S. Pemberton probably would have done. That is what most people would have done. But that is not what Candler did, and that is why there is a Coca-Cola. He did not consume his company's earnings. He reinvested them for the sake of future production.

In the area of personal transportation, there has always been a strong underlying demand in the United States. The fact that there were more than twenty million horses in the country at the turn of the century demonstrated that. There was also a demand for mechanical, inanimate transportation. Bicycle sales in the 1890s demonstrated that. But to say these things is not to say much. In the words of Adam Smith himself, "A very poor man may be said in some sense to have a demand for a coach and six. . . ."[10]

It was not underlying demand that produced the mass-marketed automobile. It was Henry Ford. There was no underlying demand specifically for the Model T. It was Ford, first and foremost, who had the vision of what a car should be. It was he who in the first decade of this century refused to go in the direction of low volume, high margin, and high prices. He and his people embraced the challenge of mass production. It was also the Ford Motor Company that first devised a workable structure to distribute mass-produced automobiles throughout the nation. Just as the company attracted the best engineers to create the miracles of the moving assembly line, it hired the best salesman in the industry, Norval Hawkins, and a cadre of people like Robert Abbott and George Banks who guided the product to the dealers.

The retail cases also provide ample illustration of the key role of the individual with insight and a sense of mission in the forging of a mass market. There was nothing inevitable about A&P's branching out from its pre–Civil War location, nor about its going into a wide variety of grocery lines, nor of John Hartford's move into economy stores prior to World War I.

John Hartford had an unbending belief in the importance of keeping the company in a position where it could deliver more quality product for less money than the competition. Adherence to that principle led him to close thousands of stores during the Depression and to transform A&P into a supermarket chain. It was the loss of this direction under the series of unimaginative conservators who succeeded Hartford that cost the company its greatness.

Sears, Roebuck also illustrates well the decisive importance of the chief executive officer and the extent to which a small number of key decisions—decisions that were not inevitable—could influence the development of a firm for years. The first such decision was Richard Sears's to go into general merchandise rather than specialize in watches. The second was the Rosenwald-Wood decision to go into retail stores. And the third was Wood's to undertake the major expansion after World War II.

All these decisions were based on an analysis of markets and long-term changes in demographics and regional population. They all sprang from a conception of Sears as America's mass marketer—serving the 80 percent of the population bracketed by the "Gold Coast" at the high end and the "junk trade" at the bottom. None of these decisions was inevitable, and each sprang in some part from the unique view of the company and of the world of the people who made them.

The term "entrepreneur" has been around for a long time. In fact, it was first used independently of association with economic activity. An entrepreneur in sixteenth-century France was a man involved in military ventures. By the eighteenth century, the word's meaning had expanded to include government contracting for public works such as roads and bridges.[11]

The entrepreneur was introduced into economic discourse in 1755, by Richard Cantillon in his *Essai sur la Nature du Commerce en Général.*[12] Cantillon described the entrepreneur as an individual who buys the means of production at certain prices in order to combine them into a product that he is going to sell at prices that cannot be known at the time he commits himself to his costs.

These ideas were refined and elaborated on by business economist Jean-Baptiste Say early in the nineteenth century. Say's entrepreneur was the agent who

> unites all means of production—the labor of the one, the capital or the land of the others—and who finds in the value of the products which result from their employment the reconstitution of the entire capital that he utilizes, and the value of the wages, the interest, and the rent which he pays, as well as the profits belonging to himself.[13]

This individual was not an economic automaton. Rather, he needed special human qualities, including

> judgment, perseverance, and knowledge of the world as well as business. He is called upon to estimate, with tolerable accuracy, the importance of the specific product, the probable amount of the demand, and the means of its production: at one time he must employ a great number of hands; at another, buy or order raw material, collect laborers, find consumers, and give at all times a rigid attention to order and economy; in a word, he must possess the art of superintendence and administration. . . . In the course of such complex operations, there are an abundance of obstacles to be surmounted, of anxieties to be repressed, or misfortunes to be repaired, and of expedients to be devised.[14]

One would imagine that a person responsible for such a wide range of critical tasks would stand at the center of the study of economics and of economic history. But this has not been the case. The main line of economic theory that has as its parent Adam Smith's *The Wealth of Nations,* published in 1776, has had little place in it for the role of the individual. In the classical and neoclassical view, the principal concern has been the examination of a general equilibrium between supply and demand resulting from the multiple reactions of businesspeople, laborers, consumers, and investors to prices. The world of high theory in economics to this day is fundamentally impersonal and timeless. Buyers do not know other buyers, buyers do not know sellers, sellers do not know other sellers; and there is perfect information. Individual variation is "cancelled out in the aggregate or suppressed by competition."[15] Social or cultural considerations can be factored into this paradigm only with difficulty, and there is not much room for unique human insight. For the neoclassical economist, the improper study of mankind is man.[16] The neoclassical paradigm has been called "perhaps the highest intellectual construction in the social sciences."[17] Brilliant work has been generated within its assumptions. But those assumptions assume away important aspects of what is plainly part of everyday reality in business.

People matter. Successful executives in similar corporations facing similar problems can devise diametrically opposed strategies to cope with them. Consider, for example, Sewell Avery and Robert Wood in 1945. Top executives within a single firm often disagree about what course to adopt. Look at the argument between Theodore Merseles and Robert Wood over retail stores at Ward in 1924. The decisions taken at these key junctures can influence companies and industries for years.[18] Timing, moreover, is critical in business. The fact that both Sears and Ward (eventually) opened stores to serve the booming Los Angeles market is far less important than the fact that Sears did so first.

Some economists have departed from the neoclassical view and attempted to find a place for the entrepreneur in their work. Most prominent among these is Joseph A. Schumpeter, who has recognized the importance of innovation and has suggested the part the entrepreneur played in its achievement. To undertake new things is difficult and constitutes

> a distinct economic function, first, because they lie outside of the routine tasks which everybody understands and, secondly, because the environment resists in many ways that vary, according to social conditions, from simple refusal either to finance or to buy a new thing, to physical attack on the man who tries to produce it. To act with confidence beyond the range of familiar beacons and to overcome that resistance requires aptitudes that are present in only a small fraction of the population. . . .[19]

In Schumpeter's view, this remarkable and essential business type was on the wane in the twentieth century because of the rise of bureaucratized big business. It "is much easier now," he wrote in 1942,

> than it has been in the past to do things that lie outside familiar routine—innovation itself is being reduced to routine. . . . [P]ersonality and will power

must count for less in environments which have become accustomed to economic change . . . and which, instead of resisting, accept it as a matter of
course.[20]

Entrepreneurship and along with it capitalism were thus slowly being
killed not by left-wing agitators who criticized their failures but rather by
their very success. Schumpeter greeted this development with distaste and
even perhaps with apprehension.

Daniel J. Boorstin, one of the leading historians of our generation,
arrived at conclusions similar to those of Schumpeter, though he approached the problem from the perspective of a different discipline.
The subtitle of the third volume of Boorstin's trilogy *The Americans* is
The Democratic Experience; but by the end of the book the word "democracy" takes on menacing connotations. Instead of being the battle
cry of each individual quest for freedom from oppression, it becomes a
morass that no one is capable of crawling out of. The future now
comes to us "on schedule." Giant organizations are bringing it to us in
a programmed fashion. At one time society concerned itself with establishing an environment in which advances in technology and progress
in general could flourish. Now, Boorstin believes, we find ourselves in
the grip of a bureaucratized "progress" beyond the reach of human
intelligence and imagination. His classic illustration is the Manhattan
Project. If the atom bomb was inventable, it would be invented. If it
was possible, it was unstoppable.[21]

Many of the entrepreneurs discussed in this book felt alienated by
bureaucratic organization. The best example, of course, is Henry Ford. He
hated organization to such an extent that he literally tried to take an ax
to his, chopping up file cabinets in moments of rage. Richard Sears did
not go that far, but he did leave his firm because the demands of organized
activity made the company that bore his name a joyless place for him.
Candler at Coca-Cola left because he felt his business was subject to
excessive regulation (this in 1916).

It would belabor the obvious to state that there are differences between
a bureaucratized big business and a small start-up. However, it does not
necessarily follow that bigness means the demise of entrepreneurship as
Schumpeter believed or that large organizations generate a mindless,
directionless momentum that the modern world mistakes for progress.

We must not read the individual out of history because even in an
organized world individuals make it. The mark of true leadership is the
ability of the individual leader to bend the large organization to his or her
will. Instead of stifling individual initiative, vision, and common sense, the
power of a well-run business can vastly leverage them.[22] Robert Wood,

for example, could move Sears into the South and West after World War II because he could exploit the organizational, mercantile, and financial power of a great American institution.

Vertical System

Many people believe that in business small is beautiful and that formal structures more often block the achievement of corporate goals than facilitate them. The wrong structure unquestionably hinders the firm. But nothing hinders it more than chaos. Effective organization is essential to great accomplishment in the business world. There can be no better example than Ford and General Motors in the 1920s.

Management of the vertical system has been a key success factor in the history of all the firms discussed in this book. When the vertical system was mismanaged—as, for example, when the cola companies, soon after World War I, found themselves at the mercy of the unpredictable whims of the market for sugar—disaster could result. When the vertical system was well managed—as, for example, it was when A&P, in its great days between the wars, backward integrated to do its own wholesaling—cost savings with attendant competitive advantages could be achieved.

Management of the vertical system might necessitate actual ownership at more than one level. The ownership option was often chosen for defensive reasons—that is, to protect needed supplies or outlets—or because only through ownership and direct managerial intervention could the necessary efficiencies be achieved. Management of the vertical chain could also entail efforts to control without owning. Examples include the franchise agreements in the soft drink and automobile industries and some aspects of Sears's specification buying program.

Defining the boundaries of the firm has received a great deal of attention from students of business. No problem is fraught with more theoretical significance because it deals directly with the relative efficiency of market versus administrative coordination of economic activity. This issue also carries practical significance of the first magnitude because it bears on where the manager will choose to invest the firm's capital.

The cases covered in this book suggest the variety of answers that firms have given to the question of their vertical boundaries. I believe there is no single answer to this problem for all historical eras, for all industries, or even for all companies within an industry.

In both the soft drink and the automobile industries, manufacturers performed some marketing functions themselves and franchised others. In the late 1880s and through the 1890s, Coca-Cola sold syrup through a network of jobbers to soda fountains around the nation. There is no indication that it ever considered doing its own wholesaling, much less integrating all the way forward into retailing.

Some problems could have been solved by ownership of soda fountains.[23] The company could have exercised greater control over how the product was advertised in the store and how it was prepared and served to customers. The consumer, it should be remembered, bought a beverage composed of syrup, carbonated water, and ice. All Coca-Cola did was ship syrup. Therefore, an important part of the "manufacture" of the end product took place off-site and was undertaken by people not employed by the company. Moreover, if Coca-Cola owned its fountains, the fountain operators could not push competing beverages offering higher margins.

The soft drink operators never integrated that far forward because the costs of these admittedly attractive benefits were excessive. Coca-Cola was an important product to the fountain but still represented only a small percentage of its income. Running a fountain was fundamentally different from producing syrup, and Coca-Cola would have had to make a large investment in personnel and capital to enter the business. Clearly, it was a better idea to try to control the retail outlet through promotion plans and dealer-training programs and by developing consumer pull through a massive, long-term advertising effort.

Bottling became a distribution option at the turn of the century. Once again, Coca-Cola had the choice of owning its own bottlers or dealing with independent firms. It chose the latter, but with a twist. It franchised parent bottlers, which in turn franchised other bottlers. The terms of the franchise agreement limited and defined the nature of the transaction. Coca-Cola supplied the syrup at a mutually agreed-upon price and worked to promote the brand. The bottlers agreed to bottle no other cola (although they could bottle other soft drinks) and to develop the local market. They held their franchises for life, and eventually they became part of their estates.

Asa Candler did not integrate forward because he did not want to make the capital investment in bottling and, more importantly, because he did not really believe in bottling. The carbonated beverage bottles he knew from early in his career often exploded, or the contents spoiled. He was a druggist; and the picture in his head of his product—part medicine and part refreshment—was of an elixir to be consumed amidst the sociability of the fountain.

Candler's decision not to go into bottling was a critical one for the company's future. The market development work of the local bottler became a key element in the mass marketing of this brand. Independent bottlers worked as well as they did, at least in part, because they were working for themselves—building their own businesses. Thus they had a large financial stake in the brand's success.

As the brand did succeed, however, Coca-Cola found itself hamstrung in some important respects by its franchise system. The bottlers could use their pricing control to dictate policy as they did in 1920. They were more interested in their local conditions than they were in Coca-Cola's market position nationwide. Why should the Baltimore Coca-Cola bottler care about share of market in Santa Fe? Why should bottlers agree to participate in a nationwide marketing program that did not meet their specific needs?

Through much of the history of both Coca-Cola and Pepsi-Cola, district managers have negotiated the many issues involved in the business with the bottlers. In recent years, these district managers have usually been young people, under 35 years of age, not long out of business school. When I interviewed some of them in 1983, I was surprised to learn how difficult such negotiations were. These young executives found themselves face-to-face with wizened bottlers, some of whom were personally worth tens of millions of dollars, whose families had been in the bottling business for a half century before the district manager was born, and who felt they knew exactly how to run their business and were in no need of advice from a 30-year-old salesperson making $35,000 a year. After a couple of days on the road, I asked one district manager how he felt about his job. He told me he was in the market for a "D.O.B." What was that? "Daughter of Bottler."[24]

The point of this story is that although every consumer in the United States knows the names Coke and Pepsi and probably not one in a thousand could name his or her local bottler, at the point of contact the bottler can be as powerful as the manufacturer. This is even truer in Pepsi's history than in Coke's. In the 1930s, Pepsi was a retailer's (Loft's) brand. By the late 1940s, it was more a bottlers' cooperative than a manufacturer's brand. Walter Mack was forced out of the company because he lost the confidence of the bottlers. Alfred Steele told the bottlers that if they trusted him they could spend their way to prosperity rather than save their way to bankruptcy. He promised to take them out of their Fords and put them into Cadillacs. This was a promise he kept, and in the process he helped make Pepsi a true manufacturer's brand.

Thus, historically the vertical system of the cola companies has been mixed. Some bottling territories have been franchised to independent entrepreneurs; others have been company owned. Even when these bottling relationships were with independent businesses, however, they were hardly market transactions in the classical sense. These relationships were long-term, characterized by exclusive agreements concerning territories and products handled.

In recent years, the soft drink companies have moved to increase their control over bottling. Where possible, they have been buying up their bottlers and consolidating operations. This trend has been pushed by a number of developments. First, the complexity of the bottling business has increased with the advent of cans and the growing number of stock-keeping units produced by beverage variations and container sizes. The era of one beverage (regular Coca-Cola) in one size (6½ ounces) is gone, never to return. It is essential that the modern bottler be up to date in plant investment and management. The cola companies cannot abide bottlers more interested in today's bottom line than in the future. Second, relations with grocery chains have demanded changes. Regional grocery chains may operate stores crossing the franchised territories of numerous bottlers. It has become more important than ever to coordinate soft drink sales with chain store trading areas. Thus, in this industry, the pressure of the differing evolutionary patterns of bottlers and the grocery trade has combined with changing economics to demand greater management of product flow by the soft drink firms.

In the automobile industry, we see a similar set of choices concerning how far forward firms should integrate toward the consumer. Should the manufacturer consign its output to a distributor, such as Sears, for example, at the factory gate? Should it wholesale but not retail? Should it wholesale and retail? Should it adopt some combination of these options?

The issues involved for Ford were staffing, investment, and control. Ford could pay the salaries needed to attract skilled professional executives to serve as headquarters sales staff, branch sales managers, assistant managers, and roadmen. Further, Ford realized that with major investments in a dozen or so branches it could exercise control over thousands of dealerships without having to hire thousands of salaried managers or to invest millions of dollars in agencies.

Like Coca-Cola with its bottlers, Ford franchised its dealers. Like the bottlers, Ford dealers did not pay an up-front fee. But there the similarity between the franchise agreements ended. Franchises to bottle Coca-Cola were permanent; automobile franchises could be terminated by either party. Coca-Cola could not raise syrup prices without the consent of the bottlers; Ford's prices were in its own hands. The bottlers had exclusive territories; Ford dealers lost their exclusives when the company unilaterally terminated exclusivity in 1921. We can thus see that the bottler franchisees had much more power than the dealer franchisees. Why?

Automobile manufacturers were more powerful in their franchise relationship than syrup (or, in the case of Pepsi-Cola, concentrate) suppliers were in theirs because the auto manufacturers did so much more for the ultimate consumer. Manufacturing an automobile was a task of great technological and engineering complexity and demanded an enormous capital investment. The end product changed the world. Manufacturing syrup or concentrate was easy. And the world would be no different if the product had never been invented.

No other product ever had the pulling power of the Model T Ford from the date of its introduction through the early 1920s. Ford owned the customer relationship; and because it did, it had the power to dictate terms to its dealers. Rare indeed must have been the automobile customer in 1915 who would have preferred purchasing any automobile from a specific dealer to purchasing a Ford from any dealer.

By contrast, plenty of people could quench their thirst with any beverage near at hand rather than save it for a half an hour to buy a Coca-Cola. That is why Coca-Cola's sales strategy required that it be within "arm's length of desire." This very necessity for universal distribution empowered the bottlers, who were so important in achieving it.

The history of manufacturer-dealer relations in the automobile industry has been marked by often bitter conflict. Yet the general industrywide problems should not obscure the differences among companies and even among divisions in companies that resulted from different product-market strategies, different philosophies of management, and different histories. For reasons such as these, there were big differences in the morale and performance of the dealer networks of Ford and General Motors in the middle and late 1920s, for example. Any static model of interfirm relations could account for such differences only with difficulty.

I have found no record in the histories of the retailers covered in this study of consideration of franchising their stores. Sears, Ward, A&P, and other big grocery chains owned their own stores; and each of them was supervised by a salaried manager.

A&P was fundamentally a retail store from early in its history. Store management was one of its competitive strengths. Its systems enabled it to simplify the task of store management, which made it easier to staff the stores with salaried managers.

For Sears and Ward, by contrast, the move into freestanding retail stores came well after the firms were founded. The problem of finding managers for these stores was a serious one. The "A" stores that Sears opened were larger than the biggest A&Ps prior to the supermarket revolution; and they were more difficult to manage in a programmed fashion because general merchandise included a wider array of goods than did groceries.

Both Sears and Ward entered into merger negotiations with J. C. Penney at the end of the 1920s because of an interest in appropriating Penney's wealth of store management talent. Penney had developed its personnel by giving them an equity interest in the firm, which is why J. C. Penney liked to refer to himself as the man with a thousand partners. Merger plans never matured, and Sears and Ward were left to work themselves through their management shortages on their own. Apparently, neither firm contemplated a franchise system such as McDonald's, which might have enabled them to tap the reservoir of entrepreneurial talent.

Store ownership was not, then, a major issue for Sears, Ward, or Penney. The extent of backward integration, on the other hand, has long been an issue for the big retailers. These three companies evolved as integrated wholesale-retail operations. By cutting out market relations at that level, the companies succeeded in sourcing goods for less and underpricing the competition.

The issue of integration further backward to manufacturing, however, was a more difficult one. If Sears, for example, invested in a supplier, it could have exclusive access to the goods that the supplier produced. Even if the supplier sold to other retailers, Sears could still guarantee itself privileged access to the product. Perhaps more important, it could gain knowledge of how and where the manufacturer sourced raw materials and of the efficiency or lack thereof of the plant. Such knowledge gave Sears matchless power to establish the terms of business. The power gained through this knowledge saved Sears from the problems of opportunism and "bounded rationality," which transaction costs theorists have cited as barriers to the efficiency of market-mediated dealings.[25] It has often been said that Sears's buyers knew more about the manufacture of what they bought than did their sources. In some lines, such as refrigerators in the 1930s, that was true. The merchants at Sears designed the product to their own specifications.

Sears's buyers sometimes exercised control of the vertical system back beyond manufacturing to the purchase of raw materials even for factories it did not own. "Naturally," Theodore V. Houser told his buyers in 1939, "the raw material content of Sears's merchandise runs into box car figures. . . ." Any reduction, however slight, in raw material prices could exercise a major impact on the bottom line. A buyer who purchased raw materials in bulk and dealt with strategically located factories could develop "a uniform product . . . built to a common specification with costs based on a common raw material. Thus you can have a nationwide sales promotion of such lines even though different stores will receive their goods from different factories."[26] A Sears buyer had the ability to create a mass market for standardized furniture, for example, even though optimum plant size and logistical costs were very different from those for refrigerators. This was possible because of the strength provided by the leverage of a great distribution system.

In some cases, where established manufacturers refused to deal with the chains, backward integration was essential. In others, merely the credible threat of backward integration disciplined suppliers, as we saw in the case of Ralston Purina and A&P in the cornflake market.

For all its advantages, the strategy of retail vertical integration had the defects of its virtues for the giant retailer. Long runs of basic items could lower production costs, but they also limited flexibility. Guaranteed orders could, over a long period of time, induce a torpor at the manufacturing level while making it impossible for the retailer to move opportunistically to make the best buys and take advantage of innovative developments. Investing in manufacturing also required added capital and management. Any retailer so doing had to question whether manufacturing was the best place to put its resources. Finally, vertical integration saddled the retailer with transfer pricing problems. What price should the manufacturing arm charge the retail arm? Where was the real source of profits or losses? Such questions could easily get lost in organizational politics.

These problems have made more difficult the strategy of vertical integration back to manufacturing for both Sears and A&P. By the late 1970s, Sears needed to move more quickly in a more competitive world. Edward Telling, Sears CEO from 1976 to 1986, pursued a policy quite different from that enunciated by Houser, in which the Sears buyer exercised the predominant influence on the investment decisions even of factories it did not own. In his book on Sears, journalist Donald R. Katz reports as a case in point the following encounter between Telling and a Sears supplier:

> Ed Telling traveled out to a screwdriver factory in Colorado . . . to hear the chief executive of the company complain that he'd built a new plant just to supply more screwdrivers to Sears, but Sears was suddenly ordering fewer screwdrivers. Telling observed that Sears already owned 40% of the screwdriver market in America, and that bumping that market share up over 50% was going to be a hell of a task. "It's your money," Telling said, "but I don't think I woulda built that new building if I were you."
> "Your own buyers *told* me to build it," the manager said.[27]

This is just one example of the pain and suffering caused when a company changes direction.

In the case of A&P, vertical disintegration was caused by a growing imbalance between the company's investment in manufacturing and its power as a distributor. Heavy investment in manufacturing was undertaken at a time when the market power of A&P's stores was diminishing. Pressure mounted for the stores to devote a higher percentage of their dwindling business to the private brands that A&P manufactured. This pressure came at a time when the power of television advertising was pulling consumers away from the private brands of a declining chain and toward nationally advertised products.

In exhibit 6–1, I have used a modified version of a chart published by Louis W. Stern and Adel I. El-Ansary in their standard textbook, *Marketing Channels,* to present a generic picture of the structure and function of the vertical system. In neoclassical economic theory, each one of these five stages interacts with its neighbor(s) through the medium of an impersonal market. In the real world of American business during the past century, the visible hand of managerial coordination has reached forward or backward, depending on the industry, to guide the flow of product from one stage to the next.

Ownership is not the only means of coordinating a vertical system. In so-called administered systems, one firm or some combination of firms develops programs that coordinate the marketing system. System members accept the leadership of the firm in question because of its power position. The contractual system takes the administered system one step further by legally formalizing these programs. Thus vertical marketing systems can be thought of as falling into four categories: conventional (the market-mediated structure of exhibit 6–1), administered, contractual, and corporate (the integrated system in which multiple levels are owned by the same firm).[28] Exhibit 6–2 arrays these four systems on a continuum to show the progression from control by impersonal market forces to control by managers. These systems are not necessarily mutually exclusive. Indeed, in many of the situations recounted in this book they coexist. Thus, in the 1920s, Coca-Cola had a conventional market relationship with sugar suppliers, a corporate relationship with some of its bottlers and a contractual relationship with others, and an administered relationship with soda fountains and food stores.

The argument of this book is that to create and organize mass markets, firms had to move away from the conventional marketing system and toward managerial coordination. This has not necessarily meant toward total vertical integration.[29] We have, in fact, seen instances of retreats from total vertical integration in the previous chapters. To choose one example, in 1905, an individual consumer could purchase a car directly

EXHIBIT 6–1

The Structure and Function of the Vertical Marketing System

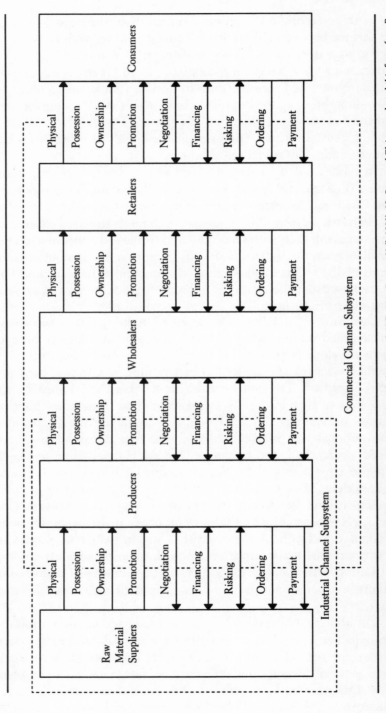

SOURCE: Adapted from Louis W. Stern and Adel I. El-Ansary, *Marketing Channels* (Englewood Cliffs, N.J.: Prentice-Hall, 1988), 12. Stern and El-Ansary adapted this figure from R. S. Vaile, E. T. Grether, and R. Cox, *Marketing in the American Economy* (New York: The Ronald Press, 1952), p. 113.

EXHIBIT 6–2

The Four Types of Vertical Marketing Systems

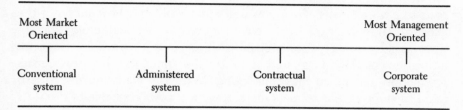

Most Market Oriented			Most Management Oriented
Conventional system	Administered system	Contractual system	Corporate system

from the Ford Motor Company. In 1917, the individual could not do so. He had to purchase from an independent retailer.

What I do want to assert is that during the past century there has been a movement away from the conventional system of marketing and toward some combination of the administered, contractual, and corporate systems. For the world of twentieth-century consumption to be brought to the American citizen, it has been essential that channel commanders create super-organizations to provide the products.[30] To use the seminal metaphor of Alfred D. Chandler, Jr., the "visible hand" of managerial coordination has been needed to supplement and to supersede the market.[31]

This assertion is contrary to the mainstream of modern economic theory and also to those aspects of public policy shaped by that theory. Yet I believe the history presented by this book can accept no other interpretation. If my interpretation is correct, the question becomes: Why? What did the visible hand of management do that the invisible hand of the market did not do and could not have done? I offer two answers, one dealing with technology and the other with human imagination.

The manufacture of many consumer products in the twentieth century demanded large plants. Think of the heavy costs involved in building Ford's plant on the River Rouge, costs that had to be absorbed prior to the generation of any revenue. When these giant works were run full and steady, the greatest stream of profits in the history of the world were within reach. Should output falter, however, losses just as great were guaranteed. The key point is that the vertical "value system," to use Michael E. Porter's term,[32] is only as strong as its weakest link. Not just the moving assembly line at the River Rouge but every step in the value system must "line out." If raw materials are unavailable, if inventory is mismanaged, if parts are not available precisely when and where needed, and if they are not of the requisite quality, the whole system fails. As the firm grows larger relative to the suppliers or distributors, vertical integration may become essential. In the meantime, the growth of the firm makes it more possible.

The genius of modern business has been the conversion of high fixed costs to low unit costs. These low unit costs could only be achieved if the fixed capital represented by the plant (or even by such marketing expenditures as advertising) were utilized as intensively as possible. Capacity utilization could not be guaranteed without volume. In other words, mass production demanded mass marketing. With the plant moving toward rated capacity thanks to mass marketing, unit costs continue to drop. As unit costs drop, unit price drops. As unit price drops, market share expands (but the market itself may expand even more quickly). With the expansion of market share by the firms that make the fixed investment in production (the plant) and/or marketing (e.g., advertising), the number of competitors declines. There is a market "shake out." The industry becomes an oligopoly. But note how this has been done—not through a conspiracy to raise prices but through investment and innovation; not through restriction of output but through its sharp increase; not through reliance on the market but through its supersession. The idea that neoclassical competition yields low prices and oligopoly yields nothing more than "monopoly rents" is a deduction killed by a fact.

Let us now discuss the second reason for managerial coordination of the vertical system: human imagination. Consider Asa Candler. He bought Coca-Cola in 1891, at a time when it was going nowhere. He believed in the product and wanted to share it with the whole country. But the world of the conventional system was a world of commodities. How could he build the Coca-Cola brand? The answer, as discussed earlier in proposition 2, was through his sales force and through advertising.

For many businesspeople in the late 1890s, advertising was a hole to throw money into. When Campbell's Soup appropriated its first funds for advertising in 1899, the secretary said to the treasurer: "Well, we've kissed that money goodbye!"[33] To the present day, the rules of accounting call for advertising to be expensed on the income statement. The reason is quite logical: It is difficult for an auditor to determine how much persuasion a given expenditure for advertising actually purchases.

Candler, however, instinctively understood that advertising was essential because the Coca-Cola brand was the only real asset his firm had. He could announce without panic in 1892 that his expenditures for advertising were not yielding returns because—unlike a financial accountant—he did not expect those expenditures to yield returns in a single fiscal year. He was investing for the future on the hunch that consumer pull would organize the distribution system without the necessity of owning it. He could approach fountains and later bottlers with a credible claim to consumer preference. If they wanted to share in that asset, they had to make a contribution in terms of an investment of their own capital in, for example, bottling equipment or wagons.

Without this key tool of vertical organization, advertising, there would have been no Coca-Cola. Without the adoption of the role of channel commander, this company could not have introduced this new product. Without the vision, drive, and willingness to assume risk of Candler, the advertising investment never would have been made.

First-Movers and Entry Barriers

The competitive contests discussed in this book show how some exceptional firms piloted by remarkable individuals managed to climb to the top of their industries. Those firms able to coordinate production and distribution to pursue the strategy of profit through volume reaped rewards in terms of return on investment of a magnitude that astounded both those involved and American society as a whole.

These returns stood forth as a beacon to competitors. Other entrepreneurs and other firms naturally wanted to have some of this bounty for themselves. Yet newcomers often found that it was not easy to build a platform from which they could compete against a company that had become solidly established as market leader.[34] All the first-movers discussed in this book sooner or later had to cope with competition, but it is noteworthy that all the first-movers are still in business today. This competitive strength and longevity result in part from first-movers' success in creating barriers to the entry of competition.

Barriers to entry are "the disadvantages that entrants face relative to incumbents"[35] and are an "inherent feature" of any market.[36] Porter lists nine general categories of barriers: economies of scale, proprietary product differences, brand identity, switching costs, capital requirements, access to distribution, absolute cost advantages, government policy, and expected retaliation.[37]

Capital requirements, especially those arising in industries where minimum efficient scale is high, are the most apparent of entry barriers. They are apparent in the literal sense; you can see them. In 1896, Henry Ford built his quadricycle in a shed in his backyard. By 1910, the plant at Highland Park was in operation. By 1913, when the moving assembly line was installed at Highland Park, Ford and General Motors already accounted for half the industry's unit sales. For any new firm to compete, it had to make a huge investment in plant; and it also had to acquire the expertise that the first-mover had already accumulated.

The giant mail-order firms also made major investments in plants. Sears's "Great Works" went up on Chicago's West Side in 1905 and was soon capable of processing 100,000 orders a day. Not long thereafter, Sears built similar establishments all over the nation. Any firm that had aspirations to enter national mail-order, general-merchandise retailing had to match Sears's investment. Not only would such distribution centers have to be built, which would invariably have meant taking on a load of debt, but somehow the expertise needed to run them had to be acquired as well. The difficulty involved here was heightened by the fact that during the course of the twentieth century, the rural market, which was the primary target of the mail-order merchants, was declining as a percentage of the national market. It is for these reasons that Robert Wood could confidently predict in 1937 that Sears and Ward would never face competition from a new entrant in the mail-order portion of their business.

It is the very absence of such capital requirements or of scale economies in manufacturing that makes the longevity of Coca-Cola's monopoly at first so puzzling. Unlike Ford with the River Rouge or Sears with its Great Works, there was no "big plant up on the hill"—no palpable barrier to entry generated by first-mover advantage—that Coca-Cola could point to. Capital assets required to build a syrup plant were not great.

And yet, Coca-Cola was by far the dominant nationally distributed product of its kind from its founding in 1886 to the 1930s. Even in the 1930s, Pepsi-Cola was able to enter the market only by giving more for less. This is often an option in business, but it is risky if based not on cost advantage but on the market leader's price umbrella. When commodity prices rose after World War II, Pepsi could not keep its own prices down. In all probability, it would have gone bankrupt had it not been saved by the brilliance of Coca-Cola-trained Alfred Steele in the 1950s.

How was it possible for Coca-Cola to maintain its position for so long? The answer is that it was able to exploit its first-mover advantages fully and to turn them into long-term barriers to the entry of competitors. What were these first-mover advantages? Let us focus on three of the barriers noted earlier: brand identity, access to distribution, and expected retaliation.

1. Brand identity was the keystone of Coca-Cola's strategy. The company quickly established the product's name throughout the nation by its commitment to intensive distribution and massive advertising expenditures. Coca-Cola managed to position itself for the mass market as the

quintessential democratic luxury. No other product ever came so completely to represent America to itself and to others around the world.

2. Access to distribution. Porter has written that the first-mover has the opportunity to

> gain unique channel access. . . . It can pick the best brokers, distributors, or retailers, while followers must either accept the second best, establish new channels, or persuade the first mover's channels to shift or divide their loyalties.[38]

This is what happened in the case of Coca-Cola. For decades following Asa Candler's purchase of the company, Coca-Cola was engaged in a laborious, town-by-town process of dealing with jobbers, with hundreds of thousands of soda fountains, and, after 1900, with hundreds of bottlers. In those fountains, Coca-Cola installed large, highly visible red dispensers, which some readers will doubtless remember. These dispensers were sold on the condition that they serve only Coca-Cola. Only Coca-Cola had a field force of service men trained and equipped to blanket the nation maintaining this equipment and teaching fountain proprietors how to use it.

As far as bottling is concerned, for more than half a century all over the country, if you were in the bottling business either you bottled Coca-Cola or you were poor. And if you bottled Coca-Cola, the franchise agreement ensured that you bottled no other cola.

3. Expected retaliation. The company protected its consumer franchise through the vigorous legal defense of its trademark.

What would Porter's list of entry barriers have looked like had his *Competitive Advantage* been published in 1880 instead of in 1985? No such list could have been compiled for most consumer products, which explains a lot about the changes that have taken place in consumer marketing over the past century. There were minimal economies of scale in manufacture, so capital requirements were trivial. With costs low, so were absolute cost advantages. There were few proprietary product differences, which made the establishment of a brand identity problematic. The consumer lived in a world not of brands but of commodities. Indeed, the consumer market in 1880 was characterized not by packaging but by packing.[39] In a world of packing, the packer was king, which is why the wholesaler was then the key functionary in marketing.[40] Other than the wholesaler, no one had effective access to distribution. There was no national distribution anyway, because the railroad network was incomplete. With no clearly defined set of national players, a new entrant did not have to fear retaliation. Finally, government policy was not a factor. There was none.

The Competitor's Options

Attracted to a market's high returns, the potential entrant finds itself blocked from them by the barriers described in the preceding section. What are the options available to it? There are two. The entrant can attempt to execute essentially the same strategy as the incumbent. Duplicating successful strategy is tempting, because "[I]ncumbents have demonstrated how to execute it and customers have shown that they accept it."[41] Success depends on whether the entrant has superior resources in terms of organization or capital to execute the same basic plan as the incumbent. Because the basis of this option is execution rather than some new strategic insight, we might label it the implementation option.

The strategic option, on the other hand, is characterized by some new view of what the market wants or some new channel configuration to link manufacturer and consumer. When skillfully executed, the strategic option can turn the incumbent's greatest strengths against it. By redefining the game, the entrant might be able to turn the incumbent's barriers to entry—a strength—into barriers to incumbent mobility—a weakness.

This book has provided examples of both types of entry strategies, as outlined in exhibit 6–3.

In the soft drink industry, Pepsi-Cola for years attempted to compete

EXHIBIT 6–3

Entry Strategies

	Soft Drinks	Automobiles	Grocery Retailing	General-Merchandise Retailing
Implementation Option	Pepsi versus Coke in the early years (1895–1920)		Kroger, First National, and other chains versus A&P (1920s)	Sears versus Ward (1890s)
Strategy Option	Pepsi price strategy (1930s); Pepsi Generation (1960s)	GM's introduction of the price pyramid and annual model change to combat Ford's Model T (1920s)	King Kullen and the other supermarket operators	Discounters and specialty stores versus Sears (1970s)

against Coca-Cola by doing what Coke did but by doing it better. Although Pepsi experienced some success in the early years of this century, its bankruptcy after World War I turned it into a dormant product for a decade. When Charles Guth bought Pepsi, it continued to languish at first. Its only sales were through Loft, of which Guth was president.

It was Guth who breathed life into this product in 1933. This he did by adopting a low-price strategy—an approach to the business fundamentally different from Coke's. "Twice as much for a nickel, too" had real impact in the Depression. Under Walter Mack, the new 12-ounce bottle was supported by highly effective radio advertising.

Given the kind of advantages enjoyed by the Ford Motor Company in 1921, how could the firm's dominant position be attacked? Not by trying to do what Ford was already doing, in the view of the Du Pont interests and Alfred Sloan. John Jacob Raskob, a Du Pont associate, described the Ford as "a special car . . . not considered by us a competitor." Sloan said that "No conceivable amount of capital short of the United States treasury" could have beaten Ford "at his own game."[42] Sloan was not going to try to make a better Model T than Ford. That is why General Motors decided to play a different game. It developed the annual model and segmented the market with the "car for every purse and purpose."

This policy brilliantly put General Motors on the path of the industry's future, as style began to play an important role in the purchase and as the used car made it imperative for the manufacturer to find new ways to obsolete the vehicles already owned. The beauty of Sloan's policy was that it enabled General Motors to gain the advantages of market segmentation on the marketing end but also of the scale economies in the factory, which were essential to maintaining a leading position in this industry. According to Arthur J. Kuhn, in *GM Passes Ford, 1918–1938*:

> Important styling variables just had to be controlled by the central headquarters staff and executives. And by 1938 divisional autonomy in styling had been restricted greatly: "Divisional originality [according to *Fortune*] gets full play in hoods, cowlings, and radiator grilles." Freedom to style hoods, cowlings, and grilles—within the constraints imposed by the interchangeable chassis parts and the corporate designed body—is not much freedom.[43]

A&P revolutionized food distribution in the early twentieth century through backward integration into wholesaling and into the processing of certain commodities and through bringing system to store management. A&P was the leading firm in the chain-store movement, which quickly spread to other lines such as drugs and, with Penney's, to soft goods.

A&P was the largest retailer in the nation for about a half century (to

1965) and the largest food merchant for longer than that (to 1973). It was not a truly national firm, since it was absent from much of the nation west of the Mississippi. One way to compete against it was to copy its strategy of vertical integration and systematic store management, but to focus on a geographic area in which it did not compete. Thus Safeway, the first grocer to grow larger than A&P, was based on the West Coast.

Attacking A&P where it was strongest was another matter. In 1930, there were numerous retailers that did precisely that. People shop for food often, and location is therefore a key to food store patronage. Even though it had 15,700 stores, A&P did not have stores on every street corner. Other chains competed using systems like A&P's.

Michael Cullen tried something new. His challenge to A&P was similar to that which Pepsi posed to Coke with the 12-ounce bottle. It changed the nature of the business fundamentally, demanding a different policy toward national brand names and in-store service and generating a different income statement.

A&P's strategy was based on the age of urban rail transport. The hub-and-spoke system of trolleys determined the company's store-location policy. That era was drawing to a close by 1930. The new age of the automobile dictated a new kind of store in a new location. Cullen recognized that and placed his firm on the path of the industry's history.

Montgomery Ward came out of the 1870s as the leading general-merchandise catalog retailer in the country. It had the endorsement of the Grangers, the kind of aid to credibility that was particularly important to a merchant whom his customers never saw.

Sears, Roebuck was founded in 1893, and had a larger share of market than Ward by 1900, a position it never relinquished. It would appear that Sears beat Ward at its own game. There was no analogue to the car for every purse and purpose, to 12 full ounces, or to the supermarket. Sears was selling the same kind of merchandise to the same class of customer. The simplest explanation for its leadership may also be the best—no one ever wrote catalog copy like Richard Sears.

Ward always had its eye on Sears and competed successfully enough to cause a lot of concern until the mid-1940s. The tragedy of its history was its failure to grasp the opportunity presented by stores in the mid-1920s. Here was the handle to the problem of beating Sears. But it was a handle Theodore Merseles chose not to grasp.

Ford, Coca-Cola, A&P, and Sears created and organized mass markets. Thus the strategic option for their new competition was market segmentation. This strategy has been mentioned a number of times, especially with regard to General Motors's attack on the Model T and Donald Kendall's attack on Coca-Cola.

Market segmentation refers to the practice of focusing on specific consumer preferences within a general product category rather than on the general category itself. Thus, for example, the Model T Ford was originally planned as the "universal" car. No General Motors car was so planned. Rather, the "car for every purse and purpose," as the phrase implies, meant selling different cars to different sets of consumers with those sets defined by how much the consumer wanted to pay and how he or she wanted to use the vehicle.

The same phenomenon can be seen in all the markets examined in this book. There has been such a resurgence in speciality stores in so many different lines that even Sears now has a specialty retailing division. Ironically, the success of many of these specialty chains was made possible by Sears's development of shopping centers. In groceries, many of the largest large chains in addition to A&P have performed poorly over the past two decades, picked apart by regional chains and local entrepreneurs who can run leaner and more efficiently.

Surely, the most remarkable example of segmentation is in the soft drink market. Within the memory of many readers of this book, the soft drink industry was dominated by one product in one bottle. Another way of saying that Coca-Cola was the "brand beyond competition" is to say that it was the "brand beyond segmentation." Coca-Cola was the universal cola just as the Model T was the universal car.

Any modern history of market segmentation must devote a lot of attention to the Pepsi Generation campaign. This targeted the young—demographic segmentation—as well as people with a certain life-style and attitude toward life—psychographic segmentation. The image of the Pepsi Generation was of a bunch of young fellows in tip-top physical condition playing football in the California surf with some of the best-looking young women in the history of the world. (Don't take my word for it. The Smithsonian Institution has a print of the "Surf Football" advertisement. Ask to see it the next time you're in Washington, D.C.) What was the "Pepsi Generation" all about? What possible connection could this advertising campaign have had with a soft drink? The answer is that Pepsi-Cola was not trying to tell customers anything about the product. It was trying to tell customers about themselves.[44]

Divisions in markets are not new. Markets have been fragmented on the basis of geography because of difficulties in transportation and communication since trade began. The process of breaking down that local, geography-based fragmentation and creating national mass markets has been the subject of this book.

But the kind of segmentation exemplified by the Pepsi Generation campaign is new. Segmentation based not on logistics or on some genuine product characteristics but on demographic and psychographic groupings carved out of the general population is an invention of late twentieth-century American marketing.

The old fragmentation was based on realities, but this new segmentation springs wholly from the imagination of the marketer. Pepsi and other such companies have been more interested in the term *segment* as a verb than as a noun. They have segmented markets, rather than merely responded to a market segment that already existed. There was no such thing as the Pepsi Generation until Pepsi created it.

Managing Change

Through the course of this book, we have observed the process by which the corporation manages change over time. We have observed the effects of exogenous changes in the infrastructure. We have seen how consumer tastes and needs with regard to particular products have changed. We have seen how new firms have tried to enter industries and how the basis of competition has changed. We have seen the exercise of individual skill and insight by observing first the creation of mass markets by first-movers and then the attempt of entrants either to beat the incumbents at their own game or to segment the market. Finally, we have seen how individual firms have changed—how they have sometimes fallen prey to forces that have aged them and robbed them of what made them great.

Of the many colas that entered the lists against Coke, only Pepsi scored a major success. Its resurrection from bankruptcy in the 1930s was made possible because in Loft it had an assured fountain outlet; and, most important, because as a bottled beverage it had what has ever proven an unquenchable appeal—twice as much for the same price.

Why did Coke not respond more forcefully? The cleverness of the Pepsi strategy was that it made standard responses difficult. Six-and-a-half ounces for 5 cents was the keystone of Coca-Cola's enviable income statement. The last thing it wanted to do was to endorse what was essentially a drastic price cut by competing on Pepsi's terms. Pepsi's move also threatened the value of the millions of 6½-ounce bottles owned by Coke's bottlers. Nevertheless, there were a number of options at Coca-Cola's disposal. It could, for example, have used coupons or other temporary consumer price promotions in market areas where Pepsi was strongest. A two-for-the-price-of-one "get acquainted" coupon might have effectively parried Pepsi's thrust. The two-bottle offer could have protected the sanctity of the "old reliable standard package" while actually giving the consumer one ounce more than Pepsi did.[45] The "get-acquainted" approach would also have put the consumer on notice that this was not a permanent price cut. It was temporary; that is, to last until Pepsi's next bankruptcy. Another option might have been a "fighting brand." Introduced at cut-rate prices and targeted where Pepsi was strongest, this might have been an effective tactic.

There is no evidence that Coke considered such possibilities. Perhaps Coke's executives felt it would be too difficult to mobilize the bottlers. One would imagine, though, that the bottlers could have been induced to take action by the appropriate financial incentives. Perhaps Coke felt that a response to Pepsi would have been expensive. And so it would have been. But a consumer franchise is a valuable thing to own and worth spending to protect. Perhaps—and this strikes me as most likely—Coca-Cola simply did not believe in Pepsi's staying power. So many colas had come and gone in the past, including the twice-bankrupt Pepsi. If this was the view of Coca-Cola's executives, they were almost right. With no cost advantages, Pepsi had to abandon its nickel price as commodity prices rose after World War II.

Pepsi's recovery in the 1950s after Alfred Steele took over is possibly more impressive than its performance in the 1930s. It had to abandon the one appeal that always scores—price—and to start playing Coca-Cola's image game. That it did so with such success under Steele and more impressively still with Donald Kendall's Pepsi Generation segmentation strategy is a tribute to both those executives. Coca-Cola's reluctance to respond vigorously also helped. It held on too long to its own marketing mind-set as the brand beyond competition.

The striking thing about the Ford-General Motors story is that Ford had the key to marketing success but then let it slip its grasp. "The old master had failed to master change," Sloan said of Henry Ford.[46] And yet Ford had understood change so well earlier in his career. He had tried eight models before settling on the Model T. He had been willing to try different marketing systems before settling on the form he chose. He had been open-minded to suggestions from dealers about how to make his product as attuned to the market as possible.

Ford's view of business had calcified by World War I. One reason for the loss of his earlier suppleness was the enormous special-purpose investment that he had made at the River Rouge for turning out Model Ts. The cost of switching over to the Model A in 1927 has been estimated in nine figures. The company had neglected to balance the need for commitment to serving the customer with the right product at the right price against the need for flexibility in the face of a changing market and competitive environment. Inadvertently, the company discovered the limits and limitations of the learning curve.[47]

Just as important as his capital commitment was the marketing mindset of Henry Ford. His allegiance to the Model T transcended the bounds of business analysis and entered the realm of the psychological if not psychiatric. He had to learn the hard way that "there is no such thing as an impregnable position of market leadership."[48]

As Sloan said, part of the credit for General Motors's success belongs to Henry Ford's failure.[49] Sloan saw that the key to leadership in the industry was the management of change. That required organizational capabilities far greater than those needed for the production of identical units year after year. With the resources at his disposal, Ford could have competed far more fearsomely against Sloan. He simply chose not to do so.

A&P's history in the 1930s shows how perspicacious executives could effectively respond to a potentially devastating competitive entry. The supermarket revolution changed the world of A&P's greatness. At first, A&P and the other chains responded the way Ford responded to the annual model change and Coca-Cola to 12 full ounces. Disbelief. The "cheapy" was a "food circus" that would die a natural death soon enough.

John Hartford's greatness lay in the fact that he was able to see beyond rationalization to the evidence in front of him. When Michael Cullen put a King Kullen near an old-style A&P, the result was disastrous; and there was no arguing with it. Hartford was also able to see beyond the outward manifestation of his company—the 15,700 stores—to its true meaning to the consumer. "It has always been our idea—we have been volume."[50] His company did not exist for the stores. The stores existed for the consumer. If the stores were not right, they had to be fixed.

And they were fixed. It took time. Not until 1938 was A&P fully committed to the supermarket strategy. It was able to move only because John's older brother George had never let it become too committed to the multiple-small-store approach. To the contrary, he kept the company on 1-year leases; and therefore it was flexible enough to move into the new format when that became necessary. A&P succeeded at the supermarket game. It went into the Depression the nation's fifth biggest industrial company and emerged from World War II still ranked fifth.

Had Robert Wood been running A&P after World War II, it might still be the nation's largest grocer. Wood moved Sears heavily into the South and the West because his foresight told him that the middle classes would be heading there. Ford did not move in the face of necessity. Hartford did move after he saw what had happened. Wood moved because he saw what *would* happen.

Wood, in 1945, did not have to launch Sears on its most daring and expensive move since going into stores. He was not pushed by the competition. To the contrary, Sewell Avery had told him that in expectation of another depression Ward was going to pursue the opposite strategy.

Wood did not wait to be under the gun to make his big move. Sears was doing quite well. No one would have criticized the company for a conservative postwar policy. If Wood had pursued such a policy, Sears would have done fine, just as Ward did fine. The problem with Avery's conservatism did not become apparent until the early 1950s. But Wood understood that the time to make a change is when you don't have to. A&P tried to change in the 1970s, but by then it was too late.

Concluding Observations

It has been the purpose of this book to show how the business firm, around the turn of the century, created and organized mass markets in a whole variety of industries and how the business firm in more recent years has created segmented markets.

I do not mean to suggest that corporations are full of manipulators who spend their time convincing people to like what they are getting rather than giving them what they really prefer. No one familiar with how business works thinks that a company can foist a product on an unwilling customer or change the will of the customer.[51] Statistics on new product failures as well as simple common sense belie such a view.

By the same token, however, I take issue with the view that consumer satisfaction is the sum and substance of the marketing task. What we have seen in this book is how a leader of vision together with an inspired organization can shape and mold a market.

Marketing is about the interplay between company and customer within the context of competition. The customer has a veto. Fortunately, we do not live in a command economy, and no customer owes any company a living. But it is the company that takes the active role, and therein lies its power. I leave this study with a heightened respect for the power of the firm and for the power of a leader within the firm.

The customer disposes. But the company proposes.

A Comparison of Chain and Independent Grocery Operations

Malcolm P. McNair estimated the gross margin of the independent grocery retailer to be 18.5 percent of net sales, or 18.5 cents out of the consumer's dollar.[1] We may thus take 81.5 cents ($1.00 − $.185) as representing the wholesaler's sales. The wholesaler's gross margin was estimated to be 11.86 percent. Since the wholesaler's sales equaled 81.5 cents, we can multiply the wholesale percentage gross margin by that dollar amount to discover how many cents out of the consumer dollar went for the wholesaler's gross margin. The result is 9.7 cents [(11.86 percent) (81.5 cents) = 9.7 cents]. This figure (i.e., 9.7 cents) added to the retail margin yields the total amount of the consumer dollar eaten up by margins in the retail-wholesale system. 18.5 cents plus 9.7 cents equals 28.2 cents. This figure (i.e., 28.2 cents) can be compared to the gross margins for all chains reporting to the Harvard Bureau of Business Research, which was 19.4 percent, or 19.4 cents out of the consumer dollar. Thus, in the case of the chains, the consumer spent 8.8 cents less on distributor margin (i.e., 28.2 cents − 19.4 cents) than in the traditional wholesale-retail system.

Now to total expense before interest. McNair estimated total expense before interest to be 16.35 percent for the independent retailer, or 16.35 cents from the consumer dollar. Total noninterest expense for the wholesale grocer was estimated at 9.54 percent. To convert this percentage to a dollar amount, it must be multiplied by 81.5 cents (see above). The result is 7.77 cents, and thus the total expenses before interest for the retail-wholesale system come to 24.12 cents (16.35 cents + 7.77 cents). This figure (24.12 cents) can be compared to the noninterest expense for all reporting chains of 17.45 cents. (As noted earlier, McNair estimated that 3.65 percent of this difference in expenses could be accounted for by the fact that the independents tended to provide delivery and credit.)

By the same methodology as that outlined above, McNair arrived at an annual inventory turnover of 3.68 times for the retail-wholesale system as opposed to 10 times for the chain system. In the case of this vital statistic, the illusion of comparing solely retailers is most pronounced. McNair estimated that retail independents turned their stock 11.75 times as opposed to 10 times for chain units. Only when the wholesaler's turn of 5.35 was added to that of the retailer did the total for the retail-wholesale system drop to 3.68.

It was turnover, probably more than any other aspect of their business, that had enabled nineteenth-century department stores to gain market share versus the older more specialized urban shopkeepers against whom they competed. The emphasis in buying strategy at Marshall Field in Chicago in the 1870s, for example, was to maintain assortments and rid the store of surplus stocks. The watchword was that "any surplus in Field's is not stock, it is cash." Field himself was quite explicit in demanding turnover.[2] Turnover meant that department stores could take a lower gross-margin percent and thus charge a lower price while achieving favorable gross-margin dollars and return on investment. Further, keeping the stock moving meant that the department stores would have fresher merchandise than their competitors and could therefore provide the steady customer with new purchase opportunities.[3] Turnover was to the department store what throughput was to the manufacturer. The importance of turnover in chain operations was recognized before World War I. So critical was it that Clyde Lyndon King predicted in 1913 that "the principle of retailing in the future will probably be to keep a limited variety of goods which can be turned over from day to day. . . ."[4] In this King was only half right. The typical supermarket in 1983 carried an average of 16,719 items,[5] which can be compared to the 270 items carried by a New York City A&P in 1911. Although the number of items had increased by a factor of more than 6,000, the importance of turnover— and this is the half of King's statement that was right—remains a primary concern of the supermarket operator.

The question of interest expense for the grocer in the 1920s relates directly to the speed of stock turnover. The typical independent retail grocer, as noted earlier, turned stock 11.75 times. The number of days in a year divided by that rate indicates that this grocer carried an average stock equal to 31.06 days' sales. The wholesaler's turnover was 5.35, which meant that they carried an average stock equal to 68.22 days. Thus it took 99.28 days to move foodstuffs from the manufacturer to the consumer through the traditional channel. This can be compared to the 36.5 days required to move merchandise by way of chain grocers, which turned their stock 10 times a year. Thus, 62.78 additional days were needed by the traditional method. The effect of this difference on interest charges can be easily imagined. We see from table 4–3 that five large, vertically integrated chains sold $1,804.8 million worth of merchandise in 1929. The cost of goods sold for these firms has been estimated at 79.5 percent (100 percent minus the estimated gross margin of 20.5 percent). Seventy-nine and one-half percent times the sales of the five chains ($1,804,781,-000) equals $1,434,800,895, which is the dollar cost of goods sold. This figure divided by 10 (the chain turnover rate) yields $143,480,090 as the average cost of inventory. Now choose an interest rate. McNair chose 6 percent. Six percent of $143,480,090 yields an interest cost of $8,608,805.

What would the interest costs have been if the merchandise these five chains handled in 1929 had moved through the traditional channels? If the wholesaler's cost of merchandise is assumed to be the same as that of the chain store that integrated wholesaling and retailing, we may begin by dividing $1,434,800,895 (which is the dollar cost of goods sold for the total retail sales of the five leading chains as calculated in the preceding paragraph) by the wholesale turnover rate of 5.35 percent. The result is an average wholesale inventory of $268,187,083. At 6 percent, interest on this amount comes to $16,091,225.

We now must determine the cost of these goods to the retailer. The wholesaler's gross margin was 11.86 percent of selling price, which equals 13.45 percent of the cost of goods sold. An addition of 13.45 percent to the wholesale cost of goods sold yields $1,627,781,615 ($1,434,800,895 + 13.45 percent). This figure divided by retail stock turn of 11.75 yields an average retail inventory valued at $138,534,606 which, multiplied by 6 percent, results in interest charges of $8,312,076. Retail ($8,312,076) and wholesale ($16,091,225) inventory interest charges add up to $24,403,301. This can be compared to chain interest charges of $8,608,805.

In this hypothetical example, the visible hand of managerial coordination saved $15,794,496 in interest charges alone over the market system. And interest charges are but a small part of the total picture, as the previous discussion and table A–1 illustrate.

TABLE A–1

Income Statement for the Chain Grocery System and the Wholesale-Retail System, 1929

	Chain	Wholesale-Retail
Retail selling price	100.0	100.0
Retail cost of goods sold	80.6	81.5
Retail gross margin	19.4	18.5
Retail expenses before interest	17.45	16.35
Retail interest expense	0.48[a]	0.46[b]
Total retail expenses	17.93	16.81
Retail net profit	1.47	1.69
Wholesale selling price	—	81.5[c]
Wholesale cost of goods sold	—	71.8[c]
Wholesale gross margin	—	9.7[c]
Wholesale expenses before interest	—	7.77[c]
Wholesale interest expense	—	0.89[c,d]
Total wholesale expense	—	8.66[c]
Wholesale net profit	—	1.04[c]

[a]Chain retail interest expense was computed by the method discussed in appendix A. The sales of the five chains in 1929 were $1,804,781,000. Total interest costs on inventory were estimated at $8,608,805. $8,608,805 ÷ $1,804,781,000 = 0.48 percent. Thus, in this instance, interest charges on inventory carrying costs alone equaled 0.48 percent of the retail selling price. In the reports of the Bureau of Business Research, total interest expenses were found to be 1.1 percent of sales for the 1924 chain grocery sample.
[b]This figure was computed in the same manner as that used above. It should be noted that a sample of retail grocers assembled by the University of Nebraska in 1929 found total interest expenses to be 0.75 percent of sales.
[c]All of these percentages are of the retail selling price.
[d]This number was computed in the same manner used above.
SOURCE: Data from Malcolm P. McNair, "Expenses and Profits in the Chain Grocery Business in 1929," *Bureau of Business Research Bulletin*, no. 84 (Cambridge, Mass.: Murray Printing, 1931).

Excerpts from Michael J. Cullen's Letter to the President of Kroger, 1930

My grocery equipment would cost two thousand five hundred dollars. My meat equipment would cost about $4,500.00 complete. A total outlay of $7,000.00 for equipment and a $23,000.00 stock of merchandise in each store. In other words, I would have an investment in each store of $30,-000.00. My operating expenses would be as follows:

1 Grocery Manager		$ 50.00 per week
1 Fruit Man		$ 25.00 per week
1 Assistant Fruit Man		$ 18.00 per week
1 Assistant Grocery Manager		$ 25.00 per week
2 Male Clerks	$18.00	$ 36.00 per week
1 Cashier		$ 15.00 per week
3 Lady Clerks	$12.00	$ 36.00 per week
1 Male Clerk		$ 15.00 per week
12 Extra Saturday Clerks	$2.50	$ 30.00 per week
Total Salaries		$250.00 per week

I expect to do a grocery business of $8,500.00 per week per store, a fruit and vegetable business of $1,500.00 per week, per store. In other words, the kind of stores I have in mind should do a grocery business of $10,000.00 a week and a meat business of $2,500.00 per week. On the grocery business, including fruit and vegetables, I can operate on a gross profit of 9%. My complete operating expenses on a $10,000.00 a week grocery business would be as follows:

Help	$250.00		2.50%
Rent	58.00		.58
Investment on Money	30.00		.30
Insurance	10.00		.10
Light-heat-water	7.00		.07
Taxes	10.00		.10
Depreciation	10.00		.10
Supervision	20.00	⅕ 5 stores	.20
Paper, bags, etc.	75.00		.75
Income tax	30.00		.30
Hauling	20.00		.20
Advertising	50.00		.50
Buying	40.00	⅕ 5 stores	.40
M. J. Cullen	40.00	⅕ 5 stores	.40
Total			6.50%

Our meat department sales per store would be at least $2,500.00 per week, and we would make a net profit of at least 3% on this meat business. This is the kind of cut-rate Chain of Wholesale selling direct to the public that I want to operate.

I want to sell 300 items at cost.
I want to sell 200 items at 5% above cost.
I want to sell 300 items at 15% above cost.
I want to sell 300 items at 20% above cost.

I want to gross 9% and do a grocery, fruit and vegetable business of $10,000.00 per week, and make a net profit of 2½% on the grocery department, and 3% on the meat department.

You need have no fear regarding the present overhead of the Chain Stores. My buying, advertising and hauling expense of $110.00 per week per store is more than enough to take care of the buying under my supervision; and this could be reduced twenty-five points after I had my fifth store opened.

I would bill all merchandise to the stores at cost, and adopt a cash register check system, that stealing or dishonesty would be impossible. I would inventory these stores every month at cost and their stock gain less all current expenses would be our net profit per month per store.

It would be a little difficult to begin with to buy for my first store, but after my fifth store was opened, I could buy the minimum shipments and ship 80% of same FOB to the store direct, thereby eliminating entirely a warehouse, which is not necessary when these monstrous stores could show a turnover such as I would get.

Can you imagine how the public would respond to a store of this kind? To think of it—a man selling 300 items at cost and another 200 items at 5% above cost—nobody in the world ever did this before. Nobody ever flew the Atlantic either, until Lindbergh did it.

When I come out with a two-page ad and advertise 300 items at cost and 200 items at practically cost, which would probably be all the advertising that I would ever have to do, the public, regardless of their present feeling towards Chain Stores, because in reality I would not be a Chain Store, would break my front doors down to get in. It would be a riot. I would have to call out the police and let the public in so many at a time. I would lead the public out of the high-priced houses of bondage into the low prices of the house of the promised land.

I would convince the public that I would be able to save them from one to three dollars on their food bills. I would be the "miracle man" of the grocery business. The public would not, and could not believe their eyes. Week days would be Saturdays—rainy days would be sunny days, and then when the great crowd of American people came to buy all those low-priced and 5% items, I would have them surrounded with 15%, 20% and in some cases, 25% items. In other words, I could afford to sell a can of Milk at cost if I could sell a can of Peas and make 2¢, and so on all through the grocery line.

The fruit and vegetable department of a store of this kind would be a gold mine. This department alone may make a net profit of 7% due to the tremendous turnover we would have after selling out daily and not throwing half the profit away, which is done at the present time in 25% of the Chain Stores throughout the land.

Then the big meat department. This would be a beehive. We would have the confidence of the public. They [would know] that every other grocery item they picked up they saved money on same, and our meat department would show us a very handsome profit. It wouldn't surprise me if we could not net 5% in this meat department.

How long are you and your Company going to sit by and kid yourself that in a few weeks this Henderson Radio Stuff and Home Owned Retailed Store propaganda will pass by?

The reason that I know that this proposition can be put over is that I have already put over a similar proposition right here in Southern Illinois. I operated Bracy's Warehouse store in West Frankfort before Bracy bought out Limerick, and did as high as $19,000.00 per week, $9,000.00 on groceries, $3,000.00 on meats and made a net profit of $15,000.00 on this one single store year before last, 1928, and I did this in a mining town of 14,000 people, mines only working half time, with A&P in the same city and Limerick doing a big business in this same city.

I was never so confident in my life as I am at the present time; and in order to prove to you my sincerity and my good faith, I am willing to invest $15,000.00 of my own money to prove that this will be the biggest money maker you have ever invested yourself in.

A salary expense of 2½%, I know seems ridiculous to you. You perhaps think this is almost impossible. I have had a great many stores under me in the past, and their weekly salary was only 3% with less than $3,000.00 sales. So this 2½% salary basis on a $10,000.00 weekly business is not only reasonable but is practical.

Again you may object to my locating two or three blocks from the business center of a big city. One great asset in being away from the business section is parking space. Another is, you can get generally the kind of store you want and on your own terms. The public will walk an extra block or two if they can save money, and one of our talking points would be, the reason we sell at wholesale prices are [sic] that we are out of the high rent district.

My other percent of store expenses I believe you will agree, are not excessive. If anything, I am a few points too high.

Don't let the buying worry you in any way whatever. I can handle the buying in fine shape. I could buy goods, ship them direct to my stores, 3% cheaper than you could buy them, store them in a warehouse, and put them all through the red tape that all Kroger items go through before they are sold. If this proposition appeals to you, there is not a question but that Reock and I could work together. It would be an asset, but what I am trying to bring out is, I would put this over without any assistance from Reock.

Before you throw this letter in the wastebasket, read it again and then wire me to come to Cincinnati, so I can tell you more about this plan, and what it will do for you and your company.

The one thought always uppermost in mind—How can I undersell the other fellow? How can I beat the other fellow? How can I make my company more money? The answer is very simple: by keeping my overhead down, and only by keeping this overhead down can I beat the other fellow.

What is your verdict?

SOURCE: Reproduced in M. M. Zimmerman, *The Super Market: A Revolution in Distribution* (New York: Mass Distribution Publications, 1955), 32–35.

Notes

Chapter 1   The All-Consuming Century: The Making of the American
Emporium

1. Quoted in Leonard W. Labaree et al., eds., "Introduction," *The Autobiography of Benjamin Franklin* (New Haven: Yale University Press, 1964), 10.

2. Labaree et al., *Autobiography*, 10–11.

3. Of course, many people, especially large numbers of enslaved Africans, did not choose to come here but were, rather, brought against their will.

4. Alexander Hamilton made a point of this in the "Report on Manufactures." See Henry Cabot Lodge, ed., *Works of Alexander Hamilton* (New York: Houghton Mifflin, 1885), 92–93. There were established churches on the state, as opposed to the federal, level until as late as 1833. See Lawrence H. Fuchs, *The American Kaleidoscope* (Middletown, Conn.: Wesleyan University Press, forthcoming).

5. David M. Potter, *People of Plenty: Economic Abundance and the American Character* (Chicago: University of Chicago Press, 1954).

6. Fuchs, *Kaleidoscope*.

7. Thomas K. McCraw and Patricia A. O'Brien, "Production and Distribution: Competition Policy and Industry Structure," in *America Versus Japan*, ed. Thomas K. McCraw (Boston: Harvard Business School Press, 1986), 77–116.

8. See the concluding chapter of Daniel Pope, "Advertising Today: The Era of Market Segmentation," in his *The Making of Modern Advertising* (New York: Basic Books, 1983), 252–98. This chapter is full of illuminating observations, many of which I elaborate upon in this book. Another important source for my characterizing Phase III as an era of market segmentation is my colleague at the Harvard Business School, Professor John A. Quelch of the Marketing Area. In two lengthy critiques of my work, which he delivered at the school's Business History Seminar, Professor Quelch emphasized the importance of market segmentation and product proliferation during the recent past.

9. See Pope's shrewd comments in *Modern Advertising*, 280.

10. For most of the material in this paragraph, I am indebted to conversations with Professor Lawrence H. Fuchs of the Brandeis University American Studies

Department. The source for Margaret Mead's observation is Donald R. Katz, *The Big Store: Inside the Crisis and Revolution at Sears* (New York: Viking, 1987), 209.

11. It is true that in the textile industry, the trend toward Phase II was well under way prior to the Civil War. Textile industry pioneer Nathan Appleton observed that the price per yard of printed cloth from the mills on the Merrimack River in Lowell, Massachusetts, declined from $.2307 in 1825 to $.0915 in 1855. Despite this precipitous decline, profits at the mills were high because costs declined even more quickly, and the market grew dramatically. See Alfred D. Chandler, Jr., and Richard S. Tedlow, *The Coming of Managerial Capitalism: A Casebook on the History of American Economic Institutions* (Homewood, Ill.: Richard D. Irwin, 1985), 167.

12. "The Top 100 Industrials: 1917, 1929, 1945, 1977," *Forbes*, 15 Sept. 1977, 128–29ff.

13. Robert H. Wiebe, *The Search for Order, 1877–1920* (New York: Hill and Wang, 1967), xiii.

14. George Rogers Taylor, *The Transportation Revolution* (New York: Harper & Row, 1951), 15.

15. Chandler and Tedlow, *Managerial Capitalism*, 173–99.

16. Ibid.

17. Alfred D. Chandler, Jr., *The Visible Hand: The Managerial Revolution in American Business* (Cambridge: Harvard University Press, 1977), 289, 297. This discussion draws heavily on Chandler's work.

18. Chandler and Tedlow, *Managerial Capitalism*, 55–82.

19. Oscar Schisgall, *Eyes on Tomorrow* (New York: Doubleday, 1981), 25–42; Editors of *Advertising Age*, *Procter & Gamble: The House That Ivory Built* (Lincolnwood, Ill.: NTC Business Books, 1988), 9–12.

20. David J. Reibstein, *Marketing: Concepts, Strategies, and Decisions* (Englewood Cliffs, N.J.: Prentice-Hall, 1985), 279.

21. Julian Lewis Watkins, *The 100 Greatest Advertisements: Who Wrote Them and What They Did* (New York: Dover, 1959), 208–209; David Ogilvy, *Confessions of an Advertising Man* (New York: Atheneum, 1963), 78–79, 116–17.

22. Thomas C. Collins, "Selecting and Establishing Brand Names," in *Handbook of Modern Marketing*, ed. Victor P. Buell (New York: McGraw-Hill, 1970), 13-75–13-76.

23. Wendy K. Smith with Richard S. Tedlow, "James Burke: A Career in American Business (A)," in *Managerial Decision Making and Ethical Values*, ed. Thomas R. Piper (Boston: Harvard Business School Press, forthcoming).

24. Ibid.

25. Chandler, *Visible Hand*, 302–305.

26. This is a theme of Alfred D. Chandler, Jr., *Scale and Scope: The Dynamics of Industrial Capitalism* (Cambridge: Harvard University Press, forthcoming).

27. Alexis de Tocqueville, *Democracy in America*, vol. 2, ed. Phillips Bradley (New York: Vintage, 1945), 105–106.

28. Daniel J. Boorstin, *The Americans: The Democratic Experience* (New York: Vintage, 1973), 89–90. For a brief critique of Boorstin's idea of consumption communities, see Michael Schudson, *Advertising: The Uneasy Persuasion* (New York: Basic Books, 1984), 159–60.

29. Pope, *Modern Advertising*, 178–79.

30. Robert L. Heilbroner, *Business Civilization in Decline* (New York: W. W. Norton, 1976), 114.

31. Chandler and Tedlow, *Managerial Capitalism*, 10.

32. Richard Wightman Fox and T. J. Jackson Lears, eds., "Introduction," in *The Culture of Consumption: Critical Essays in American History, 1880–1980* (New York: Pantheon, 1983), x.

Chapter 2   The Great Cola Wars: Coke vs. Pepsi

1. Pat Watters, *Coca-Cola: An Illustrated History* (Garden City, N.Y.: Doubleday, 1978), 13.

2. Ibid.

3. Ibid., 13–14.

4. Ibid., 15.

5. Ibid., 15–16.

6. John J. Riley, *A History of the American Soft Drink Industry* (New York: Arno, 1972), 24–26, 243–46.

7. Ibid., 248–51.

8. Ibid., 254–56.

9. J. C. Louis and Harvey Z. Yazijian, *The Cola Wars* (New York: Everest House, 1980), 25–26. The authors make much, perhaps too much, of the importance of "the crucial emphasis the revivals placed on temperance" for the growth of the soft drink business.

10. *Beverage Industry 1985 Annual Manual* (Cleveland, Ohio: Harcourt Brace Jovanovich, Sept. 1985), 24.

11. Louis and Yazijian, *Cola Wars*, 15–16.

12. Charles Howard Candler, *Asa Griggs Candler* (Atlanta, Ga.: Emory University, 1950), 115, 122–23.

13. Scott Kilman, "Coca-Cola Co. to Bring Back Its Old Coke," *Wall Street Journal*, 11 July 1985, 2. See also John Koten and Scott Kilman, "Coca-Cola Faces Tough Marketing Task in Attempting to Sell Old and New Coke," *Wall Street Journal*, 12 July 1985, 2; John Koten and Scott Kilman, "How Coke's Decision to Offer 2 Colas Undid 4½ Years of Planning," *Wall Street Journal*, 15 July 1985, 1; Timothy K. Smith and Laura Landro, "Profoundly Changed, Coca-Cola Co. Strives to Keep On Bubbling," *Wall Street Journal*, 24 Apr. 1986, 1; and Thomas Oliver, *The Real Coke, The Real Story* (New York: Random House, 1986).

14. E. J. Kahn, Jr., *The Big Drink: The Story of Coca-Cola* (New York: Random House, 1960), 22.

15. Kahn, *The Big Drink,* 106–107.

16. "To Pause and Be Refreshed," *Fortune,* July 1931, 65, 111.

17. Kahn, *The Big Drink,* 104.

18. Roger Enrico and Jesse Kornbluth, *The Other Guy Blinked: How Pepsi Won the Cola Wars* (New York: Bantam, 1986), 223.

19. Watters, *Coca-Cola,* 20.

20. For the chain of title to the product, see the Coca-Cola Company, *Annual Report,* 1922, 13, Coca Cola Archives, Atlanta, Ga.

21. Candler, *Candler,* 63. Candler did not actually buy the stock from Pemberton, who had died a pauper in 1888.

22. This sentence is the beneficiary of Theodore Levitt, "Marketing Myopia," in *Marketing Classics: A Selection of Influential Articles,* ed. Ben M. Enis and Keith K. Cox (Boston: Allyn and Bacon, 1977), 5–30. I have also benefited from discussions with Edward J. Hoff, doctoral candidate at the Harvard Business School, concerning the observations made in this paragraph.

23. "The Coca-Cola Industry," *Fortune,* Dec. 1938, 110.

24. Candler, *Candler,* 337.

25. Ibid., 343.

26. Ibid., 109.

27. James Harvey Young, "Three Southern Food and Drug Cases," *Journal of Southern History* 49 (Feb. 1983): 6.

28. Candler, *Candler,* 38–39.

29. Ross C. Treseder, "As I Remember," Coca-Cola Archives, 1973, 13.

30. Coca-Cola Company, *Annual Report,* 1896; *Annual Report,* 1907, Coca-Cola Archives.

31. Young, "Food and Drug Cases," 6.

32. Benson P. Shapiro, *Sales Program Management: Formulation and Implementation* (New York: McGraw-Hill, 1977); Benson P. Shapiro, *Instructor's Manual to Accompany Sales Program Management: Formulation and Implementation* (New York: McGraw-Hill, 1977), 10–17, 149, 277. The author provides a valuable set of questions to guide the analyst of a corporation's sales approach. My understanding of these issues has greatly benefited from the three years I spent in the First-Year Marketing Teaching Group at the Harvard Business School while Professors Shapiro and E. Raymond Corey were course heads.

33. C. F. Roland, "Trade Analysis, Supervision & Follow Up," in *Report of Sales and Advertising Conference of the Bottlers of Coca-Cola,* Atlanta, Mar. 7–8, 1923, Coca-Cola Archives, 57.

34. John Gunther, *Taken at the Flood* (New York: Harper & Brothers, 1960), 56–78.

35. Harrison Jones, "Blazing the Trail," in *Report of Sales and Advertising Conference,* 11.

36. Robert W. Woodruff, "Why Coca-Cola Abolished Its Sales Department," *Printers' Ink,* 6 Dec. 1928, 153.

37. Jones, "Blazing the Trail," 9.

38. Ibid.

39. William C. D'Arcy, "Publication and Co-Operative Advertising for 1923," in *Report of Sales and Advertising Conference,* 122.

40. S. C. Dobbs, "Aggressiveness Necessary in the Selling of Coca-Cola," *The Coca-Cola Bottler* (May 1909):5.

41. Jones, "Blazing the Trail," 11.

42. D'Arcy, "Advertising for 1923," 121.

43. Charles Howard Candler, "Thirty-Three Years with Coca Cola," typescript, 10 July 1945, Coca-Cola Archives, 16.

44. Ibid., 16–17.

45. Coca-Cola Company chronologies, Coca-Cola Archives.

46. Treseder, "As I Remember," 12.

47. Ibid., 17.

48. Asa G. Candler, "History of Coca-Cola," typescript of the proceedings of the 1909 Bottlers' Convention, Coca-Cola Archives.

49. Watters, *Coca-Cola,* 46.

50. Candler, "Thirty-Three Years," 23.

51. Ibid., 17–18.

52. Ibid., 18.

53. Ibid., 17.

54. G. A. Nichols, "Why Coca-Cola Rebuilt Its Sales Organization," *Printers' Ink Monthly* (July 1924): 20.

55. "To Pause," *Fortune,* 106.

56. Nichols, "Sales Organization," 20. The author refers both to "four co-ordinate sales divisions" and to "five sales regions." It appears that the five sales divisions were the new organizational form, judging not only from the text of this article but from corporate annual reports as well.

57. Watters, *Coca-Cola,* 129.

58. Woodruff, "Sales Department," 144ff.

59. Ibid.

60. Ibid.

61. There remain some unanswered questions about this episode due to a lack of data. For example, if, in the past, salespeople had been evaluated (we assume) on opening new accounts and increasing volume, was the former criterion merely dropped? And what of the latter? If the salespeople were not really salespeople, could they be fairly evaluated on the basis of the sales in their territories? One also wonders about the method by which this change was presented to the sales force. It seems to have been a strictly top-down decision, and it was delivered in such a way as to make starkly obvious to the employees how dependent they were on the goodwill (and perhaps the whim) of their CEO. Was this purposeful? Or was the method a sort of ritual in which all the participants knew the script?

62. "Brief Outline of Distribution System of Coca-Cola," typescript in Black Book, Coca-Cola Archives.

63. Wilbur G. Kurtz, Jr., "Joseph A. Biedenharn," *The Coca-Cola Bottler* (Apr. 1959): 95.

64. Ibid., 95, 97.

65. Ibid., 97.

66. Franklin M. Garrett, "Founders of the Business of Coca-Cola in Bottles," *The Coca-Cola Bottler* (Apr. 1959): 85–92ff.

67. Riley, *Soft Drink Industry,* 99–102.

68. A copy of the contract is available in the Coca-Cola Archives, Atlanta, Ga.

69. Watters, *Coca-Cola,* 57.

70. There were six parent bottlers by 1915. Today there are none, the last having been purchased by Coca-Cola in 1975. A brief outline of the development of the parent bottling system is available in "The Coca-Cola Company: Distribution of Bottled Coca-Cola," 27 Mar. 1940, Black Book, Coca-Cola Archives.

71. Kahn, *The Big Drink,* 73.

72. "To Pause," *Fortune,* 105.

73. Kahn, *The Big Drink,* 77–78.

74. Timothy K. Smith, "Coke, Pepsi Seek Control Over Bottling," *Wall Street Journal,* 3 July 1986, 6.

75. Kahn, *The Big Drink,* 79.

76. Melville Strauss, "How the Bottler Can Cooperate with the Salesman," in *Convention Nuggets,* Coca-Cola Archives, 1923.

77. D'Arcy, "Advertising for 1923," 123–24.

78. See, for example, Jones, "Blazing the Trail," 5–7.

79. Ibid.

80. "Developing a Home Business on Coca-Cola Through the Six-Bottle Carton," *The Coca-Cola Bottler* (Aug. 1929): 13–18; "Developing a Home Business on Coca-Cola Through the Six-Bottle Carton, Part II," *The Coca-Cola Bottler* (Sept. 1929): 13–17; "Developing a Home Business on Coca-Cola Through the Six-Bottle Carton, Part III," *The Coca-Cola Bottler* (Oct. 1929): 13–16.

81. For the problems that coolers presented to the sales force in the late 1920s, see Sanders Rowland with Bob Terrell, *Papa Coke: Sixty-Five Years Selling Coca-Cola* (Asheville, N.C.: Bright Mountain Books, 1986), 43–44, 53–56.

82. Watters, *Coca-Cola,* 129.

83. Samuel Johnson, *The Idler and the Adventurer,* ed. W. J. Bate, John M. Bullitt, and L. F. Powell (New Haven: Yale University Press, 1963), 127.

84. See the interesting treatment by Michael Schudson, *Advertising: The Uneasy Persuasion* (New York: Basic Books, 1984).

85. See Frank Presbrey, *The History and Development of Advertising* (New York: Greenwood, 1968), 1–18.

86. The following list is adapted from Paul W. Farris and John A. Quelch, *Advertising and Promotion Management: A Manager's Guide to Theory and Practice* (Radnor, Pa.: Chilton, 1981), 1.

87. The best review of the health controversies surrounding Coca-Cola in its

early years is Young, "Food and Drug Cases," 3–19. For a contemporary summary of the company's position, see the series of articles in *The Coca-Cola Bottler* by Coca-Cola lawyer Harold Hirsch: "The Coca-Cola Controversy" (Nov. 1912): 7–10; (Dec. 1912): 7–10; (Jan. 1913): 9–12; (Apr. 1913): 9–14. For the attack on Coca-Cola by Harvey W. Wiley, who had by this time left his position as chief of the Bureau of Chemistry at the Department of Agriculture, see his "The Coca-Cola Controversy," *Good Housekeeping Magazine* (Sept. 1912): 386–94. Even a casual glance through the first four volumes of Coca-Cola advertising reveals the efforts made to fight charges that the beverage posed a health risk.

88. Advertising Copy, vol. IV, Coca-Cola Archives.

89. Jones, "Blazing the Trail," 14.

90. This advertisement first appeared in the *Delineator* in July 1905. It is available in Advertising Copy, vol. I, Coca-Cola Archives.

91. Roland, "Trade Analysis," 54.

92. D'Arcy, "Advertising for 1923," 114.

93. Coca-Cola Company, *Annual Report,* 1892.

94. Daniel Pope provides a superb discussion of advertising expenditures during the era in *The Making of Modern Advertising* (New York: Basic Books, 1983), 18–61.

95. Watters, *Coca-Cola,* 97; Louis and Yazijian, *Cola Wars,* 36. The percentage rate of increase slowed thereafter; the 1929 figure was less than three times greater than that for 1912. Yet the increase in absolute terms from 1912 to 1929 of over $2.5 million was well over twice what was spent in the former year. Another way to look at these expenditures is cumulatively. From 1892 to 1929 inclusive, the Coca-Cola Company spent almost $45 million advertising Coca-Cola.

96. Coca-Cola Company, *Annual Reports,* 1894 and 1896; "Where Reciprocity Is Indicated," *The Coca-Cola Bottler* (June 1909): 5–6. For a recent treatment of trademark protection in the context of marketing history, see Susan Strasser, *Satisfaction Guaranteed: The Making of the American Mass Market* (New York: Pantheon, 1989), 29–57.

97. A suggestion of that variety can be found in two volumes, collected and published by Coca-Cola, of opinions, orders, injunctions, and decrees relating to infringement of its trademark from 1886 through 1930. See the Coca-Cola Company, *Opinions, Orders, Injunctions, and Decrees Relating to Unfair Competition and Infringement of Trade-Mark,* vol. 1, 1886–1923 (1923), and vol. 2, 1923–1930 (1939).

98. Roy W. Johnson, "Why 7,000 Imitations of Coca-Cola Are in the Copy Cat's Graveyard," *Sales Management,* 9 Jan. 1926, 28.

99. Coca-Cola Company, *Opinion, Orders,* vols. 1 and 2.

100. Johnson, "7,000 Imitations."

101. Ibid.; Roy W. Johnson, "If a Competitor Swipes Your Trade Name," *Sales Management,* 20 Feb. 1926; Kahn, *The Big Drink,* 118–19.

102. The Coca-Cola Company v. The Koke Company of America et al., 254 U.S. 146 (1920).

103. Kahn, *The Big Drink*, 121.

104. Candler, *Candler*, 144–45.

105. United States v. Forty Barrels and Twenty Kegs of Coca-Cola, 241 U.S. 995 (1916). This case lasted almost ten years. For the sociopolitical views of Candler, see Michael Shirley, "The 'Conscientious Conservatism' of Asa Griggs Candler," *Georgia Historical Quarterly* 68 (Fall 1983): 356–65.

106. "Bob Woodruff of Coca-Cola," *Fortune*, Sept. 1945, 139–40.

107. Ibid., 140.

108. "Coca-Cola Industry," *Fortune*, Dec. 1938, 66; Louis and Yazijian, *Cola Wars*, 40.

109. Louis and Yazijian, *Cola Wars*, 40.

110. Coca-Cola Company, *Annual Report*, 1921, 7.

111. "Coca-Cola Industry," *Fortune*, Dec. 1938, 66.

112. Ibid.

113. "Woodruff," *Fortune*, 139.

114. Ibid., 139–43ff.

115. Ibid.

116. Ibid.

117. Ibid., 224.

118. Allen Shepard, "The Quick-Freezing Process and the Distribution of Perishable Foods," *Harvard Business Review* 8 (May/June 1930): 339–45; G. Terry Sharrer, "Food Technology in the 20th Century," *Journal of the NAL Association* 5 (1980): 21–26.

119. Advertising Copy, vol. I, Coca-Cola Archives; Candler, *Candler*, 163.

120. "A Talk with Roberto Goizueta," *Beverage Digest*, 30 Sept. 1988, 4.

121. Quoted in Robert C. Levandoski, "Evolution of an Ad Campaign," *Beverage Industry* (May 1986): 33.

122. David M. Potter, *People of Plenty: Economic Abundance and the American Character* (Chicago: University of Chicago Press, 1954), 121.

123. Kahn, *The Big Drink*, 15.

124. Ibid., 13.

125. I would like to thank Washington attorney Reed E. Hundt for this suggestion.

126. Robert W. Woodruff, "After National Distribution—What?" *Nation's Business*, Aug. 1929, 127.

127. Coca-Cola Company, *Annual Report*, 1928, 5.

128. Coca-Cola Company, *Annual Report*, 1927, 5.

129. Coca-Cola Company, *Annual Report*, 1929; *Annual Report*, 1928, 11; *Annual Report*, 1929, 11. Unfortunately, it is unclear from these annual reports what the dollar value represented by these percentages was in these years.

130. Coca-Cola Company, *Annual Report*, 1929, 11. Once again, it is not clear what dollar value was represented by these percentages. We do know, however, that subsidiary sales accounted for 9, 10, 12, and 15 percent of total sales from 1926 to 1929, respectively. We also know that subsidiary profits accounted for 2, 9, 10, and 13 percent for these years. Canadian and export

sales were not the only sources of subsidiary profits (e.g., the company owned a carbonic acid plant), and we cannot be certain that the sales referred to in the annual reports refer to dollars rather than units (although dollar sales seem the more likely). Using what data we do have, we can derive the following table.

Coca-Cola Subsidiary Sales
and Profits, 1926–1929
(in millions)

Year	Sales	Profit
1926	$2.7	$0.17
1927	3.3	0.82
1928	4.2	1.0
1929	5.9	1.7

SOURCE: Coca-Cola *Annual Reports*, 1926–1929.

131. Bryan, Kemp and Co., "The Coca-Cola Company," Coca-Cola Archives, 8.

132. Coca-Cola Company, *Annual Report*, 1928, 3.

133. "Coca-Cola's True Earning Power in 1929," *Barron's*, 24 Feb. 1930, 10.

134. "True Earning Power," *Barron's*, 10.

135. Ibid.; Philip Palmer, "Millions from a Soft Drink," *Barron's*, 25 Jan. 1932, 12–13.

136. Coca-Cola Company, *Annual Report*, 1929, 6. *Barron's* commented on this statistic that "When it is considered that the company is operating seven syrup factories in this country, four in Canada and two in Cuba, as well as 38 warehouses, the value of $6,305,636 placed on permanent assets is extremely conservative" ("True Earning Power," 10).

137. Bryan, Kemp, "Coca-Cola," 11 (emphasis omitted).

138. "True Earning Power," *Barron's*, 10; Bryan, Kemp, "Coca-Cola," 5.

139. Henry Richmond, Jr., "A Soft Drink That Has Resisted Hard Times," *The Magazine of Wall Street*, 16 Apr. 1932, 803, 820.

140. Palmer, "Soft Drink," *Barron's*, 12.

141. Bryan, Kemp, "Coca-Cola," 10.

142. Palmer, "Soft Drink," 12.

143. Bryan, Kemp, "Coca-Cola," 8.

144. "Coca-Cola, The Highest Priced Industrial," *Barron's*, 17 June 1935, 16.

145. Bryan, Kemp, "Coca-Cola," 9.

146. Woodruff, "Sales Department," 19.

147. This estimate is based on "The Top 100 Industrials, 1929," *Forbes*, 133–34.

148. Company data are drawn from the Coca-Cola Company, *Annual Report*, 1929, 3 Feb. 1930.

149. The company made this claim as early as 1924. See the Coca-Cola Company, *Annual Report,* 1923. The only possible competition would have been the leading cigarette brands.

150. *National Markets and National Advertising* (New York: Crowell, 1930), 7, 10, 15; "Top 100, 1929," *Forbes,* 134.

151. Coca-Cola Company, Black Book, Coca-Cola Archives.

152. Coca-Cola Company, *Annual Report,* 1895.

153. Coca-Cola Company, *Annual Report,* 1929.

154. "Highest Priced Industrial," *Barron's,* 16; Coca-Cola Company, *Annual Report,* 1935.

155. Ward Gates, "A Soft Drink Unaffected by Hard Liquor," *The Magazine of Wall Street,* 15 Sept. 1934, 562.

156. United States District Court for the Eastern District of Virginia, Bankruptcy Docket, Case No. 8418. In the matter of Cussons, May & Co., Inc., et al., v. National Pepsi-Cola Corporation (alleged bankrupt); "Pepsi-Cola Company Milestones" (typescript provided by Pepsi-Cola U.S.A.).

157. PepsiCo, Inc., *Annual Report,* 1987, 36; "The Fortune 500 Largest U.S. Industrial Corporations," *Fortune,* 25 Apr. 1988, D11–D13.

158. W. Leach, "PepsiCo, Inc.—Company Report," Donaldson, Lufkin and Jenrette, Inc., 7 Apr. 1986, 2.

159. Coca-Cola Company, *Annual Report,* 1987, 38; PepsiCo, Inc., *Annual Report,* 1987, 36; "Fortune 500," *Fortune,* D–13.

160. Coca-Cola Company, *Annual Report,* 1985, 49.

161. "20-Year Retrospective: Brand by Brand," *Beverage Industry,* May 1986, 24.

162. Coca-Cola Company, *Annual Report,* 1985, 9–19. For the Slice story, see Enrico and Kornbluth, *Blinked,* 154–59.

163. PepsiCo, Inc., *Annual Report,* 1985, 8.

164. Ibid., 22–24.

165. Leach, "PepsiCo," 5.

166. In 1947, for example, Walter Mack, then the president of Pepsi-Cola, predicted that Pepsi would catch up with Coke by 1950. See E. J. Kahn, "Profiles: More Bounce to the Ounce—I," *The New Yorker,* 1 July 1950, 34.

167. Enrico and Kornbluth, *Blinked,* 235.

168. Much of the discussion that follows has benefited from and follows closely a remarkable but virtually unknown book by Pepsi-Cola executive Milward W. Martin, *Twelve Full Ounces* (New York: Holt, Rinehart & Winston, 1962), 3–44. Unfortunately, Martin's book is not footnoted. Much of it, however, appears to be based on legal documents relating to the adjudication of the ownership of Pepsi-Cola in the late 1930s. In all cases where it has been possible for me to do so, I have examined those documents, and they are often cited along with Martin's book in the notes that follow.

169. Ibid., 6–7; Louis and Yazijian, *Cola Wars,* 15–16. Note the partial text of an advertisement that appeared in the *Greensboro Daily News Sunday,* 19 Dec. 1915: "Pepsi-Cola Aids Digestion. It relieves many stomach troubles. Al-

ways the best for indigestion. It never injures the stomach no matter how much you drink of it. Children relish Pepsi-Cola and it makes them fat." This advertisement is part of a large collection of Pepsi-Cola advertising that has been donated to the National Museum of American History of the Smithsonian Institution in Washington, D.C.

170. Martin, *Ounces,* 19–21.

171. Ibid., table 2, p. 12 and table 5, p. 38.

172. Ibid., 27.

173. Ibid., 31; the photograph is reproduced in ibid., 38.

174. See ibid., 42–45.

175. Ibid., 39.

176. Ibid., 42.

177. Ibid., 31.

178. See ibid., tables 8 and 9, pp. 55 and 57.

179. This phrase was often applied to Canada Dry. See ". . . The 'Champagne of Ginger Ales' that Ate Crow and Became a Pop," *Fortune,* June 1937, 114–18; "Leading Ginger-Ale Manufacturer," *Barron's,* 12 Nov. 1937, 8. See also "Up from Pop," *Fortune,* Aug. 1931, 45–49; "Canada Dry Ginger Ale," *The Magazine of Wall Street,* 30 May 1931, 168; "Canada Dry vs. Coca-Cola," *Business Week,* 24 Aug. 1935, 14; "Now That It Has a Sponsor," *Printers' Ink Monthly* (Jan. 1939): 15ff.; and "How Will Soft Drink Companies Fare If Prohibition Ends?" *Barron's,* 25 July 1932, 26.

180. Canada Dry Ginger Ale, Inc., *Annual Report,* 1928, 16. The *Annual Reports* of Canada Dry for 1925 through 1929 are available at the Baker Library of the Harvard Business School.

181. Canada Dry Ginger Ale, Inc., *Annual Report,* 1928, 14–15.

182. In later litigation, the price of Pepsi-Cola at the bankruptcy sale was stated to be $12,000. U.S. Patent Office documents indicate that the price was $1,500 less. Martin, *Ounces,* 52.

183. Martin, *Ounces,* 46.

184. Loft, Inc., *Annual Reports,* 1919–1940, available in the Baker Library of the Harvard Business School.

185. Loft, Inc., *Annual Report,* 1929.

186. Martin, *Ounces,* 49–50; in the Court of Chancery of the State of Delaware in and for New Castle County, Loft, Incorporated v. Charles G. Guth, The Grace Company, Inc. of Delaware . . . , and Pepsi-Cola Company . . . , *Complainant's Main Brief* (cited hereafter as Chancery Court, *Complainant's Main Brief*), 252–84; Chancellor's Opinion, Loft, Inc. v. Guth, et al., New Castle County, Del., 17 Sept. 1938 (cited hereafter as Chancellor's Opinion, Loft v. Guth.) Legal briefs and other legal documents from these proceedings were kindly made available to me through the law firm of Potter, Anderson, and Corroon in Wilmington, Del.

187. Chancellor's Opinion, Loft v. Guth, 181.

188. Loft, Inc., *Annual Report,* 1931.

189. Chancellor's Opinion, Loft v. Guth, 144–45.

190. Ibid.

191. Ibid., 145–46.

192. Chancery Court, *Complainant's Main Brief,* 94.

193. Chancellor's Opinion, Loft v. Guth, 145–46.

194. Ibid., 146; Chain Store Research Bureau, *The Future of the Soft Drink Industry* (New York: Chain Store Research Bureau, n.d.), 9. This research report is available at the Baker Library of the Harvard Business School.

195. For a more elaborate calculation, see Chancery Court, *Complainant's Main Brief,* 95.

196. Chancellor's Opinion, Loft v. Guth, 151. For a discussion of that $7,000 and why Guth needed Loft to raise it, see In the Supreme Court of the State of Delaware, Guth, et al. v. Loft, no. 1 Jan. term, 1939, Brief of Loft, Inc., Appellee, 46–48.

197. Chancellor's Opinion, Loft v. Guth, 172.

198. This use of Loft to purchase and operate Pepsi-Cola was the heart of the successful effort by Loft to wrest control of Pepsi from Guth. See Chancery Court, *Complainant's Main Brief.*

199. Chancellor's Opinion, Loft v. Guth, p. 155. For the development of the Pepsi formula, see Chancery Court, *Complainant's Main Brief,* 23–40.

200. Chancellor's Opinion, Loft v. Guth, 160.

201. Martin, *Ounces,* 53; Chancery Court, *Complainant's Main Brief,* 92–100.

202. Chancellor's Opinion, Loft v. Guth, 162.

203. Ibid., 179, 165, 155.

204. Enrico and Kornbluth, *Blinked,* 17.

205. Martin, *Ounces,* 57.

206. Ibid., 58–59. For the development of the 12-ounce bottle for 5 cents, see Chancery Court, *Complainant's Main Brief,* 120–24.

207. Chancellor's Opinion, Loft v. Guth, 162.

208. For the development of a syrup distribution system and bottler network, see Chancery Court, *Complainant's Main Brief,* 120–201.

209. Joseph LaPides, "The Good Old Days," *The Pepsi-Cola World* [cited hereafter as *PCW*] 30 (Jan. 1969): 20. *The Pepsi-Cola World* from 1941 to 1984 (with the exception of a few missing years) is available in the Archives of the National Museum of American History of the Smithsonian Institution in Washington, D.C.

210. Martin, *Ounces,* 63–65. LaPides's territory included most of the states from Pennsylvania to Florida as well as Mississippi and Tennessee. He had an organization of twelve field men to manage this region. The size of this territory proved too great, and in 1941 he "agreed to return some of [it] back to Pepsi-Cola Company and let them handle it themselves." His territory was further shrunk in 1948 (LaPides, "Old Days," 22).

211. Pepsi-Cola Company, *Annual Report,* 1941, 2; Martin, *Ounces,* 84–85.

212. Loft, Inc., *Annual Reports,* 1933–1935.

213. Martin, *Ounces,* 74. One of the young lawyers in the case was Herbert Barnet, who later became Pepsi's president.

214. Chester Karrass, *The Negotiating Game* (New York: World, 1970), 57.

215. Martin, *Ounces,* 63–65; see also "Canada Dry vs. Coca-Cola," *Business Week,* 24 Aug. 1935, 14.

216. These problems led observers to believe that "Economic distribution . . . calls for a large number of plants serving a relatively small area, with trucks as the principal means of conveyance." S. L. Miller, "Carbonated Beverage Industry Highly Competitive; Plant Location Important," *The Annalist,* 20 Aug. 1937, 293ff.

217. Chain Store Research Bureau, *The Future,* 11.

218. Ibid., 22.

219. Walter Mack with Peter Buckley, *No Time Lost* (New York: Atheneum, 1982), 9, 35, 91.

220. Groves made a fortune but eventually served a term in prison. E. J. Kahn, "Profiles: More Bounce to the Ounce—II," *The New Yorker,* 8 July 1950, 36. Mack has been described elsewhere as the vice-president of Phoenix. See Martin, *Ounces,* 76. In his autobiography, however, Mack states that he told Groves he would "agree to come in and help run Phoenix as president in special situations, if you'll agree, because you own the company and you're the largest stockholder, that if I say no to a deal you won't go into it" (Mack, *Time,* 96).

221. Mack, *Time,* 95.

222. Ibid., 120–21.

223. Ibid.

224. Guth et al. v. Loft Inc., Del. Supr., 5A.2D 503 (1939).

225. Martin, *Ounces,* 92.

226. Pepsi-Cola Company, *Annual Report,* 1941, 7.

227. "Pepsi-Cola Co. (& Subs.)," *Commercial and Financial Chronicle* 149 (14 Oct. 1939): 2375–76.

228. Chain Store Research Bureau, *The Future,* 26. Like so many other estimates from these years, this is unverifiable.

229. Martin, *Ounces,* 102; LaPides, "Old Days," 23. On early Pepsi-Cola bottlers, see also "Philadelphia Pepsi-Cola Bottling Company Grows," PCW (Nov. 1941): 5–6; "Face to Face with Our Bottlers," *PCW* 3 (Mar. 1943): 6; Frank M. Lyon, Jr., "1910: The Bottling Smith Family," *PCW* 6 (Apr. 1946): 4–5ff.; Bill Martin, "Success Story," *PCW* 7 (May 1947): 10–12; Samuel S. Freeman, "The Way It Really Was," *PCW* 30 (July 1969): 32–33; "Destiny in Schenectady," *PCW* 30 (Aug. 1969): 9–17.

230. LaPides, "Old Days," 22.

231. Pepsi-Cola Company, *Annual Report,* 1941, 3–4.

232. Freeman, "Really Was," 33.

233. Many contemporary articles make this observation. See, for example, Warren E. Kraemer, "Millions in Nickels," *The Magazine of Wall Street,* 23 Mar. 1940, 737–38.

234. Philip Hinerfeld interview, 1 Feb. 1985, "Pepsi Generation" Oral History

Project, Archives Center, National Museum of American History, Smithsonian Institution, Washington, D.C. (cited hereafter as PGOHP).

235. Charles Revson, quoted in Theodore Levitt, *The Marketing Imagination* (New York: The Free Press, 1983), 128.

236. Kraemer, "Nickels," 737.

237. Ward Gates, "Profits in Fair Weather and Foul," *The Magazine of Wall Street*, 18 Dec. 1937, 285. See also Richmond, "A Soft Drink," 802.

238. Joseph D. Kelly, "The Outlook for Coca-Cola . . . ," *Barron's*, 7 Nov. 1938, 13.

239. "Distribution of Bottled Coca-Cola," Black Book, Coca-Cola Archives, Atlanta, Ga; "The Pause That Refreshes," *Business Week*, 27 Apr. 1940, 36.

240. "Coca-Cola, The Highest Priced Industrial," *Barron's*, 16.

241. "Outlay of 348 Advertisers," *Printers' Ink*, 27 Jan. 1938, 55–61ff. *Printers' Ink* estimated Coca-Cola radio advertising at $265,170 in 1937, yet the Black Book of statistics in the Coca-Cola Archives puts 1937 radio advertising at $867,123.04. See also "How Big Advertisers Divide Radio and Newspaper Appropriations," *Sales Management*, 1 May 1932, 152; "150 Leading Magazine Advertisers in 1935," *Advertising and Selling*, 16 Jan. 1936, 26ff; and "150 Leading Radio Advertisers in 1935," *Advertising and Selling*, 16 Jan. 1936, 29ff.

242. For radio advertising, see *Broadcast Advertising*, vol. 1: *A Study of the Radio Medium—The Fourth Dimension of Advertising* (New York: National Broadcasting Company, 1929); *Broadcast Advertising*, vol. 2: *The Merchandising of a Broadcast Advertising Campaign* (New York: National Broadcasting Company, 1930) (these volumes are available at the Baker Library of the Harvard Business School); Herman S. Hettinger, *A Decade of Radio Advertising* (Chicago: University of Chicago Press, 1933); Erik Barnouw, *A Tower in Babel: A History of Broadcasting in the United States to 1933* (New York: Oxford University Press, 1966), 46, 105–14, 157–60, 167–72, 202–204, 206–209, 237–45; Erik Barnouw, *The Golden Web: A History of Broadcasting in the United States*, vol. 2: *1933 to 1953* (New York: Oxford University Press, 1968), 9–18; Erik Barnouw, *The Sponsor: Notes on a Modern Potentate* (New York: Oxford University Press, 1978), 3–75.

243. Coca-Cola Company, "Estimated Number of Listeners to Various Programs for Coca-Cola," Black Book, Coca-Cola Archives.

244. "NBC Clients' Merchandising and Promotion Tied in with Broadcast Advertising," in *Broadcast Advertising*, vol. 2; Frank W. Harrold, "Telling It to the World: How Coca-Cola Is Merchandising Its Radio Program," *Printers' Ink Monthly* (Mar. 1931): 44ff.

245. Gates, "Profits," 284.

246. Coca-Cola v. Carlisle Bottling Works, 43 Fed. 2D 101 (1929). In November 1930, the Supreme Court denied Coca-Cola's petition to hear the case.

247. Chancery Court, *Complainant's Main Brief*, 7; "A Valuable Trade Name," *Barron's*, 23 May 1932, 15.

248. "Coca-Cola Victory," *Business Week*, 6 Aug. 1938, 21–22; "Pepsi Cola vs. Coca-Cola," *Printers' Ink*, 11 Aug. 1938, 13–14; "Pepsi-Cola Co. Assails

'Coca-Cola' Validity," *Oil, Paint and Drug Reporter,* 15 Aug. 1938, 3; Mack, *Time,* 124–29; Martin, *Ounces,* 99–100; The Coca-Cola Company vs. Loft, Inc. and Happiness Candy Stores, Inc., 23 T.M. Rep 167, reprinted in the Coca-Cola Company, *Opinions, Orders and Decrees Relating to Unfair Competition and Infringement of Trade-Mark,* vol. 3 (Atlanta, Ga.: Foote and Davies, 1939), 49–64.

249. Mack, *Time,* 137.

250. Ibid., 137–38.

251. Kraemer, "Nickels," 739.

252. Coca-Cola Company, *Annual Report to Stockholders,* 1955, 3. This perception was fostered by Pepsi-Cola, which noted in its *Annual Report* for 1955 that its recent sales increases had been achieved "despite revitalized, large-scale competitive activities built on the introduction of new bottle sizes in imitation of our own, and on many marketing activities similar to ours" (p. 5).

253. "Pepsi-Cola's Walter Mack," *Fortune,* Nov. 1947, 188.

254. Walter S. Mack, Jr., interview, 16 Nov. 1985, PGOHP.

255. "Walter Mack," *Fortune,* 178; see also table 2–5, p. 52.

256. Mack, *Time,* 134–35.

257. Ibid., 134.

258. Pepsi-Cola Company, *The Pepsi-Cola Story* (Purchase, N.Y., 1982).

259. Mack, *Time,* 134–35. Various versions were different lengths, but none was longer than sixty seconds. Mack remembers the jingle as lasting thirty seconds. Mack, *Time,* 134–35. A 1947 *Fortune* article states that the jingle was fifteen seconds long "[w]hen Mack first heard it" ("Walter Mack," *Fortune,* 178).

260. Randy Cohen, "Songs in the Key of Hype," *More* (July/Aug. 1977): 12.

261. Mack, *Time,* 134.

262. "Walter Mack," *Fortune,* 178.

263. Mack, *Time,* 135.

264. Cohen, "Songs," 12.

265. Mack, *Time,* 136.

266. Louis and Yazijian, *Cola Wars,* 60–61.

267. Pepsi-Cola Company, *Annual Report,* 1946, 3. For a discussion of Pepsi prices after World War II, see Martin, *Ounces,* 123–27. My figures are in nominal dollars; that is, they are not adjusted for inflation.

268. Pepsi-Cola Company, *Annual Report,* 1947, 4.

269. Martin, *Ounces,* 126.

270. Pepsi-Cola Company, *Annual Report,* 1948, 4.

271. Kahn, "Bounce—I," 32.

272. Edgar J. Higgins, "Our Progress Didn't [Just] Happen," *PCW* 15 (July 1955): 2.

273. Kahn, "Bounce—I," 40.

274. For Mack's version, see *Time,* 173–80, and his interview on deposit at the PGOHP. See also, "Pepsi-Cola Tries Out Cans," *Business Week,* 11 Mar. 1950, 100.

275. Martin, *Ounces,* 125–27; "The Steele Years," *PCW* 19 (May 1959): 5ff.;

Richard Rutter, "No Question About It; Pepsi-Cola Has Bounce," *New York Times*, 7 Feb. 1956, 39ff.

276. Alvin Toffler, "The Competition That Refreshes," *Fortune*, May 1961, 127.

277. In his interview on deposit at the National Museum of American History, Mack acknowledged that Steele was a "good showman" and a "good salesman," but asserted that "He basically didn't give a damn about anybody but himself." "I think it was fortunate for everybody," Mack said, that Steele "died when he did." (Mack interview, PGOHP.)

278. "Alfred Steele, 57, of Pepsi-Cola Dies," *New York Times*, 20 Apr. 1959.

279. Toffler, "Competition," 126.

280. Pepsi-Cola Company, *Annual Report*, 1959.

281. Pepsi-Cola Company, *Annual Report*, 1956, 4.

282. "Steele Years," *PCW*, 16; Pepsi-Cola Company, *Annual Report*, 1951, 7.

283. "Steele Years," *PCW*, 16.

284. Ibid., 5.

285. Rowland, *Papa Coke*, 186–87.

286. "Steele Years," *PCW*, 28.

287. Ibid., 10.

288. Ibid., 12. The development of the regional office system can be traced through the *Annual Reports* of Pepsi-Cola from 1950 through 1959, copies of which are available at the Baker Library of the Harvard Business School. See also, "Men at Work: The District Manager," *PCW* 17 (Oct. 1957): 5–10.

289. Rowland, *Papa Coke*, 186–87; "Steele Years," *PCW*, 24; Pepsi-Cola Company, *Annual Report*, 1951, 11.

290. "Steele Years," *PCW*, 29.

291. Peter K. Warren, formerly president of Pepsi-Cola International, personal interview, Wilton, Conn., 20 Oct. 1986; Hinerfeld interview, PGOHP; Martin, *Ounces*, 129–36. The text of Steele's speech has not survived, but it has been pieced together from these sources.

292. "Steele Years," *PCW*, 5.

293. Michael E. Porter, *Competitive Advantage: Creating and Sustaining Superior Performance* (New York: The Free Press, 1985).

294. Hinerfeld interview, PGOHP.

295. "Steele Years," *PCW*, 8; Hinerfeld interview, PGOHP.

296. Tape of Pepsi-Cola commercial in possession of the author; Hinerfeld interview, PGOHP; Enrico and Kornbluth, *Blinked*, 20.

297. "Joan Crawford Re-wed," *New York Times*, 11 May 1955.

298. "Steele Years," *PCW*, 5.

299. "Alfred Steele Dies," *New York Times*.

300. Louis and Yazijian, *Cola Wars*, 80.

301. Mack interview, PGOHP.

302. Kahn, "Bounce—I," 36.

303. An interesting effort to contrast the product focus of Coca-Cola to the

market focus of Pepsi-Cola is Michael Norkus, "Soft-Drink Wars: A Lot More Than Just Good Taste," *Wall Street Journal*, 8 July 1985.

304. This suggestion was made to me by Mr. Edward J. Hoff, doctoral candidate in business economics at Harvard University.

305. Enrico and Kornbluth, *Blinked*, 3–4, 12.

306. A recent Coca-Cola advertisement runs as follows: "I was raised on country sunshine. I'm happy with the little things. A Saturday night dance, a bottle of Coke, and the joy that the bluebird brings" (Videotape of commercial made available to me by Coca-Cola).

307. According to Hilary Lipsitz, a Pepsi-Cola advertising expert, "I can't emphasize how important California was. California was out there. And we just went out there and got all these kids" (Lipsitz, interview, PGOHP).

308. Oliver, *Story*, 42–44.

309. Ibid., 47–48, 45.

310. Ibid., 46–47.

311. Ibid., 49.

312. Enrico and Kornbluth, *Blinked*, 84.

Chapter 3   Putting America on Wheels: Ford vs. General Motors

1. Howard L. Preston, *Automobile Age Atlanta: The Making of a Southern Metropolis, 1900–1935* (Athens: University of Georgia Press, 1979), 16; "Atlanta's National Show Interests the Whole South," *The Automobile*, 11 Nov. 1909, 815–18. Samuel Candler Dobbs was chairman of the Committee on Information, which had to find lodging for over 10,000 more people than the hotels could handle. "How Atlanta Entertains Her Automobile Guests," *The Automobile*, 11 Nov. 1909, 818.

2. James J. Flink, *The Automobile Age* (Cambridge: MIT Press, 1988), 1.

3. John B. Rae, *The American Automobile: A Brief History* (Chicago: University of Chicago Press, 1965), 7.

4. Jean-Pierre Bardou, Jean-Jacques Chanaron, Patrick Fridenson, and James M. Laux, *The Automobile Revolution: The Impact of an Industry* (Chapel Hill: University of North Carolina Press, 1982), 11.

5. Flink, *Automobile Age*, 22.

6. Bardou et al., *Automobile Revolution*, 13.

7. Alfred D. Chandler, Jr., *Giant Enterprise* (New York: Arno, 1980), 5.

8. James J. Flink, *America Adopts the Automobile, 1895–1910* (Cambridge: MIT Press, 1970), 21.

9. James J. Flink, *The Car Culture* (Cambridge: MIT Press, 1975), 19.

10. Flink, *Automobile Age*, 27.

11. James J. Flink, "Automobile," in *Encyclopedia of American Economic History*, vol. 3, ed. Glenn Porter (New York: Scribner's, 1980), 1170–71; Flink, *Automobile Age*, 41.

12. Flink asserts that gasoline was widely available even at the turn of the century: "Common stove gasoline could be purchased cheaply at any general store . . ." (*America Adopts*, 242).

13. For the state of the roads at the turn of the century, see Flink, *America Adopts*, 202–13.

14. Robert F. Martin, *National Income in the United States, 1799–1938* (New York: National Industrial Conference Board, 1939), 6. Martin reports that per capita realized national income adjusted by the cost of living in 1900 was $480. Current income was $212.

15. Frederick Lewis Allen, *The Big Change: America Transforms Itself, 1900–1950* (New York: Harper & Brothers, 1952), 7.

16. U.S. Department of Agriculture, *Horses, Mules and Motor Vehicles*, Statistical Bulletin No. 5, Jan. 1925.

17. Mark Sullivan, *The Turn of the Century*, vol. 1 of *Our Times: The United States, 1900–1925* (New York: Scribner's, 1928), 26n.

18. Flink, *America Adopts*, 242.

19. Rae, *American Automobile*, 11.

20. For a discussion of these matters, see Flink, *America Adopts*.

21. Henry Ford's 1906 letter to *The Automobile* is reprinted in John B. Rae, ed., *Henry Ford* (Englewood Cliffs, N.J.: Prentice-Hall, 1969), 16–19.

22. John B. Rae, *The Road and the Car in American Life* (Cambridge: MIT Press, 1971), 43. Although Wilson's observation is often referred to, I have not been able to locate a public statement in which he specifically makes it. However, there is no question that Wilson did not like automobiles. See, for example, Arthur S. Link, ed., *The Papers of Woodrow Wilson* (Princeton, N.J.: Princeton University Press, 1966–), vol. 16, p. 320; vol. 17, pp. 609–10; vol. 21, pp. 207, 209; and vol. 23, p. 606; and Edwin A. Weinstein, *Woodrow Wilson: A Medical and Psychological Biography* (Princeton, N.J.: Princeton University Press, 1981), 135–36. I am grateful to Professor Link for bringing these citations to my attention.

23. Alfred D. Chandler, Jr., *Strategy and Structure: Chapters in the History of the American Industrial Enterprise* (Cambridge: MIT Press, 1962), 415, n. 11.

24. Rae, *American Automobile*, 23.

25. Glenn A. Niemeyer, *The Automotive Career of Ransom E. Olds* (East Lansing: Bureau of Business and Economic Research, Graduate School of Business Administration, Michigan State University, 1963), 54–93; George S. May, *R. E. Olds: Auto Industry Pioneer* (Grand Rapids, Mich.: Eerdmans, 1977), 204–85; Flink, *Automobile Age*, 35.

26. Flink, *Automobile Age*, 35.

27. Flink emphasizes that low cost without high quality could not have succeeded (*Automobile Age*, 33–39). His insistence on this point is highly persuasive. Bardou et al. emphasize the importance of the single model and contrast Ford's approach to that of the Europeans (*Automobile Revolution*, 54–76).

28. In 1979, there were 19 motor vehicles per 1,000 population in the Soviet Union and 527 per 1,000 population in the United States (Bardou et al., *Automo-*

bile Revolution, 197, 171–207, *passim*). See also "A Survey of the Motor Industry," *The Economist,* 15 Oct. 1988, 27-page insert following p. 66.

29. David L. Lewis, *The Public Image of Henry Ford: An American Folk Hero and His Company* (Detroit, Mich.: Wayne State University Press, 1976), 43, 494–95, n. 14.

30. Jonathan Hughes, *The Vital Few: The Entrepreneur and American Economic Progress* (New York: Oxford University Press, 1986), 286–89.

31. Allan Nevins with Frank E. Hill, *Ford: The Times, the Man, the Company* (New York: Scribner's, 1954), 644–45.

32. Flink, *Car Culture,* 67n. Flink cites an observation made by Reynold M. Wik.

33. Lewis, *Public Image,* 93–112.

34. Rae, *Ford,* 2.

35. David Riesman with Nathan Glazer and Reuel Denney, *The Lonely Crowd* (New Haven: Yale University Press, 1961), 13–25.

36. Rae, *Ford,* 17–18; Flink, *Automobile Age,* 33–39.

37. Rae, *Ford,* 17–18.

38. Henry Ford, *My Life and Work,* quoted in Donald Finlay Davis, *Conspicuous Production: Automobiles and Elites in Detroit, 1899–1933* (Philadelphia, Pa.: Temple University Press, 1988), 117.

39. Quoted in Federal Trade Commission, *Report on Motor Vehicle Industry* (Washington, D.C.: GPO, 1940), 59.

40. For the Selden patent controversy, see William Greenleaf, *Monopoly on Wheels* (Detroit, Mich.: Wayne State University Press, 1961); Nevins, *Ford: The Times,* 284–323, 415–44; and Flink, *Automobile Age,* 51–55.

41. "The New Model T Ford Touring Car," *Cycle and Automobile Trade Journal,* 1 Oct. 1908, 98–100, 102.

42. Henry Ford with Samuel Crowther, *My Life and Work* (Garden City, N.Y.: Garden City Publishing, 1926), 68–69.

43. Nevins, *Ford: The Times,* 509.

44. The source for the quotations and for most of the preceding description of Ford production is David A. Hounshell's outstanding *From the American System to Mass Production, 1800–1932: The Development of Manufacturing Technology in the United States* (Baltimore, Md.: Johns Hopkins University Press, 1984), 221, 216–301, *passim.*

45. Chandler, *Giant Enterprise,* 26.

46. Lewis, *Public Image,* 160–61.

47. "Ford's Fortune," *The New Republic,* 23 Mar. 1927, 131–32. For a discussion of Ford's wealth in comparison to that of the world's other richest people, see William C. Richards, *The Last Billionaire* (New York: Scribner's, 1948), 348–68.

48. Nevins, *Ford: The Times,* 480.

49. Flink, *Automobile Age,* 56.

50. "The Top 100 Industrials: 1929," *Forbes,* 15 Sept. 1977, 133.

51. An exception is Akio Okochi and Koichi Shimokawa, eds., *Development*

of Mass Marketing: The Automobile and Retailing Industries (Proceedings of the Fuji Conference) (Tokyo: University of Tokyo Press, 1981).

52. Hughes, *Vital Few,* 329. Nevins views Ford as being more involved with selling and marketing than do I (see Nevins, *Ford: The Times,* 347).

53. Theodore Levitt, *Marketing for Business Growth* (New York: McGraw-Hill, 1974), ix.

54. John B. Rae, "Why Michigan," in *The Automobile and American Culture,* ed. David L. Lewis and Laurence Goldstein (Ann Arbor: University of Michigan Press, 1983), 1–9; Merrill Denison, *The Power to Go* (Garden City, N.Y.: Doubleday, 1956), 65–76.

55. Flink, *America Adopts,* 83, 74–86, *passim.*

56. Ralph C. Epstein, *The Automobile Industry: Its Economic and Commercial Development* (Chicago: A. W. Shaw, 1928), 132–61; Lawrence H. Seltzer, *A Financial History of the American Automobile Industry* (Boston: Houghton Mifflin, 1928), 23–24; Charles M. Hewitt, *Automobile Franchise Agreements* (Homewood, Ill.: Richard D. Irwin, 1956), 18.

57. For helpful information on the distribution systems and strategies of some of the leading companies in some of these industries, see Andrew B. Jack, "The Channels of Distribution for an Innovation: The Sewing Machine Industry in America, 1860–1865," *Explorations in Entrepreneurial History* 9 (1957): 113–41; Fred Carstensen, *American Enterprise in Foreign Markets* (Chapel Hill: University of North Carolina Press, 1984); Robert B. Davies, *Peacefully Working to Conquer the World* (New York: Arno, 1976); Wayne G. Broehl, Jr., *John Deere's Company* (Garden City, N.Y.: Doubleday, 1984); Bruce Bliven, Jr., *The Wonderful Writing Machine* (New York: Random House, 1954). Harold C. Livesay discusses the extent to which the early automobile industry borrowed its marketing practices from the nineteenth-century harvester industry in "Nineteenth Century Precursors of Automobile Marketing in the United States," in Okochi and Shimokawa, eds., *Development of Mass Marketing,* 39–52.

58. For Patterson, see Roy W. Johnson and Russell W. Lynch, *The Sales Strategy of John H. Patterson* (Chicago: Dartnell, 1932).

59. Nevins, *Ford: The Times,* 249–51.

60. Ibid., 263–65.

61. Ibid., 264–65.

62. Henry L. Dominguez, *The Ford Agency: A Pictorial History* (Osceola, Wis.: Motorbooks International, 1981), 10–13; William L. Hughson, "Reminiscences," Ford Motor Company Archives, Dearborn, Mich. (hereafter, Ford Archives). Surprisingly, Hughson is not mentioned in Nevins's authoritative history of Ford.

63. Dominguez, *Ford Agency,* 12; Hughson, "Reminiscences."

64. Dominguez, *Ford Agency,* 12; Hughson, "Reminiscences."

65. For automobiles during the San Francisco earthquake, see Flink, *Automobile Age,* 32–33.

66. Hughson, "Reminiscences," 11.

67. "Domestic Branches as of July 15, 1940," Accession 68, Box 1, Ford Archives.

68. Clarence Bullwinkel, "Reminiscences," Ford Archives.

69. Ibid.; Nevins, *Ford: The Times*, 344, 403; John H. Eagal, Sr., "Reminiscences," Ford Archives.

70. "Sales to June 14 . . .," Accession 7:123, Ford Motor Company Sales, Ford Archives.

71. "Discontinuance of Retail Selling and Shop Service," general letter no. 210, 17 Nov. 1916, Accession 78, Box 1, General Letters Numbered (hereafter, GLN), Ford Archives; "An Outside Vision," *Ford Times* 10 (Oct. 1916): 106.

72. Eagal, "Reminiscences."

73. Charles C. Parlin, *The Merchandising of Automobiles* (Philadelphia: Curtis, 1915), 5.

74. "Ford to Drop Retail Sales," *The Automobile*, 17 Aug. 1916, 255; "Ford Agencies Increase Rapidly in Every City," *The Automobile*, 24 Aug. 1916, 300; "Parent Company Abandons Repair Business," *The Automobile*, 24 Aug. 1916, 300–301; "What Cooperation Is Doing for the Philadelphia Ford Dealers," *Automobile Trade Journal* (Jan. 1917): 190–91.

75. These estimates are based on an examination of a large amount of contradictory evidence. See "Outside Vision," *Ford Times*, 103; "1903—Eight Years of Ford Progress—1911," *Ford Times* 4 (June 1911): 265; "Sales to June 14 This Year . . . ," 15 June 1914, Accession 1:123, Ford Archives; List of Branches, 1 Nov. 1917, Accession 572, Box 12, Ford Archives; *The Ford Industries* (Detroit: Ford Motor Company, 1924), 125–30 (available at Ford Industrial Archives, Redford, Mich.); "Domestic Branch Organization Chart as of December 31, 1926," 8 Feb. 1927, Accession 572, Box 12, Ford Archives; "Classification of Branches," 21 Feb. 1933, Accession 572, Box 12, Ford Archives; "Retail Freight Rates in Branch Cities," 14 Jan. 1922, general letter no. 1215, Accession 78, Box 89, GLN, Ford Archives.

76. Allan Nevins and Frank Ernest Hill, *Ford: Expansion and Challenge, 1915–1933* (New York: Scribner's, 1957), 257–69.

77. Ibid., 259.

78. Lewis, *Public Image*, 127.

79. Ibid., 126–27.

80. Bullwinkel, "Reminiscences." In 1931 (a depression year), *Fortune* magazine estimated that a dealer selling a hundred cars a year in the "lower-middle" class (priced at about $700) would typically have an investment in inventory and equipment (but not occupancy costs, which this calculation expensed) of $23,400. *Fortune* calculated the average working capital investment among all dealers at $10,000 ("Automobile Selling II: The Dealer," *Fortune*, Dec. 1931, 42).

81. Nevins and Hill, *Ford: Expansion*, 110.

82. Nevins, *Ford: The Times*, 342.

83. Ibid., 342–47.

84. Roy D. Chapin, "Distributor or Branch House?" *The Horseless Age*, 15

Dec. 1916, 46, 413–14; Charles N. Davisson; "Automobiles," in *Marketing Channels For Manufactured Products*, ed. Richard M. Clewett (Homewood, Ill.: Richard D. Irwin, 1954), 83–112.

85. For the history of the automobile in Atlanta, see Flink, *Automobile Age*, 145–50; and Preston, *Automobile Age Atlanta*, especially 17–44.

86. Robert S. Abbott, personnel file, Ford Industrial Archives, Redford, Mich. I would like to thank Robert Isom and Darleen Flaherty of the Ford Motor Company for granting me access to the rich collection of material at the Ford Industrial Archives.

87. W. A. Ryan, "Sales," 23 Oct. 1918, Accession 78, Box 83, general letter (unnumbered), (hereafter GLU), Ford Archives; George I. Banks, personnel file, Ford Industrial Archives.

88. Chapin, "Distributor," 413–14.

89. This estimate is taken from Auditing Branch Reports, Accession 260, Ford Archives.

90. "Production Report: Ford Vehicles Built in Atlanta," Weismeyer papers, Ford Industrial Archives.

91. "Statistical Statement Showing Percent of Profit to Cost Per Car By Year," Fair Lane Papers, Accession 7, Box 123, Ford Archives; *Standard Catalogue of American Cars*, Collection 629.2, Box 49, Ford Archives, 530–31.

92. "The weekly report of activities submitted by each branch show [*sic*] a wide variance in the number of dealers called upon each week by individual roadmen. In some cases eight to ten dealers are called upon while in others, only three or four are visited during the entire week" ("Direction of Branch Roadmen, No. 2," general letter no. 1059, 12 May 1921, Accession 78, Box 89, GLN, Ford Archives.)

93. W. A. Ryan, "Direction of Branch Roadmen," 3 Jan. 1921, Accession 78, Box 47, GLN, Ford Archives.

94. "C. D. McKenzie," 10 Nov. 1920, Accession 78, Box 46, GLN, Ford Archives.

95. E. T. Backus, "Report on Atlanta Branch," 27 Mar. 1917, Accession 76, Box 2, Film 14503, Ford Archives.

96. Ibid.

97. Hawkins to Abbott, letter, 8 May 1917, Accession 78, Box 2, Film 14503, Ford Archives.

98. Abbott to Hawkins, letter, 11 May 1917, Accession 76, Box 2, Film 14503, Ford Archives.

99. Ibid.

100. See, for example, W. A. Ryan, "Stopping Rumors at Source," 30 Aug. 1921, general letter no. 1120, Accession 78, Box 89, GLN, Ford Archives.

101. W. A. Ryan, "Roadmen," 4 Nov. 1921, general letter no. 1186, Accession 78, Box 89, Ford Archives.

102. Arthur Pound, *The Turning Wheel: The Story of General Motors Through Twenty-Five Years, 1908–1933* (Garden City, N.Y.: Doubleday, Doran, 1934), 77–79.

103. These quotations are from the incisive portrait of Durant in Flink, *Car Culture*, 114–15.

104. John B. Rae, "The Fabulous Billy Durant," *Business History Review* 25 (Autumn 1958): 255–71.

105. Lawrence R. Gusten, *Billy Durant: Creator of General Motors* (Grand Rapids, Mich.: Eerdmans, 1973), 246.

106. John B. Rae, *American Automobile Manufacturers: The First Forty Years* (Philadelphia: Chilton, 1959), 87.

107. Quoted in Seltzer, *Financial History*, 157.

108. Arthur J. Kuhn, *GM Passes Ford, 1918–1938: Designing the General Motors Performance-Control System* (University Park, Pa.: Pennsylvania State University Press, 1986), 35–43 (Kuhn's study has proven very useful to the treatment of General Motors presented in this chapter). Alfred P. Sloan, Jr., *My Years with General Motors* (Garden City, N.Y.: Doubleday, 1972), 63–77.

109. Kuhn, *GM Passes Ford*, 34–35; Walter P. Chrysler with Boyden Sparkes, *Life of an American Workman* (New York: Dodd, Mead, 1937), 141–43, 160–61; Rae, *Automobile Manufacturers*, 138–39; Sloan, *My Years*, 28–31.

110. Kuhn, *GM Passes Ford*, 42.

111. Alfred D. Chandler, Jr., and Stephen Salsbury, *Pierre S. du Pont and the Making of the Modern Corporation* (New York: Harper & Row, 1971), 482–91; Sloan, *My Years*, 36–44.

112. Sloan, *My Years*, 45.

113. Chandler, *Giant Enterprise*, 3.

114. Seltzer, *Financial History*, 197–208.

115. John Jacob Raskob to William McMaster, letter, Du Pont Administrative Papers, Accession 1662, Box 36, File 86, Hagley Museum and Library, Wilmington, Del. This document was brought to my attention by my colleague Professor Thomas K. McCraw.

116. *Report of the General Motors Corporation for the Fiscal Year Ended December 31, 1920,* Detroit, Mich., 13.

117. Sloan, *My Years*, 19.

118. Alfred P. Sloan, Jr., *Adventures of a White Collar Man* (New York: Doubleday, Doran, 1941), 4–5.

119. Ibid., 7, 14.

120. Ibid., 18–20.

121. Ibid., 22.

122. Ibid.

123. Ibid., 24–25.

124. Ibid.

125. Ibid., 31–87.

126. Ibid., 92–93.

127. Chandler, *Strategy and Structure*, 131.

128. Ibid., 130–32; Pound, *Turning Wheel*, 173–74, 180.

129. Sloan, *My Years*, 105–106.

130. Sloan, *Adventures*, 35–36.

131. Ibid.

132. Chandler and Salsbury, *Pierre S. du Pont*, 302.

133. Ibid., 490–91.

134. Irving Bernstein, *Turbulent Years: A History of the American Worker, 1933–1941* (Boston: Houghton Mifflin, 1970), 513.

135. Chandler, *Strategy and Structure*, 130.

136. Bernstein, *Turbulent Years*, 513.

137. Ibid.

138. Sloan, *My Years*, xv.

139. Epstein, *Automobile Industry*, 105–107; 110–12.

140. Federal Trade Commission, *Motor Vehicle*, 657, 498.

141. Robert Paul Thomas, "Style Change and the Automobile Industry During the Roaring Twenties" in *Business Enterprise and Economic Change: Essays in Honor of Harold F. Williamson*, ed. Louis P. Cain and Paul J. Uselding (Kent, Ohio: Kent State University Press, 1973), 120.

142. Ibid.

143. Clare Elmer Griffin, "The Life History of Automobiles," *Michigan Business Studies* 1 (Feb. 1926): 1–3.

144. Robert Paul Thomas, *An Analysis of the Pattern of Growth of the Automobile Industry, 1895–1929* (New York: Arno, 1977), 203.

145. Ibid., 206–209. For an astute explanation of the financial problems that the used car posed to the dealer, see "Automobile Selling I," *Fortune*, Dec. 1931, 42.

146. *Automobile Selling by Practical Salesmen* (Chicago: Chicago Automobile Trade Association, 1924), 59.

147. Clyde Jennings, "What Dealers Think About Merchandising New Models," *Automotive Industries*, 10 Feb. 1921, 276–78; Harry Tipper, "Human Study a Necessary Factor in Automotive Sales," *Automotive Industries*, 9 June 1921, 1213–15; Harry Tipper, "Marketing Problems of the Automotive Industry," *Automotive Industries*, 27 Oct. 1921, 801–803.

148. Don C. Prentiss, *Ford Products and Their Sale: Book Six* (Detroit, Mich.: The Franklin Press, 1923), 743.

149. Jacob H. Newmark, *Automobile Salesmanship* (Detroit: Automobile Publishing Company, 1915), 100–102.

150. *Cadillac Dealers Manual*, n.d. (available at the Baker Library, Harvard Business School), 121–25, 128–29.

151. Ibid., 133.

152. Ibid.

153. This observation was made to me by my colleague Professor Alfred D. Chandler, Jr., who knew Sloan.

154. Nevins and Hill, *Ford: Expansion*, 266–67.

155. James Couzens, "What I Learned About Business from Ford," *System* 40 (Sept. 1921): 263–64, 360.

156. Ibid., 264.

157. Sloan, *My Years*, 186–87.

158. Couzens, "What I Learned," 360.

159. Lewis, *Public Image*, 76.

160. Administrative offices were sometimes emptied of all furniture surreptitiously at night. One group of salaried employees came to work "only to find that their desks had been chopped to pieces with an ax" (Keith Sward, *The Legend of Henry Ford* [New York: Rinehart & Co., 1948], 183). When Henry Ford II brought Ernest R. Breech to the Ford Motor Company in 1946, Breech took a look at the company's balance sheet and later recalled it as being "about as good as a small tool shop would have." The company's controller did not know the meaning of the phrase "standard volume." Breech's overall assessment was *"Really a mess"* (Allan Nevins and Frank E. Hill, *Ford: Decline and Rebirth, 1933–1962* [New York: Scribner's, 1963], 315).

161. Ford, *My Life and Work*, quoted in Davis, *Conspicuous Production*, 85.

162. Nevins and Hill, *Ford: Expansion*, 110, 159.

163. Ibid., 150–61.

164. Davis, *Conspicuous Production*, 130–31.

165. Ibid.

166. Nevins and Hill, *Ford: Expansion*, 164–65.

167. Sloan, *My Years*, 186.

168. Sward, *Legend*, 199–205.

169. Chandler, *Giant Enterprise*, 3.

170. Thomas, *An Analysis*, 216. In 1925, Chevrolet had 5,787 dealers (D. M. McDonald, "Quota System Gives Chevrolet Better Control of Retail Selling," *Automotive Industries*, 14 May 1925, 861–62).

171. Federal Trade Commission, *Motor Vehicle*, 214.

172. W. A. Ryan, "Ford's Letter to His Dealers on Used Cars," *Automotive Industries*, 7 May 1925, 820.

173. Thomas, *An Analysis*, 216, 250–52.

174. Flink, *Automobile Age*, 116.

175. See, for example, Daniel Bell, "The Company He Keeps," *New York Review of Books*, 19 Mar. 1964, 12–14; Donaldson Brown, *Some Reminiscences of an Industrialist* (Easton, Pa.: Hive Publishing Company, 1977); Chandler, *Strategy and Structure;* Chandler and Salsbury, *Pierre S. du Pont;* Chandler, *Giant Enterprise;* Alfred D. Chandler, Jr., ed., *Managerial Innovation at General Motors* (New York: Arno, 1979); Ernest Dale, "Contributions to Administration by Alfred P. Sloan, Jr., and GM," *Administrative Science Quarterly* 1 (1956): 30–61; Kuhn, *GM Passes Ford;* Sloan, *My Years;* Harold A. Wolff, "The Great GM Mystery," *Harvard Business Review* 42 (Sept.–Oct. 1964): 164–66ff.

176. Davis Dyer, Malcolm S. Salter, and Alan M. Webber, *Changing Alliances* (Boston: Harvard Business School Press, 1987), 26–27.

177. Adam Smith, *An Inquiry Into the Nature and Causes of the Wealth of Nations*, ed. Edwin Canaan (New York: Modern Library, 1937), 423.

178. Smith, *Wealth of Nations*, 61.

179. Alfred D. Chandler, Jr., describes the period prior to the 1840s as the era

of "traditional enterprise in both commerce and production" (*The Visible Hand: The Managerial Revolution in American Business* [Cambridge: Harvard University Press, 1977], 13–78).

180. Ibid., 285–376.

181. Alfred D. Chandler, Jr., *Scale and Scope: The Dynamics of Industrial Capitalism* (Cambridge: Harvard University Press, forthcoming), chap. 1.

182. Conversation with Alfred Chandler, Boston, Mass., Fall 1988.

183. Harold Katz, *The Decline of Competition in the Automobile Industry, 1920–1940* (New York: Arno, 1977), 41. The phrase "conflict among giants" was used by Walter Flanders in 1910, quoted in Flink, *Automobile Age*, 56.

184. This is the classic "marketing mix."

185. E. Raymond Corey, *Industrial Marketing: Cases and Concepts* (Englewood Cliffs, N.J.: Prentice-Hall, 1983), 2.

186. Sloan, *My Years*, 71.

187. Ibid., 67.

188. Ibid., 192–93.

189. Ibid., 190–91.

190. See, for example, Emma Rothschild, *Paradise Lost: The Decline of the Auto-Industrial Age* (New York: Random House, 1973), 26–53.

191. Sloan, *My Years*, 190.

192. Sloan, *Adventures*, 185. A comparison of Sloan's remark to this 1913 quotation from *Scientific American* illustrates well how much the focus of the industry had changed: "Although there is a greater difference in automobiles generally this year than there ever was before, it is not of the kind that the average person has as yet come to know or realize. In other words, it is not so much a difference in lines of appearances—this year's cars will appear much the same as their predecessors—as it is a deeper-rooted difference that reveals itself in greater efficiency, greater stamina and greater wearing qualities" ("The Car of 1913," *Scientific American*, 11 Jan. 1913, 26).

193. Thomas, "Style Change," 135, 120–21.

194. Sloan, *My Years*, 308.

195. Ibid., 307–24.

196. Ibid., 65–67.

197. Davis, *Conspicuous Production*, 97.

198. Sloan, *My Years*, 76.

199. Chandler and Salsbury, *Pierre S. du Pont*, 466.

200. Nevins and Hill, *Ford: Expansion*, 267–69; Martha L. Olney, "Advertising, Consumer Credit, and the 'Consumer Durables Revolution' of the 1920s" (Ph.D. diss., University of California, Berkeley, 1985), 126–28.

201. Seltzer, *Financial History*, 55; Kuhn, *GM Passes Ford*, 79–80; Sloan, *My Years*, 353–64; J. A. Estey, "Financing the Sale of Automobiles," *Annals of the American Academy of Political and Social Science* 116 (Nov. 1924): 44–49; Edwin R. A. Seligman, *The Economics of Installment Selling: A Study in Consumers' Credit* (New York: Harper & Brothers, 1927).

202. Sloan, *My Years*, 119; Pound, *Turning Wheel;* Kuhn, *GM Passes Ford,*

131–32; G. A. Nichols, "General Motors to Spend Five Million in Advertising," *Printers' Ink,* 29 Sept. 1921, 3–4ff.; Roland Marchand, *Creating the Corporate Soul: The Rise of Corporate Public Relations and Institutional Advertising* (forthcoming).

203. *National Markets and National Advertising* (New York: Crowell, 1929), 9.

204. "Farm Paper Advertising by Leaders," *Sales Management,* 21 Sept. 1929, 136; "Farm Paper Advertising by Leaders," *Sales Management,* 27 Sept. 1930, 144E; "Radio Advertising," *Printers' Ink,* 17 Jan. 1935, 63–64; "Magazine Advertising," *Printers' Ink,* 16 Jan. 1936, 68ff.; "Advertising Hits the Long Pull," *Business Week,* 18 Jan. 1936, 9–11; "Outlay of 322 Advertisers," *Printers' Ink,* 28 Jan. 1937, 63ff.; "Outlay of 348 Advertisers," *Printers' Ink,* 27 Jan. 1938, 55ff.; "Advertising Stages a Comeback," *Business Week,* 20 Jan. 1940, 38–40.

205. Johnson and Lynch, *Patterson.*

206. *Annual Report of the General Motors Corporation For . . . 1925,* 23.

207. "The Dealer," *Fortune,* 134.

208. "General Motors, Part III: How To Sell Automobiles," *Fortune,* Feb. 1939, 78.

209. "General Motors, Part I: A Study in Bigness," *Fortune,* Dec. 1938, 67.

210. "GM III," *Fortune,* 78.

211. Sloan, *My Years,* 155, 331; "General Motors, Part IV: A Unit in Society," *Fortune,* Mar. 1939, 138, 141–42.

212. Sloan, *My Years,* 325, 329.

213. Federal Trade Commission, *Motor Vehicle,* 215.

214. Sloan, *My Years,* 328–29.

215. Ibid., 326.

216. Chandler, *Giant Enterprise,* 5–7.

217. Flink, *Automobile Age,* 281.

218. Ibid., 287.

219. Ibid., 291.

220. Ibid., 288.

221. H. Ross Perot, "The GM System Is Like a Blanket of Fog," *Fortune,* 15 Feb. 1988, 48.

222. Julian Lewis Watkins, *The 100 Greatest Advertisements: Who Wrote Them and What They Did* (New York: Dover, 1959), 50–51.

223. Flink, *Automobile Age,* 288–89.

224. "The Future on Schedule" is the title of Book Four of Daniel J. Boorstin's *The Americans: The Democratic Experience* (New York: Basic Books, 1984), 523–98.

Chapter 4   Stocking America's Pantries: The Rise and Fall of A&P

1. Bureau of the Census, *Historical Statistics of the United States: Colonial Times to 1970* (Washington, D.C.: GPO, 1975), 11–12; Bureau of the Census, *Statistical Abstract of the United States* (Washington, D.C.: GPO, 1985), 22.

2. Paul W. Stewart and J. Frederick Dewhurst, *Does Distribution Cost Too Much?* (New York: Twentieth Century Fund, 1939), 15.

3. Alfred D. Chandler, Jr., and Richard S. Tedlow, *The Coming of Managerial Capitalism: A Casebook on the History of American Economic Institutions* (Homewood, Ill.: Richard D. Irwin, 1985), 310; Lewis E. Atherton, "The Pioneer Merchant in Mid-America," *The University of Missouri Studies* 14 (1 Apr. 1939): 39–46. See also Fred Mitchell Jones, "Retail Stores in the United States, 1800–1860," *Journal of Marketing* 1 (Oct. 1936): 134–42; Fred Mitchell Jones, "Middlemen in the Domestic Trade of the United States," *Illinois Studies in the Social Sciences* 21 (1937): 47–63; Gerald Carson, *The Old Country Store* (New York: Oxford University Press, 1954).

4. Atherton, "Pioneer Merchant," 39.

5. Carson, *Country Store,* 14.

6. Atherton, "Pioneer Merchant," 83. The Census of 1840 attempted to determine the number of retail stores doing business in the United States and the capital investment they represented. The Census found 57,565 retail stores with a capital investment amounting to $250,301,799. Average capital invested per store was thus $4,350, which is below the amount that Atherton suggests was necessary to be well stocked. (U.S. Department of State, *Enumeration of the Inhabitants and Statistics of the United States as Obtained at the Department of State, from the Returns of the Sixth Census* [Washington, D.C.: Thomas Allen, 1841]; Jones, "Middlemen," 44–63.)

7. Quoted in Neil Harris, *Humbug* (Boston: Little, Brown, 1973), 12.

8. Daniel Pope, *The Making of Modern Advertising* (New York: Basic Books, 1983), 31; Atherton, "Pioneer Merchant," 123. For a description of the nineteenth-century patent medicine business, see James Harvey Young, *The Toadstool Millionaires* (Princeton, N.J.: Princeton University Press, 1961).

9. Alfred D. Chandler, Jr., *The Visible Hand: The Managerial Revolution in American Business* (Cambridge: Harvard University Press, 1977), 185–376.

10. Atherton, "Pioneer Merchant," 116–25.

11. A. C. Hoffman for the Temporary National Economic Committee, *Large-Scale Organization in the Food Industries,* monograph no. 35 (Washington, D.C.: GPO, 1940), 160.

12. Atherton, "Pioneer Merchant," 121.

13. See Richard S. Tedlow, "Albert Davis Lasker," in *Dictionary of American Biography,* supp. 5 (New York: Scribner's, 1977), 410–12; and Richard S. Tedlow, "From Competitor to Consumer: The Changing Focus of the Federal Regulation of Advertising, 1914–1938," *Business History Review* 55 (Spring 1981): 35–38, 44–45.

14. Morris A. Adelman, *A&P: A Study in Price-Cost Behavior and Public Policy* (Cambridge: Harvard University Press, 1959), 25.

15. For an early discussion of the difference between shopping and convenience goods, see Melvin T. Copeland, *Principles of Merchandising* (Chicago: A. W. Shaw, 1924), 27–102.

16. Even early in the nineteenth century, there were groups of stores operated

under a single management. However, a "chain of retail stores prior to 1860 was a decided exception. Large-scale retailing did not exist in an economy characterized by slow transportation, small markets, and small-scale production" (Jones, "Middlemen," 51). See also Theodore N. Beckman and Herman C. Nolen, *The Chain Store Problem: A Critical Analysis* (New York: McGraw-Hill, 1938), 14–18.

17. Robert D. Buzzell, lecture, Harvard Business School, July 1985.

18. Ralph M. Hower, "Urban Retailing 100 Years Ago," *Bulletin of the Business Historical Society* 12 (Dec. 1938): 91–92.

19. Gene Arlin German, "The Dynamics of Food Retailing, 1900–1975" (Ph.D. diss., Cornell University, 1978), 80–81.

20. *Trends: Consumer Attitudes & the Supermarket* (Washington, D.C.: Food Marketing Institute, 1988), 22.

21. Arthur E. Goodwin, *Markets: Public and Private* (Seattle, Wash.: Montgomery Printing, 1929), 11.

22. As late as 1928—more than a decade and a half after A&P opened its first "cash-and-carry" store—an authoritative study of chains observed that, "Many of the great chain grocery systems, largely at the initiative of the local managers, hire boys to deliver in the neighborhood after school hours. . . . While the customer ordinarily does not object to taking home small purchases, when large orders are given, including such heavy items as canned goods, potatoes, or sugar, she wants to have them delivered at the back door" (Walter S. Hayward and Percival White, *Chain Stores: Their Management and Operation* [New York: McGraw-Hill, 1928], 171).

23. Thomas F. De Voe, *The Market Book,* vol. 1 (New York: Author, 1862), 35–36 [emphasis omitted]; Goodwin, *Markets,* 22.

24. J. W. Sullivan, *Markets for the People: The Consumer's Part* (New York: Macmillan, 1913), 4–13, 301–16.

25. U.S. House of Representatives, *Report of the Industrial Commission on the Distribution of Farm Products* (Washington, D.C.: GPO, 1901), 16; reprinted in Henry Assael, ed., *Early Development and Conceptualization of the Field of Marketing* (New York: Arno, 1978).

26. Quoted in Goodwin, *Markets,* 27–28. For an interesting discussion of the public markets of Boston in the 1910s, see Boston City Planning Board, *A Summary of the Market Situation in Boston,* Preliminary Report of the Market Advisory Committee (Boston: Printing Department, 1916) (document 118–1915).

27. Malcolm P. McNair, "Trends in Large-Scale Retailing," *Harvard Business Review* (hereafter cited as *HBR*) 10 (Oct. 1931): 30.

28. M. S. Rukeyser, "Chain Stores, The Revolution in Retailing," *The Nation,* 28 Nov. 1928, 568.

29. As is true with much else about A&P's early history, the date of its founding is in doubt. There is some indication that it commenced business in 1858. Roy J. Bullock, "The Early History of the Great Atlantic & Pacific Tea Company," *HBR* 11 (Apr. 1933): 289–90; Federal Trade Commission, *Chain*

Stores: Growth and Development of Chain Stores, S. Doc. 100, 72d Cong., 1st sess. (Washington, D.C.: GPO, 11 June 1932), 53.

30. Bullock, "Early History," 289–96; Edwin P. Hoyt, *That Wonderful A&P!* (New York: Hawthorn, 1969), 36–46. Apparently, one reason for the name change was that "by 1875 nearly every American city had its own 'American Tea Company' or company with so similar a name that it was hard for the public to know the difference" (Hoyt, *A&P*, 36).

31. Advertisement in *Harper's Weekly*, 23 June 1866, 399.

32. This is a reason that the company advanced. See the advertisement in *Harper's Weekly*, 27 Oct. 1866, 687; and Bullock, "Early History," 292–93. Here is the company's description of the distribution system for tea:

> To give our readers an idea of the profits which have been made in the Tea trade, we will start with the American houses, leaving out of the account entirely the profits of the Chinese factors.
>
> 1st.   The American House in China or Japan makes large profits on their sales or shipments—and some of the richest retired merchants in this country have made their immense fortunes through their houses in China.
>
> 2nd.   The Banker makes large profits upon the foreign exchange used in the purchase of Teas.
>
> 3rd.   The Importer makes a profit of 30 to 50 percent in many cases.
>
> 4th.   On its arrival here it is sold by the cargo, and the Purchaser sells it to the Speculator in invoices of 1,000 to 2,000 packages, at an average profit of about 10 percent.
>
> 5th.   The Speculator sells it to the Wholesale Tea Dealer in lines at a profit of 10 to 15 percent.
>
> 6th.   The Wholesale Tea Dealer sells it to the Wholesale Grocer in lots to suit his trade, at a profit of about 10 percent.
>
> 7th.   The Wholesale Grocer sells it to the Retail Dealer at a profit of 15 to 25 percent.
>
> 8th.   The Retailer sells it to the Consumer for *all the profit he can get.* (Advertisement, *Harper's Weekly*, 27 Oct. 1866, 687).

33. Bullock, "Early History," 291, 294, 295; Advertisement, *Harper's Weekly*, 23 June 1866, 399.

34. William I. Walsh, *The Rise and Decline of the Great Atlantic and Pacific Tea Company* (Secaucus, N.J.: Lyle Stuart, 1986), 17–18.

35. Roy J. Bullock, "A History of the Great Atlantic and Pacific Tea Company Since 1878," *HBR* 12 (Oct. 1933): 60–62.

36. Quoted in ibid., 62.

37. German, "Food Retailing," 11–12.

38. Adelman, *A&P: A Study*, 23.

39. Quoted in Bullock, "A History," 66.

40. Adelman, *A&P: A Study*, 24–25. See also U.S. Senate, *Wages and Prices Investigation*, 1911, and New York State Food Investigation Committee, *Markets and Prices*, 1912.

41. Walsh, *Rise and Decline*, 24–35, 41.

42. A&P sued the Cream of Wheat Company over this decision and lost [Great Atlantic and Pacific Tea Company v. Cream of Wheat Company, 227 Fed. 46 (1915)].

43. Adelman, *A&P: A Study,* 27; Bullock, "A History," 67.

44. Ibid.

45. Adelman, *A&P: A Study,* 27.

46. According to *Forbes,* in terms of sales, only Standard Oil (N.J.) ($1,523,-000,000), General Motors ($1,504,000,000), Ford ($1,143,000,000), and U.S. Steel ($1,097,000,000) were larger than A&P in 1929 ("The Top 100 Industrials," *Forbes,* 15 Sept. 1977, 133–34). Sales of Sears and Ward in 1929 were $403,427,008 and $267,325,503, respectively (Paul H. Nystrom, *Chain Stores* [Washington, D.C.: Chamber of Commerce, 1930], 35). Sales of J. C. Penney in 1929 were $209,690,418 (J. C. Penney Company, *Financial Statement* [31 Dec. 1929]). Despite sales of less than half that of A&P, Sears's profit was actually higher—$30,057,652.

47. "The A&P Company As a Whole," *Fortune,* July 1930, 45–46.

48. *Trends: Consumer Attitudes and the Supermarket* (Washington, D.C.: Food Marketing Institute, 1985), 13.

49. Bureau of the Census, *Statistical Abstract of the United States,* 435.

50. Bureau of the Census, *Historical Statistics of the United States,* 320.

51. Clyde Lyndon King, "Can the Cost of Distributing Food Products Be Reduced?" *The Annals of the American Academy of Political and Social Science* 48 (July 1913): 206.

52. Beckman and Nolen, *Chain Store Problem,* 171–72.

53. Ibid., 172.

54. Ibid., 171.

55. The following studies have been examined (listed in order of publication): R. S. Alexander, "Study of Retail Grocery Prices," [New York] *Journal of Commerce* 140 (2 Mar. 1929): 9, 19; Einar Bjorklund and James L. Palmer, "A Study of the Prices of Chain and Independent Grocers in Chicago," *University of Chicago Studies in Business Administration* 1 (1930): 1–55; E. Z. Palmer, "Chain and Independent Prices in Lexington, Kentucky," *Chain Store Progress,* Sept. 1930, 4–7; Malcolm D. Taylor, "Prices in Chain and Independent Grocery Stores in Durham, North Carolina," *HBR* 8 (July 1930): 413–24; Charles F. Phillips, "Chain Stores Effecting Substantial Economies," *Chain Store Progress,* May 1931; Paul D. Converse, "Prices and Services of Chain and Independent Stores in Champaign-Urbana, Illinois," NATMA (National Association of Teachers of Marketing and Advertising), *Bulletin,* Oct. 1931, Series, no. 4, 1–27; Dorothy Dowe, "Comparison of Independent and Chain Store Prices," *Journal of Business,* Apr. 1932, 130–44; R. S. Vaile and A. M. Child, *Grocery Qualities and Prices* (Minneapolis: University of Minnesota Press, 1933); Federal Trade Commission, *Chain Stores: Prices and Margins of Chain and Independent Distributors* ["Washington, DC—Grocery," 73d Cong., 1st sess., S. Doc. 62 (1933); "Memphis—Grocery," 73d Cong., 1st sess., S. Doc. 69 (1933); "Detroit—Grocery," 73d Cong., 2d sess., S. Doc. 81 (1933); "Cincinnati—Grocery," 73d

Cong., 2d sess., S. Doc. 88 (1933)]; Malcolm D. Taylor, "Prices of Branded Grocery Commodities During the Depression," *HBR* 12 (July 1934): 437–49; Charles F. Phillips, "Chain, Voluntary Chain, and Independent Grocery Store Prices, 1930 and 1934," *Journal of Business* 8 (Apr. 1935): 143–49; Theodore N. Beckman, "Prices in Chain and Independent Stores in Florida, 1935," unpublished paper, the results of which are published in Beckman and Nolen, *Chain Store Problem;* Paul D. Converse, "Prices and Services of Chain and Independent Stores in Champaign-Urbana, 1937," *Journal of Marketing* 2 (Jan. 1938): 193–200; and Mabel Newcomer and Margaret Perkins, "Price Variations Among Poughkeepsie Grocers," *Journal of Marketing* 4 (July 1939): 39–44.

56. Beckman and Nolen, *Chain Store Problem,* 81.

57. Ibid., 172.

58. Converse, "Prices and Services, 1937," 136.

59. Adelman, *A&P: A Study,* 438; Harry C. Guthmann and Kenneth E. Miller, "Some Financial Tendencies Among Leading Variety and Grocery Chains During the Past Decade," *HBR* 9 (Jan. 1931): 249; Federal Trade Commission, *Chain Stores: Invested Capital and Rates of Return of Retail Chains,* 73d Cong. 2d sess., S. Doc. 87 (Washington, D.C.: GPO, 1934), 42; Hoffman, *Large-Scale Organization,* 96.

60. Carl N. Schmalz, "Independent Stores *Versus* Chains in the Grocery Field," *HBR* 9 (July 1931): 433, n. 6.

61. Federal Trade Commission, *Gross Profit and Average Sales Per Store of Retail Chains,* 72d Cong., 2d sess., S. Doc. 178 (Washington, D.C.: GPO, 1933), 17.

62. Joseph C. Palamountain, *The Politics of Distribution* (Cambridge: Harvard University Press, 1955), 8–9.

63. Ibid., 9–12.

64. U.S. Department of Commerce, Louisville Grocery Survey—Part III—A, *Merchandising Characteristics of Grocery Store Commodities: General Funding and Specific Results,* Distribution Cost Studies—no. 11 (Washington, D.C.: GPO, 1932), 20.

65. Palamountain, *Politics,* 13.

66. Susan Strasser, "Chain Stores," Harvard Business School Case Services no. 9-386-127 (Boston: Harvard Business School, 1985), 4. The quotation is actually the statement of a retail druggist, but it could just as well have been spoken by a grocer.

67. *Bureau of Business Research Bulletin* no. 13, "Management Problems in Retail Grocery Stores" (Cambridge: Harvard University Press, 1919), 16–17.

68. Theodore Levitt, "A Heretical View of 'Management Science'," *Fortune,* 18 Dec. 1978, 50.

69. Quoted in Strasser, "Chain Stores," 4.

70. Quoted in ibid., 4–5.

71. John P. Nichols, *The Chain Store Tells Its Story* (New York: Institute of Distribution, 1940), 113.

72. See Beckman and Nolen, *Chain Store Problem,* 42–61; Paul H. Nystrom,

Economics of Retailing, vol. 1 (New York: Ronald Press, 1930), 246–60; and, Nichols, *Chain Store*, 100–15.

73. Hoffman, *Large-Scale Organization*, 66.

74. Quoted in Adelman, *A&P: A Study*, 80.

75. Malcolm P. McNair, "Expenses and Profits in the Chain Grocery Business in 1929," *Bureau of Business Research Bulletin*, no. 84 (Cambridge, Mass.: Murray Printing, 1931), 19; Beckman and Nolen, *Chain Store Problem*, 52–53.

76. Federal Trade Commission, *Chain Stores: Service Features in Chain Stores*, 73d Cong., 2d sess., S. Doc. 91 (Washington, D.C.: GPO, 1934), 62–64.

77. Ibid.

78. Ibid.

79. "Operating Expenses in Retail Grocery Stores in 1924," *Bureau of Business Research Bulletin*, no. 52 (Boston: George H. Ellis, 1925), 64–69.

80. King, "Food Distribution," 199–224.

81. Ibid., 206.

82. Bureau of the Census, *Historical Statistics of the United States*, 850.

83. Food retailers excluded from the food group were rural general stores, department stores with food departments, general merchandise stores selling food, feed-grocery stores, and many other types of stores that sold "food in relatively small amounts." See U.S. Census, Census of Distribution, *Retail Distribution (Trade Series): Food Retailing* (in 1929) (Washington, D.C.: GPO, 1934), 3. The Census also cautions that the sales of the stores in the food group "include more than the sale of food. Other principal commodities sold by food stores are cigarettes, household supplies, stationery, light gloves" (ibid., 2).

84. Federal Trade Commission, *Chain Stores: Sources of Chain Store Merchandise*, 72d Cong., 1st sess., S. Doc. 30 (Washington, D.C.: GPO, 1932).

85. Ibid.; Federal Trade Commission, *Chain Stores: Wholesale Business of Retail Chains*, 72d Cong., 1st sess., S. Doc. 29 (Washington, D.C.: GPO, 1932), 21.

86. Hoffman, *Large-Scale Organization*, 12.

87. McNair, "Expenses and Profits," 20.

88. James L. Heskett, Nicholas A. Glaskowsky, Jr., and Robert M. Ivie, *Business Logistics: Physical Distribution and Materials Management* (New York: Ronald Press, 1973), 305–306. I am much indebted to Professor Bruce Chew of the Production and Operations Management Area at the Harvard Business School for this citation and for the idea of exploring this problem in depth.

89. Neil M. Clark, "The Independent Grocer Finds 'A Way Out!' " *Forbes*, 1 Sept. 1930, 20.

90. "The A&P in Fairfield, Conn.," *Fortune*, July 1930, 42.

91. *Report of the Federal Trade Commission on Distribution Methods and Costs, Part I, Important Food Products* (Washington, D.C.: GPO, 1944), 6–7.

92. Hoffman, *Large-Scale Organization*, 68.

93. Joseph M. Fly, "Can the Chain Store Supplant the Grocery Wholesaler?" *Printers' Ink*, 23 June 1927, 146.

94. "The A&P Company As a Whole," *Fortune*, 45–49.

95. Ibid.; Hoffman, *Large-Scale Organization*, 12.

96. Federal Trade Commission, *Chain Stores: Chain Store Manufacturing*, 73d Cong., 1st sess., S. Doc. 13 (Washington, D.C.: GPO, 1935), 42.

97. Ibid., 25, 42, 52.

98. Adelman, *A&P: A Study*, 248.

99. Federal Trade Commission, *Chain Store Manufacturing*, 42.

100. Quoted in Adelman, *A&P: A Study*, 271.

101. Ibid., 256.

102. Ibid., 274.

103. Federal Trade Commission, *Chain Stores: Final Report on the Chain-Store Investigation*, 74th Cong., 1st sess., S. Doc. 4 (Washington, D.C.: GPO, 1935), 53.

104. Adelman, *A&P: A Study*, 229–43; Charles F. Phillips, "The Federal Trade Commission's Chain Store Investigation: A Note," *Journal of Marketing* 2 (Jan. 1983): 190–92. Phillips's study, based as was Adelman's work on the Commission's own data, found that no more than 16.4 percent of the independent's higher prices could be traced to their higher merchandise costs (ibid., 191). Palamountain said of the remarks quoted by the Commission that "This conclusion is clearly in error" (*Politics*, 63, n. 17).

105. Richard A. Posner, *The Robinson-Patman Act: Federal Regulation of Price Differences* (Washington, D.C.: American Enterprise Institute, 1976), 17.

106. Chandler, *Visible Hand*, 6, 286.

107. Quoted in Chandler and Tedlow, *Managerial Capitalism*, 574–75.

108. Louis Galambos, *The Public Image of Big Business in America, 1880–1940* (Baltimore, Md.: Johns Hopkins University Press, 1975), 47–48, 112–14, 118–20, 222–68. Galambos found that "opposition to big business during the progressive era was less intense than it had been during the mid-nineties" (ibid., 119).

109. Chandler carefully outlines the Standard Oil story in Chandler and Tedlow, *Managerial Capitalism*, 343–69. See also Richard S. Tedlow, "The Process of Economic Concentration in the American Economy" in *The Concentration Process in the Entrepreneurial Economy Since the Late 19th Century, Zeitschrift für Unternehmensgeschichte*, Beiheft 55, ed. Hans Pohl (Stuttgart: Franz Steiner Verlag, 1988), 107–11.

110. Alfred D. Chandler, Jr., *Scale and Scope: The Dynamics of Industrial Capitalism* (Cambridge: Harvard University Press, forthcoming), chap. 3.

111. Ida M. Tarbell, *The History of the Standard Oil Company*, vol. 2 (New York: Macmillan, 1925), 290.

112. Albro Martin, "The Troubled Subject of Railroad Regulation in the 'Gilded Age'—A Reappraisal," *Journal of American History* 61 (Sept. 1974): 349.

113. Standard Oil Company of New Jersey et al. v. United States, 221 U.S. 1 (1911); Chandler and Tedlow, *Managerial Capitalism*, 557–63; Public Law 203, 63d Cong.

114. Quoted in Thomas K. McCraw, *Prophets of Regulation* (Cambridge: Harvard University Press, 1984), 102, 104, 108–109.

115. Frank Farrington, *Meeting Chain Store Competition* (Chicago: Byxbee Publishing Co., 1922), 5.

Along these lines, the following passage from a speech, delivered by Wright Patman over network radio in 1938 is an example of vintage American demogogy and should not be lost to posterity:

One young lady [Patman was referring here to Barbara Hutton, heiress to the Woolworth fortune] inherited one of these chain store fortunes. She did not permit it to be distributed back into the different communities from whence it came by placing it in circulation here. She didn't even permit it to remain in the banks of New York City or in America, but she immediately took it to foreign countries. Her object was to use this great chain store fortune in seeking a husband, who must be a Count. She spent a large part of it and married a Count in one country. She soon discovered that this Count was no-account, so she divorced him and sought another count—whom she found and married—but later discovered that he, too, was no-account, and now she is again divorced and is taking her millions of chain store profits to other countries, looking for another Count and, I presume, hoping that he will not be of the no-account Count type. She gave up her American citizenship to save taxes.

Which will help our country more, a system that will build up huge fortunes in the hands of rich childless brothers [this charitable observation referred to John and George Hartford of A&P] and Barbara Hutton, or one that will distribute privileges and opportunities among all people? (Hoyt, *A&P,* 172.)

116. Farrington, *Chain Store Competition,* 11.

117. Hayward and White, *Chain Stores,* 491. In the late nineteenth century, the economic impact of the department store—which revolutionized competition in the lines it carried just as the chains of the interwar years did in those they carried—also became a political issue in a number of states (Nichols, *Chain Store,* 127).

118. Palamountain, *Politics,* 161. The supposed tax advantages of chains are derived from the following characteristics of their operations: "(1) Chains usually operated with a higher rate of turnover so that a tax on its stock on hand amounted to a lower proportion of total investment than it would for an independent. [It should be noted, however, that McNair found that when grocery chain retail units and independents were compared as retailers rather than as distribution systems, the independent actually had a higher rate of turn (see appendix A).] (2) Chain records may be difficult to access for local assessors and accurate data more difficult to obtain therefore. (3) A greater proportion of the chain's total investment may be intangible. (4) Assessors frequently evaluated stocks on a cost basis. Since chains purchased at wholesale, their cost of goods sold was lower. (5) Different assessment dates in different localities may have enabled chains to shift their stock to avoid taxes." [This strikes me as implausible.] (Palamountain, *Politics,* 161–62, n. 8.)

119. Charles F. Phillips, "State Discriminatory Chain Store Taxation," *HBR* 14 (Spring 1936): 350. For a comprehensive treatment of chain-store taxation to World War II, see Roy G. Blakey and Gladys C. Blakey, "Chain Store Taxation," *Taxes*, Oct. 1941, 594–602, 628 and Nov. 1941, 670–76.

120. Nichols, *Chain Store*, 129.

121. Phillips, "Discriminatory Chain Taxation," 351.

122. Palamountain, *Politics*, 162.

123. Ibid., 184–85.

124. Ibid., 176–77. To understand why the Patman Bill could justifiably be called the "Chain Store Destruction Bill," see Nichols, *Chain Store*, 163–66. (This "Death Sentence" bill should not be confused with the Robinson-Patman Act, which did, of course, become law.)

125. Quoted in Godfrey M. Lebhar, *Chain Stores in America, 1859–1962* (New York: Chain Store Publishing Corporation, 1963), 173.

126. Quoted in Strasser, "Chain Stores," 30.

127. Lebhar, *Chain Stores in America*, 171. (Michael J. Cullen specifically referred to Henderson in his supermarket proposal, which is discussed later in the chapter and which is reproduced in appendix B.)

128. Quoted in Ralph Hidy and Muriel Hidy, *Pioneering in Big Business* (New York: Harper & Brothers, 1955), 214–15.

129. Richard S. Tedlow, *Keeping the Corporate Image: Public Relations and Business, 1900–1950* (Greenwich, Conn.: JAI Press, 1979), 93.

130. Ibid.

131. Ibid., 93–96.

132. "A&P Goes to the Wars," *Fortune*, Apr. 1938, 96.

133. Lebhar, *Chain Stores in America*, 325.

134. Palamountain, *Politics*, 174. Early in the hearings on the Patman "Death Sentence" bill, Secretary of Agriculture Henry A. Wallace told the House Ways and Means Committee that "sound public policy requires that we promote efficient methods of marketing and distribution rather than discourage or prevent them by taxes such as those provided in this bill" (Lebhar, *Chain Stores in America*, 271).

135. Palamountain, *Politics*, 174, n. 36.

136. Ibid., 180.

137. Lebhar, *Chain Stores in America*, 285.

138. Chandler, *Scale and Scope*, chap. 3.

139. Frederick M. Rowe, *Price Discrimination Under the Robinson-Patman Act* (Boston: Little, Brown, 1962), 11.

140. Earl W. Kintner, *A Robinson-Patman Primer: A Businessman's Guide to the Law Against Price Discrimination* (New York: Macmillan, 1970), 10; quoted in Rowe, *Price Discrimination*, 14.

141. Quoted in ibid., 21–22.

142. Ibid.

143. Chandler and Tedlow, *Managerial Capitalism*, 653.

144. Adelman, *A&P: A Study*, 160.

145. Alan Stone, *Economic Regulation and the Public Interest: The Federal Trade Commission in Theory and Practice* (Ithaca, N.Y.: Cornell University Press, 1977), 97.

146. Morris A. Adelman wrote that the FTC's investigations of chain-store practices, which served as the research base for the Robinson-Patman Act, was in fact an investigation not of price discrimination but of price differentials. Of the Act itself, Adelman declared that it had "a single unifying principle: *to enforce discrimination against the lower-cost buyer or the lower-cost method of distribution*" (Adelman, *A&P: A Study*, 152, 160). Richard A. Posner has remarked that the "great question raised by the history and language of the Robinson-Patman Act is the extent to which Congress wanted not merely to provide more effective regulation of the types of price discriminations that are inefficient or anticompetitive in some legitimate economic sense, but also [or instead] to prevent price differences that—regardless of their possible justifications on grounds of efficiency—might be injurious to segments of the business community that were influential in the enactment of the legislation. *I regard this question as largely unanswerable*" (Posner, *Robinson-Patman*, 27 [emphasis added]). In the standard work on the subject, Frederick M. Rowe stated that the true objective of the bill was to save the grocery trades and other lines of business being transformed by chain merchandising but that legislation written forthrightly with those objectives was "constitutionally vulnerable as bald class legislation. . . . [T]he technique of amending the original Clayton Act rather than enacting a separate law was a political masterstroke which invested an anti-chain store measure with the venerable trappings of antitrust" (Rowe, *Price Discrimination*, 23).

147. Stone, *Economic Regulation*, 97–98.

148. Adelman, *A&P: A Study*, 173.

149. Ibid., 183–84.

150. McCraw, *Prophets of Regulation*, 68, 144–45.

151. "A&P Goes to the Wars," *Fortune*, Apr. 1938, 134.

152. Adelman, *A&P: A Study*, 438.

153. McCraw, *Prophets of Regulation*, 145–46.

154. Yale Brozen, "Introduction" to Posner, *Robinson-Patman*, n.p. See also Stone, *Economic Regulation*, 98.

155. For interesting and at times acerbic comments about this case and on the civil suit that followed it, see (in order of publication) Hugh M. Foster, "Monopoly in Retail Food Distribution," *Journal of Retailing*, Dec. 1941, 112–19; Robert L. Klein, "The A&P Decision," *Journal of Retailing*, Feb. 1947, 16–22; Rashi Fein, "Note on Price Discrimination and the A&P Case," *Quarterly Journal of Economics* 65 (1951): 271–79; Joel B. Dirlam and Alfred E. Kahn, "Antitrust Law and the Big Buyer: Another Look at the A&P Case," *Journal of Political Economy* 60 (1952): 118–32; Morris A. Adelman, "Dirlam and Kahn on the A&P Case," *Journal of Political Economy* 61 (1953): 436–41; Joel B. Dirlam and Alfred E. Kahn, "A Reply," *Journal of Political Economy* 61 (1953): 441–45; Joel B. Dirlam and Alfred E. Kahn, "Integration and Dissolution of the

A&P Company," *Indiana Law Journal* 29 (Fall 1953): 1–27; Morris A. Adelman, "Integration and Dissolution of the A&P Company: A Reply. Price Policy in the A&P Case," *Indiana Law Journal* 29 (Winter 1954): 367–70; and Adelman, *A&P: A Study,* especially 327–401, 526–30.

156. Adelman, *A&P: A Study,* 328–29. It is the good fortune of all students of A&P that Morris A. Adelman mastered the voluminous materials which this case generated. Adelman's work has been an essential guide to the treatment of A&P in this book.

157. Ibid., 331.

158. Ibid., 333–34.

159. Ibid., 397–401.

160. Palamountain, *Politics,* 183.

161. Ibid., 186.

162. Tedlow, "Competitor to Consumer."

163. See, in this regard, the treatment of the Federal Trade Commission's antitrust action against the manufacturers of ready-to-eat cereals in Chandler and Tedlow, *Managerial Capitalism,* 651–69; and the accompanying teaching note in Richard S. Tedlow, *Case Commentary and Teaching Technique to Accompany The Coming of Managerial Capitalism* (Homewood, Ill.: Richard D. Irwin, 1985), 314–30.

164. Chandler and Tedlow, *Managerial Capitalism,* 178, 180.

165. Phillips, "Discriminatory Chain Taxation," 349–50.

166. Posner, *Robinson-Patman,* 26.

167. M. M. Zimmerman, *The Super Market: A Revolution in Distribution* (New York: Mass Distribution Publications, 1955), 31.

168. Ibid., 32–35.

169. "What Michael Cullen Foresaw," *Super Market Merchandising,* Aug. 1955, 109.

170. Zimmerman, *Super Market,* 32–35.

171. "Michael Cullen's Story," *Super Market Merchandising,* Aug. 1955, 97.

172. All these data are calculated from Adelman, *A&P: A Study,* 254, 432, 434, 438.

Total retail sales, 1930	$1,051,978,000
Number of stores	15,700
Sales per store	67,004.97
Total investment	125,900,000
Total manufacturing investment	46,433,000
Total nonmanufacturing investment	79,467,000
Total nonmanufacturing investment per store	5,061.59
After-tax profit	30,700,000
Manufacturing profit	5,936,000
Nonmanufacturing profit	24,764,000
Nonmanufacturing profit per store	1,577.32
After-tax return on nonmanufacturing investment per store	31.16%

173. Zimmerman, *Super Market,* 32–35.

174. Ibid.

175. Carl W. Dipman, *The Modern Grocery Store* (New York: Butterick Publishing, 1931), 46.

176. Zimmerman, *Super Market,* 52.

177. Ibid., 52–53.

178. Will Soper, "Supermarkets," *American History Illustrated,* Mar. 1983, 44.

179. The operator in question was Albert Gerrard. His advertisement at his grand opening read: "Wait on yourself—no clerks. You will find everything in our store arranged alphabetically. . . . Prices never heard of before in Pomona. . . . We stretch a dollar until the eagle screams" (ibid.).

180. This operator was Clarence Saunders, owner of Piggly Wiggly (Soper, "Supermarkets," 44).

181. Zimmerman, *Super Market,* 183.

182. Terry P. Wilson, *The Cart That Changed the World: The Career of Sylvan N. Goldman* (Norman: University of Oklahoma Press, 1978), 78.

183. Ibid.

184. Ibid., 87–88.

185. Ibid., 89.

186. Stewart and Dewhurst, *Does Distribution Cost Too Much?* 7. For interesting observations on the shifting dividing line between production and consumption, see Ruth P. Mack, "Trends in American Consumption and the Aspiration to Consume," *American Economic Review* 46 (May 1956): 55–68.

187. For an example of a calculation designed to indicate the added costs incurred—in terms of time and transportation—for a consumer to drive three miles further (one way) to visit a larger and lower-priced food outlet, see Walter J. Salmon, Robert D. Buzzell, Mark S. Albion, and Marci K. Dew, "Superstore Formats of the Future," paper prepared for *Family Circle* and the Food Marketing Institute, Apr. 1985, 62–63.

188. Zimmerman, *Super Market,* 35.

189. Ibid., 110. The president of Kroger at the time was William H. Albers. A few years after this incident, Albers resigned to become president of Albers Super Markets, Inc., in Cincinnati, Ohio. He served as the first president of the Super Market Institute (today known as the Food Marketing Institute) from 1937 to 1944 (ibid., 83).

190. "The Cheapy Thrives," *Business Week,* 8 Feb. 1933, 11–12.

191. Zimmerman, *Super Market,* 39. Cullen was only 52 at the time of his death. It is said that he died of overwork. His wife, Nan Cullen, became president of the company.

192. Ibid., 40.

193. Ibid., 40–43.

194. Ibid., 43.

195. Ibid., 32–35.

196. Ibid., 21–30. An early manual issued by Piggly Wiggly summarizes Saun-

ders's approach (see *The National Standard for Piggly Wiggly Store Conduct and Maintenance* [Memphis: Memphis Linotype Printing, 1919]). The commissaries of the Ford Motor Company, though rarely cited in this connection, are an interesting example of experimentation in large outlet food retailing prior to 1930. Founded in 1919 to sell sugar, potatoes, and apples to employees, the commissaries did $12 million in volume with a net profit of $400,000 in 1926. Apparently, most of this was done out of one large site (a second store was opened on 26 August 1926, and a third at the beginning of 1927): "Instead of taking the stores to the buyers [the commissaries], through the attraction of 25% to 30% savings, depend upon attracting customers, in spite of their locations. They depend upon selling in quantities rather than one item at a time. The average purchase by each customer during recent months has been $2.78. And the success of the stores proves that the housewife can be led to plan far ahead" (Joseph E. Shafer, "The Ford Stores—A New Departure in Retailing," *HBR* 6 [Apr. 1928]: 314).

197. Zimmerman, *Super Market,* 110.

198. Charles F. Phillips, "The Supermarket," *HBR* 16 (Winter 1938): 191, n. 9. These same items were rechecked by Stanley F. Teele of the Harvard Business School in 1937. The price difference had diminished substantially, but it was still 7.6 percent in favor of Big Bear (ibid.). A 1932 *Business Week* article observed that "[t]hose familiar with the current operation of food chains contend that several systems are engaged in a gradual but continuous increase in selling prices to ensure profitable operation. Executives have come to the conclusion that attempts to keep dollar sales at last year's level merely result in increasing operating losses. They are now being converted to the theory that it is better to do less volume at a profit ("Chains' Heads Watch Sales Drop; Turn from Volume to Profit," *Business Week,* 1 June 1932, 9).

199. Henry C. Bohack, Jr., "This Chain System Finds That Price Is Losing Its Appeal," *Printers' Ink,* 19 July 1928, 26.

200. A. M. Michener, "The Chain Store in the Grocery Field," *Commerce Monthly* 10 (Dec. 1928): p. 6.

201. McNair, "Chain Grocery Business in 1929," 20. This may have been the first time McNair enunciated his famous theory in print.

202. Ibid.

203. Malcolm P. McNair, "Significant Trends and Developments in the Postwar Period," in *Competitive Distribution in a Free High-Level Economy and Its Implications for the University,* ed. Albert B. Smith (Pittsburgh: University of Pittsburgh Press, 1958), 17–18.

204. For some interesting observations, see Stanley C. Hollander, "The Wheel of Retailing," in *Marketing Classics: A Selection of Influential Articles,* ed. Ben M. Enis and Keith K. Cox (Boston: Allyn & Bacon, 1977), 315–23; Louis P. Bucklin, *Competition and Evolution in the Distributive Trades* (Englewood Cliffs, N.J.: Prentice-Hall, 1972), 119–69; and, Arieh Goldman, "The Role of Trading-up in the Development of the Retailing System," *Journal of Marketing* 39 (Jan. 1975): 54–62.

205. Schmalz, "Independent Stores," 442.

206. U.S. Census, *Historical Statistics of the United States*, 319.

207. See table 3–6, p. 155.

208. U.S. Census, *Historical Statistics of the United States*, 710. A contemporary discussion of the automobile, the paving of roads, and the resulting change in the size of trading areas can be found in Melvin T. Copeland, "Marketing," in *Recent Economic Changes in the United States*, vol. 1 (New York: McGraw-Hill, 1929), 331–42.

209. Frank J. Charvat, "The Development of the Supermarket Industry through 1950 with Emphasis on Concomitant Changes in the Food Store Sales Pattern" (Ph.D. diss., Northwestern University, 1954), 43.

210. Erik Barnouw, *The Golden Web* (New York: Oxford University Press, 1968), 220.

211. O. Fred Rost, "A Super Market X-Ray," *Advertising and Selling*, 13 Apr. 1933, 17.

212. Joel Lifflander, "Big Bear and How It Grew," *Super Market Merchandising*, Mar. 1937, 14.

213. Zimmerman, *Super Market*, 42.

214. Lifflander, "Big Bear," 14.

215. In the District Court of the United States for the Eastern District of Illinois, United States v. The New York Great Atlantic and Pacific Tea Company, Inc. et al. No. 16153 (criminal). Testimony of John A. Hartford, 20,435–36 (1945).

216. Adelman, *A&P: A Study*, 61.

217. U.S. v. A&P, Testimony of John A. Hartford, 20,438.

218. C. F. Benson, ed., *Henry James: Letters to A. C. Benson and Auguste Monod* (New York: Scribner's, 1930), 35.

219. German, "Food Retailing," 58.

220. U.S. v. A&P, Testimony of John A. Hartford, 20,438.

221. Adelman, *A&P: A Study*, 69. This phrase was the one used at the time.

222. William Applebaum, *Supermarketing: The Past, the Present, a Projection* (Chicago: Super Market Institute, 1969), 4; Ivan C. Miller, "The A&P Experiment in Supermarkets," *Advertising and Selling*, 29 July 1937, 21–22ff.

223. Adelman, *A&P: A Study*, pp. 67–69.

224. Ibid., 71.

225. U.S. v. A&P, Testimony of John A. Hartford, 20,439.

226. Estimates of the number of stores differ. The store numbers used here are from Lebhar, *Chain Stores in America*, whereas the estimates of the number of supermarkets are from Adelman, *A&P: A Study*, 434.

227. Adelman, *A&P: A Study*, 75–76.

228. Ibid., 75.

229. "A&P Goes to the Wars," *Fortune*, 97.

230. Adelman, *A&P: A Study*, 77.

231. Lebhar, *Chain Stores in America*, 395; Adelman, *A&P: A Study*, 434.

232. Little is known of the Pay-N-Takit experiment. It is not mentioned in the contemporary business periodicals I examined nor in Safeway's annual reports.

William Applebaum refers to these stores as supermarkets (*Supermarketing*, 4–5).
Judging from their name, one would assume they were self-service.

233. Ibid., 5.

234. "Safeway Stores, Inc.," *Fortune*, Oct. 1940, 61.

235. Applebaum, *Supermarketing*, 5.

236. "Looking Backwards: 25 Years of Super Market Progress," *Super Market Merchandising*, Aug. 1955, 76.

237. Applebaum, *Supermarketing*, 5.

238. Adelman, *A&P: A Study*, 81.

239. Chandler and Tedlow, *Managerial Capitalism*, 343–69; Tedlow, *Case Commentary*, 144–60.

240. Tedlow, *Case Commentary*, 236–45.

241. Walsh, *Rise and Decline*, 188.

242. "Retail Trade: Red Circle and Gold Leaf," *Time*, 13 Nov. 1950, 90.

243. Walsh, *Rise and Decline*, 75–76, 86.

244. Ibid., 79–80.

245. Ibid., 76–77, 86.

246. Ibid., 83–85.

247. Ibid., 90, 94.

248. Ibid., 129.

249. Eleanor Johnson Tracy, "How A&P Got Creamed," *Fortune*, Jan. 1973, 112, 114.

250. "The Great A&P," *Fortune*, Nov. 1947, 103.

251. Walsh, *Rise and Decline*, 132.

252. "Great A&P," *Fortune*, 249.

253. A&P, *Annual Report for the Fiscal Year Ended February 26, 1972*.

254. Tracy, "Creamed," 103–106.

255. "Great A&P," *Fortune*, 249.

256. Walsh, *Rise and Decline*, 144.

257. "A&P's Ploy: Cutting Prices to Turn a Profit," *Business Week*, 20 May 1972, 79.

258. A&P, *1972 Annual Report*. I must beg the reader's indulgence for using the rather clumsy construction "for the fifty-two weeks ending . . ." in the text. This phraseology is necessitated by a certain confusion in A&P's reporting practices during the early 1970s. This confusion is epitomized by the fact that the document entitled *1972 Annual Report* referred to in this note and the *Annual Report for the Fiscal Year Ended February 16, 1972* referred to in note 253 report results for *different* years. The *1972 Annual Report* provides results for the fifty-two weeks ending on 24 February 1973, as the text preceding this note observes.

259. A&P, *1973 Annual Report*.

260. "Will They Find the Flair at A&P?", *Fortune*, Apr. 1971, 29.

261. "Five Years for a Breath of Fresh Air," *Fortune*, Jan. 1975, 21; "Can Jonathan Scott Save A&P?" *Business Week*, 19 May 1975, 128–31ff.; "A&P's Remarkable Recovery," *Chain Store Age Executive*, Sept. 1976, 33; "Price, Pride, and Profitability," *Fortune*, Apr. 1977, 20.

262. A&P, *1975 Annual Report.*

263. A&P, *1976 Annual Report.*

264. "Price, Pride, and Profitability," *Fortune,* 20.

265. See above, p. 245.

266. "Jonathan Scott's Surprising Failure at A&P," *Fortune,* 6 Nov. 1978, 36.

267. Ibid., 40.

268. "Pride and Price Finally Get Together at A&P," *Fortune,* 12 Feb. 1979, 15–16.

269. Gwen Kinkead, "The Executive-Suite Struggle Behind A&P's Profits," *Fortune,* 1 Nov. 1982, 82.

270. "A&P Looks Like Tengelmann's Vietnam," *Business Week,* 1 Feb. 1982, 42.

271. A&P, 1988 *Annual Report.*

Chapter 5   Bringing the Mass Market Home: Sears, Montgomery Ward, and Their Newer Rivals

1. David M. Potter, *People of Plenty: Economic Abundance and the American Character* (Chicago: University of Chicago Press, 1954), 80; Francis Sill Wickwire, "The Life and Times of Sears, Roebuck," *Collier's,* 3 Dec. 1949, 18. According to Daniel J. Boorstin, "Some have called the big mail order catalogues the first characteristically American kind of book" (*The Americans: The Democratic Experience* [New York: Vintage, 1973], 128). The 1897 *Sears Catalogue* has been republished by Chelsea House (New York, 1968), edited by Fred L. Israel; the 1908 *Sears Catalogue* has been republished by Digest Books (Northfield, Ill., 1971), edited by Joseph J. Schroeder, Jr.

2. For appreciations of the cultural significance of the catalogs, see Boorstin, *Democratic Experience,* 121–29; introductory essays to the *1897 Sears Catalogue;* David L. Cohn, *The Good Old Days: A History of American Morals and Manners As Seen Through the Sears, Roebuck Catalogs, 1905 to the Present* (New York: Simon & Schuster, 1940); and Francis Sill Wickwire, "We Like Corn, On or Off the Cob," *Collier's,* 10 Dec. 1949, 21, 73–74.

3. Boris Emmet and John E. Jeuck, *Catalogues and Counters: A History of Sears, Roebuck and Company* (Chicago: University of Chicago Press, 1950), 113.

4. Donald R. Katz, *The Big Store: Inside the Crisis and Revolution at Sears* (New York: Viking, 1987), 301.

5. Sources for biographical information on Sears include the Richard W. Sears file, Julius Rosenwald papers, University of Chicago; "Human-Interest Story of Richard W. Sears," *Printers' Ink,* 8 Oct. 1914, 13ff.; Edward Dale, "Richard Warren Sears," in *Dictionary of American Biography,* vol. 16 (New York: Scribner's, 1935), 540–41; Morris Robert Werner, *Julius Rosenwald: The Life of a Practical Humanitarian* (New York: Harper, 1939), 31–45; Louis E. Asher and Edith Heal, *Send No Money* (Chicago: Argus, 1942), xi–xvii; and Emmet and Jeuck, *Catalogues and Counters,* 23–25.

6. Emmet and Jeuck, *Catalogues and Counters,* 24.

7. Asher and Heal, *Money,* xxii.

8. Ibid., 17.

9. Emmet and Jeuck, *Catalogues and Counters,* 26.

10. Emmet and Jeuck, *Catalogues and Counters,* 33; Asher and Heal, *Money,* 18.

11. For biographical information on A. C. Roebuck, see Wickwire, "Corn," 20–21.

12. Emmet and Jeuck, *Catalogues and Counters,* 172.

13. *Historical Statistics of the United States: Colonial Times to the Present,* Series A-6–8, and A-57–82 (Washington, D.C.: GPO, 1975); Robert F. Martin, *National Income in the United States* (New York: National Industrial Conference Board, 1939), 1–19.

14. Alfred D. Chandler, Jr., and Richard S. Tedlow, *The Coming of Managerial Capitalism: A Casebook on the History of American Economic Institutions* (Homewood, Ill.: Richard D. Irwin, 1985), 191.

15. Ibid., 310–26.

16. Asher and Heal, *Money,* 18.

17. Alfred D. Chandler, Jr., *Scale and Scope: The Dynamics of Industrial Capitalism* (Cambridge: Harvard University Press, forthcoming).

18. Asher and Heal, *Money,* 80. Asher was catalog editor and later acting general manager of the company. Emmet and Jeuck, *Catalogues and Counters,* 97.

19. Nathan Rosenberg and L. E. Birdzell, Jr., *How the West Grew Rich* (New York: Basic Books, 1986), 47; Robert Bartels, *The History of Marketing Thought* (Columbus, Ohio: Grid Series in Marketing, 1976), 6; George B. Hotchkiss, *Milestones of Marketing* (New York: Macmillan, 1938), 220–21; Irwin M. Heine, "The Influence of Geographic Factors in the Development of the Mail Order Business," *American Marketing Journal* (April 1936): 127–30; Katz, *Big Store,* 510. For interesting observations by a French diplomat on the New York City of 1810 as a "permanent fair," see Fernand Braudel, *The Perspective of the World* (New York: Harper & Row, 1984), 406.

20. Asher and Heal, *Money,* 75.

21. Emmet and Jeuck, *Catalogues and Counters,* 67.

22. "Sewing Machines," Box 50, Folder 11, Rosenwald papers, University of Chicago.

23. For the cream separator, see Emmet and Jeuck, *Catalogues and Counters,* 75, 112; Asher and Heal, *Money,* 87–91; Julius Rosenwald, "Why You Can't Do Too Much for the Customers," *System* 46 (Dec. 1924): 710; Julius Rosenwald to Elbert Hubbard, letter, (typed copy), Box 50, Folder 6, 24 Feb. 1909, Julius Rosenwald papers, University of Chicago.

24. Asher and Heal, *Money,* 76–77.

25. Emmet and Jeuck, *Catalogues and Counters,* 173.

26. Asher and Heal, *Money,* 27.

27. Ibid., 26–28.

28. Alfred D. Chandler, Jr., *Strategy and Structure: Chapters in the History of the American Industrial Enterprise* (Cambridge: MIT Press, 1962), 228.

29. For a different estimate—one suggesting that the average saving to the mail-order customer is closer to 15 percent—see "Montgomery Ward—History," pamphlet, p. 4, Rosenwald papers (typed copy) Box 50, Folder 10, University of Chicago. An attempt to refute the Price article, from which tables 5–2 and 5–3 are taken, is T. W. McAllister, "The Retail Merchant," *The Outlook*, 8 Mar. 1916, 580–84.

30. Paul H. Nystrom, *Economics of Retailing*, vol. 1 (New York: Ronald Press, 1930), 174–75.

31. Boorstin, *Democratic Experience*, 121–22; W. C. Brann, *The Romance of Montgomery Ward & Co.* (New York: Campbell, Starring, 1929), 5.

32. Boorstin, *Democratic Experience*, 122; Brann, *Montgomery Ward*, 4.

33. Melvin T. Copeland, *Principles of Merchandising* (Chicago: Shaw, 1927), 90.

34. Boorstin, *Democratic Experience*, 122. For a discussion of the difficulties in managing a mail-order business, see Nystrom, *Retailing*, 199–209.

35. Frank Latham, *1872–1972, A Century of Serving Consumers: The Story of Montgomery Ward* (Chicago: Montgomery Ward, 1972), 2–19.

36. Boorstin, *Democratic Experience*, 126. See also Daniel J. Boorstin, "A. Montgomery Ward's Mail Order Business," *Chicago History*, n.s. (Spring–Summer 1973): 142–52. For a selection of equally humorous and revealing letters to Sears, see Cohn, *Good Old Days*, 561–79; and Francis Sill Wickwire, "Please Rush the Gal in the Pink Corset," *Collier's*, 17 Dec. 1949, 28–29.

37. Emmet and Jeuck, *Catalogues and Counters*, 22.

38. Ibid., 180.

39. Ibid., 84.

40. Asher and Heal, *Money*, 3.

41. Ibid., 3–4; see also Wickwire, "Corn," 21, 73.

42. Emmet and Jeuck, *Catalogues and Counters*, 61.

43. Ibid., 92–93.

44. Werner, *Rosenwald*, 44.

45. Ibid., 39–40.

46. Asher and Heal, *Money*, 28–29.

47. Emmet and Jeuck, *Catalogues and Counters*, 48; Werner, *Rosenwald*, 39–40; Asher and Heal, *Money*, 8–9.

48. James M. Barker, "Reminiscences," Columbia University Oral History Collection, pp. 138–39.

49. Werner, *Rosenwald*, 21.

50. Ibid., 30.

51. Emmet and Jeuck, *Catalogues and Counters*, 66, 117.

52. Asher and Heal, *Money*, 8.

53. Julius Rosenwald, "Mail Order House, Chicago Product, Fills Public Need," typed transcription of an article published in the *Christian Science Monitor*, 10 Oct. 1923, vol. 50, folder 10, Rosenwald papers.

54. Emmet and Jeuck, *Catalogues and Counters*, 134.

55. Ibid., 132–33.

56. Ibid.

57. Ibid., 52–53, 726n.

58. Louis L. Mann, "Julius Rosenwald," in *Dictionary of American Biography*, vol. 16 (New York: Scribner's, 1935), 170.

59. The phrase is Tracy Kidder's, *The Soul of a New Machine* (Boston: Little, Brown, 1981), 3–7.

60. Werner, *Rosenwald*, 36–37.

61. Wickwire, "Life and Times," 42.

62. James M. Barker, for many years a top executive at Sears, stated that Rosenwald offered to refund the purchase price of Sears's electric belts and other such phony devices (Talk before Sears Directors' and Officers' Dinner, 25 Mar. 1968, Sears file, Wood papers, Herbert Hoover Presidential Library [cited hereafter as HHPL], West Branch, Iowa).

63. Chandler, *Strategy and Structure*, 229.

64. Werner, *Rosenwald*, 180–222.

65. Robert E. Wood, "Reminiscences," Columbia University Oral History Collection, p. 70.

66. Werner, *Rosenwald*, 229–30.

67. Chandler, *Strategy and Structure*, 229–30.

68. Ibid., 230.

69. Werner, *Rosenwald*, 236; Emmet and Jeuck, *Catalogues and Counters*, 328.

70. Emmet and Jeuck, *Catalogues and Counters*, 328–29.

71. "C. H. [*sic*] Kittle, Noted Merchant, Dead," *New York Times*, 3 Jan. 1928, 25; "Kittle's Regime Prosperous One," *Wall Street Journal*, 15 Feb. 1928, 5.

72. Quoted in James C. Worthy, *Shaping an American Institution: Robert E. Wood and Sears, Roebuck* (Urbana, Ill.: University of Illinois Press, 1984), 2–5.

73. David McCullough, *The Path Between the Seas: The Creation of the Panama Canal, 1870–1914* (New York: Simon & Schuster, 1977), 79–80, 137–47.

74. Worthy, *Institution*, 6.

75. Ibid., 7.

76. This sense of *joie de vivre* is well communicated in Wood's memoir at the Columbia Oral History Collection. For a different view of Wood, as a "frustrated citizen, criticized, misunderstood, and probably embittered," see Irving Pflaum, "The Baffling Career of Robert E. Wood," *Harper's*, Apr. 1954, 68–73.

77. Robert E. Wood, speech in acceptance of Tobe Award, 10 Jan. 1951, Sears file, Wood papers, HHPL.

78. Worthy, *Institution*, 13.

79. Ibid., 39. Wood's many prejudices are embarrassingly on display in his Columbia Oral History memoir (see, e.g., 107–108).

80. Chandler, *Strategy and Structure*, 233.

81. "Montgomery Ward," 2.

82. Rosenwald, "Mail Order House," *Christian Science Monitor*.

83. Robert E. Wood, "Merchandising Problems of the Mail Order Business," 13 Dec. 1932, Sears papers, Sears, Roebuck, Chicago, Ill., 13–14.

84. Emmet and Jeuck, *Catalogues and Counters*, 351.

85. "Montgomery Ward," 5–6.

86. Wood, "Merchandising Problems," 11.

87. Ibid., 8.

88. Ibid., 9.

89. Ibid.

90. Ibid., 10.

91. Emmet and Jeuck, *Catalogues and Counters*, 164–68; Ralph M. Hower, *History of Macy's of New York, 1858–1919: Chapters in the Evolution of the Department Store* (Cambridge: Harvard University Press, 1943), 119, 164, 269, 332–33. Other department stores going into mail order in the 1880s included Jordan Marsh; Wanamaker; Field; Strawbridge and Clothier; and Carson, Pirie, Scott (Cecil C. Hoge, Sr., *The First Hundred Years Are the Toughest* [Berkeley, Calif.: Ten Speed Press, 1988], 19).

92. Copeland, *Merchandising*, 94.

93. Emmet and Jeuck, *Catalogues and Counters*, 166.

94. Robert E. Wood to A. T. Cushman, letter, 5 Sept. 1967; Robert E. Wood to Charles H. Kellstadt, letter, 5 Sept. 1967, Sears file, Wood papers, HHPL.

95. Emmet and Jeuck, *Catalogues and Counters*, 487.

96. Sears, Roebuck and Co., *Annual Report to Stockholders*, 31 Dec. 1931.

97. Sears, Roebuck and Co., *Annual Report to Stockholders*, 31 Dec. 1931 to 28 Jan. 1933; Wood, "Reminiscences," 70–71.

98. Wood, "Reminiscences," 39; Emmet and Jeuck, *Catalogues and Counters*, 334–37, 650.

99. Wood, "Reminiscences," 40.

100. Ibid., 43.

101. Chandler, *Strategy and Structure*, 233.

102. Worthy, *Institution*, 4; Wood, "Reminiscences," 3–4.

103. Wood, "Reminiscences," 3.

104. Richard Hofstadter, *The Age of Reform: From Bryan to F. D. R.* (New York: Vintage, 1955), 23; Emmet and Jeuck, *Catalogues and Counters*, 313–16.

105. Ibid., 320–23; Nystrom, *Retailing*, 230–33; James Cash Penney, *J.C. Penney: The Man with a Thousand Partners* (New York: Harper, 1931), 29–43; Mary E. Curry, "Creating an American Institution: The Merchandising Genius of J.C. Penney" (Ph.D. diss., American University, 1980), 143–83.

106. Emmet and Jeuck, *Catalogues and Counters*, 338–40.

107. Robert E. Wood, "Past, Present and Future of the Mail Order Business," Montgomery Ward file, Wood papers, HHPL, 6–7.

108. Merseles to Wood, letter, 17 Sept. 1924; Wood to Merseles, letter, 26 Sept. 1924; Wood to Merseles, letter, 27 Sept. 1924; Ward file, Wood papers, HHPL.

109. Robert E. Wood, "R. E. Wood 'On to Chicago' Speech," 4 May 1950, Sears papers, Sears, Roebuck, Chicago, Ill., 14.

110. Emmet and Jeuck, *Catalogues and Counters*, 487, 653.

111. Ibid., 348–57, 652–53; Chandler, *Strategy and Structure*, 225–82.

112. Barker, "Reminiscences," 141–46.

113. Katz, *Big Store*, 233.

114. Wood, "Tobe Award Speech," 104; Emmet and Jeuck, *Catalogues and Counters*, 348–50; Hoge, *Hundred Years*, 104.

115. Robert E. Wood, *Mail Order Retailing: Pioneered in Chicago* (New York: Newcomen Society, 1948), 9.

116. Ibid., 10.

117. Ibid.

118. Ibid., 51.

119. Wood to Strawn, letter, 17 Aug. 1920, Montgomery Ward file, Wood papers, HHPL; Wood, "Past, Present and Future," 5. The best surviving operational data on tires in these years is given in the following table. Note, however, that these figures are only estimates, which were made by Wood in February of 1924.

Estimated Performance of Tires at Ward in 1924

	Division 61/64 (Tires, etc.)	Group "C" Metals (Included Tires)	Total Mail Order
Sales	$14,500,000	$34,100,000	$125,000,000
Percent of total	8%	27%	100%
Publicity	$772,980	$2,344,658	$11,927,500
Percent of total	6%	20%	100%
Gross profit	$3,588,750	$9,075,250	$35,657,875
Percent of sales	24.75%	26.61%	28.53%
Turnover	5.50	4.70	4.28

SOURCE: Bonus Committee to T. F. Merseles, "Bonus Plan—1924, February 18, 1924," Montgomery Ward file, Wood papers, HHPL.

120. Hoge, *Hundred Years*, 98–99.

121. Emmet and Jeuck, *Catalogues and Counters*, 390; Hoge, *Hundred Years*, 104–15. See also Michael T. French, "Structural Change and Competition in the United States Tire Industry, 1920–1937," *Business History Review* 60 (Spring 1986): 28–54.

122. Emmet and Jeuck, *Catalogues and Counters*, 437.

123. Ibid., 436–40; Katz, *Big Store*, 210; Robert E. Wood to A. T. Cushman and Crowdus Baker, letter, 28 July 1965, Sears file, Wood papers, HHPL.

124. For a list of Sears's principal retail merchandise departments, see Emmet and Jeuck, *Catalogues and Counters*, 486.

125. Wood, *Retailing*, 11.

126. Katz, *Big Store*, 228.

127. R. E. Wood, "The Company and Its Future," 17 Apr. 1934, Sears file, Wood papers, HHPL, 3.

128. Wood, "On to Chicago," 12.

129. Katz, *Big Store,* 335.

130. In 1906, Louis E. Asher dispatched J. H. Jeffries into the field to report on Ward's operations. Jeffries proceeded actually to get a job in Ward's Kansas City mail-order plant and reported that "things are not running very well." Asher responded: "I don't like the idea of your working for these people and reporting to me. I don't think that it is high class either for you or for us. . . . I don't think you could continue in your employment without injuring your self-respect" (Jeffries to Asher, letter, 7 Nov. 1906; Asher to Jeffries, letter, 9 Nov. 1906, Box 1, Folder 12, Asher papers, University of Chicago).

131. Hoge, *Hundred Years,* 21–23; Emmet and Jeuck, *Catalogues and Counters,* 172.

132. Emmet and Jeuck, *Catalogues and Counters,* 166.

133. Wood speech at Ward, 1919, Rosenwald papers.

134. Hoge, *Hundred Years,* 23–40; Emmet and Jeuck, *Catalogues and Counters,* 172.

135. Emmet and Jeuck, *Catalogues and Counters,* 295.

136. Hoge, *Hundred Years,* 80–85; Latham, *Montgomery Ward,* 63–64.

137. This firm did not survive the Depression, declaring bankruptcy in April 1932 ("Bellas Hess," *Tide,* Apr. 1932, 20).

138. Ibid.

139. Worthy, *Institution,* 17.

140. Interview with James E. Burke, Summer 1988.

141. Emmet and Jeuck, *Catalogues and Counters,* 341.

142. Ibid., 338–39, 342–44; Hoge, *Hundred Years,* 101–106; Latham, *Montgomery Ward,* 70–74.

143. Robert E. Wood to Crowdus Baker, letter, 7 May 1964, Sears file, Wood papers, HHPL.

144. "Marketing: Mail-Order Milestones," *Tide,* Apr. 1932, 18.

145. Hoge, *Hundred Years,* 116–17; "The Stores and the Catalogue," *Fortune,* Jan. 1935, 69; "Milestones," *Tide,* 18.

146. "Stores," *Fortune,* 69–80; Chapin Hoskins, "Montgomery Ward Rebuilds Business by Building Morale," *Forbes,* 15 Apr. 1932, 14–16; "Sewell Avery's Mail-Order Job Is Concerned with Man-Power," *Business Week,* 13 Jan. 1932, 24–25; "Sewell Avery Dead; Headed Ward Chain," *New York Times,* 1 Nov. 1960, 1, 39.

147. Emmet and Jeuck, *Catalogues and Counters,* 664, table 106; Montgomery Ward & Co., *Annual Report to Stockholders,* 31 Dec. 1931, 6; ibid., 1939, n.p.

148. Robert E. Wood, talk given before buyers on 5 Nov. 1936, Sears file, Wood papers, HHPL, 2.

149. Talk to be given by R. E. Wood, 30 Aug. 1938, Buying and Cataloging Forces, Sears file, Wood papers, HHPL.

150. Ibid.

151. Ibid.

152. Ibid.

153. Wood, "Reminiscences," 28.

154. Oscar E. Anderson, Jr., *Refrigeration in America: A History of a New Technology and Its Impact* (Princeton, N.J.: Princeton University Press, 1953), 8–9.

155. Anderson, *Refrigeration,* 8, 53–55.

156. Ibid., 87.

157. Ibid., 96.

158. Israel, ed., *Sears Catalogue,* 1897, 104–105.

159. Anderson, *Refrigeration,* 114–15.

160. Ibid., 209–10.

161. A. D. McKay, "Comparative Costs," National Electric Light Association, *Proceedings* (1925), 535.

162. Anderson, *Refrigeration,* 197–98.

163. I am following the version of events published in Sloan's autobiography (Alfred P. Sloan, Jr., *My Years with General Motors* [Garden City, N.Y.: Doubleday, 1963], 415). Mellowes recollected selling "about 50 machines" in the twelve months following April of 1916 (Alfred W. Mellowes, "Memo of the History of Household Electric Refrigeration," 23 July 1926, 79–10.2–14, Box 14, Frigidaire papers, General Motors Institute Alumni Historical Collection of Industrial History, Flint, Mich.).

164. Sloan, *My Years,* 413.

165. Tom Shellworth, "Report on Frigidaire's Development," 1 Feb. 1950, Section I, 79–10.1–412, Box 3, p. 4; "Results of Interview with C. F. Kettering," 30 Dec. 1948, 79–10.1–43, Box 3, "Results of Interview with Mr. John L. Pratt," 25 Mar. 1949, 79–10.1–43, Frigidaire papers.

166. "Report on Frigidaire," circa 1949, 79–10.16–21, Box 16, Frigidaire papers, 30.

167. Sloan, *My Years,* 415.

168. "Part IV: Frigidaire Product Development from 1921 to the Present," 79–10.1–45, Box 3, p. 2; "Interview with R.H. Grant," 1 Dec. 1948, 79–10.1–43, Box 3, Frigidaire papers.

169. David A. Hounshell and John Kenly Smith, Jr., *Science and Corporate Strategy: Du Pont R&D, 1902–1980* (New York: Cambridge University Press, 1988), 155; Kettering Interview; "Results of Interview with Mr. R. O. Ashton," 4 Jan. 1949, 79–10.1–43, Box 3, Frigidaire papers.

170. Hounshell and Smith, *Science,* 155–57; "Part I: Frigidaire Product Development," 13–18; "The Household Refrigerator," 79–10.1–47; "Part V: Changes in the Organization and Physical Plant from 1921 to 1949," 79–10.1–45, Box 3, Frigidaire papers, 11–13.

171. "Results of Interview with Mr. Copp," 28 Jan. 1949, 79–10.1–43, Box 3; Shellworth manuscript, circa 1950, 79–10.1–41b, Box 3, pp. 4–7; "Part VII: Frigidaire Sales and Advertising Practices," 79–10.1–45, Box 3, pp. 6–9; "Section III: Sales and Competition," Frigidaire papers, 1–4.

172. D. C. McCoy, "Frigidaire Household Refrigerators," Aug. 1964, 79–10.-16–125, Box 123, Frigidaire papers, 11, 27.

173. Report on Domestic Refrigerating Machines by Alexander R. Stevenson, Aug. 1923, General Electric Corporation, Schenectady, N.Y. This report was made available to me by Dr. George Wise; Ralph F. Roider, " 'Making It Safe to Be Hungry,' " *General Electric Review*, Sept. 1952, 37.

174. Grant Interview; McCoy, "Frigidaire," 12; C. J. Jenks, *Case Studies in Research and Innovation in General Electric*, CRO 23:57, General Electric Corp., Appliance Park, Ky., 43.

175. J. O. Downey, "General Motors and the Household Appliance Industry," 27 Mar. 1936, 79–10.5–22, Box 46; "The Frigidaire Appliance Business," Nov. 1955, 79–10.1–164, Box 11, Frigidaire papers.

176. *Historical Statistics of the United States*, part 2, 287.

177. Pynchon and Co. to National City Bank, letter, Box 1, Folder 9, Sears papers.

178. See Law Department Records, Factories and Sources, Sub-series 2, Records of the related Hercules/Servel Companies, Sears papers, Sears, Roebuck, Chicago, Ill.

179. Wood to Kittle, letter, 4 Mar. 1925; Wood to Kittle, letter, 13 Mar. 1925; Wood to Kittle, letter, 5 Aug. 1925; Contract for Sears to exchange Hercules stock for Servel stock, Box 1, Folder 4, Law Department Records, Sub-series 2, Records of the related Hercules/Servel Companies, Sears papers, Sears, Roebuck, Chicago, Ill.

180. Emmet and Jeuck, *Catalogues and Counters*, 230–32.

181. Ibid., 230–31.

182. John N. Ingham, ed., *Biographical Dictionary of American Business Leaders* (Westport, Conn.: Greenwood, 1983), 1004.

183. Private communication, Dr. A. J. Snow to James W. Button, made available to me by Mr. Button.

184. Emmet and Jeuck, *Catalogues and Counters*, 390; Ed Klingler, *How a City Founded to Make Money Made It: The Economic and Business History of Evansville* (Evansville, Ind.: University of Evansville, 1978), 87–88.

185. Coldspot typescript, Sears papers, Sears, Roebuck, Chicago, Ill.

186. Sears Spring/Summer Catalogue, 1931, 650–51.

187. Klingler, *History of Evansville*, 88.

188. Coldspot typescript, 4–5.

189. Coldspot typescript; Jeffrey L. Meikle, *Twentieth Century Limited: Industrial Design in America, 1925–1939* (Philadelphia, Pa.: Temple University Press, 1979), 4–5, 104–107.

190. Theodore V. Houser, "The Whys and Wherefores of Sears Merchandise," speech, 30 Mar. 1939. I am grateful to Professor James C. Worthy for providing a copy of this speech from his personal files.

191. Information on Dr. A. J. Snow was made available by Mr. James W. Button, former senior merchant at Sears.

192. "1934 Product Information Manual: Household Frigidaire," 79–10.2–22, Box 16, Frigidaire papers.

193. "Ford's Feat Rivaled by Coldspot: Firm Breaks New Ground in Indus-

try," *News-Graphic,* 18 Feb. 1936, 9, Box 1, Sears papers, Sears, Roebuck, Chicago, Ill.

194. Downey, "General Motors," 64–65.

195. Ibid., 68.

196. *A Market Survey of Domestic Refrigeration* (Philadelphia, Pa.: Curtis Publishing Co., 1941), 42–43.

197. Ibid., 58–73.

198. "The Nudes Have It," *Fortune,* May 1940, 104.

199. Frigidaire Marketing Research Dept., 7 Mar. 1949, 79–10.4–352, Box 43, Frigidaire papers.

200. "Have It," *Fortune,* 74.

201. *Sears Catalogue,* Spring/Summer, 1935, 577.

202. *Sears Catalogue,* Fall/Winter, 1935/1936, 585.

203. Ibid.

204. *Refrigeration and Air Conditioning Market Data for 1935* (Detroit, Mich.: Business News Publishing Co., 1935), 32.

205. "Part VII: Frigidaire Sales," 12; Downey, "General Motors," 64; "General Operating Trends in the Frigidaire Household Business," 79–10.1–52, Box 4, Frigidaire papers, 3, 6.

206. The average price is from "Have It," *Fortune,* 104. I have taken Coldspot's unit sales from the Frigidaire papers. Frigidaire figures for Coldspot sales in 1939 are 5,916 higher than the estimates in *Fortune.*

207. "Sears' War," *Fortune,* Sept. 1942, 79.

208. Robert E. Wood, "The Story in Brief," Sears file, Wood papers, HHPL.

209. For the price war into which Coldspot's entry forced the industry, see "Have It," *Fortune.*

210. Lawrence Miller, "The Demand for Refrigerators" (Ph.D. diss., Harvard University, 1956), 19.

211. Chandler, *Strategy and Structure,* 365; see also Chandler, *Scale and Scope,* chap. 6.

212. "Have It," *Fortune,* 102.

213. 1949 advertising memorandum, Frigidaire papers.

214. Robert E. Wood to Fowler McConnell, letter, 13 Jan. 1953, Box 3, Folder 4, Sears papers, Sears, Roebuck, Chicago, Ill.

215. "Note on the Major Home Appliance Industry," No. 9–372–349/Rev. 3/73 (Boston: Harvard Business School Case Services, 1973), 34.

216. Emmet and Jeuck, *Catalogues and Counters,* 664.

217. R. E. Wood Speech to merchandising staff, 23 Apr. 1946, Sears file, Wood papers, HHPL, 2.

218. "Young Sears, Roebuck," *Fortune,* Aug. 1948, 87.

219. Ibid.; Wood, "Reminiscences," 57–59; Robert E. Wood, speech to Philadelphia Chamber of Commerce, Rosenwald papers, University of Chicago. In an address given at the University of Georgia in 1939, Wood said, "If I were called on to name those portions of the country that offer the greatest opportunities, I would name the Southeast from Virginia to Mississippi and the states of Texas

and California. I venture the prediction that in the next twenty years the South-eastern states, Texas and California will grow more rapidly in wealth and popula-tion than the rest of the country. Their economic and political power will increase." (Robert E. Wood, Alumni Day Address at University of Georgia at Athens, 12 June 1939, Speeches and Articles, Wood papers, HHPL).

220. Wood, "Reminiscences," 99.

221. Katz, *Big Store*, 555.

222. "General Robert E. Wood, President," *Fortune*, May 1938, 69.

223. Ibid., 69, 104.

224. Katz, *Big Store*, 19.

225. Ibid.

226. Worthy, *Institution*, 252.

227. Katz, *Big Store*, 93–95.

228. Worthy, *Institution*, 253.

229. Wood, "Reminiscences," 98.

230. Robert Brooker with John McDonald, "The Strategy That Saved Mont-gomery Ward," *Fortune*, May 1970, 171.

231. "Montgomery Ward: Prosperity Still Around the Corner," *Fortune*, Nov. 1960, 140; Albert D. Bates, *Retailing and Its Environment* (New York: Van Nostrand, 1979), 7–8; Robert F. Hartley, *Management Mistakes* (New York: John Wiley & Sons, 1986), 119–32.

232. Hoge, *Hundred Years*, 165; "Louis Wolfson: 'How I'd Change Mont-gomery Ward's Marketing,' " *Tide*, 18 Dec. 1954, 19–21; Booton Herndon, *Satisfaction Guaranteed: An Unconventional Report to Today's Consumers* (New York: McGraw-Hill, 1972).

233. Robert E. Wood, Montgomery Ward speech, Ward file, Wood papers, HHPL.

234. Robert E. Wood, talk given before buyers, 5 Nov. 1936, Sears file, Wood papers, HHPL.

235. Robert E. Wood, "The Company and Its Future," 17 Apr. 1934, Sears file, Wood papers, HHPL, 6.

236. Worthy, *Institution*, 43–44.

237. Wood to Avery, letter, 29 Apr. 1944; Wood to Avery, letter, 2 May 1944, Sears file, Wood papers, HHPL.

238. Worthy, *Institution*, 267.

239. Ibid., 261.

240. John McDonald, "Sears Makes It Look Easy," *Fortune*, May 1964, 120.

241. Carol Loomis, "The Leaning Tower of Sears," *Fortune*, 2 July 1979, 78–85. For the impact of this article at Sears, see Katz, *Big Store*, 136–37.

242. Katz, *Big Store*, 227.

243. Ibid., 232.

244. Ibid., 275.

245. Emmet and Jeuck, *Catalogues and Counters*, 104.

246. *Chicago Tribune*, 1 Feb. 1925, 16. This advertisement was brought to my attention by Professor Roland Marchand of the University of California at Davis.

Chapter 6   Secrets of Success: Modern Marketing in Historical Perspective

1. Adam Smith, *An Inquiry into the Nature and Causes of the Wealth of Nations*, ed. Edwin Canaan (New York: Modern Library, 1937), 144.

2. "General Motors: Part I of a Study in Bigness," *Fortune*, Dec. 1938, 67.

3. This is an important theme of Daniel J. Boorstin's *The Americans: The Democratic Experience* (New York: Vintage, 1973), 89–164.

4. Quoted in David M. Potter, *People of Plenty: Economic Abundance and the American Character* (Chicago: University of Chicago Press, 1954), 135.

5. In 1951, David Riesman published a fictional story about an American bombardment of the Soviet Union with consumer goods. "Behind the initial raid of June 1 were years of secret and complex preparations, and an idea of disarming simplicity: that if allowed to sample the riches of America, the Russian people would not long tolerate masters who gave them tanks and spies instead of vacuum cleaners and beauty parlors" (David Riesman, *Abundance for What? and Other Essays* [Garden City, N.Y.: Doubleday, 1964], 67–79). After this story was published, Riesman received letters and phone calls asking for more information on the "war."

6. Quoted in Potter, *Plenty*, 135.

7. John Sculley, *Odyssey: Pepsi to Apple, A Journey of Adventures, Ideas, and the Future* (New York: Harper & Row, 1987), 336–37.

8. Charles Howard Candler, *Asa Griggs Candler* (Atlanta, Ga.: Emory University, 1950), 109.

9. Coca-Cola Company, *Annual Report, 1892*.

10. Smith, *Wealth of Nations*, 63.

11. Richard S. Tedlow, "The Business Archive: Background and Direction," in *Entrepreneurship: What It Is and How to Teach It*, ed. John J. Kao and Howard H. Stevenson (a collection of working papers based on a colloquium held at Harvard Business School, July 5–8, 1983), 258, 253–69.

12. Richard Cantillon, *Essai sur la Nature du Commerce en Général* (1755; Paris: Institut National d'Etudes Demographiques, 1952).

13. Quoted in Arthur H. Cole, "An Approach to the Study of Entrepreneurship: A Tribute to Edwin F. Gay," in *Explorations in Enterprise*, ed. Hugh G. J. Aitken (Cambridge: Harvard University Press, 1967), 32–33.

14. Ibid.

15. Thomas C. Cochran, "Entrepreneurship," in *International Encyclopedia of the Social Sciences*, vol. 5 (New York: Free Press, 1968), 88–89.

16. Jonathan Hughes, *The Vital Few: The Entrepreneur and American Economic Progress* (New York: Oxford University Press, 1986), 14.

17. Johan Arndt, "The Political Economy of Marketing Systems: Reviving the Institutional Approach," *Journal of Macromarketing* 1 (Fall 1981): 37.

18. For the role of critical incidents in the development of corporate culture, see Edgar H. Schein, *Organizational Culture and Leadership* (San Francisco: Jossey-Bass, 1985), 148–84.

19. Joseph A. Schumpeter, *Capitalism, Socialism and Democracy,* 3d ed. (New York: Harper & Row, 1950), 132.

20. Ibid.

21. Boorstin, *Democratic Experience,* 523–98.

22. This is the thesis of Harold C. Livesay, "Entrepreneurial Persistence Through the Bureaucratic Age," in *Managing Big Business: Essays from the Business History Review,* ed. Richard S. Tedlow and Richard R. John, Jr. (Boston: Harvard Business School Press, 1986), 107–35.

23. This is not as far-fetched as it might at first seem. Some brewers owned their own taverns from the 1880s through Prohibition. Daniel A. Pope, *The Making of Modern Advertising* (New York: Basic Books, 1983), 81–82.

24. Interview with soft drink company executive, Mar. 1983.

25. The leading proponent of transaction costs in recent years has been Oliver E. Williamson. See his *Markets and Hierarchies: Analysis and Antitrust Implications* (New York: Free Press, 1975); and *The Economic Institutions of Capitalism* (New York: Free Press, 1985).

26. Theodore V. Houser, "The Whys and Wherefores of Sears Merchandise," 30 Mar. 1939, papers of James C. Worthy, in his personal collection.

27. Donald R. Katz, *The Big Store: Inside the Crisis and Revolution at Sears* (New York: Viking, 1987), 411.

28. Louis W. Stern and Adel I. El-Ansary, *Marketing Channels,* 2d ed. (Englewood Cliffs, N.J.: Prentice-Hall, 1982), 306–58.

29. For an enumeration of the pros and cons of vertical integration, see Robert D. Buzzell and Bradley T. Gale, *The PIMS Principles: Linking Strategy to Performance* (New York: Free Press, 1987), 163–81.

30. Stern and El-Ansary, *Channels,* 215.

31. Alfred D. Chandler, Jr., *The Visible Hand: The Managerial Revolution in American Business* (Cambridge: Harvard University Press, 1977).

32. Michael E. Porter, *Competitive Advantage: Creating and Sustaining Superior Performance* (New York: Free Press, 1985), 34–35.

33. Pope, *Advertising,* 61.

34. For a useful review of the literature on first-mover advantage, see Marvin B. Lieberman and David B. Montgomery, "First-Mover Advantages," *Strategic Management Journal* 9 (1988): 41–58.

35. George S. Yip, *Barriers to Entry: A Corporate-Strategy Perspective* (Lexington, Mass.: D.C. Heath, 1982), 17.

36. George S. Yip, "Gateways to Entry," *Harvard Business Review* 60 (Sept.–Oct. 1982): 86.

37. Porter, *Advantage,* 6.

38. Ibid., 187.

39. Boorstin, *Democratic Experience,* 434–47.

40. For the changing role of the wholesaler in the nineteenth-century American economy, see Glenn Porter and Harold C. Livesay, *Merchants and Manufacturers: Studies in the Changing Structure of Nineteenth-Century Marketing* (Baltimore, Md.: Johns Hopkins University Press, 1971).

41. Yip, "Gateways," 87.

42. Alfred P. Sloan, Jr., *My Years with General Motors* (Garden City, N.Y.: Doubleday, 1963), 76; John Jacob Raskob to William McMaster, letter, Du Pont Administrative Papers, Accession 1662, Box 36, File 86, Hagley Museum and Library, Wilmington, Del.

43. Arthur J. Kuhn, *GM Passes Ford, 1918–1938: Designing the General Motors Performance-Control System* (University Park, Pa.: Pennsylvania State University Press, 1986), 125.

44. Daniel A. Pope has described advertisements in which "the context rather than the product becomes, in a sense, the object of the consumers' desires . . ." (*Advertising*, 280).

45. The idea of a two-for-one deal was suggested to me by Mr. Lloyd E. Cotsen, president of the Neutrogena Corporation.

46. Sloan, *My Years*, 187.

47. William J. Abernathy and Kenneth Wayne, "The Limits of the Learning Curve," *Harvard Business Review* 52 (Sept.–Oct. 1974): 109ff.'

48. Buzzell and Gale, *PIMS*, 189.

49. Conversation with Alfred Chandler, Boston, Mass., Fall 1988.

50. In the District Court of the United States for the Eastern District of Illinois, United States v. The New York Great Atlantic and Pacific Tea Company, Inc. et al., No. 16153 (criminal). Testimony of John A. Hartford, 20,439.

51. John Kenneth Galbraith, for example, overestimates the power of modern marketing in *The Affluent Society* (Boston: Houghton Mifflin, 1959). See also Charles H. Hession, *John Kenneth Galbraith and His Critics* (New York: Signet, 1972), 64–134.

Appendix A

1. Malcolm P. McNair, "Expenses and Profits in the Chain Grocery Business in 1929," *Bureau of Business Research Bulletin*, no. 84 (Cambridge: Murray Printing, 1931).

2. Alfred D. Chandler, Jr., and Richard S. Tedlow, *The Coming of Managerial Capitalism: A Casebook on the History of American Economic Institutions* (Homewood, Ill.: Richard D. Irwin, 1985), 316.

3. Richard S. Tedlow, *Case Commentary and Teaching Technique to Accompany The Coming of Managerial Capitalism* (Homewood, Ill.: Richard D. Irwin, 1985), 130.

4. Clyde Lyndon King, "Can the Cost of Distributing Food Products Be Reduced?" *The Annals of the American Academy of Political and Social Science* 48 (July 1913): 211.

5. *The Food Marketing Industry Speaks, 1984: Detailed Tabulations* (Washington, D.C.: Research Division of the Food Marketing Institute, 1984), 75.

Bibliography

Archives

Baker Library, Harvard Business School, Boston, Mass.
Coca-Cola Company, Atlanta, Ga.
Columbia University, Oral History Collection, New York, N.Y.
Federal Records Center, Suitland, Md.
Ford Industrial Archives, Redford, Mich.
GMI, Alumni Historical Collection, Flint, Mich.
General Electric Company, Appliance Division, Louisville, Ky.
General Electric Company, Schenectady, N.Y.
Hagley Museum and Library, Greenville, Wilmington, Del.
Henry Ford Museum and Greenfield Village, Archives and Research Library, Dearborn, Mich.
Herbert Hoover Presidential Library, West Branch, Iowa.
J. C. Penney, Plano, Tex.
John F. Kennedy Presidential Library, Boston, Mass.
J. Walter Thompson Company, New York, N.Y.
National Museum of American History, Oral History Collection, Smithsonian Institution, Washington, D.C.
Sears, Roebuck, Chicago, Ill.
University of Chicago, Department of Special Collections, Chicago, Ill.

Government Documents

Boston City Planning Board. *A Summary of the Market Situation in Boston.* Preliminary Report of the Marketing Advisory Committee. Boston: Printing Department, 1916.
Bureau of the Census. *Biennial Census of Manufactures, 1935.* "Beverages, Nonalcoholic." Washington, D.C.: GPO, 1936.

———. *Biennial Census of Manufactures, 1937.* "Beverages, Nonalcoholic." Washington, D.C.: GPO, 1938.

———. *Biennial Census of Manufactures,* "Nonalcoholic Beverages." Washington, D.C.: GPO, 1940.

———. *Historical Statistics of the United States: Colonial Times to 1970.* Washington, D.C.: GPO, 1975.

———. Census of Distribution. *Retail Distribution (Trade Series): Food Retailing in 1929.* Washington, D.C.: GPO, 1934.

———. *Statistical Abstract of the United States.* Washington, D.C.: GPO, 1985.

Federal Trade Commission. *Chain Stores: Chain Store Manufacturing.* 73d Cong., 1st sess., S. Doc. 13. Washington, D.C.: GPO, 1935.

———. *Chain Stores: Final Report on the Chain Store Investigation.* 74th Cong., 1st sess., S. Doc. 4. Washington, D.C.: GPO, 1935.

———. *Chain Stores: Growth and Development of Chain Stores.* 72d Cong., 1st sess., S. Doc. 100. Washington, D.C.: GPO, 11 June 1932.

———. *Gross Profit and Average Sales per Store of Retail Chains,* 72d Cong., 2d sess., S. Doc. 178. Washington, D.C.: GPO, 1933.

———. *Chain Stores: Invested Capital and Rates of Return on Retail Chains.* 73d Cong., 2d sess., S. Doc. 87. Washington, D.C.: GPO, 1934.

———. *Chain Stores: Prices and Margins of Chain and Independent Distributors,* "Cincinnati—Grocery." 73d Cong., 2d sess., S. Doc. 88. Washington, D.C.: GPO, 1933.

———. *Chain Stores: Prices and Margins of Chain and Independent Distributors,* "Detroit—Grocery." 73d Cong., 2d sess., S. Doc. 88. Washington, D.C.: GPO, 1933.

———. *Chain Stores: Prices and Margins of Chain and Independent Distributors,* "Detroit—Grocery." 73d Cong., 2d sess., S. Doc. 81. Washington, D.C.: GPO, 1933.

———. *Chain Stores: Prices and Margins of Chain and Independent Distributors,* "Memphis—Grocery." 73d Cong., 1st sess., S. Doc. 69. Washington, D.C.: GPO, 1933.

———. *Chain Stores: Prices and Margins of Chain and Independent Distributors,* "Washington, D.C.—Grocery." 73d Cong., 1st sess., S. Doc. 62. Washington, D.C.: GPO, 1933.

———. *Chain Stores: Service Features in Chain Stores.* 73d Cong., 2d sess., S. Doc. 91. Washington, D.C.: GPO, 1934.

———. *Chain Stores: Sources of Chain Store Merchandise.* 72d Cong., 1st sess., S. Doc. 30. Washington, D.C.: GPO, 1932.

———. *Chain Stores: Wholesale Business of Retail Chains.* 72d Cong., 1st sess. S. Doc. 29. Washington, D.C.: GPO, 1932.

———. *Report on Motor Vehicle Industry.* Washington, D.C.: GPO, 1940.

Hoffman, A. C., for the Temporary National Economic Committee. *Large-Scale Organization in the Food Industries,* monograph no. 35. Washington, D.C.: GPO, 1940.

New York State Food Investigation Committee. *Markets and Prices.* 1912.

Report of the Federal Trade Commission on Distribution Methods and Costs. Part I, "Important Food Products." Washington, D.C.: GPO, 1944.

U.S. Department of Agriculture, "Horses, Mules and Motor Vehicles." *Statistical Bulletin No. 5* (Jan. 1925).

U.S. Department of Commerce. "Louisville Grocery Survey—Part III—A." *Merchandising Characteristics of Grocery Store Commodities: General Findings and Specific Results.* Distribution Cost Studies—no. 11. Washington, D.C.: GPO, 1932.

U.S. Department of State. *Enumeration of the Inhabitants and Statistics of the United States as Obtained at the Department of State, from the Returns of the Sixth Census.* Washington, D.C.: Thomas Allen, 1841.

U.S. Senate, *Wages and Prices Investigation,* 1911.

Periodicals and Articles

(Articles are alphabetized by author or, when the author's name is not available, by periodical title.)

Abernathy, William J., and Kenneth Wayne. "The Limits of the Learning Curve." *Harvard Business Review* 52 (Sept.–Oct. 1974): 109ff.

Adelman, Morris A. "Dirlam and Kahn on the A&P Case." *Journal of Political Economy* 61 (1953): 436–41.

———. "Integration and Dissolution of the A&P Company: A Reply. Price Policy in the A&P Case." *Indiana Law Journal* 29 (Winter 1954): 367–70.

Advertising and Selling. "150 Leading Magazine Advertisers in 1935." 16 Jan. 1936, 26ff.

———. "150 Leading Radio Advertisers in 1935." 16 Jan. 1936, 29ff.

Alexander, R. S. "Study of Retail Grocery Prices." [New York] *Journal of Commerce* 140 (2 Mar. 1929): 9, 19.

Arndt, Johan. "The Political Economy of Marketing Systems: Reviving the Institutional Approach." *Journal of Macromarketing* 1 (Fall 1981): 37.

Atherton, Lewis E. "The Pioneer Merchant in Mid-America." *The University of Missouri Studies* 14 (1 Apr. 1939): 39–46.

The Automobile. "Atlanta's National Show Interests the Whole South." 11 Nov. 1909, 815–18.

———. "Ford Agencies Increase Rapidly in Every City." 24 Aug. 1916, 300.

———. "Ford to Drop Retail Sales." 17 Aug. 1916, 255.

———. "How Atlanta Entertains Her Automobile Guests." 11 Nov. 1909, 818.

———. "Parent Company Abandons Repair Business." 24 Aug. 1916, 300–301.

Automobile Trade Journal. "What Cooperation Is Doing for the Philadelphia Ford Dealers." Jan. 1917, 190–91.

Barron's. "Coca-Cola, The Highest-Priced Industrial." 17 June 1935, 16.

———. "Coca-Cola's True Earning Power in 1929." 24 Feb. 1930, 10.

————."How Will Soft Drink Companies Fare If Prohibition Ends?" 25 July 1932, 26.

————. "Leading Ginger-Ale Manufacturer." 12 Nov. 1937, 8.

————. "A Valuable Trade Name." 23 May 1932, 15.

Bell, Daniel. "The Company He Keeps." *New York Review of Books,* 19 Mar. 1964, 12–14.

Bernstein, Peter W. "Jonathan Scott's Surprising Failure at A&P." *Fortune,* 6 Nov. 1978, 35–44.

Beverage Digest. "A Talk with Roberto Goizueta." 30 Sept. 1988, 1–4.

Beverage Industry. "A 20-Year Retrospective: Brand by Brand." May 1986, 24.

Bjorklund, Einar, and James L. Palmer. "A Study of the Prices of Chain and Independent Grocers in Chicago." *University of Chicago Studies in Business Administration* 1 (1930): 1–55.

Blakey, Roy G., and Gladys C. Blakey. "Chain Store Taxation." *Taxes,* Oct. 1941: 594–602.

————. "Chain Store Taxation." *Taxes,* Nov. 1941: 670–75.

Bohack, Henry C., Jr. "The Chain Store Finds That Price Is Losing Its Appeal." *Printers' Ink,* 19 July 1928, 25ff.

Boorstin, Daniel J. "A. Montgomery Ward's Mail Order Business." *Chicago History,* New Series II (Spring–Summer 1973): 142–52.

Brooker, Robert, with John McDonald. "The Strategy That Saved Montgomery Ward." *Fortune,* May 1970, 168–71.

Bullock, Roy J. "The Early History of the Great Atlantic and Pacific Tea Company." *Harvard Business Review* 11 (Apr. 1933): 289–98.

————. "A History of the Great Atlantic and Pacific Tea Company Since 1878." *Harvard Business Review* 12 (Oct. 1933): 59–69.

Bureau of Business Research. "Management Problems in Retail Grocery Stores." *Bulletin No. 13.* Cambridge: Harvard University Press, 1919.

————. "Operating Expenses in Retail Grocery Stores in 1924." *Bulletin No. 52.* Boston: George H. Ellis, 1925.

Business Week. "A&P Looks Like Tengelmann's Vietnam." 1 Feb. 1982, 42–44.

————. "A&P's Ploy: Cutting Prices to Turn a Profit." 20 May 1972, 76–79.

————. "Advertising Hits the Long Pull." 18 Jan. 1936, 9–11.

————. "Advertising Stages a Comeback." 20 Jan. 1940, 38–40.

————. "Canada Dry *vs.* Coca-Cola." 24 Aug. 1935, 14.

————. "Can Jonathan Scott Save A&P?" 19 May 1975, 128–36.

————. "The Cheapy Thrives." 8 Feb. 1933, 11–12.

————. "Coca-Cola Victory." 6 Aug. 1938, 21–22.

————. "The Pause That Refreshes." 27 Apr. 1940, 36.

————. "Pepsi-Cola Tries Out Cans." 11 Mar. 1950, 100.

————. "Sewell Avery's Mail-Order Job Is Concerned with Man-Power." 13 Jan. 1932, 24–25.

Chain Store Age Executive. "A&P's Remarkable Recovery." Sept. 1976, 33–34.

Chapin, Roy D. "Distributor or Branch House?" *The Horseless Age,* 15 Dec. 1916, 413–14.

Chary, John. "Industry's Advertising Budget Reaches Huge Total." *Automotive Industries*, 21 May 1927, 751–53.

Clark, Neil M. "The Independent Grocer Finds 'A Way Out!' " *Forbes*, 1 Sept. 1930, 18–21.

The Coca-Cola Bottler. "Developing a Home Business on Coca-Cola Through the Six-Bottle Carton." Aug. 1929, 13–18.

———. "Developing a Home Business on Coca-Cola Through the Six-Bottle Carton, Part II." Sept. 1929, 13–17.

———. "Developing a Home Business on Coca-Cola Through the Six-Bottle Carton, Part III." Oct. 1929, 13–16.

———. "Where Reciprocity Is Indicated." June 1909, 5–6.

Cohen, Randy. "Songs in the Key of Hype." *More*, July–August 1977, 12.

Cochran, Thomas C. "Entrepreneurship." In *International Encyclopedia of the Social Sciences*. Vol. 5. New York: The Free Press, 1968, 88–89.

Collins, Thomas C. "Selecting and Establishing Brand Names." In *Handbook of Modern Marketing*, edited by Victor P. Buell (New York: McGraw-Hill, 1970), 13–69 to 13–76.

Commercial and Financial Chronicle 149, "Pepsi-Cola Co. (and Subs.)," 14 Oct. 1939, 2375–76.

Converse, Paul D. "Prices and Services of Chain and Independent Stores in Champaign-Urbana, Illinois." National Association of Teachers of Marketing and Advertising *Bulletin*, Oct. 1931, Series 4, 1–27.

———. "Prices and Services of Chain and Independent Stores in Champaign-Urbana, 1937." *Journal of Marketing* 2 (Jan. 1938): 193–200.

Copeland, Melvin T. "Marketing." In *Recent Economic Changes in the United States.* Vol. 1. New York: McGraw-Hill, 1929.

Couzens, James. "What I Learned About Business from Ford." *System* 40 (Sept. 1921): 261–64.

Cycle and Automobile Trade Journal. "The New Model T Ford Touring Car." 1 Oct. 1908, 98–100, 102.

Dale, Ernest. "Contributions to Administration by Alfred P. Sloan, Jr. and GM." *Administrative Science Quarterly* 1 (1956): 30–61.

Dirlam, Joel B., and Alfred E. Kahn. "Antitrust Law and the Big Buyer: Another Look at the A&P Case." *Journal of Political Economy* 60 (1952): 118–32.

———. "Integration and Dissolution of the A&P Company." *Indiana Law Journal* 29 (Fall 1953): 1–27.

———. "A Reply." *Journal of Political Economy* 61 (1953): 441–45.

Dobbs, S. C. "Aggressiveness Necessary in the Selling of Coca-Cola." *The Coca-Cola Bottler*, May 1909, 5.

Dowe, Dorothy. "Comparison of Independent and Chain Store Prices." *Journal of Business* 5 (Apr. 1932): 130–44.

The Economist. "A Survey of the Motor Industry." 15 Oct. 1988, 27-page insert following p. 66.

Estey, J. A. "Financing the Sale of Automobiles." *The Annals of the American Academy of Political and Social Science* 116 (Nov. 1924): 44–49.

Fein, Rashi. "Note on Price Discrimination and the A&P Case." *Quarterly Journal of Economics* 65 (1951): 271–79.

Flink, James J. "Automobile." In *Encyclopedia of American Economic History*, vol. 3, edited by Glenn Porter (New York: Scribner's, 1980), 1168–93.

Fly, Joseph M. "Can the Chain Store Supplant the Grocery Wholesaler?" *Printers' Ink*, 23 June 1927, 145–46.

Forbes. "The Top 100 Industrials: 1917, 1929, 1945, 1977." 15 Sept. 1977, 128–29, 133–34.

Forbes, B. C. "How Ford Dealers Are Treated, as Described by One of Them." *Forbes*, 15 May 1927, 17–19.

Fortune. "The A&P Company As a Whole." July 1930, 45–49.

———. "A&P Goes to the Wars." Apr. 1938, 96.

———. "The A&P in Fairfield, Conn." July 1930, 41–44.

———. "Automobile Selling I." Dec. 1931, 42.

———. "Automobile Selling II: The Dealer." Dec. 1931, 42.

———. "Bob Woodruff of Coca-Cola." Sept. 1945, 139–40.

———. ". . . the 'Champagne of Ginger Ales' That Ate Crow and Became a Pop." June 1937, 114–18.

———. "The Coca-Cola Industry." Dec. 1938, 64–67.

———. "The 500 Largest U.S. Industrial Corporations Ranked by Sales." 28 Apr. 1986, 182–201.

———. "Five Years for a Breath of Fresh Air." Jan. 1975, 21.

———. "The Fortune 500 Largest U.S. Industrial Corporations." 25 Apr. 1988, D11–D13.

———. "General Motors, Part I: A Study in Bigness." Dec. 1938, 40–47.

———. "General Motors, Part II: Chevrolet." Jan. 1939, 37–46.

———. "General Motors, Part III: How to Sell Automobiles." Feb. 1939, 71–78.

———. "General Motors, Part IV: A Unit in Society." Mar. 1939, 44–52.

———. "General Robert E. Wood, President." May 1938, 66–69.

———. "The Great A&P." Nov. 1947, 103.

———. "Montgomery Ward: Prosperity Still Around the Corner." Nov. 1960, 140.

———. "The Nudes Have It." May 1940, 73–75.

———. "Pepsi-Cola's Walter Mack." Nov. 1947, 126–31.

———. "Price and Pride Finally Get Together at A&P." 12 Feb. 1979, 15–16.

———. "Price, Pride, and Profitability." Apr. 1977, 20.

———. "Safeway Stores, Inc." Oct. 1940, 60–64.

———. "Sears's War." Sept. 1942, 78–83, 119–20.

———. "The Stores and the Catalogue." Jan. 1935, 69–80.

———. "To Pause and Be Refreshed." July 1931, 65.

———. "Up from Pop." Aug. 1931, 45–49.

———. "Will They Find Flair at A&P?" Apr. 1971, 29.

———. "Young Sears, Roebuck." Aug. 1948, 84–87.

Foster, Hugh M. "Monopoly in Retail Food Distribution." *Journal of Retailing* (Dec. 1941): 112–19.

Freeman, Samuel S. "The Way It Really Was." *Pepsi-Cola World* 30 (July 1969): 32–33.

French, Michael T. "Structural Change and Competition in the United States Tire Industry, 1920–1937." *Business History Review* 60 (Spring 1986): 28–54.

Garrett, Franklin M. "Founders of the Business of Coca-Cola in Bottles." *The Coca-Cola Bottler*, Apr. 1959, 85–92ff.

Gates, Ward. "A Soft Drink Unaffected by Hard Liquor." *The Magazine of Wall Street*, 15 Sept. 1934, 562–66.

———. "Profits in Fair Weather and Foul." *The Magazine of Wall Street*, 18 Dec. 1937, 283–85.

Griffin, Clare Elmer. "The Life History of Automobiles." *Michigan Business Studies* 1 (Feb. 1926): 22–27.

———. "Wholesale Organization in the Automobile Industry." *Harvard Business Review* 3 (July 1925): 424–35.

Guthmann, Harry C., and Kenneth E. Miller. "Some Financial Tendencies Among Leading Variety and Grocery Chains During the Past Decade." *Harvard Business Review* 9 (Jan. 1931): 249.

Hamilton, Alexander. "Report on Manufactures." In *Works of Alexander Hamilton*, edited by Henry Cabot Lodge. Boston: Houghton Mifflin, 1885.

Harper's Weekly. A&P Advertisement. 23 June 1866, 399.

———. A&P Advertisement. 27 Oct. 1866, 687.

Harrold, Frank W. "Telling It to the World: How Coca-Cola Is Merchandising Its Radio Program." *Printers' Ink Monthly*, Mar. 1931, 41ff.

Heine, Irwin M. "The Influence of Geographic Factors in the Development of the Mail Order Business." *America Marketing Journal* (Apr. 1936): 127–30.

Hewitt, Charles M. "The Development of Automobile Franchises." Bureau of Business Research, Indiana University School of Business, 1960.

Higgins, Edgar J. "Our Progress Didn't [Just] Happen." *Pepsi-Cola World*, July 1955, 2.

Hirsch, Harold. "The Coca-Cola Controversy." *The Coca-Cola Bottler*, Nov. 1912, 7–10.

———. "The Coca-Cola Controversy." *The Coca-Cola Bottler*, Dec. 1912, 7–10.

———. "The Coca-Cola Controversy." *The Coca-Cola Bottler*, Jan. 1913, 9–12.

———. "The Coca-Cola Controversy." *The Coca-Cola Bottler*, Apr. 1913, 9–14.

Hollander, Stanley C. "George Huntington Hartford, George Ludlum Hartford and John Augustine Hartford." In *Dictionary of American Biography*, edited by J. A. Garraty (New York: Scribner's, 1977), 276–78.

———. "The Marketing Concept: A Deja-Vu." In *Marketing Management*

Technology as Social Process, edited by George Fisk (New York: Praeger, 1986), 3–28.

———. "The Wheel of Retailing." *Journal of Marketing* 24 (July 1960): 37–42.

Hoskins, Chapin. "Montgomery Ward Rebuilds Business by Building Morale." *Forbes,* 15 Apr. 1932, 14–16.

Hower, Ralph M. "Urban Retailing 100 Years Ago." *Bulletin of the Business Historical Society* 12 (Dec. 1938): 91–101.

Hughes, Lawrence M. "Peerless May Discard Dealers and Sell Motor Cars by Mail." *Sales Management,* 29 Aug. 1931, 310–11.

———. "Sales Champion, Unrivaled, Unchallenged." *Sales Management,* 15 Oct. 1953, 30.

Jack, Andrew B. "The Channels of Distribution for an Innovation: The Sewing Machine Industry in America, 1860–1865." *Explorations in Entrepreneurial History* 9 (1957): 113–41.

Jennings, Clyde. "What Dealers Think About Merchandising New Models." *Automotive Industries,* 10 Feb. 1921, 276–78.

Johnson, Roy W. "If a Competitor Swipes Your Trade Name." *Sales Management,* 20 Feb. 1926, 254ff.

———. "Why 7,000 Imitations of Coca-Cola Are in the Copy Cat's Graveyard." *Sales Management,* 9 Jan. 1926, 27–28.

Jones, Fred Mitchell. "Middlemen in the Domestic Trade of the United States." *Illinois Studies in the Social Sciences* 21 (1937): 47–63.

———. "Retail Stores in the United States, 1800–1860." *Journal of Marketing* 1 (Oct. 1936): 134–42.

Kahn, E. J. "Profiles: More Bounce to the Ounce—I." *The New Yorker,* 1 July 1950, 32–34.

———. "Profiles: More Bounce to the Ounce—II." *The New Yorker,* 8 July 1950.

Kelly, Joseph D. "The Outlook for Coca-Cola." *Barron's,* 7 Nov. 1938, 13.

Kilman, Scott. "Coca-Cola Co. to Bring Back Its Old Coke." *Wall Street Journal,* 11 July 1985, 2.

King, Clyde Lyndon. "Can the Cost of Distributing Food Products Be Reduced?" *The Annals of The American Academy of Political and Social Science* 48 (July 1913): 119–224.

Kinkead, Gwen. "The Executive Suite Struggle Behind A&P's Profits." *Fortune,* 1 Nov. 1982, 89–90.

Klein, Robert L. "The A&P Decision." *Journal of Retailing,* Feb. 1947, 16–22.

Koten, John, and Scott Kilman. "Coca-Cola Faces Tough Marketing Task in Attempting to Sell Old and New Coke." *Wall Street Journal,* 12 July 1985, 2.

———. "How Coke's Decision to Offer 2 Colas Undid 4½ Years of Planning." *Wall Street Journal,* 15 July 1985, 1.

Kraemer, Warren E. "Millions in Nickels." *The Magazine of Wall Street,* 23 Mar. 1940, 737–39.

Kurtz, Wilbur G., Jr. "Joseph A. Biedenharn." *The Coca-Cola Bottler*, Apr. 1959, 93–97, 191.

LaPides, Joseph. "The Good Old Days." *The Pepsi-Cola World* 30 (Jan. 1969): 20–23.

Levandoski, Robert C. "Evolution of an Ad Campaign." *Beverage Industry*, May 1986, 33.

Levitt, Theodore. "A Heretical View of 'Management Science.'" *Fortune*, 18 Dec. 1978, 50–52.

Lieberman, Marvin B., and David B. Montgomery. "First-Mover Advantages." *Strategic Management Journal* 9 (1988): 41–58.

Lifflander, Joel. "Big Bear and How It Grew." *Super Market Merchandising*, Mar. 1937, 14–15.

Livesay, Harold C. "Entrepreneurial Persistence Through the Bureaucratic Age." *Business History Review* 51 (Winter 1977): 415–43.

Loomis, Carol. "The Leaning Tower of Sears." *Fortune*, 2 July 1979, 78–85.

Lyon, Frank M., Jr. "1910: The Bottling Smith Family." *Pepsi-Cola World* 6 (Apr. 1946): 4–5.

McAllister, T. W. "The Retail Merchant." *The Outlook*, 8 Mar. 1916, 580–84.

McCraw, Thomas K., and Patricia A. O'Brien. "Production and Distribution: Competition Policy and Industry Structure." In *America versus Japan*, edited by Thomas K. McCraw. Boston: Harvard Business School Press, 1986, 77–116.

McDonald, D. M. "Quota System Gives Chevrolet Better Control of Retail Selling." *Automotive Industries*, 14 May 1925, 861–62.

McDonald, John. "Sears Makes It Look Easy." *Fortune*, May 1964, 120–27.

McLay, A. D. "Comparative Costs." In *Proceedings of the National Electric Light Association* (1925), 535–36.

McNair, Malcolm P. "Expenses and Profits in the Chain Grocery Business in 1929." In *Bureau of Business Research Bulletin*, no. 84. Cambridge, Mass.: Murray Printing, 1931.

———. "Trends in Large-Scale Retailing." *Harvard Business Review* 10 (Oct. 1931): 30–39.

Mack, Ruth P. "Trends in American Consumption and the Aspiration to Consume." *American Economic Review* 46 (May 1956): 55–68.

The Magazine of Wall Street. "Companies That Are Doing Well Despite Depression: Canada Dry Ginger Ale." 30 May 1931, 168.

Martin, Albro. "The Troubled Subject of Railroad Regulation in the 'Gilded Age'—A Reappraisal." *Journal of American History* 61 (Sept. 1974): 339–71.

Martin, Bill. "Success Story." *Pepsi-Cola World* 7 (May 1947): 10–12.

Michener, A. M. "Chain Store in the Grocery Field." *Commerce Monthly* 10 (Dec. 1928): 3–12.

Miller, I. C. "The A&P Experiment in Supermarkets." *Advertising and Selling*, 29 July 1937, 21–22.

Miller, S. L. "Carbonated Beverage Industry Highly Competitive; Plant Location Important." *The Annalist*, 20 Aug. 1937, 293ff.

Newcomer, Mabel, and Margaret Perkins. "Price Variations Among Poughkeep-
sie Grocers." *Journal of Marketing* 4 (July 1939): 39–44.
The New Republic. "Ford's Fortune." 23 Mar. 1927, 131–32.
New York Times. "Alfred Steele, 57, of Pepsi-Cola, Dies." 20 Apr. 1959, 31.
―――. "C. H. [*sic*] Kittle, Noted Merchant, Dead." 3 Jan. 1928, 25.
―――. "Joan Crawford Re-Wed." 11 May 1955, 34.
―――. "Sewell Avery Dead; Headed Ward Chain." 1 Nov. 1960, 1, 39.
Nichols, G. A. "General Motors to Spend Five Million in Advertising." *Printers'
Ink,* 29 Sept. 1921, 3–4.
―――. "Why Coca-Cola Rebuilt Its Sales Organization." *Printers' Ink,* July
1924, 19–20.
―――. "What Will Take the Place of Advertising in Ford's Marketing
Scheme." *Printers' Ink,* 17 June 1926, 17–20.
Norkus, Michael. "Soft Drink Wars: A Lot More Than Just Good Taste." *Wall
Street Journal,* 8 July 1985, 12.
Oil, Paint and Drug Reporter. "Pepsi-Cola Co. Assails 'Coca-Cola' Validity." 15
Aug. 1938, 3.
Palmer, E. Z. "Chain and Independent Prices in Lexington, Kentucky." *Chain
Store Progress,* Aug. 1930.
Palmer, Philip. "Millions from a Soft Drink." *Barron's,* 25 Jan. 1932, 12–13.
Paxson, Frederick L. "The Highway Movement, 1916–1935." *American Histori-
cal Review* 51 (Jan. 1946): 236–53.
Pepsi-Cola World. "Philadelphia Pepsi-Cola Bottling Company Grows." 1 (Nov.
1941): 5–6.
―――. "Face to Face with Our Bottlers." 3 (Mar. 1943): 6.
―――. "Men at Work: The District Manager." 17 (Oct. 1957): 5–10.
―――. "The Steele Years." (May 1959): 4–29.
―――. "Destiny in Schenectady." 30 (Aug. 1969): 9–17.
Perot, H. Ross. "The GM System Is Like a Blanket of Fog." *Fortune,* 15 Feb.
1988, 48–49.
Pflaum, Irving. "The Baffling Career of Robert E. Wood." *Harper's,* Apr. 1954,
68–73.
Phillips, Charles F. "Chain Stores Effecting Substantial Economies." *Chain
Store Progress,* May 1931.
―――. "Chain, Voluntary Chain, and Independent Store Prices, 1930 and
1934." *Journal of Business* 8 (Apr. 1935): 143–49.
―――. "The Federal Trade Commission's Chain Store Investigation: A Note."
Journal of Marketing 2 (Jan. 1983): 190–92.
―――. "State Discriminatory Chain Store Taxation." *Harvard Business Review*
14 (Spring 1936): 349–59.
―――. "The Supermarket." *Harvard Business Review* 16 (Winter 1938): 188–
200.
Price, Theodore H. "The Mail Order Business." *The Outlook,* 26 Jan. 1916.
Printers' Ink. "Forty-One Advertisers; $93,462,042." 28 Jan. 1937, 106.
―――. "Human Interest Story of Richard W. Sears." 8 Oct. 1914, 13ff.

———. "Magazine Advertising." 16 Jan. 1936, 68ff.

———. "Outlay of 322 Advertisers." 28 Jan. 1937, 63ff.

———. "Outlay of 348 Advertisers." 27 Jan. 1938, 55–61ff.

———. "Pepsi-Cola vs. Coca-Cola." 11 Aug. 1938, 13–14.

———. "Radio Advertising." 17 Jan. 1935, 63–64.

Printers' Ink Monthly. "Now That It Has a Sponsor." Jan. 1939, 15ff.

Rae, John B. "The Fabulous Billy Durant." *Business History Review* 25 (Autumn 1958): 255–71.

Richmond, Henry, Jr. "A Soft Drink That Has Resisted Hard Times." *The Magazine of Wall Street,* 16 Apr. 1932, 803, 820.

Roider, Ralph F. " 'Making It Safe to Be Hungry.' " *General Electric Review,* Sept. 1952, 37.

Rosenwald, Julius. "Why You Can't Do Too Much for the Customers." *System* 46 (Dec. 1924): 709–12, 777–79.

Rost, O. Fred. "A Super Market X-Ray." *Advertising and Selling,* 13 Apr. 1933, 17–18.

Rukeyser, M. S. "Chain Stores, The Revolution in Retailing." *The Nation,* 28 Nov. 1928, 568–70.

Rutter, Richard. "No Question About It; Pepsi-Cola Has Bounce." *New York Times,* 7 Feb. 1956, p. 39.

Ryan, W. A. "Ford's Letter to His Dealers on Used Cars." *Automotive Industries,* 7 May 1925, 820.

Sales Management. "Farm Paper Advertising by Leaders." 21 Sept. 1929, 136.

———. "Farm Paper Advertising by Leaders." 27 Sept. 1930, 144E.

———. "How Big Advertisers Divide Radio and Newspaper Appropriations." 1 May 1932, 152.

Schmalz, Carl N. "Independent Stores *vs.* Chains in the Grocery Field." *Harvard Business Review* 9 (July 1931): 431–42.

Scientific American. "The Car of 1913." 11 Jan. 1913, 26.

Shafer, Joseph E. "The Ford Stores—A New Departure in Retailing." *Harvard Business Review* 6 (Apr. 1928): 313–21.

Sharrer, G. Terry. "Food Technology in the Twentieth Century." *Journal of the NAL Association* 5 (1980): 21–26.

Shepard, Allen. "The Quick-Freezing Process and the Distribution of Perishable Foods." *Harvard Business Review* 8 (Apr. 1930): 339–45.

Shidle, Norman G. "Dealers and Distribution Are Big 1924 Problems." *Automotive Industries,* 21 Feb. 1924, 378–80.

Shirley, Michael. "The 'Conscientious Conservatism' of Asa Griggs Candler." *The Georgia Historical Quarterly* 68 (Fall 1983): 356–65.

Silk, Alvin J., and Louis William Stern. "The Changing Nature of Innovation in Marketing: A Study of Selected Business Leaders, 1852–1958." *Business History Review* 37 (Autumn 1963): 182–200.

Smith, Timothy K. "Coke, Pepsi Seek Control Over Bottling." *Wall Street Journal,* 3 July 1986, 6.

Smith, Timothy K., and Laura Landro. "Profoundly Changed Coca-Cola Co. Strives to Keep on Bubbling." *Wall Street Journal*, 24 Apr. 1986, 1.

Soper, Will. "Supermarkets." *American History Illustrated*, Mar. 1983, 40–44.

Sprague, Jesse Rainsford. "Confessions of a Ford Dealer." *Harpers*, June 1927, 26–35.

Super Market Merchandising. "Looking Backwards: 25 Years of Super Market Progress," Aug. 1955, 68–86.

―――. "Michael Cullen's Story." Aug. 1955, 91ff.

―――. "What Michael Cullen Foresaw." Aug. 1955, 109ff.

Taylor, Malcolm D. "Prices in Chain and Independent Grocery Stores in Durham, North Carolina." *Harvard Business Review* 8 (July 1930): 413–24.

―――. "Prices of Branded Grocery Commodities During the Depression; Chain and Independent Grocery Stores in Durham, North Carolina." *Harvard Business Review* 12 (July 1934): 437–49.

Tedlow, Richard S. "Albert Davis Lasker." In *Dictionary of American Biography*, supplement 5. New York: Scribner's, 1977, 410–12.

―――. "Automobile Marketing in the Context of American Business History." In *Business Management in Historical Perspective*, edited by Maurice Lévy-Leboyer and Patrick Fridenson. Cambridge, Eng.: Cambridge University Press, forthcoming.

―――. "From Competitor to Consumer: The Changing Focus of the Federal Regulation of Advertising, 1914–1938." *Business History Review* 55 (Spring 1981): 35–58.

―――. "The Process of Economic Concentration in the American Economy." In *The Concentration Process in the Entrepreneurial Economy since the Late 19th Century, Zeitschrift für Unternehmensgeschichte*, Beiheft 55, edited by Hans Pohl. Stuttgart: Franz Steiner Verlag, 1988, 107–11.

Tide. "Bellas Hess." Apr. 1932, 20.

―――. "Marketing: Mail-Order Milestones." (Apr. 1932), 18.

―――. "Louis Wolfson: 'How I'd Change Montgomery Ward's Marketing.'" 18 Dec. 1954, 19–21.

Time. "Retail Trade: Red Circle and Gold Leaf." 13 Nov. 1950, 90.

Tipper, Harry. "Dealer Mortality in Automotive Field Not Exceptionally Large." *Automotive Industries*, 27 Apr. 1922, 928–29.

―――. "Distributing Channels Important Marketing Factors." *Automotive Industries*, 29 Dec. 1921, 1282–83.

―――. "Distributors or Factory Branches, Part I." *Automotive Industries*, 19 Jan. 1922, 140–41.

―――. "Human Study a Necessary Factor in Automotive Sales." *Automotive Industries*, 9 June 1921, 1213–15.

―――. "Marketing Problems of the Automotive Industry." *Automotive Industries*, 27 Oct. 1921, 801–803.

Toffler, Alvin. "The Competition That Refreshes." *Fortune*, May 1961, 124–28.

Tracy, Eleanor Johnson. "How A&P Got Creamed." *Fortune*, Jan. 1973, 104–106, 108, 112, 114.

Wall Street Journal. "Kittle's Regime Prosperous One." 15 Feb. 1928, 5.

Weil, Mrs. J. B. "Harold Hirsch." *The Coca-Cola Bottler,* Apr. 1959, 138ff.

Whitehorne, Earl. "A Message from the Sales Managers." In *Proceedings of the National Electric Light Association* (1929), 137–48.

Wickwire, Francis Sill. "The Life and Times of Sears, Roebuck." *Collier's,* 3 Dec. 1949, 18–19, 42–43.

———. "Please Rush the Gal in the Pink Corset." *Collier's,* 17 Dec. 1949, 28–29, 48–50.

———. "We Like Corn, On or Off the Cob." *Collier's,* 10 Dec. 1949, 20–21, 73–74.

Wiley, Harvey W. "The Coca-Cola Controversy." *Good Housekeeping,* Sept. 1912, 386–94.

Wolff, Harold. "The Great GM Mystery." *Harvard Business Review* 42 (Sept.–Oct. 1964): 164–66.

Woodruff, Robert W. "After National Distribution—What?" *Nation's Business,* Aug. 1929, 125–26.

———. "Why Coca-Cola Abolished Its Sales Department." *Printers' Ink,* 6 Dec. 1928, 144ff.

Yip, George S. "Gateways to Entry." *Harvard Business Review* 60 (Sept.–Oct. 1982): 86.

Young, James Harvey. "Three Southern Food and Drug Cases." *The Journal of Southern History* 49 (Feb. 1983): 3–36.

Books, Pamphlets, and Transcribed Interviews

Abernathy, William J., Kim B. Clark, and Alan M. Kantrow. *Industrial Renaissance: Producing a Competitive Future For America.* New York: Basic Books, 1983.

Adelman, Morris A. *A&P: A Study in Price-Cost Behavior and Public Policy.* Cambridge, Mass.: Harvard University Press, 1959.

Advertising Age Editors. *Procter & Gamble: The House That Ivory Built.* Lincolnwood, Ill.: NTC Business Books, 1988.

Aiken, Hugh G. J., ed. *Explorations in Enterprise.* Cambridge, Mass.: Harvard University Press, 1967.

Allen, Frederick Lewis. *The Big Change: America Transforms Itself, 1900–1950.* New York: Harper & Brothers, 1952.

Allen, Michael. *Ford Model T: Super Profile.* Newbury Park, Calif.: Haynes Publishing Group, 1987.

Anderson, Oscar, E., Jr. *Refrigeration in America: A History of a New Technology and Its Impact.* Princeton, N.J.: Princeton University Press, 1953.

Applebaum, William. *Supermarketing: The Past, the Present, a Projection.* Chicago: Super Market Institute, 1969.

Asher, Louis E., and Edith Heal. *Send No Money.* Chicago: Argus, 1942.

Assael, Henry, ed. *Early Development and Conceptualization of the Field of Marketing.* New York: Arno Press, 1978.

Automobile Quarterly Editors. *The Buick: A Complete History.* Princeton, N.J.: Princeton Publishing, 1985.

Automobile Selling by Practical Salesmen. Chicago: Chicago Automobile Trade Association, 1924.

Automobiles of America. Detroit: Automobile Manufacturers Association, 1961.

Bardou, Jean-Pierre, Jean-Jacques Chanaron, Patrick Fridenson, and James M. Laux. *The Automobile Revolution: The Impact of an Industry.* Chapel Hill, N.C.: University of North Carolina Press, 1982.

Barker, James M. "Reminiscences." Oral History Collection, Columbia University, 1951.

Barnouw, Erik. *The Golden Web: A History of Broadcasting in the United States, 1933–1953.* New York: Oxford University Press, 1968.

————. *The Image Empire: A History of Broadcasting in the United States from 1953.* New York: Oxford University Press, 1970.

————. *The Sponsor: Notes on a Modern Potentate.* New York: Oxford University Press, 1978.

————. *A Tower in Babel: A History of Broadcasting in the United States to 1933.* New York: Oxford University Press, 1966.

Bartels, Robert. *The History of Marketing Thought.* Columbus, Ohio: Grid, 1976.

Bates, Albert D. *Retailing and Its Environment.* New York: Van Nostrand, 1979.

Beasley, Norman. *Main Street Merchant: The Story of the J. C. Penney Company.* New York: McGraw-Hill, 1948.

Beckman, Theodore N., and Herman C. Nolen. *The Chain Store Problem: A Critical Analysis.* New York: McGraw-Hill, 1938.

Benson, C. F., ed. *Henry James: Letters to A. C. Benson and Auguste Monod.* New York: Scribner's, 1930.

Bernstein, Irving. *Turbulent Years: A History of the American Worker, 1933–1941.* Boston: Houghton Mifflin, 1970.

Beverage Industry 1985 Annual Manual. Cleveland, Ohio: Harcourt Brace Jovanovich, Sept. 1985.

Bliven, Bruce, Jr. *The Wonderful Writing Machine.* New York: Random House, 1954.

Boorstin, Daniel J. *The Americans: The Democratic Experience.* New York: Vintage, 1973.

Brann, W. C. *The Romance of Montgomery Ward & Co.* New York: Campbell, Starring, 1929.

Braudel, Fernand. *The Perspective of the World.* New York: Harper & Row, 1984.

Broadcast Advertising: A Study of the Radio Medium—The Fourth Dimension of Advertising, vol. 1. New York: National Broadcasting Company, 1929.

Broadcast Advertising: The Merchandising of a Broadcast Advertising Campaign, vol. 2. New York: National Broadcasting Company, 1930.

Broehl, Wayne G., Jr. *John Deere's Company.* Garden City, N.Y.: Doubleday, 1984.

Brown, Donaldson. *Some Reminiscences of an Industrialist.* Easton, Pa.: Hive Publishing Co., 1977.

Bucklin, Louis P. *Competition and Evolution in the Distributive Trades.* Englewood Cliffs, N.J.: Prentice-Hall, 1972.

Burlingame, Roger. *Henry Ford.* Chicago: Quadrangle, 1955.

Bury, Martin H. *The Automobile Dealer.* Philadelphia: Philpenn, 1961.

Buzzell, Robert D., ed. *Marketing in an Electronic Age.* Boston: Harvard Business School Press, 1985.

———, and Bradley T. Gale. *The PIMS Principles: Linking Strategy to Performance.* New York: The Free Press, 1987.

Cadillac Dealers Manual. Detroit: Cadillac Motor Car Company, n.d.

Cain, Louis P., and Paul J. Uselding, eds. *Business Enterprise and Economic Change: Essays in Honor of Harold F. Williamson.* Kent, Ohio: Kent State University Press, 1973.

Candler, Charles Howard. *Asa Griggs Candler.* Atlanta, Ga.: Emory University, 1950.

Cantillon, Richard. *Essai sur la Nature du Commerce en Général.* Paris: Institut National d'Etudes Demographiques, 1952 [1755].

Carson, Gerald. *The Old Country Store.* New York: Oxford University Press, 1954.

Carstensen, Fred V. *American Enterprise in Foreign Markets.* Chapel Hill, N.C.: University of North Carolina Press, 1984.

Chain Store Research Bureau. *The Future of the Soft Drink Industry.* New York: Chain Store Research Bureau, n.d.

Chandler, Alfred D., Jr. *Giant Enterprise.* New York: Arno, 1980.

———. *Managerial Innovation at General Motors.* New York: Arno, 1979.

———. *The Railroads: The Nation's First Big Business.* New York: Harcourt, Brace and World, 1965.

———. *Scale and Scope: The Dynamics of Industrial Enterprise.* Cambridge, Mass.: Harvard University Press, forthcoming.

———. *Strategy and Structure: Chapters in the History of the American Industrial Enterprise.* Cambridge, Mass.: MIT Press, 1962.

———. *The Visible Hand: The Managerial Revolution in American Business.* Cambridge, Mass.: Harvard University Press, 1977.

———, and Richard S. Tedlow. *The Coming of Managerial Capitalism: A Casebook on the History of American Economic Institutions.* Homewood, Ill.: Richard D. Irwin, 1985.

———, and Stephen Salsbury. *Pierre S. du Pont and the Making of the Modern Corporation.* New York: Harper & Row, 1971.

Chrysler, Walter P., with Boyden Sparkes. *Life of an American Workman.* New York: Dodd, Mead, 1937.

Clewett, Richard M., ed. *Marketing Channels: For Manufactured Products.* Homewood, Ill.: Richard D. Irwin, 1954.

Coca-Cola Company. *Opinions, Orders, Injunctions, and Decrees Relating to Unfair Competition and Infringement of Trademark.* Vol. 1, 1886–1923. Atlanta, Ga.: Foote & Davies, 1923.

————. *Opinions, Orders, Injunctions, and Decrees Relating to Unfair Competition and Infringement of Trademark.* Vol. 2, *1923–1930.* Atlanta, Ga.: Foote & Davies, 1939.

————. *Opinions, Orders, Injuctions, and Decrees Relating to Unfair Competition and Infringement of Trademark.* Vol. 3, *1931–1938.* Atlanta, Ga.: Foote & Davies, 1939..

Cohn, David L. *The Good Old Days: A History of American Morals and Manners As Seen Through the Sears, Roebuck Catalogs, 1905 to the Present.* New York: Simon & Schuster, 1940.

Collier, Peter, and David Horowitz. *The Fords, an American Epic.* New York: Summit Books, 1987.

Copeland, Melvin T. *Principles of Merchandising.* Chicago: Shaw, 1924.

Corey, E. Raymond. *Industrial Marketing: Cases and Concepts.* Englewood Cliffs, N.J.: Prentice-Hall, 1983.

Cowan, Ruth Schwartz. *More Work For Mother: The Ironies of Household Technology from the Open Hearth to the Microwave.* New York: Basic Books, 1983.

Davies, Robert B. *Peacefully Working to Conquer the World.* New York: Arno, 1976.

Davis, Donald Finlay. *Conspicuous Production: Automobiles and Elites in Detroit, 1899–1933.* Philadelphia, Pa.: Temple University Press, 1988.

Day, George S. *Analysis for Strategic Market Decisions.* St. Paul, Minn.: West Publishing Company, 1986.

Denison, Merrill. *The Power To Go.* Garden City, N.Y.: Doubleday, 1956.

DeVoe, Thomas F. *The Market Book,* vol. 1. New York: Author, 1862.

Dictionary of American Biography. New York: Scribner's, 1935.

Dictionary of American Biography, Supplement Five, 1951–1955. New York: Scribner's, 1977.

Dipman, Carl W. *The Modern Grocery Store.* New York: Butterick Publishing, 1931.

Dominguez, Henry L. *The Ford Agency: A Pictorial History.* Osceola, Wis.: Motorbooks International, 1981.

Dyer, Davis, Malcolm S. Salter, and Alan M. Webber. *Changing Alliances.* Boston: Harvard Business School Press, 1987.

Eastman, Joel W. *Styling vs. Safety: The American Automobile Industry and the Development of Automotive Safety, 1900–1966.* Lanham, Md.: University Press of America, 1984.

Emmet, Boris, and John E. Jeuck. *Catalogues and Counters: A History of Sears, Roebuck and Company.* Chicago: University of Chicago Press, 1950.

Enis, Ben M., and Keith K. Cox, eds. *Marketing Classics: A Selection of Influential Articles.* Boston: Allyn & Bacon, 1977.

Enrico, Roger, and Jesse Kornbluth. *The Other Guy Blinked: How Pepsi Won the Cola Wars.* New York: Bantam, 1986.

Epstein, Ralph C. *The Automobile Industry: Its Economic and Commercial Development.* Chicago: Shaw, 1928.

Farrington, Frank. *Meeting Chain Store Competition.* Chicago: Byxbee Publishing Co., 1922.

Farris, Paul W., and John A. Quelch. *Advertising and Promotion Management: A Manager's Guide to Theory and Practice.* Radnor, Pa.: Chilton, 1981.

Fine, Sidney. *Sit Down: The General Motors Strike of 1936–1937.* Ann Arbor, Mich.: University of Michigan Press, 1969.

Fischer, David Hackett. *Historians' Fallacies: Toward a Logic of Historical Thought.* New York: Harper & Row, 1970.

Flink, James J. *America Adopts the Automobile, 1895–1910.* Cambridge, Mass.: MIT Press, 1970.

———. *The Automobile Age.* Cambridge, Mass.: MIT Press, 1988.

———. *The Car Culture.* Cambridge, Mass.: MIT Press, 1975.

The Food Marketing Industry Speaks, 1984: Detailed Tabulations. Washington, D.C.: Research Division of the Food Marketing Institute, 1984.

Ford, Henry, with Samuel Crowther. *My Life and Work.* Garden City, N.Y.: Garden City Publishing, 1926.

Fox, Richard Wightman, and T. J. Jackson Lears, eds. *The Culture of Consumption: Critical Essays in American History, 1880–1980.* New York: Pantheon Books, 1983.

Fuchs, Lawrence H. *The American Kaleidoscope.* Middletown, Conn.: Wesleyan University Press, forthcoming.

———. *Family Matters.* New York: Warner Books, 1974.

Galambos, Louis. *The Public Image of Big Business in America, 1880–1940.* Baltimore, Md.: Johns Hopkins University Press, 1975.

Galbraith, John Kenneth. *The Affluent Society.* Boston: Houghton Mifflin, 1959.

Garraty, John A., ed. *Encyclopedia of American Biography.* New York: Harper & Row, 1974.

Goodwin, Arthur E. *Markets: Public and Private.* Seattle, Wash.: Montgomery Printing, 1929.

Green, Constance M. *Eli Whitney and the Birth of American Technology.* Boston: Little, Brown, 1956.

Greenleaf, William. *Monopoly on Wheels.* Detroit: Wayne State University Press, 1961.

Gunther, John. *Taken at the Flood.* New York: Harper & Brothers, 1960.

Gusten, Lawrence R. *Billy Durant: Creator of General Motors.* Grand Rapids, Mich.: Eerdmans, 1973.

Handlin, Oscar. *The Uprooted.* New York: Grosset & Dunlap, 1951.

Harris, Neil. *Humbug.* Boston: Little, Brown, 1973.

Hartley, Robert F. *Management Mistakes.* 2d ed. New York: John Wiley & Sons, 1986.

Hayward, Walter S., and Percival White. *Chain Stores: Their Management and Operation.* New York: McGraw-Hill, 1928.

Heasley, Jerry. *The Production Figure Book for U.S. Cars.* Osceola, Wis.: Motorbooks International, 1977.

Heilbroner, Robert Louis. *Business Civilization in Decline.* New York: W.W. Norton, 1976.

Herndon, Booton. *Satisfaction Guaranteed: An Unconventional Report to Today's Consumers.* New York: McGraw-Hill, 1972.

Heskett, James L., Nicholas A. Glaskowsky, and Robert M. Ivie. *Business Logistics: Physical Distribution and Materials Management.* New York: Ronald Press, 1973.

Hession, Charles H. *John Kenneth Galbraith and His Critics.* New York: Signet, 1972.

Hettinger, Herman, S. *A Decade of Radio Advertising.* Chicago: University of Chicago Press, 1933.

Hewitt, Charles M. *Automobile Franchise Agreements.* Homewood, Ill.: Richard D. Irwin, 1956.

Hidy, Ralph, and Muriel Hidy. *Pioneering in Big Business.* New York: Harper & Brothers, 1955.

Hoge, Cecil C., Sr. *The First Hundred Years Are the Toughest: What We Can Learn from the Century of Competition Between Sears and Ward's.* Berkeley, Calif.: Ten Speed Press, 1988.

Hofstadter, Richard. *The Progressive Historians.* New York: Vintage, 1968.

———. *The Age of Reform: From Bryan to F.D.R.* New York: Vintage, 1955.

Hotchkiss, George B. *Milestones of Marketing.* New York: Macmillan, 1938.

———, and Richard B. Franken. *The Leadership of Advertised Brands.* New York: Doubleday, Page, 1923.

Hounshell, David A. *From the American System to Mass Production, 1800–1932: The Development of Manufacturing Technology in the United States.* Baltimore, Md.: Johns Hopkins University Press, 1984.

———, and John Kenly Smith, Jr. *Science and Corporate Strategy: Du Pont R&D, 1902–1980.* New York: Cambridge University Press, 1988.

Hower, Ralph M. *History of Macy's of New York, 1858–1919: Chapters in the Evolution of the Department Store.* Cambridge, Mass.: Harvard University Press, 1943.

Hoyt, Edwin P. *That Wonderful A&P!* New York: Hawthorn, 1969.

Hughes, Jonathan. *The Vital Few: The Entrepreneur and American Economic Progress.* New York: Oxford University Press, 1986.

Ingham, John N., ed. *Biographical Dictionary of American Business Leaders.* Westport, Conn.: Greenwood, 1983.

Jackson, Kenneth T. *Crabgrass Frontier.* New York: Oxford University Press, 1985.

Jardim, Anne. *The First Henry Ford: A Study in Personality and Business Leadership.* Cambridge, Mass.: MIT Press, 1970.

Jenks, C. J. *Case Studies in Research and Innovation at General Electric.* Appliance Park, Ky.: General Electric Corp., CRO23:57.

Johnson, Samuel. *The Idler and the Adventurer,* edited by W. J. Bate, John M. Bullitt, and L. F. Powell. New Haven, Conn.: Yale University Press, 1963.

Johnson, Roy W., and Russell W. Lynch. *The Sales Strategy of John H. Patterson.* Chicago: Dartnell, 1932.

Kael, Pauline. *The Citizen Kane Book.* New York: Bantam, 1971.

Kahn, E. J., Jr. *The Big Drink: The Story of Coca-Cola.* New York: Random House, 1960.

Kao, John J., and Howard H. Stevenson, eds. *Entrepreneurship: What It Is and How to Teach It.* Collection of working papers based on a colloquium held at Harvard Business School, July 5–8, 1983.

Karrass, Chester. *The Negotiating Game.* New York: World, 1970.

Katz, Donald R. *The Big Store: Inside the Crisis and Revolution at Sears.* New York: Viking, 1987.

Katz, Harold. *The Decline of Competition in the Automobile Industry, 1920–1940.* New York: Arno, 1977.

Kidder, Tracy. *The Soul of a New Machine.* Boston: Little, Brown, 1981.

Kintner, Earl W. *A Robinson-Patman Primer: A Businessman's Guide to the Law Against Price Discrimination.* New York: Macmillan, 1970.

Klingler, Ed. *How a City Founded to Make Money Made It: The Economic and Business History of Evansville, Indiana.* Evansville, Ind.: University of Evansville, c. 1978.

Kotler, Philip. *Marketing Management: Analysis, Planning and Control.* 5th ed. Englewood Cliffs, N.J.: Prentice-Hall, 1984.

Kuhn, Arthur J. *GM Passes Ford, 1918–1938: Designing the General Motors Performance-Control System.* University Park, Pa.: Pennsylvania State University Press, 1986.

Labaree, Leonard W. et al., eds. *The Autobiography of Benjamin Franklin.* New Haven: Yale University Press, 1964.

Latham, Frank. *1872–1972, A Century of Serving Consumers: The Story of Montgomery Ward.* Chicago: Montgomery Ward, 1972.

Lebergott, Stanley. *The American Economy: Income, Wealth, and Want.* Princeton, N.J.: Princeton University Press, 1976.

———. *The Americans: An Economic Record.* New York: W.W. Norton, 1984.

Lebhar, Godfrey M. *Chain Stores in America, 1859–1962.* New York: Chain Store Publishing Corporation, 1963.

Levitt, Theodore. *Marketing for Business Growth.* New York: McGraw-Hill, 1974.

———. *The Marketing Imagination.* New York: Free Press, 1983.

Lewis, David L. *The Public Image of Henry Ford: An American Folk Hero and His Company.* Detroit: Wayne State University Press, 1976.

———, and Laurence Goldstein, eds. *The Automobile and American Culture.* Ann Arbor, Mich.: University of Michigan Press, 1983.

Link, Arthur S., ed. *The Papers of Woodrow Wilson.* Princeton, N.J.: Princeton University Press, 1966–   ), vols. 16, 17, 21, 23.

Livesay, Harold C. *Andrew Carnegie and the Rise of Big Business.* Boston: Little, Brown, 1975.

Long, John C. *Roy D. Chapin.* Author, 1945.

Louis, J. C., and Harvey Z. Yazijian. *The Cola Wars.* New York: Everest House, 1980.

McAusland, Randolph. *Supermarkets: 50 Years of Progress.* Washington, D.C.: Food Marketing Institute, 1980.

McCracken, Grant. *Culture and Consumption: New Approaches to the Symbolic Character of Consumer Goods and Activities.* Bloomington, Ind.: Indiana University Press, 1988.

McCraw, Thomas K. *Prophets of Regulation.* Cambridge, Mass.: Harvard University Press, 1984.

———, ed. *The Essential Alfred D. Chandler: Essays Toward a Historical Theory of Big Business.* Boston: Harvard Business School Press, 1988.

———, ed. *America versus Japan.* Boston: Harvard Business School Press, 1986.

McCullough, David. *The Path Between the Seas: The Creation of the Panama Canal, 1870–1914.* New York: Simon & Schuster, 1977.

McNair, Malcolm P., and Eleanor G. May. *The Evolution of Retail Institutions in the United States.* Cambridge, Mass.: Marketing Science Institute, 1976.

Mack, Walter, with Peter Buckley. *No Time Lost.* New York: Atheneum, 1982.

Marchand, Roland. *Advertising the American Dream: Making Way for Modernity.* Berkeley, Calif.: University of California Press, 1985.

———. *Creating the Corporate Soul: The Rise of Corporate Public Relations and Institutional Advertising.* Forthcoming.

A Market Survey of Domestic Refrigeration. Philadelphia: Curtis Publishing Co., 1941.

Martin, Milward W. *Twelve Full Ounces.* New York: Holt, Rinehart & Winston, 1962.

Martin, Robert F. *National Income in the United States, 1799–1938.* New York: National Industrial Conference Board, 1939.

Maxim, Hiram Percy. *Horseless Carriage Days.* New York: Dover, 1962.

May, George S. *R. E. Olds: Auto Industry Pioneer.* Grand Rapids, Mich.: Eerdmans, 1977.

Meikle, Jeffrey L. *Twentieth Century Limited: Industrial Design in America, 1925–1939.* Philadelphia, Pa.: Temple University Press, 1979.

Meyers, Marvin. *The Jacksonian Persuasion: The Politics and Belief.* Stanford, Calif.: Stanford University Press, 1957.

Mirsky, Jeanette, and Allan Nevins. *The World of Eli Whitney.* New York: Macmillan, 1952.

Myers, John G., William F. Massy, and Stephen A. Greyser. *Marketing Research and Knowledge Development: An Assessment for Marketing Management.* Englewood Cliffs, N.J.: Prentice-Hall, 1980.

National Automobile Chamber of Commerce. *Facts and Figures of the Automobile Industry*. 1920.

National Markets and National Advertising. New York: Crowell, 1930.

The National Standard for Piggly Wiggly Store Conduct and Maintenance. Memphis, Tenn.: Memphis Linotype Printing, 1919.

Nevett, Terence, and Ronald A. Fullerton, eds. *Historical Perspectives in Marketing: Essays in Honor of Stanley C. Hollander*. Lexington, Mass.: D.C. Heath, 1988.

Nevins, Allan, and Frank E. Hill. *Ford: Decline and Rebirth, 1933–1962*. New York: Scribner's, 1963.

———. *Ford: Expansion and Challenge, 1915–1933*. New York: Scribner's, 1957.

———. *Ford: The Times, the Man, the Company*. New York: Scribner's, 1954.

Newmark, Jacob H. *Automobile Salesmanship*. Detroit: Automobile Publishing Co., 1915.

Nichols, John P. *The Chain Store Tells Its Story*. New York: Institute of Distribution, 1948.

Niemeyer, Glenn A. *The Automotive Career of Ransom E. Olds*. East Lansing, Mich.: Bureau of Business and Economic Research, Graduate School of Business Administration, Michigan State University, 1963.

Nystrom, Paul H. *Chain Stores*. Washington, D.C.: U.S. Chamber of Commerce, 1930.

———. *Economics of Retailing*, vol. 1. New York: Ronald Press, 1930.

Ogilvy, David. *Confessions of an Advertising Man*. New York: Atheneum, 1963.

Okochi, Akio, and Koichi Shimokawa, eds. *Development of Mass Marketing: The Automobile and Retailing Industries*. Tokyo: University of Tokyo Press, 1981.

Oliver, Thomas. *The Real Coke, The Real Story*. New York: Random House, 1986.

Palamountain, Joseph C. *The Politics of Distribution*. Cambridge, Mass.: Harvard University Press, 1955.

Parlin, Charles C. *The Merchandising of Automobiles*. Philadelphia: Curtis, 1915.

Penney, James Cash. *J. C. Penney: The Man with a Thousand Partners*. New York: Harper, 1931.

"Pepsi Generation" Oral History Project. Interview with Philip Hinerfeld, 1 Feb. 1985. Washington, D.C.: Archives Center, National Museum of American History, Smithsonian Institution.

"Pepsi Generation" Oral History Project. Interview with Walter S. Mack, 16 Nov. 1985. Washington, D.C.: Archives Center, National Museum of American History, Smithsonian Institution.

Piper, Thomas R., ed. *Managerial Decision Making and Ethical Values*. Boston: Harvard Business School Press, forthcoming.

Pollay, Richard W., ed. *Information Sources in Advertising History*. Westport, Conn.: Greenwood Press, 1979.

Pope, Daniel A. *The Making of Modern Advertising.* New York: Basic Books, 1983.

Porter, Glenn, and Harold C. Livesay. *Merchants and Manufacturers: Studies in the Changing Structure of Nineteenth-Century Marketing.* Baltimore, Md.: Johns Hopkins University Press, 1971.

Porter, Michael E. *Competitive Advantage: Creating and Sustaining Superior Performance.* New York: The Free Press, 1985.

————. *Competitive Strategy: Techniques for Analyzing Industries and Competitors.* New York: The Free Press, 1980.

Posner, Richard A. *The Robinson-Patman Act: Federal Regulation of Price Differences.* Washington, D.C.: American Enterprise Institute, 1976.

Potter, David M. *People of Plenty: Economic Abundance and the American Character.* Chicago: University of Chicago Press, 1954.

Pound, Arthur. *The Turning Wheel: The Story of General Motors Through Twenty-Five Years, 1908–1933.* Garden City, N.Y.: Doubleday, Doran, 1934.

Prentiss, Don C. *Ford Products and Their Sale.* Detroit: The Franklin Press, 1923.

Presbrey, Frank. *The History and Development of Advertising.* New York: Greenwood, 1968.

Preston, Howard L. *Automobile Age Atlanta: The Making of a Southern Metropolis, 1900–1935.* Athens, Ga.: University of Georgia Press, 1979.

Rae, John B. *The American Automobile: A Brief History.* Chicago: University of Chicago Press, 1965.

————. *American Automobile Manufacturers: The First Forty Years.* Philadelphia: Chilton, 1959.

————, ed. *Henry Ford.* Englewood Cliffs, N.J.: Prentice-Hall, 1969.

————. *The Road and the Car in American Life.* Cambridge, Mass.: MIT Press, 1971.

Refrigeration and Air Conditioning Market Data for 1935. Detroit: Business News Publishing Co., 1935.

Reibstein, David J. *Marketing: Concepts, Strategies and Decisions.* Englewood Cliffs, N.J.: Prentice-Hall, 1985.

Richards, William C. *The Last Billionaire.* New York: Scribner's, 1948.

Riesman, David. *Abundance for What? and Other Essays.* Garden City, N.Y.: Doubleday & Co., 1964.

————, with Nathan Glazer and Reuel Denney. *The Lonely Crowd.* New Haven, Conn.: Yale University Press, 1961.

Riley, John J. *A History of the American Soft Drink Industry: Bottled Carbonated Beverages, 1807–1957.* New York: Arno, 1972.

Rosenberg, Nathan, and L. E. Birdzell, Jr. *How the West Grew Rich.* New York: Basic Books, 1986.

Rothschild, Emma. *Paradise Lost: The Decline of the Auto-Industrial Age.* New York: Random House, 1973.

Rowe, Frederick M. *Price Discrimination Under the Robinson-Patman Act.* Boston: Little, Brown, 1962.

Rowland, Sanders, with Bob Terrell. *Papa Coke: Sixty-Five Years Selling Coca-Cola.* Asheville, N.C.: Bright Mountain Books, 1986.

Schein, Edgar H. *Organizational Culture and Leadership.* San Francisco: Jossey-Bass, 1985.

Schisgall, Oscar. *Eyes on Tomorrow.* Garden City, N. Y.: Doubleday, 1981.

Schlesinger, Arthur M. *A Thousand Days.* Boston: Houghton Mifflin, 1965.

Schudson, Michael. *Advertising: The Uneasy Persuasion.* New York: Basic Books, 1984.

Schumpeter, Joseph A. *Capitalism, Socialism and Democracy.* 3d ed. New York: Harper & Row, 1950.

Sculley, John, with John A. Byrne. *Odyssey: Pepsi to Apple, A Journey of Adventures, Ideas and the Future.* New York: Harper & Row, 1987.

Sears Catalogue, 1897. Edited by Fred L. Israel. New York: Chelsea House, 1968.

Sears Catalogue, 1971. Edited by Joseph J. Schroeder, Jr. Northfield, Ill.: Digest Books, 1971.

Seligman, Edwin R. A. *The Economics of Installment Selling: A Study in Consumers' Credit.* New York: Harper & Brothers, 1927.

Seltzer, Lawrence H. *A Financial History of the American Automobile Industry.* Boston: Houghton Mifflin, 1928.

Shapiro, Benson P. *Instructor's Manual to Accompany Sales Program Management: Formulation and Implementation.* New York: McGraw-Hill, 1977.

———. *Sales Program Management: Formulation and Implementation.* New York: McGraw-Hill, 1977.

Shih, Ko Ching, and C. Ying Shih. *American Soft Drink Industry and the Carbonated Beverage Market.* Brookfield, Wis.: W. A. Krueger, 1965.

Sloan, Alfred P., Jr. *Adventures of a White Collar Man.* Garden City, N.Y.: Doubleday, Doran, 1941.

———. *My Years with General Motors.* Garden City, N.Y.: Doubleday, 1963.

Smith, Adam. *An Inquiry into the Nature and Causes of the Wealth of Nations.* Edited by Edwin Canaan. New York: Modern Library, 1937.

Smith, Albert B., ed. *Competitive Distribution in a Free High-Level Economy and Its Implications for the University.* Pittsburgh, Pa.: University of Pittsburgh Press, 1958.

Sorensen, Charles E., with Samuel T. Williamson. *My Forty Years with Ford.* New York: W.W. Norton, 1956.

Stern, Louis W., and Adel I. El-Ansary. *Marketing Channels.* 2d ed. Englewood Cliffs, N.J.: Prentice-Hall, 1982.

Stewart, Paul W., and J. Frederic Dewhurst. *Does Distribution Cost Too Much?* New York: Twentieth Century Fund, 1939.

Stone, Alan. *Economic Regulation and the Public Interest: The Federal Trade Commission in Theory and Practice.* Ithaca, N.Y.: Cornell University Press, 1977.

Stover, John F. *American Railroads.* Chicago: University of Chicago Press, 1961.

Strasser, Susan. *Never Done: A History of American Housework.* New York: Pantheon Books, 1982.

————. *Satisfaction Guaranteed: The Making of the American Mass Market.* New York: Pantheon Books, 1989.

Sullivan, J. W. *Markets for the People: The Consumer's Part.* New York: Macmillan, 1913.

Sullivan, Mark. *The Turn of the Century,* vol. 1 of *Our Times: The United States, 1900–1925.* New York: Scribner's, 1928.

Sward, Keith. *The Legend of Henry Ford.* New York: Rinehart & Co., 1948.

Tarbell, Ida M. *The History of the Standard Oil Company,* vol. 2. New York: Macmillan, 1925.

Taylor, A. J. P. *The Second World War.* New York: Putnam, 1975.

Taylor, George Rogers. *The Transportation Revolution.* New York: Harper & Row, 1951.

————, ed. *The Turner Thesis.* Boston: D.C. Heath, 1956.

Tedlow, Richard S. Case Commentary and Teaching Technique to Accompany The Coming of Managerial Capitalism. Homewood, Ill.: Richard D. Irwin, 1985.

————. *Keeping the Corporate Image: Public Relations and Business, 1900–1950.* Greenwich, Conn.: JAI Press, 1979.

Tedlow, Richard S., and Richard R. John, Jr., eds. *Managing Big Business: Essays from the Business History Review.* Boston: Harvard Business School Press, 1986.

Thomas, Robert Paul. *An Analysis of the Pattern of Growth of the Automobile Industry, 1895–1929.* New York: Arno, 1977.

Tocqueville, Alexis de. *Democracy in America.* Edited by Phillips Bradley. Vol. 2. New York: Vintage, 1945.

Trends: Consumer Attitudes and the Supermarket. Washington, D.C.: Food Marketing Institute, 1985.

Trends: Consumer Attitudes and the Supermarket. Washington, D.C.: Food Marketing Institute, 1988.

Vaile, R. S., and A. M. Child. *Grocery Qualities and Prices.* Minneapolis, Minn.: University of Minnesota Press, 1933.

Walsh, William I. *The Rise and Decline of the Great Atlantic and Pacific Tea Company.* Secaucus, N.J.: Lyle Stuart, 1986.

Watkins, Julian Lewis. *The 100 Greatest Advertisements: Who Wrote Them and What They Did.* New York: Dover Publications, 1959.

Watters, Pat. *Coca-Cola: An Illustrated History.* Garden City, N.Y.: Doubleday, 1978.

Weinstein, Edwin A. *Woodrow Wilson: A Medical and Psychological Biography.* Princeton, N.J.: Princeton University Press, 1981.

Werner, Morris Robert. *Julius Rosenwald: The Life of a Practical Humanitarian.* New York: Harper, 1939.

Wiebe, Robert H. *The Search for Order, 1877–1920.* New York: Hill and Wang, 1967.

Williamson, Oliver E. *The Economic Institutions of Capitalism.* New York: The Free Press, 1985.

————. *Markets and Hierarchies: Analysis and Antitrust Implications.* New York: The Free Press, 1975.

Wilson, Terry P. *The Cart That Changed the World.* Norman, Okla.: University of Oklahoma Press, 1978.

Wood, Robert E. *Mail Order Retailing: Pioneered in Chicago.* New York: Newcomen Society, 1948.

————. "Reminiscences." Oral History Collection, Columbia University, 1961.

Worthy, James C. *Shaping an American Institution: Robert E. Wood and Sears, Roebuck.* Urbana, Ill.: University of Illinois Press, 1984.

Yip, George S. *Barriers to Entry: A Corporate-Strategy Perspective.* Lexington, Mass.: D.C. Heath, 1982.

Young, James Harvey. *The Toadstool Millionaires.* Princeton, N.J.: Princeton University Press, 1961.

————. *The Medical Messiahs: A Social History of Health Quackery in Twentieth-Century America.* Princeton, N.J.: Princeton University Press, 1967.

Zaleznik, Abraham, and Manfred F. R. Kets De Vries. *Power and the Corporate Mind.* Boston: Houghton Mifflin, 1975.

Zimmerman, M. M. *The Super Market: A Revolution in Distribution.* New York: Mass Distribution, 1955.

Unpublished Doctoral Dissertations

Charvat, Frank J. "The Development of the Supermarket Industry Through 1950 with Emphasis on Concomitant Changes in the Food Store Sales Pattern." Ph.D. diss., Northwestern University, 1954.

Curry, Mary E. "Creating an American Institution: The Merchandising Genius of J.C. Penney." Ph.D. diss., American University, 1980.

German, Gene Arlin. "The Dynamics of Food Retailing, 1900–1975." Ph.D. diss., Cornell University, 1978.

Miller, Lawrence. "The Demand for Refrigerators." Ph.D. diss., Harvard University, 1956.

Olney, Martha L. "Advertising, Consumer Credit, and the 'Consumer Durables Revolution' of the 1920s." Ph.D. diss., University of California, Berkeley, 1985.

Sass, Steven Arthur. "Entrepreneurial Historians and History: An Essay In Organized Intellect." Ph.D. diss., Johns Hopkins University, 1977.

Harvard Business School Cases, Legal Cases and Other Material

The Coca-Cola Company v. The Koke Company of America et al., 254 U.S. 146 (1920).

Great Atlantic and Pacific Tea Company v. Cream of Wheat Company, 227 Fed. 46 (1915).

In the Court of Chancery of the State of Delaware in and for New Castle County, Loft, Incorporated v. Charles G. Guth, The Grace Company, Inc. of Delaware . . . , and Pepsi-Cola Company . . . , *Complainant's Main Brief;* Chancellors's Opinion, Loft, Inc. v. Guth et al., New Castle County, Delaware, 17 Sept. 1938.

In the District Court of the United States for the Eastern District of Illinois, United States v. The New York Great Atlantic and Pacific Tea Company, Inc. et al. No. 16153 (criminal) (1945).

Leach, W. "PepsiCo., Inc.—Company Report." Donaldson, Lufkin and Jenrette, Inc., 7 Apr. 1986.

"Note on the Major Home Appliance Industry." Case No. 9–372–349/Rev. 3/73. Boston: HBS Case Services, 1973.

Salmon, Walter J., et al. "Superstore Formats of the Future." Paper prepared for *Family Circle* and The Food Marketing Institute, Apr. 1985.

Smith, Wendy K., with Richard S. Tedlow. "James Burke: A Career in American Business." Boston: Harvard Business School Case Services, Case No. 389–177, 1989.

Standard Oil Company of New Jersey et al. v. United States, 221 U.S. 1 (1911).

Strasser, Susan. "Chain Stores." Harvard Business School Case Services, No. 9–386–127. Boston: Harvard Business School, 1985.

United States District Court for the Eastern District of Virginia, Bankruptcy Docket, Case No. 8418. In the matter of Cussions, May & Co., Inc., et al., v. National Pepsi-Cola Corporation (alleged bankrupt).

United States v. Forty Barrels and Twenty Kegs of Coca-Cola, 241 U.S. 995 (1916).

Index